Tenth Edition

DEATH, SOCIETY, and HUMAN EXPERIENCE

Robert J. Kastenbaum

Arizona State University

Allyn & Bacon

Boston • New York • San Francisco
Mexico City • Montreal • Toronto • London • Madrid • Munich • Paris
Hong Kong • Singapore • Tokyo • Cape Town • Sydney

Editor in Chief: Karen Hanson
Series Editorial Assistant: Courtney Shea
Senior Marketing Manager: Kelly May
Production Supervisor: Beth Houston
Editorial Production Service: Pre-Press PMG
Manufacturing Buyer: Debbie Rossi
Electronic Composition: Pre-Press PMG
Photo Researcher: Poyee Oster
Cover Administrator: Joel Gendron

For related titles and support materials, visit our online catalog at
www.pearsonhighered.com.

Between the time website information is gathered and then published, it is not unusual
for some sites to have closed. Also, the transcription of URLs can result in typographical
errors. The publisher would appreciate notification where these errors occur so that they
may be corrected in subsequent editions.

At press time, CIP data was not yet available.

**Credits appear on page 544, which constitutes an extension of the copyright
page.**

Printed in the United States of America

10 9 8 7 6 5 4 3   RRD-OH   12 11 10

**Allyn & Bacon
is an imprint of**

ISBN-13: 978-0-205-61053-2
ISBN-10:   0-205-61053-6

For Cynthia

and for those

you have loved . . .

CONTENTS

3   THE DEATH SYSTEM *71*

4 DYING *109*

5   HOSPICE AND PALLIATIVE CARE   *147*

6   END-OF-LIFE ISSUES AND DECISIONS   *175*

9 EUTHANASIA, ASSISTED DEATH, ABORTION, AND THE RIGHT TO DIE *271*

10 DEATH IN THE WORLD OF CHILDHOOD 309

11 BEREAVEMENT, GRIEF, AND MOURNING 351

12 THE FUNERAL PROCESS *393*

13   DO WE SURVIVE DEATH?   *439*

PREFACE

The first business of life is to stay alive. Ask the blades of grass that struggle up to the sunlight through the hard surfaces of a city street. Ask our resourceful adversaries, the virus and the microorganism, who continue to reinvent themselves whenever we launch a new pharmacological assault. Ask the child of a devastated homeland who has already experienced massive loss, stress, and deprivation but is determined to survive it all, and does. Ask nurses, paramedics, and physicians who have seen people make remarkable recoveries, seemingly because they had such a strong will to live. Ask firefighters why they risk their own lives to save people they've never met.

Even at its most resourceful and fortunate, though, life does not succeed indefinitely. That is a pretty good reason for having books and courses focused on dying, death, and grief. For many years, society clung to the strategy of ignoring death and, unfortunately, the dying and the grieving person. The rule of silence created more problems than it solved. There was little comfort for the dying or grieving person, and little counseling for the troubled mind of the suicidal person. Inadequate communication interfered with potentially supportive relationships. Health care professionals had their own share of misery: responsible for care of the "incurable" (as dying people often were known), yet not prepared to deal with mortality in their own thoughts and feelings.

Many people participated in the systematic avoidance of death. They paid the price in anxiety, burdensome defenses, and hard knocks from a reality that could not be forever disguised and avoided. Other people brooded alone, haunted by death-related anxieties. Still others challenged death by risky actions; these episodes turned passive anxiety into active thrills but, too often, resulted in serious injury or death. Few had the opportunity to reflect on dying and death with the help of a sensitive instructor and knowledge-based writings. There was little peer support for the nurse who dared to "get involved" with dying patients by actually being with them, the teacher who allowed students to discuss their death fears and bereavement experiences, or the researcher who had wandered so far from the mainstream as to pursue questions about our response to mortality. Funny thing, though: let death come a little too close to one's own life, and the same people who had looked askance at the local "death lady" now approached her for counsel and comfort.

The field of research and practice sometimes known as *thanatology* started to take shape in the 1960s, mostly in Western Europe and North America (Chapter 14). Like the other early "deathniks" back then, I had to learn most everything on the go. Our professional training had prepared us for a lot, but not for encounters with mortality. The first time I stepped into a death and dying classroom was as the instructor, and the same would hold true for many other death educators who followed. It still seemed odd to be studying death. Eventually I figured out that *thanatology* was actually the study of life—but with death left in. As the 1970s started, we had the emerging hospice movement, a scattering of classes and workshops, media attention, and *Omega*, the first peer-reviewed journal devoted to death and dying.

We didn't have a textbook, though, so I wrote one. I thought then, as I think now, that we should call on experiences, knowledge, and insights from many perspectives. No field had all the answers, and most had been reluctant even to raise the questions. Easy generalizations had already appeared in both public and professional discourse: Whoa, let's be careful! Let's not become overly attached to conclusions that satisfy our wish for wish-fulfillment, or seem to confirm the assumptions we have dragged along with us. This meant offering detailed analysis and critical perspective when appropriate, even if it disobliges the page-flippers and skimmers.

I thought a lot about the people who would read this book. Some people would be working toward or engaged in a human services career. Others would be following their curiosity about a subject that had been so curiously ignored. There would also be people—many—who had experienced one or more traumatic death-related situations that continued to trouble them. Perhaps it was time to find a new way to come to terms with this lingering issue. For other people, death-related issues would be ongoing: a roommate is suicidal, a family member is dying, they might themselves have a life-threatening condition. There is a give-and-take in the classroom that no book can accomplish on its own. Nevertheless, an author can respect the diverse life experiences and circumstances that people bring with them.

ABOUT THE TENTH EDITION

This book is intended to contribute to your understanding of your relationship with death, both as an individual and as a member of society. For example, you will learn:

- How our thoughts and feelings about death develop from childhood's hour and how we struggle with anxiety and denial, but move toward a mature and effective view of death.
- How baby boomers are experiencing the later years of their life course and coming to terms with mortality as expressed through aging and death anxiety, suicide, and faith in an afterlife.
- What very different ideas and meanings have been associated with death throughout the centuries.
- How and why the Undead have survived into our own times.
- How and why the ideas of "death" and "dead" have become unsettled in our own time.

- How social forces and events affect the length of our lives, how we grieve, and how we die: in nations ravaged by disease, poverty, and violence, as well as in more prosperous and fortunate nations.
- How dying people are perceived and treated in our society and what can be done to provide the best possible care.
- How the "Good Death" is a difficult but valuable ideal.
- What are continuing developments and challenges to hospice (palliative care).
- What choices and decisions we have about the way we are treated at the end of our lives.
- What stresses and risks are experienced by many caregivers to terminally ill people and their families.
- How people respond to the sorrow and anxiety of grief and the challenge of moving on with their lives.
- Why the funeral and memorialization process is still with us today after so many centuries, and how it is changing.
- Who is most at risk for suicide and who is most likely to become either a killer or a victim of homicide.
- What is happening in the continuing controversy over euthanasia and physician-assisted death.
- What is becoming of faith and doubt about an afterlife.
- How we can help others cope with their death encounters.

These and many other topics are presented as interactions between the individual and society. It is true that we live and die as individuals. However, it is also true that we live and die within a particular society during a particular time in world history. Preoccupation with our thoughts and feelings as individuals could lead us to lose sight of the larger picture in which social dynamics often influence the timing, mode, and experience of dying as well as our basic interpretations of life and death.

We draw upon the best available scholarship and research, as well as upon the words of people who have found themselves in the middle of death-related situations. Often we will note the limitations of present knowledge and offer alternative interpretations. It is our intention to present information clearly but without undue simplification.

I welcome you personally to this book and to the course to which this book may contribute. Take advantage of your instructor's expertise. Do not hesitate to ask your questions and share your experiences. Explore the ever-growing literature on the human encounter with mortality. Discover what observers from many different perspectives can offer us. Now join us in one of humankind's oldest—and newest—voyages of discovery.

ACKNOWLEDGMENTS

I appreciate the comments offered by the following reviewers: Patrick Ashwood, Hawkeye Community College; Gregory T. Busch, West Virginia University; and Michelle M. Loudermilk, Fayetteville Technical Community College. It was also good to hear from other instructors and readers who had useful suggestions to make.

I hope you will find this book to be helpful in your explorations of death, society, and human experience.

A NOTE FROM THE PUBLISHER ON SUPPLEMENTS

Instructor's Manual and Test Bank. Includes learning objectives, chapter summaries, key terms with definitions, lecture and project suggestions, and test questions in multiple-choice, true-false, short answer, and essay formats.

PowerPoint Lecture Slides. Outlines major points from the text and features graphs and tables from the text. PowerPoint lecture slides are available online for download.

Computerized Test Bank. The printed Test Bank is also available through Allyn & Bacon's online testing system, MyTest. The user-friendly interface allows you to view, edit, and add questions; transfer questions to tests; and print tests. Search and sort features allow you to locate questions quickly and to arrange them in whatever order you prefer.

Study Guide for the Annenberg/CPG Telecourse—*Death: A Personal Understanding*. This telecourse, consisting of ten one-hour programs, is based on Kastenbaum's text, and is available from Annenberg/CPG **(www.learner .org).** The Study Guide, produced by Allyn & Bacon, is available online to adopters using the telecourse and using *Death, Society, and Human Experience*, Tenth Edition.

Faculty Guide for the Annenberg/CPG Telecourse—*Death: A Personal Understanding*. Free upon request to adopters using the telecourse and *Death, Society, and Human Experience*, Tenth Edition.

Snorting death thunders a few steps behind these revelers in Pampola, Spain's Sanfermines Fiesta. This 400 year-old tradition of risking one's life for a sporting high continues. Taunting death is sometimes describe as an incredible thrill—by those who survive.

chapter 1

AS WE THINK ABOUT DEATH

. . . we are taught not to contemplate the possibility that all being is ephemeral—including our own. But san men remind us of it every day: as our trash goes, so one day, go we. No wonder we need to hate them.
—Robin Nagel (2008)

I felt like we were going to get thrown out of the car numerous times (loose belts, for sure), and I had zero control in anticipating which direction we were thrown next. Ben didn't fare much better, although he didn't put his hands on his knees sucking in some air, as I had to re-orient myself after we got off. He did convince me to get right back on (no line at this time) in the front car, which led to a much more controlled but still thrilling ride than before. I'm glad we hit it again before I could think about it or I might not have done her again.
—Anonymous rollercoaster enthusiast (2008)

One man was stretchered away after he was hit in the back by a bull with its horn and another man who had tripped had a lucky escape when the animal simply tripped over him. . . . "You're not even thinking. You're just sprinting. The elation at the end of it. You're just ecstatic," said a 23-year-old accountant from Adelaide, Australia, Jim Atkinson.
—CNN (2004)

"His brow was perfectly calm. No scowl disfigured his happy face, which signifies he died an easy death, no sins of this world to harrow his soul as it gently passed away to distant and far happier realms."
—Civil War Confederate soldier, quoted by Drew Gilpin Faust (2008, p. 21)

Estimates of self-immolations in Afghanistan are hard to come by, especially in the largely lawless northern and southern regions. Doctors at the Herart Public Hospital said they had received more than 100 female burn cases this year, with most of the women dying soon after arrival. . . . Some female deaths may be ascribed to suicide in order to cover up for "honor killings"—when women deemed to have "dishonored" their family are killed—or to dowry deaths—when brides are burned for not bringing adequate dowries into their in-laws' households.
—Leela Jacinto (2002)

We did not tell our participants they were particularly good or worthy—we simply had them write about what was important to them, without evaluating their ideas and without asking them to evaluate themselves. As a result, they became less defensive in response to reminders of death. . . .
—Brandon J. Schmeichel and Andy Martens (2005, p. 665)

In the land of the Uttarakurus grows the magic Jambu tree, whose fruit has the property of conferring immunity from illness and old age, and, by means of this fruit, they lengthen their lives to a thousand years or even, in some accounts, to eleven thousand years . . . among other things, their realm includes landscapes of precious stones and trees from whose branches grow beautiful maidens.
—Gerald J. Gruman (2003, p. 33)

So death, the most terrifying of ills, is nothing to us, since so long as we exist, death is not with us, but when death comes, then we do not exist. It does not then concern either the living or the dead, since for the former it is not and the latter are no more.
—Epicurus, Third century B.C.

Life is supposed to go on. Yes, there is death, but not here, not now, and surely not for us. We wake to a familiar world each day. We splash water on the same face we rinsed yesterday. We talk with people whose faces are familiar. We see so much of what we have seen many times before. It is so comforting . . . this ongoingness of daily life. Why disturb this pattern? Why think of death? Why make each other anxious? And why do anything that would increase our risk of dying before our time? Here are a few quick, if perhaps not entirely satisfying, answers:

• We can't help but think of death. It's the fault of the sanitation workers who haul our garbage away. That is the considered opinion of New York City sanitation worker Robin Nagel, who is also a professor of anthropology. She notes that we live in a high-consuming, rapid-disposing culture. Furthermore, we are

Sanitation workers in New York City are just doing their job, but anthropologist (and fellow employee) Robin Nagel observes many people anxiously associate the disposal of trash with their own mortality in a throw-away society that has difficulty in facing the realities of impermanence and death.

a culture that tries to keeps death and the dead at the farthest margins of our physical and emotional space. We sort of know what we are doing, enough to realize that there is no permanence in our lives. Today's bargain purchase is tomorrow's garbage. I, who have purchased, used, and discarded so much will myself be hauled off some day, and then what? What will it all have meant? We don't have to agree with Professor Nagel. But if we want to know "Why We Love to Hate San Men" (op. cit.) well, she has just told us.

- It's hard to resist the opportunity to be scared out of our wits on a diabolical rollercoaster or by being gored and trampled by a bull. Each year so many people crowd into the northern Spanish town of Pamplona that they become almost as much a menace to each other as the six bulls and six steers who rush down cobblestone streets. The ecstasy of outrunning death is hard to understand for those who organize themselves around the avoidance of mortal anxiety (see also Chapter 15). Our friend "Anonymous" has the proper attitude for a person who tries out the biggest and baddest rollercoasters over and over again. It's the thrill of terror and the joy of survival. Are these people actually risking death? Accidents do occur and are usually attributed to inadequate attention to safety issues (Johnson & Williams, 2007). Furthermore, the cardiovascular risk is serious enough to elicit medical warnings (Peck, 2005). Healthy volunteers experienced sharp rises in blood pressure during a brief rollercoaster ride, and several had potentially life-threatening cardiac responses. People with cardiovascular conditions are placing themselves at risk on the more daunting amusement park rides—as are those with previously undetected medical problems. Apparently, then, we like to avoid unnecessary risk and mortal terror—except when we don't. Why? Because there's fun in the intensified feeling of being alive when we dance along the edge of survival (see *edge theory,* this chapter).

- In mid nineteenth-century United States, people thought often and intensely about death. No family was secure from the threat of virulent epidemics and lethal infections, especially during or after childbirth. Fortunately, people knew how they were supposed to think about death. Guidebooks for Christian living and dying were relied on by many people—and families were becoming relied on ever more, along with religion, as the center of one's life. The Civil War brought death on an unprecedented scale and in horrifying forms. The loss of young lives was devastating to families on both sides of the conflict. What made these losses all the more unbearable was that sons, brothers, husbands, and fathers had died far from home, bereft of familial comfort and spiritual ministry, and possibly in a despairing state of mind. The Confederate soldier quoted by Faust (p. 21) was providing a welcome service when he described his cousin's death in such positive terms in a condolence letter. It was best if his relatives could be made to believe that their young man had ended his life at peace with himself and with God. How people died had much to say about how they had lived and what would be their estate in the afterlife (see also the *good death* in Chapter 15).

- Young women, even girls as young as 11, have set themselves on fire, choosing extremely painful deaths over lives enslaved to men they did not want to marry. Such events are still occurring in Afghanistan, and in other places where females are still treated as disposable property. Some of these deaths are finally coming to general attention, as when Shakiba, a 19-year-old Afghan woman, was interviewed on television from the hospital bed in which she would soon die. Shakiba's family sold her to become a man's second wife. "My family was selling me and I didn't know what else to do." Women between 14 and 20 years of age who were desperately trying to escape marriages to older men have carried out most of the self-immolations. These women were being married off for a "bride price" intended to help the rest of the family survive. But the families themselves have also been accused of killing their women for being uncooperative or for having violated their society's rigid sexist code of conduct. Not only death, but death in youth, and death preceded by intense suffering were chosen by these women over lives that seemed even worse.

- Death anxiety has been studied extensively in recent years. Some researchers focus on our response to *mortality salience.* How do we feel, think, and behave when we encounter a situation that has an association with death? The Schmeichel & Martens study (op. cit.) is one of several that have found that we are less disturbed by mortality salience when we are feeling confident about ourselves. This is part of a larger approach to *terror management* that we will be exploring later in this chapter.
- Epicurus has it all figured out—or does he? According to his logic, neither the living nor the dead should be concerned about death. Is that a philosophy we can or should live by today?
- Through the centuries, most people died before what we now would consider to be mid life. Many, in fact, did not survive childhood. Perhaps, this is one reason why the folklore and legends of ancient times are filled with stories about fortunate people who lived so long that they hardly needed to think about death. The Uttarakurus were supposed to live in the far north of India, but similar tales flourished in Greek, Persian, Teutonic, Hindu, and Japanese lore, among others. One of the oldest Hebrew legends speaks of the River of Immortality, which some scholars believe provided the background for Christ being identified with the Fountain of Life. The idea that in a faraway place there were refreshing waters that could extend life and perhaps, also renew youth was still credible enough to gain funding for Ponce de León's 1513 expedition to Florida. Fear of dying could be attributed to the prevailing short life expectancy, but the relatively few prosperous and powerful elders of the past also sought ways to postpone death. If only we could do something about death, we wouldn't have to be thinking about it so often!

The preference for life over death takes other forms as well. For example, many families today have fading photographs of relatives who died years ago of pneumonia, tuberculosis, cholera, typhoid, scarlet fever, infantile paralysis, and other widespread diseases. These people wanted to live. One hoped to survive the diseases that threatened children and young adults alike. One hoped for the chance to realize personal dreams for a good life. While today people still hope for a good life, perspectives have changed about what to do when life isn't so good. There are now increasing demands for release from life when the quality of that life has been reduced by painful or incapacitating illness. Death, once viewed as the problem, is being regarded as the answer by a growing number of people.

In this chapter we begin our exploration of thoughts, knowledge, attitudes, and feelings about death. Although our focus is on the United States, we will also consider dying, death, grief, and suicide in other societies. It is not enough, though, to attend only to the way other people think about death, therefore, this chapter also provides the opportunity to take stock of our own thoughts, knowledge, attitudes, and feelings.

NOT THINKING ABOUT DEATH: A FAILED EXPERIMENT

As a society, we have tried not thinking about death. Most of us completed our school days without being exposed to substantial readings and discussions about dying, death, grief, and suicide. Who would have taught us anyway? Our teachers were products of the same *never-say-die* society. Death did surface occasionally as an event remote from our own experiences. For example, X many gunmen murdered each other in a famous shoot-out. Some king or other died in Europe and somebody else grabbed the throne on a date we might need to remember for the exam.

Those students who persevered until they had a graduate degree received only further lessons in death avoidance. Nurses, physicians, psychologists, social workers, and others who would be relied on to provide human services were not helped to understand their own death-related feelings and attitudes, let alone anybody else's. During these long years, even clergy often felt unprepared to cope with the death-related situations they would face. Few of their instructors had themselves mastered the art of ministering to the dying.

The media also cooperated. Nobody died. Nobody had cancer. Lucky "Nobody"! Instead, people would "pass away" after a "long illness." Deaths associated with crime and violence received lavish attention, then as now, but silence had settled over the everyday deaths of everyday people. When a movie script called for a deathbed scene, Hollywood would offer a sentimental and sanitized version. A typical example occurs in *Till the Clouds Go By* (1946), a film that purported to be the biography of songwriter Jerome Kern. A dying man tries to communicate to a friend his realization that this will be the last time they see each other, but Kern's character obeys the Hollywood dictum that deception is the best policy: even mature adults cannot face the reality of death, so it is best to pretend death doesn't exist. As a result, the friends never actually connect, never offer significant words of parting to each other. A physician then enters the room and nods gravely to the friend, who immediately departs. Another mortal lesson from Hollywood: The moment of death belongs to the doctor, not to the dying person and the bereaved. Audiences today see this scene as shallow and deceptive. One student spoke for many others in complaining, "It was as phony as can be—what a terrible way to end a relationship!" A new question has arisen, though: Does the public fascination with grisly corpses and mangled body parts on television programs such as *CSI* literally depersonalize death?

Not thinking about death was pretty much a failure. People continued to die, and how they died became an increasing source of concern. Survivors continued to grieve, often feeling a lack of understanding and support from others. Suicide rates doubled, then tripled among the young, and remained exceptionally high among older adults. Scattered voices warned us that in attempting to evade the reality of death, we were falsifying the totality of our lives. Who were we kidding? Neither an individual nor a society could face its challenges wisely without coming to terms with mortality.

It is still difficult to think about death, especially when our own lives and relationships are involved. Nevertheless, enforced silence and frantic evasion seem to be less pervasive now. There is an increasing readiness to listen and communicate about this once-taboo subject.

Listening and Communicating

"Doctor, I want to die. Will you help me?" This question is the title of an influential article by Timothy E. Quill, M.D. He advised that:

Dying patients need more than prescriptions for narcotics or referrals to hospice programs from their physicians. They need a personal guide and counselor through the dying process—someone who will unflinchingly help them face both the medical and the personal aspects of dying, whether it goes smoothly or it takes the physician into unfamiliar, untested ground. Dying patients do not have the luxury of choosing not to undertake the journey, or of separating their person from their disease. Physicians' commitment not to abandon their patients is of paramount importance (1993, p. 872).

Statements of this kind have become increasingly common. More physicians are now listening and communicating. Patients and family members feel more empowered to express their concerns, needs, and wishes. Physicians feel more compelled to take these concerns, needs, and wishes into account.

Some people have a ready-made answer that dismisses an open discussion of death: "There's nothing to think about. When your number's up, it's up." This idea goes back a long way. It is part of that general view of life known as *fatalism*. Outcomes are determined in advance: There's nothing we can do to affect the outcomes, so why bother? There is something to be said for respecting the limits of human knowledge and efficacy, but there is also something to be said for doing what we can to reduce suffering and risk within our limits. The person who is quick to introduce a fatalistic statement often is attempting to end the discussion before it really begins. It is what communication experts call a *silencer*.

Fatalistic attitudes in today's world are perhaps more dangerous than ever. As we will see, many deaths in the United States can be attributed to lifestyle. Our attitudes, choices, and actions contribute to many other deaths across the entire life span. Ironically, it is the belief that there is no use in thinking about death and taking life-protective measures that increase the probability of an avoidable death.

YOUR SELF-INVENTORY OF ATTITUDES, BELIEFS, AND FEELINGS

We have touched briefly on a few of the death-related questions and beliefs that are current in our society. Perhaps some of your own thoughts and feelings have come to mind. One of the most beneficial things you can do for yourself at this point is to take stock of your present experiences, attitudes, beliefs, and feelings. This will give you not only a personal data baseline, but will also contribute further to your appreciation of the ways in which other people view death.

Before reading further, please begin sampling your personal experiences with death by completing Self-Inventories 1–4. Try to notice what thoughts and feelings come to mind as you answer these questions. Which questions make you angry? Which questions would you prefer not to answer? Which questions seem foolish or make you want to laugh? Observing your own responses is part of the self-monitoring process that has been found invaluable by many of the people who work systematically with death-related issues.

Each of the inventories takes a distinctive perspective. We begin with your knowledge base, sampling the information you have acquired regarding various facets of death. This is followed by exploring your attitudes and beliefs. We then move on to your personal experiences with death. Finally, we look at the feelings that are stirred in you by dying, death, and grief. Our total view of death comprises knowledge, attitudes, experiences, and feelings—and it is useful to identify each of these components accurately. For example, if I fail to distinguish between my personal feelings and my actual knowledge of a death-related topic, I reduce my ability to make wise decisions and take effective actions.

Please complete the self-inventories now.

INVENTORY #1:
YOUR KNOWLEDGE BASE

Fill in the blanks or select alternative answers as accurately as you can. If you are not sure of the answer, offer your best guess.

1. Most baby boomers:

   a. Do not believe in Heaven
   b. Believe in Heaven, but not in ghosts
   c. Believe in Heaven, but do not expect to go there
   d. Believe in Heaven, and expect to go there

2. How many deaths are there in the United States each year?

3. The leading cause of death for the population in general is _____ .

4. A person born in the United States a century ago had an average life expectancy (ALE) of about _____ years.

5. A person born in the United States today has an ALE of about _____ years.

6. Around the world, who has the higher ALE, females or males?

7. In the nation of _____, ALE has dropped from 63 to only 34 years over the past quarter of a century. Why?

8. There is a new entry among the 10 leading causes of death in the United States. This is _____ .

9. What is the leading cause of fatal injuries in the United States? _____

10. A seriously ill person is in the hospital and not expected to recover. How much time is this person likely to spend alone each 24-hour day?

INVENTORY #1:
(continued)

---

11. Homicide rates in the United States have been consistently highest in:

    New England ——————
    Mountain states ——————
    Southern states ——————
    West north central states ——————

12. Does your state recognize an advance directive for end-of-life medical care as a legal and enforceable document?

    Yes   No

13. A suicide attempt is most likely to result in death when made by a:

    a. Young woman
    b. Young man
    c. Elderly woman
    d. Elderly man

14. Cryonic suspension is a technique that is intended to preserve a body in a hypothermic (low-temperature) state until a cure is discovered for the condition from which that person suffered. How many people have actually been placed in cryonic suspension, and how many have been revived?

15. The earliest childhood memory reported by most adults is an experience of ——————————.

16. —————————— is the first, and so far the only, state to legalize physician-assisted death under specified conditions.

17. Palliative care most often has relief from —————————— as its top priority.

18. What was placed inside the chest of a royal Egyptian mummy and why?

19. In the United States, cremation is now chosen by about one person in ——————————.

20. Near-death experience reports have several key elements in common with G-LOC. What is G-LOC?

21. Jack Kevorkian, M.D., "assisted" in the death of more than 100 people. How many of these people were terminally ill?

22. Periodic mass extinctions have eliminated many species and taken a tremendous toll of life. The three most recent mass die-offs are thought to have been caused by ——————————.

23. The Harvard Criteria offered an influential guide to the diagnosis of ——————

24. PTSD has been receiving increased media attention lately. What is it?

25. —————————— is the philosopher who turned down the opportunity to escape his unjust execution, and instead used the occasion to explain to his friends why death should not be feared.

Answers to self-inventory questions are found later in this chapter. Please don't peek!

INVENTORY #2:
MY ATTITUDES AND BELIEFS

Select the answer that most accurately represents your belief.

1. I believe in some form of life after death:

   Yes, definitely _____
   Yes, but not quite sure _____
   No, but not quite sure _____
   No, definitely _____

2. I believe that you die when your number comes up. It's in the hands of fate:

   Yes, definitely _____
   Yes, but not quite sure _____
   No, but not quite sure _____
   No, definitely _____

3. I believe that taking one's own life is:

   Never justified _____
   Justified when terminally ill _____
   Justified whenever life no longer seems worth living _____

4. I believe that taking another person's life is:

   Never justified _____
   Justified in defense of your own life _____
   Justified when that person has committed a terrible crime _____

5. I believe that dying people should be:

   Told the truth about their condition _____
   Kept hopeful by sparing them the facts _____
   Depends upon the person and the circumstances _____

6. In thinking about my own old age, I would prefer:

   To die before I grow old _____
   To live as long as I can _____
   To discover what challenges and opportunities old age will bring _____

7. To me, the possibility of nuclear weapon warfare or accidents that might destroy much of life on Earth has been of:

   No concern _____   Little concern _____
   Some concern _____   Major concern _____

8. To me, the possibility of environmental catastrophes that might destroy much of life on Earth has been of:

   No concern _____   Little concern _____
   Some concern _____   Major concern _____

9. Drivers and passengers should be required to wear seat belts.

   Yes, agree _____   Tend to agree _____
   Tend to disagree _____   No, disagree _____

10. The availability of handguns should be more tightly controlled to reduce accidental and impulsive shootings.

    Yes, agree _____   Tend to agree _____
    Tend to disagree _____   No, disagree _____

11. A person has been taken to the emergency room with internal bleeding that is likely to prove fatal. This person is 82 years of age and has Alzheimer's-type dementia. What type of response would you recommend from the ER staff?

    Comfort only _____
    Limited attempt at rescue _____
    All-out attempt at rescue _____

12. You have been taken to the emergency room with internal bleeding that is likely to prove fatal. You are now 82 years of age and have Alzheimer's-type dementia. What type of response would you hope you receive from the ER staff?
    Comfort only _____
    Limited attempt at rescue _____
    All-out attempt at rescue _____

13. Another round of chemotherapy has failed for a woman with advanced breast cancer. The doctor suggests a new round of experimental therapy. She replies, "I wish I were dead." What do you think should be done—and why?

    _____

    _____

INVENTORY #3:
MY EXPERIENCES WITH DEATH

Fill in the blanks or select the most accurate alternative answers.

1. a. I have had an animal companion who died. Yes No
    b. How I felt when my pet died can be described by words such as ———— and _____ .

2. The following people in my life have died:

    Person   How Long Ago?

    A. _____

    B. _____

    C. _____

    D. _____

    E. _____

3. The death that affected me the most at the time was _____ .

4. How I felt when this person died can be described by words such as _____ and _____ .

5. This death was especially significant to me because _____ _____ .

6. In all the circumstances surrounding this person's death, including what happened afterward, my most positive memory is of _____ .

7. My most disturbing memory is of _____ _____ .

8. I have conversed with dying people.
    Never ——   One person ——
    Several people ——   Many people ——

9. I have provided care for a dying person.
    Never ——   One person ——
    Several people ——   Many people ——

10. I have known a person who attempted suicide.
    Not to my knowledge _____
    One person _____
    Several people _____

11. I have known a person who committed suicide.
    Not to my knowledge _____
    One person _____
    Several people _____

12. I have known a person who died in an accident.
    Not to my knowledge _____
    One person _____
    Several people _____

13. I have known a person who was murdered.
    Never _____
    One person _____
    Several people _____

14. I have known a person who died of an AIDS-related disease.
    Not to my knowledge _____
    One person _____
    Several people _____

15. I know a person who has tested positive for the AIDS virus.
    Not to my knowledge _____
    One person _____
    Several people _____

INVENTORY #4:
MY FEELINGS

Select the answer that most closely represents your feelings.

1. I would feel comfortable in developing an intimate conversation with a dying person.
    Yes, agree _____   Tend to agree _____
    Tend to disagree _____ No, disagree _____

2. I would hesitate to touch someone who was dying.
    Yes, agree _____   Tend to agree _____
    Tend to disagree _____ No, disagree _____

3. My hands would tremble when I was talking to a dying person.
    Yes, agree _____   Tend to agree _____
    Tend to disagree _____ No, disagree _____

4. I would have more difficulty in talking if the dying person was about my age.
    Yes, agree _____   Tend to agree _____
    Tend to disagree _____ No, disagree _____

5. I would avoid talking about death and dying with a person who was terminally ill.
    Yes, agree _____   Tend to agree _____
    Tend to disagree _____ No, disagree _____

6. I would avoid talking with a dying person if possible.
    Yes, agree _____   Tend to agree _____
    Tend to disagree _____ No, disagree _____

7. I have had moments of anxiety in which I think of my own death.
    Never _____   Once _____
    Several times _____ Often _____

8. I fear that I will die too soon.
    Yes, agree _____   Tend to agree _____
    Tend to disagree _____ No, disagree _____

9. I have no fear of death as such.
    Yes, agree _____   Tend to agree _____
    Tend to disagree _____ No, disagree _____

10. I have no fears associated with dying.
    Yes, agree _____   Tend to agree _____
    Tend to disagree _____ No, disagree _____

11. I feel good when I think about life after death.
    Yes, agree _____   Tend to agree _____
    Tend to disagree _____ No, disagree _____

12. I am anxious about the possible death of somebody I love.
    Yes, agree _____   Tend to agree _____
    Tend to disagree _____ No, disagree _____

13. I am grieving over somebody who has already died.
    Yes, agree _____   Tend to agree _____
    Tend to disagree _____ No, disagree _____

14. I have a hard time taking death seriously. It feels remote to me, not really connected to my own life.
    Yes, agree _____   Tend to agree _____
    Tend to disagree _____ No, disagree _____

15. I have some strong, even urgent, feelings regarding death these days.
    Yes, agree _____   Tend to agree _____
    Tend to disagree _____ No, disagree _____

Note: Questions 1–6 are part of a scale introduced by Hayslip (1986–1987).

SOME ANSWERS—AND THE QUESTIONS THEY RAISE

Here are the answers to Self-Inventory #1:

1. Most members of the baby boomer generation believe in ghosts and in their own acceptance into Heaven, though they judge that many other people will not make it (Chapter 13).
2. More than 2 million people die in the United States each year. The most recent data (2002) document 2,443,387 deaths (Chapter 3).
3. Heart disease continues to be the leading cause of death in the United States (Chapter 3).
4. A person born in the United States *in 1900* had an ALE of 47 years (Chapter 3).
5. A person born in the United States *today* has an ALE of nearly 78 years (Chapter 3).
6. Females outlive males almost everywhere throughout the world (Chapter 3).
7. Zimbabwe, beset by AIDS, poverty, and societal disorder, has suffered a severe reduction in ALE (Chapter 3), after having previously achieved one of the highest levels ever in Africa.
8. Alzheimer's disease has become the eighth leading cause of death in the United States, an unfortunate consequence of the aging of the population and the limited success so far in preventing or treating this condition (Chapter 3).
9. Motor vehicle accidents have long been the most common cause of fatal accidents in the United States. Among elderly people, falls are the second most common type of injury fatality (Chapter 3).

More women than men dining in this upscale restaurant? No surprise. Females most often outlive males.

10. Seriously and terminally ill people were alone almost 19 hours a day according to a hospital study (Chapter 4).
11. Homicide rates have been consistently the highest in southern states (Chapter 9).
12. Yes—all states do! (Chapter 6).
13. A suicide attempt is most likely to be fatal when it is made by an elderly man (Chapter 7).
14. Fewer than 100 human bodies have been placed in cryonic suspension worldwide, and no known attempts have been made to resuscitate them (Chapter 6).
15. A death or other loss experience is most often the earliest childhood memory recalled by adults (Chapter 10).
16. Oregon is the only state at present to have legalized a form of physician-assisted death (Chapter 9).
17. Relief from pain is most often the top priority for palliative care or hospice programs. Relief from other symptoms is also provided as much as possible (Chapter 5).
18. The royal physicians replaced the heart with a scarab, a carved stone that represented the dung beetle, whose mysterious work of helping to bring life back from death was regarded as intrinsic to the great cycle of being (Chapter 12).
19. About one person in four in the United States now chooses cremation. There is much variation in frequency of choosing cremation within the United States and among nations (Chapter 12).
20. G-LOC is a sudden loss of normal consciousness that is experienced by pilots under acceleration stress. Tunnel vision and bright lights are among the perceptual changes that resemble near-death experiences (Chapter 13).
21. Less than a third of the patients whose lives Kevorkian helped to end were actually terminally ill at the time (Chapter 9).
22. Scientists now believe that asteroids were responsible for the three most recent mass die-offs or extinctions (Chapter 15).
23. The Harvard criteria have been applied to determine whether a nonresponsive person should be considered brain-dead (Chapter 2).

24. Post-traumatic stress disorder is a disabling condition that is related to overwhelming experiences, such as warfare and disaster (Chapter 3).
25. Socrates (Chapter 15)

Attitudes, Experiences, Beliefs, Feelings

Attitudes refer to our action tendencies. I am ready to act or I am not ready to act. I am ready to approach or to avoid this situation. *Beliefs* refer to our worldview. *Fatalism,* as already mentioned, is one type of belief. *Feelings* provide us with qualitative information or a status report on our sense of being. I feel safe or endangered, happy or sorrowful, aroused or lethargic. Two people may hold identical beliefs and attitudes but differ greatly in their feelings. On Self-Inventory #2, question 10, for example, these two people may answer, "Yes, I agree: The availability of handguns should be more tightly controlled to reduce accidental and impulsive shootings." However, one of these people may have relatively little feeling attached to this view. Perhaps this person thinks that it is risky to have a lot of handguns around on general principles. The other person might be the widow of a physician who was shot to death by an emotionally disturbed person who did not even know him. Her feelings could hardly be more intense. (This is a real person, the former owner of a home my wife and I purchased. Incredible as it may seem, the young widow herself became the recipient of death threats because she spoke up in favor of gun control.)

Personal *experience* influences our attitudes, beliefs, and feelings. For example, people who have had near-death experiences while in a life-threatening situation often develop a different perspective on life and death (Chapter 14). A paramedic who has responded to a thousand motor vehicle accidents is likely to have a stronger attitude and more intense feelings when noticing children without seat belts in a car. A person who has never suffered the death of a loved one may be more impatient with a bereaved colleague who does not seem to "snap back" right away.

There is a profound experiential difference between people who have had a personally significant death and those for whom death has remained a distant topic, or even just a word. Death stopped being just a word for a graduate student of social work when both her parents were killed in an automobile accident. She could not go on with her own life until she fully realized their deaths as well as her own mortality. "Before all this happened, it was just a word to me, death. I could hear death. I could say death. Really, though, it was just a word. Now it's like something under my own skin, if you know what I mean." Simply knowing intellectually that people die was not enough; she now had to connect death with life in a very personal way.

This challenge is ours as well. If we have experienced a death that "got" to us—whether the death of a person or an animal companion—then we are also more likely to realize what other people have been going through. This is one of the most powerful dynamics at work in community support groups. Organizations such as Compassionate Friends and Widow-to-Widow provide emotional support for bereaved persons from those who have already experienced the sorrow and stress of loss. New support groups continue to be formed to help people with specific types of death-related stress such as for parents whose child has been killed by a drunk driver or for persons with AIDS.

However, there are limits to the value of experience. Just because a person has had a particular kind of loss experience does not necessarily enhance their ability to support others. Furthermore, some people have proven helpful to the dying, the grieving, and the suicidal even if they have not had very similar experiences in their lives. The basic point to consider is whether at this time in your life you are someone who has experienced death in an undeniably personal and significant way, or whether you still have something of an outsider's perspective.

Some people have an inner relationship with death that goes beyond basic realization. The sense of being dominated or haunted by death can emerge from one critical experience or from a cluster of experiences. Perhaps you have mourned the deaths of so many people that you could not even list them in the space provided. Perhaps you knew several people who died unexpectedly at the same time. Perhaps you are still responding strongly to the death of one person who had been

at the center of your life. The question of whether or not your life is being highly influenced by death-related experiences cannot be answered by examining a simple list. We would need to appreciate what these people meant to you, and what lingers in your mind regarding the deaths themselves, the funeral, and the memorialization process. Furthermore, we would need to examine your own involvement in the situation. For example, people who have provided direct personal care for a dying friend or relative have a different set of experiences than those who have not. Perhaps you have a vivid memory of your last visits with a person who was a very important part of your life. On the other hand, perhaps you were thousands of miles away when this person died and had no opportunity to be with your loved one. We may be much influenced by how a person has died as well as by the fact of death itself. A death by suicide, for example, has often been considered tainted, resulting in additional stress and social isolation for the remaining family.

These are but a few of the ways in which our past experiences with death can influence us in the future. Paramedics who have rushed to many accident scenes and other emergencies are likely to respond differently to the next death-related situation they encounter than people who have never seen death and dying close-up. Because everyone does not respond in the same way when encountering a death-related situation, then it is probably not really the "same" situation for each of us.

How Does State of Mind Affect Death-Related Behavior?

Much remains to be learned about the link between what goes on in our minds and how we actually behave in death-related situations. Here are a few studies that have addressed specific aspects of this question:

• *The living will: why most of the living won't.*
  The document known as the *living will* (Chapter 6) has been available since 1968. Although this document was designed to meet the growing public interest in controlling end-of-life decisions, most people did not choose

to use it. Why? VandeCreek and Frankowski (1996) found that most people had not thought much about their own deaths and also believed that their last days were a long way off. The authors conclude that "completing living wills connotes personal death, and this appears to be a substantial barrier to completing the document" (1996, p. 80). Avoidance of death thoughts was therefore closely associated with missing a significant opportunity to influence their situation when the last days do come. In the past few years there has been an increase in the number of people signing an advance health care directive (a successor to the living will) because this option is now part of established hospital policy—but many hospital personnel still have not completed their own document because, well, they'd rather not think about it!

- *Should I sign an organ donation card?*

  All states, as well as the District of Columbia, have enacted some version of the *Uniform Anatomical Gift Act* (Chapter 6). Despite the widespread availability of the organ donation option in association with the driver's license, relatively few people sign and carry organ donor cards (Lock, 2002). Personal attitudes play a major role in this decision. Nondonors tend to be more anxious about death and to have the specific fear of being declared dead prematurely (Robbins, 1990). Additionally, people who think of themselves as effective and self-reliant are more likely to sign the donation cards. The decision to donate organs to save another person's life seems closely related to the individual's general attitude and personal fears and anxieties.

- *Stepping off the curb.*

  Is there a relationship between state of mind and risk-taking behavior in everyday life? Laura Briscoe and I (1975) observed 125 people as they crossed a busy street between the Detroit Art Institute and Wayne State University. There were equal numbers of street crossers in five risk categories. People classified as Type A, the safest pedestrians, stood at the curb until the light changed in their favor, scanned traffic in both directions, entered the crosswalk, moved briskly across the street,

and checked out traffic from the opposite direction lanes before reaching the halfway point. At the opposite extreme were Type E pedestrians who crossed in the middle of the block, stepped out from between parked cars with the traffic lights against them, and did not look at traffic in either direction. (Miraculously, all 25 in this study did survive their crossings.) All street crossers were interviewed when they reached the other side. The observed street-crossing behavior was closely related to their general attitudes toward risk taking. For example, the high-risk pedestrians also classified themselves as high-risk drivers, and judged that they put their lives in jeopardy about 16% of the time in an average week, as compared with only 2% for Type A crossers. The Type E crossers were four times more likely than the Type A crossers to have contemplated or attempted suicide. They also reported a higher level of frustration with life. Within the limits of this study, it was clear that people's general attitudes and feelings can be expressed in behavior choices that either increase or decrease the probability of death.

- *In God they trust.*

  Cardiovascular surgery has come a long way in recent years. Many distressing symptoms have been relieved, and many lives have been extended. Nevertheless, the recovery and rehabilitation process is effortful and sometimes punctuated by medical complications or episodes of discouragement. A recent study (Ai et al., 2007) followed patients through their postoperative period and found that those with "positive religious coping styles" experienced less pain and distress. These people were secure in their faith, trusting in a higher and benevolent power. They were also able to draw on social support from other people who shared their faith and helped to sustain their hope. Other studies have also hinted at improved health outcomes, including reduced mortality, for people with secure religious faith and peer support. Doubt and conflict in religious belief seems to have a negative effect on health outcomes, although more research is needed to firmly establish these findings.

MAN IS MORTAL: BUT WHAT DOES THAT HAVE TO DO WITH ME?

Our attitudes toward life and death are challenged when a person close to us dies. In *The Death of Ivan Ilych* (1886), Leo Tolstoy provides an insightful portrait of the complexities, confusions, and urgencies that can afflict survivors, as well as the dying person. Consider just one passage from a novel that has lost none of its pertinence and power over the last century:

The thought of the sufferings of the man he had known so intimately, first as a schoolmate, and later as a grown-up colleague, suddenly struck Peter Ivanovich with horror . . . "Three days of frightful suffering, then death! Why, that might suddenly, at any moment, happen to me," he thought, and for a moment felt terrified. But—he himself did not know how—the customary reflection at once occurred to him, that this had happened to Ivan Ilych and not to him. . . . After which reflection Peter Ivanovich felt reassured, and began to ask with interest about the details of Ivan Ilych's death, as though death were an accident natural to Ivan Ilych, but certainly not to himself (pp. 101–102).

Peter Ivanovich is a responsible adult who presumably knows that we are all called mortals for a good reason. Yet he is playing a desperate game of evasion. Consider some of the elements in Peter Ivanovich's response:

1. He already knows of Ivan Ilych's death; otherwise he would not have been participating in the obligatory paying of respects. But it is only on viewing the corpse that the realization of death strikes him. There is a powerful difference between intellectual knowledge and emotional impact or realization. For one alarming moment, Peter feels that he himself is vulnerable. How could that be!

Count Leo Tolstoy, author of *The Death of Ivan Ilych* and other powerful novels, entrances his grandchildren with a more lighthearted story.

2. Peter Ivanovich immediately becomes concerned for Peter Ivanovich. His feelings do not center on the man who has lost his life or the woman who has lost her husband.

3. Yet he cannot admit that his outer line of defenses has been penetrated, that his personal anxieties have been triggered. He is supposed to show concern for others, not let them see his own distress. Furthermore, he hopes to leave this house of death with the confidence that death has, in fact, been left behind.

4. Peter Ivanovich's basic strategy here is to differentiate himself from Ivan Ilych. Yes, some people really do die, but not people like himself. The proof was in the fact that Peter was the vertical and mobile man while Ivan (that luckless, inferior specimen) was horizontal and immobile. We witness Peter Ivanovich, then, stretching and tormenting his logic in the hope of arriving at an anxiety-reducing conclusion.

5. Once Peter Ivanovich has quelled his momentary panic, he is able to discuss Ivan Ilych's death. Even so, he is more interested in factual details than in feelings and meanings. He has started to rebuild the barriers between himself and death. Whatever he learns about how his friend died will strengthen this barrier: all that was true of Ivan obviously is not applicable to him.

These evasive strategies, and others, are not confined to the pages of a Russian novel. You may well have the opportunity to see them in operation when people in your life are confronted by what researchers today refer to as *mortality salience*. And how will you deal with these situations yourself?

ANXIETY, DENIAL, AND ACCEPTANCE: THREE CORE CONCEPTS

Three concepts that are central to understanding death attitudes are interwoven through this excerpt from Tolstoy's masterpiece. Peter Ivanovich felt tense, distressed, unwell, and apprehensive. *Death anxiety* is the term most often applied to such responses. Anxiety is a condition that seeks its own relief.

To reduce the painful tension, a person might try many different actions—taking drugs or alcohol, for example, or fleeing from the situation. One form of avoiding death anxiety has received most of the attention from counselors and researchers: *denial*. This is a response that rejects certain key features of reality in the attempt to avoid or reduce anxiety. Peter Ivanovich denies the basic fact that he is as mortal as Ivan Ilych in order to distance himself from the death.

Many writers have urged that we should accept death. However, it is not always clear what they mean by acceptance: How does this response differ from resignation or depression? Precisely what should we accept—and on whose authority? And what is it that makes acceptance the most desirable response? Does a "good death" (Chapter 15) require acceptance? In Tolstoy's novel, Ivan Ilych eventually does achieve a sense of acceptance, but Peter Ivanovich seems to be as self-deceived and befuddled as ever.

Anxiety, denial, and acceptance are not the only death attitudes that we encounter, although most research has concentrated on these concepts. People often experience depression and a sense of loss when death is near. Although sorrow and anxiety are both distressing states of being, neither can be reduced to the other. Sorrow is oriented toward the past, anxiety toward the future. Still another strategy is to identify with death: Some people attempt to reduce their own death anxieties by joining forces with death, by killing others, whether in reality or in games and fantasies. How much harm have people done to each other when they have tried to control their own anxiety by becoming instruments of death?

STUDIES AND THEORIES OF DEATH ANXIETY

Death anxiety has attracted much attention from researchers and theorists. After identifying limitations of the prevailing methodology, we will review the main findings, and then acquaint ourselves with the theories and their implications.

Self-report questionnaires are widely used in studies of death anxiety. The measures first introduced to study death anxiety usually provided only a total score based on the number of answers that are keyed in the direction of anxiety (e.g., "I am very much afraid to die"). A later generation of measures provides more specific information, but the earlier findings established the baseline. Self-report instruments have the advantage of brevity, convenience, and simple quantitative results. There are limitations to what we can learnfrom them, however (Kastenbaum, 2000b):

1. Little is learned about the respondent's overall attitude structure or belief system; therefore, death anxiety is taken out of context and difficult to interpret.
2. Low scores on death anxiety scales are difficult to interpret. Do they mean low anxiety or high denial?
3. How high is high anxiety, and what is a "normal" level? The fact that an individual's score is higher than those of most others does not by itself demonstrate that it is "too high"—too high for what? Little has been learned about the level of death anxiety that is most useful and adaptive in various situations.
4. Respondents often are selected opportunistically. College students continue to be overrepresented, and members of ethnic and racial minorities continue to be underrepresented.
5. The typical study is a one-shot affair. How the same respondents might express their attitudes at another time or in another situation is seldom explored.

Despite these limitations, some findings have been obtained repeatedly and are worth our attention. Death anxiety research has also become somewhat more sophisticated in recent years.

MAJOR FINDINGS FROM SELF-REPORTS OF DEATH ANXIETY

Several patterns have emerged from self-report studies of death anxiety.

How Much Do We Fear Death?

Self-report studies consistently find a low to moderate level of death anxiety. Should we take these results at face value? Or should we suspect that most people are in the habit of suppressing their anxieties, trying to convince themselves and others that death holds no terror for them? However we interpret the results, it appears that most people do not consider themselves to be very anxious about death as they go about their everyday lives. I am inclined to believe that the self-report instruments measure death anxiety only when the scores are very high: when the respondent is in a genuine state of alarm.

One of the few studies to seek death anxiety in the laboratory found that people could be cool, calm, and collected on the verbal level while at the same time experiencing a strong emotional response on the neurophysiological level (Feifel & Branscomb, 1973). We are limited to the direct question verbal level in the mainstream self-report research, however, so can only speculate about what the respondents were feeling when they were providing their moderate replies.

Are There Gender Differences in Death Anxiety?

Women tend to have higher death anxiety scores on self-report scales. This pattern has now been confirmed by a survey of studies conducted in fifteen nations (Lester, et al., 2006–2007). Does this mean that women tend to be "too" anxious? Probably not. There is some evidence that women are more comfortable than men in dealing openly with their thoughts and feelings on many emotionally intense subjects, not only on those that are death-related.

Over the years I have observed that women almost always outnumber men decisively in seminars and workshops that deal with dying, death, and grief. I have met many more women than men in hospice and other caregiving situations as well (also see Chapter 5). If this is anxiety, perhaps we should be grateful for it, since relatively few "low death anxiety" men have responded to these challenges. Research findings reveal a gender difference, but do not demonstrate that women are *"too"*anxious. Most nurses reported a higher level of death anxiety than the general population, yet they also accepted death as an integral part of life. Furthermore, some of this anxiety could be attributed to their limited training in caring for people with life-threatening or terminal conditions (Brisley & Wood, 2004). Level of death anxiety tells us something, but not everything, about the way a person interprets and responds to death-related situations.

Are There Age Differences in Death Anxiety?

Does anxiety increase as the distance between ourselves and death decreases? If so, then elderly adults might be expected to express a higher level of death anxiety. Not so. Studies show either no age differences or somewhat lower death anxiety for older people. Having seen and learned much from life, many people have come to terms with death as they move through their later years. The fear of becoming helpless and dependent on others may increase, but death itself regarded as a natural ending to their lives. Episodes of intense death anxiety in elderly people often are related to relationship loss, increased health concerns, or uncertainties and also often can be relieved when the person is helped to feel safe again (Kastenbaum, 2000a).

There is still another side to death anxiety in the later adult years: Some people experience so much distress from bereavement, social isolation, financial concern, and physical ailments that they feel ready to have their lives come to an end (Kastenbaum, in press). This attitude is also reflected in the high completed suicide rates for elderly white men. Low death anxiety might then be related to dissatisfaction with the quality and prospects of life.

Death anxiety tends to be relatively high in adolescence and early adulthood. Twelker (2004) found that young adults worried more about dying. The younger respondents also had more specific worries about dying before they could do everything they wanted to do, dying alone, not being remembered, and what to expect after death. It is possible that such concerns are moderated as one's life becomes more settled and predictable. On the other hand, it is also possible that death anxiety goes underground through much of the adult life course, not so much overcome as sent back to the closet. Death anxiety is apt to rise again in later middle age, perhaps occasioned by the death of friends and family and the physical signs of one's own aging. After this rise, there is a decline to a new low in death anxiety for people in their seventies.

A recent study by Russac et al. (2007) noted that death anxiety peaked at around age twenty for both men and women. It was also found that women—but not men— experienced a secondary peak in death anxiety as they entered their fifties. Death anxiety decreases for women as they enter their sixties, and continues to be relatively low for men. Why? The researchers suggest that for many women, the age fifty spike corresponds to the end of their reproductive careers and is therefore a depressing reminder that she is growing older. They also note that the peak of death anxiety occurs at the same time that men and women reach the height of their reproductive capabilities. These are the researchers' speculations. What do you think?

Here Come the Boomers

Most of the studies reviewed here are cross-sectional. In the Russac et al. (2007) study, for example, researchers were not able to wait for twenty-year-old respondents to become fifty or eighty. It is possible, even probable, that there are generational as well as age differences at work. The baby boomer generation is a case in point. This term has usually been applied to people in the United States and the United Kingdom who were born between 1946 and 1964. Experts, however, see two population waves with significantly different cultural experiences (e.g., Gillon, 2004). Those individuals born soon after the end of World War II are the true boomers because there are so many of them. They are the product of a spike in the birthrate from 1945 until 1955. They became the first television-from-the-cradle and rock-and-roll generations and came of age during the Vietnam War era with its social tensions and unrests. By the mid 1960s, the population increase had subsided, no doubt with assistance from the newly available birth control pill.

The oldest of the boomers are now already eligible for Social Security benefits. Many have earned the right to be called the *sandwich generation* because they have had the challenge of caring for their long-lived parents as well as for their children. Aging is not especially popular with this active and achieving generation that has been keen to continue the vigor and appearance of youth. They are not the first generation with the preference to stay young and live forever (Grossman, 2000), but are perhaps the most dynamic in trying to accomplish this feat.

Boomers are falling into the many nets laid about by researchers. Benton et al. (2007) have found a close connection between aging anxiety and existential death anxiety. These researchers found that for the baby boomers retirement can reduce social status and amputate part of one's identity. Other losses follow, including the loss of family members and friends, and the physical changes that the mirror impudently reports. Age-related losses forecast further age-related losses, and then there's that *death thing* that does not seem to belong in the typical boomer's game plan. There will be more research and more insights from the boomers themselves, but it is clear that belonging to a particular generation influences our view of death as well as our style of life.

Is Death Anxiety Related to Mental Health and Illness?

Death anxiety that is high enough to be disabling is a problem at any age and may warrant the attention of professional caregivers. Generally, self-reported death anxiety is higher in people with diagnosed psychiatric conditions. It is not uncommon for mental health workers to observe panic reactions centering around death fears. Death anxiety can rush to the surface when the affected person's ego defenses are weakened and can no longer inhibit the impulses, fears, and fantasies that are ordinarily suppressed.

We should bear in mind, however, that death concern is not limited to people who are emotionally disturbed, nor to any one type of person. For example, it is not unusual to experience an upsurge of death anxiety when we realize how close we have come to being killed in a motor vehicle accident. The sudden, unexpected death of another person can have a similar effect. Situations in which people feel alone and unprotected can also arouse a passing sense of separation anxiety, which for most purposes is indistinguishable from death anxiety.

There are reasons to be both anxious about death and to keep our anxiety within bounds. People with a sound mental health status have learned to avoid the extremes of too much anxiety and too heavy a reliance on defenses against anxiety. It has also been found that people with a knack for regulating their thoughts in general are less likely to have anxious and defensive responses to death-related situations (Gailliot et al., 2006).

Does Religious Belief Lower or Raise Death Anxiety?

The influence of religion in death anxiety has been a subject of controversy for many years. Bronislaw Malinowski (1948), a pioneering anthropologist, concluded that religion has the basic function of reducing the individual's intense fear of death. A fellow anthropologist, A. R. Radcliffe-Brown (1952) came to just the opposite conclusion: Religion gives rise to fear of evil spirits, punishment, torment, and hell. Both observations are primarily based on preliterate societies and beg the question of whether or not religion serves the same function in societies at a higher level of general development.

There are substantial differences in religious belief among societies. In many tribal societies, death is believed to be followed by a life similar to the one that has just been concluded (Chapter 13). There may be anxiety about the journey through death to the next life (Kastenbaum, 2004), but the outcome is neither annihilation nor some frightening new state of being. By contrast, spirit possession is a major component in some religions, so interactions between the living and the dead are vital concerns. Fear of the dead may be more intense than fear of death, as J. G. Frazer (1933/1966) observed from his review of numerous anthropological reports. People in one society may fear eternal damnation, while in another there might be an intense taboo against contact with a dead body.

A longitudinal study in the United States studied the relationship between religiousness and fear of death and dying from youth to later adulthood (Wink & Scott, 2005). No support was found for the assumptions that highly religious people would report the lowest level of death anxiety in their later adult years. Within the limits of this study, strong religious belief did not provide an effective buffer against fear of dying and death. People who firmly believe or firmly disbelieve in religion and an afterlife report less anxiety than those with overall doubts or a "moderate belief."

Religion seems to enter into our death orientations in a complex manner. From a practical perspective, we would probably be more effective by learning how religion and death are associated for a particular person or family.

Situational Death Anxiety

The apprehension and restlessness we carry around with us in everyday life is sometimes called *trait anxiety* (Lee, W. E., Wadsworth, M. E. J.,

"High anxiety" has two meanings: fear of heights and a general state of elevated apprehension and dread. This steel worker 750 feet above New York City's famous Broadway district seems well equipped, mentally and equipment-wise to cope with at least the first type of high anxiety.

& Hotopf, M. (2006). Some of us are more "antsy" than others. However, there are situations that tend to make most people more anxious. We are gradually learning more about situational factors in death anxiety. The observations drawn upon here come primarily from clinical experience (Kastenbaum, in press).

Transitional situations often lead to a spike in death anxiety. The situations themselves may not have a direct relationship to death, but they threaten our sense of security. A list of transitional situations might well begin with separation, divorce, and other types of relationship loss. Even the exercise of imagining separation from a relationship partner can lead to more death-related thoughts (Mikulincer et al. 2002). Feeling abandoned increases our sense of vulnerability, which, on the emotional map, is not far from fear of mortality. Heightened death anxiety might pervade society during periods of financial distress, violent episodes, family separation because of military action, and whatever shakes a society's confidence in its values and competence.

Exposure to death might seem to be a situation that will increase our anxiety. Often, though, we seal off such episodes before they penetrate our awareness. Most of us have strategies for limiting the impact of an exposure to death. For example, it's too bad about the neighbor who died of pulmonary disease, but we reason that since we don't smoke the same brand of cigarettes, there is no cause to worry. However, a delayed stress reaction often arises some time after our brush with death. We might have nightmares or sudden moments of distress without quite knowing the reason or reasons. Often, this is the death-related experience getting through to us. A severe response of this type is now recognized as Post Traumatic Stress Disorder (PTSD).

The death of another person sometimes becomes the wake-up call that reminds us of our own mortality. Often it is the death of a parent, or some other significant person in our life, whom we had let ourselves assume always would be there.

Life-threatening illness can persist for weeks, months, even years. During this extended period, people are likely to have a variety of thoughts and feelings about their situations. The first jolt often occurs when people discover that their illnesses are life-threatening or terminal. Suicidal thoughts might occur at this time. A second period of anxiety arousal may occur later, accompanied by depression, as a result of continuing physical decline and fatigue. At this point the anxiety may be focused more on the fear of abandonment and suffering for no good reason, rather than on death itself. Other moments of anxiety can develop when a new medical complication arises or a new treatment is proposed. Nevertheless, drawing upon their own resources and support from family and friends, many people can cope with a life-threatening situation without experiencing intense anxiety. Effective communication, symptom relief, and a positive worldview contribute much to anxiety reduction. Family members also are under stress and can experience death-related anxiety (Adelbratt & Strang, 2000). The anxieties of patient, family members, and professional caregivers can form a continuous loop of mutual distress.

THEORETICAL PERSPECTIVES ON DEATH ANXIETY

There are two classic theories of death anxiety, and they could hardly be more opposed to each other.

Early Psychoanalytic Theory

Sigmund Freud reasoned that we could not really be anxious about death:

> Our own death is indeed quite unimaginable, and whenever we make the attempt to imagine it we can perceive that we really survive as spectators . . . at bottom nobody believes in his own death, or to put the same thing in a different way, in the unconscious everyone of us is convinced of his own immortality (1913/1953, p. 304).

Our "unconscious system" does not respond to the passage of time, so the end of personal time through death would not register. Again, on the unconscious level, we do not have the concept of negation, so there is no death to cancel out life. Furthermore, we have not actually experienced death. When we express death anxiety, it is only a cover story. For many years psychoanalysts spoke of *thanatophobia* as the expressed fear of death that serves as a disguise for the actual source of discomfort. Their mission was to dig, dig, dig until unearthing the underlying fear.

What, then, do we fear, if it is not death? Freud's answer was not exactly his finest moment: thanatophobia derives from the castration anxiety experienced during our normally abnormal psychosexual development. In a nutshell, boy loves his mother and fears that his father will cut him down to size for expressing this desire. Freud's description of the Oedipus complex has enjoyed a flourishing career in fiction, drama, and popular psychology, but it does not succeed here. There are numerous flaws in this explanation. For example, if people have not been dead before, it is also the case that very few have been castrated. To use Freud's own reasoning, how could they then be afraid of this calamity? Castration anxiety is even more a stretch when applied to females. The assertion that girls feel they have already been castrated because they don't have what boys have deserves all the ridicule it has reaped over the years.

However, Freud's castration–death anxiety theory could be interpreted more generously. He admitted to making up little stories as a way of expressing new ideas. In this case, Freud might well have been suggesting that the source of death anxiety is the fear of losing value, love, and security by being less than a whole person. People who feel they are losing or have lost their sense of security in the world might well experience this generalized confusion and fear as death anxiety. This is an interpretation that does ring true with clinical observations. People who feel they cannot control the frightening things that are happening (or might happen) to them often experience an upsurge in death anxiety (Kastenbaum, 2000a).

The bottom line for the early psychoanalytic position is clear, even if the explanation is open to question: Way down deep, we cannot comprehend our own annihilation; therefore, our anxieties can only seem to be about death.

The Existential Challenge

The *existential* position takes the opposite approach: Awareness of our mortality is the basic source of anxiety. Our fears take many forms but they can be traced back to our sense of vulnerability to death. Ernest Becker (1973) believed that death anxiety is at the root of severe psychopathology, such as *schizophrenia*. People with schizophrenia suffer because they do not have enough insulation from the fear of death. The rest of us might share the schizophrenic's panic if our society did not work so hard to protect us from the *ontological confrontation*—the awareness that we are always and acutely mortal.

Society's primary function is to help us all pretend that life will continue to go on and on. This is accomplished by a belief system that is supported with rituals and symbols that produce a sense of coherence, predictability, and meaning. It is a comforting illusion in which most of us are willing participants. We feel that we are part of something bigger, more powerful, and more durable than ourselves. Monumental edifices throughout the world contribute to the illusion of our invulnerability. From this standpoint, the destruction of the World Trade Center towers would be thought to have had a profound, unsettling effect on all of us by allowing our death anxiety to break through the cracks in society's protective posture.

Becker's writings stimulated the development of *terror management theory* (Tomer, 2002), which suggests that we try to control our death anxiety by socially sanctioned evasions and fantasies. There are two facets to this strategy: Keep up our own self-esteem, and become an integral part of an entity greater than ourselves. Religious belief and practice could go a long way to meeting this collective need. However, faith can be undermined by disasters that overtake society (e.g., virulent epidemics, famine) as well as by radically changing circumstances (e.g., the rise of science and technology). Fortunately, we have the alternative strategy available: to feel so confident and competent about ourselves that we can master death threats through our own strengths. And we are doubly protected when we feel strong personally in a strong society. If one of these foundations is shaken, then it is time to depend on the other foundation.

A productive series of studies has refined and supported terror management theory (Pyszezynski et al., 2004 for a review of the pioneering research). Most of the results are consistent with the proposition that exposure to mortality salience is defended by the most available strategy: counting on one's own resources, or holding on tighter to society. Helping to strengthen people's self-esteem seems to decrease death anxiety. Other studies have found that people tend to become more defensive when reminded of their mortality and then try to control their anxiety by focusing on the worldviews from which they draw comfort (Tomer, 2002). Schmeichel and Martens (2005) summarize the terror management approach for us: Cultural worldviews buffer us from fearful preoccupation with our own impermanence, vulnerability, and mortality (p. 658).

Terror management theory is continuing to guide a variety of interesting studies and has shown the flexibility to modify its working hypotheses as the results come in. Two concerns have not yet been addressed, however: (1) Are these studies actually tapping into the depths of existential terror—or (2) are they just arousing a little discomfort in the usual suspects (college students) who are responding to the research cues within the relatively safe academic environment? It seems a long way from the anguish and despair of mortal terror to the controlled setting and circumstances of the research. The other concern is the assumption that society is devoted 100 percent to the amelioration of death anxiety. This proposition has been contradicted repeatedly by societies that have deliberately promoted death anxiety in order to incite the population into violence against a supposed demonic enemy, or for other power-control purposes. Terror management can be a tool used either to raise or lower anxiety level.

Edge Theory

Both the Freudian and the existential positions on death anxiety make basic assumptions that seem beyond empirical investigation. How can we know with any degree of certainty what the unconscious system knows or does not know (even if we accept the reality of unconscious processes)? How can we prove all anxieties have their roots in the fear of nonbeing? Why is it that most people do not report a high and disabling level of death anxiety but also do not completely deny such feelings? The typical report of a moderate level of death anxiety supports neither the psychoanalytic nor the existential positions. There are many useful observations in the writings of insightful psychoanalysts and existentialists, but their propositions are open to question.

There is room for other theories as well. I have proposed an *edge theory* that distinguishes between our everyday low level of death anxiety and the vigilant state that is aroused when we encounter danger (Kastenbaum, 2000b). The experience of death anxiety is the self-awareness side of a complex organismic response to danger. Anxiety has its survival function; it is not always something to be sedated or rebuked. We feel ourselves to be at the very edge of the safe and known, perhaps just one step away from disaster. Edge theory emphasizes our survival and adaptation functions—the ability to detect sources of potential harm both through built-in biomechanisms and through the development of cognitive and social skills. There is no need to be anxious all the time; in fact, this would be an exhausting and ineffective way to function. However, there are dangerous situations in this world, and we might save our own or somebody else's life by moving quickly to an emergency footing when confronted by a significant threat.

The first emergency responders to the World Trade Center attacks showed a remarkable blend of alarm and control. They neither ignored nor faltered in the face of an overwhelming threat to life. Most of us do not have their training and experience to cope with emergent disasters, but we can hone our own danger response systems to provide enough anxiety to provoke our attention but also to exercise enough control and balance to survive the situation.

Whatever reduces our everyday stress level is likely to improve our ability to detect and respond to actual threats. A relaxed attitude is also more likely to free us to discover opportunities for adventure, creativity, and more rewarding relationships. Despite their differences, all the theories mentioned here agree that feeling at peace with ourselves and secure—but not overconfident—in our abilities can reduce death anxiety without compromising our ability to cope with threats.

ACCEPTING AND DENYING DEATH

We now focus on death-related feelings, attitudes, and actions within our everyday lives.

Sitting in his favorite chair after dinner, the man suddenly went pale. He felt severe pain in his chest, and had to gasp for breath. His wife was by his side in a moment. "What's wrong? Oh! I'll get the doctor, the hospital." The man struggled for control and waved his hand feebly in a dismissive gesture. "It's nothing—really. . . . I'll just lie down till it goes away."

This scene, with variations, has become familiar to health care professionals. The concept of denial comes to mind when a person has delayed seeking diagnosis and treatment for a life-threatening condition, as well as in other situations in which the mortality salience is not acknowledged. Accepting the reality of serious illness can increase anxiety but also increase the chances of survival. There is often a subtle interplay between our impulses to accept and deny death-related events.

Is It Really Denial?

"Acceptance" and "denial" are used in a variety of ways and their meanings can become blurred and misleading. From a psychiatric standpoint, denial is regarded as a primitive defense. It rejects the existence of threat. This strategy may be effective for a short period of time and for situations in which there is an overwhelming threat. However, denial becomes increasingly ineffective when prolonged or used repeatedly: We do not survive long in the world when we ignore crucial aspects of reality. Denial is most often found in a person who is suffering from a psychotic reaction, or as any person's first response to crisis and catastrophe.

Denial in this fundamental sense is not usually part of our everyday repertoire of coping strategies. But we do engage in a number of behaviors that have some resemblance to denial. "Oh, she's just in denial!" people say, when the individual in question has only engaged in a strategic evasive action. By using

For Better or For Worse®

this term as a buzzword, we often come to glib and premature conclusions. Often, people are not denying in the psychiatric sense of the term: a primitive and ineffective mechanism. Rather, they are coping with difficult situations in the most resourceful ways they can discover at the moment. This will become clearer as we distinguish among several processes, all of which can be mistaken for denial (Box 1-1):

1. *Selective attention.* Imagine a situation in which many stimuli and events are competing for our attention. We cannot give equal attention to everything that is going on. A person who has never been in a hospital before, for example, might find many new, interesting, and challenging things to observe. These may seem more vivid than something as abstract as the diagnosis and prognosis that eventually will be made. This often happens with children. The individual is not in denial, but simply directing his or her attention to whatever seems most salient in the immediate situation.

2. *Selective response.* A person exhibiting this behavior may have significant thoughts and feelings about death. However, the person has judged that this is not the time or place to express them. The person may think, I'm not going to open up to this young doctor who looks more scared than I

am, or there is nothing more I can do about the situation at this moment, so I will talk about something else, or just keep quiet. The person may also decide that there is something very important I must accomplish while I still have the opportunity, and it must take priority over dealing with my approaching death. Therefore, the person who may seem to be denying death might actually be working very hard at completing tasks in full awareness that time is running out.

3. *Compartmentalizing.* The person is aware of being in a life-threatening situation, and is responding to some aspects. But something is missing: the connection between one aspect of the situation and another. For example, the person may know that their prognosis is poor. This is an accurate perception: No denial is involved. The person may also be cooperating with treatment and rationally discussing the situation (adaptive response, and there's still no denial). Yet this same person may also be making future plans that involve travel or an exercise program, as if expecting to be around and in good health for years to come. In compartmentalizing, much of the dying and death reality is acknowledged, but the person stops just short of *realizing* the situation. All the pieces are there, but

---

BOX 1-1   DENIAL AND DENIAL-LIKE RESPONSES TO DEATH

- *Selective attention*
  "I will feel less anxious if I don't allow myself to notice some things."

- *Selective response*
  "It would be better if I did not let others know how I feel right now."

- *Compartmentalizing*
  "One subtracted from one will not be zero as long as I keep these two numbers separate from each other."

- *Deception*
  "I will deliberately mislead you in order to reduce your anxiety and mine."

- *Resistance*
  "Of course I know that my life is in danger—but I'm not going to give in to it in any way."

- *Denial*
  "A touch of indigestion, that's all."

the individual resists putting them together to complete the whole picture.

4. *Deception*. People sometimes deliberately give false information to others. This takes place in dying and death situations, too. When people are telling each other lies (for whatever purpose), it makes sense to acknowledge this deceptive action for what it is and not confuse the issue with the buzzword *denial.*

5. *Resistance*. People who are in stressful situations may recognize their danger but decide not to "give in" to it. Some people in war-torn Bosnia, for example, decided to go about their daily rounds of shopping and visiting, although these activities increased their vulnerability to snipers. They were not denying the death risk. Rather, they had resolved to defy the war and keep their spirits up by not becoming prisoners to fear. A person who has been diagnosed with an incurable medical condition might become angry instead of anxious and adopt an "I'll show them!" attitude. And sometimes, as we all know, a person with an apparently terminal condition does recover. There is a significant difference between the person who cannot accept the reality of his or her fate and the person who comprehends the reality but decides to fight for life as long as possible.

6. *Denial* (the real thing). This is the basic defensive process that was defined earlier in this chapter. The person is not just selecting among possible perceptions and responses, limiting the logical connections between one phenomenon and the other, or engaging in conscious deception. Rather, the self appears to be totally organized against recognizing its death-laden reality. Such an orientation can be bizarre and may accompany a psychotic reaction. It does not have to be that extreme, however. We can sometimes detect the existence of a true denial process that weaves in and out of other, more sophisticated, ways of coping.

Temporary denial responses can be experienced by anybody who is under extreme stress. Denial responses are often seen in the wake of overwhelming catastrophes. For example, a woman was discovered intently sweeping the floor of her home after a tornado had passed through the city; the floor was practically all that was left of her home. Another woman was so debilitated by her long illness that she could no longer take nourishment by mouth or carry out other basic activities of everyday life. She had participated actively in decisions about her impending death: cremation, a simple memorial service, gifts to her church's youth program in lieu of flowers, and so forth. One morning, though, she astonished her visitors by showing them a set of travel brochures and her new sunglasses. She spoke of feeling so much better and was as eager as can be to take a long-delayed vacation. Two days later, however, she was dead.

The Interpersonal Side of Acceptance and Denial

Each person in a dying and death situation influences and is influenced by the others. The acceptance/denial process is interpersonal as well as intrapsychic. Furthermore, both the immediate situation and the historical background must be considered. One man may come from an ethnic background that treats dying and death in a straightforward manner (e.g., the traditional Amish). But suppose that person finds himself dealing with a medical establishment where death is still a high-anxiety taboo topic. Here is a potential death accepter trapped among the deniers. The reverse can also happen. Consider a woman who grew up learning how to deny death, especially the deeper emotions that it evokes. Suppose she becomes a patient in a health care establishment where the staff is relentless in practicing its belief that we must be open and sharing with each other. Here, then, is the death denier confronted by the accepters. We need to be aware of the forces operating in the present situation and the individual's previous life pattern in order to understand what is taking place between the dying person and the caregiver.

Weisman (1972) has observed that a person does not usually deny everything about death to everybody. More often, a selective process is involved. We must go beyond the question, "Is this person denying death?" It is more useful to ask instead, "What aspects of dying or death are being shared with what other people, under what circumstances, and why?" The same questions could be asked about acceptance—a person might "deny" with one friend and "accept" with another. Apparent denial on the part of the patient may derive from a lack of responsive people in their environment.

A related point has to do with the function of denial. The purpose of denial, according to Weisman, is not simply to avoid a danger, but to prevent the loss of a significant relationship. All of the adaptive processes that have been described here might be used, then, to help the other person feel comfortable enough to maintain a vitally needed relationship. The individual faced with death may have to struggle as much with the other person's anxiety as with his or her own. Instead of placing the negative label of denial upon these adaptive efforts, we might instead appreciate the care and sensitivity with which they are often carried out.

Anxiety, Denial, and Acceptance: How Should We Respond?

Anxiety is an uncomfortable, at times almost unbearable, condition. It would be a mistake, however, to consider anxiety in completely negative terms. Small doses of anxiety can alert us to danger: "Something's wrong here, what?" Anxiety can also prepare us for action: "I've been on stage a thousand times and a bundle of nerves a thousand times—but that's just how I want to feel before the curtain goes up!"

The response strategies of acceptance and denial likewise are not necessarily good or bad in themselves. We must examine the contexts in which these processes are used and the purposes they seem to be serving. If what we are calling denial really is denial, then we may be dealing with someone who is making a desperate stand against catastrophe. The person has been forced to fall back on a primitive defense process that rejects important aspects of reality. This individual needs psychological help and, quite possibly, other types of help as well.

On the other hand, the person may not be denying so much as selectively perceiving, linking, and responding to what is taking place. The coping pattern might include evasion, but there is also method, judgment, and purpose at work. Even flashes of pure denial may contribute to overall adaptation, as when challenges come too swiftly, last too long, or are too overwhelming to meet in other ways. A little later, the individual may have found another way to deal with the same challenge, once the first impact has been partially deflected and partially absorbed.

I suggest that we proceed with the following set of premises:

1. Most of us have both acceptance and denial-type strategies that are available for coping with stressful situations. These strategies may operate within or outside our clear awareness, and one strategy or the other may dominate at various times.
2. States of total acceptance and total denial of death do occur, but usually in extreme circumstances: when the individual is letting go of life after achieving a sense of completion and having struggled as long as struggling seemed worthwhile, or when the individual is resisting the first onslaught of catastrophic reality. These experiences can have a profound spiritual resonance.
3. Much that is called denial can be understood more adequately as adaptive processes by which the person responds selectively to various aspects of a difficult situation.
4. Our pattern of adaptation should be considered within the context of our interpersonal network. Do we interact mostly with people who share and listen, who avoid conversations on difficult issues, or who are quick to pass judgment? Family, friends, and colleagues can make it either easier or more difficult to find our way through the anxiety of life-threatening situations.
5. Acceptance and denial can be evaluated only when we are in a position to understand what the person is trying to accomplish and what he or she is up against.

In the Shade of the Jambu Tree

At the start of this chapter, we made a brief visit to the exotic land of the Uttarakurus where the magic Jambu tree grows and people live 1,000 or perhaps, 11,000 years. Sounds good—especially if we want to keep the thought of death as distant as possible. Attempts to remove the sting from the prospect of death have stimulated more than beguiling legends. Influential worldviews have been formed around the core issue of what should be done with death. A significant example is Taoism, a major philosophical-religious system that developed in ancient and medieval China and continues to contribute to world thought and culture. Our eyes see a diversity of forms and activities as well as a relentless process of change. It is up to our minds to comprehend what cannot be so easily perceived: the basic unity of nature. Tao (pronounced "dow") is translated as *The Way*. It is the force that both moves and unites all that exists. We, in the western world, may be in the habit of separating mind from matter, for example, but both are within the flow of the Tao.

What we call life and what we call death are also facets of the Tao as the same reality underlies both. This sense of an affinity or communion between life and death is part of the Taoist answer to death. There is also a more activist dimension; though. Life can be prolonged by drawing upon the power of the Tao. In practical terms, this ancient philosophy led to forms of exercise, diet, and the use of natural substances (such as herbs) that were thought to strengthen health and preserve life. Present-day fitness regimes were prefigured in Taoist philosophy and practice.

Chemistry, biology, pharmacology, metallurgy, and other sciences and technologies also were given impetus by Taoist philosophy (Gruman, 2003). Nature has secrets that might be divined by patient study and moments of inspired observation. We can live longer and better and therefore, keep the simmering pot of death anxiety from boiling over. Chinese alchemy devoted much of its attention to the prolongation of life, and this also became one of the prime goals of alchemy when it developed in Western culture. (Transforming base metals into precious metals was also an ardent pursuit, but a life free from death anxiety was the true gold standard.)

Thinking of life, we are also at least implicitly thinking of death. Thinking of death, we are attracted to the idea of a life that somehow flourishes, continues, and renews despite a universe that seems to have other plans. Perhaps, each of us can find our own comfort zone in which life can be enjoyed while death is given its due.

SUMMARY

Not thinking about death has often been a failed experiment throughout human history. Listening and communicating are far more helpful approaches. You monitored your own knowledge, attitudes, beliefs, and feelings about death in a series of self-inventories. These exercises provided you with a stronger base for looking at the way other people think about death and how state of mind can affect death-related behavior.

We reminded ourselves that our personal orientations toward death are far from simple. For example, although the survival motive is powerful, sometimes we delight in risk-taking behaviors. The dynamics of accepting and denying death were explored with the help of characters in Leo Tolstoy's probing novel *The Death of Ivan Ilych*. We then looked carefully at the core concepts of anxiety, denial, and acceptance. Freudian and existential theories offer competing ideas about death anxiety and its place in our lives. Recent studies have supported terror management theory, derived from Ernst Becker's existential approach. Cultural worldviews and personal self-esteem seem to be important buffers against the experience of intense death anxiety, but both sources of support are subject to breakdown. We respond differently when reminded of death (*mortality salience*), and even more so when our vulnerability to death is exposed by a threatening situation. Most people report themselves to have a low to moderate level of death anxiety, with women having somewhat higher scores.

The baby boomer generation is now experiencing the challenges of aging and the prospect of death. It is probable that generational influences on the ways we negotiate life and death will become more evident from now on. We also saw that denial is a generalizing term with regards to death. Some responses that are misinterpreted as denial are better understood as selective attention, selective response, compartmentalizing, deception, or resistance. Attention was also given to the kind of interactions we have with each other in death-related situations, and some suggestions were offered. The ancient philosophical-religious system of Taoism provides an influential example of thinking about life and death as unified in the reality underlying all that exists.

REFERENCES

Adelbratt, S., & Strang, P. (2000). Death anxiety in brain tumor patients and their spouses. *Palliative Medicine, 14,* 499–507.

Ai, L. A., Park, C. L., Huang, B., Rodgers, W., & Tice, T.N. (2007). Psychosocial mediation of religious coping styles: A study of short-term psychological distress following cardiac surgery. *Personality and Social Psychology Bulletin, 33,* 867–882.

Becker, E. (1973). *The denial of death.* New York: Free Press.

Benson, J. F., Christopher, A. N., & Walter, M. I. (2007). Death anxiety as a function of aging anxiety. *Death Studies, 31,* 337–350.

Brisley, P., & Wood, L.-M. (2004). The impact of education and experience on death anxiety in new graduate nurses. *Contemporary Nurse, 17.*

CNN (2004, July 7). Several trampled by Pamplona bulls. http://cnn.com/2004/WORLD/Europe/07/07/spain.Pamplona

Epicurus. In Warren, J. (2004). *Epicurus and his critics.* New York: Oxford University Press.

Feifel, H., & Branscomb, A. B. (1973). Who's afraid of death? *Journal of Abnormal Psychology, 81,* 282–288.

Frazer, J. G. (1966). *The fear of the dead in primitive religion.* New York: Biblo & Tannen. (Original work published 1933.)

Freud, S. (1953). *Thoughts for the times on war and death.* In *Collected works* (Vol. 4, pp. 288–317). London: Hogarth. (Original work published 1913.)

Gailliot, M. T., Schmeichel, B. J., & Baumeister, R. F. (2006). Self-regulatory processes defend against the threat of death: Effects of self-control and trait self-control on thoughts and fears of dying. *Journal of Personality and Social Psychology, 91,* 49–62.

Gillon, S. (2004). Boomer nation: *The largest and richest generation ever and how it changed America.* Glencoe, Ill: Free Press.

Grossman, T. (2000) *The baby boomers' guide to living forever.* Golden, Colorado: Hubristic Press.

Gruman, G. J. (2003). *A history of ideas about the prolongation of life.* New York: Springer.

Jacinto, L. (December 11, 2002). Death by fire. Forced marriages are driving some women to self-immolation. ABCNEWS.com

Johnson, J., & Williams, C. (October 7, 2007). Roller coaster still stalling, riders injured. *Washington Post,* p. CO3.

Kastenbaum, R. (2000a). Counseling the elderly dying patient. In V. Molinari (Ed.), *Professional psychology in long term care* (pp. 201–226).

Kastenbaum, R. (2000b). *The psychology of death.* (3rd ed.). New York: Springer.

Kastenbaum, R. (2004). *On our way. The final passage through life and death.* Berkeley: University of California Press.

Kastenbaum, R. (In press). Death anxiety. In G. Fink (Ed.), *Encyclopedia of stress.* (2nd ed.). New York: Academic Press.

Kastenbaum, R., & Briscoe, L. (1975). The street corner. A laboratory for the study of life-threatening behavior. *Omega, Journal of Death and Dying, 7,* 351–359.

Lee, W. E., Wadsworth, M. E. J., & Hotopf, M. (2006). The protective role of trait anxiety: A longitudinal study. *Psychological Medicine, 36,* 345–351.

Lester, D., Templer, D. I., & Abdel-Khalek, A. (2006–2007). A cross-cultural comparison of death anxiety: A brief note. *Omega, Journal of Death and Dying, 54,* 255–260.

Lock, M. (2002). *Twice dead. Organ transplants and the reinvention of death.* Berkeley: University of California Press.

Malinowski, B. (1948). *Magic, science, and religion and other essays.* Garden City, NJ: Doubleday.

Mikulincer, M., Florian, V., Birnbaum, G., & Malishkevich, S. (2002). The death-buffering function of close relationships: Exploring the effects of separation reminders on death-thought accessibility. *Personality and Social Psychology Bulletin, 28,* 287–299.

Peck, P. (November 16, 2005). American Heart Association: Thrill-a-Minute Roller Coaster rides may be dangerous to our hearts. http://medpagetoday.com/cardiology/arrythmia/tb/2159

Quill, T. E. (1993). *Death and dignity.* New York: Free Press.

Radcliffe-Brown, A. R. (1952). *Structure and function in primitive society.* New York: Free Press.

Robbins, R. A. (1990). Signing an organ donor's card: Psychological factors. *Death Studies, 14,* 219–230.

Russac, R. J., Gotliff, C., Reece, M., & Spottswood, D. (2007). Death anxiety across the adult years: An examination of age and gender effects. *Death Studies, 31,* 549–561.

Schmeichel, B. J., & Martens, A. (2005). Self-affirmation and mortality salience: Affirming values reduces worldview defense and death-thought accessibility. *Personality and Social Psychology Bulletin, 31,* 658–667.

Tolstoy, L. (1960). *The death of Ivan Ilych.* New York: The New American Library. (Original work published 1886).

Tomer, A. (2002). Terror management theory. In R. Kastenbaum (Ed.), *Macmillan encyclopedia of death and dying* (Vol. 2, pp. 885–887). New York: Macmillan.

Twelker, P. A. (2004). The relationship between death anxiety, sex, and age. www.tiu.edu/psychology/deathanxiety.htm

VandeCreek, L., & Frankowski, D. (1996). Barriers that predict resistance to completing a living will. *Death Studies, 20,* 73–82.

Weisman, A. D. (1972). *On dying and denying.* New York: Behavioral Publications, Inc.

Wink, P., & Scott, J. (2005). Does religiousness buffer against the fear of death and dying in late adulthood? Findings from a longitudinal study. *Journal of Gerontology, 60B,* 207–214.

GLOSSARY

Collective Representations: The symbols and themes that convey the spirit and mood of a culture.

Death anxiety: Emotional distress and insecurity aroused by encounters with dead bodies, grieving people, or other reminders of mortality, including one's own thoughts.

Denial: An extreme response in which one attempts to cope with danger or loss by ignoring important features of reality.

Edge theory: A theoretical approach that emphasizes the survival function of death-related anxiety.

Existentialism: A philosophical position that emphasizes people's responsibilities for their own lives and deaths.

Fatalism: The belief that future events have already been determined; therefore, one is powerless to affect the future.

Living will: A document that instructs medical personnel on an individual's wishes should a situation arise in which that person cannot communicate directly. Often involves the request for limiting the type of medical interventions. The living will is one of a class of documents known as advance directives (Chapter 6).

Mortality salience: A situation that is likely to bring thoughts of death to mind. Related to *Ontological confrontation* but is often not as threatening.

Ontological confrontation: A situation that sharply reminds people of their personal vulnerabilities to death.

Post-traumatic stress disorder: A delayed response to a death or other disturbing experience that has occurred under extremely stressful conditions. The traumatic event is re-experienced repeatedly, and other disturbances of feelings, thoughts, and behavior are also likely to occur.

Schizophrenia: A form of mental, and perhaps biomedical, illness in which a person is out of contact with reality and emotionally alienated from others.

Taoism: An ancient and still-influential Chinese philosophical-religious system that sees life and death as linked in a fundamental reality that underlies the apparent diversity, change, and disorder of the observable world.

Terror management theory: A theory based on the proposition that many of our sociocultural beliefs, symbols, and practices are intended to reduce our sense of vulnerability and helplessness in prospect of death.

Thanatophobia: Fear of death.

Uniform anatomical gift act: A law that permits people, upon their own deaths, to designate their bodily organs for transplantation to other people.

ON FURTHER THOUGHT . . .

Useful Reference Books for Exploring Death-Related Topics

Bryant, C. D. (Ed.). (2003). *Handbook of death and dying.* Two volumes. Thousand Oaks, CA: Sage.

Kastenbaum, R. (Ed.). (2002). *Macmillan encyclopedia of death and dying.* Two volumes. New York: Macmillan.

Stroebe, M. S., Hansson, R. O., Schut, H., and Stroebe, W. (2008). Handbook of bereavement research and practice. Washington, D.C.: American Psychological Association.

Stroebe, M. S., Hansson, R. O., Stroebe, W., & Schut, H. (Eds.). (2001). *Handbook of bereavement research.* Washington, DC: American Psychological Association.

Taylor, R. P. (2000). *Death and the afterlife. A cultural encyclopedia.* Santa Barbara, CA: ABC-CLIO.

Scholarly and Professional Journals

Death Studies   www.tandf.co.uk
Illness, Crisis, and Loss   www.baywood.com
Mortality   www.tandf.co.uk
Omega, Journal of Death and Dying   www.baywood.com
Suicide and Life-Threatening Behavior   www.guilford.com

Shiva, the Hindu Lord of Dance, is represented here in an eleventh-century statue on display at London's Royal Academy of Arts. There is a god of death and a god of regeneration: Shiva is both.

chapter **2**

WHAT IS DEATH?

What Does Death Mean?

I shouldn't smoke. I need a smoke. I shouldn't smoke.
Why shouldn't you?
The burning is so painful. It hurts the tobacco so much.
Does the tobacco feel pain?
It has a soul. Everything has a soul. Everything feels pain. But I need to smoke! (Tears of anguish in his eyes)
Are you feeling pain, too?
(Registering surprise at the question.) Dead men don't feel pain.
I need a smoke
—Author's conversation with psychiatric patient (1958)

Before he died he said that his skin had come on fire, with the feeling of insects crawling beneath it. A scar he bore on his right cheek just to the edge of his mouth had been caused by a nail driven through the coffin.
—Reported by Wade Davis (1988)

In all the darkest pages of the malign supernatural there is no more terrible tradition than that of the Vampire, a pariah even among demons. Foul are his ravages; gruesome and seemingly barbaric are the ancient and approved methods by which folk must rid themselves of this hideous pest.
—Montague Summers (1928)

I collected the instruments of life around me, that I might infuse a spark of being into the lifeless thing that lay at my feet. It was already one in the morning; the rain pattered dismally against the panes, and my candle was nearly burnt out, when, by the glimmer of the half-extinguished light, I saw the dull yellow eye of the creature open; it breathed hard, and convulsive motion agitated its limbs.
—Victor Frankenstein, in Mary Shelley's *Frankenstein* (1818/1977, p. 72)

I carefully noted the simulated positions of seventeen different kinds of insects belonging to different genera, both poor and first-rate shammers. Afterwards I procured naturally dead specimens of some of these insects . . . others I killed with camphor by a slow easy death; the result was that in no instance was the attitude exactly the same, and in several instances the attitudes of the feigners and of the really dead were as unlike as they could possibly be.
—Charles Darwin's notebook as quoted by Carrington & Meader (1921)

Plastination reveals the beauty beneath the skin, frozen in time between death and decay.
—Dr. Gunther von Hagens (2005)

You are the nurse. Or the physician, hospital administrator, clergyperson, or lawyer. Perhaps instead you are the family member. The person in this bed does not seem responsive or able to survive without intensive care. Make your diagnosis:

Akinetic mutism?	*Brain damage?*
Brain-dead?	*Catatonia?*
Coma?	*Locked-in Syndrome?*
Minimally conscious state?	*Permanent vegetative state?*
Persistent vegetative state?	*Transient vegetative state?*

—A situation that is occurring more often

Even though a person may be "dead" because his heart stops working, some muscle, skin and bone cells may live on for many days. So, while the entire person as a functioning organism is dead, parts of the biologic organism live on for varying periods of time. The amount of time these cells and tissues live depends on their ability to survive without oxygen and other nutrients, and with an increasing amount of metabolic waste products building up within them. . . . Then when is a person dead?
—Kenneth V. Iserson, M.D. (2001, p. 3)

Death is NOT to be ruled by the mere lifting of life support until it is certain that the soul has departed the body.
—Dr. Bakr Abu Zaid (2002, p. 3)

Then, when lust hath conceived, it bringeth forth sin; and Sin, when it is finished, bringeth forth death.
—New Testament, James: 1:15

Death? It's a change of clothes. That's all!
—Interview respondent

Death? I see him as very patient and very polite. He waits for each of us some place, just around a corner or even at the foot of our bed. I think of him as being there all the time, but only when we can see him is he there for us. He doesn't have to say anything and neither do we. He knows what he's here for and he knows we know.
—Respondent in a study of death personification

IDEAS ABOUT THE NATURE AND MEANING OF DEATH

Death is the end of life, right? But wait—perhaps death is what begins *after* the end of life. Anyhow, it is clear that we are either alive or we are dead. Existence, nonexistence, it's digital! What else do we know for sure? Some of us know for sure that death is the implacable enemy of life. Others of us know for sure that death is the portal through which we enter a higher form of existence. And, yes, some of us are capable of holding both these beliefs at the same time without the frown of a doubt.

In the preceding paragraph we muddled through several of the dominating assumptions in mainstream Western tradition. We might have difficulty in realizing that life and death are regarded quite differently by many other people. In Hindu philosophy, for example, birth, death, rebirth, and, then again, death are linked in a constantly recurring cycle (Kramer, 2003). We are born to die, but we die to be reborn. For another example, there is a resilient ancient tradition that recognizes intermediate conditions between alive and dead.

What we mean by "death" becomes of practical importance when we when we draw upon these assumptions in making life decisions or communicate with others who have a different conception. We begin, then, by exposing ourselves to competing ideas about the nature and meaning of death. We ask: What is this death that one person accepts and another person denies? That one person seeks and another person avoids? That one person cannot stop thinking about and another person believes is hardly worth thinking about?

Not only do individuals differ in their attitudes and feelings, but the same person may differ from situation to situation—as when I noticed that the starboard engine of the ancient DC-3 had burst into flames. *Death* was no longer a word for scholarly contemplation, but the enlivening prospect of a rapid plunge into the green hills of West Virginia. Years later as pretty much an inert lump on an intensive care unit, I felt death to be already with me. He was being slow and casual about his work and somehow not as interesting as I would have supposed (Kastenbaum, 2004). Many survivors of near-death experiences have reported an enduring change in their conceptions of death and life alike (Chapter 13). There are practical consequences resulting from the fact that death can mean different things to different people, or different things to the same person at different times. If you and I hold varying assumptions about the nature of death, then we may also take different courses of action at decisive moments.

We return now to the opening quotations to become more familiar with the variety of ways in which death has been conceived.

The psychiatric patient was housed in a high security building on the campus of a Veterans Administration Hospital. Nobody seemed to know precisely what he had experienced as a lieutenant in the Pacific island phase of World War II combat, but he had returned broken in body and mind. Now he had his health back, but now he was also neither eating nor speaking. Just looking at him, you could see he had been through hell and brought hell back with him. Somehow we bonded. The cigarette episode was one in which he expressed himself with a deeply wounded innocence.

> I see tears in your eyes. You are feeling pain now.
> Touch your cheeks,
> Feel your tears.
> Are those my tears?
> It hurts so much to be alive.
> (Pause. Lights cigarette. Pause.)
> (With great deliberation, as though each word cost him something.)
> No more war.

This man felt deadened and sometimes felt dead. Nevertheless, there was still a roiling desperation that might come out some time in a violent action, or given the chance to filter through in a way that might improve his quality of life. Feeling dead is an exhausting way of going through life, and it not that uncommon for people with major emotional distress.

A "dead man walking" condition can also be a cultural as well as an individual phenomenon. Clairvius Narcisse could be classified as a recovered zombi. He recovered first from being a corpse, and then from being a drudge laborer who had only the ability to follow simple orders. Unlike the unfortunate lieutenant, Narcisse had literally returned from the grave (if the evidence be trusted). He seemed to have taken something of death back with him, although eventually recovering his personality.

The vampire is perhaps the most spectacular creature who commutes between life and death. Today our image of the vampire is strongly conditioned by the Hollywood and television versions, including an apparently unlimited supply of parodies. Montague Summers re-introduced the earlier and earthier version in his classic *The vampire and his kith and kin* (1928). The vampire still has something to teach us, and so we will meeting him/her again, along with the revenant and the zombi in a section devoted to the undead.

The elegant and agile Archer depicted in this chapter is a remarkable example of a new way to appreciate life through death. Anatomist Gunther von Hagens developed a tissue preservation technique known as *plastination*. Death has always been associated with decay. Plastination replaces the fluids and lipids in biological tissues with polymers (such as silicone, epoxy, and polyesters). The result is a dry, odorless and durable specimen that can be studied by generations of medical students. Often the focus is on a particular body part, such as a region of the nervous system. However, von Hagens also created a gallery of life-like figures from plastinated corpses. Like her companion figures, The Archer offers a distinctive opportunity to view both the human body in an action position and a special anatomical feature: Her brain is situated above the skull for easier viewing. Two traveling BodyWorlds exhibits have impressed and educated millions of museum visitors in Asia, Europe, and North America. Dr. von Hagen's stated objective includes respect for the human body in life and death is also evident. It is in this context that he suggests "Plastination reveals the beauty beneath the skin, frozen in time between death and decay."

DEATH AS OBSERVED, PROCLAIMED, AND IMAGINED

Both Victor Frankenstein and his monster were created by an 18-year-old woman whose own life had been born through death. Mary Shelley's mother was an independent thinker who wrote powerfully about the rights of women 200 years ago. Mary Wollstonecraft's death soon after childbirth had an enduring effect on the daughter who would later marry poet Percy Shelley and go on to live a creative, adventuresome, but tragedy-marked life. In addition to her own curiosity about death, Mary Shelley came of age at a time when "galvanic" (electrical) experiments were a conspicuous part of the new scientific enterprise; doctors were procuring corpses by suspicious means to improve the quality of medical education and knowledge, and reports were circulating about people having been buried alive (Bondeson, 2001).

Shelley's novel brought the growing excitement and fears into sharp focus. Perhaps the dead could be reanimated. Perhaps death is not necessarily permanent and irreversible. And perhaps the age of the "modern Prometheus" was about to begin. Just as Prometheus pilfered fire from the gods as a gift to humans, so a Victor Frankenstein might harness lightning to the alarming project of creating life. Mary Shelley knew, however, that Prometheus suffered a terrible punishment for his disobedience. Frankenstein's creation turned out to be painfully and pitifully flawed—a warning to all scientists of the future, reaching to the gene splitters and cloners of today. Attitudes toward death—and the dead—became more complex with the introduction of *Frankenstein,* as well as Bram Stoker's *Dracula* (1975) and many other works that dared to test the boundaries.

Unlike Victor Frankenstein, Charles Darwin was a real scientist, and on his way to transforming our understanding of life on earth, in water, and in sky. When not making discoveries ashore, he conducted many small experiments aboard his ship, *The Beagle.* Darwin could distinguish clearly between insects that were either looking dead or actually were dead. *Thanatomimesis* is the simulation of death, often to avoid being killed (Kastenbaum, 2003), although it also is used in children's play to master death-related anxiety (Chapter 10). It is possible that the lieutenant's occasional conviction that he was dead also had the protective function of escaping being killed again. Darwin's observations contribute to the unsettling realization that the dead may be only apparently so (Bondeson, 2001).

Medical Professor Kenneth V. Iserson does his part to keep us off balance by discussing death not as a sudden and massive event but as a complex process that takes place over time. Even as the physician signs a death certificate, there may still be biologic activity throughout the body. Tradition, society, and science have decided on the criteria for pronouncing death, but nature does not entirely agree.

Islam does not agree either. A thousand years ago, the most learned and effective physicians were in Islamic lands, writing treatises that guided other European doctors for centuries to come. Dr. Bakr Abu Zaid is well aware of current practices in the definition of death and life support systems. Nevertheless, he cautions against taking a purely materialistic or objective approach. According to Islamic teachings, death is certain and final only when the soul has left the body. Neither Dr. Zaid nor Islam is alone in this belief. The people of many world societies have long believed that death is marked by the separation of soul from body. One would surely want to pay attention to EEG and other observations of a faltering body, but one would also have to be sensitive to the less tangible event of soul/body separation.

We enter still other realms of death perspectives when we open books of ancient philosophy or the New Testament. In the third century B.C., Epicurus offered a philosophy that has continued to influence many people from ancient times to the present. (A good way to become familiar with this view is to read *On the Nature of Things*, the narrative poem in which Lucretius articulates many of Epicurus's ideas.) Epicurus, agreeing with another philosopher, Democritus, argued that the universe comprises atoms in motion and that our own actions—indeed, our innermost thoughts and feelings—are shaped by the pattern of past events. We live and die in a materialistic universe. What, then, is death? It's really not much of anything—simply one more event in a long sequence of events that has no intrinsic meaning or value. We never actually experience death, and the fact of death does not violate any contract we might imagine that the gods have cosigned with us.

How, then, should one live, Epicurus? Wise people appreciate life and maintain a sense of balance and proportion. We are not major players in a great cosmic drama. We just happen to be here for a while, then again will become part of the vapor from which we arose. A depressing view? Not for Epicurus, at least. He formed a community known as The Garden, in which like-minded people—women as well as men, poor as well as rich, slaves as well as free citizens—lived in equality and friendship (this community endured for about 500 years). He offered a model for harmonious living within a universe that does not seem to care about either our lives or our deaths, but most people have preferred a version in which the universe is rule abiding and purposeful, and in which human lives and deaths do count for something.

The Christian version has met this need for many people over many years. The New Testament story is told somewhat differently from one gospel to the next. The faithful can encounter a bewildering variety of interpretations from preachers and scholars. The Christian message regarding death can be read as simple or complex. The quotation from James at the beginning of this chapter delivers one facet of this message. Lust—sexual feeling, thought, and activity—is intimately associated with death. Before the emergence of Christianity, other religions in the ancient world had emphasized a connection between withering away and fertility. Life was regenerated through death (was that a vampire slithering by?). Careful observance of rituals might persuade the gods to allow crops to succeed and babies to thrive. Sacrifices (animal or human) could also help matters along—a little death here and there as payment for life.

Christianity, however, specified that sexuality itself is sinful and carries the death penalty. Virginity and abstinence take on theological resonances. Suicide and martyrdom, especially in earlier eras, were seen by some Christians as an appropriate alternative to sexual indulgence. Not only the "deathification of sex," but also the "sexualization of death" have been consequences of the concept put forth in the gospel of James and other passages in the New Testament. A passionate and mystical union with God became an increasingly dominant theme in the version of Christianity that became known to the world through the interpretations of *Paul the Convert* (Segall, 1990). At the same time, sexual union between two humans and their bonds of attachment were seen as less spiritual and worthy. Long before celibacy became a requirement for priests, there was already pressure for choosing religious devotion over sexual relationships. Not all Christians favor this intertwining view of death and sexuality, but it is undeniably an influential part of the tradition.

The man who said death is "a change of clothes. That's all!" perhaps identifies himself with the New Age movement. Those within this movement view life as a journey through multiple lives. Death is a transition, a door through which one passes on the way to the next life. This conception clearly differs from the others. Unlike

Epicurus and other atomists, life and death are regarded as purposeful—there is a point to it all and a progression. Unlike the New Testament view, death is not a punishment for sexuality or for anything else. A flat EEG is not impressive, because the life and death of the spirit are not seen as byproducts of brain activity. This view has some commonality with Islam and other religious traditions that believe in a soul principle that is not entirely dependent on the physical body.

Death becomes less abstract when represented as a person. The college student who envisioned death as "very patient and very polite" was stepping away from the more common American view of death as an enemy whose presence should be denied as long as possible. Instead, she pictured death as a kind of watchful companion who knows and respects us throughout our lives and whom we should not be surprised to see when the time comes.

Death as Symbolic Construction

What is death? It is an idea, a concept. Some contemporary scholars see death as a *symbolic construction*. Something our minds have constructed from our experiences, our guesswork, our needs, and our ignorance. Death is therefore subject to the same rules and limitations as any other concept. This does not mean that death is unreal or fictitious. Death is a concept we need because it has so many important referents, associations, and consequences. Water is also a concept. We look at ice, snow, mist, rain, standing pools, and flowing streams and write the formula H_2O on the board and call them all water, even though their forms look so different. Water is not simply something that presents itself to our eyes, but a useful concept. When we try to determine the difference between "alive" and "dead" and to define death itself, we are dealing with symbolic constructions. We are working with the words, concepts, and ways of thinking that are available to us in a particular society at a particular time.

"Dead" and "death" are concepts that are still under construction—still subject to question, challenge, and revision. For example, I have often had to sort out my own impressions when at the bedside of an unresponsive person who is not expected to recover. If I judge that this person is dead (as a person), then why even try to communicate? If, however, I cannot be sure of this person's state of being, then I might try to attempt to communicate as best I can. Symbolic constructions of death can lead us either to increased or reduced interactions.

Some of the most influential constructions of death in our society come from movies and television, with the Internet so coming on strong. The average person today is less likely to have direct, unfiltered encounters with dying and death than in the past. At the same time, we are frequently exposed to constructed depictions of dying and death in the movies and on television. Schultz and Huet (2000–2001) examined popular and award-winning films. Most deaths in these films were presented in a sensational and violent manner. Seldom were we shown the actual course of dying and death that is experienced by most people in our society. Encouragingly, perhaps, films that had received awards were much more likely to include expressions of sorrow and sadness. Gender differences were striking. Male characters were six times more likely to instigate death, and female characters were twice as likely to be the victims. The authors conclude that "in American film, death is distorted into a sensational stream of violent attacks by males, with fear, injury, further aggression and the absence of normal grief reactions as the most common response" (p. 149). The male as slayer and female as slain is consistent with homicide patterns in the United States (Chapter 9).

We will see (Chapter 10) that it takes a while for children to understand that death is not just intentional or accidental but will befall everybody in one way or another. The child's attempt to understand the nature and meaning of death is certainly not assisted by the aggressive and violent constructions of death in popular movies.

The ideas about death that we have sampled have recently taken on a more urgent aspect. Is this person "dead enough" to have organs removed and transplanted to save another person's life? To have the life-support system removed? The ancient question, What is death? has been joined by an even more pressing concern—When is dead? We turn, then, to biomedical approaches to answering these related questions.

BIOMEDICAL APPROACHES TO THE DEFINITION OF DEATH

Death is "certified" thousands of times every day by physicians. This process meets society's need for verifying that one of its members has been lost. It is also a signal to the bereaved survivors and society. The survivors are now expected to start reorganizing their lives around the fact of this loss, while society makes its arrangements. Insurance benefits are to be paid, the deceased will not be eligible to vote at the next election, and this unique death will become part of mortality statistics. The *"When* is dead?" question takes a practical form: "Under what conditions should a person be considered dead?"

Traditional Determination of Death

The most common signs of death have been lack of respiration, pulse, and heartbeat, as well as failure to respond to stimuli such as light, movement, and pain. Lowered body temperature and stiffness are also expected to appear, followed later by bloating and signs of decomposition.

In the past, a competent physician usually had no need for technology. Nevertheless, errors could be made. Victims of drowning and lightning, for example, would sometimes be taken for dead, when in fact their vital functions had only been suspended. Those who suffered a stroke, epileptic seizure, or diabetic coma might also be pronounced dead instead of receiving treatment. The same fate could befall a person gifted in the once popular art of hysterical fainting. "Madame Fluffington fainted dead away at the distressing news!" (She might have kept one eye open.)

The possibility that people might be pronounced dead while still alive was an unsettling one, and Edgar Allan Poe seized upon this fear for some of his most scary and therefore popular writings. One of my favorite articles from the past was published in the land where, as popular mythology has it, the undead have been most active. Writing in the *Transylvanian Journal of Medicine* in 1835, Dr. Nathan Shrock reports that his own uncle had almost been buried alive

until, at the last minute, he showed faint signs of life. Shrock then leads the reader through the traditional signs of death and explains how even the lack of moist breath on a mirror held in front of the nose and mouth, can be misleading.

Mark Twain (1883/1972) claimed to have visited a municipal "dead house" in Munich:

Around a finger of each of these fifty still forms, both great and small, was a ring; and from the ring a wire led to the ceiling, and thence to a bell in a watch-room yonder, where, day and night, a watchman sits always alert and ready to spring to the aid of any of that pallid company who, waking out of death, shall make a movement— for any, even the slightest movement will twitch the wire and rings that fearful bell. I imagined myself a death-sentinel, drowsing there alone, far into the dragging watches of some wailing, gusty night, and having in a twinkling all my body stricken to quivering jelly by the sudden clamor of that awful summons! (p. 189)

A more professionally trained observer devoted himself to exploring the what and when of death some years later (Kastenbaum, 2000a). A pathologist working in a Detroit hospital, he instructed nurses to call him when a patient's death was imminent. He wanted to be there at the moment of death. The physician's name would not become well known for some time yet, but Jack Kevorkian, M.D., was already drawn to the mysterious transition between life and death. Kevorkian was one of the few physicians in our own time who wrote about the status of the eye at death. He believed the condition of the eye provided the most reliable basis for determining whether or not the person was dead (and, if dead, for how long). He reported his observations with 51 consecutive cases (1957) and discussed his method and overall findings in a later paper (1961). Specifically, he found that the status of the eye at death included (a) segmentation and interruption of blood circulation, (b) a haziness of the cornea, and (c) appearance of homogeneity and paleness. Kevorkian urged other physicians to follow his lead by examining dying patient's eyes with an ophthalmoscope. Few took up his suggestion. Health care providers as well as the general public were not ready to look death in the face.

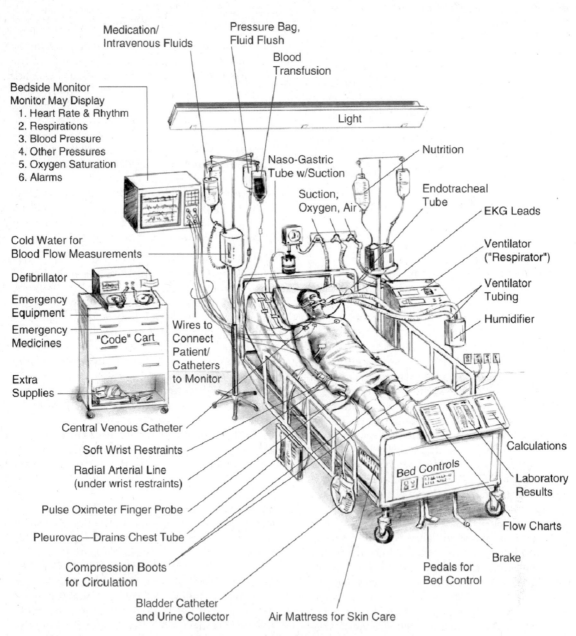

Medication/
Intravenous Fluids

Pressure Bag,
Fluid Flush

Blood
Transfusion

Bedside Monitor
Monitor May Display
1. Heart Rate & Rhythm
2. Respirations
3. Blood Pressure
4. Other Pressures
5. Oxygen Saturation
6. Alarms

Light

Nutrition

Naso-Gastric
Tube w/Suction

Suction,
Oxygen, Air

Endotracheal
Tube

EKG Leads

Cold Water for
Blood Flow Measurements

Ventilator
("Respirator")

Defibrillator

Ventilator
Tubing

Emergency
Equipment

Humidifier

Emergency
Medicines

"Code" Cart

Wires to
Connect
Patient/
Catheters
to Monitor

Extra
Supplies

Central Venous Catheter

Calculations

Soft Wrist Restraints

Laboratory
Results

Radial Arterial Line
(under wrist restraints)

Bed Controls

Pulse Oximeter Finger Probe

Flow Charts

Pleurovac—Drains Chest Tube

Brake

Compression Boots
for Circulation

Pedals for
Bed Control

Bladder Catheter
and Urine Collector

Air Mattress for Skin Care

A comatose patient lies in a critical care unit room. While equipment might vary in appearance at different hospitals, its function to monitor and support vital functions remains the same.

Ways of Being Dead

Medical advances have made it possible to maintain the body of a nonresponsive individual for an indefinite period of time. The heart continues to beat; the respiratory system continues to exchange its gases. Reflex responses may also be elicited. The *person,* however, no longer seems to be there. Under such circumstances, we may hesitate to evoke either category, alive or dead. Eventually, though, a decision might have to be made, and it will require a definition of "deadness," if not of death. Consider the following brief examples, each dependent on a firm definition of death:

1. Family members and the attending physician agree that the life-support system should be withdrawn because the patient is unresponsive and has no chance to recover. Would "pulling the plug" constitute murder? Or is the person already dead? And, if we cannot murder the dead, is it nevertheless a crime of some sort because vegetative functions could have continued indefinitely?

2. Another patient is also comatose and unresponsive but vegetative processes continue even in the absence of an elaborate life-support system. (Intravenous fluids are being given, but there is no ventilator to maintain respiration.) Elsewhere in the hospital, an organ transplant team is urgently seeking a kidney that might keep somebody else alive for many years. The needed kidney could be liberated by ruling that the comatose patient is dead. The organ must be removed while the host body is still relatively intact if it is to have its best chance to function in the other patient. Removal of the kidney is a procedure that will be fatal for the comatose patient. Would this operation be a crime, or is it laudable because it might help one person and cannot harm the one who is dead or all-but-dead?

3. The vegetative functioning of a comatose woman is being maintained by elaborate life-prolonging procedures. However, there is a living fetus within the woman. The fetus will not survive unless society decides to keep the woman's vegetative processes intact until it has become more viable. Does this mean that society is keeping a dead person alive? And does it mean that society knowingly kills that dead person in order to deliver a baby who has a fighting chance to survive?

Either the similarities or the differences among these conditions could be emphasized. How vital is the distinction between cessation of bodily processes and loss of the person as a person? What difference, if any, is there between the "deadness" of a body that continues to function on a vegetative level with or without an elaborate life support system? Who or what is it that no longer lives—perhaps still a person but not the same person?

Brain Death and the Harvard Criteria

By the 1950s, it was recognized that some unresponsive patients were "beyond coma," that is, no electrophysiological activities could be detected from the brain. Postmortem examinations revealed extensive destruction of brain tissue. This condition came to be known as *respirator brain.* The implication was clear: some patients who were connected to ventilators had lost their brain function—and therefore should be considered dead. At first, the concept of brain death served mainly to help physicians decide that additional medical procedures would be of no benefit to the patient. Soon, however, the concept was being used in a new and controversial way: ". . . the practice of undertaking organ removal from beating-heart donors rather than waiting upon the cessation of effective pumping of blood by the heart . . . (McCullagh, 1993, p. 9).

Here was a remarkable change in the construction of deadness. The heart is still beating—in fact, physicians make sure the heart is still beating—but the patient is, let's say, "dead enough" to be classified as an appropriate organ donor. Biomedical advances had led us into a twilight zone in which ethical standards and value priorities had become elusive and ambiguous. Both the health care and the justice systems felt the need for guidance. A committee of the Harvard Medical School faculty issued an opinion (Ad Hoc Committee, 1968) that has since served as primary guide for determination of brain death. The first three criteria (which

Death in life, or life in death? The Archer is one of many three-dimensional figures created by anatomist Gunther von Hagens from corpse tissue. Plastination produces durable specimens for study by medical and nursing students. Museum tours of von Hagens' plastinates demonstrate technology's continuing adventuring across the boundaries between life and death.
Copyright: Gunther von Hagens, Institute for Plastination, Heidelberg, Germany (www.bodyworlds.com).

follow) would have come as no surprise to physicians of an earlier generation. It is the last two criteria, dependent on technological advances, that introduce new considerations.

The Harvard Criteria

1. *Unreceptive and unresponsive.* No awareness is shown for external stimuli or inner need. The unresponsiveness is complete even when ordinarily painful stimuli are applied.
2. *No movements and no breathing.* There is a complete absence of spontaneous respiration and all other spontaneous muscular movement.
3. *No reflexes.* The usual reflexes that can be elicited in a neurophysiological examination are absent (e.g., when a light is shined in the eye, the pupil does not constrict).
4. *A flat EEG.* Electrodes attached to the scalp elicit a printout of electrical activity from the living brain. These are popularly known as brain waves. The respirator brain does not provide the usual pattern of peaks and valleys. Instead the moving stylus records a flat line: the absence of electrophysiological activity.
5. *No circulation to or within the brain.* Without the oxygen and nutrition provided through blood circulation, brain functioning soon terminates.

The first three criteria—the traditional ones—usually serve the purpose. The Harvard report was not intended to require the use of the EEG in all cases, only those in which a question remains and the traditional criteria may not be sufficiently reliable. It was recommended that in such situations the tests of brain functioning should be repeated about 24 hours later.

The Current Scene

Brain death became an official diagnostic category in 1981. It was defined as a condition in which irreversible known damage has permanently destroyed all functional brain activity, including loss of the brainstem's capacity to enable spontaneous breathing. This definition was crafted to avoid a mistaken diagnosis. The nature and extent of the brain damage should be known. The possibility that there is residual brain functioning that is "on hold" rather than destroyed must be ruled out. It must be established that the patient's condition had not been caused by drugs, severe metabolic or endocrine disturbances, or hypothermia (cold shock).

This is a conservative approach that gives benefit of doubt to the possibility of recovery. Some have argued that permanent loss of functioning in the cerebral cortex should be enough to diagnose brain death. The networks of highly differentiated cells in the upper reaches of the brain are considered essential for experience, thought, and personality. Massive and nonreversible damage to the cerebral cortex dissolves the person, even though flickerings and reflexive movements may continue to be produced by nerve centers in the brainstem. It is destruction of both cerebral cortex and brainstem, however, that has become established as the criterion for brain death. This condition is known as *whole brain death*.

The Harvard Criteria and the decision to require whole brain failure as the criterion for brain death have provided useful structure and guidance. Complications have arisen, though, with the improvement of neurological assessment techniques and the recognition of variant states of brain dysfunction. Several concepts are now being applied and researched, as exemplified in Table 2-1. It is possible that there will continue to be significant new developments in this complex area of research and diagnosis.

Distinctions between these states require up-to-date knowledge of neuroscience and adequate practical experience. Physicians in general practice can make some of these distinctions reliably, but specialists are needed in other situations. Accurate diagnosis is essential, because each condition has its own implications for decision making, management, and outcome. Several of these conditions could be mistaken for brain death by uninformed observers. This could happen readily in observing patients with akinetic mutism, catatonia, coma, or the locked-in syndrome with its harrowing similarity to being buried alive. Each of these conditions is essentially different from the others, but all can give the impression of terminal nonresponsiveness. By contrast, we might be impressed by the nonpurposive reflexes and grimaces of a person in a persistent or permanent vegetative state and thereby persuade ourselves that the person is still there.

TABLE 2-1
Brain Death and Related Concepts

Akinetic Mutism	Sensorimotor pathways are preserved but cannot initiate actions or speak. Bilateral frontal lobe dysfunction and possibly other brain injuries are involved.
Brain Damage	General term that has become of limited usefulness.
Brain Death	Prolonged nonreversible cessation of all brain activity with complete absence of voluntary movements, response to stimuli, brain stem reflexes, and spontaneous respirations.
Catatonia	Immobility, muscular rigidity, mutism, posturing, grimacing, stupor; sometimes giving way to sudden outbursts of violence, panic, or hallucination. Considered to be a neuropsychiatric disorder.
Coma	A deep state of unconsciousness from which the individual cannot be aroused. Usually associated with injury or dysfunction involving both cerebral hemispheres or the brain stem.
Locked-In Syndrome	Neurological condition in which a person is conscious and able to think but cannot move any part of the body except the eyes, which can be used for communication.
Minimally Conscious State	Severe impairment that can be distinguished from coma or vegetative state by occasional and limited behavioral evidence of awareness.
Permanent Vegetative State	All cognitive functions, including awareness, are absent, even if eyes are open and sounds and nonpurposive movements are made. Sleep-wake cycles, autonomic control, and respiration continue. Condition is of long duration.
Persistent Vegetative State	(See Transient and Permanent Vegetative States.) The condition is known to have been caused by brain damage that might be moderated or reversed.
Transient Vegetative State	(See Persistent Vegetative State.) Condition has been caused by drugs, extreme cold, or injury with possibility of recovery.

Sources: Burns, Login, Bruno, Kimura, Crisci, Saosnik, Beslac-Bumbasirevic, Ercegovac, & Wijdicks (2004); Giacino, Ashwal, Childs, Cranford, Jennett, Katz, Kelly, Rosenberg, Whyte, Zafone, & Zasler; (2002); Iserson (2003); Jennett (2002); Wade & Johnston (1999); Wijdicks (2001).

The less familiar diagnosis of "minimally conscious state" is receiving increasing attention in the hope of identifying more cases in which recovery has some likelihood (Giacino et al., 2002). Success in identifying these cases depends much on the ability of physician or psychologist to identify behavioral clues to the patient's mental state. The diagnosis of persistent vegetative state can be set aside once a patient has shown the ability to follow simple commands, answer questions with word or gesture, and make a purposeful movement. The phenomena surveyed here will be encountered again when we explore euthanasia and the right to die (Chapter 9).

EVENT VERSUS STATE

We create some of our own difficulties by using the same word for two different, though related, ideas. Death is sometimes treated as though an event—that is, something that occurs in a specific way and at a specific time and place. When it is death as event that concerns us, it is often possible to be factual and precise. ("This is the room where the victim was found. There is the blunt instrument. The clock was toppled over and still shows the exact moment that this dastardly act was committed!")

Quite different is our use of the same word in referring to the state that follows the event. Life has ceased (death as event). What happens from now on? The answer to this question is much less accessible to ordinary sources of information. Some interpretations of death as a state follow, including a challenging new construction that is, well, still under construction.

WHAT DOES DEATH MEAN?

Let's take an example before looking systematically at the meanings that are summarized in Table 2-2.

The soloist in Bach's haunting Cantata No. 53 sings:

Schlage doch, gewunschte Stunde,
brich doch an gewunschter Tag!
Strike, oh strike, awaited hour,
approach thou happy day!

TABLE 2-2

Meanings That Have Been Given to Death

- Death is an enfeebled form of life.
- Death is a continuation of life.
- Death is perpetual development.
- Death is waiting.
- Death is cycling and recycling.
- Death is nothing.
- Death is virtual and, therefore, not really death after all.

The hour that is awaited eventually will be displayed on the face of an ordinary clock. It belongs to public, shared, or mortal time. The hour and day of death will be entered into the community's vital statistics. What the devout singer anticipates, however, is entry into a new realm of being in which the time changes of terrestrial life no longer apply.

The survivors will continue to measure their own lives by clock and calendar. They may remember that the deceased has been dead for 6 months, 5 years, and so on. But this conventional manner of marking time has no bearing upon the deceased, who will have entered Heaven. The death event will have cleaved the deceased from the community's shared time framework at the same instant that it transports this individual to eternity. The hour that strikes refers to death as event; the heavenly blessing that follows refers to death as state.

This, however, is only one interpretation of death as a state. Let us now consider other meanings that have emerged throughout history.

INTERPRETATIONS OF THE DEATH STATE

Here are competing interpretations of the death state that have long been influential— plus a new interpretation that has been emerging in our society and deserves consideration.

Enfeebled Life

Young children often think of death as a less vigorous form of life. The people who "live" in the cemetery don't get hungry, except once in a while. The dead are tired, sad, bored, and don't have much to do. A 3-year-old girl who was saving her comic books for grandmother,

worried that she might have forgotten to take her bifocals with her to the grave.

The child of today who offers this interpretation is in a sense carrying forward the belief system common in Mesopotamia thousands of years ago. The deceased person is gradually submerged into the underworld. There the deceased is transformed into a repulsive and pitiable creature one might expect to find today in a horror movie. The mightiest ruler and the fairest maiden lose all power, all beauty. The dead become equal in their abysmally low estate.

The decremental model ruled throughout much of the ancient world. Abandonment, depletion, and endless misery were the lot of all mortals— with the possible exception of mighty rulers and those of very special merit. The idea that the death state can be influenced by pious belief or moral conduct had not yet taken firm hold.

Continuation

Passage from life on earth has often been interpreted as a transition to more of the same. We are accustomed to the idea of a profound change, a transformation. The cessation of life is extraordinary, so it must also lead to something extraordinary. Some tribal societies have pictured the dead as going on with life pretty much as usual. One hunts, fishes, plays, makes love, becomes involved in jealousies and conflicts, and so forth. The afterlife can even include the risk of death! The individual faces challenges and crises just as before, including the possibility of a final annihilation. For example, the Dayak of Borneo believed that the soul returns to earth after its seventh death and there enters a mushroom or fruit near the village. This returned soul invades the body of a woman who chances to eat the morsel, and one is therefore reborn. One may be less fortunate, however. A buffalo, deer, or monkey might find this delicacy first, and the soul will then be reborn as an animal, losing its human identity in the process.

Perpetual Development

Suppose that the universe itself is not completely determined, that all of existence is en route to making something else of itself. Suppose further that what we make of our lives is part of this universal process. What might be the death state in such a flowing, changing universe? This possibility emerged first from the prophets and philosophers of evolution. These visionaries either anticipated or built upon Darwin's discoveries in proposing a radically different view of life and its place in the universe. For example, philosophers Samuel Alexander (1920) and Lloyd Morgan (1923) suggested that evolution applied not only to species but to the universe as a whole. Life itself is an emergent quality from a universe that continues to transform itself. Mind is a further quality that has emerged from life. In Alexander's words, the universe itself is in the process of "flowering into deity": God is still being created. In this view, the relationship between life and death also continues to evolve. The basic law is continued development both for individual minds and for the universe at large.

One of the most striking conceptions was offered by a man who also made enduring contributions to scientific methodology. Back in 1836, Gustav Theodor Fechner proposed a Hindu-influenced model of the death state itself as perpetual development. Death is a kind of birth into a freer mode of existence in which continued spiritual growth may occur. The death state is not the same for everybody. Death is not the same for everybody. Individuals differ in the stage of spiritual development they have achieved up to the moment of the death event, and this difference will influence their developmental course after death. Furthermore, the death state not only varies for different people, but is itself subject to change as the universe continues to evolve. In a sense, then, the death state provides everyone with at least the opportunity to become more alive than ever.

Do these ideas seem merely quaint? Evolutionary biologists today operate on the premise that the future state of a system cannot be entirely predicted from knowledge of its starting point (Goldsmith & Zimmer, 2001). In other words, change is real (or reality is change). Biological systems are subject to change within the larger system we call the universe, which is itself subject to change. What we call life and death are not exceptions to the apparent transformation and unpredictability of the universe. As goes the universe, so goes the very nature of life and death.

Enthusiasm for developmental conceptions of the death state might be dampened if we attend to current theories regarding the fate of the universe. Cosmologists are questing for a theory of everything-everywhere-everywhen. They do not comfort us with a vision of an evolving universe that will become ever more congenial to human purposes. Instead, in their view, the universe will do itself in, or, rather, do itself out by expansion that will eventually dissolve the flowing structures of energy and matter. Any "part" of the universe will be like any other part and no place will be any place. Planets, solar systems, and galaxies are doomed to become just a memory. Beyond that: There will be nobody left to remember. No life forms will be around even to experience the terminal phase. There are ingenious competing theories about the precise end-phase scenario. Holographic theory (Talbot, 1992) offers a possible exception: Mind and matter are both to be considered as holographs that interact to construct reality. We would need to do some serious rethinking about the nature of life and death if the holograph theory should happen to prevail.

Waiting

What happens after the death event? We wait!

In Western society, this waiting period is often regarded as having three phases: suspension, judgment, and disposition. During the first phase, the souls or spirits are in a transitional state between the end of earthly life and entry into their new realms of being. The Day of Judgment arrives, and the sleepers awaken, receive salvation or damnation, and take their places either for "eternity" or "for all times" (concepts that often are treated as though identical, although philosophers hold them to be sharply different).

These three phases are given different priorities by particular individuals and societies. Some Christians, for example, emphasize the taking-a-good-long-rest phase. Others focus attention upon the critical moment of judgment. Still others contemplate that ultimate phase when sorrows and anxieties will have passed away, when the just are rewarded and everlasting radiance and peace prevail. Some believers have embellished this phase by predicting that

Zits®

their own redemptions will be accompanied by the punishment of unbelievers. In ancient Egypt, by contrast, the act of judgment occurred promptly after death. More emphasis was placed on judgment and final disposition than on the preceding state of suspended animation.

I have characterized this general conception of the death state as waiting in order to emphasize its implications for time, tension, and striving. A tension exists between the death event itself and the end state. The dead may seem to be at rest— but it is actually a time for watchful waiting. Judgment and final disposition are still to come.

Furthermore, the sense of waiting hovers on both sides of the grave. The aged and the critically ill are sometimes regarded as waiting for death. In this view, death is not simply the cessation of life, but a kind of force, perhaps a kind of deliverance as well. From a broader perspective, all the living, healthy though they may be, are only "putting in time" until they too move through the event into the state of death. The waiting is not over until all souls have perished and then awakened for judgment and final disposition. Not everybody shares this view of death. However, it has been around long enough in Western society to exert a powerful influence. Perhaps some of our daily tension derives from this apprehension that fate will not be determined until the end of the end . . . beyond death.

In Christian thought, there is a complexity and ambiguity that is not easily resolved. Leon-Dufour's (1986) analysis of *Life and Death in the New Testament*, notes that the man who most

forcefully interpreted Jesus' message himself wavered between radically different alternatives. Paul at first conceived that the Kingdom of Heaven would not open its gates until the end of time (i.e., when the last generation of life on earth had perished). Later, he expressed the belief that one would experience the gratifications of eternal life immediately after death. Paul regarded death both as welcome release and catastrophic event. However one chooses to interpret the interpretations, the concept of waiting both for death and for the final outcome of death may have more influence on us than we usually realize.

Cycling and Recycling

One of the most popular conceptions of the death state is also one of the most radical. Death comes and goes, wending in and out of life. This view is often expressed by children. After a person has been dead for a while, that person will probably get up again and go home. Sure, the bird was dead Friday, but maybe it's been dead long enough. Some adults also have regarded death as a temporary condition that alternates with life. Death is just one position on a constantly revolving wheel, the great wheel of life and death. (The "Bankrupt" place on "The Wheel of Fortune" television program comes to mind.)

In his classic *The Wheel of Death* (1971), Philip Kapleau points out that the wheel is a core symbol of Buddhism. Another important symbol is a flame passing from lamp to candle. This signifies rebirth. Kapleau also reminds us of the phoenix, "a mythical bird of great beauty who lived for five hundred years in the desert. It immolated itself on a funeral pyre and then rose from its own ashes in the freshness of youth, living another cycle of years" (p. viii). The phoenix represents both death and regeneration. Some funeral rituals also encourage the regeneration or recycling of life through death (Block & Parry, 1996).

Kapleau argues that the cyclical view of life and death is more rational than many people in Western society are willing to grant:

> The assertion that nothing precedes birth or follows death is largely taken for granted in the West, but however widely believed, it is still absurd from a Buddhist viewpoint. Such an assertion rests on the blind assumption—in its own way an act of faith—that life, of all things in the universe, operates in a vacuum (p. xvii).

Kapleau's comparison between the states of prebirth and postdeath also makes me think of the all-too-bright 10-year-old who attended one of my classes with his mother. At the end of the class, I asked him if there was anything he would like to say. "Just a little question. I mean, what are we *before* life and where are we or is it only nothing and would that be the same nothing we are after life or a different kind of nothing and . . . ?" As you will not be surprised to learn, I have since grown more cautious in asking 10-year-olds for their questions!

The recycling of life through the death state was an article of faith for many peoples in the past. This idea regained popularity in recent years in the United States with the emergence of the Aquarian or New Age movement, which has retained its attraction for many people. A typical statement by a follower: "Death is simply a transition from one life to another. We all live many lives."

Nothing

Perhaps we are deceiving ourselves when we imagine death to be any kind of state at all. To *be* dead could be considered a linguistic fallacy, a contradiction in terms. This self-deception is further encouraged when we fail to distinguish between dying and death. Dying is something.

There are significant bodily changes, and these changes have consequences for thought, feeling, and social interaction. The death event is also something: the final cessation of life processes. But is death itself a *state*? One might think instead of death as total absence: absence of life, absence of process, absence of qualities. The more we say about death, the more we deceive ourselves and use language to falsify. Even when I say, "This person is dead," I may be slyly contradicting myself. This person *is*? No, the whole point is that this person *isn't*. Our language forms lead us repeatedly into subtle affirmations of being even when we are trying to acknowledge nonbeing.

The concept of death as nothing is repugnant to many people. It seems too barren and devoid of hope. Furthermore, it is difficult to cope with the concept of nothing. Calling it *nothingness* is a futile exercise that reifies a reification, making a bigger somethingness out of nothing. We know little if anything about nothing. Our minds do not know what to do with themselves unless there is at least a little something to work with. Yet the difference between even a little something and the concept of nothing is enormous. Furthermore, we tend to become anxious when faced with formlessness and with experiences that do not fit into our usual fixed categories of thought.

Sometimes we try to deal with this anxiety by calling death a "void" or a "great emptiness." It feels reassuring to give things a name: Perhaps giving nothing a name can be helpful, too. Nevertheless, even terms such as void screen the recognition of death as a nonstate. How resourcefully we construct images that are intended to conceal the possibility of nothing!

Few people seem to care for the definition of death as nonstate, and fewer still exercise the mental rigor it would require to adhere consistently to this view. But as much as we ignore or reject the idea of nothing, it refuses to vanish into, well, nothingness.

Virtual, Therefore Not Death

Many of us have become involved with people who are not exactly either here or there. We also see, hear, and interact with beings, scenes, and events that never were nor will be. *Virtual reality* first came to general attention through audio-video devices that delivered impressions so vivid that our brains were tempted to suppose them real. Virtual reality is opening new opportunities for learning, experiencing, and achieving—and escapism.

Death has not been neglected. The joy of killing is featured in many popular games. People living, people dead, and people computer generated can interact. Virtual cemeteries have blossomed on the Internet, where the dead can be accessed 24/7 by families, friends, and curious strangers. The body of the deceased has become less crucial to some funeral rites and memorialization. The Internet now offers itself as either another dimension of remembrance or a possible replacement for traditional interactions with the dead. No exhausting and expensive trips to distant cemeteries. No complicated scheduling. No concern that the burial site will have deteriorated because of neglect, vandalism, or a depressing environment. No standing in the rain. No having to put up with certain relatives one does not especially cherish. No physical aura of death and decay. On the other hand, by not actually visiting the grave, there is less opportunity to speak privately to a deceased family member and no opportunity to place a flower on the actual gravesite.

The dead are "there," in whatever sense that cyberspace is a place. It is a different kind of dead, though, and takes some getting used to. The fact that younger generations grow up with computer skills increases the likelihood of increased virtual interaction with the dead. What will we have gained and what will we have lost when virtual interaction with the dead becomes a larger element in our death system?

The more we become accustomed to remote interactions, the less our senses and feelings are guided by the breath and presence of people who really live and can really die. The more we become engrossed in virtual reality, the greater may be the temptation to see death as also something that is without dimension and place. Virtual reality has the compelling characteristic of being everywhere and nowhere at the same time. It can also be shuttled back and forth between existence and nonexistence at our pleasure. The virtual universe can go dark at our command and return in all its glory whenever we choose to access it again. It is not as messy as real life and

death, and offers the illusion of control without asking very much of us in return. Will it eventually become an alternative to traditional spiritual approaches to life and death? How freely these images float; how they move and morph and sport! What a model for out-of-body experiences and the desire to transcend the limits of our physical being! Here, then, is a new modality for the ultimate make-over: converting death into something safer, less disturbing, less consequential, and less personal. People sometimes regard the images on television and movie screens as more real than the people and events in their own lives. Virtual reality may result in a quantum leap in the tendency to see both life and death as somewhere else.

Implications of the Ways in Which We Interpret Death

How we interpret the state of death can influence our thoughts, feelings, and actions. A person may refuse to approach a corpse, even though it is that of a much beloved individual. The ancient Babylonians, Egyptians, and Hebrews revered and attempted to comfort their aged. But who among them would want to be contaminated by a body that was beyond the pale of life? Elaborate decontamination rituals were prescribed for those who inadvertently or by necessity had touched a corpse:

> Whoever touches the dead body of anyone will be unclean for seven days. He must purify himself with water on the third day and on the seventh day. . . . Whoever touches the dead body of anyone and fails to purify himself . . . must be cut off from Israel . . . (Old Testament: Num. 19)

By contrast, death might be regarded as a tranquil state of awaiting a restful sleep. Yet the prospect of waiting would be anything but tranquil for the person who is attuned to the moment of judgment instead of the interlude between the death event and final state. Two terminally ill people who are equally firm in their religious convictions might differ in their specific anticipations of death and therefore in their moods and behaviors. A terminally ill person who believes that death is simply a passage to the next reincarnation may be less concerned about the moment of judgment than either of the foregoing people; the terminally ill person may be more interested in what is to come than the life that will be left.

These are but a few implications of the ways in which we interpret death as a state. Because of the difficulty of trying to interpret death as any kind of state, humankind has often used a supplementary approach—comparing death to conditions with which we have more direct knowledge.

CONDITIONS THAT RESEMBLE DEATH

We can liken death to something else or we can liken something else to death. Exploring death analogies will help not only in continuing the task of defining death, but will also lead us into several problem areas that deserve further attention.

Inorganic and Unresponsive

Fire, lightning, whirlpools, floods, earthquakes, and other natural phenomena have always impressed humankind. But we can also be impressed by lack of activity in the world. This perception may contribute to a sense of comforting stability: Gaze at those everlasting mountains! They were here in the days of our ancestors and will continue to tower above our children's children! At other times, however, silent and inert surroundings may elicit a sense of deadness. "Stone cold dead in the marketplace" is a phrase that has not yet been retired. The parallel with the stiff form of a cadaver is obvious. "Stone cold" reinforces the deadness of the dead.

The hard, unyielding surface of a rock contrasts with our vulnerable flesh and sensitive feelings. A person exposed to stress and danger may envy the durability of the rock. A person accused of misdeed might "stonewall it," creating a shield of unresponsiveness that emulates the lifeless character of the rock. Stone was also used as a representation of death in mythology. Mythological unfortunates were transformed from flesh and blood into insensate rock by incident or unwise action—a glimpse of Medusa's terrifying visage on one of her "bad hair days," or that fatal backward glance made by Orpheus upon leaving Hades.

We live in an invented, as well as a natural, world. We say things like, "The motor has died" and "Perhaps the battery went dead." We age, and our machines wear out. Ancestors who lived close to the rhythms of earth had fire and stone to inspire their representations of life and death. We have added the mechanical and electronic apparatus, from windmill to computer and beyond. For example, stand at the bedside of a critically ill person who is connected to an external support system with multiple lifelines. Is this a living person? Or is it a set of machines functioning? Or can the situation best be understood as an integrated psychobioelectromechanical process in which the human and nonhuman components have merged to form a special system of their own? While we are considering this situation, it ends. The monitor reveals a flat line: Life activity has ceased. But what has ended? Do we say the machines failed or the body, or—?

We usually recognize that we are dealing in an evocative figure of speech when we liken death to the hard, cold unresponsiveness of a stone. But the distinction between analogy and fact is easy to blur. Failure of the machine can be seen as the failure of the machine that is the person as well. "Pulling the plug" is a revealing phrase that bridges analogy and fact. But the fact is that the machine is far from an adequate representation of the person.

Sleep and Altered States of Consciousness

Sleep has long served as another natural analogy to death. The ancient Greeks pictured sleep (*Hypnos*) as the twin brother of death (*Thanatos*). Sleep and death remain entwined with cultural traditions. Orthodox Jews, for example, on arising from sleep in the morning, thank God for restoring them to life again.

Some people today still replace the word *death* or *dead* with *sleep* when they speak to children. However, when children are told that a deceased person is "only sleeping," we may question what message is coming across. The young child is not likely to have a firm grasp on the distinction between sleep and death. The analogy, therefore, may register as reality. Late in the evening, the child is told, "Go to sleep!" by the same parent who said that grandmother is asleep or that death is a long sleep. It should not be a surprise if the child has difficulty falling asleep that night. Children do experience insomnia and nightmares in which death-related themes are prominent.

Adults as well as children may experience insomnia when death intrudes in their lives. While working in a geriatric hospital, for example, experience taught me to expect nocturnal disturbances on any ward where a patient had died unexpectedly. An aged man or woman might speak matter-of-factly about the death and seem not to have been personally affected but then awaken in terror and confusion that night, seeking a living face and a comforting word.

Whether used wisely or foolishly, however, sleep remains one of the most universal and easily communicated analogies to death. Myth and fairy tale abound in characters who, believed dead, are actually in a deep, enchanted sleep. Snow White and Sleeping Beauty are perhaps the best known examples.

Altered states of consciousness occurring in sleep or resembling sleep have also been used as analogies to death. People may dream they are dead and feel frozen, immobilized, or powerless to act (see also Chapter 13):

> My dream was going along OK, for a dream. Then it was suddenly not my dream. It was something that was happening, and I couldn't do anything. I couldn't move anything. Not my hand, not one finger. The more I thought about it, the worse it got. The harder I tried to move, the worse, it got. I was in a panic, frozen in a panic. My heart was pounding like mad and I still couldn't do anything. I remember thinking, "Yeah, maybe I'm dead in my grave and this is just what it's like, thinking you can do something, you should do something, but you can't" (dream report from a client in counseling who was experiencing several types of situational stress).

Drug- and alcohol-induced states of mind also sometimes are likened to death, whether as a joyful or a terrifying "trip." The now rarely employed technique of insulin coma therapy was known to generate terrifying death-like experiences.

Normal sleep differs from the altered states of consciousness that can result from disease,

trauma, drugs, alcohol, or other special circumstances. The coma of the seriously ill person, for example, is not likely to represent the same neural state as normal sleep. The temporary loss of consciousness in some epileptic seizures has at times been interpreted as a deathlike state, but, again, the status of the brain during these episodes differs markedly from both normal sleep and cerebral death.

Beings Who Resemble or Represent Death

In Homer's epic, *The Odyssey,* Ulysses ties himself to the mast of his ship to protect himself from enormous bird-like creatures with the heads of women. Some are perched on a rock, trying to lure the sailors with sweet song; others are circling near the vessel. The hybrid bird-person has been a compelling figure in art and mythology for many centuries. Often these winged creatures were associated with death. Post-Homeric Greeks had to contend with both *sirens* and *harpies.* Sirens brought death, and harpies obliterated memory. Death, then, might come with or without loss of memory, as represented by two different fabulous beings.

The winged hybrid at other times was depicted as a soul bird. This represented the spirit leaving the body at the time of death, hinting at resurrection. Later the bird-people were joined by fish-people, many of whom were also associated with death. The hybrid death-beings usually were portrayed as females. There was a tendency for peaceful death to take masculine form, whereas painful and violent death came through female agents. This characterization hardly seems fair: Consider how many people have died violently in man-made wars and how many have been comforted in their last days by women. The Muses, arriving a bit later in history than the sirens and harpies, were females who were depicted in a more kindly light. The Muses would sing at funerals and guide departed souls on their journeys through the underworld. Some also inspired artists, writers, and musicians in their creative ventures.

Orpheus was regarded as fabulous for his powers rather than his appearance. A master musician, Orpheus represented power over death.

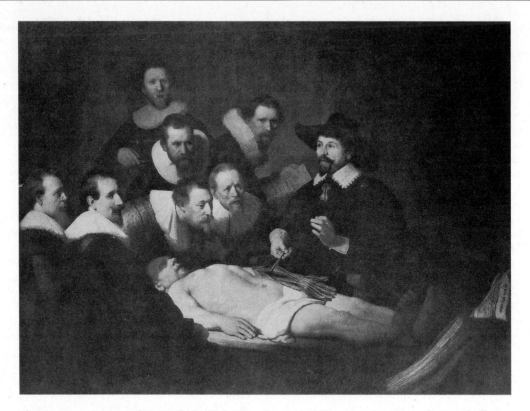

The Anatomy Lesson of Dr. Nicholus Tulp (Rembrant, 1632) was at the time a daring challenge to beliefs that the human corpse is too fearsome or too sacred to touch.

He charmed the fearsome guardians of the underworld with his music. Orpheus not only liberated his beloved Eurydice from Hades through his song but also brought rocks and trees to life. (Unfortunately, as you probably know, Orpheus could not resist looking back at Eurydice as she followed him out of Hades, so, because he disobeyed the god, their reunion came to a sudden end.)

The skeleton has also enjoyed a long career as a deathly being. Examples can be found throughout the ancient world. Artifacts from the buried city of Pompeii include a modern-looking depiction of a skeleton boxed inside a black border, suggesting a symbolic depiction of death. The skeleton flourished in medieval Europe, appearing in numerous works of art from approximately the thirteenth through the fifteenth centuries. We see the skeleton, for example, bearing a scythe on its shoulder and confronting young men, with the world behind them and hell gaping open underneath. This depiction appears on the title page of one of many books of the time called *Ars Moriendi* (*The Art of Dying*). The skeleton is also a prominent figure in van Eyck's rendering of *The Last Judgment.*

The animate skeleton did not simply pose for pictures. It danced. One whirl was enough for any mortal. Images of the Dance of Death flourished during the fourteenth and fifteenth centuries when the effects of the bubonic plague (the "Black Death") were keenly felt. Skeletal death was a measured and sedate dancer; frenzy and terror were not depicted in its moves.

We have not entirely forgotten this representation of death even today. The skeleton still dangles from doors on Halloween, although with lessening frequency because it has been placed on the politically incorrect list. The image of skull and crossbones appears on bottles containing poisonous substances, highway safety brochures, and in old Errol Flynn, or newer Johnny Depp, pirate films. The skeleton is especially conspicuous on the *Day of the Dead,* celebrated in Mexico and in Mexican American communities in the United States. The living and the dead greet each other and renew old acquaintances on this day. Special religious services are held in private homes, churches, and graveyards, and skull-shaped candies are among the delicacies of the day (perhaps not what the pious quite had in mind when singing "Come sweet death").

These are but a few of the shapes that humans see as resembling and representing death. The next shape to consider is the human form itself.

DEATH AS A PERSON

The field glitters in the intense sunlight. A solitary worker is attempting to harvest the crop with his scythe. He is:

> a vague figure fighting like a devil in the midst of the heat to get to the end of his task—I see in him the image of death, in the sense that humanity might be the wheat he is reaping. So it is—if you like—the opposite to that sower I tried to do before. But there's nothing sad in this death; it goes its way in broad daylight with a sun flooding everything with a light of pure gold (as quoted by Gottlieb, 1959, p. 161).

This was Vincent van Gogh's own interpretation of his painting. Other artists have also represented death as a person or person-like figure. Death has also had a starring role in movies. In two of death's most notable film appearances, we find the figure in a monk's robe in Ingmar Bergman's *The Seventh Seal* and as Mr. Brink in Paul Osborne's *On Borrowed Time.* In these films, a determined knight delays the death monk's victory in a chess match, and an elderly man captures Mr. Brink in a tree. Nobody can be taken by death while these serious games are in progress.

Personifications of death can be found throughout the spectrum of human expressive activity from ancient times to the present (Aries, 1981; Tamm, 2003). For example, death has often participated in children's games through the centuries. Hide-and-seek is a game that has thrilled children the world over, possibly because the child who is "it" can be understood as a stand-in for death and will catch the unwary. The child who is tagged can later enjoy taking a turn as the impersonator of death (Opie & Opie, 1969).

Personifications can help individuals and societies to cope with death by (a) objectifying an abstract concept that is difficult to grasp with the mind alone; (b) expressing feelings that are difficult to put into words; (c) serving as a coin of communication among people who otherwise would hesitate to share their feelings; (d) absorbing some of the shock, pain, anger, and fear that is experienced as a result of traumatic events; and (e) providing symbols that can be repeatedly reshaped to stimulate emotional healing and cognitive integration.

How We Personify Death: The First Study

Studies of death personification can tell us something useful about the ways in which both the individual and society are interpreting death. We are now in a position to compare young adults' personifications of death at two points in time: 1971 and 1996. Four types of personification were offered most frequently by participants in the first (1971) study. The *macabre* personification vividly depicted ugly, menacing, vicious, and repulsive characters. One undergraduate stated:

> I see Death as something I don't want to see at all. He or she—I guess it's a he, but I'm not sure—has jagged, sharp features. Everything about how he looks is sharp and threatening, his bony fingers with something like claws on the end of all of them, even a sharp nose, long, sharp teeth, and eyes that seem as though they can tear and penetrate right into you. Yet all this sharpness is almost covered over by . . . hair, bloody, matted hair.

A young nurse had difficulty in personifying death at first and then said:

> I can imagine him, Death, being nearby. It makes me feel trembly and weak, so I don't want to take a good look at him. No look at him could be good, anyhow, if you know what I mean. I feel his presence more than actually see him. I think he would be strong, unbelievably

*"Happy fortieth. I'll take the muscle tone in your upper arms,
the girlish timbre of your voice, your amazing tolerance for caffeine,
and your ability to digest French fries. The rest of you can stay."*

strong, and powerful. It could make your heart sink if you really had to look at him. But if he wanted you, there wouldn't be anything you could do about it.

Macabre personifications sometimes included outright physical deterioration. It was common for the respondents to express emotional reactions to their own images—for example, "When I look at this person—don't think it isn't possible—a shivering and nausea overwhelm me." The macabre personification often was an old person and almost always a terrifying being who is the sworn enemy of life. The relationship between age and personification is not so simple, however, as the next image reveals.

The *gentle comforter* could hardly be more different. Although usually pictured as an aged person, there was little physical and no psychological resemblance to Mr. Macabre. The gentle comforter was the very model of serenity and welcome. People who gave this kind of personification generally were those who also found the task easiest

and least threatening. The following typical example is from a registered nurse:

A fairly old man with long white hair and a long beard. A man who would resemble a biblical figure with a long robe which is clean but shabby. He would have very strong features and despite his age would appear to have strength. His eyes would be very penetrating and his hands would be large. Death would be calm, soothing, and comforting. His voice would be of an alluring nature and, although kind, would hold the tone of the mysterious. Therefore, in general, he would be kind and understanding and yet be very firm and sure of his actions and attitudes.

Another depiction suggests the respondent has been working toward an accepting attitude regarding her mortality:

*Death, I see him as very patient
and very polite. He waits for
each of us some place, just*

around a corner or even at the foot of our bed. I think of him as being there all the time, but only when we can see him is he there for us. He doesn't have to say anything and neither do we. We know what he's here for and he knows we know.

The *gay deceiver* is usually seen as a young fascinating individual. (The term does not refer to a homosexual orientation: Gay deceiver was applied to this form of death personification before *gay* became widely used as a synonym for male homosexuality.) The personification can be either male or female, often with sexual allure. The gay deceiver tends to be an elegant and worldly person who can guide one into a tempting adventure. But, as one study respondent noted, "One could not trust him. He would be elusive in his manners, hypocritical, dishonest, persuasive. Death would first gain your confidence. Then you would learn who he really is, and it would be too late."

One young woman described death in the following manner:

She is beautiful, but in a strange way. Dark eyes and long dark hair, but her skin is pale. She is slender and she is sophisticated looking. . . . I imagine her beckoning me to come with her. She will take me to a new circle of people and places, a lot fancier, more exotic than what I have in my own life. I feel sort of flattered that she would want my company, and I sort of want to go with her, to discover what I may have been missing. . . . But I am scared, too. How will this evening end?

The gay deceiver is unique for its mixture of allure, excitement, and danger. Death remains the outcome, but at least the getting there is interesting.

The *automaton* does not look like anything special. He is undistinguished in appearance. One might pass him on the street and not really notice him. The automaton tends to be dressed conservatively. There are no striking mannerisms. If there is any distinctive quality at all, it is a sort of matter-of-fact blandness, a blank expression. This "ordinariness" is an important facet of his personality and meaning. One woman, for example, characterized him as:

having no feeling of emotion about his job—either positive or negative. He simply does his job. He doesn't think about what he is doing, and there is no way to reason with him. There is no way to stop him or change his mind. When you look into his eyes you do not see a person. You see only death.

The automaton appears in human guise but lacks human qualities. He does not lure, comfort, or terrify; he just goes about his business as might any bored but competent functionary. It has always seemed to me that there is something rather modern about this depersonalized personification—Does he represent a quality of alienation in mass society?

Respondents were most likely to see death as "a gentle, well-meaning sort of person." The "grim, terrifying" image was the least frequently selected. Death usually was personified as a relatively old person. Masculine personifications were given much more frequently than feminine. In more recent samples, the percentage of feminine personifications has increased across all categories. Masculine representations continue to remain most common, however.

The Follow-Up Study

Much has changed in our society since the first study. For example, there are now many more death education courses, grief counselors, peer support groups, and hospice care programs—as well as a raging controversy over physician-assisted death. There are also larger societal changes, such as the reduction of a nuclear war menace, the increase in terrorism, transformations in electronic communication, and continued progress in the empowerment of women. Have our personifications of death also changed in some way?

In a follow-up study, Kastenbaum and Herman (1997) found that:

- Death is still represented predominantly as a male—but there is a sharp increase in female personifications from female respondents.
- Men and women now differ more in the type of personality they attribute to death. Women

continue to favor the image of death as the gentle comforter. Men, however, now most often describe death as a "cold and remote" person. The men were also more likely than the women to see death as "grim and terrifying." More than three fourths of the men but a little less than half of the women saw death as either cold or grim.

- There is still a tendency for the gentle comforter to be viewed as an elderly person, but this is no longer true of the other personifications.

After completing the death personification items, respondents were asked to identify Jack Kevorkian. He was at that time in the news almost every day for his advocacy and practice of physician-assisted death. Almost all respondents correctly reported that he is the physician who "puts people out of their misery" and who always seems to be in court defending his right to do so. We had wondered if Dr. Kevorkian's central role in the public controversy on physician-assisted death might have produced a new or modified personification, one that might be modeled after him. The answer was clear. Nobody mentioned Dr. Kevorkian as a person who came to mind when they thought about their death personifications. Despite his media image as "Doctor Death," Kevorkian did not influence death personifications. Perhaps our personifications come from deeper levels of the mind, as discussed by Jung (1959) and Neumann (1971), and therefore cannot easily be moved aside by passing faces and events. Perhaps there are other reasons. What do you think? Why did the next generation of young men have more negative images of personified death than those who were young a quarter of a century ago—while young women continue to feel that death is gentle and comforting? Perhaps it is time for another study.

CONDITIONS THAT DEATH RESEMBLES

"That was an awfully dead party," we might say, just as actors might remark when the final curtain drops, "Whew! What a dead house tonight!" Or we say comment, "Look how tired she is—she's dead on her feet!" These are examples of using death or dead as metaphors to describe other things. Here are some other ways in which deadness serves as an instructive way of acknowledging certain aspects of life.

Social Death

You are with other people but nobody is paying attention to you. You might as well not be there at all. *Social death* is identified by observing how a person is treated by others. The individuals themselves may be animated enough. They may even be desperately seeking interaction. Despite their readiness for recognition and contact, they are being disconfirmed and excluded. The concept of social death recognizes that when we die in the eyes of others, we may become somewhat less of a person.

Social death can be seen in ways such as the following:

- A person has violated one of the taboos of the group. As a result, the individual is "cut dead." This could be the West Point cadet who is given the silent treatment or the child who married somebody of the "wrong" religion, race, or socioeconomic echelon.
- A member of the tribe violates a taboo and is ritualistically expelled, a symbolic execution. In a bone-pointing ceremony, the tribal community certifies one of its errant members as dead. This public ritual does not harm a hair on the offender's head but terminates the individual's life as a group member. The offender's property may be redistributed, and his or her name may be discarded or assigned to somebody else after it has become decontaminated. A parallel process sometimes occurs in mainstream Western society. For example, when an agency supervisor was dismissed on the basis of sexual harassment charges, a corporate official issued a command to all the agency employees: This man's name was never to be mentioned again. Here was bone pointing, minus the bone. The law may also strip a person of the rights of citizenship, and the church may excommunicate.
- The social transformation of a living person into custodial object can occur in modern facilities with cheerful decor as well as grim and decrepit institutions. Even the old person who lives independently in the community can be victim of the socially dead treatment (e.g., being passed over while trying to get the atten-

tion of a store clerk or being placed at the bottom of medical or educational priorities). Exclusionary actions have also operated against people who have developed feared diseases such as AIDS, or against those who make others uncomfortable because of scars or physical infirmities. A person whose face has been severely burned in an accident, for example, may discover that others avert their eyes and keep a greater distance.

- A dying person may be treated as though already dead. An elaborate pattern of aversive and person-denying behavior may be generated around a living person whose demise is anticipated. This pattern is likely to include little or no eye contact, reluctance to touch, and talking to others in the presence of the person as though he or she were not there. What makes this kind of situation even more unfortunate is that the person taken for dead may still be very much alive, alert, and capable of meaningful interaction.

Phenomenological Death

Concentrate now on what is taking place inside the person. Regardless of society's attitudes and actions, is the individual alive to himself or herself? There are two types of phenomenological death. First, part of the person may die in the mind of the surviving or observing self. Partial death can range in personal significance from the trivial to the profound. Two examples follow:

- A young man undergoes surgery that saves his life but results in the loss of the capacity to father children. In his own mind, one part of his total self has died. He will never be a parent. Although much else about his own self remains alive to me, there is now the mental and emotional challenge of working through the loss of one of his most valued potential roles and sources of satisfaction.
- A young athlete is physically fit by most standards. But she has suffered an injury in athletic competition that is just disabling enough to end her career. She is a runner with bad knees. She was an accomplished athlete both in her mind and in the minds of others. Now she has to remake her identity, while still mourning privately for the athlete who has perished.

In the first example there is a surviving self who recognizes the loss of one or more components of the total self. "I am still here, but I am not the person I once was or might have become." There is an element of mourning for the lost aspect of the self. The other type of phenomenological death is quite different. Here, the total self takes on a deadened tone. The person does not experience life as freshly or intensely as in the past. Pleasures do not really please. Even pain may fail to break through the feeling of dulled indifference.

Feeling dead to yourself is a quality of experience that can shade into depersonalization: "I have no body," or "This body is not mine." Some psychotic people present themselves as though they were dead, as we have already seen. This can be either in the sense that they have actually died or through the impression that they do not relate to their own bodies and biographies as though they belong to living persons. This may be accompanied by a depersonalized attitude toward other people as well. The person may be mute, slow moving, and given to maintaining a rigid posture for protracted periods (as in the catatonic form of schizophrenia).

The sense of inner deadness or fading out sometimes is experienced with the use of alcohol or other drugs. It can also accompany other alterations in bodily state. Whatever the cause, the circumstances, or the outcome, we must recognize a state of mind in which the person becomes dead to himself.

People sometimes choose pain over sedation to avoid the sense of being dead to themselves (Baider, 1975):

Mrs. A. was a 62-year-old Puerto Rican woman who constantly refused to take any medicine, even when in great pain. Her rationale was similar to that of other Puerto Rican patients (with far advanced cancer) I met. Doctors don't know as much as they think they do about the person's body. Each body has a soul, and if the doctor cannot see the soul, then he cannot see the body. "I know, I know that my family does not want that I suffer . . . but suffering is part of life . . . and without it you are not a man. No medicine can help with any pain . . . or, sometimes it could help putting all your body asleep . . . like a baby . . . and then it takes away my pain . . . but it also takes away all that I feel and see. If I could feel the pain I can also feel my body . . . and then I know I am still alive (p. 378).

One person, perhaps in good physical health, reduces the sense of aliveness in an effort to avoid emotional pain. Another person, perhaps in extremely poor health, accepts intense physical pain as a link to life itself. These differences in our relationships to phenomenological aliveness and deadness are but two of the variations that must be acknowledged as we continue our exploration into the human encounter with death.

THE UNDEAD

The borderline between "alive" and "dead" has been crossed many times by human imagination, accompanied variously by hope, fear, curiosity, and downright thrill seeking. The vampire is one of the earliest and most enduring characters in this tradition. Although well represented in fiction, drama, and parody, the vampire also has had a featured role in fertility rites, religious thought, and world folk culture. The *revenant* and the *zombie* are other creatures who reside in the shadowlands between life and death. We have already seen that biomedical developments sometimes blur the distinction between alive, and how our use of metaphoric language can foster ambiguity. The Undead, then, are not quite as far out as they might seem to rational people like us. (We are rational, aren't we?)

In visiting The Undead it would be best to leave behind our media-saturated images and stereotypes. With all respects to Bela Lugosi, Vincent Price, George Montgomery, Vampira, Buffy, and other stars of the genre, we really need to learn what we can about the birth, history, and perhaps fate of The Undead.

The Fertile Dead

Life gives way to death. This stubborn fact was recognized by our most remote ancestors. But death also gives way to life. The dry, wilted field awakens to the bird song of spring. A soul passes out of this life, and a new—or recycled—soul appears. Agricultural people such as the ancient Egyptians were embedded in the procession of seasons, their survival dependent on renewal by sun and flood. Farmers encouraged their crops

with deconstructed organic materials that became known as fertilizers. Rituals were performed to persuade the gods to keep the good times coming. Sacrifices were crucial to fertility rituals in many parts of the world: A particularly effective sacrifice involved elevating a member of the society into a transcendent role: "You are king! No, wait! You are god!" This promotion was, in the truest sense, short-lived. The hero-king-god would be ritually murdered, and his remains offered to that always ravenous mega-creature, *The Great Mother.* Neumann (1963, pp. 148–149) lays this out for us:

> In the myths and tales of all people, ages, and countries—and even in the nightmares of our own nights—witches and vampires, ghouls and specters, assail us, all terrifyingly alike. . . . This Terrible Mother is the hungry earth, which devours its own children.

Here we have come to the heart of what we might call *The Undead Complex.* This is a culturally-shared, emotionally-charged belief configuration with the following components:

- Something mysterious happens between life and death and between death and life. What was living loses breath and blood, becomes pale and stiff. What is buried under ground sprouts new life. People, too?
- This is scary stuff, because the decomposition of the body is so repulsive.
- This is also sacred stuff because gods control the life and death cycle. Somebody or something must be at work underground to digest and reconstruct the dead. The Egyptians identified the scarab (aka dung beetle) as a significant intermediary.
- We should therefore cherish the intermediaries between life and death, no matter how their work and their persons might offend our sensibilities. At the same time, it is prudent to beware of creatures that scuttle back and forth from the grave—especially when they sport human-like features, distorted, mocking images of ourselves.

From Beast to Dark Lover

Vampire is derived from a Slavic word that also meant werewolf (Perkowski, 1989). And, indeed, there was an earthy and bestial quality to the vampires who haunted the imagination of European peasants through many centuries.

They were often crude, smelly creatures who were more likely to attack a cow than seduce a lady in her boudoir. This primitive vampire was at home in superstition and folk tale. The people of the village knew he was real, though: who else could account for those savage attacks, and look at how this grave has been disturbed!

An upgraded vampire started to emerge in the early eighteenth century, and a broader public took notice. This version was a lot more interesting, if for all the wrong reasons. He (and occasionally, she) had an inordinate craving for blood. This intensified obsession coincided with the introduction of transfusions that, in themselves, raised hopes, fears, and fantasies. Experiments with electricity were also starting to test the possibility of reanimating the dead—so the vampire now had a larger stage on which to slither. Now clearly more human than animal, the vampire was at home in two places where most were not: the night and the grave. The dark side of respectable non-vampires was weirdly receptive to this terrible, and also naughty creature.

The decisive step up the cultural ladder occurred when the vampire went literary. Several stories had already made the rounds, but it was Bram Stoker's *Dracula* (original 1897; in Wolf, 1975) that established the vampire as the model to whom all others must aspire. Count Dracula was a sophisticate of royal blood whose horrifying nocturnal activities included more than a hint of forbidden sexuality. Stoker fashioned Dracula from Slavic folk materials. Stage productions drew huge audiences who cringed with horrified delight. The film industry, when it arrived, made him into a star. Ordinary leading men, let alone the average fellow in the audience, were confronted by a rival who could outdo them in just about every department that counted (other than political correctness). Women were properly appalled and improperly thrilled.

It did not take long, though, for nervous laughter to arise as a putdown. Dracula proved to be a reliable source of comic material, from vaudeville to contemporary film and television. Even Halloween children could master the master of darkness by impersonating him with plastic fangs and cape. Don't be scared, folks. Scholars, bold creatures that they are, also ventured to net the vampire in their treatises (interesting examples include Auerbach's (1995) *Our Vampires, Ourselves,* and Wilcox's (2006), *Why Buffy Matters.* The vampire would now be deconstructed for us in feminist, political, and psychoanalytic terms.

The vintage vampire is not yet on the endangered list, but does have to find his and her way through the complexities of postmodern life. The many novels by Anne Rice and other popular writers have invited us to understand and perhaps feel a little compassion for those who find it as hard to die as to live. In doing so, perhaps we might also accept the invitation to revisit the darker side of our own natures where life and death do not necessarily obey the rules of strict rationality.

Bringing the Vampire Down to Earth

We have bypassed the most obvious question about vampires in order to present this brief survey of their origins in the human mind and their reputed behaviors. This question is, of course: *Are they real?* Paul Barber (1988) has offered a persuasive analysis that will serve until/unless a better one comes along. He notes that people have been mighty curious and mighty disturbed about what might be going on in the grave. We see people die and we bury them—but then what? Hardly anybody knew the details of decomposition, the sequence of changes that a corpse undergoes in the grave. Fantasies find it easy to arise from this ignorance. Most of the reports that fostered the vampire legend came from rural areas of Eastern Europe and featured unnatural happenings (our cow's milk turned sour!) and untidy graves. Barber explains the untidy grave as follows:

- Animals dig up bodies from shallow graves: that's why it's empty!
- Flooding uncovers bodies from shallow graves: he didn't excavate himself!
- Grave robbers, well, they rob graves, looking for anything useful, including marketable body parts.
- The corpse probably did move a little. That's what happens when gasses form and expand.
- This corpse looks in better than expected condition, but check the temperature and the soil chemistry.

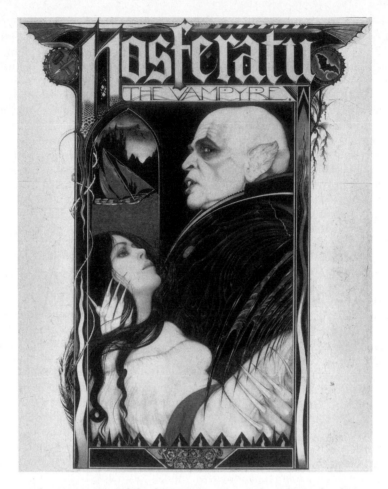

Nosferatu was one of the first vampires to make it big in books, on stage, in movies. He has been largely replaced by more recent versions, but still invades the nightmares of people with long memories.

The null hypothesis is, as ever, a tough proposition to prove. Neither Barber nor anybody else can say—for sure—that there never was or never might be an authentic vampire, but positive evidence for their existence is not abundant. The situation is similar for revenants—sad, wandering spirits still in their human form. It is likely that figures matching that description have been encountered, but less likely that they are dead men walking. Zombies have been described in somewhat similar terms. A true zombie has returned from his grave with a diminished capacity for thought and feeling. Unlike revenants and

vampires, zombies have been associated largely with the voodoo religion and Creole culture as practiced in Haiti, West Africa, and areas of the U.S. South. The available evidence seems sufficient for conjecture, but insufficient for firm conclusion. A leading hypothesis (Davis, 1988) is that so-called zombies are people who slipped into a nonresponsive trance after being deliberately poisoned with a serving of puffer fish (yes, that Japanese delicacy!). They might have been buried before recovering or they might have interpreted their lapse of consciousness as death. Tradition has it that zombies can also be created through religious rituals that might or might not include drugs. Zombies have a secure place in our repertoire of fringe beings and continue to work steadily in the motion picture industry. Much larger and sometimes much scarier than the humble Egyptian dung beetle, they do lack the luminosity of the sacred.

Today's Undead still bear some marks of their sacred, bestial, and gothic-romantic ancestry. It might only be in our nightmares, however, that we catch a whiff of their mysterious mission between the living and the dead.

DEATH AS AN AGENT OF PERSONAL, POLITICAL, AND SOCIAL CHANGE

The meanings of death often can be encountered in public as well as personal life. How we interpret death can either support the status quo or hasten political and social change. The following are major examples of death at work within society.

The Great Leveler

Since ancient times, people have been sorting each other out by class, caste, sex, physique, race, geography—and whatever I've left out. The result is a structure of dominance and submission. For example, the latest wave of immigrants to the United States from "the old country" often were looked down upon by those who had made the same transition a little earlier. Those who have themselves been victims of discrimination on the basis of religious or racial identities sometimes discriminate against people within their own groups (e.g., as "too orthodox" or "too liberal" or as looking too much like, or too much different from, those in the mainstream). How far does the urge to discriminate go? Does it at least end with death?

On the eve of his execution in 1672, Peter Patrix (1910) wrote these lines in his dungeon cell. He would be thrilled if you would read them aloud with a proper sneer:

I dreamt that, buried in my fellow clay,
Close by a common beggar's side I lay.
And, as so mean a neighbor shock'd my pride,

Thus, like a corpse of quality, I cried,
"Away, thou scoundrel! Henceforth touch me not;
More manners learn, and at a distance rot!"
"Thou scoundrel!" in a louder tone, cried he,
"Proud lump of dirt! I scorn thy word and thee.
We're equal now, I'll not an inch resign;
This is my dunghill, as the next is thine." (p. 292)

Yes, death has often been used in an ironic and forceful manner to support the cause of equal worth and rights during life. It is unsettling for the ruling class to concede that death has equal power over the mighty and the lowly. Shakespeare expresses this realization in a speech he gives to King Richard II:

Within the hollow crown
That rounds the mortal temples of a king
Keeps Death his court; and there the antick sits,
Mocking his state, and grinning at his pomp;
Allows him a breath, a little scene,
To monarchize, be fear'd, and kill with looks;
Infusing him with self and vain conceit—
As if this flesh, which walls about his life,
Were brass impregnable; and humor'd thus,
Comes at the last, and with a little pin
Bores through his castle wall, and—
farewell king!
(III: 2)

This speech probably did not increase the comfort level of crowned heads the world over. With no weapon other than his pen, Shakespeare had advanced the cause of a society in which the living as well as the dead might regard each other as people with certain inalienable rights.

Works of art commissioned during medieval times often displayed the theme of death as the great leveler. Gallant knights and beauteous maidens are interrupted on their journeys by death, often in the form of a skeleton. Skulls stare sightlessly from tables, shelves, and nearly hidden corners of the room as scholars ponder their books or marriage rites are performed. In such ways did the elite remind themselves that pride and triumphs are fragile commodities.

The enormous toll of lives taken by the bubonic plague during its several major visitations temporarily unseated both the aristocracy and the church. Death did not seem impressed with the powers-that-be on earth. Peasants observed how royalty and church officials either fell prey to the disease or scurried away, unable to exercise any control. The first clumsy revolutions were attempted, and a few reforms were achieved (only to be lost when the power establishment had recovered itself). Many years later, a new and more equitable social order would take hold. As the winds of social change swept through Europe, death the leveler had a distinctive role, emboldening the common person to resist the established system. Peter Patrix would have liked that.

The Great Validator

Society can also use death to measure the value of its deceased members. Funereal splendor is an obvious way of using death to demonstrate the worth of individuals—and, perhaps more importantly, their survivors. A Midwestern funeral director described the situation as he sees it:

> I do what you want me to do. You come in here and say you want simple arrangements, and that is exactly what I will provide. You know what you want, and I am here to meet your needs. . . . But let me tell you why I sell some of the more expensive items—it's because the people themselves want it that way! . . . They are not satisfied until they feel they are getting the best funeral for their loved one that they can afford. . . . If everybody wanted bare-minimum funerals, that is what we would be providing. When you see a big, a magnificent funeral, you are seeing what the family felt it truly must have.

Interestingly, the tradition of a "big funeral" in which no expense is spared has its roots in early American tradition. In colonial days, families sometimes spent themselves to the verge of poverty. Religious leaders such as Cotton Mathers decried the lavish funerals much as critics do today, but many of his brethren remained intent on proving their piety and worth by funereal displays.

The opportunity for survivors to affirm their own worth through the funeral process (Chapter 10) has been seized upon throughout the centuries. The heroine in a Greek tragedy risks her own life by arranging for the proper burial of her outcast brother. Committees meet in closed session to decide whether a deceased person is distinguished enough to deserve burial in sacred soil. And the legendary cowboy simply implores, "Bury me not on the lone prairie."

We have found that obituary notices in Boston and New York newspapers give more space and more often use photographs in reporting the deaths of men as compared with women (Kastenbaum, Peyton, & Kastenbaum, 1977). Studies by other researchers in the United States and the United Kingdom have confirmed this finding (Moremen, 2003). It has also been found that most of the obituaries were written by men. Do your own study today and you might find that the gender gap in honoring the dead is decreasing as more women have become prominent in society.

Death Unites/Separates

Death radically alters our relationships with others. It can be seen either as the ultimate act of separation or the opportunity to rejoin others who have gone before us. Occasionally death has even been seen as a way of bringing friends and foes together. Alexander Pope wrote in the seventeenth century:

> The grave united, where even the great find rest
> And blended lie the oppressor and oppressed.
> (Lines 315–316)

Two centuries later, a British soldier imagined his own battlefield death—an event that soon thereafter actually happened as World War I neared its end. Wilfred Owen (1918) concluded his antiwar poem with this poignant stanza:

> I am the enemy you killed, my friend.
> I knew you in this dark, for so you frowned
> Yesterday through me as you jabbed and killed.
> I parried; but my hands were loath and cold.
> Let us sleep now (p. 1).

The despairing or dying person may yearn to become united with God. This hope is expressed in many hymns and carols. Typical is this verse included in a popular collection of 1844, *The Original Sacred Heart:*

Northfield
How long, dear Savior, O how long
Shall this bright hour delay?
Fly swift around, ye wheels of time,
And bring the promised day.

This promise, however, was not without its threatening aspect. The gravestone marker for Miss Polly Coombes of Bellingham, Massachusetts, (dated 1785) takes a somber and challenging tone:

READER ATTEND: THIS STATE
WILL SOON BE THINE
BE THOU IN YOUTHFUL HEALTH
OR IN DECLINE
PREPARE TO MEET THY GOD

Perhaps the most common form of the union-through-death theme is the wish to be with loved ones who are "on the other side." An old woman dreams that she has become a little girl once again and is being welcomed by her father. A boy wrestles privately with thoughts of suicide so that he can join the big brother he misses so much. The survivor of a random, drive-by shooting consoles herself with the expectation of being reunited some day with her slain family member. Although some of us may find comfort in the prospect of reunion with loved ones through death, the more obvious consequence is separation. The familiar face of someone who has died is not to be seen again. One has lost a treasured companion, and the pain of separation can be overwhelming.

"I felt like part of me had been pulled apart. Like I wasn't a whole person any more. And then I went numb. Like I was in shock, with loss of blood, just like I had lost an arm or a leg or worse." This is the way a young woman felt when she learned that her husband had been killed in Vietnam. He had been alive to his loved ones until the message came, although in objective fact he had been dead for an indeterminate period of time. The moment that his wife learned of their final separation is the moment when the death event occurred for her. The moment we as survivors feel the shock and anguish of separation may be the most significant moment of death. The shock and pain of sudden loss was experienced again by thousands of Americans after the terrorist attacks of September 11, 2001. Family and friends of terrorist victims had some comfort in knowing that the nation shared in their grief: Those bereaved by the Vietnam War had much less support because the war itself had been opposed by many people.

This sense of separation can occur in advance of the actual death and linger long afterward. For example, some families face the probable death of their living children while still suffering from the loss of one or more who have already died:

The family were still grieving Ann's death when Roy began to exhibit symptoms of the same disease. . . . Adam has a similar form of the same illness. . . . "We know it all now—we shall be left with nothing—no children—nothing" (Atkin, 1974, p. 66).

Children also experience the sorrow of separation from each other, even if they do not fully understand the concept of death:

He had lost one sibling and was facing the experience a second time. His sister, in the latter stages of her illness, seemed unaware and unresponsive. Yet her little brother seemed to evoke some faint recognition. She appeared to smile with her eyes—a last window into the darkness. He said: "I don't mind if you don't talk to me. It's lonely without you. I can talk to you." He prattled on about his rabbit, his cars, and his wish to have a party on his birthday (p. 69).

The difficulty in understanding death, coupled with the strong need to continue the relationship, can lead both children and adults to behave at times as though final separation had not really taken place (see also Chapters 8 and 11). The deceased person may still be spoken of in the present tense ("Jimmy only likes smooth peanut butter"), and interaction patterns may seem to include the expectation that the deceased has been only temporarily detained.

The Ultimate Problem or the Ultimate Solution?

Death is sometimes regarded as either the ultimate problem or the ultimate solution. As individuals or as a society we may even hold both views at the same time.

A dark jest made the rounds in the aftermath of the French Revolution: "Come and see the wonderful new machine—a miracle! One treatment by the good Dr. Guillotine and—phoof!—never again a headache!" The Guillotine brothers were actually appalled by public executions and suggested the device as a replacement for slower and more painful methods. But why have public executions in the first place? Are there no other ways to resolve conflicts and protect the legitimate interests of society?

Death as ultimate solution has been applied on a mass level as well (Chapter 9). Hitler's "final solution of the Jewish problem," translated into the genocidal murder of more than 6 million men, women, and children—Jews and large numbers of Romani (gypsies) and others despised as "non-Aryan." Unfortunately, the attempt to solve a problem by killing others neither started nor ended with the Holocaust. Angola . . . Burundi . . . Haiti . . . Somalia . . . The Sudan—these are among the names of nations from which reports of mass violence continue to reach us. Never mind history; we need read only today's news.

Opposing this theme is the conviction that death, far from being the final solution, is humankind's worst enemy and most profound problem. Death may be seen as the ultimate problem because it ends our opportunity to achieve. This is certainly a threat in a society in which the need to achieve has been a dominant motive. ("I can't die just yet—I have so much to do!")

Death may also be seen as the ultimate problem because it brings the curtain down the theater of inner experience. We will have no more thoughts, no more feelings. Consciousness, awareness, will be extinguished. Still again, death may be seen as the ultimate problem because it defies understanding. Faith may be sufficient for some people, but others may be frustrated because the human intellect seems incapable of penetrating the mystery of death. The last words of the dying are sometimes given special attention in the hope that those who are closest to the mystery might also be closer to the answer and somehow able to impart this answer to us. Unfortunately, this logic is questionable

(Kastenbaum, 1993, 2002a). We can learn much from the strength and resourcefulness of many people as they cope with the dying process, but they do not necessarily understand death any better than the rest of us.

The Ultimate Meaningless Event

Random, senseless death might be regarded as the ultimate meaningless event. A young man fires an automatic weapon into a group of people working out in a health-and-fitness facility. A person who will later be described as a "disgruntled former employee" returns to the workplace and fires at everybody who happens to be there. A retired man with a grudge against a homeowners' association blasts away at neighbors enjoying themselves at a community center. The family, friends, and colleagues of these victims suffer not only the grief of loss, but also the shock and confusion that accompany an event that is outside one's normal frame of reference. We can understand why violent death might occur in the course of criminal activities or dysfunctional relationships. Some deaths, however, appear to make no sense at all, especially those in which the killer did not know the victim or have anything palpable to gain from the act of murder.

Fatal accidents can also raise the question of meaninglessness. A man survives many hazardous battle situations but is killed by a neighbor backing her car out of the driveway. An infant is left unattended for a few minutes and drowns in a bathtub that contained only a few inches of water. Two children are playing quietly on a sidewalk near the school when a van swerves over the curb, strikes them dead, and then plows into another group of people. The consequences of a few minutes of inattention or a disregard for safety precautions seem so tremendously out of proportion to the "little" error that was involved. As with the victims of random killings, accidental deaths may seem to violate our basic expectations about life. This is not the way things are supposed to happen, not the way that lives are supposed to end.

Most people are reluctant to conclude that there is no answer. It is difficult to accept the proposition that a death could be meaningless, because this implies that life, too, might not be part of a meaningful, rational, and coherent universal pattern. Perhaps we are misled at times by faith in rationality. There has to be a good explanation for everything—even death. Everything has to make sense; everything (even nothing) has to be logical.

But—maybe not!

SUMMARY

There are many competing answers to the related questions: What is death? What does death mean? Epicurus (third century B.C.) held that the universe consisted fundamentally of atoms in motion without any guiding principle or purpose. In this indifferent universe, neither life nor death had any special meaning. Christianity entered with a powerful message of hope—a sanctified life after death—but also with the complications of death itself as punishment for sin. For people who are often described as "New Agers," death is not meaningless, punishment, or salvation. It is simply one of the way stations in a long, perhaps infinite spiritual journey across many lives. Fantasy (Victor Frankenstein) and actual (Charles Darwin) scientists of the past explored the uncertain boundaries between life and death, and this endeavor continues to flourish today. The competing ideas about death can be seen as symbolic constructions, drawn from our experiences, our needs, and our guesswork. It would be difficult to do without a concept of death, but it seems almost as difficult to agree on the specifics.

The biomedical approach is more complex and tends to focus on the question: When (under what conditions) is a person dead? The development of life-support systems and organ transplantation procedures has created more situations in which questions can arise. The Harvard Criteria for determining brain death have become useful guidelines to decision making. Nevertheless, it is a challenge to recognize such distinctions as persistent, permanent, and transient forms of vegetative state, as well as the minimally conscious syndrome and several other conditions, all of which have implications for decision making.

Several interpretations of the death state were examined. The traditional interpretations are death as (1) enfeebled state, (2) continuation of life, (3) perpetual development, (4) waiting, (5) cycling and recycling, and (6) nothing. We also considered an emerging new interpretation: death as virtual and, therefore, not really death at all. We also explored objects and conditions that resemble death. These include inorganic and unresponsive objects, sleep and altered states of consciousness, and beings who resemble or seem to personify death. The most commonly given death personifications were identified and discussed. There are also conditions that death resembles, such as social and phenomenological death.

The Undead have flourished since ancient times as mysterious, frightening, yet perhaps essential components of the life-into-death-into-life cycle. The vampire's transition from bestial predator to dark lover reveals how society can do a make-over on its symbolic constructions. We are also reminded that a purely rational approach to the interplay of life and death would distort the reality of darkness and light.

Death has often served as an agent of personal, political, and social change. It has taken the form of the great validator that measures the social value of deceased people, but death has also been seen as uniting or separating people, representing the ultimate problem, the ultimate solution, or the ultimate meaningless event.

REFERENCES

Ad Hoc Committee of the Harvard Medical School to Examine the Definition of Brain Death. (1968). A definition of irreversible coma. *Journal of the American Medical Association, 205,* 337–340.

Alexander, S. (1920). *Space, time, and deity:* Vols. 1–2. London: Macmillan.

Aries, P. (1981). *The hour of our death.* New York: Knopf.

Atkin, M. (1974). The "doomed family": Observations on the lives of parents and children facing repeated child mortality. In L. Burton (Ed.), *Care of the child facing death.* London & Boston: Routledge & Kegan Paul.

Auerbach, N. (1995). *Our vampires, ourselves.* Chicago: University of Chicago Press.

Baider, L. (1975). Private experience and public expectations on the cancer ward. *Omega, Journal of Death and Dying, 6,* 373–382.

Barber, P. (1990). *Vampires, burial, and death: Folklore and reality.* New Haven, CT: Yale University Press.

Block, M., & Parry, J. (Eds.). (1996). *Death and the regeneration of life.* Cambridge, UK: Cambridge University Press.

Bunson, M. (1993). *The vampire encyclopedia.* New York: Gramercy.

Burns, J. M., Login, I. S., Bruno, M. K., Kimura, C., Crisci, G., Saposnik, L., Beslac-Bumbasirevic, S. G., Jovanic, D., Ercegovac, M., & Wijdicks, E. F. (2002). Brain death worldwide: Accepted fact but no global consensus in diagnostic criteria. *Neurology, 59,* 470–471.

Davis, W. (1988). *Passage of darkness: The ethnobiology of the Haitian zombie.* Chapel Hill: University of North Carolina Press.

Fechner, G. T. (1977). *The little book of life after death.* (Reprinted by New York: Arno.) (Original work published 1836.)

Giacino, J. T., Ashwal, S., Childs, N., Cranford, R., Jennett, B., Katz, D. I., Kelly, J. P., Rosenberg, J. H., Whyte, J., Zafonte, D. O., & Zasler, N. D. (2002). The minimally conscious state. *Neurology, 58,* 349–353.

Goldsmith, T. H., & Zimmer, W. F. (2001). *Biology, evolution, and human nature.* New York: Wiley.

Gottlieb, C. (1959). Modern art and death. In H. Feifel (Ed.), *The meaning of death* (pp. 157–188). New York: McGraw-Hill.

International Society for Plastination. http://edis.at/plast

Iserson, K. V. (2003). Persistent vegetative state. In R. Kastenbaum (Ed.), *Macmillan encyclopedia of death and dying:* Vol. 2 (pp. 668–669). New York: Macmillan.

Jennett, B. (2003). *The vegetative state: Medical facts, ethical and legal dilemmas.* New York: Cambridge University Press.

Jung, C. G. (1959). *Four archetypes.* Princeton, NJ: Princeton University Press.

Kapleau, P. (1971). *The wheel of death.* New York: Harper & Row.

Kastenbaum, R. (1993). Last words. *The Monist. An International Journal of General Philosophical Inquiry, 76,* 270–290.

Kastenbaum, R. (2000a). Looking death in the eye: Another challenge from Doctor Kevorkian. In K. K. Kalman (Ed.), *Right to die versus sacredness of life* (pp. 279–286). Amityville, NY: Baywood.

Kastenbaum, R. (2000b). *The psychology of death* (3rd ed.). New York: Springer Publishing Co.

Kastenbaum, R. (2002a). Last words. In R. Kastenbaum (Ed.), *Macmillan encyclopedia of death and dying:* Vol. 2 (pp. 515–518). New York: Macmillan.

Kastenbaum, R. (2003). Thanatomimesis. In R. Kastenbaum (Ed.), *Macmillan encyclopedia of death and dying:* Vol. 2 (p. 888). New York: Macmillan.

Kastenbaum, R. (2004). *On our way. The final passage through life and death.* Berkeley: University of California Press.

Kastenbaum, R., & Herman, C. (1997). *Death personification in the Kevorkian era. Death Studies, 21,* 115–130.

Kastenbaum, R., Peyton, S., & Kastenbaum, B. (1977). Sex discrimination after death. *Omega, Journal of Death and Dying, 6,* 33–44.

Kevorkian, J. (1957). Rapid and accurate ophthalmoscopic determination of circulatory arrest. *Journal of the American Medical Association, 164,* 1660–1662.

Kevorkian, J. (1961). The eye in death. *CIBA Clinical Symposia, 13,* 51–62.

Kramer, K. P. (2003). Hinduism. In R. Kastenbaum (Ed.), *Macmillan encyclopedia of death and dying:* Vol. 1. (pp. 410–44). New York: Macmillan.

Leon-Dufour, X. (1986). *Life and death in the New Testament.* New York: Harper & Row.

McCullagh, P. (1993). *Brain dead, brain absent, brain donors.* New York: Wiley.

Moremen, R. D. (2003). Gender discrimination after death. In R. Kastenbaum (Ed.), *Macmillan encyclopedia of death and dying:* Vol. 1 (pp. 311–314). New York: Macmillan.

Morgan, L. (1923). *Emergent evolution.* London: Williams & Norgate.

Neumann, E. (1971). *The origins and history of consciousness.* Princeton, N.J.: Princeton University Press.

Opie, I., & Opie, P. (1969). *Children's games in street and playground.* London: Oxford University Press.

Owen, W. (1918). Strange meeting. www.illyria.com/owenstr-html

Patrix, P. (1910). In F. P. Weber (Ed.), *Aspects of death and correlated aspects of life in art, epigram, and poetry.* London: H. K. Lewis & Co., Ltd., 292.

Perkowski, J. L. (Ed.) (1976). *Vampires of the Slavs.* Cambridge, MA: Slavica Publishers.

Pope, A. (Original work published 1746). *Windsor-Forest.* http://andromeda.rutgers.edu/-ilynch/tests/windsor.html

Schultz, N. W, & Huet, L. M. (2000–2001). Sensational! Violent! Popular! Death in American movies. *Omega, Journal of Death and Dying, 42,* 137–150.

ScienceSpace (no date). vrinfo@gmu.edu

Segall, A. (1990). *Paul the convert.* New Haven: Yale University Press.

Seifert, J. (1993). Is "brain death" actually death? *The Monist. An International Journal of General Philosophical Inquiry, 76,* 175–202.

Shelley, M. (1977). *Frankenstein, or the modern Prometheus.* In L. Wolf (Ed.), *The annotated Frankenstein.* New York: Potter. (Original work published 1818.)

Shrock, N. M. (1835). On the signs that distinguish real from apparent death. *Transylvanian Journal of Medicine, 13,* 210–220.

Stoker, B. (1975). *Dracula.* In L. Wolf (Ed.), *The annotated Dracula.* New York: Potter. (Original work published 1897.)

Summers, M. (1928). *The vampire and his kith and kin.* New York: E. P. Dutton.

Talbot, M. (1992). *The holographic universe.* New York: HarperPerennial.

Tamm, M. E. (2003). Personifications of death. In R. Kastenbaum (Ed.), *Macmillan encyclopedia of death and dying:* Vol. 2 (pp. 669–671). New York: Macmillan.

Twain, M. (1972). *Life on the Mississippi.* Reprinted by Norwalk, CT: Heritage. (Original work published 1883.)

Von Hagens, G. (March 27, 2002) in Chris Hogg, Body Parts. http://news.hbc.co.uk1/hi/t21Greg.Point/Forum/1888662.stm.

Wade, D. T., & Johnston, C. (1999). The permanent vegetative state: Practical guidance on diagnosis and management. http://bmj.bmjjournals.com/cgi/content/full/319/7213/841

Wijdicks, E. F. M. (2001). The diagnosis of brain death. *New England Journal of Medicine, 344,* 1215–1221.

Wilcox, R. (2006). *Why Buffy matters.* London: I. B. Tauris.

Zaid, B. A. (2002). The Islamic ruling on brain death and life support. TheModernReligion.com/misc/hh/braindeath.html

GLOSSARY

Brain death: A condition in which vegetative processes of the body may continue, although the capacity for thought, experience, and behavior has been destroyed.

Catatonia: A neuropsychiatric disorder that at times takes the appearance of stupor, rigidity, immobility, and mutism.

Coma, comatose: A deep state of unconsciousness from which the individual cannot be aroused.

EEG: The electroencephalogram presents a visual display of the ongoing electrical activity of the brain.

Intravenous fluids: Liquids that are introduced directly into the veins to restore metabolic balance and provide nutrition, avoid dehydration, or treat infections.

Martyrdom: The heroic sacrifice of one's life for a cause or faith.

Minimally conscious state: Severe impairment distinguished from coma or vegetative state by occasional and limited evidence of awareness.

Respirator brain: Physical destruction of the brain as observed in postmortem examinations.

Revenant: An undead wanderer who does not necessarily behave like a vampire.

Transient vegetative state: Characteristics are those of the *Vegetative State* but caused by drugs, extreme cold, or injury that has some potential for recovery.

Vampire: A nocturnally reanimated corpse who seeks fresh blood.

Vegetative state: Sleep-wake cycles, respiration, and other vital autonomic activities continue, but awareness and thought are absent. A persistent vegetative state may be reclassified as a permanent vegetative state after long duration.

Virtual reality: Computer-generated scenes, beings, and events that simulate actual or possible versions of the world.

Zombie: A reanimated corpse whose death and resuscitation involved sacred rituals but perhaps also drugs. He or she now functions in a lifeless and automatic way. Associated primarily with West African, Haitian, and Creole voodoo practice.

ON FURTHER THOUGHT:

Argue against one of the main themes of this chapter! Under what conditions might we be better off if we did not think about death? Think about not thinking—and when you come up with something good, please pass it around!

Good news, indeed! Cigarettes are not only an attractive symbol of the liberated woman, but never, ever, will do harm. Not so! The post World War II tobacco advertisement campaign resulted in a continuing high lung cancer mortality among women who emulated role models such as depicted here.

chapter 3

THE DEATH SYSTEM

"You've come a long way, Baby!" (1968)
"It's a woman thing!" (1995)
—Virginia Slims advertising slogans

"I thought about suicide every day after Cheyenne's birth. I loved this baby; I went through all the physical pain of delivering her. I had her baby book prepared, with the place for her birth certificate."
—Joanne Cacciatore, quoted by Lamar Lewin (May 22, 2007)

"The findings, including a new 14-year additional follow-up in old age, revealed that conscientiousness, measured independently in childhood and adulthood, predicted mortality risk across the full life span."
—Leslie R. Martin, Howard S. Friedman, & Joseph E. Schwartz (2007)

Dhanu, the single name of a young woman, is the most famous Tamil Tiger suicide bomber. On May 21, 1991, she hid a girdle of grenades beneath her gown, presented a garland to Rajiv Gandhi, India's top political figure, and exploded, instantly killing them both. Dhanu has become a heroine to the women of Sri Lanka's Hindu Tamil minority.
—Robert A. Pape (2005, p. 226)

The blood-stained cloak allegedly worn by Mary Todd Lincoln on the night of the assassination. Locks from Elvis' GI haircut. Pieces of Beethoven's corpse. Albert Einstein's brain. This odd array of historical artifacts is at the center of a new ethical conflict for life scientists.
—Lori B. Andrews et al. (2004, p. 215)

Everybody needs to die in 2010 if they don't want to pay estate tax.
—Larry Dace, certified public accountant

I watch Fellers creep around the pond, his beard dripping, his burly form crouched over his waders, a net in his hand and a flashlight in his mouth. Taking care not to let the frog see his moon shadow, Fellers inches forward, pauses, inches closer—and then whips the net down in a splash. It comes up full of slimy stuff that he pulls out, a handful at a time, until he reaches the frog at the bottom.
—W. Wayt Gibbs (2002)

In the early 1990s the Parsis started to notice that there were fewer birds at the tower. At first they assumed that the vultures had simply gone elsewhere. . . . But researchers in other parts of India began to observe a similar condition . . . about forty vulture deaths in a colony in Keoladeo National Park. . . . Many of the vultures had exhibited a strange behavior before dying, hanging their heads so low that their beaks nearly touched their bellies.
—Stephen Bodio (2001)

Seven newborn boys, six of whom were black, were injected with radioactive iodide *in the early 1950s at a hospital in Memphis, Tenn., as part of a study funded by the federal government . . . it was one of at least five done around the country on a total of 235 newborns and older infants.*
—Scripps Howard, December 22, 1993

Simon was the family angel. He was handsome. He was perfect. Everybody loved him. Of course, he got more attention than I did, but you couldn't get angry at him. Then he died. It was diphtheria. Most people today don't even know that word. Diphtheria was just terrible. My mother's sister died about the same time after delivering her second baby. That baby died, too, or was born dead, I don't know which. Ellie came down with rheumatic fever. She made it to her 15th birthday, and couldn't even blow out the candle; that's a fact. The graveyard kept filling up with family. When I was about 10 or so, I remember coming back from the graveyard and thinking: "Why, there are as many of us here as home." Maybe that's why I've always felt at home at graveyards.
—A man of 93, reflecting on his childhood

Everything that makes a collection of individuals into a society and keeps that society going has implications for our relationship to death. In this chapter we will be looking more systematically at the *death system*. These diverse examples serve as our introduction.

• A few women smoked a few cigarettes in the first half of the twentieth century. They would light up a single cigarette once or twice a week on social occasions, and seldom, if ever, inhaled. Many more women started smoking many more cigarettes in the post World War II years, largely as the result of advertising campaigns that associated this activity with what they were assured was the new, liberated woman. Their emancipation was self-declared every time they flamed up an Eve, a Virginia Slim, or, even more daringly, one of the rugged male brands. The impressive increase in female smoking was soon shadowed by an equally impressive rise in their lung cancer rates and mortality (Surgeon General's Report, 2001; Cancer Facts & Figures, 2008). The morbidity and mortality rate is still increasing for women who smoke. There is no doubt that the manipulation of cultural symbols in a saturated advertising campaign has cost many women their health and lives. The end of life experiences for each of these women can be studied from medical, palliative care, and spiritual perspectives, as can the grief of their family and friends. But we would be missing a big part of the picture if we neglected the way in which the tobacco industry penetrated our society's death system, and was allowed to continue. Furthermore, the process is still ongoing. As Anna Quinlan (2007, p. 92) observes, "Younger women have to be constantly created to fill the death gap," and so Camel No. 9 has been introduced as a "cute and cool" cigarette to lure teenagers. The quest for gender equality and the profit motive co-exist within the same society and have made their way together in the death system.

• When the state office of vital records mailed a death certificate instead, Cacciatore said, "I literally dropped it. When I called and asked for my daughter's birth certificate, the woman asked how she died, and when I told her, she said I didn't have a baby, I had a fetus, and I couldn't get a birth certificate." Appalled by this response, Cacciatore persuaded Arizona to become the first state to provide birth certificates for stillbirth. The death system's bureaucracy had been operating on the premise that a stillborn infant had never entered the lives of family and society. This often resulted in *disenfranchised grief* (Chapter 11): the loss was not considered significant enough to be mourned, therefore increasing the burden on the bereaved parents. Cacciatore—now a professor—would go on to establish the M.I.S.S. Foundation for prevention and peer support of stillbirth and infant death. Bureaucratic procedure reaches into many lives and deaths. A woman sitting near me in a Social Security office would agree with this statement: She was dead, according to government records. Phone calls and correspondence having failed, she hoped that by showing up—again—at the office, it might be decided that she was still among the living. (They gave her more papers to fill out.)

- In this and following chapters we will come upon many examples of societal influence on how long we live and the way in which we die. However, as individuals we are not passive and powerless. We have a role in shaping our own destiny. A series of studies by health psychologists supports this proposition. For example, Martin et al, (2007) found that people with a strong conscientiousness component in their personalities excelled in avoiding mortality risks from childhood onward. Among other things, conscientious people were much less likely to become smokers and thereby expose themselves to a multitude of health risks. Self-discipline and dutifulness might be regarded as quaint characteristics in today's opportunistic and media-saturated society—but these "old school" virtues seem to be adding years to lives.

- Dhanu, described as a "remarkably beautiful young woman in her late twenties" (Pape, p. 226), is thought to have been the first attacker to use a suicide belt—years before this tactic became part of Middle East and North African violence. Patient and disciplined, Dhanu was active in a political movement that had taken up terrorist methods in an effort to establish independence from India. There was also something intensely personal involved. Dhanu had been gang-raped by Indian soldiers who killed her four brothers. Rape and murder have since become increasingly common terror techniques in Darfur (Sudan) and other places where populations are sharply divided on political, economic, ethnic, and religious issues. Dhanu and other members of the Black Tigress unit have broken from a nearly universal cultural tradition in which women were regarded as the bearers of fertility and nurturers of life. It remains to be seen whether a society can revert to traditional gender expectations after killing has become a mission for women as well as men.

- Being dead does not automatically exclude a person from society. There are numerous cultural traditions of invoking the dead and attempting to communicate with them (Chapter 13). Today it is science and scholarship that is at the forefront of attempts to learn from the dead. Lori Andrews and her colleagues (2004) call attention to the need for ethical guidelines for studying the dead. Does our curiosity justify inquiries into the dead? The authors urge that research on human remains be conducted in consultation with all relevant people and organizations, including family members and descendants. It should also conform to all applicable state, federal, and international regulations regarding treatment of the dead. They also suggest requiring researchers to make a case that the (deceased) individual would have agreed to testing for that purpose. Would Beethoven have wanted to find out if some of his odd behavior late in life, and perhaps even his deafness, had been caused by sipping lead-laced wine?

- "Nothing is certain except death and taxes" has been a familiar bromide for many years. There are, in fact, many links between the two. An example was brought to my attention by the accountant who noticed my eyes had glazed over as we went through forms and numbers. With the mere hint of a smile, Dace pointed out that a new law would provide the maximum benefits to pass on to survivors in

Vultures await their next assignment as part of nature's program of recycling life through death. Pesticides are threatening the lives of vultures in India, arousing public health concerns as well as disrupting the established order of life-death transition.

the year 2010. Conscientious people should do their best to die in that one golden year to take advantage of this one-time opportunity. The law was due to expire after that, so the prudent person would expire before that deadline.

- Frogs and vultures. We think of these creatures as belonging to the natural order of things. They don't have Social Security numbers and e-mail addresses, and they don't pay taxes (at least, not yet). Nevertheless, they are very much a part of the death system in every nation where they flick their tongues for flying insects or keep watch for carrion. The connection has turned lethal in recent years. Many ponds where the lusty songs of frogs were a sure sign of spring have gone silent. Grossly deformed frogs have also turned up in great numbers, and some species seem to have disappeared from their habitats.

Meanwhile vultures, those large and awesome scavengers, have also been dropping to their own deaths in alarming numbers. Why "alarming"? For centuries in India, vultures have been relied upon to strip the corpses of humans as well as animals. Tibetan Buddhists have also assigned vultures a key role in "sky burial":

> Although the Parsis continue to stack their dead within the towers (their religion, Zoroastrianism, forbids them to contaminate earth, fire, or water with their corpses), the bodies remain unmolested except by the gradual effects of the elements (Bodio, 2001, p. 26).

Furthermore, with vultures now in short supply, India's sacred cattle—living and dying on the streets—are being left to rot because Hindus are forbidden to touch their corpses. The remains of other dead animals will also remain longer. Outbreaks of tuberculosis, anthrax, and other diseases can occur under these circumstances, and the situation could also spread to Africa.

Two elements are especially significant in the frog and vulture die-off: (1) the most probable cause: pesticides, especially DDT; and (2) religious attitudes and practices that have enhanced the role of vultures. The possible impact of frog extinction is less obvious but perhaps even more significant in the long run, because it could be part of a much broader pattern of endangerment to many biological species, a cascading process with effects of unknown breadth and magnitude.

And what should we make of the deaths of the creatures who themselves seem to have been designed by nature to assist the dead in recycling new life forms?

• The act of injecting newborn infants with radioactive iodide as part of a government-funded study met with severe criticism by physicians and ethicists as soon as the facts came out (after nearly 40 years of silence). John Gofman, a leading expert on the dangers of low-level radiation, stated that this experiment increased the risk of cancer for these children: "It's like saying, 'We're going to visit cancer on some of you— not necessarily all of you—but we have increased the risk individually and some of you will get it.' It's not a nice thing to do with children" (Scripps Howard, 1993). The fact that this was an official government project exposes still another type of conflict within our society's death system. Here was the government playing an active role in increasing the probability of illness and death—and for newborns! Furthermore, the Memphis study was disturbing in its revelation that "liberty and justice for all" may not have been applied to infants of color. Racism in life prepares for racism in death. Was this an isolated episode from the past? Or could medical racism still be happening today? We will be updating this issue later in the chapter.

• The man of 93 was part of a diminishing generation that remembered when childhood was a time of ever-present risk for disabling illness and death. The local cemetery was an extension of the neighborhood where so many promising and cherished family resided. Dramatic changes in longevity and life expectation are usually expressed in statistics, but we will not want to forget that advances in public health are really about giving individuals the opportunity to survive well into their adult years.

These are but a few of the conflicts and complications that are found in any society's death system. Perhaps we should make things simpler for ourselves—why don't we just get rid of death?

A WORLD WITHOUT DEATH

Suppose that the world is just as we know it, with one exception: Death is no longer inevitable. Disease and aging have been conquered. How would people respond to this situation, individually and as a society? How would the quality of life change?

Think first of the effects of the no death scenario on the world at large. In the left side of Box 3-1, write down the changes you think would be likely to happen.

Think next of how the no death scenario would influence your own life. In the right side

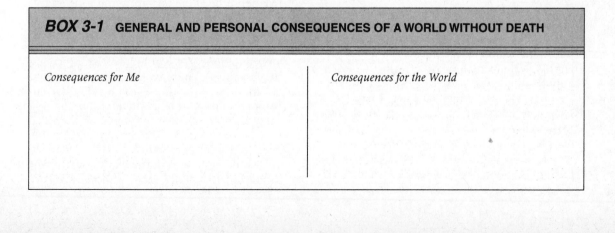

BOX 3-1 **GENERAL AND PERSONAL CONSEQUENCES OF A WORLD WITHOUT DEATH**

Consequences for Me	*Consequences for the World*

of the box, describe some of the major ways the no death situation would be likely to influence you. None of us can know for sure what would actually happen if this hypothetical situation became reality. Nevertheless, many plausible and interesting predictions can be offered. Compare your ideas with those that follow, as given by other students who have completed this exercise.

General Consequences

- Overcrowding would lead to infringements on privacy, mobility, and other individual liberties. "Space would be incredibly precious." "People would develop new mental and physical habits to keep others at an emotional distance." "Turf mentality would be all-powerful." "After a while, nobody would feel comfortable being alone even if you could be." "I don't see how people could still be individuals."
- Birth control would be enforced. This control would be an exercise of power and prestige. "It will all depend on what the elite want people bred for." "If basketball coaches get control, they'd want to breed for 7-foot centers." "Every group of crackpots and bigots would try to use selective birth control to exterminate the kind of people they don't happen to like."
- New laws would be needed because relationships between people will have changed so much. "Inheritance might not mean anything any more. The younger generation couldn't expect anything from the older generation unless we cooked up new laws." "I think that babies with genetic or with birth defects might not be allowed to survive because there would be room for so few babies when adults are not dying off."
- Society would become very conservative and slow to change its ways. "Old people would outnumber young people so much that anything new would hardly have a chance." "The world wouldn't really have a future. There'd only be a terrific bias to keep things as they are or even to roll things back to the past."
- The economic structure of society, however, would change. "Life insurance—who would need it? And then, what would happen to that whole industry?" "People wouldn't have to put money away for their funerals. In fact,

there would be hardly any money to be made on the dead." "Doctors might not make as much money because there wouldn't be all this fear of death. But maybe they'd make even more money with plastic surgery and fancy ways to try to keep people looking young. Who knows?"
- Moral beliefs and practices might also change in many ways. "That would be just about the end of marriage, and maybe of divorce, too. People would think, hey, what's the point of being married to just one person forever and ever. Everybody'd either screw around a lot with everybody else or maybe just get tired of it after a couple of thousand years and play video games instead."
- Death would take on a different aspect. "Religion is mostly getting people to shape up or go to Hell. If we're not going to die, then who's going to listen and what's going to happen to religion?" "Death has always been the enemy. Now it might be the biggest friend ever. We might hire people to kill us in some really decisive way, like blowing us to pieces. I think I would buy shares in the Mafia. Or maybe governments would arrange special wars only for the purpose of getting a lot of people killed." "I really don't think we can do without death psychologically. Society would find some way to make death possible, and this would be considered the right thing, not an evil thing."

Personal Consequences

- We would organize our lives differently. "I don't know if I would have the same ambitions and make any progress on them. As it is now, about the only way I get anything done is when a deadline is staring me in the face, which happens all the time in my classes. If there's all the time in the world, there wouldn't be any pressure, and I might not ever get anything done." "I would just give up trying to plan ahead. There would be just too much ahead, so much that it would be very hard to comprehend." "I'd be really afraid of making some terrible mistake in what I do, because the consequences could follow me I guess forever, for centuries anyhow."
- We would be free from the fear of death. "If I found out that there really and truly wasn't

going to be any more death, I would feel light and free for the first time and I could really enjoy life. I hope I'm not kidding myself either, but even the thought of a no-death world makes me feel wonderfully free." "My brother's got himself almost killed at least three times. He's into being a macho risk-taker. I'm a lot more careful. I would probably take more chances with my life, and do some more exciting things, because it really wouldn't be taking such a chance, would it? I wonder what my brother would do?"

- Our personal relationships would extend indefinitely, creating new opportunities and new challenges. "It's a crazy idea, but I like it. The people I care about would always be with me." "I find it hard to think of becoming an old person and being an old person right along with my parents and grandparents. Would I still feel like a child. What would become of generations if we all spent most of our lives being old together?"

- Our ideas about the purpose and meaning of life might change. "It would be a hard idea to get used to, especially with all that I have always believed as a Christian. I would want to keep my beliefs—I would have to—but it might make some difference, there not being natural death and therefore not being eternity and heaven. Or would there still be? It could be confusing." "I have to wonder what value anything would have anymore. Maybe the only thing I would value is how to fill all that time . . . how to fill all that time."

A world without death would differ in many ways from the world we know today. You may have thought of some consequences that go beyond those presented here, and the list certainly could be extended. *The main point is that our individual and societal patterns of functioning are connected with death in one way or another.* Life insurance, for example, depends also on the profit motive, and the profit motive in turn arises from complex ideological and social conditions. Yet, as respondents often observed, no death means no life insurance. Take as another example the relationship some respondents have predicted between the elimination of death and the establishment of stringent birth control measures. "If nobody dies, then nobody can get born."

Individual implications of our relationship to death cannot easily be separated from the general consequences. Consider, for example, those who fear they would lose their drive for accomplishment if time were endless. This is a personal matter, but connected with a cultural ethos in which the achievement motive is highly valued. Social philosophers have argued that one of the most powerful driving forces in Western society is the need to achieve a kind of salvation through achievement. We accumulate material goods and acquire status to demonstrate that we should be among the blessed. A bumper sticker that had its day in the sun once advised us that "The winner is the one who dies with the most toys."

Lessen the need to achieve and acquire and we alter our relationship with time and death. The lifestyle oriented toward work and achievement has been increasingly challenged by enthusiasm for a leisure lifestyle. Baby boomers sometimes work very hard at play as signs of aging and the shadow of mortality arise. One boomer may have spoken for many others when he confided to me, "If I work any harder at playing and staying young, I'll be old before my time and kill myself for sure." And then he was off jogging again under brilliant Arizona skies.

This no-death thought experiment raises many questions that require us to think of society as well as the individual. The death system concept provides a way of doing so.

BASIC CHARACTERISTICS OF THE DEATH SYSTEM

How serious is *my* health problem? What should *I* say to my neighbor whose child was killed in an automobile accident yesterday? Would *I* be better off dead than old? These personal challenges take place within a dynamic society. It is true that we live and die as individuals, but it is also true that we are linked with each other by language, expectations, customs, and needs. In this section, we shift our focus to the ways in which our confrontations with death are systematically influenced by our participation in society.

We face death alone in one sense, but in another and equally valid sense, we face death as part of a society whose expectations, rules, motives, and symbols influence our individual encounters. This will become clearer as we turn our attention now to the components and functions of the death system.

COMPONENTS OF THE DEATH SYSTEM

The death system is made up of people, places, times, objects, and symbols.

People

All of us are potential components of the death system. Tomorrow I might be called on suddenly to use the techniques I learned in a cardiopulmonary resuscitation course, or somebody else may be called on to use these skills on me. (I hope we've both learned well!) Most of us phase in and out of the death system as circumstances dictate. Some of us though, such as people working in the funeral and memorial industry, serve as core participants. How they are perceived by others is often strongly influenced by their profession.

One funeral director described the typical situation members of this trade must contend with: "When I walk into a room, Death walks in with me. That is how people react to me." The fact that many of us find it difficult to think of a funeral director as a normal and distinct individual testifies to this individual's embeddedness in the death system.

The agent who sells life insurance is also very much part of the death system. The same may be said for all the clerks, adjusters, marketing people, and executives involved in life insurance. The members of the custodial staff who clean up the high-rise offices of MegaMoolah Insurance Company late in the evening are unlikely to reflect on their role in the death system, but their paychecks have their origin in somebody's decision to make a financial investment in anticipation of death. The premiums we pay to guarantee death benefits are part of a complex network of investments. The death money may be used to create new jobs or abolish old ones, support a local business or challenge it with a competitor, and so on.

The florist is also part of the death system. Floral tributes help flower growers and merchants stay in business. The lawyer who meets clients to draw up wills and living trusts is another involved person. Such meetings are some of the few situations in which a healthy adult is likely to sit down and discuss personal death-related issues. Even so, many lawyers report that their clients often prefer to delay making a will or living trust as long as possible because of the obvious connection with death.

People working in a variety of occupations earn their livelihoods from death-related services. A consumer movement that encourages less elaborate and costly funerals (Chapter 12) affects the funeral director, the florist, the cemetery association, and so on. The trend toward merged families with "his, her, and our" children can complicate the inheritance process. The availability of life care retirement communities can reduce the amount of money that can be passed along to children and therefore also influence estate planning and will-making.

Other people associated with the death system might not come so readily to mind. Think, for example, of the big truck you saw pull up behind a supermarket the other day. It was filled with pet food, case after case. Every can in every case depicts a contented dog or cat, while the inside contains some type of meat product. All that meat, of course, came from what once were living creatures. The truck driver, the person who shelves the cans, the assistant store manager who makes sure they are priced correctly, and the clerk at the checkout register are but a few of the people who participate in the death system through their processing of pet food. Those who raise, those who slaughter, and those who process a variety of living animals to become food for pets also should be included. The people in the canning factory should be included, as should the accountants, the executives, and the advertising agency. The cat that meows so convincingly for its favorite brand on television is also part of the death system—as is the cat at home that, unimpressed by the advertising programs, sniffs disdainfully at the food dish, turns up his or her tail, and walks away with an offended air. As purchasers of this product, are we not all part of this complex network as well, a network that requires the death of animals to feed other animals?

Still unmentioned are the health professions and the clergy, all of whom have important roles in the death system. It would not do to leave out the scientists who are designing lethal weapons, cloning crops and creatures, or trying to prevent or even reverse the extinction of species. Now that Dolly the sheep has come and gone, should we also clone the extinct Tasmanian tiger (Tinkler, 2002) to keep it company, or perhaps rescue the wooly mammoth from the dead as a theme park feature ("Wildlife Park," 2002)?

At any moment, you or I might become drawn actively into the death system. A friend unexpectedly reveals to us that she has a fatal illness. We are in an automobile accident in which somebody dies. A funeral procession interrupts our cruise down the street. Perhaps it is the insurance agent gently inquiring if we have made adequate provisions for the education of our children. The points of entry are numerous, and, of course, when we exit, we are all part of the death system.

Places

Certain places have become identified with death. The cemetery and the funeral home are obvious examples. There are other places whose associations with death depend on the ideas and experiences we carry around with us. Today people come and go from the hospital all the time. It is the place where babies are born, life-saving procedures are performed, and accident victims are treated. It is also still the place where people die sometimes, but is only one facet of the modern medical center. People with long memories, however, give a different perspective. A spry woman of 93 explained:

> The doctors would say, "We're taking you to the hospital, Mike." And Mike he would directly close his eyes and turn his face to the wall. Then the doctor would say, "Now, now Mike. Don't take on like that. We're going to make you well at the hospital." And Mike he wouldn't say a word. But when the doctor walked out the room, Mike he would say, "I'm a dead man." Everybody knew it. You went to the hospital to die. . . . And even to walk by the hospital, you would shudder right down to your shoes. And you'd walk a little faster.

In a modern hospital, death is often granted its small, isolated territory in return for promising to stay within those bounds. Here the patients with the most severe life-threatening conditions reside.

However, any room on any unit can become a death place when a patient unexpectedly "goes sour." It can take months before the ward feels safe again. In the meantime, you can see a variety of decontamination rituals as those associated with the ward attempt to rid the environment of its newly acquired "deathness." Similar measures have been taken in private homes as well: a bed may be given away because it is the one in which Uncle Otto "expired," and its continued presence somehow keeps the unwelcome aura of "deathness" in the household atmosphere.

Historical battlefields often are thought of as death places for centuries, as is the Tower of London, that grim edifice by the banks of the Thames where royal murders occurred. Ford's Theater in Washington DC is remembered mostly as the place where Lincoln was assassinated. A pathway in the woods may be spoken of in hushed tones by the schoolchildren who discovered a human corpse while on a nature walk. Even a familiar house across the street can be a death place in the minds of neighbors who now feel uncomfortable as they pass by. Once a place has become associated with death, we no longer think and feel the same way about it. We have but to think of Oklahoma City and New York City, where people perished and buildings collapsed as a result of domestic and foreign terrorism. The people of Oklahoma City will long remember how a major downtown building suddenly became a place of death.

Times

Death also has its times or occasions. Memorial Day, for example, is a regularly occurring time set aside in the United States to honor those who have fallen in defense of the nation. In some tribal societies, several days are devoted to communal mourning for all who have died during the preceding year. (Simpler burial rituals are held immediately after the deaths.) The Days of the Dead in Mexican tradition (Rosales, 2003) can startle the unprepared visitor who expects death observances to be somber and restrained. The public carnival atmosphere of *Dia de los Muertos* suggests an easy familiarity with the dead—and the visitor might not be aware of the more reflective and somber rituals that are conducted at the family level. This celebration is thought to have roots in

DEATH'S DISPENSARY.

OPEN TO THE POOR, GRATIS, BY PERMISSION OF THE PARISH.

The discovery that a polluted water pump in an impoverished area of London was the source of a cholera epidemic intensified the demand for public health reforms from the middle of the nineteenth century forward.

Aztec festivals, is further shaped by Roman Catholic belief and practice, and in some places by Halloween (Taylor, 2000). Claudio Lomnitz (2005) offers a powerful interpretation of Mexican culture in which death imagery has been a pervasive influence through centuries of turbulence and into the present day. Many societies have established periodic occasions when death is granted dominance over everybody's thoughts and feelings. Just as we might grant death its own space in return for death not invading ours, so we might set aside special times for death, hoping that death will not steal the time of our lives.

Prayers for the dead are offered on regular occasions—for example, by Jewish and Japanese Americans who are keeping the faith, and by Catholics who are celebrating Mass. December 29 is observed in honor of the Sioux annihilated by the Seventh Cavalry at Wounded Knee, South Dakota, in 1890. Anniversaries of the disasters in Waco, Texas; Oklahoma City; and the three sites of the September 11, 2001 terrorist attacks are still being observed by many of those who were affected. Some of us also acknowledge a death time that has deep personal significance that might not be shared by others. This can take the form of a valuable spiritual reflection or, more problematically, what psychiatrists call an anniversary reaction, in which the survivor falls ill, behaves erratically, or suffers an "accident."

The clock and the calendar treat each passing moment, each passing day, with equal disinterest. For the individual and for society, however, certain times seem to fall under the particular auspices of death, and we respond to these times in a special manner.

Objects

Death has its objects and things as well as its people, places, and times. The hearse and the death certificate are among the conspicuous objects in the American death system. Death notices have their own separate section in newspapers. Taxidermists have converted hunting trophies and beloved animal companions into still life (or still death) souvenirs. Freeze-drying could be the technique of the future (Bryant & Shoemaker, 2003). The noose, the gallows, and the electric chair are also among our more obvious images of death. The spraying device that "kills bugs dead" is an object in our society's death system; the same may be said of the nuclear "devices" that we aimed at potential enemies for years while they aimed theirs back at us.

Objects whose intended uses have little to do with death may produce lethal effects through accidents or misuse. Both the automobile and the cigarette have been spoken of as instruments of death, although not conceived for that purpose. Alcoholic beverages and other pharmacological substances have also served as instruments of death, although, again, not intended for such a purpose. Things, like people, places, and times, can be recruited into the death system, and when this happens their meanings are transformed, even though the objects themselves remain the same.

Symbols

Language and other symbols play a major role in death systems. In Western culture, the black armband tells a story. Funeral directors generally provide black limousines for the funeral procession and black garb for themselves. Not all societies symbolize death with dark colors, but we soon learn to recognize the particular colors

and other symbols meant to convey death-related messages in a given culture. In some neighborhoods, closing the shutters has been a traditional signal of a death within, although this practice continues to fade. Administration of the priestly ritual for the sick often is associated with impending death, although not officially described as "last rites."

Death symbols tell us something about a culture's attitudes toward death. The choice of music is one example (Kastenbaum, 2003). Slow, solemn music intoned on an organ suggests an orientation different from that of a simple folk song with guitar accompaniment and is different again from a brass band strutting down the street playing "When the Saints Go Marching in." The Catholic requiem mass encompasses both a plea for the Lord to grant the dead eternal rest in His perpetual light, and, in the *Dies irae* section, a terrifying evocation of the Day of Wrath and its call to judgment. When gang members decided to organize the funeral for a slain member, they included a rap song written in his memory (Holveck, 1991). By contrast, when Queen Mother Elizabeth died in her 101st year:

> Slow drumbeats punctuated the shrill bagpipe lament of nearly 200 regimental musicians. Soldiers of the Royal Horse Artillery in gold-trimmed black tunics rode six black horses pulling a gun carriage that bore the coffin (Associated Press, 2002, April 10).

That soldiers and a gun carriage should be so integral to the funeral services also tells us something about a society's associations with death.

The words we use and those we refrain from using can also reveal something about a culture's death system. For many years in our society, people "passed on," "expired," or "went to their reward." I have noticed a decrease in euphemisms and an increase in brusque expressions in recent years, for example, "She OD'd" (overdosed) and "He croaked." Both the euphemistic and the dysphemistic approach serve to distance the speaker from the raw reality of death. Currently, health care professionals prefer the objectivistic "terminally ill" to the still uncomfortably emotional "dying."

Although today more people discuss death openly, we still tend to code the topic with indirect, symbolic, and sometimes downright evasive language. In one major hospital system, for example, a deceased patient is still spoken of as having been transferred to "Tower Nine." There are eight towers or units in this hospital; the ninth is not of this world. Notice with what linguistic garments people clothe their communications about dying and death, and you will also be observing something important about their underlying attitudes.

FUNCTIONS OF THE DEATH SYSTEM

We have surveyed the components of the death system. Next, we will become acquainted with the major functions.

Warnings and Predictions

A core function of society is to protect its members. All societies issue warnings and predictions intended to stave off threats to life. These warnings and predictions can be based on folk customs, science, pseudoscience, organized religion, or individual revelation. The threats that are forecast may be accurate, exaggerated, or completely imaginary. Society may choose either to respond to or to ignore the alarms. Cassandra's plea to destroy the horse that the Greeks left as a gift at the gates of Troy is a classic example of a warning unheeded and its disastrous consequences. Investigation of the FBI and CIA responses to warnings of a terrorist attack are more recent examples (National Commission on Terrorist Attacks, 2004). Even more recently, governmental agencies have come under severe criticism for allegedly ignoring warnings about safety issues in the aviation industry (Levin, 2008) and for the formaldehyde contamination of trailers provided to victims of Hurricane Katrina (Evans, 2008).

It can be difficult to determine which warnings should be taken seriously. A central problem for our times is how to navigate between the extremes of constant hypervigilance and smug neglect. How much of our attention should be devoted to the recently surfaced threats posed by terrorism, and how much to the continuing problem of air and water pollution and global warming? To the possible effects of overhead high-voltage wires? To radon, asbestos, and lead in our homes and workplaces? Are we tempting death if we drive across one of the nation's many bridges that are considered hazardous?

"Small-craft warning" and "tornado watch" are familiar phrases in some parts of the United States. In Arizona, we hear occasional "flash flood" warnings: it is not easy to imagine that a dry ravine might suddenly resound to the roar of a raging current of water. We expect to be advised of impending floods, blizzards, and dust storms, as well as of avalanche conditions. There are also frequent announcements of possible hazards associated with consumer goods and services. Evaluating all these warnings is a full-time job in itself.

The death system provides warnings and predictions to specific individuals as well as to larger units of society. The physician may hesitate before interpreting that laboratory report to us. The mechanic may fix us with a hard look: "Your car is an accident ready to happen."

Hearing that there is a threat to our well-being does not end the story. We must still decide what we are going to do about it. Mr. Macho Guy and Ms. Lucky Goose might well ignore all the warnings, as might those who live life by the numbers and figure that there is nothing they can do when their own numbers come up.

Preventing Death

All death systems have strategies that are intended to prevent death. In Western society, we tend to think of health professionals, firefighters, police, and researchers striving for cures or safety improvements. One of the great public health accomplishments has been the control of contagious diseases that once took a high toll, especially among the very young and the very old. Unfortunately, this benefit has been limited primarily to developed nations; many people die worldwide each year from contagious diseases whose prevention and treatment has been well established.

Hard-won medical victories create rising expectations. As a physician with more than 40 years of experience explained:

> People don't want much these days. All they expect is to live forever and, well, maybe to be young forever, too. . . . I guess it's our fault for knocking off typhoid, scarlet fever, diphtheria, tuberculosis, and whatever. They expect us to cure everything now. I guess we almost expect it, too.

There are life expectancies, and then there are life expectancies!

Source: Zits Partnership 2008. King Features Syndicate. (Published 5/21/08.)

"Making war" on death and disease has been a popular phrase for a while now. There are problems with this conception, however. The war against death often is conducted in a selective manner, following society's general paths of discrimination and unequal opportunity. Whatever makes some people appear to have high social value in general makes them more favored candidates for death-prevention efforts. "If you are going to have a heart attack, make sure you are wearing a good suit and are in the right part of town—also, try to be young and white!"

Cynical comments of this type unfortunately retain a core of truth even today, as disclosure of the radioactive iodide studies has reminded us. For example, poor women in the United States are still less likely to be diagnosed and treated for breast cancer and are therefore more likely to die from this ailment. It could also be said that the war against death includes a war against ourselves because many lives now end as a result of lifestyle practices and decisions (e.g., using tobacco and alcohol or engaging in practices that increase the risk of HIV-AIDS transmission).

Medical Apartheid

The Memphis iodide injection experiment was but one of many abuses of black Americans from colonial times onward, as documented by Harriet A. Washington (2006). Medical apartheid, the term proposed by Washington, was far more extensive than reported by the mainstream media, and it was not limited to the United States. Perhaps the most extreme examples that have come to light were a series of projects intended to create epidemics in South Africa's black townships during that nation's apartheid period. Among other methods, the surgeon general—the surgeon general!—authorized:

> laced flyers, chocolate, letters, and cigarettes with anthrax and saturated T-shirts with poisons . . . [and] infused township water supplied with treatment-resistant strains of cholera (Washington, p. 378).

One does not want to believe such reports. It is even more difficult, though, not to believe what participants in an international conference on death and dying heard from two distinguished health care experts who had first hand experience with the situation. "They thought the country would be better off with fewer blacks, and were quite open in saying so. Lethal diseases were welcome. Prevention and treatment was not. AIDS was an instrument of policy."

Medical apartheid in the United States was brought under substantial though not complete control as new regulations were established and enforced. Even a prestigious hospital or university that crossed the line was subject to embarrassment and punishment. Public outrage at the abuse of black Americans in medical research was the most powerful force in correcting the situation.

But the motivation to conduct research without annoying regulations has led to the outsourcing of dubious projects:

> The use of poor people of color abroad by American scientists today enables researchers to escape both the strictness of institutional review boards and the gaze of the FDA (Food and Drug Administration). Medications considered far too dangerous or too hopelessly tainted for testing in the West have been introduced into clinical trials with unsuspecting African patients. Within the past decade, even the infamously tetragenic drug thalidomide has been tried on Africans as a treatment for leprosy—forty years after it produced twelve thousand horribly deformed babies around the world. Third World women subjects of thalidomide trials for leprosy and AIDS were not warned of the horrible birth defects the drug can cause (op.cit., pp. 390–391).

Most health care professionals are outraged and appalled when they encounter abuse or neglect of vulnerable populations. Doctors Without Borders is one example of many that represent an active and positive approach. Nevertheless, medical apartheid has proven to be a resistant strain within society's overall effort to save lives from premature death.

Caring for the Dying

A staff member in one of the world's most sophisticated medical research centers was describing her work to me in a completely professional manner. Suddenly, tears of sorrow and frustration intruded as she tried to explain what happens when the decision is made to shift from "cure" to "comfort" care:

> Sometimes the point comes when the doctors decide that's it. There's nothing we can do—or should do—all the cards have been played, and there's just no way we can really hope to arrest the illness. The brakes screech! We all have to come to a full and sudden stop. We may have been doing everything in the world to keep this person alive for months and now we have to stop all that and change what we do, but it is a lot harder to change how we feel about the patient and ourselves, about what we're doing. I

don't think human thoughts and feelings were made for such sudden stops and starts!

Fortunately, the transition between trying to prevent death and providing care to a dying person is not always this drastic. Prevention and comforting can be encompassed within the same philosophy and carried out by the same people in many situations. Patients and their families may play an active part in the decision making, and health care providers may function as a team (e.g., hospice care; see Chapter 45).

How can the various health professionals (each with distinctive skills, points of view, and needs), the family, and the life-threatened person work together harmoniously if some of them persist in the objective of prevention while others believe that comfort and relief should take precedence? Should prevention of death continue to be the overriding goal until the very end, or are there circumstances in which the emphasis should shift to comfort?

Advocates of both positions can be found in the ranks of all those associated with terminal care. There are physicians who take quite literally the never-say-die orientation—so long as life has any chance, it is the physician's responsibility to do all within his or her power to support this chance. Other physicians more readily accommodate their efforts to the signs of impending and inexorable death. This attitude seems to be more in keeping with earlier medical practices when physicians had fewer options to work with and were inclined to see themselves as nature's assistant. There is reason to believe, however, that the United States is working seriously toward a revision of its philosophy and practice for caring for the dying (Chapters 4 and 5).

Disposing of the Dead

"Disposing of the dead" is a heartless-sounding phrase, but it is a task that all societies must perform. At the very minimum, there is a need to dispose of the physical remains. Seldom, however, is a society content with the minimum. The funeral and memorialization process (Chapter 12) tells much about the overall stability and cohesiveness of a culture as well as what that society makes of death.

Here are a few examples from American society:

- A minister dies unexpectedly. His wife and children are stunned, then grief stricken. Forced to think of funeral arrangements, they find themselves in perfect agreement. The minister had been a family-oriented person who preferred the simple, the intimate, the natural. The funeral, then, should be without ostentation. Only the family and a few special friends should be involved. But this plan offends the congregation. A small, simple, private commemoration would fail to symbolize the deceased's significant place in the community. It would, in effect, diminish the status of the congregation itself. The congregation would also be deprived of this opportunity to express its respect for the departed spiritual leader. It just wouldn't be right to let this death pass without a conspicuous public ceremony. The power of the many prevailed in this instance. The disposal of this man's body and the accompanying ritual became a public event. It was a "beautiful" funeral, with participation from community leaders as well as the congregation.

  How did the family feel? They reacted as though not only the husband and father had been taken away from them but his death as well. What they experienced deeply as private loss and grief had become a public exhibit. And yet the community felt that it, too, had strong rights and needs. Just as much of this man's life had been devoted to the public sphere, so his death should be shared. This is one of many examples that could be given of the contest between private and public "ownership" of the deceased. Some death systems emphasize one side, some the other, but the private-versus-public dialectic seems to be present in all of them.

- Two young men are pushing a gurney through the corridors of a large modern hospital. This action has been planned to take as little time as possible and to attract little or no attention from others. Soon they have reached the service elevator and the door closes behind them. The casual observer will have noticed only an empty stretcher. A more sophisticated observer will know or guess that this is a false-bottomed device that is designed expressly for disguised

transportation of the dead. A society whose health care establishment goes out of its way to wrap a cloak of invisibility around the dead is telling us something about its fundamental attitudes toward the meaning of life. Do we think of the dead as fearful, disgusting, or dirty? Are we as afraid of being "contaminated" as members of any preliterate society? Such questions arise when we observe avoidance-of-the-corpse rituals even within the corridors of the modern hospital system.

- The old man has died. Family converge from everywhere. There is a problem, however. The oldest generation, including the widow, expect a strictly traditional observation of the death. All the time-honored rituals must be observed. The younger generations, however, are more Americanized and consider the old way too formal, too consuming of time and money, and generally not to their liking. The funeral director is caught squarely in the middle. The death of a respected family patriarch, then, threatens to bring a bitter intergenerational conflict to the surface.

  Our death system undergoes change with every new generation. And, since three- and four-generation families are becoming increasingly common in the United States, we face the challenge of understanding each other's viewpoints when dealing with body disposal and other death-related decisions. Whatever improves intergenerational communication and understanding will help our death system to function in a more harmonious and effective manner.

- The rain and floods that devastated large sections of the United States in the summer of 1993 created problems for the dead as well as the living. In Hardin, Missouri, flood waters churned through the local cemetery. This burial ground had been used for about 200 years and was a core of the community's history. Hundreds of bodies were unearthed from their graves. Despite the pressing need to deal with flood recovery, the community showed no less concern for making things right with the dead. They did all they could to identify the corpses and return them to their designated burial places. Anthropologists, *pathologists*, and other outside experts offered their assistance.

Eventually, approximately 100 bodies were identified; the others, still anonymous, were provided with caskets and given a mass burial. Members of the community spoke of their relief in helping their loved ones "rest in peace."

Our diverse American society includes subgroups whose lifestyles are rather distinctive. The Amish way of life and death provides an instructive example of alternative approaches (Bryer, 1977; Hostetler, 1993). There are approximately 80,000 Amish people in the United States, descendants of Swiss Anabaptists who were persecuted for their beliefs until granted refuge and religious liberty by William Penn in 1727. The Amish maintain a family-oriented society that emphasizes religious values, a simple agrarian lifestyle, separation from the non-Amish world, and a strong doctrine of mutual assistance. The infirm and the mentally ill are looked after in the community rather than in institutions. The Amish people function "at the same unhurried pace as . . . their forefathers, using horses instead of automobiles, windmills instead of electricity, and facing death with the same religious tenets and steadfast faith of their fathers" (Bryer, 1977, p. 256).

Family members dress the deceased in white garments (Bryer, 1977):

> It is only at her death that an Amish woman wears a white dress with the cape and apron which were put away by her for the occasion of her death. This is an example of the lifelong preparation for the facing of death, as sanctioned by Amish society. The wearing of all white clothes signifies the high ceremonial emphasis on the death event as the final rite of passage into a new and better life (p. 254).

The funeral is home-oriented. A large room is cleared for the simple wooden coffin and the hundreds of friends, neighbors, and relatives who will soon visit. The coffin is placed in the center of the room; there are no adornments to distract from the basic fact of death. The funeral service is held in the house or barn, a practice of the Amish for many generations. Neighbors dig the grave, and all watch in silent prayer as the coffin is lowered and the grave filled with earth. Other families see to it that the mourners are fed. The Amish response to death is very much in keeping with the Amish way of life. This is expressed, for example, by the old woman who carefully washes, starches, and irons her own funeral clothing so it will be ready when the time comes. A death may occasion grief and lead to hardships for an Amish family like any others, but many of the doubts, tensions, and conflicts that have become commonplace in the larger death system seem to be absent for these people, who have developed and perpetuated a distinctive lifestyle of their own.

Social Consolidation After Death

Death does not merely subtract an individual from society. It can also challenge society's ability to survive. In relatively small societies, the impact of every death threatens the integrity of the entire group. In a mass society, this usually becomes obvious only when death unexpectedly strikes down a powerful leader.

The terrorist attacks of September 11, 2001, had the short-term effect of bringing people together in grief, compassion, and determination. The continuing effect is more complex and still ongoing. Social consolidation, once achieved, does not necessarily endure, at least not in its initial form. For example, the government moved quickly to approve financial compensation for families of World Trade Center (WTC) victims. One year later, though, this program was subjected to fierce criticism: Few survivors had actually received benefits, and the application process seemed unduly complicated and, perhaps most disturbingly, appeared to regard some victims as deserving of more financial benefits than others (LeSure, 2002; Ridley, 2002). The government's mathematical formula was criticized as treating some lives as more valuable than others, thereby increasing the emotional pain of many survivors. Whatever the merits and flaws in this plan, social consolidation after the WTC deaths has been seriously disrupted.

Before the terrorist attacks, there were the assassinations of John F. Kennedy, Martin Luther King Jr., and Robert Kennedy, which exemplified the types of death that shake even the largest and most powerful nations. Each of these men represented political power as well as something on a more personal and emotional level to millions of others. The manner of their deaths intensified the impact. The sudden, unexpected death of a significant person makes ordinary people feel vulnerable. Furthermore, each of these deaths was not only sudden but also violent, and not only violent but also intentional. People were shaken by the realization that even the most powerful among us were vulnerable.

One major function of the death system, then, is to meet the challenges posed to individual and group by loss of a member. This challenge may be of broad scope, as in a terrorist attack or the violent death of a powerful leader, or it can be as silent and personal as a death in the family:

> The realtor's illness didn't appear serious, but he died a day after entering the hospital, even before testing could be completed. From that point on the family hardly seemed to be a family anymore. They went their own ways, found things to do that kept them from being home at the same time, and seldom took a meal together. At first the 16-year-old son appeared to be the least affected. He continued his usual routines, although he did spend even more time behind the closed door of his room. Within a few months, though, it was obvious that the young man was really not doing so well after all. Most of the time he barely spoke, but then he would explode in anger without known reason and stalk away. An observant teacher noticed that the only time he mentioned his father he used the present tense, as though he were still alive.

This is an example of the temporary failure of social consolidation after a death. The family had fragmented. Relatives, friends, and neighbors had not provided useful support. For contrast, consider again the Amish. Consistent with their general orientations toward life and death, the Amish provide direct and long-term support to those whose lives have been disrupted by the death of a loved one. It is not a case of many people coming by to express sympathy for a short period and subsequently disappearing; instead, relatives or friends may take over vital functions in the home for months, until the family can get back on its feet. Social consolidation after death is vital if the survivors are to continue as confident and competent members of the culture.

The dead may or may not become well integrated into society. Traditional cultures are more likely to find a place for their ancestors. In the United States it takes something special to be included in the social consolidation process. Elvis Presley was definitely special in the hearts of many people, and he is honored not only with the shrining of his home, but also with a postmortem income approaching $40 million per year (www.forbes.com).

Some people have been so valued by society that they continue to flourish in the economy as well as in collective memory. While the social memories of some people fade almost instantly upon their deaths—or even before—others become even more treasured. Learning how and why these choices are made is a provocative topic that could tell us much about the way in which society uses, abuses, or dismisses its dead.

Making Sense of Death

Our efforts to explain death to each other constitute another important function of the death system. Some explanations are handed down from generation to generation in the form of philosophical statements, poetry, and commentaries on holy scriptures. There are also famous last words and scenes that have been attributed (and often misattributed) to heroes, leaders, and other celebrated people of the past. Authentic last words seldom meet the listener's need to discover or affirm a coherent meaning of death (Kastenbaum, 1993a; 2002a). Nevertheless, a popular assumption has been that, at the last moment, people have a privileged insight into the meaning of life and the mystery of death. End-of-life conditions today, sedation included, are not especially conducive to memorable last words, although many caregivers will have had such an experience on occasion.

Laconic statements such as "Nobody lives forever!" hardly qualify as explanations. However, much of our discourse on the subject of death is on this superficial level. Such statements might reduce the anxiety of the person who makes them through bridging what would otherwise be a tense and awkward silence. Perhaps hearing any words at all on the subject has some value to the recipient.

I spent several days in a hospital waiting area unobtrusively listening to conversations among visitors of terminally ill friends and relatives. The conversation was usually on other matters, and most of the death-oriented talk was limited to clichés. The visitors seldom, if ever, seemed to say anything new or thought provoking to each other—as if by mutual agreement. Nevertheless, there was some comfort taken and some comfort given, however, in exchanging words.

Consider the alternative: Not to have words spoken might confirm the fear that death is unspeakable, and, therefore, perhaps unthinkable as well. We would feel more helpless and alienated than ever. When we can at least go through the motions of exchanging words in this difficult situation, then we are showing the ability to function under stress. We are trying to make sense of death, and this mental and emotional activity helps keep us going.

At other times, however, we are not searching for just any words about death. We are looking for the most cogent and powerful understanding possible. The kind of explanation is related to the particular questions we have in mind. A child, a young adult, and an aged adult might have different questions in mind as well as different ways of evaluating possible answers. So, too, a person deeply rooted in Asian tradition and one with equally strong roots in the Western world are likely to differ in their approaches.

Making sense of death becomes an especially high-priority activity for us when a death undermines the basic way in which we interpret the world. Unexpected death, especially of a child, might shake our guiding assumptions about life. Most of us can easily call upon the range of explanations that are available to us within our particular death systems. It is more challenging, however, to examine the credentials of these various explanations and more challenging still to work toward our own explanations.

Animal and human sacrifice were practiced throughout many world cultures both before and after the biblical period. Caravaggio (1603) portrays the Sacrifice of Isaac as described in the Old Testament.

KILLING

All death systems have another major function: killing. It is a decisive way for the regime to demonstrate its power and authority. This function is carried out in many ways. Here we will focus on sacrifice, war, and *capital punishment*.

Sacrifice: Killing for Life

Seldom, if ever, does a single function of the death system operate by itself. Sacrifice is a major example of several functions coming together with both death and life the intended outcomes.

Blood sacrifice has been an integral part of many world societies for about as long as historical record can tell us. Ancient sites in Asia, Europe, North Africa, and South America have given evidence of human sacrifice (Benson & Cook, 2001; Carrasco, 1999; Davies, 1981; Eliade, 1978; Green, 2001). Sacrifice was intended to persuade the gods to look with favor on their people. Often sacrifice was at the core of rituals to encourage fertile crops or protect against disaster. Sometimes the sacrifices were in the service of expeditions for conquest, war, or trade. Food, drink, objects, and animals were commonly dedicated to the gods, but human sacrifice was the most compelling offering.

Each society had its own configuration of beliefs and circumstances for sacrifice. Nevertheless, at the core was the belief that life can be traded for life if this transaction is mediated by death. Give the gods the vibrant lives they seek, and in return they may award continued life to society.

One of the most disturbing facets of human sacrifice was also one of the more common: the ritual murder of children. Skeletal remains of sacrificed children have been found enclosed within gates, walls, fortresses, and other structures. Child sacrifice is specified in Judeo-Christian history as well. The Book of Kings tells us that when Joshua destroyed Jericho he made an ominous prophecy. The man who dares to rebuild that city "shall lay the foundation stones thereof upon the body of his first born and in his youngest son shall he set up the gates thereof." This is precisely what happened, again, according to scriptures, when Heil sacrificed his oldest and youngest sons as

he rebuilt Jericho. A central episode in religious history is Abraham's preparation to obey god by sacrificing his son, Isaac (who, at the last moment, is replaced by an animal). Less often discussed is the fate of Jephtha's daughter. Jephtha asked God for victory in battle, vowing that he would sacrifice the first living creature he saw when returning home. Upon his victorious return, Jephtha was greeted by his daughter. His daughter (whose name is not mentioned) became a burnt offering to God: No last minute reprieve here.

Inca and Aztec rituals centered on the sacrifice of a great many people; new findings continue to be discovered (notably in Peru and northern Argentina). Young females were frequently the victims in Inca ceremonies; Aztec practices required such a large supply that their warriors were kept busy bringing back captives. Drinking the blood and eating the flesh of sacrificial victims was thought to transfer the vital energies of one person to another, while the heart and other choice offerings were dedicated to the gods. In other cultures, such as ancient China and Egypt, family, government officials, and household servants were entombed along with a deceased royal personage of the first rank, the better to continue their service and companionship in the next life.

Human sacrifice diminished considerably through the centuries. Human victims were largely replaced by animals and, then, often, by symbols, such as the small figurines placed in the later Egyptian tombs. How recently human sacrifices have been conducted and by whom is a matter of controversy. It is possible that occasional murder/sacrifices are still occurring at the hands of deranged people rather than established societies (Kastenbaum, 2002b).

Carolyn Marvin and David W. Ingle (1999) have stirred another controversy with their analysis of patriotism. They suggest that totem-thinking still occurs in contemporary society, with national flags playing a significant role in both representing and licensing blood sacrifices through war. Their analysis and conclusions are almost certain to be repugnant to people who see patriotism as a pure and positive value, but their ideas may nevertheless stimulate some thoughtful reflection and discussion.

War as a Function of Society

Warfare has brought death to millions through the centuries. Fundamental questions are raised about human nature. Are we killers at heart? Is there a deep-rooted aggressive instinct that must find expression in bloody triumphs? Or does war arise from situational pressures that could be reduced by improved knowledge, skills, and social organization? Does the commandment "Thou shalt not kill" express our real moral position, or is it undermined by a more basic conviction that we have the right to take the lives of others?

War has often been considered the natural state of affairs. It was taken for granted that one group would raid another's lands to steal the cattle and other valuables, and that the other group would retaliate as opportunities arose. Much of the routine fighting would take the form of raids and skirmishes. Killing and being killed were possible outcomes but not necessarily the main objectives. It was so much easier if we could surprise and scatter the enemy in order to loot at our leisure and return unharmed. However, there would also be raids of reprisal in which a previous death on one side would have to be avenged by killing somebody on the other side.

War also held true as a normal fact of life for the most sophisticated civilizations. The ancient Greek city-states were following the examples of their own gods when they took the field to sack and subdue another people. Had not their own deities triumphed over the Titans after the most awesome battles? Rome sent its legions on missions of conquest, and its successors, the Holy Roman Empire and the Byzantine Empire, both excelled in the military arts. Their holy men generally affirmed that deadly force was a right, indeed a responsibility, of the state. When the devout Thomas More published *Utopia* (1516) many centuries later, he affirmed the legitimacy of war and its attendant taking of life: The Utopian must simply kill in a thoughtful and cost-effective manner.

By the eighteenth century, a great philosopher, Immanuel Kant, wrote *Perpetual Peace* (1795/ 1932), convinced that peace is an absolute necessity and could be achieved by international organization and cooperation. Years later, however, Karl von Clausewitz (1832/1984) could still persuade many that the capacity to make war is vital to the success of any nation. The psychological dimensions of war were examined in a memorable exchange of correspondence between Albert Einstein and Sigmund Freud (1933). The physicist believed that the most critical problem facing humanity was not the nature of the physical universe but our own propensity for violence. The psychoanalyst agreed that an aggressive instinct did exist and was not likely to be rooted out of our nature. We might, however, learn to love the other in ourselves and ourselves in the other person—in other words, to experience and respect our common humanity. Having survived "the war to end all wars," Freud believed that civilization had one more chance to channel its aggressive tendencies to more constructive use. Alas, a few years later he was an old man dying in a foreign land (England) because the unthinkable second world war had already flamed out from his own country to engulf the world. The physicist who had feared so deeply for our ability to survive our own warlike nature would soon be known as godfather of the nuclear bomb.

Examples can be found to support almost any theory of war and human violence. Religion, for example, has provided visions of universal human kinship and perpetual harmony—but also incitement for the most relentless and pitiless slaughter. War has taken the aspect of a rational instrument of state policy—but also of a catastrophe we blunder into from time to time for any number of trivial reasons. No simple answer encompasses all the themes, motives, and events that have issued from warfare.

A Deadly Species

We have become ever more a deadly species as we have become more "civilized." The invention of the standing army, for example, made it possible to wage war in any season and extend the duration of the hostilities. The application of assembly line tactics for raising livestock ensures that about 17 million chickens are hatched each day and rapidly moved along from egg to fast-food sandwich without ever having seen a barnyard. (Take a job on the chick-sexer line and you will become an extreme serial killer: those of the "wrong" gender for that line will be terminated without delay.) Improved technology has made it possible to conduct night warfare against each other and, as a spin-off, to increase the hunter's advantage over his prey. Killing on behalf of society or special interest groups is a function of the death system that thrives on organizational expertise.

The state's systematization of killing can be seen in the specification of precisely how executions are to be conducted in relationship to the crime. Consider the following verdict passed on a thirteenth-century Englishman (cited in Jankofsky, 1979):

> Hugh Dispenser the Younger . . . you are found as a thief, and therefore shall be hanged; and are found as a traitor, and therefore shall be drawn and quartered; and for that you have been outlawed by the king, and . . . returned to the court without warrant, you shall be beheaded and for

that you abetted and procured discord between the king and queen, and others of the realm, you shall be embowelled, and your bowels burnt. Withdraw traitor, tyrant and so go take your judgment, attained wicked traitor (p. 49).

This example of "overkill" was not a random emotional outburst but a deliberate attempt to strengthen those in power. A respected individual who had taken the wrong (losing) side in a conflict or who was a member of the aristocracy might simply have his head severed. As a special privilege, the head of the executed might not be placed on a spike of the city gates. Capital punishment, then, could either inflict agony and heap disgrace on the condemned or be content with taking life but not reputation.

Capital punishment has long been a controversial issue; both the sentence itself and the way in which it is carried out. Thomas Edison introduced the electric chair as a more humane method, but also as a way of promoting his own business interests. Unfortunately, the early electric chairs had effects that were agonizing for the prisoner and horrifying for the observers. The scene depicted here is from 1908.

Killing by the death system—or, to put it another way, society turned killer—can take more subtle forms, and it is these forms that actually result in more deaths than capital punishment. Infant mortality in the United States, for example, has consistently been higher in families who live below the poverty level. Nonwhite subpopulations have an exceptionally higher risk, with respiratory illnesses being the most frequent specific cause of death. Excessive risk of death follows impoverished and socially disadvantaged people throughout their lives. For example, toxic waste dumps are often placed in areas whose residents are people who are already at greater than average risk for death because of poverty and discrimination. Whether or not the term *kill* is used, the outcome of systematic deprivation may be premature death.

Capital Punishment

Execution has been practiced by many, but not all, cultures, with widely varying criteria for the conditions under which a person should be put to death. In recent years, there has been a strong international trend, especially in Western nations, to eliminate capital punishment. At present, eighty-four nations have abolished the death penalty, and another thirty-three have not executed any one in more than a decade (Death Penalty Information Center, 2008). No European nations enforce a death penalty. The nations with the most confirmed executions in 2007 were China (470, though considered an underestimate), Iran (317), Saudi Arabia (143), Pakistan (135), and the United States (42).

English criminal law, upon which much of our own legal system is founded, made death the punishment for an astonishing array of offenses —but, in practice, relatively few were actually executed. The death penalty conveys a mighty theme even when it is responsible for few deaths: This same society that on many occasions functions to protect and prolong life will on certain occasions act on behalf of death. Capital punishment is as susceptible to local circumstances and general social forces as any other function of the death system. For example, execution was a public spectacle in the early years of the United States (Masur, 1989). Offenders brought to justice were presented as

reminders of how pious and responsible people should behave:

> The last words and dying confessions hinged on the warning typically given toward the close of the ceremony. The minister's lengthy sermon rebuked behavior that defined republican government and defied social relations; the prisoner's terse warnings catalogued vices and absolved society of responsibility for criminal behavior (op. cit., p. 34).

Who is the governing authority with the right to inflict capital punishment has not always been clearly and effectively established. Lynchings far exceeded legal executions in Southern states following the Civil War. In Northwest Tennessee there were eleven mob lynchings for every legal execution. White supremacy attitudes continued extralegal executions into the first two decades of the twentieth century. Along with more vigorous law enforcement efforts, public concern about the brutalizing effect of capital punishment contributed to Tennessee's rejection of both legal and extralegal executions, and the state has executed only one inmate since 1960.

Some states have abolished capital punishment while their neighbors have not (e.g., North Dakota and South Dakota). Additionally, there are differences in the types of crime that are punishable by death. In Missouri, for example, capital punishment applies to those who commit murder in the hijacking of public conveyances or who murder employees of correctional facilities. Maryland has a concise rule: Subject to the death penalty are those who commit "first degree murder, either premeditated or during the commission of a felony." In contrast, Alabama lists "murder during kidnapping, robbery, rape, sodomy, burglary, sexual assault or arson; murder of a peace officer, correctional officer, or public official; murder while under a life sentence; contract murder; murder by a defendant with a previous murder conviction; murder of a witness to a crime."

Supreme Court Decisions

A series of Supreme Court decisions continues to affect application of the death penalty in the United States (www.deathpenaltyinfo.org/article. php?did=127&seid=30 and www.law.cornell.

edu/topics/death_penalty.html; Sherman, 2008). In response to criticism of perceived excessive use of the death penalty, the Court ruled that:

- The death penalty is excessive punishment for the rape of an adult woman.
- Mentally retarded criminals should not be executed because this practice constitutes "cruel and unusual punishment," as prohibited by the Eighth Amendment to the Bill of Rights.
- The death penalty can no longer be applied to juvenile offenders because teenagers have diminished culpability for their crimes because of their assumed lack of maturity, incomplete character development, and vulnerability to negative influences.
- The jury rather than the judge must make a finding of "aggravated factors" that would justify imposition of the death penalty rather than a lesser punishment.

More recently, the Court agreed to consider another issue that has come to the fore. Lethal injection has become the most common method of execution and is used in thirty-five states. It was introduced as a more efficient and humane measure than the gas chamber or electrocution. Opponents of this method argue that it can be an exceptionally inhuman method because it is subject to inept application. Three drugs are administered. Theoretically, the first drug produces unconsciousness, and the second stops breathing and causes paralysis. It is the third drug that has the lethal effect of stopping the heart. Presumably, at that time the condemned prisoner would not feel the intense burning of the drug through his or her veins. Critics identified instances in which they alleged the inmate had remained conscious and experienced intense suffering—but, paralyzed, could not communicate the agony.

Scheduled executions in several states were put on hold until the Supreme Court made its decision. On April 16, 2008 the Supreme Court, in a 7-2 split decision, ruled that the plaintiffs had not shown that lethal injection constituted cruel and unusual punishment. Advocates of the death penalty believed the real issue here was the gradual abolishment of

capital punishment, even though it was only a method that was at stake. Opponents prepared to offer more extensive evidence for another try, noting that the three-drug combination had been rejected by most veterinarians and outlawed for use with animals in many jurisdictions. It has also been observed that a sufficient dose of a barbiturate alone (the first drug in the mix) would result in painless death, although it would take longer.

Please see Table 3-1 for a summary of the controversy. And please consult your own moral perspective on the larger issue of capital punishment. Should we abide by "Thou shalt not kill," or by the law of the talion: "An eye for an eye, a tooth for a tooth . . . a death for a death?"

TABLE 3-1
The Lethal Injection Controversy

The drugs	Intended effect
Sodium thiopental (barbiturate)	Produce unconsciousness
Pancuronium bromide	Stop breathing Produce paralysis
Potassium chloride	Stop heart; cause death

The problem

The barbiturate can fail to produce unconsciousness, while the bromide does produce paralysis, leaving the prisoner vulnerable to agonizing pain that cannot be expressed as the potassium chloride runs through his or her veins, hence, "cruel and unusual punishment," a violation of basic rights.

TSUNAMI, CYCLONE, EARTHQUAKE, AND HURRICANE KATRINA— CHALLENGES TO THE DEATH SYSTEM

"Natural disaster" clearly suggests that human activity was not responsible for the loss of life and property. Four of the most devastating disasters in recent history, however, reveal again that attitudes and priorities can affect prevention and certainly do affect support and survival after the event.

Tsunami: A Stealth Wave and Its Impact

The tsunami of December 2004 resulted in enormous loss of life. The death toll has been estimated as within the 200,000 to 300,000 range. Although many people were killed by the tsunami, few people were injured or dying. The tsunami was ruthlessly exact in its selection of victims; most people either drowned or escaped unhurt. "We saw very few serious injuries," an official said. "There was no in-between" (Goodman, 2005, p. A-1). The caring function of the death system had no opportunity to aid dying and life-threatened victims. More than a million survivors were burdened with grief, and entire communities found themselves without homes and means of earning income.

Tsunami comes from the pairing of the Japanese words for harbor (*tsu*) and wave (*nami*). It has often been described as a "tidal wave" but has little to do with tidal rhythms. A tsunami can pass without notice in the sea because of its very long wavelength, but becomes a powerful destructive force as it concentrates in the shallows approaching landfall. Tsunamis are generated by underwater landslides, earthquakes, volcanic eruptions, and other naturally occurring events. Most tsunamis lose their force before reaching land and therefore are seldom detected.

There was no general warning of the killer tsunami, although at least one villager recognized the danger at the last moment and was able to save almost all his neighbors (Herman, 2005). This lack of warning could be regarded as a major failure of the death system in nations bordering the Indian Ocean: Indonesia, India, Sri Lanka, Thailand, Malaysia, Somalia, Kenya, and Tanzania. It might not be a fair assessment, however. Devastating tsunamis are rare. It is a special challenge for a society to maintain a high state of alertness for a rare, though overwhelming catastrophe. Learning from disaster is perhaps a more appropriate measure of a death system's effectiveness. Within six months of the tsunami, plans were well advanced for an early international warning system (Kettlewell, 2005, June 24). Community response drills were also introduced to prepare beach observers to notice signs of possible tsunami activity.

The tsunami could not have been prevented by any known technology. This fact might be more difficult to accept in nations that rely on advanced technology for the solution to life's problems. Nature reminds us that technology has its limits. The fishing villages and occasional tourist destinations along the Indian Ocean coast have relied primarily on their own traditional efforts with less expectation of technological solutions, and the survivors did not blame anybody for the catastrophe.

TABLE 3-2

The Tsunami and the Death System

Function	Comment
Warning and predicting	No general warning, prediction, or preparation.
Preventing	The tsunami could not have been prevented, but thousands of lives could have been saved by an effective warning system.
Caring for the dying	Most died within a few minutes or escaped. Few were dying after the sudden catastrophe.
Disposing of the dead	Finding and identifying the dead were difficult and frustrating efforts, only partially successful.
Social consolidation after death	Total or near loss of entire families and communities limited intimate support, as did prevalence of other survivors with their own grief and needs.
Making sense of death	Generally recognized as an act of nature and a risk associated with coastal living.
Killing	No killing directly associated with the tsunami, but preexisting political violence continued in some areas.

The 9/11 terrorist attacks on the United States (Chapter 8) also resulted in swift death, with very few injured or dying survivors. In both instances, much of the effort turned immediately to identifying victims and disposing appropriately of their remains. Many victims of the tsunami and of 9/11 could not be identified, although for different reasons. The bodies of tsunami victims that were found could have been the source of dangerous contagions. The shortage of safe drinking water and adequate sanitation could have opened the way to cholera and typhoid epidemics. Local authorities and international assistance averted these threats with prompt attention to the human remains, provision of safe drinking water, and immunizations. Competent attention to the dead almost certainly saved lives.

The memorialization process was limited because so many family and friends who would have participated in these events had themselves perished. The overall process of social consolidation after death could not readily follow traditional practices because the local communities with their support potential had been seriously damaged and, in some cases, completely destroyed. Nevertheless, two healing processes were promptly introduced (Nakashima, 2005, January 12; Nakashima, 2005, January 25). Displaced children, many of them orphaned, were placed in schools that immediately offered emotional support and a sense of belongingness, along with useful activity. The other process has resulted from the tsunami's selective mortality. Often the men from the affected areas were either farming in high country or fishing well offshore when the tsunami occurred. In either case, they were spared the disaster. Their wives, sisters, and mothers, along with many children, were in the tsunami path. Husbands suddenly found themselves widowers. They experienced not only intense grief, but also a sense of disorientation. These were "family men." Life without their wives and other family members was incomplete and baffling: These rugged men had to grapple with unfamiliar roles, dependent on one another and uncertain about what comes next. With their families gone, some say their lives have lost purpose (Nakashima, 2005, January 25, p. A01). Over time, many of the men found ways

to reconstitute their lives. This process involves more bonding and sharing with each other and also a gradual reaching out to find other possible wives and construct other families.

Making sense of death is sometimes the most difficult challenge. Genocide and other acts of violence have often caused people to question their basic assumptions about God, justice, and their fellow humans. This existential anxiety does not seem to have afflicted most of the tsunami survivors. They knew the disaster was not devised by enemies, nor was it interpreted as divine punishment for some sin or failing. It was just a terrible thing that happened to happen. The primary concern was how to make sense of life: the life that has been lost and the altered kind of life that was now upon the survivors. The fact that many people are in the same situation was supportive.

The tsunami took many lives, but the death system itself did not become a killer. The international community responded with services and supplies, suggesting that compassion does continue to cross boundaries in this world, despite all the personal agendas and competing interests.

Hurricanes Katrina And Rita

On August 23, 2005, the National Hurricane Center in Miami, Florida, issued an advisory about a weather system forming over the Bahamas, about 350 miles east. It was the 12th tropical depression of the turbulent season. The storm strengthened to become Hurricane Katrina. It made land on the Gulf Coast the next day. In the midst of widespread destruction, New Orleans mayor Ray Nagin estimated that as many as 10,000 people might have died. Two very different societies attempted to cope with these onslaughts, and, in so doing, illustrated their death systems in action. (Please see Tables 3-3 and 3-4 for summaries.)

Fortunately, the death toll from Hurricane Katrina was well below the early estimates. Even so, many died. Louisiana suffered 1,035 storm-related fatalities, Mississippi had 228, Florida 14, Alabama 2, Georgia 2 (AP MAINSTREAM, 2005). Conflicting interpretations of the disaster and intense criticism of government response became the dominant story in national media. The anger and sorrow continue to this day. We begin with the basic facts.

The Katrina Timeline

Experts in atmospheric disturbances were alarmed about the threat of a colossal hurricane a month before it struck the Gulf Coast (Revkin, 2005). A week before the impact, local, state, and federal agencies heard reports that Katrina could be the long-feared "big one" that could destroy New Orleans. Nonstop conference calls were confirmed that all emergency plans were in place, and National Guard troops outside of Louisiana were placed on ready alert (Zwerling & Sullivan, 2005). Some observers would later comment that Hurricane Katrina was the most predicted natural disaster in history.

The storm reached the Gulf Coast on August 29. The levees protecting New Orleans had been rated as able to withstand winds up to 130 mph. Katrina had weakened to sustained winds of 95 mph when it punched through New Orleans levees and flooded most of the city (Kaye, 2005). St. Bernard Parish was quickly under 10 feet of water. This suggested that New Orleans's protection was much weaker than supposed. A natural disaster was declared.

Most residents of New Orleans obeyed the mayor's announcement of mandatory evacuation. Roads were jammed. Some people chose not to leave, however, and others had no means of transportation. Residents of low-income areas were trapped in the flood. The media almost immediately raised the issue of implicit racism: blacks had been consistently marginalized and this placed them at higher risk in a disaster.

New Orleans was out of control. Early efforts to plug the levee breaches failed, so it was not long before about 80 percent of New Orleans was underwater. A patchwork of rescue teams in boats and helicopters was working hard to find people trapped by the toxic waters with their mix of biological and chemical pollutants. Thousands of people did find their way to the Superdome. A typical report of the situation that developed there:

> They had flocked to the arena seeking sanctuary from the winds and waters of Hurricane Katrina. But understaffed, undersupplied and without air-conditioning or even much lighting, the domed stadium quickly became a sweltering and surreal vault, a place with overflowing toilets and no showers. Food and water, blankets and sheets, were in short supply. . . . By Wednesday the stink was staggering. Heaps of rotting garbage in bulging white plastic bags baked under a blazing Louisiana sun on the main entry plaza, choking new arrivals as they made their way into the stadium after being plucked off rooftops and balconies. "They're housing us like animals," said an Army veteran, dripping with perspiration, unable to contain her fury and disappointment (Treaster, 2005, p. 1).

Extensive media coverage documented both rooftop rescues and corpses that nobody had time to remove. Police and other security personnel were seldom on the scene. It would later be confirmed that 249 of the city's 1,500 police officers had abandoned their posts during the emergency (Bolstad & Spangler, 2005). News cameras repeatedly documented an apparent disconnect between the distress and outrage of people trapped in the city and the frequently bland and hesitant response of local and federal officials. It would be nearly a week before personnel and supplies arrived in force to the shattered city. "Crisis and Chaos: New Orleans' Descent into Despair" (Thomas, 2005) was not an exaggerated title for a magazine article. Federal and local bureaucracy, expected to protect the population in times of emergency, had itself had contributed much to the risk and suffering.

Many survivors of the storm remained anxious about the fate of family and friends whose safety and whereabouts were still unknown. Many had deaths to mourn. Many had lost homes, neighbors, schooling, church, employment—so much of what had connected them to their personal worlds. Some people would have the opportunity to renew much of their previous lifestyle; others would suffer losses that could never be replaced. Failure of the nation's death system in the Gulf Storm disaster continued with confused and ineffective responses to grieving and displaced survivors. For example, the low-income residential areas of New Orleans have received little rehabilitation, and the trailers provided for homeless survivors were polluted with a toxic substance. Lessons not well learned.

Hurricane Katrina and the Death System

The response of the U.S. death system to the massive Gulf Coast hurricane is hinted at in Table 3-3. It would take a book of its own to describe and draw lessons from this catastrophe. I offer three key points that might contribute to further inquiry and understanding:

- *Frame of reference—everyday or emergency?* Most of us most of the time operate within our everyday frame of reference. By contrast, paramedics, firefighters, and other people who have training in coping with life-or-death situations can switch quickly and efficiently into emergency mode. People in a fragile emotional condition tend to operate as though "ordinary" situations are threats and emergencies—and sometimes they are more perceptive than those who are dulled into routine. Organizations as well as individuals tend to slip into a self-perpetuating everyday frame of reference. Signs of an impending emergency might be absorbed into organizational routine.
- *Switching into emergency mode has its cost.* We must put aside our routines, obligations, and pleasures. Furthermore, we are also admitting to vulnerability, as well as taking the risk that it is really not much of an emergency at all, so we will just look foolish. It is also difficult to sustain the vigilance and activation over a period of time. A crucial question, therefore, is who will switch to an emergency framework and under what circumstances? For residents of New Orleans, there had been many hurricanes, and residents would probably keep surviving them. Local officials displayed this attitude as well. It would be too expensive to upgrade the levees and upgrade other protective measures. The very fact that one had not yet fallen victim to catastrophe can serve to deaden the survival impulse. Previously, many Galveston, Texas, residents and visitors also had ignored evacuation announcements, and on one day—September 8, 1900—8,000 died as a result. When should we hold onto our everyday frame of reference, and when should we switch to emergency mode?
- *Turf issues: Who is in charge here?* Survivors of the tsunami for the most part had to rely on themselves. An isolated fishing village is not usually encased in an elaborate bureaucratic network. By contrast, the response to Hurricane Katrina involved a large number of local, state, and federal agencies. Each of these agencies had its own mission and its own internal hierarchy. Many of the documented failures to respond effectively were related to the drag of the bureaucratic process and to uncertainty and conflict regarding each agency's responsibilities and authority. It becomes difficult to respond to emerging situations as organizations become larger and more

TABLE 3-3

Hurricane Katrina and the Death System

Function	Comment
Warning and predicting	• Long-standing recognition of vulnerability. • Clear advance warning of impending disaster.
Preventing	• Hurricane itself could not be prevented. • Loss of life, social disorganization, and massive property destruction could have been sharply reduced by improved advance planning and emergency response.
Caring for the dying	• Medical care interrupted and undermined by damage to hospitals and communications.
Disposing of the dead	• Delay in recovering bodies; major problems in identifying corpses.
Social consolidation after death	• Community support shattered by evacuation, scattering of family members, limited response by overwhelmed human service agencies.
Making sense of death	• Intense criticism of governmental agencies whose alleged failures contributed to death and destruction.
Killing	• Reports of a spike in lethal violence were later found to be inaccurate.

hierarchical. How can organizations learn to cooperate for the common cause instead of becoming caught up in turf wars?

- *Community can make the critical difference in emergency situations.* New Orleans, for example, is not a generic Any City. It is distinctive for its location, history, ethnic mix, and vibrant culture. Outsiders can make significant errors, as in assuming that low-income people experienced themselves as victims mired in poverty, when in fact they had a secure sense of place and meaning. Scholar and New Orleans native Judith Wester (2005) offers the example of military crashing through front doors to rescue the inhabitants for their own good:

> Why did they not simply knock on the door and say: "We do not understand this Area, we need your help in saving it. Can you guide us?" In this way they could have engaged the inhabitants in their own salvation rather than condemn them with their beliefs and attitudes about poverty.

Fortunately, there were also many instances of compassionate and effective response in both societies. Volunteer nurses and Red Cross workers were among those who worked tirelessly under stressful circumstances to help injured and distraught survivors. Cities across the nation provided housing and other assistance, including employment and schooling opportunities, for people forced out of their communities. Some lessons were learned—and quickly Hurricane Rita became comparable in force to Katrina, but governmental and private agencies were much better prepared and helped to limit casualties and offer prompt support (Gibbs, 2005).

A Cyclone and an Earthquake

Two devastating natural disasters struck in May, 2008. Thousands died as Cyclone Nargis blasted through the western coast of Myanmar (Burma), and thousand died as a powerful earthquake destroyed schools and many other structures in the Chengdu region of China. Many died in the immediate carnage; others needed help if they were to survive. There could hardly be a more striking contrast in the response of their respective death systems.

China immediately sent an estimated 100,000 soldiers for rescue efforts. Hospitals and other local service providers quickly moved into action, supported by throngs of volunteers and generous donations. There was little doubt that coming to the aid of earthquake victims was the number-one national priority. By contrast, the ruling military regime of Myanmar persisted in preparing for and holding a scheduled referendum vote intended to continue and strengthen their control. Orphaned and homeless children were evicted from shelters so they could be used for the referendum. The international community responded quickly with offers of material aid and skilled emergency workers. There followed weeks of frustration and anguish as the regime blocked most relief efforts while victims struggled for survival. Preventing death, caring for the suffering, and reconstructing a damaged society was a much lower priority than a dictatorial regime's self-interest.

HOW OUR DEATH SYSTEM HAS BEEN CHANGING—AND THE "DEATHNIKS" WHO ARE MAKING A DIFFERENCE

We have completed an overview of the death system, with particular attention to the United States. Now we ask where this system has been and where it is going. We begin with the kind of people who have emerged as counselors, educators, researchers, and change agents in the death system.

Changing Ways of Life, Changing Ways of Death

There is a strong connection between ways of life and ways of death in every culture in every epoch. (For useful historical examples, see Aries, 1981; Eire, 1995; Huizinga, 1926/1996; Laungani, 1996.) Here we use a more narrow focus. First, we will identify one of the main influences on death systems throughout history—the ways in which people died. In the next section, we see how the "deathniks" and *thanatology* (the study of death) have emerged and contributed to the current death system.

Many societies have been dominated by a particular image of death. I have noticed that these images of death are influenced by the types of catastrophic dying with which a society has become intimately familiar. Table 3-4 presents some of the major forms of catastrophic dying that human societies have been experiencing through the centuries, along with the markers and signifiers associated with each (Kastenbaum, 1993b).

How people die has an effect on our images and concepts of death. For example, tuberculosis was a realistic source of intense anxiety from the nineteenth century well into the twentieth century. People who felt helpless as loved ones lost their vitality, suffered, became emaciated, and died also had reason to fear that they might have the same fate as a result of a disease that is more readily contagious than AIDS. The avoidance of death that became so entrenched in our culture was certainly influenced by experiences with people who died the harrowing death of a tuberculosis victim. We have already touched on one of the forms of dying that is making an impact on our current death system—the persistent vegetative state (Chapter 1). Our feelings and ideas about death often are influenced by what we know or think we know about how people die. As one or another mode of dying becomes more prominent in society, the death system is likely to change in response. Similarly, as sociocultural conditions change, the types of death that are most prominent are also likely to change. There may be no logical connection between how people die and what death means. Nevertheless, we are all likely to be influenced by the circumstances that surround death. Yesterday, the death systems of most societies were organized around the prospect of death at an early age as a result of contagious diseases and infections. Today, many deaths are related to lifestyle (smoking, drinking, murder, suicide, motor vehicle accidents) and to conditions associated with advanced age have become salient. And tomorrow?

The Beginnings of Death Education, Research, and Counseling

The death system in the United States (and in many other nations) was once devoted to avoiding even the thought of death. This situation started to change after the end of World War II. The reality of violent death could not easily be denied, nor could the loss and grief survivors experienced. Reflective people also wondered anew about this strange race known as *Homo sapiens* that periodically devotes its resources and

TABLE 3-4

Modes of Dying and the Images of Death They Have Encouraged

Condition	Markers and Signifiers
The Black Death	Agony, disfiguration, partial decomposition while still alive, putrefaction > *human vanity and pride, punished and abandoned by God.*
Syphilis	Facial disfiguration, dementia, moral degradation > *wages of sin.*
Tuberculosis	Death steals our breath; blood flows from our bodies, which increasingly become skeletonized > *curse of the cities and factories, but also romantic exit for beautiful, brilliant, doomed youth.*
Live burial	Imagined and occasionally actual fate of some who fainted, seized, or otherwise lost consciousness > *terror of life in death.*
Cancer	Pain, anxiety, body damage, and distortion > *insidious attack by an enemy from within.*
Persistent Vegetative State	Profound helplessness, inability to think or act on one's own behalf > *terror of death in life.*
AIDS	Symptoms and stigma of many of the earlier forms of catastrophic dying—blood and body fluid related, disfiguration, dementia, skeletonization, respiratory distress, plus linkage with taboo sexuality > *Death encompasses the most frightening experiences and outcomes that have ever haunted the imagination.*

Source: Kastenbaum (1993b, pp. 84–85).

passions to killing each other. People of religious faith were hard-pressed to discover purpose, redeeming value, and God's love and mercy in a slaughterhouse world. From the devastating experience of war and its lingering aftereffects, there arose insistent questions about the meaning of life, death, and personal responsibility. More and more thinkers came to the conclusion that one had to come to terms with death in order to live a coherent and positive life.

There was also an increasing awareness of the private sorrows many people experienced. There were not only people who had lost loved ones in the war, but also a great many who had to remain silent about their grief because there were so few people who were willing and able to listen. Mental health specialists started to recognize that unresolved grief was a major factor in some of the behavioral and emotional problems that came to their attention.

Meanwhile, another massive problem was also working its way to the surface. Many people who would have died quickly of virulent diseases and uncontrolled infections made prompt recoveries with the newly developed antibiotic and other "wonder drugs." However, biomedical advances had achieved only limited results with other life-threatening conditions, such as many types of cancer and progressive neurological disorders. More and more people were therefore being maintained in the borderlands between life and death, often suffering pain, social isolation, and despair. The state of the art in medicine could not restore health, but it could keep people alive in stressful circumstances. Some health care professionals and members of the general public became distressed and outraged by this situation. Why should people be made to suffer in this way—especially in a society that considers itself humane and technologically competent?

These were some of the issues that forced themselves into public and professional awareness. Instrumental in this movement were people from various backgrounds who broke through the taboo against acknowledging death. There were few if any "experts" in death half a century ago (although there were people with skills in specific areas, such as the funeral director). The people who taught the first classes on dying and death had never taken such courses themselves. The people who provided counseling to dying or grieving people had never received professional training for these services. The people who designed and conducted the first research projects likewise had to develop their own methods, theories, and databases. Included among these people were anthropologists, clergy, nurses, physicians, psychologists, sociologists, and social workers. Many had to overcome deeply entrenched resistance before they could offer educational or therapeutic services or gain entry for research. These pioneers of thanatology were hardy people, however, and gradually made themselves understood and welcome in many quarters. Some described themselves as thanatologists (from the Greek, *thanatos,* for death); others smiled and accepted the appellation "deathnik." Mostly, they did not believe that a whole new profession had to be created. Instead, the mission was to bring concern for the human encounter with mortality into the awareness of caregivers, educators, and researchers within existing disciplines. The "nurse-thanatologist," for example, must first be a knowledgeable and skillful nurse. Few workers in this field would claim that the mission has been fully accomplished, but there is a growing cadre of people with expertise to give a hand. We will catch up again with death educators and counselors in later chapters and will continue to share useful contributions from researchers throughout the book.

CAUSES OF DEATH: YESTERDAY, TODAY, AND TOMORROW

A child born in the United States in 1900 had a life expectancy of about 47 years, a little more if a female, but considerably less (about 33 years) if "Black and other." By the middle of the twentieth century, life expectancy at birth had increased about another 20 years for citizens of all racial backgrounds. For infants born today, the ALE is just below 78 years. It is estimated that by 2015 the ALE in the United States will have edged above 79 years. Most fortunate today is the newborn in Japan with an estimated ALE of 82. Unfortunately, this remarkable benefit does not extend to millions of children in hard-pressed Third World nations. The tragedy of Zimbabwe is that not long ago it was one of the most prosperous countries in Africa. Now ravaged by HIV/AIDS, economic meltdown, and internal strife, Zimbabwe has the lowest ALE in the world: 37 years for men, 34 years for women (Nordqvist, 2006). The world regional differential in ALE is presented in Table 3-5.

Three patterns have existed in the United States since the modern era of population statistics:

• Females have a longer life expectancy than males from birth onward. Currently, the differential at birth is about five years.
• Whites have a longer life expectancy than blacks from birth onward. The differential at birth is about five years.
• Life expectancy continues to increase in the United States at all age levels and for both race categories that are in common use. Today's 99-year-old is more likely than ever to celebrate a centennial birthday. Every year the lives of about 2.5 million people in the United States come to an end, but each year more people survive to bring out a new calendar.

TABLE 3-5
Life Expectancy at Birth in World Regions

Area	All	Females	Males
Africa	54	55	52
Asia	67	68	65
Developed nations	75	79	72
Europe	74	78	74
Latin America (and Caribbean)	71	74	68
Less developed nations	64	66	63
North America	80	74	74

Source: World Health Organization, Population Reference Bureau (2004).

BASIC TERMS AND CONCEPTS

Several terms are used frequently in presenting mortality data. *Mortality* refers to deaths, as distinguished from *morbidity,* which refers to illness. Here are several other key terms and concepts:

Life expectancy: The estimated number of years remaining in a person's life at a particular time (e.g., birth). It is useful to keep in mind that half of this population is expected to live longer and half is expected to live shorter lives than the mythical average person.

Longevity: The average number of years between birth and death. This statistic is based on lives that have ended, as distinguished from life expectancy, an estimate of years yet to be lived.

Cause of death: This determination is made by a physician and recorded on the death certificate. There are three general categories: degenerative biological conditions, disease, and socioenvironmental (such as accident, suicide, and murder). In practice, these categories may overlap, and the completeness and accuracy of cause of death information is subject to question.

Mortality rate (also known as *death rate*): This is a measure of the proportion of people who have died within a particular time-period to the number of people in the population. The mortality rate is calculated on the basis of number of deaths either per 1,000 individuals or per 100,000 individuals within a 1-year period unless otherwise specified. (Unfortunately, both 1,000 and 100,000 are used in various statistical reports: We must be careful!). It is important not to confuse the mortality rate with a percentage that is reckoned on a base of 100.

Age-standardized mortality rate (ASMR): The ASMR does make adjustments for age. When data are presented in this form, we can make more reliable comparisons between the death rates of various populations, or even the same nation, at different times. Developing nations, for example, often have a higher proportion of younger people because fewer reach the advanced adult years. Their death rate from cancer is likely to be lower but mainly because many die of other causes first.

For the United States, census data provide the most comprehensive and accurate information on causes and rates of death. These data themselves age somewhat in the decade between census reports; therefore, various techniques have been devised to provide useful estimates for the intervening years. The most recent official data available often go back several years.

With this background information in mind, we can now look at changing patterns of mortality.

Leading Causes of Death in the United States Today

There have been changes not only in the death rate but also in the most common causes of death. In 1900, pneumonia and influenza (considered together) and tuberculosis were the leading causes of death, almost equal in their toll. The third most common cause of death at this time was a set of intestinal illnesses in which diarrhea and enteritis were frequent symptoms. Twenty years later, these intestinal maladies had vanished from the list of major causes of death and have never returned. Pneumonia/influenza still topped the list—in fact, the nation and much of the world were trying to recover from a devastating epidemic of influenza. Tuberculosis was still a major threat to life, but its death toll had declined markedly (from 194.4 to 113.1 per 100,000 between 1900 and 1920).

By 1940 heart disease had become the leading cause of death in the United States, and so it has remained. Why? Fewer people are dying young of infectious diseases. More people are living long enough to develop physical problems in various organ systems, many of these problems having an impact on the functioning of the heart and of the entire cardiovascular system. Additionally, changes in diet, activity, and stress patterns put more people at risk for heart problems—a risk that in recent years is being reduced by increased attention to diet and exercise. Cancer is another condition that people become more vulnerable to with increasing adult age. By 1940 cancer had become the second most common cause of death in the United States, and this also remains true today. The emergence of cancer cannot be attributed entirely to the "graying" of the population, however. For example, the use of tobacco products is linked to lung cancer as well as to a variety of other life-threatening conditions. Lung cancer is the number-one cause of cancer deaths. Cancer death rates for children have been reduced by an estimated 60 percent since 1950, with slighter declines for young and middle-aged adults.

The pathway from health to death has lengthened for many people. Biographies, memoirs, and novels written a hundred or more years ago often depict people going through intense life-or-death crises. People would either die or pull through within a matter of days, and there was not much the physician could do in most cases, except to join in the prayers. In our own times, people often live for years with a life-threatening condition (see "lingering trajectory," Chapter 4). The protracted and uncertain course of heart disease and cancer has even unsettled the way in which we speak of the at-risk person. Is this woman "dying" if, in fact, she operates a business from her home and continues to do much of the child care? Is this man "terminally ill" if he gets by with just a little assistance here and there and still enjoys a rewarding family life? Both people are afflicted with the condition that will probably be cited eventually as cause of death. Although it is likely that their lives are being foreshortened, they do not function from day to day as "terminally ill" or "dying" persons. Essentially, they are people who are trying to make the best of their lives under difficult circumstances.

We may also think of people in their late eighties or nineties who are alert and active yet frail. These people also are not terminally ill or dying, and it would be inappropriate to apply these terms to them. They, too, are trying to make the best of each day for as long as they can. We need to develop a new vocabulary and new concepts for describing the slow procession from vigorous life to death. A simple dying/not dying distinction is not very useful in a society in which so many people move through life resourcefully despite a variety of stresses and constraints.

Changes in causes of death and mortality rates have many implications for the way we interpret and respond to people who are at particular risk for their lives. With these considerations in mind, we now look at the major causes of death in the United States (Table 3-6).

Alzheimer's disease has become one of the leading causes of death for the first time as the population continues to age. It should be kept in mind, though, that many people live with Alzheimer's for years, at various levels of functioning, before death. Heart disease, cancer, stroke, influenza and pneumonia, and homicide have become somewhat less frequent causes of death.

TABLE 3-6
The 12 Leading Causes of Death in the United States

Cause	Rate	Deaths
1. Heart Disease	247.8	700,142
2. Cancer	196.0	553,768
3. Cerebrovascular*	57.9	163,538
4. COPD**	43.7	123,013
5. Accidents	35.7	101,537
6. Diabetes mellitus	25.3	71,372
7. Pneumonia, Flu	22.0	62,034
8. Alzheimer's disease	19.1	53,852
9. Kidney disease	14.0	39,480
10. Septicemia	11.4	32,238
11. Suicide	10.7	30,622
12. Liver Disease	9.5	27,035

*Stroke" and related conditions.
**Chronic Obstructive Pulmonary Disease.

Source: National Vital Statistics Reports (2005).

What Will Be the Cause of My Death?

This is a question we might prefer not to ask. However, as students of thanatology, perhaps we should inform ourselves regarding the leading causes of death at a particular time of life. One more statistical table, then (Table 3-7)!

We see that the three leading causes of death for young adults are the result of human decisions and actions. Here is a golden opportunity for reducing the risk of death by improving our decision making. Accidents and suicide continue to be among the highest death risks for adults who are 25–44 years old. Motor vehicle fatalities continue to be the most frequent type of deaths that are classified as accidental. Taking seriously the familiar but too often neglected injunction, "If you drive, don't drink" would greatly reduce this toll. From the mid forties onward, heart disease and cancer become the leading causes of death. Young adults might take a moment to appreciate their low overall death rate: A look ahead makes it clear that the risk increases markedly in future years.

TABLE 3-7
Leading Causes of Death by Age

Age group	Overall death rate
15–24 years	**80.1**
• Accidents	
• Homicide	
• Suicide	
• Cancer	
• Heart disease	
25–44 years	**153.0**
• Accidents	
• Cancer	
• Heart disease	
• Suicide	
• HIV/AIDS	
45–64 years	**636.1**
• Cancer	
• Heart disease	
• Accidents	
• Diabetes	
• Cerebrovascular disease	
65 years and over	**5,022.8**
• Heart disease	
• Cancer	
• Cerebrovascular disease	
• COPD*	
• Alzheimer's disease	

*Chronic Obstructive Pulmonary Disease.
Source: National Vital Statistics Reports, (2005).

Causes of Death in the Future?

Public health advances have tamed some of the threats to life that ravaged world populations throughout history. Antibiotics have saved many lives from infections that previously would have been fatal. Yellow fever, malaria, cholera, typhoid, plague, diphtheria, tuberculosis, and smallpox are among the contagions repeatedly afflicting society, and are especially deadly for infants, young children, and elders. These diseases have been brought under various levels of control in developed nations. However, people in some regions remain highly vulnerable to epidemics. Malnutrition, unsafe water, lack of medical services, and the stress of violence lower resistance to a wide variety of illnesses.

Diseases can now spread rapidly through the world, so an illness once restricted to a small and isolated area can rapidly enter the mainstream. It is not only familiar conditions such as malaria that remain active in local areas and therefore potentially a worldwide threat. Previously unknown conditions have also been emerging. The prevention function of the death system was alerted by the emergence of AIDS and has since given heightened attention to other potential threats. The Ebola virus, spread by blood, saliva, and feces, was discovered in 1976 when a lethal outbreak occurred in a small community in Zaire. This virus is fast working and deadly. There are fears that it might re-occur and spread to large population centers. Three other viruses have demonstrated their lethality and aroused international attention. The mosquito-borne West Nile virus is being monitored as a possible major threat to life. Less known is the Marburg virus discovered in Angola, where nearly two hundred people died from it in a month (LaFraniere, 2005). The Marburg virus is a variant of the Ebola virus and thought to have passed to humans from infected monkeys. Most attention has been given to a condition called *severe acute respiratory syndrome* (SARS). It is thought to have its source in infected poultry in several Asian nations and has proved both highly contagious and life threatening. Up to this point, there have been relatively few known human fatalities from SARS, but health experts are aware that continuing vigilance is essential to prevent and/or control possible future outbreaks. The alarm level has been raised because flocks of migrating geese are spreading the disease to other birds in Burma, India, and perhaps elsewhere (Manning, 2005).

There is still another prospect that has public health authorities very much concerned: The antibiotics that have been so valuable in subduing infections are starting to lose their effectiveness. Some viruses and other microorganisms have developed resistances to the most frequently used antibiotics. The unwise use of antibiotics for minor ailments and the public's more-than-occasional failure to use them as directed may also be responsible for the loss of effectiveness. Perhaps we will be lucky. But perhaps the evolution of infectious diseases (Ewald, 1994) and emerging viruses (Morse, 1993) will result in a catastrophic increase in death rates. There have already been bioterrorism alarms that focus on the dangers of anthrax and smallpox, diseases with a lethal history that have been controlled by medical research and public health practices. But these diseases could be unleashed again by those who identify with the killing rather than the preventing and healing functions of the death system.

SUMMARY

Everything that makes a collection of individuals into a society and keeps that society going has implications for our relationship to death, as we have seen through many examples. At first we tried to imagine a world without death. This helped us to freshen our perspective on the world in which we live as mortals and the death system in which we participate. We may think of the death system as the interpersonal, sociophysical, and symbolic network through which an individual's relationship to mortality is mediated by society. The death system of any society can be analyzed in terms of its components and functions. The components include people, places, times, objects, and symbols (including language) that have special death-related meanings. The functions include warnings and predictions, preventing death, caring for the dying, disposing of the dead, social consolidation after death, making sense of death, and killing. Each of these functions was illustrated with key examples that often revealed conflicts, biases, and strains in society (e.g., unequal protection from life-threatening conditions, the influence of lifestyle on vulnerability to death, war, and blood sacrifice). Medical apartheid was identified as a racial bias that has made its way into the health care system all too frequently, although public awareness and enforced regulations have reduced the problem to some extent. The tsunami that took the lives of an estimated 200,000 people on December 26, 2004, revealed the strengths and limitations of the death systems within the affected societies.

A brief historical review showed how various modes of dying (e.g., the Black Death, syphilis, and tuberculosis) have influenced society's images of death itself. We also became familiar with the beginnings of death education, research, and counseling.

Leading causes of death were examined after we solidified our knowledge of terms such as mortality and morbidity, and the various ways in which mortality (death) rates are reported. We saw that the general mortality (death) rate in the United States continues to decrease, decreased throughout the twentieth century, and accompanied, as we would expect, by increases in life expectancy. Females and whites continue to have higher life expectancies than males and blacks. The leading general causes of death were identified (heart disease is still number one), as well as the leading causes of death for various age groups. It was noted that the three leading causes of death for youth (ages 15–24) in the United States are related more to lifestyle than to medical factors. New risks to life may be on the horizon, particularly emerging viruses with the potential for causing worldwide epidemics.

REFERENCES

Andrews, L. B., Buenger, N., Bridge, J., Rosenow, L., Stoney, D., Gaensslen, R., et al. (2004). Enhanced: Constructing ethical guidelines for biohistory. *Science, 304*, 215–216.

Aries, P. (1981). *The hour of our death.* New York: Knopf.

Associated Press. (2002, April 3). Poor called more likely to die of breast cancer. *The Arizona Republic.*

Associated Press. (2002, April 10). Thousands pay solemn respects to Queen Mother. *The Arizona Republic.*

Benson, E. P., & Cook, A. G. (2001). *Ritual sacrifice in ancient Peru: New discoveries and interpretations.* Austin: University of Texas Press.

Bodio, S. (2001, September). India's disappearing vultures. *The Atlantic Monthly, 288,* 25–27.

Bolstad, E., & Spangler, N. (2005, September 28). Embattled New Orleans police leader calls it quits. *East Valley Tribune,* p. A8.

Bryant, C. D., & Shoemaker, D. J. (2003). Dead zoo chic. Some conceptual notes on taxidermy in American social life. In C. D. Bryant (Ed.), *Handbook of death and dying:* Vol. 2 (pp. 1019–1026). Thousand Oaks: Sage.

Bryer, K. B. (1977). The Amish way of death. *American Psychologist, 12,* 167–174, 254–256.

Carrasco, D. L. (1999). *City of sacrifice: The Aztec empire and the role of violence in civilization.* Boston: Beacon.

Clausewitz, K. V. (1984). *On war.* Princeton, NJ: Princeton University Press. (Original work published 1832.)

Davies, N. (1981). *Human sacrifice in history and today.* New York: Morrow.

Einstein, A., & Freud, S. (1933). Why war? In C. James & S. Grachen (Eds.), *Collected papers of Sigmund Freud:* Vol. 4 (pp. 273–287). London: Hogarth.

Eire, C. M. N. (1995). *From Madrid to purgatory: The art and craft of dying in sixteenth-century Spain.* Cambridge, UK: Cambridge University Press.

Eliade, M. (1978). *A history of religious ideas.* Chicago: University of Chicago Press.

Evans, B. (April 1, 2008). Scientist; CDEC bosses ignored warning. http://myearthlink.net/article/nat?guid= 2008401/47flc150_13345200804018360553

Ewald, P. W. (1994). *Evolution of infectious disease.* Oxford, New York: Oxford University Press.

Gibbs, N. (2005, October 3). Act two: Hurricane Rita. *Time,* pp. 30–42.

Gibbs, W. W. (2002). On Cemetery Pond. www.sciam.com

Goodman, P. S. (2005, February 3). Tsunami's unpredictable outcome: Few injuries. *Washington Post,* p. A01.

Green, M. A. (2001). *Dying for the gods: Human sacrifice in Iron Age and Roman Europe.* Charleston, SC: Tempus.

Herman, W. (2005, January 14). The man who saved his village. *Arizona Republic,* p. A2, 18.

Holveck, J. (1991). Grief reactions within the adolescent gang system (project paper). Tempe: Arizona State University. Department of Communication.

Hostetler, J. A. (1993). *Amish society* (4th ed.). Baltimore: Johns Hopkins University Press.

Huizinga, J. (1996). *The autumn of the Middle Ages.* (Corrected version). Chicago: The University of Chicago Press. (Original work published 1926.)

Jankofsky, K. (1979). Public execution in England in the late Middle Ages: The indignity and dignity of death. *Omega, Journal of Death and Dying, 10,* 433–458.

Kant, I. (1932). *Perpetual peace.* Los Angeles: U.S. Library Associates. (Original work published 1795.)

Kastenbaum, R. (1993a). Last words. *The Monist, an International Quarterly Journal of General Philosophical Inquiry, 76,* 270–290.

Kastenbaum, R. (1993b). Reconstructing death in postmodern society. *Omega, Journal of Death and Dying, 27,* 75–89.

Kastenbaum, R. (2002a). Last words. In R. Kastenbaum (Ed.), *Macmillan encyclopedia of death and dying:* Vol. 2 (pp. 515–518). New York: Macmillan.

Kastenbaum, R. (2002b). Sacrifice. In R. Kastenbaum (Ed.), *Macmillan encyclopedia of death and dying:* Vol. 1 (pp. 733–737). New York: Macmillan.

Kastenbaum, R. (2003). "Arise, ye more than dead!" Culture, music, and death. In C. D. Bryant (Ed.), *Handbook of thanatology:* Vol. 2 (pp. 1008–1018). Thousand Oaks, CA: Sage.

Kaye, K. (2005, October 4). New data suggests Katrina was a less intense category 3 storm. *South Florida Sun-Sentinel, 1.*

Kettlewell, J. (2005, June 25). Tsunami aid "went to the richest." http://news.bbc.co.uk/hi/world/south_asia/4621365.stm

Laungani, P. (1996). Death and bereavement in India and England: A comparative analysis. *Mortality, 1:* 191–212.

LeSure, E. (2002, September 17). WTC firm poses objections to victim compensation fund plan. Associated Press. www.ap.org/WTC

Levin, A. (April 4, 2008). FAA inspectors allege threats. *Arizona Republic,* p. A4.

Lewin, T. (May 22, 2007). A move for birth certificates for still-born children. *New York Times.*

Lomnitz, C. (2005). *Death and the idea of Mexico.* New York: Zone.

Manning, A. (2005, July 7). Bird flu could spread to humans. *Arizona Republic,* p. A7.

Martin, L. R., Friedman, H. S., & Schwartz, J. E. (2007). Personality and mortality risk across the life span: The importance of conscientiousness as a biopsychosocial attribute. *Health Psychology, 26,* 428–436.

Marvin, C., & Ingle, D. W. (1999). *Blood sacrifice and the nation. Totem rituals and the American flag.* Cambridge, UK: Cambridge University Press.

Masur, L. P. (1989). *Rites of execution. Capital punishment and the transformation of American culture, 1776–1865.* New York & Oxford: Oxford University Press.

More, T. (1975). *Utopia.* New York: Norton. (Original work published 1516.)

Morse, S. S. (Ed.) (1993). *Emerging viruses.* Oxford, New York: Oxford University Press.

Nakashima, E. (2005, January 12). Indonesian children go back to school. *Washington Post,* p. A14.

Nakashima, E. (2005, January 25). For men of seaside village, lonely and unfamiliar roles. *Washington Post,* p. A01.

Nakashima, E. (2005, January 28). Indonesia offering "olive branch" to rebels. www.washingtonpost.com/wp-dyn/articles/A42800-2005Jan23.html

National Commission on Terrorist Attacks Upon the United States. (2004). *The 9/11 Commission report.* New York: Norton.

National Vital Statistics Reports. (2005).

O'Connor, A. (2004). U.S. infant mortality rate rises slightly. www.nytimes.com/2004/02/12/health/

Pape, R. A. (2005). *Dying to win.* New York: Random House.

Quinlan, A. (October 1, 2007). Killing the consumer. *Newsweek,* p. 92.

Revkin, A. C. (2005, September 27). Gulf currents that turn storms into monsters. www.nytimes.com/2005/09/27/science/earth

Ridley, A. (2002, December 11). WTC victims: What's a life worth? *Time Online Edition.* www.time.com/time/nation

Rosales, F. A. (2003). Days of the dead. In R. Kastenbaum (Ed.), *Macmillan encyclopedia of death and dying:* Vol. 1 (pp. 204–206). New York: Macmillan.

Scripps Howard. (1993, December 22) Babies in U.S. study got radioactive shots. www.shns.com/shns/g/index.

Taylor, R. P. (2000). *Death and the afterlife. A cultural encyclopedia.* Santa Barbara: ABC-CLIO.

Thomas, E. (2005, September 12). Crisis and chaos: New Orleans' descent into despair. *Newsweek,* pp. 42–46.

Tinkler, E. (2002, May 29). Extinct tiger tapped for cloning. *The Arizona Republic,* p. A15.

Treaster, J. B. (2005, September 1). Superdome: Haven quickly becomes an ordeal. www.nytimes.com/2005/09/01/national special

Washington, H. A. (2006). *Medical apartheid.* New York: Doubleday.

Wester, J. R. (2005). To help or harm: Misperceptions of the relief worker in Post-Katrina New Orleans. Paper presented at Death, Dying, and Deposition Conference, Bath, England.

Wildlife park to add mammoth attraction. (2002, August 21). www.cnn.com/2002/TECH/8/21/clone.mammoth

Zwerdling, D., & Sullivan, L. (2005, September 26). Katrina timeline: Unexecuted plans. www.npr.lrg/templates/story.php?storyID54839666

GLOSSARY

Age-standardized death rate: A mortality rate in which the age of a population is statistically controlled so that it does not affect interpretation of the numbers.

Capital punishment: Execution carried out by the legal system in accordance with the death penalty.

Cardiovascular resuscitation (CPR): The process of reestablishing respiration and heart action by opening the airway, rescue breathing, and compression of the chest, as required by the circumstances.

Cerebrovascular accident (CVA): Commonly known as stroke. Primary effects on speech and voluntary movement. Can be fatal.

COPD: Chronic obstructive pulmonary disease. Includes emphysema and chronic bronchitis, both of which progressively create "air hunger" (dypsnea).

Death system: The interpersonal, sociophysical, and symbolic network through which society mediates the individual's relationship to mortality.

Life expectancy: Estimated length of time between a specified point in time (e.g., birth) and death.

Longevity: Number of years between birth and death.

Morbidity: Illness.

Mortality: Death. Also: the condition of being vulnerable to death.

Mortality rate: Proportion of people in a particular population who die within 1 year, based on number of deaths per 1,000 or 100,000. Also known as death rate.

Pathologists: Physicians who specialize in the study of living or dead cells and tissues.

Radioactive iodide: A substance used in diagnosing and treating disorders of the thyroid gland.

Thanatology: The study of death and death-related phenomena.

Tsunami: A series of extremely long waves generated by earthquakes, landslides, or underwater volcanic eruption. Previously known erroneously as "tidal wave."

ON FURTHER THOUGHT . . .

- *Does your state have a death penalty? If so, for what offenses?* www.deathpenaltyinfo.org/article.php?did51218scid:11 For further information: Bureau of Justice Statistics www.ojp.usdodj.gov/bjs/pubal2.htm#C
- *More about tsunamis? Excellent online article in Wikipedia (really!):* http://en.wikipedia.og/wiki/Tsunami For an illuminating account of an historical volcanic eruption and tsunami, find a copy of *Krakatoa: The day the world exploded* (2003) by Simon Winchester.

- *More about hurricanes, including Katrina and Rita?* Google the extensive coverage from late August through September 2005 in *New Orleans Times-Picayune, New York Times, Washington Post.* *Time* magazine, October 3, 2005, for theories of hurricane origins and trends.

Other Useful Online Resources

CDC National Prevention Information Network
   www.cdcnpin.org
DeathNet
   www.rights.org/deathnet/open.html
Ethics Updates
   www.ethics.sandiego.edu/Applied/DeathPenalty/
Kearl's Guide to Sociology of Death and Dying
   www.trinity.edu/mkearl/death.html
Sociology Online Library
   www.fisk.edu/vl/Sociology/Overview.html
Thanatolinks
   http://lsds.com/death/
Webster:
   www.katsden.com/death/index.html
World Health Organization
   www.who.int
Yahoo's Death Page
   www. yahoo.com/Society_and_Culture/Death

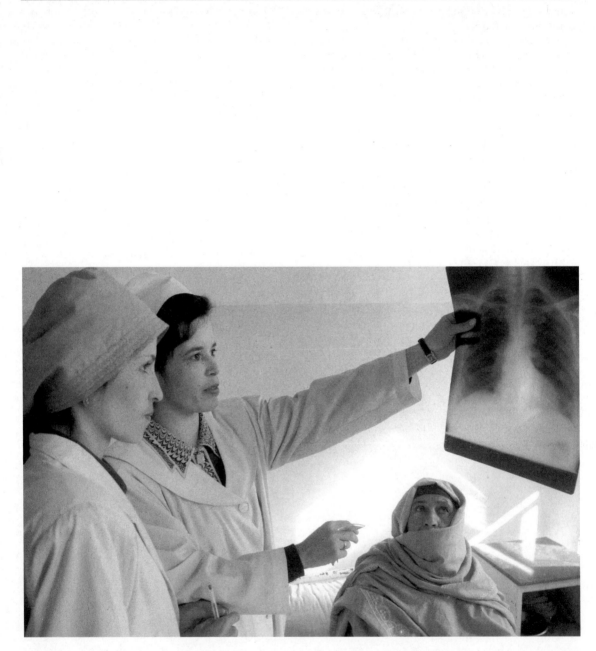

Two Afghanistan physicians examine an X-ray that could confirm the patient's diagnosis and prognosis. The patient anxiously endures her waiting time. What are her chances? Will the doctors tell her everything? Communication is often difficult for everybody in a life-or-death situation.

chapter

DYING

Transition from Life

No believer should die alone and abandoned.
—Pope Benedict XVI (2008)

*Civil War soldiers had many opportunities to die and a variety of ways in which to do so. . . .
As men became soldiers and contemplated battle, they confronted the very real possibility of
death. They needed to be both willing and ready to die, and as they departed for war, they
turned to the resources of their culture, codes of masculinity, patriotism, and religion to
prepare themselves for what lay ahead.*
—Drew Gilpin Faust (2008, pp. 4–5)

Woe is me. I think I am becoming a god.
—Vespasian (A.D. 79)

Don't let it end like this. Tell them I said something.
—Pancho Villa (1923)

*This is going to sound terrible. It is terrible. I wanted to shake her. Shake her and say, "Are
you in there? Are you IN there?" I didn't, but I wanted to: that's still terrible, isn't it?*
—Daughter whose aged mother had died in a geriatric facility

*On average, patients spent 18 hours, 39 minutes per day alone. These seriously ill patients
with poor prognoses spent most of their time in the hospital alone. Staff visits were frequent but brief. . . . Patients with advanced dementia and minority patients appear to
have less bedside contact.*
—Daniel P. Sulmasy (2000, p. 289)

*When a person looks at you and says, "I'm going to die," they usually do die. That's what
my experience has been. Somehow they know that their life is going to pass. What I found
is going to help them the most is to be in there with them. From a medical perspective,
we've always been taught to save everybody—get in there, resuscitate everyone. It's not
always going to save them. Sometimes you're the last person they're talking to. What I've
learned is: get that family member, get that husband, get the wife, get the daughter, get the
grandson, whoever that significant person who's waiting in that waiting room so anxiously, get them in there. So their last few breaths or conversation can be with that family
member—not with someone who doesn't really know them.*
—Noreen Levison, told to Studs Turkel (2001, p. 42)

My father died in his ninety-third year. He was alert, comfortable, and still very much himself. What he said most often to everybody was, "Thank you, thank you, thank you."
—Yohei Sasakawa, private communication (1996)

Over the centuries, traditions have arisen for interpreting and responding to the dying process. Pope Benedict XVI recently reaffirmed "the life and dignity of the seriously ill and dying." He emphasized the value of spiritual faith, social support, and medical expertise at the end of life. Of particular concern to him was the plight of elderly people isolated in large cities and at risk of being abandoned when approaching death. Much different was the prospect of dying that faced men becoming soldiers in the Civil War. They were for the most part young and healthy. Some regarded the war as necessary or exciting (at least, at the start), but many could not see the sense of it. The longer the bloodshed and debilitating war-related illnesses continued, the less meaningful it all seemed. Was "doing your duty" enough reason to die miserably far too soon and far too away from home? There was, nevertheless, an underlying similarity between the isolated elderly people mentioned by the Pope and the soldiers marching off to war: both faced the prospect of ending their lives in the company of strangers, if with any company at all.

Today there are significant changes taking place in the conditions of both life and death. We are faced with the challenge of deciding what lessons we should keep from the past and what new lessons might need to be learned. A useful place to begin is at the end: the moment of death where philosophical issues of meaning come down to the here-now of a unique individual's unique situation.

THE MOMENT OF DEATH: IS IT VANISHING?

The moment when life passes into death has long been charged with passionate meanings. In Irish tradition, a death invoked a spirit known as the *banshee,* who pierced the air with its wild lament. Among the Lugbara of central Africa, it was a designated member of the community who uttered the *cere,* a whooping kind of melody that was sounded only at the moment of a death. For centuries, the deathbed scene was regarded as the climax of the Christian drama on earth, with salvation or damnation suspended in the balance. In a modern hospital room, a wife transformed into widow hurled herself onto the body of her husband with screams and racking sobs.

Each of these responses is linked to a distinctive aspect of the dying person's situation. The banshee's cry announced the painful transition of a soul from the world of the living to the realm of the spirits. In contrast, the Lugbara's *cere* signaled a shift in communal arrangements: the deceased person's assets and obligation were now to be redistributed according to tradition. The Christian deathbed scene attempted to provide a model for righteous living and faith that might earn salvation in the afterlife (Bell, 2005; Paxton, 2003). The numerous family members I observed overcrowded in their dying patriarch's hospital room were of Romani (gypsy) heritage. Here it was the anguish of loss and separation from a loved one that dominated the scene. The fiercely expressed sorrow was alarming to some of the staff but an essential response on the part of the family.

Last words have often been seized upon as emblems of meaning. Vespasian was an up-from-the-ranks general who succeeded Nero as Roman emperor and attempted to restore integrity to the regime. Becoming a god was the hope of every Roman emperor, but Vespasian did not welcome this transformation because he still had so much work to do. Pancho Villa was both a notorious Mexican bandit and a beloved folk hero who retired in good graces, only to be assassinated by a rival. A media favorite, Villa was chagrined to realize that he had nothing "famous" to say as he lay dying, hence his request that reporters invent something interesting that he might have said. Vespasian and Villa felt the need to offer spontaneous "exit interviews" from their lives. The emperor left us with a glimpse of a reluctant god; the bandit left us with the anxiety of a person who was for once at a loss for words while the world was waiting to listen.

In their various ways, these examples demonstrate the impulse to draw meaning from the last moment of life. Even if we were not present, it could be inspiring to hear, for example, that the person "passed away peacefully," that loving words were exchanged, that it was felt to be "the right time," that dignity was preserved. A positive memory image might also help the survivors come to terms more easily with their own mortality. What we would not want to hear is that "all that suffering was for nothing" or "What's life if it ends like this?"

Up to this point we have been reviewing tradition—but what is happening today? The woman whose mother died in a geriatric facility had an experience that is becoming increasingly common. There was no obvious transition from life to death. The aged woman had slipped deeper and deeper into a nonresponsive condition. Her daughter had continued to visit, although her mother no longer recognized her, and now there was hardly a flicker of awareness. Was her mother still somewhere "inside" that passive form on the bed? The daughter wanted her mother back—but she also ached for relief from the tension of being with somebody who was not quite there. There was no obvious transition from life to death when the end did come. No deathbed scene. No last words. No ceremony. No ripple through society.

The Slipping Away

This is how many aged people ended their lives in geriatric facilities from about the middle of the twentieth century onward. Even more lives are now ending this way: an almost imperceptible slipping away from a condition of progressive impairment. Our traditional ideas about the dying process are becoming less descriptive of today's ideas. Why is this so?

- Medical advances are making it possible to help people survive longer with conditions that formerly had been considered terminal.

The person now has a "life-threatening" condition but is not "dying." It has become more difficult to determine the point at which the progression of a long-term illness should be considered dying. Ask not for whom the bell tolls: It is probably the beep of a monitor when vital signs cease.

- There is still a tendency for physicians to experience a patient's death as their failure and, therefore, a tendency to avoid contact with the patient when "the case is hopeless."
- With the aging of world populations, Alzheimer's disease and related dementias more often accompany people in their last phase of life. Afflicted individuals might not seem present at their deaths.
- Preterminal and terminal sedation can reduce awareness and responsivity so that communication is also impaired and the passage from life to death less conspicuous. There is also a zone of indeterminacy in which a person might be unable to respond to the family or staff member, yet still be cognizant of the situation.
- Often the person dies alone. Family might have visited on occasion, but do not happen to be there at the last moment. Being with a minimally responsive terminal patient is seldom a high priority for hospital systems, a situation intensified by the frequent shortage of nurses. The nurses who have provided attentive care might be strongly motivated to be with the patient through the end phase but will probably be under pressure to serve other patients. Sulmasy's (2000) study is one of several to document the limited amount of personal contact a hospitalized patient is likely to experience. I have tried repeatedly to obtain accurate statistics about presence or absence of a staff member at the time of death, only to be defeated by bureaucratic resistance. As a former hospital administrator myself, I can understand why few people really want to know how many people in our society exit from life without another person in attendance.

The "moment of death" is still being nurtured by compassionate health care providers (e.g., Turkel, 2001) and in hospice settings (Chapter 5). Valentine (2007) reports that few of the terminally ill patients in her study were

The deathbed scene of George Washington (1791) is attended by pulse-taking physicians rather than the angels and priests that were often depicted in the demise of celebrated people in earlier times.

known to have offered last words. However, some patients "took charge of their own dying and leave-taking" and "recovered their own characteristic selfhood . . . in some cases becoming more than themselves, to assume an enhanced aliveness, presence, and relatedness to loved ones" (p. 233). Yohei Sasakawa, executive director of one of Japan's major philanthropic organizations, has the cherished memory of his aged father's last words. His simple but eloquent "Thank you, thank you" has become a family treasure.

In this chapter, we consider dying not so much as an abstraction but as an experience that takes many forms, depending on the nature and management of the illness, the social support system available, and the unique person whose life is in jeopardy. How and when we die is influenced by societal practices as well as physical disorders. For example, it has been found that hospitalized patients are more likely to die when members of either an understaffed nursing (Aiken et al., 2002) or medical (Provonost et al., 2002) service have excessive demands on their time and energies. But why do hospitals often have fewer nurses and physicians available than called for by the situation? Furthermore, why do some of the best academic teaching hospitals provide relatively little care for patients in end-of-life situations and little education in terminal care for the next generation of physicians (Meier, 2005)? To answer questions such as these, we will need to explore the economics of health care and the prevailing attitudes within the medical community. In other words, we will become more familiar with the way the American death system works. We will also be touching on how personal lifestyles affect the timing and manner of our deaths. For example, negative emotions have been found to endanger health by undermining or overwhelming our immune systems (Kiecolt-Glaser et al. 2002). If negative emotions are part of our daily experiences, we are more likely to encounter life-threatening experiences, and more likely to lose that battle. It is unlikely that we can understand dying by focusing only on dying: We must also consider the total pattern and meaning of the life that is coming to an end.

Dying as Transition

Dying is one of many transitions that we experience in our lives. This means that we can call upon what we already know from other transitional situations. In a sense, we are already "practicing death" with bedtime rituals in childhood and in other temporary separations of daily life (Kastenbaum, 2004; Chapter 10). In growing up, we experience our first day of school, our first romantic adventure, our first solo ride behind the wheel of a car, our first day on the job. Many of us move on to such other memorable transitions as the first time we have held our baby or discovered a gray hair on our own head. Some transitions are long awaited ("At last, I'm old enough for my driver's license!"). Some may have been dreaded ("Do I actually have to support myself now?"). Many transitions are tinged with ambivalence ("I'm kinda ready to get married, sort of, but sort of not").

The transition from life itself is unique because the separation is complete and final. However, like other experiences of transition, the dying process includes interactions that can either be upsetting or comforting, communications that can either inform or confuse, and self-evaluations that can either undermine or strengthen one's sense of identity. It follows that the transition from life is unique for every individual. No two people bring the same thoughts, feelings, accomplishments, and illness-related experiences. Furthermore, no two people have the same set of relationships. The quality of life during the final illness depends much on the quality of the individual's relationships with others and the availability of those who are most capable of providing comfort and support.

We give attention first to the basic question of what dying is and when it begins, following up on our opening discussion. Next, we look at some of the "trajectories" or forms the dying process can take and their consequences for patients, family, and staff. The challenge of communicating well throughout the dying process is then explored, including problems that have been well documented in the health care system. The influences of age, gender, interpersonal relationships, disease, treatment, and environment are considered. This is followed by an exploration of stage theory and other models of the dying process, including a multiple perspective approach that identifies important parallels between dying and other experiences with which most of us are more familiar. We conclude with attention to ongoing efforts intended to improve care of the dying.

This is a good time to pause and consider dying from a very personal perspective. I suggest that you give your attention now to the thought exercise outlined in Box 4-1. Why not try this exercise right now? It has proved helpful to other people who were also starting to study dying and terminal care. The questions raised in this exercise are taken up later in the text, and your instructor will have other observations to add.

WHAT IS DYING, AND WHEN DOES IT BEGIN?

Individual and Interpersonal Responses

What is dying, and when does it begin? The knowledge that "I am dying" can transform the individual's view of self and world.

A New England artist (Lesses, 1982–1983) who was terminally ill described the comfortable familiarity of her home:

> I live with an oak coffee table
> beside my bed where
> my silver-framed clock ticks hard
> through the night
> like my cat when she purrs.

But this sense of comfort could not disguise the fact that her life had changed decisively:

> I hate every morning
> hating it
> with my stomach jumping
> before I've had a chance to think
> of anything I awake non-thinking and I am
> like a small animal backed into the corner
> of a cage to escape from the hand clutching,
> reaching through the wire door
> I feel the power of the hand's grasp
> and fear it
> without knowing what the power is.

Other terminally ill people have different experiences to report, but the feeling that "How I live now is not as I lived before" is hard to escape. Friends and relatives also are affected, and their responses in turn affect the terminally ill person. Consider Greg, for example, a college student I remember well through the years. Greg lived more than two years with the knowledge that he would probably die in the near future. He suffered from a form of leukemia that was unusually puzzling to his physicians. Greg recognized that the disease was his central problem, but often he was more concerned about how other people related to him:

> I have had to develop almost a whole new set of friends. My good old buddies just felt awfully uncomfortable around me. They couldn't be themselves anymore. I realized they'd be relieved if I would just sort of drift away from them.

What disturbed Greg's friends most was the discrepancy and ambiguity. His sturdy appearance made it difficult to accept that he was in the grip of a life-threatening disease. None of the "good old buddies" could relate to both facts: that Greg looked healthy and functioned well and that he was also terminally ill. Most of his friends and family chose to relate only to the healthy young man. According to Greg:

> I guess it was my own fault. If I wanted to make things easier for everybody, I could have just shut up about my condition. But I didn't think I had to. I mean, you talk about important things with your best friends, don't you? I didn't go on and on about it. When something new happened, or I started feeling shaky about it, I would say something. Oh, man—they just couldn't handle it!

When Greg had an acute episode, he would be in the hospital. Afterward he would keep to himself for a while. "I didn't like to show my face around when I felt rotten," he said. This pattern crossed his friends' expectations. Everybody knew that a dying person looks different, so Greg should have looked different. Similarly, it was assumed that dying was the last thing a dying person would want to talk about. A young man might be expected to be especially keen to preserve his macho image by concealing any signs of pain, weakness, or fear. Greg was a deviant, then, in behaving as a dying young man should not.

BOX 4-1 YOUR DEATHBED SCENE

A Thought Exercise

They are planning a movie about your life. This film is intended to be as faithful as possible to the facts. Help them plan the deathbed scene. Describe the ending of your life in as much detail as you can, based upon what you expect is most likely to happen. It would be best if this description is complete enough to help locate the setting, the time, who else might be on the scene, and anything else that is needed. (Yes, of course—they're giving you lots of money for your cooperation, but you are in control of planning this scene according to your best guess at what the future will bring.)

Please use a separate sheet of paper for this exercise.

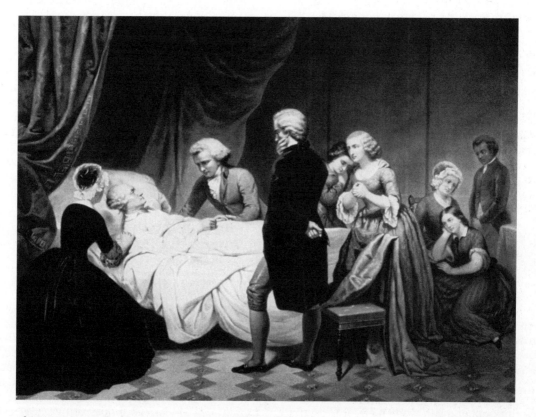

This is George Washington's other deathbed scene—here surrounded by family in portrait-appropriate formal clothing, including wigs for the gentlemen. This version, carefully staged for posterity, takes liberties with the actual deathbed scene. Both verbal and pictorial constructions of deathbed scenes are subject to influence by societal values.

By contrast, Matilda D. was depleted by many years of illness and seemed too frail to survive much longer (Kastenbaum et al. 1981). She was admitted to a geriatric hospital at age 86, suffering from painfully advanced rheumatoid arthritis, anemia, and difficulty in eating and drinking. Attentive nursing care enabled her to remain relatively stable for several months, but Matilda's condition gradually worsened. Most of her time was spent sleeping or lying on her bed in considerable discomfort. At this point, she was regarded as failing but not dying. This was a meaningful distinction to staff members because it indicated what pattern of care would be most appropriate. They did not face the ambiguity that Greg's friends had to contend with. Furthermore, the staff and Matilda's daughter also expected that dying and death would soon follow for Matilda. This again contrasts with Greg and the chemotherapy patients for whom there was some hope of remission.

Matilda was officially considered a dying person when her lungs started to fill with fluid and her general condition weakened. The next "proper" action was to relocate Matilda to the intensive care unit (ICU). Some patients were treated successfully for a medical crisis on the ICU, but it also served as the exit ward. Matilda's status change to a dying person meant that she would be moved to a death place. When a facility has an agreed-upon death place, then it is possible to maintain the illusion that death will not visit elsewhere. Her new status could also be seen in an altered pattern of staff interactions. Basic care was still provided in a conscientious, professional manner, but the contacts were now briefer and more mechanical. The subtle change from a living to a dying person had taken place in the perceptions and actions of staff members. The certainty of her death made it easier for staff to shift their patterns.

Fortunately, Matilda's life did not end with isolation and dehumanization. My hospital colleagues and I had started a therapeutic companion program to help provide residents with a core relationship through which they might regain their sense of personhood and control. Andrea George (a folk singer by profession) had formed a close relationship with Matilda. There had been time to discover Matilda's personal qualities and values. Her therapeutic companion and her daughter continued to relate to Matilda as a distinctive human being, even when she could no longer respond in words. Matilda's favorite music was sung and played to her, and she died literally in touch with two people for whom she had remained a unique and valued person.

We often treat people differently when they are perceived as dying, even if we are not aware of this difference. A classic study by LeShan (1982) found that nurses took a significantly longer time before going to the bedside of a dying patient as compared with other patients on their unit. The nurses were surprised and upset when told of this differential response pattern. They would not have knowingly withdrawn from terminally ill patients. The nurses resolved to respond promptly to terminally ill patients. After a few weeks, however, the original pattern reinstated itself. As much as they wanted to treat all patients equally, the nurses found it difficult to avoid being influenced by society's ingrained fear of contact with dying people.

Onset of the Dying Process: Alternative Perspectives

The point when dying begins depends on our frame of reference. The proposition that *we die from the moment we are born* could be useful in developing a personal philosophy of life, but it also encourages evasion. It is also questionable as a direct statement of fact. It is true that there is a continual sequence of death among the cells that comprise our bodies. The outer layer of the skin, for example, is composed of dead cells that are replaced in turn by other dead cells. Programmed cellular death (*apoptosis*) expresses itself in the life course from the perinatal phase onward. The loss of the umbilical cord after birth is an obvious example. It would be misleading to insist that the normal turnover of cells and the atrophy of unnecessary structures constitute a process of dying for the organism as a whole. Should the term dying be used so loosely, we would simply have to find a new term to represent the very different processes observed when life actually is in jeopardy.

A more challenging concept has been with us for many years. Three centuries ago Jeremy Taylor, chaplain to King Charles I of England, likened aging to a form of terminal illness (Taylor, 1651/1977). He suggested that aging might be regarded as slow dying and dying as fast aging. However, elderly people cannot be described as dying without ignoring the vigor and vitality that many continue to express at an advanced age. It is also difficult to equate dying with aging when we look at the details. For example, a young person could die of a specific bodily failure (e.g., an unexpected drug reaction), although otherwise in good health and not resemble an aged person at all.

Dying usually begins as a psychosocial event. Organ systems fail, but it is in the realm of personal and social life that dying occurs. To put this a little differently: we construct the idea of "dying" from many experiences, communications, and related concepts. Let us now consider some of the contexts in which the onset of dying is discovered or certified.

1. *Dying begins when the facts are recognized.* A doctor's waiting room might include essentially healthy people who have been convinced for years that they are dying, but also people showing up for a routine checkup who are not yet aware of their life-threatening conditions. Perhaps, then, the dying process begins when a physician concludes that the patient is afflicted with a terminal illness. The physician might fear that the patient has been on a "terminal trajectory" for some time before the diagnostic evaluation was established. But this had not been "official" dying; it is only now that the person is considered a dying patient. This might be a reasonable basis for establishing the onset of dying, but it excludes people with the same terminal illness who have not consulted a physician, as well as the possibility of a flawed diagnosis. Furthermore, a person might have a terminal disease, but still remain relatively symptom free and functional for some time to come.

2. *Dying begins when the facts are communicated.* Perhaps, though, it would make more sense

to date the onset of the dying process from the moment at which the physician informs the patient. This can be a complicated situation. There is likely to be an interval between the physician's determination of the prognosis and the time when it is shared with the patient. Physicians seldom break the news at the same instant that they reach their conclusions. There may be a delay of days, weeks, or even months before the physician tells the patient what has been found. Furthermore, sometimes the physician never does tell the patient—or the patient does not "hear" the unwelcome information.

3. *Dying begins when the patient realizes or accept the facts.* More than one nurse has returned from the bedside of a patient almost bursting with anger at the physician. "Why hasn't he leveled with this patient? This man is dying, and nobody has told him what's going on!" At times this concern is well justified. The physician has not provided the terminally ill patient with a clear statement of the condition. At other times, however, the patient was told but "didn't stay told." Somehow the patient was able to forget or misinterpret the central facts, or perhaps the physician said one thing with words and something else with facial expression and tone of voice. Studies reviewed by Kaufman (2005) find that patients tend to overestimate their probability of survival and are therefore not dying to themselves. Weisman (1972) adds that our realization of a terminal illness often is partial and floating, what he calls "middle knowledge." Similarly, I have known terminally ill people who have tried out different interpretations of their situations from day to day. What we think we understand about the patient's state of mind might apply only to a particular moment in time as the situation and interpretation continue to alter.

The physician's communication can be subtle or direct, couched in clear language or obscured by technical jargon. The patient may go away either with a clear understanding or in a state of uncertainty and confusion. There can be another time lag, then, between communication and realization of terminal illness. For examples of poor and competent physician-patient communication, see Box 4-2.

It can be difficult to determine how much the patient does understand. Many aged patients who appeared to be completely unresponsive were capable of responding when approached with patience and touch-enhanced communication (Kastenbaum, 2000). People with advanced Alzheimer's disease may not be able to understand that they are dying but nevertheless be appreciative of compassionate human contact. Ann Hurley and Ladislav Volicer (2002) urge that family and other caregivers of people with Alzheimer's prepare them to cope with the progression of the disease in the early stages; those with the disease should learn ways of asking for help so they may best understand what is being communicated. Improved

family-physician communication is also being urged (Associated Press, 2008) in deciding what treatment and comfort measures should be selected as a person with dementia approaches the end of life.

Disagreements may also arise because the terminally ill person, like anybody else, behaves differently depending on the situation. A different attitude toward the illness may be expressed to a member of the immediate family than to a physician, a colleague, or a stranger. Most of the health care staff may be under the impression that the patient does not know of the terminal illness, but one nurse may realize that he is keenly aware of the situation because he has selected that nurse as the person with whom to share his innermost thoughts and feelings. Weisman (1993) adds that our realization of a terminal illness often is partial and floating, what he

---

BOX 4-2   "BREAKING THE BAD NEWS": PHYSICIAN–PATIENT COMMUNICATION

How Not To	**✓ A Better Way**
Give the bad news right away and get it over with.	✓ Take the time to establish a relationship with the patient and family.
Give all facts at one time.	✓ Share a fact, see how the patient responds, and wait until one fact is digested before going on.
Impress patients and family with your medical knowledge.	✓ Keep it simple. Don't "snow" them with details unless they ask for more details.
Tell the diagnosis, then move on.	✓ Take the time to discover what this diagnosis means to the patient: Explain and educate.
End the session after you have told what you consider enough.	✓ Allow pauses, breathing spaces, so patient/family can ask questions.
Make sure you have broken through denial.	✓ Respect what might seem like denial: The message will be heard when the patient is ready.
Stretch the truth if necessary to cheer up the patient.	✓ Do not say anything that is not true; this destroys trust and sets up later anger and sorrow.
Make it clear that there is nothing more we can do for the patient.	✓ Make it clear that you will be with the patient and respond to his or her needs.

calls "middle knowledge. Similarly, I have known terminally ill people who have tried out different interpretations of their situations from day to day. What we think we understand about the patient's state of mind might apply only to a particular moment in time as the situation and interpretation continue to alter.

4. *Dying begins when nothing more can be done to preserve life.* The physician might not have classified the person as dying, despite the diagnostic signs, because avenues of treatment remain open. "I haven't tried all possible combinations of drugs," the physician may reason, or "Building the patient up with transfusions might make her a better candidate for another surgical procedure."

Perhaps this patient could be one of the rare survivors. This often happens when the medical and nursing staff has an exceptionally strong motivation to keep the patient alive (e.g., a child or a person of their own age and background). This reluctance to define a patient as dying can stand in the way of discussing the possibility of hospice care (see Chapter 5). Furthermore, the family physician may have an opinion that is different from that of the specialist—and one specialist might differ from another.

The judgment that a person is dying could be considered premature if it discourages actions that might have lead to recovery. As late as the eighteenth century in a city as sophisticated as London, special efforts had to be

Isabel Spinoza was placed on dialysis when her kidneys failed. She is not a U.S. citizen and faced termination of her life-prolonging treatment because of budget problems in the Arizona health care system. The state did continue to fund her treatment, but economic issues continue to influence the care of life-threatened people throughout the nation (see also Chapter 5).

made to persuade the establishment that victims of drowning could be restored by prompt treatment. By contrast, we might conclude that the classification of a person as dying has been delayed too long if painful and socially isolating treatments are continued beyond reasonable hope of success and therefore, prevent the person from living his or her final days as he or she might have chosen.

When to shift from "prevention of death" to "care of the dying" and how to accomplish this shift in an effective and humane manner are questions that hinge in part upon our definition of dying.

TRAJECTORIES OF DYING: FROM BEGINNING TO END

We have been exploring the onset of the dying process as interpreted by the various people involved. Chapter 5 examines in detail the hospice approach, with its emphasis on the home and family. Here the emphasis is on what are still the most common pathways to death—those that conclude in a health care facility.

A series of pioneering studies by Barney Glaser, Anselm Strauss, and Jean Quint Benoleil (1966, 1968) observed interactions with dying people in six medical facilities in the San Francisco area. Keep in mind that field researchers did not have the responsibility for patient care that occupies the energies of the hospital staff. Furthermore, the researchers were not the husbands, wives, or children of a dying patient. This emotional distance gives field researchers a limited but unique perspective.

The research team organized many of its observations according to the concept of *trajectories of dying*. All dying processes take time; all have certain paths through time. For one person, the trajectory could be represented as a straight downward line. For another, it might be represented more accurately as slowly fluctuating, going down, leveling off, declining again, climbing a little, and so on. Be patient with the description of these varying trajectories: they provide a useful introduction to the real life and real death circumstances in which most of us will find (or lose) ourselves.

Certainty and Time

Staff members must answer two questions about every patient whose life is in jeopardy: Will this patient die? If so, when? These are the questions of certainty and time. The questions are important because the attitudes and actions of the health care staff are based largely on what they take to be the answers. It is uncomfortable when a patient's condition does not lend itself to straightforward expectations such as "This man will recover" or "This woman will die but not for some time." In the emergency room, the staff's initial uncertainty can change to certainty in just a few minutes. The fate of a premature baby may be determined in a few hours or a few days, but the outlook for a cancer patient may remain indeterminate for months.

Together, certainty and time yield four types of death expectation:

1. Certain death at a known time.
2. Certain death at an unknown time.
3. Uncertain death but a known time when certainty will be established.
4. Uncertain death and an unknown time when the question will be resolved.

Staff interaction with patients was closely related to their expectations about time and certainty of death. Especially important are situations in which expectations change. One of their examples is a physician's decision to discontinue blood transfusions. The nurses may reject this hint and continue to do everything in their power to give the patient still another chance. The subtle pattern of communication among staff in such a case affects everybody (Glaser & Strauss, 1968):

> Since the doctor had said nothing official, even nurses who believe the patient is dying can still give him an outside chance and stand ready to save him. They remain constantly alert to counterclues. "Everybody is simply waiting," said one nurse. If the doctor had indicated that the patient would die within the day, nurses would have ceased their efforts to save him, concentrating instead on giving comfort to the last, with no undue prolonging of life (p. 11).

This physician did not carelessly forget to instruct the nurses to alter their approach. By putting nothing into words, the physician allowed a little leeway for others to continue their efforts to maintain life against the odds. We can become more familiar with the varying patterns of communication that accompany the dying process by considering three of the dying trajectories identified by the Glaser-Strauss-Benoleil research team: lingering trajectory, expected quick trajectory, and unexpected quick trajectory.

The Lingering Trajectory

The caregivers display a characteristic pattern when a patient's life is slowly fading. Seldom is there a dramatic rescue scene. Staff members try to keep the patient comfortable but feel that they have already done "all that we can" and that the patient has "earned" death after a long struggle. It would be unusual to find a team of specialists rushing into the geriatric ward to perform heroic measures. A quiet fading away seems to be accepted by the staff as a fit conclusion to the lingering trajectory.

Perhaps the death that terminates a lingering trajectory is more acceptable because the person was considered socially dead. The more responsive patients are considered more alive. Staff members also become attached to some patients more than others. More people on the lingering trajectory are aware of their social death than might be realized. "You're as good as dead when they put you behind the fence. That's why they went and put up the fence!" That observation was made to me by the resident of a large geriatric facility that, in fact, had recently been fenced off from the community. "Life's on that side. We're on the other." From what I was starting to see, he was filing an accurate report.

Visits from family members often fall off sharply with the lingering trajectory. The slowly dying person seldom speaks of final things to family and friends—or to anybody. Staff members tend to assume that the patient is moving rather gently toward death (Glaser & Strauss, 1968):

These patients drift out of the world, sometimes almost like imperceptibly melting snowflakes. The organization of work emphasizes comfort care and custodial routine, and is complemented by a sentimental order emphasizing patience and inevitability (p. 64).

But the picture is not always so tranquil. It is not uncommon for somebody in the situation to deny or resist the impending death. Sometimes this is a temporary reaction as, for example, an adult son has a difficult time realizing that the mother he has known as a vigorous, can-do person is now debilitated, exhausted, and inching toward death (Kaufman, 2005). There can also be a more aggressive attitude on the part of a family member. As Proulx and Jacelon (2004) would later observe, there can be "tremendous societal pressure on a dying person to be a 'good patient' while trying to experience the 'good death'" (p. 119). Glaser, Strauss, and Benoleil noticed incidents in which a next of kin would upset the staff by showing "too much emotion" after the patient died. Strong reactions to a patient's death sometimes challenge the staff's assumption that there is little social loss in the passing of a "lingerer."

The patience of family and/or staff may be strained when a patient fails to die on schedule. My first experience with this phenomenon occurred many years ago when the daughter of an aged patient strode angrily back from his ward and complained, "They said he was on the death list, so I came here as soon as I could. And there he was—you can see for yourself! Sitting up in bed and playing cards. And winning!" There had been a misunderstanding. A member of the hospice staff had informed the daughter that her father was on the "D. L.," a term that actually means *Danger List*. Nevertheless, the main problem was that the daughter did have reason to believe that her father was close to death and had organized her emotions accordingly. After a few minutes of cooling off, she made it clear that she did not really want her father dead but that it was difficult to keep thinking of him as all but dead and waiting "for the other shoe to drop."

The lingering trajectory allows both the patient and the family time to grow accustomed to the idea of dying, make plans, work through old conflicts and misunderstandings, and review the kind of life that has been lived. But this trajectory also can have the disadvantage of attenuating relationships and creating situations in which the person is perceived as being in limbo—not quite alive and not quite dead. The lingering trajectory has become a typical pattern in Western society, especially in nursing care facilities.

The Expected Quick Trajectory

Time is truly of the essence on an expected quick trajectory. The staff organizes itself to make the most effective use of the time that remains. This contrasts vividly with the leisurely pattern of care and staff organization that surrounds the patient on a lingering trajectory. Staff definitions of the situation can change rapidly. For example, "He is out of immediate danger but probably will not survive very long" changes to "I think he has passed the crisis point and has a real chance of pulling through."

Several types of expected quick trajectories were observed, each accompanied by a different pattern of staff interaction. In a *pointed trajectory,* the patients are exposed to risky procedures that might either save their lives or result in death. The staff often has enough advance time to organize its efforts properly. The patient may also have the opportunity to exercise some control and options (e.g., share precious minutes with a loved one, see that certain personal matters are acted upon). By contrast, the *danger-period trajectory* requires more watching and waiting. The question is whether the patient will be able to survive a stressful experience such as high-risk surgery or a major heart attack. The patient may be unconscious or only partially aware of the surroundings as compared with the alert state of a patient with a pointed trajectory. The danger period can vary from hours to days. This is the type of situation in which the family may remain at bedside or in the corridor, with doctors, nurses, and monitoring devices maintaining their vigilance.

The *crisis trajectory* imposes still another condition on everybody involved. The patient is not in acute danger at the moment, but the individual's life might suddenly be threatened at any time. The tension will persist until the patient's condition improves enough so that the danger passes or until the crisis actually arrives and rescue efforts can be made.

Different from all of these is the *will-probably-die trajectory.* The staff believes that nothing effective can be done. The aim is to keep the patient as comfortable as possible and wait for the end to come, usually within hours or days. In more recent years, there has been increasing administrative pressure to move will-probably-die patients to facilities that require less expensive resources: "Open this bed for somebody who really needs it!" People who are not quite ready to die may be perceived as taking up expensive space in a cure-oriented medical center. Unfortunately, this pressure can result in transferring an aged person to a geriatric facility that lacks the staff to offer expert preterminal care. The transfer process itself can add to the distress of a patient who has already experienced discontinuities in care.

Other problems can also arise in connection with the expected quick trajectory. What should those people in the waiting room be told? Who should tell them? Is this the time to prepare them for the bad news, or can it be postponed a little longer? Should all the family be told at once, or is there one person who should be relied on to grasp the situation first? What should we do if the family itself is in conflict, making conflicting requests and demands? This situation challenges the staff's stamina, judgment, and communication skills. However, the presence of the family can also make a positive difference to a person for whom death seems to be in near prospect.

The most salient features of the expected quick trajectory are time urgency; intense organization of treatment efforts; rapidly shifting expectations; and volatile, sensitive staff-family interactions. In the midst of this pressure, errors can be made. For example, as Glaser, Strauss, and Benoleil observed, there may be attempts to save patients from medical problems they do not have. A person may arrive at the hospital in critical condition with no medical history available to guide the staff. The pressure of time may then force medical personnel to proceed on the basis of educated guess rather than secure knowledge. Imagine the pressure the staff faces when it has to cope with several expected quick trajectories while also caring for patients with different needs.

Whether or not there is a chance to save the patient's life sometimes depends on the resources that are available at the crucial time in a particular hospital or unit. The lack of a trauma response team or advanced diagnostic equipment could make the difference between the will-probably-die trajectory and one with more hope. Ask around in your own area: *Where would health care professionals themselves prefer to be taken if they were in a serious accident or had some other type of medical emergency?* They will probably identify significant differences in equipment and staffing that could make a life-or-death difference. The perceived social value of the endangered person can also spell the difference between an all-out rescue attempt and a do-nothing orientation. "When a patient is not 'worth' having a chance," say Glaser and Strauss (1968), "he may in effect be given none." Social stereotypes that hold that one person is more important than another (whether on the basis of age, sex, race, occupation, economic status, or whatever) can play a decisive role in the death system when quick decisions must be made about priority and extent of life-sustaining effort.

The Unexpected Quick Trajectory

The significance of the interpersonal setting in which dying takes place is emphasized again by the *unexpected quick trajectory.* The experienced emergency room team adjusts quickly to situations that might immobilize most other people. However, the appearance of the unexpected quick trajectory in other areas of the same hospital can spark a crisis. On these wards, there is less preparation for emergency, and personnel may experience a "blow up" (Glaser & Strauss, 1968, p. 121). Perhaps Weisman's concept of *middle knowledge* should be applied to personnel as well as to terminally ill patients. The staff in nonemergency areas know but do not believe that a life-or-death situation might arise at any moment. In this sense, something really does blow up when a patient unexpectedly enters a crisis phase on the "wrong" ward—the staff's comforting myth of an orderly and manageable universe.

Some unexpected deaths are more disturbing than others. The "medically interesting case" is one of the most common examples. The staff is more likely to be upset by the death of a patient who presented unusual features and challenges. Personnel also tend to be affected more by the death of a patient whose life they had tried especially hard to save. Glaser and Strauss report that it is the "poor physician who tried so hard" who receives the sympathy of other staff members rather than the patient. The patient may have never seemed like an individual human being to the staff during their intensive life-saving efforts. The patient who dies for the wrong reasons also dismays and alarms the staff. Treatment may have been focused on one critical aspect of the patient's condition, while death was approaching through a different route.

The staff's need to shield itself against surprise is a major theme that runs through the unexpected quick trajectory. Everybody in a life-threatening situation has a need to exercise control—professional staff as well as patient and family. This need often drives persistent efforts to maintain the illusion of control. Patients have reported how hard they have worked to bolster the doctors' impressions that they have everything under control (Kastenbaum, 1978). Unfortunately, the well-practiced defenses of the hospital staff may become dangerously exaggerated or suddenly give way when reality punctures the illusion.

The hospital itself can precipitate an unexpected quick trajectory. Glaser and Strauss observed confusion in the mobilization of treatment resources, the turning of attention away from other patients to concentrate on an urgent case, accidents attributable to carelessness or poor safety practices, and a variety of problems that can arise when a hospital is understaffed. Problems attributable to understaffing and staff turnover have become even greater in the years following the Glaser-Strauss pioneering studies.

The combination of time pressure and surprise can lead to what Glaser and Strauss term *institutional evasions.* For example, there may not be time to bring a physician to the bedside. If nurses carry out the potentially life-saving procedures without direct medical supervision, then they will have exposed themselves to the possibility of criticism and liability action—but if they do not act promptly, the patient may die before the physician arrives. Evasions of institutional rules may be minor or substantial. The institution itself may choose either to notice or to carefully ignore the infractions. One extra source of tension within the unexpected quick trajectory, then, is the conflict between doing what seems to be best for the patient without delay and abiding strictly by the regulations.

Life-or-Death Emergencies

There is another type of "quick trajectory" that can occur any time, any place. A person in good health may suddenly become the victim of an automobile accident, a small child may fall into a swimming pool, an "unloaded gun" may discharge, a restaurant patron may choke, a person with a history of heart disease may sustain another attack. These are just a few of the emergency situations that can result in death.

Several types of problems are more likely to arise when there is a life-or-death emergency in a community setting as compared with a health care facility:

- *Panic*: "This can't be happening! What should we do?"
- *Inappropriate action:* "Let's get him on his feet."
- *Misinterpreting the situation:* "Stop whining and go back to bed!"
- *Minimizing the danger:* "I don't need a doctor. It's just a little indigestion."
- *Preoccupied by own concerns:* "I'd better clean this place up before I call anybody."

There have been many examples of prompt and competent response from family members, neighbors, colleagues, and passersby. For example, a man in his eighties had the presence of mind and the skill to perform cardiac pulmonary resuscitation (CPR) on a toddler who had fallen into a pool—an all too frequent occurrence in Arizona. This child recovered, but many have died or suffered permanent injury. Errors and poor decisions sometimes occur within health care settings also, but the risk is greater in community settings. A camper's friends, for example, may think they are doing the right thing by carrying out a snake bite remedy that has been passed along for generations—but they should be rushing the victim to a poison control center instead.

Emergency medical technicians and paramedics are often called upon when life-endangering situations arise in the community. Trained to provide front-line response to emergent health crises, these men and women may have more encounters with disaster in two or three days than most people do in a lifetime. Dale Gladden recalls one of his first experiences as a paramedic (Kastenbaum, 1993–1994, pp. 6–7):

> It was at a (community fraternal club). There was a dance going on—lots of loud music, dim lights. No one dancing. Everyone was just standing around. An elderly man had collapsed. . . . Communication was bad. We would give medicine, then call a physician on the phone and tell him the situation and what we had done. The man had gone into ventricular fibrillation. I intubated him, and the RN with me tried to get an IV in him—it was hard for her because of the bad lighting. He was a diabetic. IV (intravenous) was hooked up and we started defibrillation. There was that smell of burning hair associated with defib machines. We got a pulse and blood pressure back. Got an ambulance. The man was breathing fine so I took the tube out and we transported him to the hospital. He survived and was very thankful to me.

This man almost certainly would have died without the prompt and skilled intervention. Sometimes, however, no amount of skill and effort can save a life. It is not unusual for paramedics to find one or more people already dead on the scene. Even though the paramedic knows that a person is beyond resuscitation, it may be necessary to carry out *CPR* and other procedures in order to conform with regulations. At such times, the paramedic is likely to feel—as Gladden did after responding to another call—that it is wrong "to go through all this trouble for a dead person, why not let her be at peace? I had lots of questions why we went through the whole routine when she was already dead."

There is another odd situation that can arise when a person dies suddenly in a community setting. Although paramedics or nurses on the scene may know that the person is dead, the legal declaration of death may not be made until the body has been transported to a medical facility. This means that some of the deaths that are reported as having occurred in a hospital actually occurred elsewhere. Hospital physicians simply confirmed the ER team's assessment that the patient was beyond resuscitation. In many communities, emergency response personnel are now following "Field Termination of Resuscitation Guidelines" that enable them to forego useless procedures when it is obvious that the person has no chance of survival. Just such an incident was reported soon after the new provisions were approved in Mesa, Arizona. A chronically ill 90-year-old woman refused breakfast one morning, sat in her favorite chair, and stopped breathing. Her son later commented that "We didn't know what to do. She wanted to die at home. We wanted to handle it as quietly as we could." The paramedics who came to the home honored the family's wishes. Instead of performing unwanted and ineffective resuscitation procedures, they stayed to talk with the family and help them deal with their first wave of grief and make arrangements for disposition of the body. The Mesa paramedics also receive training in the basics of grief support—certainly a good idea for police officers as well and all people who may be called upon when a death occurs.

In some jurisdictions, it is possible for people to complete a medical care directive that forbids resuscitation measures. Where this law applies, paramedics and EMTs can refrain from performing resuscitation procedures without exposing themselves to legal risk. What is the law in your state and community? Your local department of health, hospital, or medical association can answer this question for you.

GUARDED FEELINGS, SUBTLE COMMUNICATIONS

Most of us do not say everything on our minds to whomever we happen to be with in every situation. We speak more openly with those we have learned to trust. Furthermore, we take the other person's state of mind into account: Should we alarm somebody who is already anxious or who has a difficult task to perform that requires complete concentration? And how should we get a message across? Should we be as quick and direct about it as possible? Or should we work our way up, starting with something relatively neutral and gradually getting to the point? How we communicate with another person depends on our own personality style, who that other person is, and what is at stake in the immediate situation.

Difficulties in Communication

We should not be surprised, then, to find that feelings may be guarded and communications subtle among people faced with the prospect of death. One might assume—mistakenly—that the dying person does not know what is happening or is unwilling to discuss it. Often the implicit rules make honest communication very difficult. For example, while working in a geriatric hospital, I found that personnel usually responded to patients' direct communications about death in a manner that quickly ended the interaction. The odds were about three to one against the staff member being willing to listen to what the patient had to say. Giving false reassurance ("Oh, you'll outlive me, Charlie!"), changing the subject, and a variety of other evasive responses were more common than an openness to what the dying person really wanted to communicate.

This attitude is still prevalent in many places. Aged patients on a lingering trajectory frequently are treated as though socially dead and are therefore denied even the opportunity to die as a person. I have heard staff members make remarks such as the following in the presence of the patients (Kastenbaum, 1984):

"This one, she can't talk. She doesn't know what you are saying."
"You should have seen her when she first came here, but look at her now!"
"The poor thing would be better off going in her sleep" (p. 6).

These remarks were not only degrading but erroneous. There was independent evidence that these patients, although vulnerable and failing, did understand what was being said over their (socially) dead bodies. One example that I will always remember occurred during an inspection of an extended care facility. This facility (operated by a state agency) was under court orders to improve its physical plant and its treatment program. The whistle had already been blown, time had been provided to improve care, and my visit as a consultant for the federal government was expected. However, there was no evidence of improvement, or motivation to do so. I was told that "these people (the patients) don't understand anything anyhow."

I asked the staff to show me the most impaired, uncomprehending patient on the ward. This request seemed to throw them into confusion, so I walked to the furthest corner of this large, dark, and filthy ward. An old, pale, scrunched-up woman was lying in bed, her hair tangled and untended, her body smelling of neglect. I asked for the patient's name and some information about her background. Did she have a husband, children, visitors? What had been her interests, activities, and achievements before she came here? All the staff knew was her name, and the fact that her husband or somebody visited once in a great while.

I stood by the woman's bed, took her hand, and spoke to her, using the small bits of information I had been given. In less than a minute she had painfully faced around and squeezed my hand in return. In another few minutes she was speaking and moaning. I could not make out all the words, but there was no mistaking that she knew somebody was trying to communicate with her and that she had the need and a limited ability to respond. She was still there as a person. The staff noted this interaction and retreated from it. But at the end of the inspection visit, the charge nurse turned to me and muttered, "If you're going to write anything about this, I'd better tell you that this is not the patient I told you it was. I mixed the patients up somehow. That was Mrs.__, not Mrs.__."

This story is not told to criticize geriatric facilities in general. The situation on this particular unit was the outcome of systematic neglect of the frail elderly and of those who provide care for them. Having their own sense of horror to contend with, the staff responded by erasing the patients' individuality and humanity. This woman had almost no opportunity to communicate to anybody about anything. It is not simply that we often have difficulty communicating about "mortal matters": There are many people close to death who are deprived of the opportunity for normal social interaction of any kind. And how unnecessary!

Doctor-Patient Communication: The SUPPORT Study

The health care system is still unsettled from the results of a major study conducted back in 1998. This project is known by the acronym SUPPORT: Study to Understand Prognoses and Preferences for Outcomes and Risks of Treatment (SUPPORT, 1995). The SUPPORT project was intended to help physicians make better decisions about end-of-life issues and to prevent "a mechanically supported, painful, and prolonged process of dying." The results could hardly have been more discouraging. More than 9,000 adult patients with life-threatening diseases were studied in five teaching hospitals. Half the patients and their doctors were observed for two years; the other half were included in a two-year intervention phase that attempted to improve communication and care. Box 4-3 summarizes the unsettling results of both phases.

The observation phase found that physicians seldom showed interest in the patients' own preferences. Cardiopulmonary resuscitation (CPR) would be performed regardless of the patient's stated preference. Giving patients the opportunity to express their preferences seemed to be only an empty gesture that had little or no effect on what would actually be done. Pain control was also ineffective, despite continuing advances in methods of relief. Many patients therefore were exposed to unrelieved pain and aggressive treatment, and many also spent at least 10 days on life support equipment in the ICU.

The intervention phase of the study attempted to improve this situation by providing the physicians with more information about their patients' preferences as well as their physical status. Nurses with special training made multiple contacts with patient, family, physician, and hospital staff. They encouraged attention to pain control and to better physician-patient communication to contribute to better decisions in planning the course of treatment. Unfortunately, these interventions did not work. Communication remained flawed; physician preferences for aggressive treatment were not modified in light of patients' preferences; pain control was as poor as before.

BOX 4-3 THE SUPPORT STUDY OF SERIOUSLY AND TERMINALLY ILL HOSPITALIZED PATIENTS: MAJOR FINDINGS

I. The Observation Study

1. Half of the patients who died during the course of the study had moderate or severe pain during their final three days of life.

2. Physicians often used jargon that the patient did not understand when talking about cardiopulmonary resuscitation (CPR) and often (41 percent) never even discussed this subject with their patients.

3. In 80 percent of the cases, physicians misunderstood what the patients wanted with respect to the use of CPR.

4. Physicians often did not follow the patients' stated preference to avoid the use of CPR: In about 50 percent of the cases, the physician did not write a do-not-resuscitate (DNR) order.

II. The Intervention Study

1. There was no increase in discussions between physicians and patients.

2. Physicians often continued to disregard patients' preferences to have CPR withheld, even when these preferences were known to them.

3. There was no improvement in pain control.

4. Computer projections of the patients' prognoses were no more accurate than those made by the attending physicians.

5. Much of the patient information generated during the intervention phase failed to reach the physicians because of various communication problems.

The findings were disturbing enough to prompt an immediate editorial response from the *Journal of the American Medical Association* ("Improving Care," 1995). The anonymous editorial writer urged other physicians:

> Don't project our concept of a good death onto patients. . . . Respect for patient autonomy means that physicians must allow informed patients to determine what value they place on such a chance of survival and what risks they are willing to undergo (p. 1635).

Since publication of the SUPPORT findings, there have been additional efforts to encourage physician respect for the stated preferences of terminally ill people and to provide more effective pain relief. This process continues to face resistance from entrenched attitudes and habits. Encouragement is to be found in the rapid growth of palliative care programs within hospitals (Meier, 2005) and in the more receptive approach to patient communication by the current generation of medical students on their way to becoming physicians.

Improving Communication

It has been known for years that most people in a life-threatening situation would prefer to have open discussions with their physicians and family members (Hayslip & Peveto, 2005). This need for honest communication was expressed by most of the terminally ill people whose outcomes were followed in the SUPPORT study. Furthermore, the need for improved communication is expressed by terminally ill people who prefer the continuation of active treatment as well as those who prefer that aggressive treatment be discontinued as death approaches. This is often accompanied by the urgent request for alleviation of pain (Laakkonen, Pitkala, & Strandberg, 2004). For example, one woman who realized that the end of her life was near wished that the doctors would communicate with her so that

> I would get the information, whether there is anything that can help. Whether I will get some treatment. Even though I have lived this long and seen quite enough, it's amazing how one wants to cling to life. That's how it is always (p. 121).

A study by physicians has also confirmed that terminally ill patients and their caregivers found it helpful to discuss death, dying, and bereavement (Emanuel et al., 2004). The authors concluded that it is a misguided practice to discourage or even forbid people from discussing death with terminally ill patients. This conclusion is not exactly breaking news, however. That many dying people welcome the opportunity to discuss this situation was established by Herman Feifel (1959) in the early days of the death awareness movement. Apparently, we still need to keep making this discovery.

Here are a few other suggestions about communicating with people who are in life-threatening situations.

First, *be alert to symbolic and indirect communications,* as illustrated by the following examples:

1. *Sharing dreams.* People may prepare themselves for their final separation through dream work before conscious thoughts and direct interpersonal communications occur. Dreams reported by terminally ill cancer patients have been found to differ from those of healthy older people (Coolidge & Fish, 1983–1984). Among these differences was a greater frequency of death content in dreams, but the dreamer usually saw somebody else as dead. The dreamer often attempted to discover the identity of this person:

   > I dreamt of a funeral and in the funeral was a little girl going to be buried in her coffin. I couldn't get to her so I tried to open it to see who it was and it was one of my daughters. Little Antonette. She was lying on her side and the lid was falling in the coffin. . . . I went to fix the lid. . . . I kept on doing things that would upset the coffin. I felt like a criminal that didn't belong there (p. 3).

   Listening to each other's dreams can be a valuable way to supplement and enrich interpersonal communication for people who are comfortable with their own dream life. It is not essential that the patient or the listener come up with the "right" interpretation of these dreams. Simply being able to

share these inner experiences with another person can provide an additional supportive line of communication.

2. *Symbolic and indirect language.* While dreams provide a treasury of symbolic language and actions, such characteristics can also appear in everyday speech. Following is an example that came to our attention during a research project in a geriatric hospital (Weisman & Kastenbaum, 1968).

   > The 75-year-old former stonemason had lost some of the vigor he had shown earlier in his hospital stay, but otherwise appeared to be in stable condition and doing well. One morning he asked for directions to a cemetery near his former home. Although he made the direct statement that he was expecting the undertaker, this was not taken up by the staff as a clue to impending death. It was just a statement that didn't make much sense. The next day, he told several people that his boss (going back many years, in reality) had called for him: he was supposed to help dig graves for eight people. The delusion now became persistent. He insisted on staying around the ward so he could be available to the people who would come to take him back to the cemetery.

   > Two days before he died, the patient had several teeth extracted (a procedure that was seen as having little risk because of his good condition). He then told staff that it was time to call his sisters—about whom he had never before said a word. His death came as a surprise to the staff although, apparently, not to himself. Cause of death was determined to be cerebral thrombosis. Despite all the clues this man had given, no notice had been taken. His "crazy talk" seemed even less crazy when a subsequent review indicated that the old stonemason had outlived seven siblings—his reference to digging a grave for eight people no longer seemed to be arbitrary (p. 16).

   After a number of experiences such as this one, both our clinical and research staffs markedly improved their ability to identify patients whose death was more imminent than might have been expected and learned to pay close attention to what was said, whether in direct or symbolic language.

Much of physician-family communication about death is indirect. This tendency was made clear again in a study that found discussions of a terminally ill patient's condition often avoided direct mention of death and instead touched on what will probably be happening in the future (Rodriguez et al. 2006). This apparently slight difference in language allows each of the participants to comprehend the situation in their own way but within the bounds of reality.

3. *Leave-taking actions.* Deeds as well as words can help. My colleagues and I in both institutional and community settings have observed such behaviors as sorting through possessions and giving some away; creating the occasion for one last interaction of a familiar kind, such as playing checkers or going fishing together; and terminating mutual obligations and expectations (e.g., "Thanks for the loan of the bowling ball. I won't be needing it anymore"). Most people who are aware of their terminal illnesses do hope to have the opportunity to bid farewell to the important people in their lives—but not necessarily all in the same way. It is wise to take our cue from the dying person rather than impose a particular kind of farewell scene that happens to appeal to us.

Second, *help to make competent and effective behavior possible.* Illness, fatigue, and reduced mobility make it difficult to continue functioning as a competent person. This is true whether or not the individual is suffering from a terminal condition. The progressive nature of terminal illness, however, increases the individual's dependency on others and limits the range of spontaneous action. The person attempting to cope with terminal illness often retains a strong need to be competent, effective, and useful to others. Family, friends, and other caregivers cannot only improve communication, but also help to support the dying person's sense of self-esteem by striking a balance between meeting the realistic needs associated with dependency and creating an environment in which the person can continue to exercise some initiative and control.

Timely and appropriate support is needed, not a total takeover of the dying person's life. Attentive listening and observing are required to match the style, level, and intensity of care with the individual's physical condition and psychosocial needs. By accomplishing one side of the communication process—listening and observing—it becomes more probable that the patient can maintain a core of competent and effective behavior and continue to communicate needs and attentions.

Third, *recognize that the dying person sets the pace and the agenda.* There is no schedule that has to be met, no set of tasks that the dying person must accomplish—unless the dying person has established a schedule and set of tasks. This is no time for listeners to impose their own needs or to expect the dying person to behave in accordance with preconceived ideas of just what it is that a dying person is supposed to do. Although the patient will usually introduce thoughts concerned with dying and death, there are individual differences regarding when and how this topic is brought up. For example, during a particular interaction the patient may choose to say nothing about death. This does not necessarily mean that the patient is "denying" or is "behind schedule." The patient may just be taking a little "vacation" from this overwhelming topic or be more concerned at the moment with some other matter. Furthermore, one terminally ill person might choose to discuss specific death-related issues (e.g., reviewing funeral plans or the distribution of property) while another is more focused on feelings and relationships. I have known many dying people who had not much left to say about death because they had already had all the time they needed to settle their thoughts and communicate their concerns and desires. These people still had need for supportive everyday communication but did not need to be reminded that they were dying!

Fourth, *do not confuse the dying person's values and goals with our own.* Communication can be distorted or even broken off when others project their own needs on the dying person. We have already seen that substituting our needs and values for those of the patient is a major problem in medical care of dying people. Requiring the dying person to move along from one "stage" to another also imposes an additional burden on everybody in the situation. Another stress can be introduced if we insist that the patient give up "denial." As noted earlier (Chapter 1), denial has become an overused and often misused term. There are many reasons why a person might not acknowledge his or her terminal condition at a particular time and to a particular individual. Furthermore, denial-like behaviors may be useful strategies. Connor's (1992) research with terminally ill cancer patients found confirmation that the supposed "deniers" were downplaying the seriousness of their illness because this strategy was helping them to maintain their most significant interpersonal relationships. Connor also makes the important point that some people have had a dysfunctional lifestyle for many years and continue to make excessive use of denial-like behaviors in their terminal illness. Other people have functioned well until confronted with the loss, stress, and uncertainties associated with a life-threatening illness. To say that a person is denying seldom tells us all that would be useful to understand and may, in fact, misrepresent the situation.

INDIVIDUALITY AND UNIVERSALITY IN THE EXPERIENCE OF DYING

Does everybody die in the same way? If so, then it might be possible to discover general laws or regularities upon which care and management can be based. Or does everybody die in a unique way, depending on many different factors? We are more likely to be good observers and useful caregivers if we understand the specifics of each situation. The discussion begins, then, with respect for both universal factors and individual dimensions of dying.

Factors That Influence the Experience of Dying

Attention will be given to some of the ways in which age, gender, interpersonal relationships, disease, treatment, and environmental context influence the experience of dying.

Age

Age by itself is an empty variable that exercises no direct influence. Nevertheless, chronological age serves as an index for a variety of factors that can make a significant difference throughout life, including the process of dying.

- *Comprehension of dying and death.* Our intellectual grasp of death is related both to the level of development we have achieved and to our life experiences (see Chapter 10). At one extreme is the young child who is keenly sensitive to separation but who does not yet comprehend the finality and irreversibility of death. At the other extreme is an aged adult who not only recognizes the central facts of death but has seen many close friends and relations die through the years. The "same" experience will be different for people with varying life histories and cognitive structures.
- *Opportunity to exercise control over the situation.* Children are accorded fewer enfranchised rights than adults. Even the "natural death" acts passed by state legislatures do not directly strengthen the child's position as a participant in decision making. The traumatic experiences of young Marie (Chapter 6) illustrate a serious problem that has not yet been entirely remedied.
- *Perception and treatment by others.* Perceived social value differs with age. Elderly patients often are victimized by the assumptions that (a) they are ready to die and (b) nobody would miss them much. Both professional caregivers and the general public have tended to act upon these assumptions without first inquiring into their accuracy. For example, doctors are much more likely to withhold resuscitation efforts in patients older than age of seventy-five, even though they are likely to force CPR on younger patients.

It is all too easy to mistake a depressive reaction for a terminal course. Many circumstances can lead to depression among elderly adults, including bereavement, social isolation, fatigue, and chronic though not life-threatening conditions. Expertise in assessing and treating depression is required, along with the independence of mind to break free of the "ready to die" stereotype and look carefully at each individual's situation. Unfortunately, every day there are depressed elderly men and women whose chances for survival as well as a renewed quality of life are diminished by society's inclination to see stressed and depressed older adults as ready for the grave.

Misperceptions often occur at the other extreme of the age range as well. For example, there remains a stubborn belief among some physicians that infants do not experience pain to any appreciable extent. Bone marrow samples are taken, needles are inserted into the spine, and burn dressings are changed without adequate analgesia. A life-threatened infant may undergo very painful procedures repeatedly. Although this attitude is gradually changing, it may be difficult to eliminate because the belief that infants do not experience pain serves anxiety-reduction purposes for physicians and nurses who are responsible for their treatment.

Gender

A man with cancer of the prostate may be concerned with the threat of becoming impotent as well as with the risk to his life. Cervical cancer may disturb a woman not only because of the life risk but also become one of the treatment possibilities—hysterectomy—would leave her unable to become pregnant. Both the man and the woman may be troubled about the future of their intimate relationships even if the threat to their lives is lifted. Some people interpret physical trauma affecting their sexual organs as punishment for real or imagined transgressions. Others become preoccupied with their physical condition in a way that interferes with affectionate and sexual relationships. "I'm no good any more" may be a self-tormenting thought for either the man or the woman, each experiencing this in his or her own way. These are not the only types of reactions that people express to cancer of the reproductive system; these simply illustrate some of the many possible interactions between sex role and disease.

When a woman is faced with a life-threatening illness, she is likely to have concerns about the integrity and well-being of her family. Will the children eat well? Can her husband manage the household? What most troubles the woman/wife/mother may be the fate of her family as much, or even more than, her own. The man/husband/

father in the traditional family is likely to have distinctive concerns of his own. Has the illness destroyed his career prospects? Will he lose his job or his chance for advancement even if he makes a good recovery? Has he provided well enough for his family in case he doesn't pull through? Is he, in effect, a "good man" and a "real man" if he cannot continue to work and bring in the money? There may be a crisis in self-esteem if he is confined to hospital or home for a protracted time, away from the work situations that support his sense of identity.

Gender differences are important from the standpoint of professional caregivers as well as the patient. Direct care to the dying person is usually provided by women, often nurses, licensed practical nurses, aides, or technicians. Responsibility for the total care plan, however, still is often in the hands of a male physician. The physician may be more time conscious and personal achievement oriented, characteristics that favor survival of the rigors of medical training. He may therefore be more persistent in cure-oriented treatments but also quicker to withdraw when death is in prospect. The nurse may be more sensitive to the patient's relationship with significant people in his or her life and less apt to regard impending death as a failure.

Changing patterns of sex roles in Western society are showing up in adaptation to terminal illness. It is more likely now than in past years, for example, that the wife is also a wage earner and familiar with financial management. Similarly, the husband of today may have had more time with the children and more responsibility for running the household than in the past. Furthermore, the healthy partner may be more attuned to the needs and concerns of the sick partner because there has been more commonality in their experiences. It is likely that there will be many other effects of changing sex roles on the management of terminal illness. For example, as more women enter or reenter the workforce, the number of people available to serve as volunteers and informal helpers may decline.

Interpersonal Relationships

It is difficult to overestimate the importance of interpersonal relationships in the terminal phase of life. Clinical experience has further supported the findings of an influential early study (Weisman & Worden, 1975). Among hospitalized patients who were likely to die within a few months, those who maintained active and mutually responsive relationships survived longer than those with poor social relationships. The patients who died rapidly also tended to have fewer friends, more distant relationships with their families, and more ambivalent relationships with colleagues and associates. They became more depressed as treatment failed. The investigators noted that the patients with poor relationships often expressed the wish to die, but that this did not represent an actual acceptance of death: It was a product of their frustration and disappointment with life. The same investigators (Weisman & Worden, 1976) later found that the terminally ill patients who were experiencing the most distress also were those with the most interpersonal difficulties. Not only the length of survival, then, but also the quality of life was associated with the kind of interpersonal relationship enjoyed or suffered by the patient. Fortunately, there is now more recognition of the role of family relationships in a person's end-of-life experiences (e.g., Hickman, Tilden, & Tolle, 2004).

There are situations in which it is the family who needs the most support. For example, an elderly man on a lingering trajectory toward death was at home, under the care of his wife, with assistance from other family members. Mr. Tchinsky was in a semi-comatose state, not suffering either physical or emotional distress. His wife, however, was struggling with anxiety and guilt. In actuality, Mrs. Tchinsky was a loving and attentive caregiver, but she had difficulty in controlling the leakage from his *colostomy bag*. This relatively small problem was the source of great distress because to Mrs. Tchinsky it meant that she was failing her husband in his time of need. A visiting nurse identified and responded tactfully and effectively to this problem. Within a short time, Mrs. Tchinsky was again secure in her role as loving wife and caregiver, and the rest of the family was also relieved. This intervention did not involve the application of either high technology or counseling: A caring family just needed a little timely help to fulfill its obligations toward the dying man (Kastenbaum & Thuell, 1995).

Final conversations between people in close relationships can be profoundly valuable both for the dying person and the survivor. Keeley's (2007) interviews with people who recall final conversations with family members or friends reveal parting messages that confirmed love, strengthened identity, validating religious or spiritual beliefs, achieved reconciliation, or emphasized the depth of their abiding relationship. Sometimes the messages were simple and direct, e.g., "I love you," repeated several times during the conversation. A daughter and her dying father used American Sign Language to communicate "I love you" when he lost his ability to speak. Words of affection often were accompanied by nonverbal actions, such as taking the dying person's hand and looking at each other. Final conversations often helped the survivor to have a sense of closure and completion. Keeley's study and the experience of many end-of-life caregivers make it clear that the opportunity for final conversations should be made available, even in situations that are not conducive to intimate personal interactions.

Where and How We Die—From the Abstract to the Particular

We die in a particular place that contributes to our comfort, misery, or both. Similarly, the particular services we receive also have a significant effect on our experience. Discussions of the dying process sometimes become so abstract and generalized that we neglect the specific medical problems involved. Think, for example, of the difference between a person whose likely cause of death will be kidney failure and its complications and a person suffering impairment of respiratory function (perhaps a coal or uranium miner). The person with kidney failure may fade away as waste products accumulate in the body. Over time, the patient may become more lethargic and less able to sustain attention and intention. There may be intermittent periods of better functioning when the patient seems more like his or her old self. The final hours or days may be spent in a comatose condition.

By contrast, a degenerative respiratory condition is likely to produce more alarming symptoms and experiences. Perhaps you have seen a person with advanced emphysema struggle for breath. An episode of acute respiratory failure is frightening to the individual and likely to arouse the anxiety of others. Once a person has experienced this kind of distress, it is difficult to avoid apprehension about future episodes.

Some conditions are accompanied by persistent pain and discomfort unless very carefully managed. Other conditions can reach peaks of agony that test the limits both of the individual and the state of medical comfort giving. Nausea, weakness, and a generalized sense of ill-being may be more dominant than pain for some terminally ill people. It is difficult to be serene when wracked by vomiting or diarrhea. *The point is that we do not die abstractly.* We bring our distinctive life history to the situation, and the situation itself is distinctive and almost certain to change over time. As we consider theoretical models of the dying process, then, it is useful to keep in mind that death comes down to the unique individual within a complex and shifting situation. Abstract perspectives can be useful, but we will always want to keep the actual person and situation well in mind.

THEORETICAL MODELS OF THE DYING PROCESS

People hesitate to interact with dying people for many reasons. One of these reasons can be the lack of a coherent and useful perspective. What does it mean to be dying? What can be expected? Several conceptual approaches have attempted to deal with questions of this kind (Corr, Doka, & Kastenbaum, 1999). In this section, you are invited to consider several additional perspectives.

Do We Die in Stages?

Two stage theories of the dying process have been especially influential. Both regard dying as a sequence of psychological or spiritual stages. The differences are also substantial, however.

A Buddhist Perspective

Buddhists have long been aware of individual differences in the way people die. Some

people are killed instantly in an accident, and others slowly decline and outlive their mental powers. In such situations, there is no opportunity to progress through the stages. Furthermore, some people are anxious and beset by emotional conflict as death nears. These people are also unlikely to proceed through the stages of spiritual enlightenment. His Holiness, Tensin Gyatso, the fourteenth Dalai Lama, states that not all people move through the stages as they die (Gyatso, 1985). One must have sufficient time and be in a state of mind that is conducive to spiritual development. Those who have developed spiritual discipline throughout their lives are more likely to experience the entire cycle of stages.

For Buddhists, there is a complex relationship between mind and body. At death, the coarse connections between mind and body are severed—but the very subtle connections continue. There is also a broad philosophical conception that becomes especially significant as death approaches. As expressed by the Dalai Lama: "When you are able to keep impermanence in mind—seeing that the very nature of things is that they disintegrate—most likely you will not be greatly shocked by death when it actually comes" (p. 170).

There are eight stages in the Buddhist journey toward death. Perhaps our first surprise is that these stages occur in ordinary life as well. "In more subtle form, the eight transpire each time one goes in or out of sleep or dream, sneezes, faints, or has an orgasm" (Gyatos, 1985, p. 98). Only the sensitive and disciplined person is aware of these subtle forms of dying that occur in everyday life.

What are the fundamental changes that occur as one moves from the first to the final stage of dying?

Stage 1. Eyesight dims, but one begins to have mirage-like visions.

Stage 2. Hearing diminishes. There is a new internal vision: of smoke.

Stage 3. The sense of smell disappears, and there is now an internal vision that is "likened to fireflies in smoke." The dying person is no longer mindful of other people.

Stage 4. Sensation is lost from the tongue and the body. The dying person is no longer mindful of his or her own concerns. Breathing ceases. (At this point the person would be considered dead by a Western physician but not so to the Buddhist.)

Stage 5. This is the first of the pure visionary stages. White moonlight is perceived.

Stage 6. The person experiences visions of red sunlight.

Stage 7. The person experiences visions of darkness, faints, and then awakens into the final stage.

Stage 8. The clear light of death appears. This unique state of consciousness persists until death.

The Buddhist stages, then, all focus on the experiential state or phenomenology of the dying person and are divided equally into those that occur while the person is still alive by ordinary standards and those that occur when the person would appear to be dead to most observers. This model of dying served as a guide to Buddhists for many centuries before the current death-awareness movement arose in Western society. (There is also a somewhat less elaborate stage theory of dying within the Islamic tradition [Kramer, 1988].) We turn now to the stage theory that has become most familiar to readers in the Americas and Western Europe.

Kübler-Ross: The Five Stages

Five stages of dying were introduced by Elisabeth Kübler-Ross in her book *On Death and Dying* (1969). These stages are said to begin when a person becomes aware of his or her terminal condition. The stages are presented as normal ways of responding to the prospect of death and the experience of dying. The patient begins with a stage known as denial and moves through the remaining stages of anger, bargaining, depression, and acceptance. Some people do not make it all the way to acceptance. Progress may become arrested at any stage along the way. Furthermore, there is often some slipping back and forth between stages, and each individual has a distinctive tempo of movement through the stages. This conceptualization, then, emphasizes a universal process that allows for a certain amount of individual variation.

Stage 1. Denial is the first response to the bad news. "No, not me, it can't be true!" The denial stage is fueled by anxiety and usually runs its course in a short time. It could also be described as a "state of shock from which he recuperates gradually" (p. 37).

Stage 2. Anger wells up and may boil over after the initial shock and denial response has passed. "Why me?" is the characteristic feeling at this time. Rage and resentment can be expressed in many directions—God not excluded. The patient is likely to become more difficult to relate to at this time because of the struggle with frustration and fury.

Stage 3. Bargaining is said to be the middle stage. The dying person attempts to make a deal with fate. The individual may ask for an extension of life, just long enough, say, to see a child graduate from high school or get married. The bargaining process may go on between the patient and caregivers, friends, family, or God.

Stage 4. Depression eventually follows as the person experiences increasing weakness, discomfort, and physical deterioration. The person can see that he or she is not getting better. The symptoms are too obvious to ignore. Along with stress, strain, and feelings of guilt and unworthiness, there may be explicit fear of dying at this stage. The person becomes less responsive and his or her thoughts and feelings are pervaded by a sense of great loss.

Stage 5. Acceptance, the final stage, represents the end of the struggle. The patient is letting go. Despite the name, it is not a blissful state. "It is almost void of feelings. It is as if the pain had gone, the struggle is over, and there comes a time for 'the final rest before the long journey' as one patient phrased it" (Kübler-Ross, 1969, p. 100).

Interwoven through all five stages is the strand of hope. Realistic acknowledgment of impending death may suddenly give way to hope for a miraculous recovery. Hope flickers back now and then throughout the entire sequence. In addition to describing these stages, Kübler-Ross indicates some of the typical problems that arise at each point and suggests ways of approaching them. She emphasizes, for example, the need to understand the patient's anger during the second stage rather than to retaliate and punish the patient for it.

Evaluating the Stage Theory

We first consider shortcomings of the stage theory, followed by observations that are more supportive.

First, *the existence of the stages as such has not been demonstrated.* Although four decades have passed since this model was introduced, there is no clear evidence for the establishment of stages in general, for the stages being five in number, to be those specified, or to be aligned in the sequence specified. Dying people sometimes do use denial, become angry, try to bargain with fate, or lapse into depression or a depleted, beyond-the-struggle way of being. However, the reality of these moods or response sets has nothing necessarily to do with stages. Dying people have many other moods and responses as well. These include, for example, expressions of the need to control what is happening and to preserve continuity between themselves and those who survive them. For a particular person at a particular moment, any of these needs may take highest priority. Kübler-Ross did not provide the kind of clear definitions of the stages that lend themselves to research, and results from the few studies that have examined facets of stage theory have not supported this model. Textbooks on nursing as well as the mass media continue to focus on the five stages despite the lack of evidence, and often to the exclusion of other aspects of the dying process. The theory won acceptance and continues to have its adherents despite the lack of data. This casual attitude regarding the factual basis of a theory suggests that it meets social or emotional needs rather than scientific criteria.

Second, *no evidence has been presented that people actually do move from Stage 1 through Stage 5.* Brief clinical descriptions of various patients are given in the Kübler-Ross book as examples of the stages. But evidence that the same person passed through all the stages was not offered either at that time or subsequently. One might as well offer snapshots of five different people in five different moods as proof that these moods occur in a particular sequence.

Third, *the limitations of the method have not been acknowledged.* The conclusion that there are five stages in the terminal process was based on psychiatric-type interviews conducted by one person and interpreted by the same person. This is a reasonable way to gather information, gain insights, and develop hypotheses to be tested within the structure of a formal research project, a potentially useful beginning. However, the research effort never moved past this beginning, and its inherent flaws and limitations were never transcended. Furthermore, what the dying person says and does in the presence of a psychiatrist is a highly selective behavior sample. The nurse who cares regularly for the patient's physical functioning often sees other aspects of the personality that do not show up in an interview, and the same may be said of physicians, ministers, family members, and friends. Behavioral studies might reveal still another different perspective, as might a diary kept by the patient. One limited source of information about the experiences and needs of the dying patient has taken the place of extensive, multilevel, cross-validated approaches.

Fourth, *the line is blurred between description and prescription.* Stage theories in general often fail to distinguish clearly between what happens and what should happen. Kübler-Ross repeatedly cautioned against trying to rush a person through the stages. Nevertheless, many people did assume that the patient should be hustled "on schedule" from denial right through to acceptance, and that it is a mark of failure for everyone concerned if the timing is off. This expectation added unnecessary pressure to the situation and also enshrined "acceptance" as the universally desired outcome of the dying person's ordeal. The concept of universal stages lends itself to misuse by those who find their tasks simplified and anxieties reduced through a standardized approach to the dying person.

Fifth, *the totality of the person's life is neglected in favor of the supposed stages of dying.* The supposed universality of the stages sometimes leads to the dying person being treated as a specimen moving along predetermined paths rather than as a complete human being with a distinctive identity. However, each dying person is male or female, of one ethnic background or another, and at a particular point in his or her life. The nature of the disease, its symptoms, and its treatment can all have a profound effect on what the dying person experiences. Perhaps most important of all, who the person is deserves prime consideration in this situation as in any other. Even if the stage theory were clarified and proved, it would not account for as much of the dying person's experience as has been widely assumed. We take the entire course of our lives with us into the final months and weeks. Emphasis on the hypothetical stages of reaction to terminal illness tends to drain away individuality or at least our perception of it.

Finally, *the resources, pressures, and characteristics of the immediate environment can also make a tremendous difference.* There are still medical environments in which almost everybody denies death almost all of the time. When the terminally ill person denies, it may be an attempt to conform to the implicit social rules of the situation rather than a manifestation of either individual personality or the hypothetical sequence of stages. Why waste one's depleted energies by fighting the system? The same terminally ill person might respond quite differently in a community hospital, a major medical center, an Amish community, or a hospice program. Environmental dynamics, mostly neglected in stage theory, have much to do with the experiences and responses of terminally ill people.

Nevertheless, Kübler-Ross did much to awaken society's sensitivity to the needs of the dying person. Accepting the stage theory is not essential for appreciation of her many useful observations and insights. Some of the practical problems that have arisen in the wake of Kübler-Ross' presentations should be attributed to their hasty and uncritical application by others. Kübler-Ross' contributions might be most valuable for their emphasis on communicational interactions. She demonstrated that it is not only possible, but helpful, to converse with terminally ill people. Many nurses and social workers were inspired by her lectures and workshops. With these examples in mind, they were able to overcome the prevailing societal taboos against open and honest communication with dying people.

A Developmental Coping Model of the Dying Process

Charles A. Corr (1993) has proposed an alternative perspective that is intended to move beyond the flaws and limitations of the stage theory. He believes that "an adequate model for coping with dying will need to be as agile, malleable, and dynamic as is the behavior of each individual" (p. 77). People may try out certain coping strategies only to reject them firmly, or may pursue several strategies at the same time, even if they are not compatible. Furthermore, people will differ in the tasks and needs that are important to them as well as in their methods of coping. The model must respect individuality as well as universality, and it must offer practical guidelines for caregivers. It is not enough just to identify a coping process and give it a name.

Corr identifies four challenges that dying people encounter: the physical (satisfying body needs and reducing stress), the psychological (feeling secure, in control, and still having a life to live), the social (keeping valued attachments to other individuals and to groups and causes), and the spiritual (finding or affirming meaning, having a sense of connectedness, transcendence, and hope). We face challenges throughout the course of our lives, so we can draw upon what we have already learned and achieved when we must cope with the challenges of the dying process.

Above all, Corr advocates greater empowerment for the dying person and for those who are intimately involved in caregiving. With open communication and trusting relationships, we might feel less need for simple theories of the dying process. It is also a useful approach for recognizing that the dying person remains a living person who is attempting to cope as resourcefully as possible with challenges and stresses, and for including the full range of factors that influence the experience and course of the dying process.

The Dying Person's Own Reality as the Model

The patient's own reality is at the heart of another alternative theory. The emphasis here shifts from the observer's frame of reference, away from stage or developmental tasks that an outsider might find useful to make sense of the dying process. Instead, the challenge is to learn how dying people interpret their own situation. In this view, there may be as many theoretical models of dying as there are dying people. Interest in the way terminally ill people interpret their experiences has been growing in recent years. For example, Debbie Messer Zlatin (1995) found that terminally ill people had a variety of different life themes to share. She also observed that there are important differences between people who do and who do not have integrated life themes to call upon as they face the stress of the dying process. Neris Diaz-Cabello (2004) found that within Hispanic culture there are a variety of individual and family perspectives on dying and death. Xolani Kacela (2004) identified significant differences between "religiously mature" and less mature people in interpreting their end-of-life experiences. Patient narratives collected by Barnard (2000) and Lawton (2000) offer additional examples of the ways in which terminally ill people interpret their own experiences.

An in-depth example has been provided through the journal kept by a distinguished researcher during the last weeks of his life (Kastenbaum, 1995–1996). William McDougall, a British-born physician, was a founder of the field of social psychology and an influential thinker in several other areas of scholarly activity. His terminal illness was a painful ordeal, occurring in 1938, years before palliative care techniques became widely available. The last weeks of his life centered on this confrontation between relief of pain and his determination to exercise his will power as long as possible. When his pain was at its most intense, the exercise of his intellect was also at its most inspired. He could avoid becoming what he perceived as a passive and defeated victim as long as he could maintain his intellectual effort against pain. Occasionally, McDougall and his will power were victorious: "How far can an intellectual effort diminish pain? It can throw fairly severe pain into the background and keep it there pretty steadily for an hour or two. And I think one gains confidence and success in the effort" (p. 142).

McDougall's intellectual approach to the dying process is at odds with the current emphasis on emotions, relationships, and peaceful acceptance, and he does not subscribe to any standard list of "developmental tasks." Such reliance on intellectualism and will power would have made McDougall guilty of a politically incorrect response, if we apply the "shoulds" that became popular when the death awareness movement emerged in the 1970s. McDougall, though, continued to be McDougall—even more so—as he called upon all his knowledge and skills to integrate dying and death into his overall view of self and world. A person who decided to treat McDougall from an outsider's perspective would have very likely failed to understand and, therefore, respond usefully to this man's distinctive interpretation of the dying process.

A Multiple Perspective Approach

For many years I was focused on what might be unique about the dying process. Eventually, though, I realized that much of what the dying person experiences has its counterpart in other situations. The more clearly we recognize the similarities, the more we can draw upon knowledge of more familiar phenomena to help us understand and support the dying person. This multiple perspective approach asks us first to identify these other processes one at a time and then to gradually put them together to form both a more comprehensive and detailed understanding of the dying person's situation. The central fact that the person is terminally ill would then be added to complete the picture (Kastenbaum, 2000).

Seventeen partial models of the dying process are identified in Box 4-4. By "partial model" I mean that each offers a framework for observing and responding to one aspect of the dying person's situation. Which of these partial models would be most useful for understanding what a particular person is experiencing will depend on that particular person and his or her situation.

It would be unusual to go through life without experiencing some of these situations, perhaps repeatedly. A person with a progressively life-threatening condition is almost certain to have many of these sources of concern—in addition to concerns that are associated specifically with the prospect of death. We can draw upon our own life experiences and observations to help us understand and respond effectively to what a dying person is experiencing. We will be careful, of course, to avoid assuming that the other person must be interpreting the situation the same way we did. Here are brief comments regarding a few of the partial models. Draw upon your own observations and reflections to go beyond what space permits us to present here (see also Kastenbaum, 2000).

BOX 4-4 PARTIAL MODELS OF THE DYING PERSON'S SITUATION

Model	Brief Description
1. Restricted activity	I can do less and less.
2. Limited energy	I must conserve what is left of my strength.
3. Damaged body image	I do not look and feel as I should.
4. Contagion	You act like you would catch something bad from me.
5. Disempowerment	I have lost the ability to influence you.
6. Attributional incompetency	You think I can't do anything right.
7. Ineffectuance	I can't make things happen the way I want them to.
8. Stress response overload	My defenses have become so intense that they are causing problems of their own.
9. Time anxiety	I fear it's too late to do all I must do.
10. Performance anxiety	How am I doing? How do you think I am doing?
11. Loss and separation	I am losing contact with everything that is most important to me.
12. Disengagement	I feel like withdrawing from interactions and responsibilities.
13. Journey	I am going some place I have never been before.
14. Closing the book	I am doing everything for the last time; it will soon be over.
15. Endangered relationship	I fear I am losing your love and respect.
16. Struggling brain	My mind is not working as it should; the world is slipping away from me.
17. Storying	I must come up with the best possible story of all that has happened, is happening, will happen.

1. *The restricted activity model.* We are likely to become frustrated, angry, and depressed when circumstances prevent us from doing what we usually do and from what we feel very much needs doing. Some people become tense and agitated when confined to bed for just a few days. Some people in perfect physical health either stew or feel helpless when their activities are restricted by external circumstances (such as bad weather, bureaucratic delay, or insufficient funds). Part of the tension and frustration experienced by dying people can be attributed to restricted activity. Everything we know and everything we can devise to help people deal with a restricted activity situation could relieve some of the dying person's stress.

2. *The damaged or altered body image model.* You have never been upset because the mirror suggests you might be too thin or too heavy. You have never had a bad hair day. You will certainly not be concerned when your hair begins to silver and wrinkles and age spots appear. And certainly you felt just as good about yourself as ever when you had that runny nose or outbreak of zits. Many of the rest of us, though, do respond with concern when our body no longer looks the same. Our anxiety tends to increase further when our body no longer performs the same. We may experience anything from mild to severe distress as we experience both visual and biological feedback that suggests we are not now as we were. The dying person is subject to prolonged and ever-intensifying feedback that is hurtful to self-image and confidence. What do we know about coping with distorted and altered body image? What can we do to help? These are among the constructive questions we could set our minds to when we want to be helpful to a dying person.

3. *The disempowerment model.* Other people are now making all the decisions. You are pretty much out of the loop. Life is going along without you. Once you were at the center of things; now you are a disenfranchised outsider, not really abused but not really taken seriously as a real player, either. People experience disempowerment

in many situations: The one-hit pop singer, the executive whose leverage disappeared during the latest corporate reorganization, the wife who has become a widow and lost much of her social status along with her husband. Some people are relieved to relinquish positions of power in the family, community, and workplace, but others feel rejected, abandoned, and bitter. There is often a period of doubt and seeking regarding one's own identity: "Who am I now, and am I worth anything?" Many dying people experience disempowerment in various forms. If we can heighten our awareness of this phenomenon, we put ourselves in a better position to be helpful.

4. *The time anxiety model.* Will you ever get it done in time? How can you write all those term papers, and prepare for all those exams with so little time left? Schedules and deadlines are ever present in the lives of many people. It is not unusual to face several sets of schedules and deadlines at the same time as personal, family, social, and work demands converge on us. Everything seems to be moving too fast, and we feel tense and irritable as we look for some way out of the dilemma. The situation is intensified when we have too little time to accomplish something that is of great importance to us. Dying people sometimes find themselves in precisely that situation. They may have such crucial end-of-life issues as making financial arrangements to benefit the family or rescuing an intimate relationship that had come apart. We might be more helpful if we recognized that a dying person might be struggling with a foreshortened future and pressing needs to accomplish some things.

5. *The journey model.* The idea of journey is embedded in most if not all world cultures (Cole, 1992). Galen, Aristotle, and other voices from ancient times described the life course as a journey from one age or stage to the next. Christian theologians spoke of "spiritual ages," and in our own time Erik H. Erikson's (1950) "Eight Ages of Man" is among the more influential updates of the

journey idea. Rituals have long been closely associated with journeys. It is risky to leave our present situation and venture forth. The real and symbolic distance between where we are and where we are going is full of danger. Ritual protects. Anybody who has ever moved into a new relationship, new job, or new community has probably experienced something of the anxiety that can be associated with even a positive change. Dying people are in transition from the world they have known (Kastenbaum, 2004). Some of their thoughts and feelings might well be understood in these terms. Are there forms of ritual that would be meaningful and supportive to this person on the final journey?

Most of us do not come to the dying process as complete strangers. We have had experiences such as those identified in Box 4-4, and perhaps we have learned something useful from them.

Your Deathbed Scene

Perhaps you took a crack at the deathbed scene exercise suggested in Box 4-1. Following is some information on the way that other people participating in death-related classes have depicted their own deaths (Kastenbaum & Normand, 1990). The typical respondent:

- Expected to die in old age
- At home
- Quickly

- With the companionship of loved ones
- While remaining alert and
- Not experiencing pain or any other symptoms.

What was the most common alternative response? Those who did not expect to die in the manner summarized instead saw themselves as perishing in an accident, usually on the highway and while they were still young. In fact, those who thought their lives would end in a fatal accident tended to expect these accidents to occur in the near future. Almost all thought they would be alert and experience no pain or other symptoms as they neared death, whether death happened at home in old age or on the road in youth.

These deathbed scene expectations by mostly young college students will take on more meaning when we continue our exploration of the dying process in the next chapter with the focus on hospice care. You can enhance the personal meaning of the next chapter by pausing to answer the questions raised in Box 4-5.

Improving End-of-Life Care

That too many people die in pain, isolation, and despair has been known for a long time by those close to the situation. The hospice and palliative care movement (Chapter 5) developed in response to this need. There is now more widespread recognition of the need to improve end-of-life care, although policy decision makers and major societal institutions still have responded somewhat laggardly.

BOX 4-5 A THOUGHT EXERCISE

The following questions were included in the National Hospice Demonstration Study (in a slightly different form). In the next chapter you will learn how terminally ill people responded to these questions and some of the implications for hospice care.

Now imagine yourself nearing the end of your life, and give the answers that best describe your own thoughts and feelings. Write your answers on a separate piece of paper.

1. Describe the last three days of your life as you would like them to be. Include whatever aspects of the situation seem to be of greatest importance.

2. What will be your greatest sources of strength and support during these last days of your life?

A national survey commissioned by Last Acts (2002) found that Americans judge that end-of-life care is inadequate and should be improved. This critical judgment was given by people of all racial/ethnic backgrounds, education levels, ages, places of residence, and of both genders. Most of the respondents reported having lost a family member or friend during the past five years, and their low ratings of end-of-life care were similar to those of people who had not been recently bereaved.

There was an obvious disconnect between the way in which most Americans wanted their lives to end and what usually did happen. For example, seven of ten people said they would prefer to die at home, surrounded by family and friends—but more than seven in ten died in a hospital. There was also a disconnect between the hospice/palliative care philosophy and what occurs in medical training and facilities. Six of ten physicians still had not received formal training for end-of-life care, and few U.S. hospitals had programs designed to support and comfort terminally ill people. Improved care for dying people is still somewhere between vision and reality.

The National Institutes of Health (2005) conducted a more recent inquiry into the status of care for terminally ill people in the United States. The NIH report notes that many questions and issues were not yet been resolved. For example, very little has been learned about the end-of-life situations for children and their caregivers and for persons with severe cognitive or other communication disorders. Minorities have remained underrepresented in end-of-life research as well as in access to and use of health care options. There is also little evidence on the management of symptoms other than pain. Furthermore, most of the research has focused on people with terminal cancer, so relatively little has been learned about the experiences of people with other types of terminal conditions. Congestive heart failure, end-stage renal disease, chronic obstructive pulmonary disease, and liver failure are among the life-limiting conditions that have rarely been studied from the end-of-life perspective. The experiences and stresses of professional caregivers at the end of life have also not been studied sufficiently.

Several of the conclusions and recommendations especially deserve our attention here (National Institutes of Health, 2005):

- Spiritual well-being has achieved recognition as a goal in end-of-life care. The limited information currently available suggests that families as well as patients benefit from programs that support dignity, purpose, and meaning. There is much yet to do if such programs are to be developed throughout the nation and their positive outcomes confirmed.
- The level of staff training varies across settings of care (e.g., nursing, homes, community hospitals, university hospitals, and hospices). More attention is needed on identifying the types of care that are most beneficial in each setting and on providing adequate end-of-life training for all care providers.
- There is a need to heighten awareness of ethical questions "regarding such things as the concept of a good death, and identify and resolve ethical problems in end-of-life care that arise from conflicting needs of care givers and care receivers" (p. 6).
- "Current end-of-life care includes some untested interventions that need to be validated" (p. 7).
- "Current end-of-life care is often fragmented among providers and provider settings, leading to a lack of continuity of care and impeding the ability to provide high-quality, interdisciplinary care" (p. 7).
- "Enhanced communication among patients, families, and providers is crucial to high-quality end-of-life care" (p. 7).

The obvious positive is that there is now enough experience and accomplishment to make end-of-life care a national priority. Whether or not there will be enough support to reach the next level of quality care remains to be seen.

SUMMARY

This chapter has considered dying as part of our total life experience while at the same time attending to what is distinctive about living with terminal illness. We have noted that the process of dying has been changing somewhat, along with broader changes in society and medical technology. The "last moment," for example, is less likely to pass as a salient and memorable occasion (though see Chapter 5 for the hospice approach). You were given the opportunity to imagine your own deathbed scene before we turned to the fundamental questions: What is dying, and when does it begin? How we answer these questions is consequential because a person is often treated very differently by others when defined as dying or terminally ill. Several competing alternatives were identified. Dying might be said to begin when (1) the physician draws this conclusion, (2) the physician informs the patient, (3) the patient accepts this conclusion, or (4), nothing more can be done to preserve life.

The transition from life to death can take one of several different trajectories, as described by Glaser and Strauss. We gave particular attention to the lingering trajectory, the expected quick trajectory, and the unexpected quick trajectory. Hospital staff members usually feel and respond differently to people who are on different trajectories. Awareness of these differences can help us to provide more effective support to patients, family, and staff. Familiar terms such as healthy, dying, and terminally ill do not apply to all individuals.

Some people end their lives in social isolation because of inadequate communication with others. Studies have documented continuing gaps in communication between many physicians and their terminally ill patients. The physician's inability or unwillingness to listen to the patient's statements all too often leaves the patient with uncontrolled pain and violates the patient's preferences for end-of-life management. Suggestions are made for improving communication with dying family members and friends.

We reminded ourselves that dying is both a universal and an individual experience. Age, gender, interpersonal relationships, the nature of the disease and its treatment, and the environmental setting were considered as influences on the individual's experience of dying.

Theoretical models of the dying process include two stage theories that have originated in markedly different contexts: the ancient Buddhist conception and the clinical observations made by Kübler-Ross. The eight-stage Buddhist model is intimately related to that religion's view of the ever-changing and disintegrating process we call everyday life. The last four of these stages are said to occur past the point at which a western-trained physician would have certified death. The Kübler-Ross model consists of a sequence of responses that moves through denial, anger, bargaining, depression, and acceptance. Individuals do not always proceed through all the stages in either of these models. The Kübler-Ross stage theory is carefully evaluated. Attention is also given to three more recent theoretical approaches: a developmental coping model, accepting the dying person's own reality as the model, and a multiple perspective model in which many different physical, personal, and interpersonal processes are considered separately and then brought together. We then revisited the deathbed scene you created and invited you to consider some further questions about how you might feel in the last days of your life.

In conclusion, we drew upon reports from Last Acts and the National Institutes of Health that documented continuing challenges to the improvement of end-of-life care in the United States.

REFERENCES

Aiken, L. H., Clarke, S. P., Sloane, D. M., Sochalski, J., & Silber, J. H. (2002). Hospital nurse staffing and patient mortality, nurse burnout, and job dissatisfaction. *Journal of the American Medical Association, 288,* 1987–1993.

Associated Press (February 2, 2008). Fatal dementia cases raise ethical issues. *Arizona Republic,* p. A9.

Barnard, D. (2000). *Crossing over: Narratives of palliative care.* New York: Oxford University Press.

Bell, R. J. (2005). "Our people die well": Deathbed scenes in Methodist magazines in nineteenth century Britain. *Mortality, 10,* 210–223.

Cole, T. R. (1992). *The journey of life.* Cambridge: Cambridge University Press.

Connor, S. R. (1992). Denial in terminal illness: To intervene or not to intervene. *The Hospice Journal, 8,* 1–15.

Coolidge, F. L., & Fish, C. E. (1983–1984). Dreams of the dying. *Omega, Journal of Death and Dying, 14,* 1–8.

Corr, C. A. (1993). Coping with dying: Lessons that we should and should not learn from the work of Elisabeth Kübler-Ross. *Death Studies, 17,* 69–84.

Corr, C. C., Doka, K. J., & Kastenbaum, R. (1999). Dying and its interpreters: A review of selected literature and some comments on the state of the field. *Omega, Journal of Death and Dying, 39, 239–261.*

Diaz-Cabello, N. (2004). The Hispanic way of dying: Three families, three perspectives, three cultures. *Illness, Crisis, & Loss, 12, 239–255.*

Emanuel, E. J., Fairclough, D. L., Wolfe, P., & Emanuel, L. L. (2004). Talking with terminally ill patients and their caregivers about death, dying, and bereavement. *Archives of Internal Medicine, 164, 1999–2004.*

Erikson, E. H. (1950). *Childhood and society.* New York: Norton.

Faust, D. G. (2008). *This republic of suffering. Death and the American Civil War.* New York: Alfred A. Knopf.

Feifel, H. (Ed.) (1959). *The meaning of death.* New York: McGraw-Hill.

Glaser, B. G., & Strauss, A. (1966). *Awareness of dying.* Chicago: Aldine.

Glaser, B. G., & Strauss, A. (1968). *Time for dying.* Chicago: Aldine.

Gyatso, Tensin, the 14th Dali Lama. (1985). *Kindness, clarity, and insight.* (J. Hopkins, Trans.). Ithaca: Snow Lions.

Hayslip, B., Jr., & Peveto, C. A. (2005). *Cultural changes in attitudes toward death, dying, and bereavement.* New York: Springer.

Hickman, S. E., Tilden, V. P., & Tolle, S. W. (2004). Family perceptions of worry, symptoms, and suffering in the dying. *Journal of Palliative Care, 20, 20–27.*

Hurley, A. C., & Volicer, L. (2002). Alzheimer's disease. "It's Okay, Mama, if you want to go, it's okay." *Journal of the American Medical Association, 288, 2324–2331.*

Improving care near the end of life: Why is it so hard? [Editorial] (1995). *Journal of the American Medical Association, 274, 1634–1636.*

Kacela, X. (2004). Religious maturity in the midst of death and dying. *American Journal of Hospice & Palliative Medicine, 21, 203–208.*

Kastenbaum, R. (1978). In control. In C. A. Garfield (Ed.), *Psychosocial care of the dying patient* (pp. 227–244). New York: McGraw-Hill.

Kastenbaum, R. (1984). The changing role of the physician with the terminally ill elderly. In I. Rossman (Ed.), *Clinical geriatrics* (3rd ed., pp. 618–620). New York: Lippincott.

Kastenbaum, R. (1993–1994). Dale Gladden: An Omega interview. *Omega, Journal of Death and Dying, 28, 1–16.*

Kastenbaum, R. (1995–1996). "How far can an intellectual effort diminish pain?" William McDougall's journal as a model for facing death. *Omega, Journal of Death and Dying, 32, 123–164.*

Kastenbaum, R. (2003). *The psychology of death* (3rd ed.). New York: Springer.

Kastenbaum, R. (2004). *On our way: The final passage through life and death.* Berkeley: University of California Press.

Kastenbaum, R., Barber, T., Wilson, S., Ryder, B., & Hathaway, L. (1981). *Old, sick, and helpless.* Cambridge, MA: Ballinger.

Kastenbaum, R., & Normand, C. (1990). Deathbed scenes as expected by the young and experienced by the old. *Death Studies, 14, 201–218.*

Kastenbaum, R., & Thuell, S. (1995). Cookies baking, coffee brewing: Toward a contextual theory of dying. *Omega, Journal of Death and Dying, 31, 175–188.*

Keeley, M. P. (2007). "Turning toward death together": The functions of messages during final conversations in close relationships. *Journal of Social and Personal Relationships, 24, 225-253.*

Kiecolt-Glaser, J. K., McGuire, L., Robles, T. F., & Glaser, R. (2002). Emotions, morbidity, and mortality: New perspectives from psychoneuroimmunology. *Annual Review of Psychology, 53, 83–107.*

Kramer, K. (1988). *The sacred art of dying.* New York: The Paulist Press.

Kaufman, S. R. (2005). *. . . And a time to die. How American hospitals shape the end of life.* New York: Scribner.

Kübler-Ross, E. (1969). *On death and dying.* New York: Macmillan.

Laakkonen, M. L., Pitkala, K. H., & Strandberg, T. E. (2004). Terminally ill elderly patients' experiences, attitudes, and needs: A qualitative study. *Omega, Journal of Death and Dying, 49, 117–130.*

Last Acts (2002). *Means to a better end: A report on dying in America today.* Princeton, N. J.: Robert Woods Johnson Foundation.

Lawton, J. (2000). *The dying process. Patients' experiences of palliative care.* London: Routledge.

LeShan, L. (1982). In M. N. Bowers, E. N. Jackson, J. A. Knight, & L. LeShan (Eds.), *Counseling the dying* (pp. 6–7). New York: Nelson.

Lesses, K. (1982–1983). How I live now. *Omega, Journal of Death and Dying, 13, 75–78.*

Meier, D. E. (2005). Variability in end of life care. Bmj. Bmjjournals. com/ cgi/ content/ full/ 328/ 7449/ E296

National Institutes of Health (2005). Improving end of life care, http://consensus.nih.gov/ta/023/Eol.final021805.html

Paxton, F. S. (2003). Christian death rites, history of. In R. Kastenbaum (Ed.), *Macmillan encyclopedia of death and dying:* Vol. 1 (pp. 163–167). New York: Macmillan.

Pope Benedict XVI (February 25, 2008). Pope reaffirms Church's stance against Euthanasia. www.catholic.org

Proulx, K., & Jacelon, C. (2004). Dying with dignity: The good patient versus the good death. *American Journal of Hospice and Palliative Medicine, 21, 116–120.*

Provonost, P. J., Angus, D. C., Dorman, T., Robinson, K. A., Dremisov, T. T., & Young, T. L. (2002). Physician staffing patterns and clinical outcomes in critically ill patients, *Journal of the American Medical Association, 288,* 2151–2162.

Rodriguez, K. L., Gambio, F. J., Butow, W., Hagerty, R., & Arnold, R. M. (2006). Pushing up daisies: Implicit and euphemistic language in oncologist-patient communication. *Supportive Care in Cancer, 15,* 153–161.

Sulmasy, D. P. (2002). I was sick and you came to visit me: Time spent at the bedsides of seriously ill patients with poor prognoses. *American Journal of Medicine, 111,* 385–389.

SUPPORT. (1995). A controlled trial to improve care for seriously ill hospitalized patients. *Journal of the American Medical Association, 274,* 1591–1599.

Taylor, J. (1977). *Holy dying.* New York: Arno Press. (Original work published 1651.)

Turkel, S. (2001). *Will the circle be unbroken?* New York: The New Press.

Vespasian (A.D. 79). In last words of real people, www.geocities.com/Athens/Acropolis/6537/real-t.hm

Villa, P. In last words of real people, www.geocities.com/Athens/Acropolis/6537/real-t.hm

Weisman, A. D. (1993). Avery D. Weisman: An Omega interview. *Omega, Journal of Death and Dying, 27,* 97–104.

Weisman, A. D., & Kastenbaum, R. (1968). *The psychological autopsy: A study of the terminal phase of life.* New York: Behavioral Publications.

Weisman, A. D., & Worden, J. W. (1975). Psychosocial analysis of cancer deaths. *Omega, Journal of Death and Dying, 6,* 61–65.

Weisman, A. D., & Worden, J. W. (1976). The existential plight in cancer. Significance of the first 100 days. *International Journal of Psychiatry in Medicine, 7,* 1–16.

Zlatin, D. M. (1995). Life themes: A method to understand terminal illness. *Omega, Journal of Death and Dying, 31,* 189–206.

GLOSSARY

Apoptosis: Cell death that is programmed into the biology of the life course.

Cardiopulmonary resuscitation (CPR): Massage, injection, or electrical stimulation intended to restore heart and breath.

Colostomy bag: A container for the collection of feces, attached to an abdominal opening following a surgical procedure on the bowel.

Danger list (D.L.): A classification used by some health care systems to indicate that a patient is at risk for death.

Institutional evasions: Techniques used by staff members to bypass the rules in order to get through a difficult situation.

Middle knowledge: A state of mind in which the person has some awareness of death but shifts from time to time in acknowledging and expressing this awareness.

Stage theory: Holds that the phenomena in question occur in a fixed sequence of qualitatively different forms.

Trajectories of dying: The distinctive patterns through time that can be taken by the dying process, for example, a long fading away (lingering trajectory) or unexpected (quick trajectory).

ON FURTHER THOUGHT . . .

Useful online resources:

AIDS Caregivers Support Network
www.wolfenet.com/acsn

The ALS Association*
www.alsa.org
(*amyotrophic lateral sclerosis, also known as Lou Gehrig's disease)

American Cancer Society
www.cancer.org

American Lung Association
www.lungusa.org

Last Acts
www.lastacts.org

Leukemia and Lymphoma Society
www.leukemia.org

National Alliance for Children with Life-Threatening Conditions
www.nacwltc.org

National Association of People with AIDS
www.napwa.org

National Stroke Association
www.stroke.org

Partnership for Caring
www.partnershipforcaring.org

An emerging issue: Personal needs or community risk?

An outbreak of severe acute respiratory syndrome (SARS) in Hong Kong in 2004 was a warning of possible larger scale health crises to come. Specifically, authorities had to choose between isolating the victims to prevent an out-of-control epidemic or giving in to family members' urgent pleas to be with their dying loved ones. Suppose you were on the spot; what decision would you make and why? Be as clear as possible about both your feelings and your reasoning. A reference:

Kastenbaum, R. (2005). Emerging ethical issues in the 21st century. In K. J. Doka, B. Jennings, & C. A. Corr (Eds.), *Ethical dilemmas at the end of life.* Washington, DC: Hospice Foundation of America.

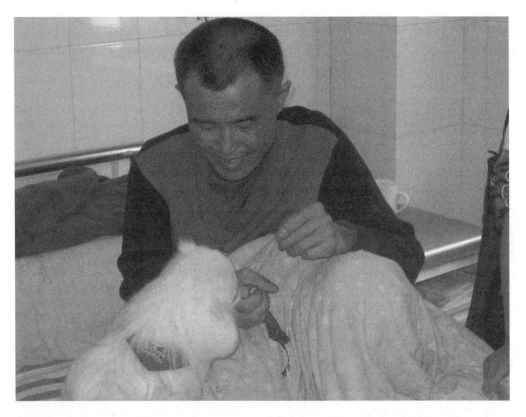

Yes, this is a hospice—a hospice that encourages family participation and a homelike atmosphere while providing quality medical and nursing care. Dr. Liu, however, director of this Chinese hospice program, would prefer that the dog keep all paws on the floor.

Source: IAHPC NEWS ONLINE. (March 2006). Online newsletter of the International Association for Hospice & Palliative Care, 7, 3. http://www.hospicecare.com/news/03-06/

chapter 5

HOSPICE AND PALLIATIVE CARE

They're just the most caring, loving, compassionate group of people I've ever known, and they can talk to me openly about death, and they can use the word "terminal" and look me in the eye . . . and I mean, we're able to talk about it.
—A woman with heart disease describes her hospice experience (Caroline Pevey, 2005, p. 131)

Hundreds of hospice providers across the country are facing the catastrophic consequences of what would otherwise seem a positive development: their patients are living longer than expected.
—Kevin Sack, 2007 (p. 3)

. . . it's that which is so frightening . . . it feels . . . it feels roughly like . . . running on a treadmill . . . and there right at the front on the treadmill . . . there's it's like death . . . you fight and you fight but . . . but you don't get away and well I can't explain it in a better way.
—A woman with terminal cancer describing her fatigue (Olav Lindqvist, Anders Widmark, & Brigit H. Rasmussen, 2004, p. 241)

To feel safe. To be with people who know and care about you. To have the attention of expert caregivers who respect your wishes and those of your family. Palliative care offered an alternative to the typical medical management approach to terminally ill people when it was established in the United Kingdom and introduced to North America with the New Haven (later renamed Connecticut) Hospice in 1974.

Through its relatively short history, modern hospice care has been changing as well as expanding. Even the terminology has shifted. *Hospice* too often suggested a place, not a program care, and this term also had existing negative meanings in France and some other societies. We now hear more of *palliative care*. This term was suggested by Canadian physician Balfour Mount (2003) in the 1970s and has continued to gain favor. As Mount notes, the word *palliative* derives

from *pallium*, the Latin for cloak. The term evolved to refer to interventions that reduce suffering.

Hospice has come a long way toward fulfilling its promise. The National Hospice and Palliative Care Organization (NHPCO, 2008) estimates that currently about 1.3 million people a year in the United States receive services through a hospice program. About one person in three chooses palliative care as the end of life nears. Some people—more than 200,000—recover sufficiently to be discharged. Hospice has been found to protect and enhance patients' quality of life (Anonymous, 2005) as well as to provide cost savings for Medicare when compared with traditional medical management (Raduluvic, 2007). Nevertheless, palliative care has not become an entirely secure part of the human services system, nor is it meeting all the needs of all the people who might benefit. This chapter identifies obstacles, limitations, and challenges as well as achievements.

Consider, for example, the shifting configuration of conditions with which people enter hospice care. Terminal cancer was by far the most common illness among hospice patients from the beginning. Now, however, palliative care is also being provided for an increasing number of people with life-threatening heart conditions. Betty Specter, the woman quoted above who so warmly appreciated hospice care, is among those with a cardiac condition who have enrolled in a palliative care program. Hospice services are proving helpful. But there is a catch, as noted by Sack (2007) and others. Hospice patients with cardiac conditions often live longer than expected by Medicare regulations and budgeting provisions. Should patients with terminal heart disease be ejected from hospice care even if they are receiving a superior level of care? Or should regulations and budgeting be revised to accord with the new situation? If forced out of hospice by restrictive regulations, the cardiac patients would still require care, and that care would still cost money. At present, the regulations are holding firm. In fact, hospices that have cared for people who lived "too long" are being required to reimburse the government. This imposes a severe financial burden on hospice organizations, especially those in rural areas with marginal resources. It is likely that some hospices will have to close, and that many will be hard pressed to offer their services. Effectively meeting human needs at the end of life does not guarantee a hospice organization that it will be given realistic support by the health care bureaucracy.

This ongoing situation reminds us that hospice care is more than an arrangement between terminally ill people, their families, and compassionate caregivers: it is part of a complex health management system in which political and economic agendas play a powerful role. Palliative care made it into this system in relatively short order, but thereby became vulnerable to a massive bureaucracy that will sometimes assist and sometimes threaten its mission. Perhaps political will and a more flexible bureaucracy will rescue hospice from this dilemma; perhaps it will get worse. Continued public advocacy for palliative care could make the difference. On the positive side, the medical establishment, after a period of

hesitation, is making significant contributions to the palliative care movement. A subspecialty in palliative medicine was approved in 2006, and major programs have been launched to educate physicians and nurses in terminal care (e.g., Harvard Medical School, 2008).

Let's go back to Kim, the woman with terminal cancer who was experiencing a debilitating sense of fatigue:

> if I can have a reasonably tolerable life . . . but to take one step and then you have to rest and then one step and then it hurts in your chest . . . and . . . well then then then I can feel it sometimes that . . . yes, if you could just, bang, fall asleep then . . . and it was all over . . . (sigh) although I don't really want that (sad) (p. 241).

The palliative care movement recognizes that a great many people eventually find themselves in situations that take them to the edge of hope and endurance. There is a continuing effort to develop improved care techniques. Hospice must also keep itself alive and well even when confronted by daunting challenges. The vitality and resourcefulness of the hospice movement is itself an achievement worth celebrating.

HOSPICE: A NEW FLOWERING FROM ANCIENT ROOTS

Temples of healing ministered to the psychological and physical ailments of the Greeks. Priests and other healers recognized that health and illness involved the whole person. The temples were designed to soothe, and encourage the anxious and ailing people who journeyed to them. Every effort was made to restore the patients through an appealing physical environment, music, therapeutic conversation, positive imagery, bathing, massage, and walks in the countryside. Later, imperial Rome established hospitals for military personnel. The bureaucratic style of organization in these early hospitals would be recognized today. However, neither the temple nor the hospital was designed primarily for the care of the dying person.

Some compassionate people did provide comfort to the dying. The earliest examples of palliative care have bequeathed only hints to the historian. Perhaps in the *harem* of a Byzantine

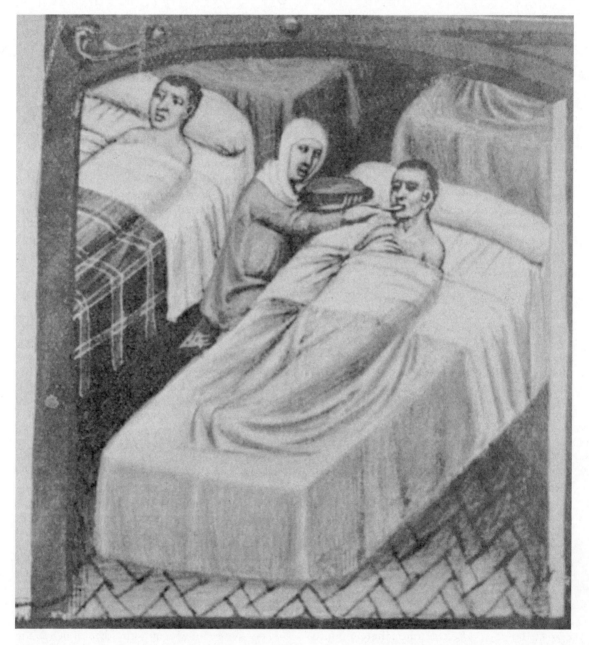

It is a woman who provides care for disabled and life-threatened men in this thirteenth-century illustration, and it is still most often women who serve at the bedside of terminally ill people.

ruler there were women with special skill in caring for the dying. Perhaps some wealthy families in Syria or Athens saw to it that the poor were treated well in their last days of life. The documentary trail becomes clearer with the advent of the Christian era. Public infirmaries *(nosocomeia)* were established in Greek-speaking areas of Christianity during the fourth century. These facilities cared for people dying of epidemics as well as those who were likely to recover. The Roman emperor Julian, an opponent of the upstart Christian movement, acknowledged that these hospices had made a very favorable impression on everybody "owing to the humanity evinced by Christians toward outsiders" (Phipps, 1988). Julian resolved to establish his own hospice in every city, but his own death aborted this plan.

The hospice movement spread to western Europe near the end of the fourth century through the influence of Fabiola, a wealthy Roman widow who had been inspired by the care for the sick that she had witnessed in monasteries in the Holy Land (Phipps, 1988). Fabiola brought this concept back with her to Italy, not only supporting hospices financially but also serving as a nurse herself. St. Jerome knew Fabiola and honored her contributions, writing that "Often too she washed away the matter discharged from wounds which others, even though men, could not bear to behold . . . She gave food with her own hand and even when a patient was but a breathing corpse she would moisten his lips with liquid" (cited by Phipps, p. 93). And so Fabiola, this woman who lived and died about 1,600 years ago, may have given an enduring gift to humankind that in our own time has been renewed as the modern hospice program.

A type of hospice became well established in the fifth century. The term itself derives from the Latin *hospitium* that has also given us such words as *host* and *hostess*. The medieval hospice was usually a house in which people in need could find food, shelter, and other comforts under Christian auspices. Care of the homeless dying was but one function of the medieval hospice, which most commonly served those undertaking the arduous pilgrimage to the Holy Land. Certain religious orders became especially known for their hospice care. Established by Benedictine monks in the sixth century, the Monte Cassino monastery included one of the most noted hospices (unfortunately, destroyed during World War II). Throughout the medieval period the hospice functioned as one of the purest expressions of Christian piety: here the hungry were fed, the thirsty given water, the naked clothed, the homeless sheltered, and the sick provided care and comfort. Medical treatment was minimal—probably just as well, considering how ineffective or even dangerous most "remedies" were at that time.

Unfortunately, something went very much wrong between the time that the early hospices flourished and the beginning of the modern hospice movement. During the intervening centuries the original hospice tradition clung to life in only a few scattered facilities. Phipps suggests that hospices became an innocent casualty of the Protestant Reformation and then were replaced by state-run institutions with different types of personnel and philosophies. Whatever the reasons, bureaucracy and technology-oriented medicine gradually took over the scene. The emerging approach to health care had neither a strong religious foundation nor interest in people who persisted in dying even though receiving the latest fashions in treatment.

A renewed hospice approach made its appearance in the nineteen century. Again, the leaders were women who recognized the need to provide compassionate and effective care for people at the end of their lives. Jeanne Garnier inspired other young widows to establish L'Association des Dames du Calvaire in Lyon, France in 1842. Her influence spread to other cities where organizations were established that anticipated modern hospice care (Clark, 2000). Another major step forward was Mary Aikenhead's establishment of St. Vincent's Hospital in London. In her memory, Our Lady's Hospice for the Dying started in 1879 at a nearby convent. In 1905, London's St. Joseph's Hospital introduced improvements in pain relief and general medical care. The worldwide hospice movement today owes much to the women who created such caregiving institutions despite their initial lack of financial resources and political influence. For some time, however, these programs remained small and isolated as industrial and technological development continued to transform society. They were also deeply embedded in religious belief systems and church practices (Humphreys, 2001).

The hospice movement took its next major step forward when a medical officer at St. Joseph's Hospice improved pain control for dying people. This was Dr. Cicely Saunders, who, in 1967, founded St. Christopher's Hospice in London, which has since served as inspiration and model for many others. Starting out as a student of philosophy, politics, and economics, Saunders enrolled in a nurse training program during World War II. A back injury made it difficult for her to continue as a nurse, so she became a social worker, and then a physician. This triple perspective liberated Saunders from seeing the dying person from the limitations of any one health provider standpoint. Her vision of hospice care emphasized contributions and interactions from people of diverse backgrounds.

I asked Dame Saunders about the circumstances that led to her introduction of modern hospice care. The inspiration provided by two people was especially important. Lillian Pipkin, a Salvation Army matron, taught her the basics of pain management for terminally ill patients, which she was then able to apply for the first time herself at St. Joseph's and, subsequently, at St. Christopher's. Pipkin was also a role model for Saunders in understanding and communicating with dying patients. The other person was David Tasma, a dying man who

> needed not only symptom relief, but also the time, space, and atmosphere in which to come to his own terms with his life. At this point, David was feeling that his life had been unfulfilled and perhaps meaningless. Something emerged during our long conversations that not only sparked the inspiration for hospice but also made possible his own quiet peace . . . David had made a personal peace with the God of his forefathers before he died, and he left me with the assurance that he had found his answers— and with the belief that all our caring must give total freedom to others to make their own way into meaning (Saunders, 1993).

Tasma also contributed his small legacy to Saunders for what would become the hospice project.

And what was the first response of physicians and nurses to her innovations? Would they be dubious and resistant?

I was therefore soon able to demonstrate to an increasing number of visitors that dying patients could be alert, as well as free from pain, and very able to do the teaching themselves. Without this opportunity, I do not think the modern hospice movement would have been established and I am everlastingly grateful to the patients and Sisters of St. Josephs who, together with David Tasma and the patients of St. Luke's, I see as the true founders (Saunders, 1993).

These personal reflections convey the spirit in which the hospice movement was conceived:

- From Fabiola onward, women have been the prime movers in attempting to improve the care of dying people.
- Unique personal interactions and relationships have been crucial to the development of hospice. Hospice has grown from the efforts of a few highly motivated individuals rather than as part of a formal plan hatched by bureaucratic committees.
- The stereotype that doctors "know better" than their patients has been reversed in hospice philosophy. All care providers are invited to learn from the people who really know what it feels like to cope with the physical and psychological stresses of dying: the patients themselves.
- Although hospice leaders often are people with strong religious belief, the emphasis is on giving "total freedom to others to make their own way into meaning." This was evident at the start in the interaction between a Christian physician and her Jewish patient (Tasma).

STANDARDS OF CARE FOR THE TERMINALLY ILL

An International Work Group on Death and Dying (IWG), including Dr. Saunders and other pioneers, saw the need to develop guidelines for hospice care. The task force decided first to identify the unspoken assumptions that governed the care of the terminally ill. The items on the following list were seen as the typical pattern of a "good" or "successful" death from the perspective of the facility in which terminally ill people spent the final days of life. In other words— these were the hidden rules that hospice intended to replace.

Hidden or Implicit Standards of Care

1. The successful death is quiet and uneventful. The death slips by with as little notice as possible; nobody is disturbed.
2. Few people are on the scene. There is, in effect, no scene. Staff is spared the discomfort of interacting with family and other visitors whose needs might upset the well-routined equilibrium.
3. Leave-taking behavior is at a minimum: no awkward, painful, or emotional good-byes to raise the staff's anxiety level.
4. The physician does not have to involve him- or herself intimately in terminal care, especially as the end approaches.
5. The staff makes few technical errors throughout the terminal care process and few mistakes in medical etiquette.
6. Attention is focused on the body during the care-giving process. Little effort is wasted on the unique personality of the terminally ill individual.
7. The patient expressed gratitude for the excellent care received.
8. The person dies at the right time, that is, after the full range of medical interventions has been tried out before the onset of a long period of lingering on.
9. After the patient's death, the family expresses gratitude for the excellent care received.
10. The staff is able to conclude that "we did everything we could for this patient."
11. Physical remains of the patient are made available to the hospital for clinical, research, or administrative purposes (via autopsy permission or organ donations).
12. A memorial (financial) gift is made to the hospital in the name of the deceased.
13. The cost of the terminal care process is determined to have been low or moderate, i.e., money was not wasted on a person whose life was beyond saving or, more importantly, the hospital came out ahead after expenses were compared with reimbursements.

The task force itself proposed a very different set of standards!

Proposed Standards Recommended by the International Task Force

- Patients, family, and staff all have legitimate needs and interests.
- The terminally ill person's own preferences and life-style must be taken into account in all decision making.

These were the basic guidelines. Examples of more specific standards include the following:

Patient-Oriented Standards

1. *Remission of symptoms is a treatment goal.* Even if the patient is expected to die within hours or days, efforts should be continued to maintain functional capacity and relieve pain and anguish. A dying person should not be made to endure thirst, for example, or gasp for breath when a change of position might afford relief.
2. *The patient's intentions will be respected as one of the main determinants of the total pattern of care.* The rights and responsibilities of family, staff, and society as represented by the legal system must also be taken into account. The point is the willingness of family and health care providers to take seriously any document through which patients express their own wishes. (Advance directives, see Chapter 7, would later come into being.)
3. *Patients should feel safe.* They should not have to live in apprehension of unexpected diagnostic or treatment procedures, brusque interactions, or breakdown in medication and meal routines.
4. *Opportunities should be provided for leave-takings with the people most important to the patient, and for experiencing the final moments in a way that is meaningful to the patient.* This requires flexibility in visiting hours and rules for admitting visitors (for example, children were often excluded). There should be privacy, and freedom from interruption. The patient should also have the opportunity to take leave of other patients and staff members if desired.

Hospice care offers a more personal and comforting approach to helping terminally ill people.

Family-Oriented Standards

1. *Families should have the opportunity to discuss dying, death, and related emotional needs with the staff.* It is not acceptable for the staff to disregard requests for information or expressions of the need to share feelings.
2. *Families should have the opportunity for privacy with the dying person both while living and immediately after death.* This might include their participation in dressing the corpse and accompanying it to the funeral home. Or it might include simply being alone with the dead spouse, sibling, or parent for an hour or so without interruption by staff.

Staff-Oriented Standards

1. *Caregivers should have adequate time to form and maintain personal relationships with the patient.* This is not a priority in most medical facilities, Hospital scheduling practices seldom make it possible for a nurse or other staff member to maintain a steady relationship with a patient.
2. *A mutual support network should exist among the staff.* Care for the terminally ill can become an emotionally depleting experience, especially if staff is given little opportunity to share their experiences and feelings.

These guidelines were subsequently incorporated into the Medicare specifications for a full service hospice and the standards adopted by the National Hospice and Palliative Care Organization. A more detailed version was later developed in a cooperative project by several organizations concerned with improving end of life care. (An executive summary and the full text are available through Info@NationalConsensusProject.org).

THE HOSPICE IN ACTION

Should we choose hospice or traditional care?"
is a key question. We will be in a better position
to consider this question after exploring just
what it is that hospice does. The following are a
few examples of how a hospice actually works.

Entering St. Christopher's

The first example is an observation I had the
opportunity to make during a visit to St. Christopher's. Word was received that a person was arriving for admission. A station wagon had just
pulled up to an entrance facing the hospice's attractive garden plaza. The patient-to-be was a
frail, emaciated woman who looked to be in her
60s. She was accompanied by a younger man.
Dr. Saunders and the woman greeted each other
as sunlight propitiously broke through the cloudy
London skies. The woman smiled and said, "Well,
I finally made it!" On her face there was the mark
of physical ordeal, but no indication of anxiety,
anger, depression, or confusion.

The patient was immediately introduced to
the nurse who would be responsible for much
of her care and then assisted her to what would
be her own bed (which had been transported
by elevator to the ground-entrance). Just a few
minutes later while touring the hospice, we
came on this woman again. She was already
settled into her own place, sipping tea with the
man who had driven her to the hospice. As it
turned out, he was her husband. The debilitating effects of advanced cancer had given her an
aged and emaciated appearance.

This simple incident tells us something about
the aims and techniques of the hospice. The patient and her family had already been well acquainted with the hospice before time of admission. Consequently, there was a sense of having
made the next logical stop on her journey
through life rather than a jarring transition from
home to an impersonal institution. Much of St.
Christopher's effort is devoted to its home-care
program. With the guidance of hospice personnel,
some families are able to provide high-quality
care to their terminally ill members throughout
the course of the illness. Patient and family know
that the inpatient facility would be there when
and if they needed it.

*A hospice can be thought of more aptly as a process
and as a spirit of mutual concern rather than as a
place.* The sociophysical environment of the
hospice or palliative care facility is designed for
life as well as death. For example, staff recognized the importance of the first few minutes of
the admission process. Efficiency was improved
by having the patient's own bed ready to meet
her, an innovation at that time. Most important
was the affirmation of human contact by both
the medical director and the nurse. The prompt
welcoming of the husband through the tea service further signified the hospice's interest in
encouraging the maintenance of interpersonal
relationships and comforting habits.

The philosophy of care encompasses the entire
family unit. Many family members not only visit
with their own kin but also befriend other patients. This much reduces the likelihood of social
isolation for the patient and the sense of helplessness for the family. It does raise the possibility,
however, that the family might spend so much
time and effort at the inpatient facility that they
neglect their own needs. To place a friendly limit
on family involvement, St. Christopher's established a weekly "family's day off." This allows the
family a brief vacation without any sense of guilt
attached. At the end of this day I finally noticed
what was missing among the residents of
St. Christopher's: anxiety, shame, or despair. They
did not have much life left to them, but their dignity and security were intact.

Mother's Last Moments: A Daughter's Experience

Another example comes from an American
hospice program in Miami and expresses the
viewpoint of the young adult daughter of a
woman who had been terminally ill for several
months. The woman was being cared for at
home during what proved to be the final phase
of her illness.

The next day I woke up and went in to see my
mother. I noticed the difference immediately. She
had this rattle in her throat. She kept trying to
talk, but all her words were garbled by the mucus
in her throat. . . . And I called the doctor and he
gave me a good idea of what was happening. It

was very hard for me to believe that she was so close ("to death" were the words implied but not spoken by the daughter). She looked so calm and serene. In her room and among all her things. She looked really OK. She didn't look like she was in distress. *She looked like she was just glowing.* And my sister came over. She brought over a tape made by a priest on death and dying. We put it on and we let my mother listen to it; isn't that awful? And it was talking about acceptance of death and it seemed to be quite appropriate at the time. And then my sister went to the movies and I stayed around. And my sister had left a picture of her little boy so my mother could see him. And it was just as if everything was in preparation.

I got out her make-up and lotion and started to make her up. Put lotion all over her skin. She knew what I was doing, because she held out her arm like this, and moved a little here and there to make it easier to make her up. But I was afraid in touching her body. She was so frail, I was afraid her skin might break if I touched her too hard to hug her. Before this time, she hadn't wanted to be touched, because it hurt. But now it didn't seem to hurt her at all; her pain had diminished. I put blush on her face . . . and lipstick on . . . and I brushed her hair.

As I bent down to hug her, she—her body—I don't know how to describe it: she opened her mouth as I was holding her, and blood came out. And I thought at first, "What's wrong, what's happening?" And Emma, our temporary housekeeper said, "It's okay. It's nothing. She'll be okay. Why don't you go out? A break would be good for you." But it was hard for me to let go of her. A part of me felt like "that was it," but, oh, no, it couldn't have happened. When I looked at her again, she looked—beautiful. She was glowing. She was just—beautiful. It was the only time I saw her look so beautiful during her whole illness. And when I came back the hearse was in front of our house.

And I said, "Oh, no! You're not going to take my mother away!" And my father was there and the people who were supposed to be there; the things that were supposed to happen . . . I resented it all.

They're not going to go into the room. I'm going into the room first!" I wanted to touch her. I wanted to be alone with her. I went in and closed the door. And I touched her all over, and took her all in. And then I realized, I realized . . . she had gone without a struggle. It was really right, it was all right, you know? She looked very good. She looked as if it was right. It wasn't painful. It was the right time, and she was ready to go.

This is part of just one person's experience with death. Other family members responded in their own distinctive ways. The father, for example, did much planning and managing—his way of coping with the impending loss. Family members could respond in ways true to themselves, instead of being constricted by a traditional hospital situation.

There were other positive features as well. This woman died free of pain and suffering. She felt safe. The final impression that "it was right" helped the daughter integrates her mother's death into her own ongoing life. She would not have to live with regret, self-recrimination, or anger about her own actions. Would she have felt comfortable applying lotion and make up to her mother if they had been in a hospital? Would this even have been permitted? Would she have been allowed to return for a few minutes of privacy with her mother after death?

The Hospice of Miami was an important source of support, but there was also strength in the intact and affectionate family itself. This does not mean, however, that the relationship between hospice and family was smooth at all times. At first, there was resistance because the introduction of palliative care confronted them with the realization that they would soon lose the mother/wife to death.

The daughter's life had changed at the moment she first learned of her mother's terminal illness some months before. The circumstances of her mother's death and dying influenced so much that she selected a career in the human services so she can provide care and comfort to others.

Dying from Two Worlds

Hospice had its primary roots in a white Christian tradition. Today, many people in the United States draw on multiple traditions. How hospice can respond to these diverse and individual situations is exemplified by Barbara, a woman who had lived an active and useful life in two worlds. She was deeply rooted in her Native American culture and also a distinguished university faculty member. This strong and vibrant woman was diagnosed with ovarian cancer at the age of 46 and within a few years would lose the battle for her life (Staton, Shuy, & Byock, 2001). Her many friends as well as her family were resolved to help her end her days in a way that would respect both her traditions as well as her unique personality. During most of her final illness Barbara received care either at her or at her sister Irene's home. She would go to Missoula's Hospice House when needed.

One day Barbara stopped eating and drinking. She now had a faraway look in her eyes. Irene asked her: "Have you started your journey to the other side?" Barbara replied with a smile "so big. And I told her, 'I'm here with you. I'm not going to leave you. You don't have anything to be afraid of. I want to thank you for this opportunity to see through your eyes to the other side.'" The sisters shared Native American traditional beliefs in which ancestors would come to escort them to the other side, but also drew comfort from the Bible, which Irene read to her near the end.

> I always read her the Psalms—Psalm 23—and then I would burn smudge for her. I hung my eagle fan above her head because our belief is that's the dream world. And that when you lay down to rest, that eagle spirit is going to help you to have good dreams (op. cit., p. 276).

From the hospice's first contact with Barbara through the memorial services there was a natural meld of Native American culture with Christian tradition and modern palliative care techniques. No religious spokesperson on either side demanded a pure or exclusionary approach. The Bible and the eagle feather, the hospice and the home were meaningfully related through the life of Barbara and her friends.

Adult Respite Care

Hospice programs usually provide care at the patient's home and in medical care facilities, as needed. There is a third alternative: respite care. At some point in the course of a terminal illness, the patient may feel more comfortable in a respite care setting than either at home or in a hospital. For example, Walter, a robust businessman with "never a sick day in his life," had to admit to a persistent feeling of fatigue and discomfort. When finally persuaded by his family to see a doctor, he learned that he had an advanced and incurable cancer.

Once it was clear that there was no realistic hope for recovery, the family agreed to select the hospice alternative. Walter's condition was stabilized for several weeks. He took advantage of this time to work out a satisfactory business deal with his partner, say his good-byes to old friends, and immerse himself in the daily life of his very supportive family. His functional capacity then declined sharply. With great tact, Walter suggested that he be given "a few days off" until he recovered his strength. In retrospect, the family and the hospice nurse realized that he had wanted to relieve the unremitting pressure on his family—and that he sensed his death was imminent.

At his suggestion, Walter was taken to a respite care center, housed in a comfortable home-like setting. He thanked his wife and son and gently ordered them to take good care of each other and the rest of the family until he perked up a little and could come home. About an hour later the hospice nurse came by to see how he was doing. "I can go now," he smiled, "and so can you." He died peacefully within a few minutes.

In this instance the respite care center did not have to offer any special services. What Walter needed was a way of establishing a little distance between himself and his loving family at the very end of his life. It is not unusual for a dying person to feel that he or she has "taken care of business" and expressing personal feelings to the people who most matter. The availability of an adult respite care center can give family members a valuable relief from constant responsibility, even though this may be for only a few days. These brief "vacations" can be useful to the terminally ill person as well as the family. As one woman confided within a week of her death: "I try my best to keep their spirits up, but it's getting harder and harder. I don't like to be alone either, but at least when I'm alone I don't have to perform." A few days with considerate and expert caregivers who are not part of one's interpersonal network can liberate the dying person from investing the limited available energy in meeting the needs and expectations of others.

Hospice-Inspired Care for Children

Consider this description of an episode in the life of Marie, "a ghostlike seven-year old" who had already undergone three unsuccessful kidney transplants from cadavers and was being kept on dialysis treatment until a fourth transplantable organ could be located:

As Marie sat on the child-life worker's lap, she ground her teeth with great intensity and anxiously shifted the position of her blood-pressure cuff. She incessantly scratched and picked at the gauze pads which guarded her old abdominal wounds. 'My tummy hurts! My tummy hurts!' she announced, in hope that she would be permitted a day off. After Marie's blood pressure was read, she reenacted the procedure, detail by detail, with the child-life worker. Marie methodically placed the cuff on the child-life workers arm, pumped forcefully, and, stethoscope in hand, engagingly admonished her to be still and not to cry. Satisfied with her work, Marie carefully folded the cuff and put it away. She took the child-life worker's hand and hesitantly hobbled toward the scale where she was weighed. . . .

When the preparations for dialysis were over, reality robbed Marie of her tenuous control over her experience. Her dialysis rituals could no longer protect her, and her fear was apparent in her eyes. As the staff placed Marie's papoose, or restraint, under her back, she frantically pleaded, 'Have to make pee-pee. . . . Mommy coming? . . . Bleeding! Give me something to put me to sleep!' Three adults . . . wrestled with Marie as in panic she squirmed and fought to release herself from the papoose. Marie's right hand, the only part of her body free of restraint, blindly gripped the child-life worker's fingers. . . . Marie's mother would not be waiting for her after the ordeal had ended. Sedatives would not be used to ease the passage of time (Meagher & Leff, 1989–1990).

This was a typical experience in Marie's life. She suffered physical and emotional pain throughout her final hospital stay—during which she was, to all purposes, abandoned by her family because they could no longer tolerate the stress themselves. Astoundingly, the medical staff systematically denied Marie the partial relief she might have experienced from pain-killing medication. Instead they attempted to deceive her by pretending to inject medications into her tubing. Why? So that she would not become a drug addict!

Marie experienced the torment of pain and abandonment in addition to the ravages of her disease. Her caregivers were not evil or unfeeling people, but they were working within the framework of aggressive, cure-oriented medicine. This "pull out all the stops" approach often reaches its peak of intensity when the patient is a child. The death of a child is an exceptionally powerful blow and violates our expectations in a society where so many people survive into advanced adult years. Sometimes this approach is successful; more often the child dies anyway, but experiences more suffering and less comfort than would have been provided if a hospice-inspired program of care had been selected.

It is very difficult in the case of a child to say, "let her go with love and comfort" as long as there seems to be any chance at all to prolong her life. This is probably the main reason that hospice care for dying children has not become more common. The decision to select hospice care involves recognition of impending death, a recognition that is usually avoided by family and caregivers as long as possible (and even a little longer).

Children's Hospice International (www.chionline.org) has taken a leadership role in advocating state of the art palliative care for terminally patients and educating other professionals. It is largely through their efforts that almost all hospice programs in the United States now are open to accepting children as patients. There is also a growing advocacy for including children in discussions about hospice and other medical care situations (Hinds, Bradshaw, Oakes, & Pritchard, 2002).

More than a million infants and children are afflicted with life-threatening illness in the United States each year. Efforts are being made to establish federally funded pediatric palliative care benefits as parallel to those already available for adults (Dabbs, Butterworth, & Hall, 2007). Meanwhile, home care can be arranged for many terminally ill children. The opportunity to stay at home may be even more important for children than adults, to avoid the anxiety of separation. Parents can continue to be parents to their ailing child, but they will need assistance from health care providers who have the communication skills to deal resourcefully with this difficult situation. Care might be furnished either by a hospice organization or by a growing number of hospitals that have introduced palliative care into their own programs. These comprehensive, patient-and-family palliative programs are not only improving the quality of life for seriously ill children, but also enabling many to survive longer than expected (Ward, 2007). There is now also an expanding clinical and research literature that focuses on palliative care for children (Brown, Warr, & Schibman 2007; Carter & Levitown, 2004; Goldman, Hain, & Liben, 2006).

Hospice Care for People with AIDS

A person whose HIV infection has converted to an active case of AIDS might encounter the same sources of stress as does any person afflicted with any terminal illness. These include (1) the progressive loss of functions; (2) pain, fatigue, and other symptoms; (3) disruption and potential loss of interpersonal relationships; and (4) a future in which hopes, plans, and ambitions become replaced by the prospect of death. Palliative care and effective management often reduce the stress level and maintain a higher degree of comfort and individual lifestyle during the final phase of the illness.

There were barriers, however, to hospice care for persons with AIDS, including the following:

- Willingness of the community to support hospice operations through volunteer services and fundraising if hospice programs accept AIDS patients.
- Willingness of hospice staff and administrators to provide services to AIDS patients.
- Willingness of AIDS patients to select the hospice option and willingness of their families to serve as participating caregivers.

- Willingness of the health care system to make whatever adjustments might be necessary in admission and management of AIDS patients.

Hospice programs did make themselves available to AIDS patients. There was at first the risk that volunteers and other forms of community support would fall away if AIDS patients were accepted. By and large, though, the community maintained its support, although troubled by the association between AIDS and a promiscuous lifestyle. More accustomed to helping patients with terminal cancer, hospice programs had to devise new procedures for dealing with AIDS, a complex condition with many *symptoms* to treat and difficult treatment decisions to make. As time went on, almost all hospice programs reported that people with AIDS were receiving their full range of palliative care and support services.

HIV/AIDS remains a significant cause of illness and death in the United States and throughout much of the world. However, more people with HIV now live for years without symptoms. New drugs have made important contributions to this development. Some people with AIDS are reluctant to enter hospice care because they either hold out hope for *remission* or have been denying the severity of their illness. There is a zone of uncertainty about individual prognosis, so people differ in how they evaluate their situations. Nevertheless, hospice care often can manage their complex physical and emotional needs more adequately than traditional medical practice.

Hospice Care on the International Scene

Desperate refugees flooded the nation by the hundreds of thousands. Hospitals and rehabilitation centers were overwhelmed by the number of wounded people. The mass media was filled with reports of killing, torture, and extreme suffering physically, emotionally, socially, and spiritually. The question was raised: does it make any sense to speak about 'dying with dignity' amid so many terrible and extremely humiliating deaths? Is it realistic to speak about dying decently in a country where so many persons now cannot live decently (Jusic, 1997, p. 126).

Anica Jusic, M.D. was founder of the first palliative care unit in Croatia just before his country was invaded by the Serbian/Yugoslav army. Hospice pioneers in other nations have also encountered chaotic and dangerous situations, along with a lack of understanding and responsiveness from the ruling establishment. In Columbia, for example, the authorities were intent on denying morphine derivatives to ease the pain of terminally ill patients—at the same time that the illicit drug trade was perhaps the nation's most prosperous industry. Every hospice established within a particular cultural and geographical setting has its story to tell. Humane and effective care for dying people is a universal challenge, and people are finding ways to develop palliative care service that is realistic and acceptable in a particular setting.

An International survey of hospice programs (Wilson & Kastenbaum, 1997) found that:

- Hospice programs are growing rapidly throughout much of the world.
- The programs vary greatly. Some hospices serve small populations in a sprawling rural area with difficult road access, few telephones, and limited health care facilities. Other hospices serve a large but compact population in a technologically developed urban area. What works well for one hospice organization may not be feasible for another,
- Throughout the world, the largest number of hospice patients fall within the sixty to seventy-nine age group, with only about one patient in nine being under the age of forty. Men and women are using hospice services more or less equally, with some local variations.
- Home care is the type of service most often received by hospice clients in every world region—often in nations or areas in which there had been no previous home care services of any type.
- All world cultures are proving to have traditional strengths that can contribute to the success of a palliative care program. Traditional cultures may at first resist hospice services, but reports indicate that love and concern for dying members of the family eventually brings forth a warm and caring response.
- The early phases of hospice development invariably encounter resistance from some medical practitioners and governmental officials, as well as a public that has long avoided open discussion of the "taboo" topics of dying and death. The United States has not been alone in its reluctance to deal with death. Similar response have been reported by hospice pioneers in Africa, Asia, Near and Middle East, and South America.
- Pain relief remains the central objective of palliative care, no matter how the program is structured or what cultural group it serves. Most hospice programs around the world have had to work strenuously to persuade physicians and lawmakers that it is possible to relieve the suffering of terminally ill people without creating drug addicts or causing premature death. Unfortunately, there is still considerable resistance to effective pain relief from people who have not informed themselves about the actual facts of palliative care.
- Education of the general public, human service professionals, and governmental decision makers has been recognized as a high priority by hospice programs around the world. Palliative care requires a host society that is able to integrate dying and death into its conception of the life course.

Despite notable progress, many people throughout the world continue to suffer for lack of palliative care. David Clark (2007–2008, p.107) characterizes the situation as "desperate. Where the need is the greatest, the fewest hospice and palliative care services exist. There is unrelieved suffering on a mass scale and the efforts of a handful of activists to promote palliative care globally are often ignored and unsupported. One million people die each week. It is estimated by the World Health Organization that 60 percent of these could benefit from palliative care. Yet at present only a tiny proportion of dying people ever receive the support of hospice and palliative care services."

RELIEF OF PAIN AND SUFFERING

Alleviation of pain and suffering is the primary goal of palliative care programs. Why is pain control so important?

- Pain is, by definition, a stressful experience.
- Pain reduces the ability to give attention to other matters, thereby isolating the sufferers and reducing their opportunities to reflect, interact, and accomplish.

- Pain can intensify other symptoms such as weight loss, insomnia, pressure sores, and nausea.
- Fear and anticipation of pain can also be demoralizing. "Will the pain return?" "Will it get worse?" "Will I be able to endure it?" For many people, anxiety about the level of pain that might be yet to come can be even more disturbing than the pain that is already being experienced.
- Pain contributes much to anxiety about the dying process. Some people assume that dying is "all pain" and unavoidable. This expectation can generate emotional distress, impair communication, and lead to thoughts of suicide. ("I'd kill myself first!").

Temperature, pulse, respiration and blood pressure. Those are the four *vital signs* that physicians and nurses throughout the world have been monitoring for many years. Recently, there is a fifth vital sign: *pain*. The hospice movement has made pain control a major priority in terminal care. More health care providers are also trying to determine the level of pain experienced by patients with any medical condition. Although not yet universally practiced, the establishment of pain as the fifth vital sign is a significant contribution from the palliative care movement. It remains difficult to assess level of pain—and, therefore, level of relief, because it is essentially a qualitative and subjective experience. Nevertheless, progress is being made in pain assessment and there is a gradual increase in the number of health care providers who are skilled in this process.

Much of the hospice success in pain control derives from superior knowledge of available medications and their optimal use. This effectiveness accords with hospice philosophy: People should be as pain-free as possible as the end of life approaches, to allow them the opportunity to complete projects, engage in leave-takings, or just to find some enjoyment and meaning in each remaining day. Patients and their families should not have to endure pain as long as possible until forced to beg for relief.

The hospice team has particular expertise in controlling what otherwise would be unremitting pain. Traditionally, the medical profession has had only intermittent focus on pain relief, often limited to short-term or acute pain situations. This approach is seldom effective with terminally ill cancer patients (Davis, 2004). Hospice practice and research have demonstrated that most people can receive significant relief from pain throughout the dying process. There are still times, however, when the available techniques do not bring adequate pain control, so innovation and research remain a key priority.

Many of the failures in pain relief throughout the health care system are failures to apply knowledge that is already available (Davis & Walsh, 2004). For example, it has been found that hospital-based nurses and physicians did not have the correct facts about pain relief in terminally ill people even though they held generally favorable attitudes toward hospice (Kinzel, Askew, & Goldbole, 1992).

Only 35 percent of nurses and 56 percent of physicians recognized that the total dose of narcotic to provide equivalent pain relief would be less with a regular dosing schedule than on an as-needed basis in this (a palliative care) setting. Only 10 percent of nurses and 38 percent of physicians were able to correctly order four narcotic analgesics according to potency. None of the physicians or nurses correctly identified 'more than 960 milligrams' as the correct response on a multiple choice question regarding the maximum safe dose of morphine sulfate that can be given orally over 24 hours (p. 88).

Physicians have reported that they do not have adequate education and training in providing relief from pain. They did not prescribe adequate medication to relieve the acute suffering of dyspnea (difficulties in breathing) and erred seriously by ordering forced feedings for patients with lack of appetite. Patients with advanced cancer under the care of these physicians would have suffered the anxiety of dyspnea without relief because of the widespread fear in the medical profession that opioids, the drug of choice for this problem, would turn the patients into addicts. Inflicting forced feeding on a person with advanced cancer would add another torment without providing real benefit. Physicians with more experience were no more competent than those with less experience. Unfortunately, physicians who themselves were not skilled in managing pain and other symptoms were the models for younger physicians.

Effective pain management requires more than a textbook knowledge of drug effects (especially since some of the textbooks themselves are out of compliance with clinical experience). The needs and pain tolerance of the particular individual must be considered, and the course of treatment must be subject to prompt review whenever problems arise.

Knowledgeable caregivers acquaint themselves with the family's concerns and show them how they can be part of the pain relief effort. Family-oriented care can reduce their stress, and therefore the patient's as well. Attention to the family's needs has also been shown to help them cope with grief after the death has occurred (Kissane, Lichtenthal, & Zaider, 2007–2008). Another key to alleviating pain in terminally ill patients is to reduce the mental distress that is associated with illness, dependency, loss of function, and concern about the future. The personality and mental state of the patients and the interpersonal setting in which they are located can influence sensitivity to pain. Some people have difficulty with the concept that pain can be all too real and at the same time related to one's mental and emotional state. A related tradition also can interfere with adequate pain relief. Since the middle of the twentieth century it has been fairly common practice for physicians to use a set of specific observations to distinguish "real" (organic) from "fake" (psychological) pain. It turns out that the frequently used Waddell observational signs *do not* reliably distinguish organic from psychological pain, but do underestimate the amount of pain that is actually experienced (Fishbain, Cole, Cutler, Rosomoff, & Rosomoff, 2003).

Other techniques for relieving pain have included massage, application of heat, cold, menthol, and electrical nerve stimulation to the skin; careful positioning and exercising; hypnosis; guided imagery and aromatherapy. These methods, reminiscent of the ancient Greek temples of healing, have been applied along with drugs and surgery. The comforting presence of companion animals has also been found helpful (Geisler, 2004). Most of these techniques can be used safely by informed caregivers and provide comfort without themselves producing stress or side effects.

Some people whose distress has led them to contemplate suicide or physician-assisted death have responded well to noninvasive pain alleviation techniques and respite care programs.

Other Symptoms and Problems

Pain is not the only problem that can beset a dying person. Other symptoms include:

- Nausea
- Vomiting
- Dyspnea (respiratory difficulties)
- Pressure sores
- Insomnia
- Incontinence
- Weakness
- Fatigue
- Confusion and Dementia
- Depression

Effective care requires attention to the prevention or alleviation of all these problems. A patient-centered approach with frequent interactions is required for palliation. For example, Foubert and Vaessen (2005) consider nausea to be a much neglected symptom, although it is often a side effect of chemotherapy. Despite the best care, however, the terminally ill person is likely to become weaker and more fatigued as the end approaches. Fatigue to the point of exhaustion is a symptom of terminal decline that often has not received the attention it deserves. Little is known about the relationship between a patient's experience of exhaustion and the accompanying physical condition, nor has there yet been much development of palliative measures. Furthermore, symptoms that might be noted separately on a checklist often are interlinked. A woman struggling with terminal cancer was quoted earlier in this chapter: ". . . but to take one step and then you have to rest and then one step and then it hurts in your chest." Exhaustion, pain, and depression are all part of this experience.

There is another common symptom that is only now starting to receive the attention it deserves. "Confusion," "delirium," and "dementia" are the terms most often applied to the disordered mental states that appear in some terminally ill patients as well as in other situations. The terms are sometimes used interchangeably, but it is useful to recognize the differences. *Confusion* (from the Middle English for "mingled together") is a state of mind in which there is a lack of clarity and organization, along with a difficulty in making accurate judgments. A person can be confused momentarily because of circumstances. Effective communication (e.g., explaining a medical procedure in a way the patient can understand) is sometimes sufficient to dispel the confusion. *Delirium* is an agitated and incoherent state of mind that could be described as a fit of madness. It is often associated with intoxication and other physical disorders. Wildly fluctuating moods often occur. Careful evaluation of medical status is essential. Delirium can be part of an acute life-threatening episode. It is a common, though far from universal, syndrome in the last few days of life. Unlike the other terms, *dementia* signifies a long-term, perhaps permanent mental-and-brain decline that cripples memory and renders the person unable to provide competent self-care. Alzheimer's disease has become the most widely known type of dementia.

Effective care for one symptom can help reduce the stress of other symptoms, but the direction will continue toward less energy and functional ability. Palliative care is ongoing, resourceful, and realistic in its expectations. Hospice patients are less likely to be restricted to their beds until death is very close, but eventual decline must be expected. Findings from the landmark *National Hospice Study* (Mor, Greer, & Kastenbaum, 1988) indicate that the social quality of life remained high for hospice patients during their final weeks and days as compared with patients receiving traditional medical care. Despite the inescapable fact of continued physical deterioration, patients receiving hospice care maintained their intimate relationships and avoided the social isolation that has often befallen the dying person. The data also suggested that the personality and values of the person before becoming terminally ill also had a major influence on experiences during the last weeks of life. The difference between hospice and traditional types of care is significant, but so are individual differences in personality and social support system.

The Last Three Days of Life: From Patients' Perspective

Recall the thought questions raised at the end of Chapter 4. You were asked first to describe the last three days of your life as you would like them to be. Reflect on your own responses as you learn how terminally ill people participating in the National Hospice Discharge Survey (NHDS) answered the same questions (suggested by Beatrice Kastenbaum). The following types of answers were most common (in order of frequency):

- I want certain people to be here with me.
- I want to be physically able to do things.
- I want to feel at peace.
- I want to be free from pain.
- I want the last three days of my life to be like any other days.

The support offered by hospice care makes it possible for many patients to be at home and enjoy the company of the "certain people" who mean the most to them. Similarly, with the advice and support of hospice volunteers and staff, the patient could still control some activities of daily life. Remaining in their environment provided a context for feeling at peace and having each day keep something of the feeling of a comforting routine. The patients' goals and the goals of hospice care were identical.

It is interesting to note some of the *least* frequently mentioned wishes for the last three days of life. Only about one person in 20 cared about "completing a task" or being "mentally alert." Even fewer hoped to "accept death," and fewer still wanted to "know when death is imminent," "to be able to bear pain," or "live until a certain time or event." This collection of low-incidence items includes many of the most dramatic wishes that are sometimes attributed to the dying person. By far the greater number of terminally ill people simply wanted the comfort of familiar faces and the ability to continue to do a little for themselves and have a sense of peaceful routine. The goal of accepting death philosophically or demonstrating the ability to tolerate pain was seldom stated.

These findings invite reflections such as the following: (1) what most people wanted was no more and no different from what hospice care tries to achieve and (2) it is wiser to learn from each individual what really matters than to attribute motives and themes picked up elsewhere. The question on *sources of strength* was also included in the NHDS. Following are the most frequent responses.

- Supportive family or friends
- Religion
- Being needed
- Confidence in self
- Satisfied with the help received

There appears to be a good match in general between what terminally ill cancer patients' hopes for their last days and what hospice is designed to provide. The dying person's quality of life depends much on the social support that has been available to that person. Competent management of pain and compassionate attention from both family and hospice caregivers is helping many a terminally ill person to find continuing meaning and value in life. Palliative care can address the "partial models of the dying person's situation" (Kastenbaum, 2000) reviewed in Chapter 4. Terminally ill people will still experience, for example, restricted activity, limited energy, and damaged body image, but they can also experience the support and understanding of professional and family caregivers who can help them continue to feel secure and valued.

Your Deathbed Scene, Revisited

Think again about the personal deathbed scene you imagined while reading the preceding chapter. Now that you have read more about the dying process and terminal care, it might be instructive to review your own expectations. Was your deathbed scene similar to those of most students? If so, then you came up with a sanitized image that is at odds with the way that most people actually die. Most dying people have pain and a variety of other symptoms, perhaps fortunately controlled by skilled and compassionate caregivers. Most college students portray themselves as dying without pain and without other symptoms (Kastenbaum & Normand, 1990). Additionally, most students indicated that they wanted to and actually *would* "go

quickly." By contrast, most people actually die over a longer period of time. Some terminally ill people do "slip away quietly" in their sleep, but this is often preceded by months of declining health and increased functional limitations. Realistically, most of us will live for sometime with our final illness, and so will our loved ones. How should we balance wishful fantasy and reality?

What does it mean if even those self-selected people who have chosen to enroll in a death-focused class have unrealistic ideas about their probable condition at the end of life? Your reflections are invited.

HOSPICE ACCESS, DECISION MAKING, AND CHALLENGES

Palliative care takes place within a complex and shifting mix of circumstances: cultural, political, and economic, as well as medical. It's not at all simple. Here we summarize the basic procedure for hospice access, and then identify several ongoing issues of concern to service providers, patients, and their families.

Choosing the Hospice Option

Hospice care in the United States is available as an optional program under Medicare (Part A). A person with what is described as a "life-limiting illness" can choose to receive traditional hospital-based medical care, or enroll instead in an approved hospice organization. To be certified and reimbursed, a hospice must meet a firm set of standards. These include having its services available 24/7, staffed by a team of qualified professionals and trained volunteers. There are also patient eligibility requirements; patients must be Medicare eligible.

Gaining access to a hospice program is most direct for patients who are eligible for Medicare (Part A) hospital insurance. A physician is required to certify that the patient has a life expectancy of six months or less. Most physicians are troubled by this requirement, which does not seem adequately to represent the ambiguities of the medical situation. When this certification has been made, the patient signs a statement that confirms selection of hospice care for the terminal illness. This *Medicare hospice benefit* then replaces the standard Medicare benefit. The coverage is quite extensive: The services of physicians, nurses, home health aide, homemaker, and pastoral counselor are all included, as are rentals of medical equipment and medications. Generally, at-home expenses are fully covered, but there may be some expenses associated with in-hospital stays. Unfortunately, bereavement services are seldom adequately funded, so individual hospices vary in the support they can offer to families after the death.

Access to hospice can be more difficult if a patient does not have a primary physician with whom a strong trusting relationship has been established, or is not eligible for Medicare hospital benefits. These and other possible obstacles often can be overcome after discussion with a hospice director or social worker. It is useful to allow some time to explore the situation, have one's questions answered, and solve problems that might stand in the way of access. The most common barriers to hospice service include:

- Physicians' difficulty with hospice admission criteria, reluctance to lose control of their patients, and, in some cases, restrictions on the number of pain control prescriptions they are allowed to write.
- Insufficient family cooperation with hospice. As one nurse commented: "Many times, the patient is ready for hospice and the family is not . . ."
- Inadequate communication between managed care health staff and terminally ill patients and their families. As expressed by another hospice nurse:

> Doctors don't take the time to discuss with patients and families. This is particularly true for the County system and HMO's. Patients have seen so many doctors, they don't have a particular doctor. They feel so trashed, because they feel like they've been bumped from person to person, and now they have to choose hospice.

- Late referral of patients to hospice care. This is a persistent problem throughout most of the world. Patients are sometimes referred to hospice when they have only a few days to live, thereby severely restricting the ability

of palliative care providers to help them. At its most extreme, patients are not referred for hospice care until death is only hours away. Most often, it is the physician who is criticized for reluctance to admit "failure," and acknowledge that the time for comfort care has come, or resistance to transferring a patient. Sometimes, though, it is the family that is not ready to accept the proximity of death and continuing in its demand for the physician to do everything possible (Sanders et al. 2004).

- Availability of family support. The basic hospice model involves a dying person, that person's family and home, and the services provided by professional and volunteer caregivers. Ideally, there is an intact family that wants the dying person to be at home as much as possible and whose members are ready and willing to participate in the daily care. That each hospice patient must have a primary family caregiver (e.g., spouse or child) became a requirement in the federal regulatory and funding system. There are a growing number of exceptions, however, and regulatory agencies appear to a little more flexible in this regard. Hospices, neighbors, and others can sometimes be very creative in coming up with a primary caregiver and a home environment. In deciding about hospice care, then, it is useful to give attention to the availability of family and, if necessary, additional caregiver support.

Unequal Access to Hospice Care

It has already been noted that the international hospice movement, for all its efforts, reaches only a very small proportion of terminally ill people throughout the world. There are significant access problems within the United States as well. Gorospe (2006) judges palliative care to be an essential public health intervention that is presently seldom available to ethnic minorities. His focus is on Native Americans whose general health services have long been rated as insufficient. Public health advances have contributed to lengthening of life, but also to lengthening periods of decline and suffering. Other people rarely given the opportunity for palliative care include impoverished residents of both inner city and rural areas, and migrants. The "have-not's" in society are likely to be excluded from palliative care as well as other services and opportunities.

Studies have shown there is not equal access and utilization of palliative care. Homeless people encounter discrimination from many sources, and are seldom consulted about their end of life preferences by health care providers. "Relationship-centered care, characterized by compassion and respectful, two-way communication, was . . . absent" (Tarzian, Neal, & O'Neill, 2005, p. 36). Members of racial and ethnic minorities less frequently choose hospice care (Lyke & Colon, 2004). Other people, such as the homeless, have very little contact with the health care system throughout their lives. Still others do not meet the Medicare requirements for participation.

The end of life takes place in a nursing home for about one person in five, and this frequency has been increasing in recent years. Unfortunately:

> Dying residents experience high rates of untreated pain and other symptoms. They and their family members are isolated from social and spiritual support. Hospice improves end-of-life care for dying nursing home residents by improving pain control, reducing hospitalization, and reducing use of tube feeding, but it is rarely used (Zerezan, Stearns, & Hanson, 2000).

The "done-bads" have also been neglected. The population of prison inmates has continued to age, along with the general population. Hospice programs—especially those that provide comprehensive and high quality services—are still a rarity in prisons, although awareness of this problem is gradually increasing.

Patient Care Issues

Palliative care providers, attuned to individuals and their distinctive circumstances, cope with a variety of challenges every day. There are some concerns, however, that are either increasing in scope and intensity or not yet given sufficient attention.

Continuity of care is one of these issues. Ward & Gordon (2006–2007) observe that the intimate bond so important in hospice care seems to be in jeopardy because of economic and organizational pressures. The patient and family sense of safety, security, and comfort depends much on the establishment and maintenance of trusting relationships. Hospice philosophy has consistently emphasized the value of compassionate and dependable relationships at the end of life. A changing cast of care providers, all under time pressure, makes it very difficult for intimate bonds to form and endure. In their case study of a nonprofit, stand-alone hospice, Ward & Gordon find that forced organizational restructuring has jeopardized the organization's ability to continue with its labor-intensive, high staff to patient ratio. The restructurings were forced by Medicare regulations and intensifying competition from large, profit-making health care organizations. The result was a renewed "medicalization of death" that allowed little latitude for supportive interactions and a spiritual perspective. Many other hospice organizations have been experiencing the same pressured shift from original purpose and method to "a more businesslike and clinical culture" (Ward & Gordon, p. 10). One of the defining characteristics of palliative care—a situation of safety and trust with continuity of relationships—is at considerable risk today.

Spirituality, already mentioned, has been a cherished theme for many hospice pioneers. It was often rooted in Christian belief, but not limited to any one faith. St. Christopher's Hospice, for example, was alert to the spiritual needs of all its patients and families, including those with agnostic or atheistic worldviews. Today in the "more businesslike and clinical culture" of health care organizations, hospices are having some difficulty in protecting the spiritual core of their mission. But what is spiritual care in practice? Pulchaski (2007–2008, p. 42) offers this example:

> To be able to sit in silence as someone grapples with the unknown, and through the silence and the compassionate presence facilitate healing of that person, that is a profound act of love and of honoring the dignity of each person we treat.

It remains to be seen whether spirituality can be integrated into the care of seriously and terminally ill people within a mega-health care system that has other priorities and processes.

Two other issues challenge hospice philosophy and practice. The "difficult patient" is well known to health care providers. Nurses are often skilful in dealing with resistant and ill-tempered patients. The really difficult patient can test caregivers to their limits, however, a situation that one does not ordinarily associate with hospice service. "Mr. A" is an example discussed by Reeves et al. (2007). As a nursing home resident, he insulted the staff, frequently with racial and sexual slurs. He disrupted the facility, accused the staff of neglect, and hassled the other residents. If his behavior pattern is still in doubt, we learn that "On eight occasions he has tried to assault people with his motorized wheelchair, once leaving the facility and attempting to hit people on a busy street until police intervened" (p.13).

Palliative care programs believe in giving everybody a chance, so a person such as Mr. A. can sometimes bring his behavioral problems into a hospice. The added stress of just one person with a significant behavior problem can be a significant burden. Additionally, there is a challenge to the basic hospice principle of patient autonomy. Terminally ill people are not to be over-managed, not made to conform to standard operating procedure. What should be done when a patient's abusive behavior affects the care of other patients and demoralizes compassionate care providers? The conflict between rights of the individual and the rights of other people occurs

Dame Cicely Saunders (1918–2005), founder of the international hospice movement.

in many situations. Hospice, with its intensive service to seriously ill people and their families, is still seeking ways to approach and resolve this challenge.

There is another situation that also can be unsettling. Theoretically, terminally people enroll in hospice care for expert symptom relief and comprehensive care, as distinguished from continued, all-out aggressive treatment. In practice, though, some people change their minds. A person, feeling stronger through hospice care, might transfer to the basic Medicare benefit for another round of cure-oriented treatment. This choice does not run counter to hospice philosophy and practice. What does generate concern is a patient's wish to hasten death. Palliative care is intended to help people through their last days, not to shorten their lives. It has taken years of public education to dispel the fear that hospice is an agency of euthanasia or assisted suicide. There are special circumstances in Oregon, the only state in which physician-assisted suicide (PAS) is legal (see Chapter 9). Hospice staff in Oregon might be divided in their personal attitudes toward a PAS request, but the existence of an established process at least removes concern about possible violation of the law (Harvarth et al. 2006). In all other states, a hospice patient who expresses the wish to hasten death thereby raises the acute issue of individual autonomy versus communal law and established practice. The ethical and public opinion standing of hospice could be endangered whatever response is made. Patients sometimes resolve the dilemma for themselves, either by working past the impulse to hasten death, or voluntarily refusing food and fluids. Experienced care providers understand that a person's mindset can shift significantly as they cope with the physical, mental, and spiritual challenges of the final passage.

A simple but fundamental piece of advice is offered by Dr. Robert Twycross, a pioneer in the development of pain relief procedures for terminally ill people: "*Truth may hurt but deceit hurts more*. Being sensitively honest with one's patients has always been a key characteristic of palliative care" (2007–2008, p. 13).

DAME CICELY SAUNDER'S REFLECTIONS ON HOSPICE

The founder of the international hospice movement inspired palliative care programs worldwide. Dame Cicely Saunders (1918–2005) agreed to respond to some fairly personal questions about her own experiences as a way of inviting you to continue your interest in this ongoing project.

Q: *How do you get used to death and to losing people you have cared for—and then having to do it all over again the next day?*

A: An auxiliary nurse who has worked in St. Christopher's told me recently, "You miss some people a lot, but next day there is a new patient and family to get to know and help." Both of us, and everyone else I have talked with, have mentioned "team" or "community" as a major positive as well as the continued learning of new ways to help. Above all, the patients remain the inspiration. Meeting people of great maturity facing life's end with endurance, humanity and faith in various forms is a great encouragement.

Q: *How do hospice caregivers renew their own spirits? What do you do in your own life to keep going? What are your sources of strength and commitment?*

A: For myself, my Christian commitment, together with constant learning, reading, and traveling to other teams/units have been forms of renewal. I also have a great support system of friends and colleagues. A physiotherapist (after 30 years working in the field) says, "We know we cannot cure our patients but we can still maximize their remaining potential . . . the patients keep me sane and focused. We are pioneers in an unexplored field." My colleagues all have an indefatigable capacity for new thinking and developing together as a team.

Q: *Women provide direct care to terminally ill people in the United States far more often than men . . .*

A: The preponderance of women in the field seems to be common around the world. But some men have made invaluable contributions to caring. Many have a spiritual dimension as a basis for their commitment.

Q: *Two situations are often highly stressful both to caregivers and family—the patient who has no realistic hope of survival but wants to keep fighting, and the family who insists on having "everything done," although there is really nothing effective yet to be done . . .*

A: This is not such a desperate dilemma. Patients who want to go on fighting are likely to return to their oncologist, who will advise and counsel. Otherwise, really skilled listening and discussion with the palliative care specialist may resolve a situation. We find most people will gradually learn to let go. Cultural differences require explanation and understanding. Families likewise need careful communication from the first contact. Once trust is established these problems can be approached if and when the time comes.

Q: *What is the "worst" death you have come across, and what made it so?*

A: A patient refused all pain control on principle and died slowly and painfully over several weeks. The doctors and nurses anguished over this. When he was semi-conscious and groaning, the psychiatrist maintained he was not suffering from any psychiatric symptoms and was competent to make that choice. It was felt ethically correct to respect the patient's decision, although the nurses were most unhappy and the team was split.

Q: *How does a "good death" affect the family survivors and the health care providers?*

A: I think my husband (aged 93) achieved a good death. After many years of caring as he went from one life-threatening illness to another,

we had to accept his statement that "I have done what I had to do in my life and now I am ready to die." But when he was desperately breathless with a chest infection he asked me, "Can't you help me to die? I said, "It will be in God's time" and he then replied, "I agree." A few days later the breathlessness passed and he had two peaceful weeks, still alert and gradually less talkative, except for flirting with the nurses! On the last afternoon, two of his former art pupils visited him. One wrote to me afterwards. "He seemed very peaceful but as if he was in touch with something beyond where we were." He slipped away just before I returned from home that night, but that was all right for me too, because I knew he was not alone.

Q: *Dr. Kevorkian . . .*

A: What Dr. Kevorkian did seemed to me to be totally unprofessional and careless of true human compassion and skill.

Q: *The international hospice movement has come a very long way in a short time. What can we all do to help the hospice philosophy fulfill its potential?*

A: We need people to conduct more research into palliative care for people dying of other diseases, more research, more skills development, more education of health care professionals outside of hospice specialists, and more understanding of the values and commitment of developing countries.

Many people have discovered a way to become active in the hospice movement by serving as volunteers. Interested? See Box 5-1.

BOX 5-1 SHOULD I BECOME A HOSPICE VOLUNTEER? A DIALOGUE

- *Does my local hospice need volunteers?*
  Probably so. A hospice usually has a director of volunteers and will welcome your call.

- *What should I expect when I meet the director of volunteers?*
  A friendly but professional interview. The hospice has responsibility for exercising good judgment in the selection of volunteers.

BOX 5-1 (continued)

• *You mean they might not accept me?*
This is a possibility. Has someone very close to you died recently? Many hospices ask people who have had a recent bereavement to wait a while before becoming a volunteer. Or the interviewer may judge that you have a disorganized life style.

• *Hey, I'm going to get organized, starting tomorrow!*
Fine! But the volunteer director will need to be convinced that you are a reliable person who keeps appointments. And should you come across like a person who needs to impose your own religious beliefs on others—or use hospice in the service of your own fantasies and problems—then you might receive a polite but firm refusal.

• *That won't happen to me. I'm taking this great class on death and dying, and reading this really terrific textbook. So after I'm accepted as a volunteer, will they give me some guidance and supervision?*
Definitely. You will be asked to attend a series of training sessions before you are activated as a volunteer. Most people find this to be a valuable learning experience. You will receive guidance and supervision all the way along the line, and you will always have somebody to call if problems arise.

• *What kind of things would I do as a volunteer?*
There are many possibilities. You might be a companion for a patient in his or her home for a few hours so that others in the household have the opportunity to shop or take care of business. You might drive the patient to an appointment or to visit an old friend. You might help the patient write letters or e-mails. You might help prepare a meal when family or friends visit. You might help the patient or a family member complete a special project.

And at times you might just "be there." A hospice volunteer can wind up doing many different things, depending upon the needs of the individual families (Willis, 1989). And some volunteers devote themselves to keeping the hospice system going, rather than working with patients. They do office work, fund-raising, and other things depending upon the needs of the individual families.

• *What are the other volunteers like?*
I've been fortunate enough to know many hospice volunteers. As a rule, they are bright, mature, and neighborly people who have been rather successful in life. Many feel that through hospice they can give something back to other people. Some are health care professionals who believe strongly in the hospice philosophy.

• *Like nurses and medical social workers?*
Yes, some volunteers are well-qualified professionals. Some have been very successful in other lines of work, but are new to health and social care. And you will find other students as well—looking for an opportunity to help others while acquiring valuable personal experience.

• *Anything else I should know?*
Before you contact hospice, reflect on your own motivation: Do you have a passing curiosity or a firm resolve to help others? Will you be available to serve as a volunteer after you complete the course? Even though hospice may ask you to give only a few hours of your time per week, people will be counting on you to come through. If you have further questions at this time, you might ask your local hospice to put you into contact with several of their experienced volunteers.

• *See you at the hospice office!*
Go easy on those donuts.

SUMMARY

Hospice care is intended to provide comfort, relief, and a sense of security for terminally ill people and their families. It differs from traditional medical management in several important ways: (1) expertise in the control of pain and other symptoms; (2) centered around the situation, needs, and desires of the particular dying person and family; (3) including family members and volunteers as part of the caregiving system. The hospice approach to terminal care has its roots in shelter houses established in the fourth century for the comfort of pilgrims, the ill, and the dying. After a period of neglect, hospice activity started again in the late nineteenth century and took its modern form with the establishment of St. Christopher's Hospice (London) in 1967. Connecticut Hospice (New Haven) was the first such program in the United States (1974). About one person in three in the United States now selects the hospice care option for end of life care. Standards of care for hospice programs include the well-being patient, family, and staff. Adult respite programs can provide a useful temporary alternative to hospital and home care. Palliative care for children is becoming increasingly available. Case histories offered some idea of how hospice care is offered and its benefits for dying persons and their families.

Hospice programs have most often served adults with advanced cancer or progressive neurological dysfunction. Today, though, Increasing numbers of people with life-threatening heart disease are selecting palliative care. Hospice is adapting well to providing care for cardiac patients, but this is producing a disconnect with Medicare: patients are living "too long." An open question is whether the health care system will adjust to changing circumstances, or endanger hospice's ability to continue its high quality programs. There is also concern that the original hospice mission, with its emphasis on enduring and trusting relationships, spirituality, and patient-oriented care might be at risk from a more business-like and clinical orientation. We looked at several other applications of hospice philosophy and practice: for children, people with AIDS, and people of diverse ethnic backgrounds. Hospice programs are developing rapidly throughout the world, finding welcome in nations with very different cultural and religious patterns. Nevertheless, only a very small number of terminally ill people can turn to palliative care in developing nations.

Research and clinical experience indicate that hospice care often does prevent and relieve suffering. Pain relief is most often the highest priority. The gradual acceptance of pain as the fifth vital sign in health care contacts with all patients is one of the remarkable achievements of the hospice movement, Unfortunately, though, what has been discovered about effective pain relief in palliative programs has not always been applied by physicians operating outside of the hospice framework. Many physicians are still inadequately trained to provide effective pain relief for dying people, and many still have unrealistic anxieties about turning a person into a drug addict through the administration of morphine and related medications. Fatigue and nausea are among the other distressing symptoms that require attention in palliative care. The relief of suffering also requires attention to the mental distress that can be associated with illness, dependency, loss of function, and concern about the future.

We concluded by sharing an interview with international hospice movement pioneer Dame Cicely Saunders, a brief revisit to your imagined deathbed scene, and an introduction to the volunteer's role in hospice care.

REFERENCES

Anonymous. (2005). Hospice costs Medicare less and patients often live longer, new research shows. *Journal of Hospice & Palliative Nursing, 7*, 10–11.

Brown, E., Warr, B., & Schribman, S. (2007). *Supporting the child and family in pediatric palliative care.* London: Jessica Kingsley.

Carter, B. S., & Leveton, M. (2004). *Palliative for infants, children, and adolescents.* Baltimore: Johns Hopkins Press.

Centers for Disease Control and Prevention. (2001). *HIV/AIDS Surveillance Supplemental Report, 2000.* Rockville, MD: CDCP.

Clark, D. (2000). Palliative care history: A ritual process. *European Journal of Palliative Care, 7:* 50–55.

Clark, D. (2007–2008). End-of-life-care around the world: Achievements to date and challenges remaining. *Omega, Journal of Death & Dying, 56,* 101–110.

Dabbs, B., Butterworth, L., & Hall, E. (2007). "Tender mercies": Increasing access to hospice services for children with life-threatening conditions. *American Journal of Maternal/Child Nursing, 32,* 311–319.

Davis, M. P. (2004). Acute pain in advanced cancer: *American Journal of Hospice & Palliative Medicine, 21,* 47–50.

Davis, M. P., & Walsh, D. (2004). Epidemiology of cancer pain and factors influencing poor pain control. *American Journal of Hospice & Palliative Medicine, 21,* 137–142.

Fishbain, D. A., Cole, B., Cutler, R. B., Lewis, J., Rosomoff, H. L., & Rosomoff, R. S. (2003). A structured evidence-based review on the meaning of nonorganic physical signs: Waddell signs. *Pain Medicine, 4,* 141–181.

Foubert, J., & Vaessen, G. (2005). Nausea: The neglected symptom. *European Journal of Oncology Nursing, 9,* 21–32.

Geisler, A. N. (2004). Companion animals in palliative care: Stories from the bedside. *American Journal of Hospice & Palliative Medicine, 21,* 285–288.

Goldman, A., Hain, R., & Liben, S. (2006). *Oxford textbook of palliative care for children.* New York: Oxford University Press.

Gorospe, E. C. (2006). Establishing palliative care for American Indians as a public health agenda. *Internet Journal of Pain, Symptom Control, & Palliative Care, 4,* 1528–8227.

Harvard Medical School. (2008). Harvard Medical School Center for Palliative Care. Pallcare@partners.org

Harvarth, T. A., Miller, L. L., Smith, K. A., Clark, L. D., Jackson, A., & Ganzini, L.(2006). Dilemmas encountered by hospice workers when patients wish to hasten death. *Journal of Hospice & Palliative Nursing, 8,* 200–209.

Hinds, P. S., Bradshaw, G., Oakes, L. L., & Pritchard. M. (2002). Children and their rights in life and death situations. In R. Kastenbaum (Ed.), *Macmillan encyclopedia of death and dying:* Vol. 1 (pp. 139–147). New York: Macmillan.

Humphreys, C. (2001). "Waiting for the last summons": The establishment of the first hospices in England 1878–1914. *Mortality, 6:* 146–166.

Jusic, A. (1997) Palliative medicine's first steps in Croatia. In C. Saunders & R. Kastenbaum (Eds.), *Hospice care on the international scene,* pp.125–129. New York: Springer.

Kassine, D., Lichtenthal, W., & Zaider, T. (2007–2008). Family care before and after bereavement. *Omega, Journal of Death & Dying, 56,* 21–32.

Kastenbaum, R. (2000). *The psychology of death,* 3rd ed. New York: Springer.

Kastenbaum, R., & Normand, C. (1990). Deathbed scenes as expected by the young and experienced by the old. *Death Studies, 14:* 201–218.

Kastenbaum, R., & Wilson, M. (1997). Hospice care on the international scene: Today and tomorrow. In C. Saunders & R. Kastenbaum (Eds.), *Hospice care on the international scene* (pp. 262–272). New York: Springer.

Kinzel, T., Askew, M., & Goldbole, K. (1992). Palliative care: Attitudes and knowledge of hospital-based nurses and physicians. *Loss, Grief & Care, 6:* 85–95.

Lindqvist, L., Widmark, A., & Rasmussen, B. H. (2004). Meanings of the phenomenon of fatigue as narrated by 4 patients with cancer in palliative care. *Cancer Nursing, 27,* 237–243.

Lyke, J., & Colon, M. (2004). Practical recommendations for ethnically and racially sensitive hospice services. *American Journal of Hospice & Palliative Medicine, 21,* 131–133.

Meagher, D. K., & Leff, P. T. (1989–1990). In Marie's memory: The rights of the child with life-threatening or terminal illness. *Omega, Journal of Death and Dying, 20:* 177–191.

Mor, V., Greer, D., & Kastenbaum, R. (1988). *The hospice experiment.* Baltimore: Johns Hopkins University Press.

Mount, B. (2003). Palliative care: A personal odyssey. *Illness, Crisis, & Loss, 11,* 90–103.

Movementbuilding. (n.d.). Understanding prison health care: Elder & end-of-life care. www.movementbuilding. org/prisonhealth/elder.html

National Hospice and Palliative Care Organization (2008). NHPCO facts and figures: Hospice care in America. www.nhpco.org/research

Pevey, C. (2005). Patient speaking: Hospice patients discuss their care. *American Journal of Hospice & Palliative Medicine, 22,* 129–133.

Phipps, W. E. (1988). The origin of hospices/hospitals. *Death Studies, 12,* 91–100.

Puchalski, C. M. (2007–2008). Spirituality and the care of patients at the end-of-life: An essential component of care. *Omega, Journal of Death and Dying, 56,* 33–46.

Radulovic, J. (2007). Hospice care saves money for Medicare, new study shows. http://nhpco.org/i4a/pages/ Index.cfm?pageID=5386

Reeves, R. R., Douglas, S. P., Garner, R. T., & Reynolds, M. D. (2007). The individual rights of the difficult patient. *The Hastings Center Report, 37,* 13–15.

Sack, K. (2007). Hospice care: Longer lives mean money lost. *New York Times.* http://infoweb.newsbank.com. ezproxy1.lib.asu.edu/iwsearch/we/InfoWeb?actionp_

Sanders, B. S., Burkett, T. L., Dickinson, G. E., & Tournier, R. E. (2004). Hospice referral decisions: The role of physicians. *American Journal of Hospice & Palliative Medicine, 21,* 196–202.

Saunders, C. (1993). Dame Cicely Saunders: An Omega interview. *Omega, Journal of Death & Dying, 27,* 263–270.

Staton, J., Shuy, R., & Byock, I. (2001). *A few months to live. Different paths to life's end.* Washington, DC: Georgetown University Press.

Tarzian, A. J., Neal, M. T., & O'Neill, J. A. (2005) Attitudes, experiences, and beliefs affecting end-of-life decision-making among homeless individuals. *Journal of Palliative Medicine, 8,* 36–48.

Twycross, R. (2007–2008). Patient care: Past, present, and future. *Omega, Journal of Death & Dying, 56,* 7–20.

Ward, E. G., & Gordon, A. K. (2006–2007). Looming threats to the intimate bond in hospice care? Economic and organizational pressures in the case study of a hospice. *Omega, Journal of Death & Dying, 54,* 1–18.

Ward, G. (2007). More hospitals offering sensitive end-of-life care. *Daily News Journal* (Murfreesboro, Tenn). http://dnj.midsouthnews.com/apps/pbcs.Dll/article?AID=/20071228/BUSINESS

Willis, J. (1989). Hospice volunteers. In R. Kastenbaum & B. K. Kastenbaum (Eds.), *Encyclopedia of death* (pp. 147–149). Phoenix: The Oryx Press.

Wilson, M., & Kastenbaum, R. (1997). Worldwide developments in hospice care: Survey results. In C. Saunders & R. Kastenbaum (Eds.), *Hospice care on the international scene.* NY: Springer.

Zerzan, J., Stearns, S., & Hanson, L. (2000). Access to palliative care and hospice in nursing homes. *Journal of the American Medical Association, 248,* 2489–2494.

GLOSSARY

Hospice: (1) A program of care devoted to providing comfort to terminally ill people through a team approach with participation by family members. (2) A facility in which such care is provided.

Medicare hospice benefit: A federal reimbursement program that enables eligible people to select hospice care as an alternative to traditional medical management during their terminal illness.

National hospice study: A major project (1982–83) that compared traditional and hospice care for terminally ill people in the United States. The Medicare Hospice Benefit was established as a result of this study.

Palliative care: Health services intended to reduce pain and other symptoms to protect the patient's quality of life.

Physician-assisted suicide (PAS): Termination of a person's life by a physician through lethal injection or other means, at that person's request. (Illegal except in Oregon when in compliance with the state's Death with Dignity Act).

Remission: The disappearance or relief of symptoms.

Symptom: An observable sign of dysfunction and/or distress (e.g., pain, fever).

Terminal illness: Defined in the Medicare Hospice Benefit as an illness that is expected to end in death within six months or less. In other contexts, the specific definition of terminal illness is open to discussion and controversy.

Vital signs: Body functions that are routinely assessed by physicians and nurses. Traditionally included temperature, pulse, respiration, and blood pressure. Now also includes patient's experience of pain.

ON FURTHER THOUGHT . . .

Useful online resources:

American Academy of Hospice and Palliative Medicine
www.aahpm.org
American Hospice Association
www.americanhospice.org
Canadian Palliative Care Association
www.cpca.net
Children's Hospice International
www.chionline.org
European Association for Palliative Care
www.eapcnet.org
Hospice and Palliative Nurses Association
www.hpna.org
Hospice Association of America
www.nahc.org
Hospice Foundation of America
www.hospicefoundation.org
Hospice Information (international)
www.hospiceinformation.info
National Hospice and Palliative Care Organization
www.nhpco.org
National Hospice Work Group
www.nhwg.org
Stop Pain.Org
www.stoppain.org

An unsettled question:

The modern hospice movement was incubated by caregivers with a strong religious orientation, largely Christian. What should be the role of religion in palliative care today? In thinking about this question, take into account people with a terminal illness whose religious orientations differ from mainstream Christianity, or those who have no religious affiliations, or who belong to ethnic and racial groups that have not expressed much interest or comfort with the idea of hospice care. Can hospice care fulfill its promise without a strong religious orientation? Is "spirituality" identical with or significantly different from association with an established religion?

Paramedics and other first responders must bring their training, experience, and personal judgment to bear in emergency situations. This can include deciding which of several lives can be saved.

chapter 6

END-OF-LIFE ISSUES AND DECISIONS

Do you have an Advance Directive (power of attorney for healthcare or living will)?
—Ronald S. Go et al, (2007, p. 1490)

Rather than waiting for organs, why don't people with failures band together, pool their risk and draw lots to determine who among them should be killed for the sake of their organs?
—Gerhard Overland (2007, p. 355)

A devoted family surrounded this elderly gentleman, who was in the last stages of severe cerebrovascular disease. They had visited him regularly and were quietly reconciled to losing their father as he became progressively moribund. Suddenly, a daughter who lived in another state stormed in, loudly demanding heroic measures that would do no good. Ironically, she had never visited her father since he entered the hospital and was obviously driven by guilt.
—Stephen D. Gresham and Glen E. Gresham (2005, p. 1)

After two years of nursing home care, Millie Morrisey developed pneumonia and respiratory distress. As had been its custom, the nursing home staff called an ambulance. Documentation of preferences—which included foregoing antibiotics, mechanical ventilation and tube feeding—were neither sought nor readily accessible in her chart. The hospital quickly admitted her to the ICU, initiated antibiotics and mechanical ventilation, and used physical restraints so that she would not dislodge the tubes and lines to which she was connected. She mostly did not seem to understand what was happening and was agitated and tearful.
—Marilyn J. Field and Christine K. Cassel (1997, pp. 93–94)

Ordinarily, the dead have a right in Islam to the sanctity and wholeness of their body, but the need to save a life overrides this injunction. . . . While saving a life is of paramount importance in Islam, the family of the deceased must consent and are in no way obliged to consent to organ donation even if it involves the death of another person who is alive but gravely ill.
—Mohammad Mehdi Golmakani, Mohammad Hussein Niknam, and Kamyar M. Hedayat (2005, p. RA 106).

*Ask me what I'm fixing for supper tonight, I can't tell you. So, what kind of party I'm
planning to throw for the end of my life—go away!*
—A woman talking back to a television program

FROM DESCRIPTION TO
DECISION MAKING

I don't know what we're having for supper
tonight, either, but supper will probably happen. Death certainly will. Perhaps we should
think some about end-of-life issues and decisions. We have prepared ourselves by observing how hospice care (Chapter 5) is attempting
to provide safe conduct through the dying
process (Chapter 4). Each day many people
face the decision either to continue with cure-
oriented treatment or to choose symptom relief
and comfort care. This end-of-life decision, like
the others that will be considered in this chapter, depends much on the adequacy of communication among health care professionals, terminally ill patients, and their families. Another
type of end-of-life decision will be considered
in its own chapter. Physician-assisted death,
also known as assisted suicide (Chapter 9)
raises legal, medical, and ethical issues that require special examination. Here we will concentrate on a broad range of basic end-of-life
decisions that we are likely to encounter either
directly or indirectly. These include the unusual option of cryonic suspension and the
challenge of organ donation.

We begin with a brief inquiry into the whole
idea of planning for the end of our lives. This is
followed with a reflection on our own ideas and
feelings as we trace the development of advance
directives for controlling care during a terminal
illness.

WHO SHOULD PARTICIPATE
IN END-OF-LIFE DECISIONS?

There has been a turnabout in public attitudes toward end-of-life decision making. The
idea that we ourselves should have the final
say did not gather force until our society

started a renewed dialogue about dying and
death, stimulated by the increasingly widespread application of life support systems and
the emergence of the hospice care movement.
Patient self-determination had to overcome the
habit of leaving such matters to the medical
system.

Today there is more opportunity for us to
express our wishes. Informed consent is an established principle. A variety of advance directives are available. But are people being offered
the option of increased control over the last
days of their lives—or being confronted with
unsettling and confusing choices that many
prefer to avoid?

The question about having an advance directive or living will becomes more interesting
when it is put to health care professionals. The
respondents in this Mayo Clinic study (Go,
Hammes, Lee, & Mathiason, 2007) represented a
broad range of experienced health care professionals such as physicians, physician-assistants,
nurse practitioners, social workers, and specialized therapists. The findings—as you might well
have guessed—indicate that "Despite work experience with patients who have a high mortality
rate, health care professionals at our cancer center do not adequately communicate end-of-life
planning decisions to their own primary care
physicians" (p. 1407). The results probably surprised few health care professionals and social
scientists: there is still a lot of resistance to facing
end-of-life decisions. Experience with terminally
ill people does not seem to encourage health
care providers to work through their own
thoughts and feelings.

It is startling to discover a bioethicist raising
the prospect of sacrificial killing (Overland,
2007). Nevertheless, that is one way to call attention to the hard realities of organ donation
(or "anatomical gifts"). The people on the long
waiting lists generally have little opportunity to
do anything but hope.

The option of donating organs or tissues has raised ethical and religious, as well as scientific and technical, questions. These issues arise throughout the world. Muslims, for example, have to find their way between two fundamental beliefs that could lead to divergent responses: the high value placed on dignity and sanctity of life, and the perhaps even higher value placed on salvation through obedience to divine decrees (Golmakani, Niknam, & Hedayat, 2005). Debate continues among Islamic scholars, but in practice many Muslim nations practice organ transplantation with the requirement that family offer consent without coercion. In today's highly mobile world where people of diverse backgrounds often interact, it would be useful to develop a consensus on organ transplantation among the varied religious traditions. Organ donation and its controversies will be explored further in this chapter.

The daughter who came storming into the end-of-life scene most likely did not participate in family discussions and decision making. Discordant events of this kind are common. Ideally, the person whose life is coming to an end and all family members would develop a shared understanding: "This is what would be best. This is what would be right for all of us." Doctors and nurses who are called upon to serve the terminally ill patient must cope with mixed messages and family conflict when end-of-life considerations have not been discussed and resolved.

Fortunately, every day there are people who are discharged alive and viable after an episode in an intensive care unit (ICU). Every day, however, there are people whose lives end in an ICU, despite all that medical and nursing care can offer. The end-of-life literature has been silent about the use of physical restraints in critical care settings. Nevertheless, the possibility of physical restraints might well be added to the elements of end-of-life decision making. Local hospital policy and practice has much to do with use of restraints, as do staffing patterns and patient characteristics such as advanced age, presence of invasive devices, and cognitive impairment (Mathisen,

2005). The decision to seek continuation of aggressive medical care increases the possibility that restraints might be used. Millie Morrisey's final days (Field & Cassel, 1997) would have been less frightening and more comforting in a palliative care setting.

Some people find decision making stressful. Others characteristically make and unmake decisions with their minds in a revolving-door mode. Furthermore, the increased emphasis on individual autonomy is hard on people who are accustomed to relying on others or discussions with family or friends. The idea that all individuals should make decisions for themselves has a lot of appeal in societies that laud individual personality and achievement. Not everybody shares that view, however.

There are many world cultures within which the family is clearly the center of life. Furthermore, respect for the past may be no less important than what one achieves in the future. This way of life may be accompanied by the deeply held belief that people can do little to alter their fate: It is in the hands of the gods. An overemphasis on individual decision making, then, runs the risk of making "deviates" or "failures" of a great many people who are simply moving along a well-trodden path as did many generations before them.

Suppose, though, that we are people who are interested in having our own wishes expressed and honored. How would we go about it? We would become familiar with the opportunities afforded by advance directives.

THE LIVING WILL AND ITS IMPACT

Advance directives are instructions for actions to be taken in the future if certain events occur and if we are not able to speak for ourselves at the time.

The living will was the first advance directive to receive general attention in the United States. It was introduced in 1968 by a nonprofit organization that was ahead of its time in educating public and professionals about end-of-life options. (Then known as the Euthanasia Educational Council, it later was renamed

Concern for Dying.) The original living will is presented in Box 6-1.

People were encouraged to add other specific statements between the introductory text and the signature, although few did. The living will played a valuable role in stimulating awareness of death-related issues. Communication increased somewhat between individuals and their families, physicians, nurses, ministers, and lawyers. Over the years there has been increasing public acceptance of the living will in principle, although at the most about one person in five has actually completed the document.

The living will, however, proved to have limited effectiveness. Its lack of specificity made it difficult for physicians to respond. It could be difficult to honor the patient's wishes as generally expressed in the document and at the same time exercise one's medical judgment in the actual ongoing situation. Even physicians who were in sympathy with the patient's request felt uncertain about the legal and ethical implications of withholding procedures that might extend life.

BOX 6-1   THE LIVING WILL

My Living Will

To My Family, My Physician, My Lawyer, and All Others Whom It May Concern

Death is as much a reality as birth, growth, maturity, and old age. If the time comes when I can no longer take part in decisions for my own future, let this statement stand as an expression of my wishes and directions, while I am still of sound mind.

If at such a time the situation should arise in which there is no reasonable expectation of my recovery from extreme physical or mental disability, I direct that I be allowed to die and not be kept alive by medications, artificial means, or "heroic measures." I do, however, ask that medication be mercifully administered to me to alleviate suffering even though this may shorten my remaining life.

This statement is made after careful consideration and is in accordance with my strong convictions and beliefs. I want the wishes and directions here expressed carried out to the extent permitted by law. Insofar as they are not legally enforceable, I hope that those to whom this Will is addressed will regard themselves as morally bound by these provisions.

DURABLE POWER OF ATTORNEY (optional)

I hereby designate _____ to serve as my attorney-in-fact for the purpose of making medical treatment decisions. This power of attorney shall remain effective in the event that I become incompetent or otherwise unable to make such decisions for myself.

Signed _____

Optional Notarization: Date _____

"Sworn and subscribed to Witness before me this _____ day of _____ 20 ____"

Witness Address _____

Notary Seal Address _____

(Optional). My Living Will is registered with Concern for Dying

(Number _____).

The standard living will did not address questions of this specificity.

Furthermore, the fact that a person had completed a living will did not guarantee that it would come to the attention of physicians and other health care personnel when it really counted. Having a document registered by the office of a New York–based organization did not necessarily mean that a physician in Pocatello, Idaho, or a paramedic in Nashville, Tennessee, would have this information readily available. Newer types of advance directives have attempted to provide more specific guidance to care providers and to integrate the information more securely in health care systems.

RIGHT-TO-DIE DECISIONS THAT WE CAN MAKE

The living will stirred up interest, hope, and anxiety. As we will see in Chapter 9, troubling questions arose about the right to refuse treatment and the kind of evidence that should be required as proof of the person's intentions. The right to refuse treatment gained support as courts upheld the principle of informed consent, which requires that in all situations patients receive adequate information about the nature of the procedures and the potential risks as well as benefits. It was no longer a process limited to life-threatened or terminally ill individuals.

We consider now some of the major developments in advance directives since the introduction of the original living will.

From Living Will to Patient Self-Determination Act

State legislatures hesitated, and then complied with, the public's request to have a legal foundation placed under the living will declaration. Starting with California in 1976, every state passed a "natural death act" (also known as "death with dignity" and "living will" acts). Two significant transfers of power from the state to the individual are embodied in these measures:

- The law recognizes a mentally competent adult's right to refuse life support procedures (such as machines to assist respiration and circulation).

- Individuals are entitled to select representatives who will see that their instructions are carried out if the individual is not able to do so. A patient who can no longer speak, for example, should be able to count upon his or her appointed health care agent to safeguard the terms of the advance directive. These agents are often known as health care proxies. The responsibility assigned to this person is usually known as durable power of attorney for health care. It is not required, however, that the agent or proxy actually be an attorney.

Even these significant new laws, however, did not guarantee that the intentions would be respected in practice. Part of the problem can be traced to the health care system's previous unfamiliarity with such documents. Physicians and hospital administrators were not accustomed to having patients tell them what they could and could not do. There was also the problem of integrating an advance directive into the health care communication system. Where should the document itself be located? How many copies should be made? How can patients be sure that anybody will actually look at their living wills when the time comes? These problems were especially common in the early days of the living will and are still encountered today.

The lack of clarity and detail in the living will itself remained a problem. Newer advance directive forms therefore encouraged people to be more specific. This opportunity requires a willingness to think about end-of-life issues and also to gain some familiarity with medical concepts and issues. It has become clear that many people (including professional care providers) do not complete advance directives. Members of ethnic groups with a tendency to distrust the health care system and a reluctance to disclose their feelings to strangers have a low rate of participation in the advance directive process (Searight & Gafford, 2005). Cultural traditions of avoiding discussion of death and dying also contribute to this reluctance. People with decisional incapacity often have difficulty in comprehending advance directives and, therefore, do not participate in the process (Hardin & Yusufaly, 2004). Useful suggestions have been offered for making advance directives easier to comprehend, including the substitution of oral statements to physicians in place of written directives. Whatever the decision we reach, we will probably know ourselves better and be in a better position to help family and friends who may also be considering this option.

We can begin the process immediately by responding to the questions presented in Table 6-1. These questions explore our readiness to consider and discuss end-of-life issues in general.

In prefacing *The Rules and Exercises of Holy Dying* (1651/1970), Jeremy Taylor observed that:

> It is a great art to die well, and to be learned by men in health, by them that can discourse and consider, by whose understanding and acts of reason are not abated with fear or pains: and as the greatest part of death is passed by the preceding years of our life, so also in those years are the greatest preparations to it . . . (p. iv–v).

Taylor's advice is perhaps even more relevant today because the options for technological prolongation of life have so greatly increased and, as we have seen, the legal and moral dimensions have also become more complex.

We are ready now for Table 6-2, which presents several of the key decision points that should be specified in an advanced health care directive if we want to convey specific instructions to health care providers. It might be stressful to think our way through each of these decision points, but doing so will reduce the stress and ambiguity for the health care service providers who we depend upon to honor our requests. Put bluntly, we need to take responsibility to make and communicate our own decisions in the clearest possible manner if we expect others to take responsibility for respecting these decisions.

College Students' Attitudes Toward End-of-Life Issues

The last item in Table 6-2 is taken from a study of college students in history of medicine and sociology classes at the University of Rochester (Karnik, Kamel, & Harper, 2002).

Most of the respondents did choose one or more of the life-sustaining options. Major surgery, perhaps the most familiar of the choices, was also the choice most frequently made. There were no significant differences in choices made by the women and the men. There were differences, though, in relationship to ethnic background.

TABLE 6-1

My Readiness to Explore and Discuss Personal End-of-Life Issues

Yes	No	
___	___	1. I feel ready to consider all the issues that are related to the end of my life.
___	___	2. I intend to discuss at least some of these issues thoroughly with at least one other person whose views matter to me.
___	___	3. I intend to require of my physicians that they provide me with all the information I need to guide my decision making in a prompt, comprehensive, and honest manner.
___	___	4. I intend to select or create a document that communicates my preferences regarding treatment during the terminal phase of life.
___	___	5. I intend to designate a person to represent my preferences and interests in the event that I become incapacitated.
___	___	6. I intend to review and, if appropriate, modify my will and other legal instruments to ensure that they represent my final wishes in an effective way.
___	___	7. I intend to review my most significant relationships and take whatever steps are needed to resolve lingering problems and to renew and strengthen mutual ties.
___	___	8. I intend to do all that is possible to provide the opportunity for meaningful leave-taking interactions with the people in my life.
___	___	9. I intend to convey my preferences regarding burial/cremation and funeral services to those who will be responsible for making the arrangements.
___	___	10. I intend to review and reflect upon what is of most importance to me in life and to devote much of my remaining time and energies to these core values.

TABLE 6-2
Advance Directive Requests

Yes	No	
——	——	1. I want all life-sustaining treatments to be discontinued if I become terminally ill and permanently incompetent.
——	——	2. I want all life-sustaining treatments to be discontinued if I become permanently unconscious, whether terminally ill or not.
——	——	3. I want all life-sustaining treatments to be discontinued if I become unconscious and have very little chance of ever recovering consciousness or avoiding permanent brain injury.
——	——	4. I want to be kept alive if I become gravely ill and have only a slight chance of recovery (5% or less) and would probably require weeks or months of further treatment before the outcome became clear.
——	——	5. I want to have fluids and nutrition discontinued if other life support measures are discontinued.
——	——	6. Five types of possible life-sustaining options are listed below. If you were seriously ill, which of these options would you choose? (You can choose more than one.)

Choose	Do Not Choose	
——	——	Ventilator or other artificial means
——	——	Artificial nutrition or hydration
——	——	Kidney dialysis
——	——	Major surgery
——	——	Do not resuscitate order

African Americans (72%) were the most likely to request life-sustaining measures in general—but least likely to ask for a do not resuscitate (DNR) order. (The researchers here seemed to have stumbled a bit in classifying DNR as a life-sustaining option: By rejecting DNR, the African American students were in effect saying that they did want resuscitation efforts.) Hispanics (47%) were the least likely to request life-sustaining measures, with whites (59%) in the middle. There was also an Asian sample but from such diverse nations and cultures that it did not seem appropriate to consider them as a unitary group.

What about religious faith? Atheists were the least likely to request a DNR order. In other words, they preferred to take advantage of a last chance to continue this life. There were only small differences in life-sustaining option choices among Catholics, Jews, and Protestants.

The researchers have additional comments to offer as they draw upon interviews with the participants and results of other studies. They note that African Americans tend to receive less intense medical care than whites and to be more negatively stereotyped than other patients. There is concern that the quality of care would be further diminished if a DNR were posted. Mexican American families are reported as having more hope for recovery, so families would feel guilty if they declined any life support measure.

Students of nursing were the most reluctant to accept life-prolonging treatments and the most supportive of DNR orders. "Nursing students were probably the most familiar with the concept of DNR . . . and the limits of modern medicine, and thus approached the questions more from a health care provider's point of view" (p. 5).

Advance Medical Directives: What Should We Do?

Many people think an advance medical directive is a good idea, but relatively few have actually taken this step. (Confession: It is only by this tenth edition that the author of this textbook got around to preparing his advance directive, and then only because he heard the "rustle of angel wings.")

Useful guidance to advance directives is offered by attorney Charles P. Sabatino (2005). He sets several pertinent facts in front of us:

• Advance directives are legal in every state.
• An advance directive legal in one state generally will be legal in all others. There may be

some difference in terminology between the versions, but adjustments are made so that the basic expressed wish of the patient is respected.

- Advance medical directives do not restrict treatment efforts within generally accepted medical standards. Pain control and comfort care are continued, as is any treatment that does not attempt to keep patients alive against their wishes.
- We can use a form approved by our home states or can revise it to better express our own concerns and preferences. Sabatino (2005) declares that "it is a mistake to pick up an 'official' form and just sign it unchanged, without first being sure that it truly reflects one's specific wishes" (p. 1).
- A lawyer is not needed to complete a legal and effective form, though could be a useful resource if questions arise.
- Doctors and other health care providers are legally obligated to follow an advance directive. This was not the case in the past, notably with the living will (LW). Medical providers cannot treat us against our wishes. Having said this, we should recognize that there are complexities and ambiguities in the link between preparing a directive and guaranteeing that it will be honored. We can improve the chances by expressing ourselves precisely and selecting a competent health care proxy. Even so, a sudden life-or-death crisis might not make it possible to retrieve and apply the directive. In many states, paramedics are still required to resuscitate and stabilize accident victims to rush them to the hospital. This situation might change in the next few years.

Sometimes the patient and family must take the initiative to encourage health care personnel to discuss end-of-life experiences with them. There is a lingering fear in the medical tradition that people just cannot deal with dying and death. Research says otherwise (e.g., Emanuel et al., 2004), as does more than three decades of experience in the death awareness movement.

Sabatino and others recommend that our first decisive step should be the selection of a health care proxy, a person with the ability to represent our wishes and see that they are fulfilled if we are unable to do so ourselves. The next formal step is completion of the advance directive itself. We can

obtain a valid form by contacting the American Bar Association or its local chapter, our state's department of health services, or our medical service provider. I would also suggest that you visit the Aging with Dignity website (www. agingwithdignity. org) and become familiar with its version of the advance directive. Valid in many but not all states, this document is instructive for the opportunities it offers to consider our options and preferences.

The Combined Advance Directive

A promising new development might encourage more people to complete an advance directive (AD) and also improve the chances that it will be readily available when needed. The combined advance directive (CAD) is more comprehensive than the forms previously available. It therefore provides the opportunity for people to consider the full range of end-of-life options and share their questions and views with their families, friends, and professional service providers. Because all the individual's preferences are included in a single document, it is easier to put on record and distribute.

Several versions of the CAD have been developed by concerned and informed citizens, and additional versions can be expected. The instrument articulated by the Vermont Ethics Network (2006) is particularly worth considering for clarity and accessibility. The complete form with instructions is available as a download (www.vtethicsnetwork.org).

The first of five sections offers a guide to selecting an agent and alternative for making health care decisions if the situation should arise. The second section presents treatment wishes: preferences for accepting or stopping treatment to keep one alive under certain circumstances. The items are clear and detailed which is an improvement over the vague language in some previous documents. The basic list is augmented by "specific care wishes near the end of my life." Here one can address three significant issues: (1) "I want sufficient pain medication even though it may hasten my death; (2) I want hospice care when I am dying, if possible and appropriate; (3) I prefer to die at home, if this is possible." A person can

Baseball great Ted William's death was followed by controversy and outrage when his head was separated from his body and placed in liquid nitrogen storage.

check any, all, or none of these options. Another feature of this section is the opportunity to share one's spiritual and other care concerns. This has been somewhat neglected in previous documents.

Organ donation is the subject of the third section. It is not as detailed as some documents that have been devised specifically for organ donation, but is concise and informative. Section four takes us to "My wishes for disposition of my remains after my death," and the concluding section presents the "signed declaration of wishes." It also includes the important reminder to list people and locations that will have a copy of this document.

With and Without an Advance Directive

The SUPPORT study (1995) delivered a double dose of disappointment for those concerned with advance directives and the larger issue of patient-physician communication. As summarized in Chapter 5, the study first documented a pervasive pattern of medical indifference to the wishes of life-threatened and terminally ill people. An intervention was then conducted to improve medical responsivity, but it failed rather miserably. A research team has recently examined the role of advance directives more than a decade after both the SUPPORT study and introduction of the Patient Self-Determination Act (Teno et al., 2007). Focus was on people who died in a nursing home, in a hospital, or at home with hospice, with a total sample of more than fifteen hundred individuals. The follow-up information was obtained from bereaved family members or other knowledgeable informants.

Most of these people—about seven out of ten—did have an advance directive (AD). Those who died in a hospital were the least likely to have an AD. There were two clear differences in the experiences of people with and without an AD during their end-of-life period. Fewer people with an AD were on a respirator or intubated for feeding. This differential can be interpreted as more compliance with a patient's wish to limit medical interventions; it can also be interpreted as receiving more efficient care to avoid the need for respirator and feeding tube. Physician communication with patient and family was perceived as more problematic when no AD had been prepared. Bereaved family members in these situations more often felt that the physicians were not keeping them well informed.

This study suggests that there are advantages to completing and presenting an AD. Nevertheless, even with an AD, about one of four patients experienced inadequate pain control, and half were reported to have received inadequate emotional support. The researchers note that much still remains to be done if terminally ill people are to receive the highest possible quality of care.

A RIGHT *NOT* TO DIE? THE CRYONICS ALTERNATIVE

Do we have a right *not* to die? Even if we are dead? Did Walt Disney make this choice, and should "The Splendid Splinter" have been given the opportunity to stand again in the late-inning shadows of Fenway Park and glare at a nervous pitcher? The answer to the first question is clear: Disney was not placed in cryostasis, despite rumors to the contrary. The second question runs afoul of the persistent issue of who might deserve a second chance of life, and who should make the final decision.

The cryonics alternative has been available since 1967 when the first person chose to have his certified dead body placed in a hypothermic (frozen) condition for possible of resuscitation at a later time. I did not meet Dr. James H. Bedford personally, but paused for a moment by the aluminum chamber that holds his physical remains at the Alcor Life Extension Foundation in Scottsdale, Arizona. Bedford, a psychologist, was the first person to test the possibilities of cryonic preservation and restoration with his own body. Stephen Bridge, former Alcor director, helped to transfer Bedford from his original cylinder to a newer model in 1984. He observes that Bedford looked as "healthy" as when first placed into cryostasis. Bedford is 1 of about 50 at that facility (precise numbers are difficult to pry from cryonic sources). One of the others is the mother of R. C. W. Ettinger whose best-selling book, *The Prospect of Immortality* (1966) brought keen but fleeting attention to the subject. Most other people in cryostasis with Alcor or other facilities have requested that their identities be kept confidential.

Relatively few people were aware of the cryonics movement until the controversy following Ted Williams' death in 2002. There were conflicting reports about Williams' own intentions, and dissension among his surviving family members. The sports community was appalled by the unseemly family dispute, but even more by the image of the near-legendary baseball player's body being "kept on ice," as some erroneously characterized the process. The situation took a bizarre turn in 2003 when a former Alcor employee charged that Williams' head had been damaged by careless treatment. These charges were denied and not clearly resolved, but the president of the organization resigned and the state of Arizona imposed additional regulatory authority over Alcor. It is not clear to what extent this episode has damaged the reputation of the cryonics alternative, but it was certainly not the kind of publicity that was desired. The cryonics alternative is worth considering here as a counterbalance to the current emphasis on the right to die. It is also instructive for what the public's response might tell us about our attitudes toward life and death.

Historical Background

The desire to extend our lives is one of the most enduring themes in human history. In pretechnological times it was attempted through physical ordeals, magical spells, secret rituals, and experiments with a variety of substances and concoctions. The impulse for life extension has often been associated with the quest for eternal or restored youth (Gruman, 1966; Kastenbaum, 1995). An ancient Egyptian papyrus offers instructions on how to transform a person of eighty into a youth of twenty (reportedly, some of the suggestions have become incorporated into the modern cosmetic industry). Alchemists whose work eventually prepared the way for the physical sciences hoped to convert base metals such as lead into gold—but hoped even more fervently that they could find the elixir to keep people alive and healthy for many more years. Importing the essence of monkey glands into one's body, or having a coil or two of one's intestines removed was the leading edge of medical optimism well into the twentieth century: no more successful than the ancient maneuvers. So—what does the cryonic approach have on offer?

Rationale and Method

Advocates of the cryonic approach believe it possible to maintain "deceased" people at very low temperatures for long periods of time. Eventually, medical breakthroughs will cure the conditions that led to their "death" (Drexler, 1991). Some believe that resuscitation should wait even longer—until science has turned off or reversed the aging process. Until recently there were two levels of vision: (1) restoring "dead" people to continue their lives where they had left off and (2) not only raising the dead, but equipping them with bodies that will be resistant to aging and mortality. An even more ambitious scenario is now being proposed: growing new bodies from "neuro" preparations preparations (brains only).

This scenario has often been introduced in movies and works of fiction. Nevertheless, there is some connection to demonstrable reality. Surgeons routinely lower the patient's body temperature, especially for lengthy operations. Human sperm and embryos have been maintained in a frozen condition until use— perhaps some readers of this book were given their lives in this manner. There has been some success in preserving body parts and even whole animals in a hypothermic state. In short, cryonic procedures have a significant place in biomedical procedures. These applications, however, are a long way from preservation and revival of a certifiably dead human being.

The basic rationale is that we have a right to live, and to seek extended survival. Cryonicists are sensitive about the criticism that it is selfish to desire a second chance at life. The fact that this alternative seems limited to people with adequate financial resources is troubling from the ethical standpoint: perhaps cryonics would turn out to be another example of elitism and discrimination? Is the cryonic alternative a legitimate exercise of individual rights, or a demonstration of excessive ego?

The cryonics procedure cannot begin until a physician has certified the patient as dead. To begin the procedure earlier could be considered homicide. A team of cryonicists immediately lower the body temperature and give injections to protect vital organs, while a heart–lung machine circulates the cryoprotectant agents that are intended to protect against the hypothermic process. The body is brought to the nearest cryonics facility, where further preparations are made and the cooled and wrapped body is placed into a cylinder filled with liquid nitrogen. The cryonic organization maintains the level of liquid nitrogen (which is subject to evaporation over time) and ensures the integrity of the protective chamber. And sooner or later, or perhaps never, biomedical advances will make it possible to thaw, resuscitate, and cure the person of "temporary death."

No such attempts have yet been reported at Alcor, the largest of the life extension foundations, or any other facility. Medical and scientific advisors to the cryonic movement have thus far stated that resuscitation techniques have not yet advanced to the point where such an attempt would be feasible.

Heads of Stone: A Radical New Development

The methods already described have been improved somewhat over time, notably in the effectiveness of the cryoprotectants to prevent formation of crystals as a result of freezing. More recently, there have been two major changes: (1) neural (head-only) preservation has replaced whole-body preservation, and (2) the cooled tissues are vitrified (transformed into a stone-like substance).

Why preserve only the head? Less cost, takes less space. And it is the brain, not the head, that is the focus.

What is vitrification? It's a process that replaces the fluid inside cells with antifreeze compounds. The temperature is then dropped way down, to − 130°C. The result is a rigid stone-like structure that is actually a form of glass. The vitrified tissues are considered to be no longer subject to biochemical processes and are expected to remain stable indefinitely. Vitrification has had other uses in medical research and education (including Dr. von Hagen's plastinates, Chapter 2), so it is a new application rather than a new process. Like earlier forms of cryostasis, though, no attempts have yet been made to reverse the process.

Vitrification requires an extra leap of faith .Two leaps, actually—first, that an entire body can be regenerated from neural DNA and, second, that glass can again become flesh. Cryonicists believe that whole-body regeneration will become feasible as cloning experiments continue. In the past, people who considered the cryonic alternative could at least envision a whole body (head and all) keeping cool until the time came for resuscitation. It is asking much more of people to imagine a glass–stone head that will morph a new or renewed person.

The switch to vitrification has been defended as a more refined, as well as less expensive, procedure. Alexander (2003), however, offers a critical perspective. He reports that by the end of the twentieth century cryonicists admitted to themselves that:

> People frozen before the late 1990s were goners. The old methods were just too crude. Alcor and the other cryonic outfits kept them frozen out of a sense of sacred duty, respect for the pioneers, and the slim chance that in some great technological leap, all the cells popped by ice crystals, all the cracked, mushy organs could somehow be repaired. . . . But when they weren't putting on a brave face, even the boundless optimism of the most ardent cryonicist gave way to the recognition that the prospects for even the more recently chilled were pretty iffy (pp. 232–233).

More Questions

Here are some other questions that are far from settled. What do you think? Should we regard cryostasis:

1. As body preservation, like mummification?
2. As body disposal (cryo-remains)?
3. As an affront to God and Nature or just one more life-prolongation effort among others?
4. As *denial* of, or *resistance* to, death?
5. As the potential realization of a long-cherished human desire or just a fantasy that affluent people can afford?
6. As a new chapter in the ancient mythology of the journeys of the dead or in the related stories of a sleeping beauty waiting to be warmed by a lover's kiss?
7. As a fantasy addition to a category of "sleepers" who are neither living nor dead in the traditional senses of the terms?

Having left so many questions for your own consideration, I will venture an observation on one more issue. Counting all of Alcor's guests, there seem to be fewer than 100 cremains in the entire world. Although several hundred people have reportedly signed up for possible cryostasis, this is an astoundingly small number of people who have attempted to overcome death with this technological option. Few of the cryonic organizations that were established in the early days of the movement seem to be operational today. Social and behavioral scientists have given little attention to this phenomenon. I must rely upon a study I conducted back in the 1960s, in which most respondents firmly rejected cryonic suspension even though they were open to many other end-of-life possibilities. "Freeze—wait—reanimate!," the slogan of the time, was a bad idea, and also a scary one.

The tragedy of a fatal motor vehicle accident can sometimes result in the availability of organs to save another person's life. Quick action is necessary to make this a possibility.

Often mentioned was the fear of overstepping the human domain: It's not for us to challenge the mortality to which God has consigned us. There was also much concern about loss and distortion of relationships. ("If I come back young, and my wife is old . . ."; "I wouldn't want to come back alone, without my people.") Others were distressed by the idea of losing so much control, along with being distrustful of how their fate would be managed by others. Although few said so explicitly, there was also a fear akin to being buried alive. It must also be said that more than four decades after Dr. Bradford's venture into cryospace, there has still not been anything resembling a breakthrough in demonstrating the effectiveness of this procedure.

ORGAN DONATION

Organ donation stands in marked contrast to the hope of cryonic resuscitation. Registering one's self as an organ donor improves the chances of another person's survival. The organs most sought for transplantation are kidneys and livers. Hearts, heart–lung sets, intestines, and pancreas are also on the waiting list. Unfortunately, the demand is far greater than the supply. Many people wait anxiously for their turn—which might or might not come in time. Approximately 75,000 people are on the waiting list in the United States at any point in time, and approximately 6,000 die each year while waiting (Joyce & Williams, 2003).

Successful Organ Transplantation

Five factors clearly have restraining influences on the number of successful transplantations: (a) willingness of people to donate, (b) condition of the donated organs, (c) biological match between donor and recipient to avoid rejection, (d) whether the overall condition of the recipient is strong enough to ensure survival with the new organ, even if it is not rejected, and (e) expense and timely delivery. Furthermore, health care professionals may be caught in a stressful situation: required by federal regulations to ask families for permission, yet hesitant to impose on the grieving survivors, especially when the death occurred in a sudden and unexpected manner.

Organs are sometimes donated by living people who are likely to survive their anatomical gift (often a kidney). In these circumstances, it is possible to plan carefully for the future. Most often, living people donate organs to family members or others they know, but anonymous donations to unknown recipients are becoming less uncommon. There has been a steady increase in the number of living donors, but this still amounts to only approximately 7,000 people a year. Cadaveric donations remain the most common source for transplants. (The occasion for cadaveric donations often arises with little or no advance notice and requires prompt identification and action.) Victims of fatal motor vehicle accidents are some of the most available sources. Organ donations by the living have increased over time, but the dead still contribute a little more than half of the organs transplanted each year (United Network for Organ Sharing, 2004). The situation is further complicated by the revelation that about a third of the people listed as waiting for an organ transplant are not eligible because of health or other complications (Stein, 2008).

Competition, Tension, Controversy

Competition has spurred conflict. For example, should an available organ go to the person who is in the most need and has the highest probability of surviving with it—or to a person who resides in the local area from which the donation was received? There is also concern that some potential recipients face discrimination. Charges of discrimination against recipients on the basis of ethnicity or race have been made from time to time, but such a practice would violate accepted standards of care.

There is also concern that disadvantaged people may be selling their organs for use by those who are more affluent. Authorities in India remain concerned about the illegal but prospering sale of organs from living human donors (Devraj, 2002). Authorities condemn this practice both on ethical and biomedical grounds: the donors, already suffering hardships and deprivations, increase their own risks of death. How common and widespread this practice may be has not yet been determined. It does stand as a compelling example of how a society's death system can virtually cannibalize itself.

Anthropologist Margaret Lock offers a penetrating analysis of organ transplantation from a sociocultural standpoint in *Twice Dead* (2002). In Japan, for example, the exchange of gifts is closely woven into the social fabric. Although a kidney is a distinctive and nontraditional gift, the offer nevertheless occurs within a strong pattern of exchange and therefore might constitute an expected kind of behavior. Within Christianity, organ donation can accord with "the biblical sense of charity." There are aspects of organ donation, however, that can create confusion and frustration. For example, many Americans prefer having the opportunity to choose who will receive their organs. This desire runs counter to the needs and practices of the health care system. Prejudices can also complicate a prospective transplantation gift. People may have difficulty, for example, accepting voluntary organ donations from death-row prisoners. Lock quotes a transplant surgeon regarding this situation:

> He said to me, with some embarrassment, "I wouldn't like to have a murderer's heart put into my body," then added hastily, glancing at my tape recorder and trying to make a joke out of the situation, "I might find myself starting to change" (p. 320).

Most recipients are matter-of-fact about the source of their organs, but some feel emotionally linked to the donors and believe that their lives have changed because of this intimate connection with another person.

The organ donation and distribution system continues to be marked by tension and controversy. The relationship between organ donation and the diagnosis of brain death has been a subject of concern for years (Chapter 2): Would the pressure for quick harvesting of organs lead to premature certification of death? This issue has become more salient in recent years because of a practice known as "donation after cardiac death" (DCD). Previously, most organs were removed only after a patient was certified as brain dead. The new procedure, advocated by federal health officials, transplant surgeons, and organ banks, involves removal within minutes after the heart stops beating (Stein, 2007). It is used most frequently when family members have agreed to have life-support efforts terminated after a motor vehicle accident or stroke. The number of DCD procedures is rapidly increasing. Health care organizations are faced with the question of whether or not this practice should be allowed in their facilities. Advocates point to the opportunity for harvesting more usable organs and distributing them more rapidly to those who so urgently need them. However, some doctors and bioethicists fear that transplant surgeons might pressure families to discontinue treatment, thereby compromising their terminal care, or even hastening their deaths. At present, many hospital organizations are in the process of deciding about the advisability of using the DCD procedure.

Another approach was mentioned at start of this chapter: how about operating a survival lottery for people in need of an organ or issue transplant? Several types of lottery have been proposed since the mid 1970s. In its most dramatic form, everyone in the waiting pool would be a potential donor for everybody else (Harris, 1994). This donor would be selected by a random and presumably fair process, the anatomical gift then made available to another person in the waiting pool, again by random drawing. Needless to say, this plan has not yet been put into action (as far as is known). It has remained, though, as a stimulus to bioethicists who are searching for some fair way out of the supply/demand dilemma. Overland (2007) has recently taken up this challenge. He suggests there is still merit in the survival lottery proposal, though there are prickly details to be resolved. Is this a direction that should be encouraged? Would you welcome a survival lottery for yourself or your loved ones if on a list for organ transplantation?

Becoming a Donor

"Should I register as a prospective organ or tissue donor?" This is obviously a personal decision that is likely to be influenced by our life experiences and worldview. Sometimes, though, the decision is clouded by uncertainties regarding the process. Fortunately, there is detailed and reliable information readily available. It is widely recognized that acquiring and distributing anatomical gifts is a sensitive process that needs to be regulated in the best interests of everybody involved. You will find an authoritative presentation of the Revised Uniform Anatomical Gift Act (National Conference, 2006, revised 2007) available for download (http://law. upenn.edu) and at other sites. It is also worth checking out the version of this Act that has been adopted by your state government (e.g., State of Arizona, 2007). It is probable that most of your questions will be answered by these documents; if not, inquiries can be made to your local government and organ banks.

One point is particularly worth noting: the participation of a *disinterested witness* is required when a person "makes, amends, revokes or refuses to make an anatomical gift" (State of Arizona, p. 1). This is a person who is not eligible to receive an anatomical gift and is not a relative or guardian of the person making the decision. This provision is among the safeguards to protect the independence of decision making.

It is useful to think ahead of time regarding details of the donation. Do you wish to donate any and all organs or tissues, or are there some you would prefer to exclude? Do you wish to make this anatomical gift available for whatever purpose it proves to be most suitable: therapy, education, or research? Or would you prefer to limit the use? These can be difficult questions to consider, but a little easier to deal with when given advance thought.

FUNERAL-RELATED DECISIONS

The funeral and memorialization process is discussed in Chapter 12. Individual decision making, though, can benefit from acquiring specific information, exploring alternatives, and discussing the situation with the important people in our lives. We will focus on the practical matters of funeral and burial costs and arrangements.

It sounds rather cold to think of ourselves as "consumers" of funeral and burial services, but this is part of the reality. Here are several useful suggestions that have been passed along by the American Association for Retired People (AARP) as well as other public interest groups:

- Funeral homes are required to provide price lists at their place of business and some will mail the information. Although prices can also be disclosed by telephone, it is a good idea to have a written list that includes all options.
- Do thorough comparison shopping. The differences can be significant. Look at separate price lists for general services, caskets, and outer burial containers, rather than only at an overall cost estimate.
- Be aware of additional charges for additional services and products. For example, many funeral homes will prepare obituary notices or provide music, but for an additional charge.
- Do not hesitate to inquire about simple and immediate burials or about cremation. Again, check to learn what services are included in the basic fee.
- The most expensive single item in a traditional funeral is the casket. Be aware that you can choose to purchase a casket from the Internet or other outside source and that a funeral home cannot charge you extra for this.
- Resist agreeing to add-on services or products unless these are what you and your family really want.

There has been increasing pressure on the public in recent years to plan funerals well in advance and often to commit their money in advance as well. This development is part of a major change in the funeral industry. The family-owned community funeral home is rapidly being taken over or displaced by corporate expansion. Even though a familiar family name might still be seen on signs and advertisements, it could be that your local funeral home has become a franchise operation with national or international headquarters elsewhere. Funeral director Thomas Lynch (1997) is among the critics of this trend:

> The firm in the next town was bought out last year by Service Corporation International (SCI)—The Big Mac of the mortuary trade. They own most of Paris and Australia, a lot of London and Manhattan. They buy guys like me. They want the brick and mortar, the fifty years of trading on the family name. They want to be like one of the family, mine and yours. At the moment these multinational firms own a fifth of the mortuary dollar volume in the United States. They are in a hurry to own more and more (pp. 174–175).

Many others are concerned about the mega-corporate influence on funeral services. Funeral directors were once among the most respected citizens in small town America (Holloway, 2002). Their families did know the families who came to them in time of need. Prepaid funeral and burial arrangements can be useful to some people, but caution is recommended.

A Perspective on End-of-Life Decisions

Society is actively engaged in rethinking and restructuring the ways in which we treat each other near the end of life. Both the general public and health care professionals may at times feel uncomfortable because the rules have been changing. We are now being asked to make decisions that usually seemed to have made themselves. The physician generally was in the position of unquestioned decision maker. These decisions often flowed from the belief that one should do everything that might be done to extend life, even if there was little or no hope of success. On occasion the decision could be made (quietly, unobtrusively) to withhold or withdraw cure-oriented treatment to spare the patient further suffering. Now the physician is expected to share decision making with patient and family and to be responsive as well to other health care professionals and legislative measures.

The new social and medical climate for end-of-life decisions favors strengthened participation, communication, and patients' rights. More physicians themselves have become active in this cause. And Millie Morrisey's distress was soon alleviated. The nursing home staff did become aware of her wishes and quickly removed the ventilator and offered her comfort care that resulted in a peaceful death a few days later (Field & Cassel, 1997). Furthermore, shaken by this experience, the nursing home made changes in its policies and practices to prevent such a situation from happening again.

We are in a difficult but promising situation: More people are concerned about making end-of-life decisions that respect patient and family wishes, but how to do this in an effective and timely way is a challenge that still must be addressed by the health care system as well as individuals. There may also be crucial personal situations to resolve. Should the terminally ill

person try to overcome years of grudges and negative feelings toward a family member or friend? Is it better to hold onto the anger or to seek resolution? Or is it the terminally ill person's relationship with God that needs to find resolution one way or another? Still again, there may be a strong need to complete a project or mission. Near the end of his life, J. S. Bach (1685–1750) was so weakened by illness that his family tried to persuade him to remain in bed. He wouldn't have that. Instead he devoted practically every waking hour to *Art of Fugue*, one of the most remarkable compositions from one of the world's most remarkable composers. His mental and emotional powers remained at their peak despite his rapidly failing health. There are not many J. S. Bachs with such a monumental project to complete near the end of their lives, but there are others among us who have endeavors they are deeply committed to seeing through as long as possible. End-of-life decisions can take many

Johann Sebastian Bach continued to compose his monumental
Art of Fugue until very nearly his last breath.

forms, so we are well advised to be sensitive to the special needs of every individual.

SUMMARY

The responsibility for end-of-life decisions was once largely in the hands of physicians and the health care system. Today there is more opportu-nity for patients and their families to participate in decision making. However, not everybody feels prepared to exercise control over the medical interventions that should be attempted near the end of their lives. Some people most highly value the option of individual choice; others function within a tradition that favors family or faith-based decision making. There is growing awareness that more attention should be given to patient and family ethnic background and values.

The *living will* was the first advance directive to gain wide attention. This document stimulated widespread discussion of end-of-life issues. All states now have enacted legislation based upon the *living will* concept that people should have the right to limit the kind of treatment they receive near the end of their lives. Courts established the principle of *informed consent,* which supports individual choice. The federal government subsequently enacted the *Patient Self-Determination Act,* with the intention of increasing patient participation and hospital compliance. All these measures have had some success in providing patients and families with more choice in end-of-life health care options, but difficulties still persist. Research indicates that people who have prepared an advance directive do receive a pattern of terminal care that is closer to their own preferences. The *combined advance directive* is a new development that enables a person to express end-of-life preferences across a comprehensive range of issues: treatment wishes (including spiritual concerns), organ donation, and funeral arrangements. This document holds promise for encouraging more reflection and discussion of the end-of-life situation, as well as providing a single source for those who will be responsible for carrying out the individual's wishes.

The right to request limitation or termination of treatment was contrasted with the desire to do everything possible that might extend or renew life. The cryonic approach (earlier carrying the slogan, "Freeze—wait—reanimate!") was discussed as one of the more salient and extreme examples.

Organ donations (also known as anatomical gifts) are a much more demonstrably effective end-of-life option that has contributed directly and indirectly to the survival of many people. However, there is a chronic shortage of organs and tissues. People in need can wait only so long for the organ or tissue that could keep them going. The limited supply of available organs and tissues has generated intense anxieties and controversies. One example is the accelerated process for removing organs immediately after cardiac failure: praised for its efficiency, and criticized for a possible bias toward "premature harvesting" and disregard for the dying person. Proposals for a "survival lottery" are receiving a mixed reception, but many people are seeking ways to improve the current stressful situation of organ transplant distribution.

REFERENCES

Aging with Dignity. www.agingwithdignity.org

Alexander, B. (2003). *Rapture.* New York: Basic Books.

Devraj, R. (2002). HEALTH-INDIA: Legal ban fails to check kidney "exports." www.oneworld.org/ips2/dec00/11

Drexler, K. E. (1991). *Unbounding the future.* New York: Morrow.

Emanuel, E. J., Fairclough, D. L., Wolfe, P., & Emanuel, L. L. (2004). Talking with terminally ill patients and their caregivers about death, dying, and bereavement. *Archives of Internal Medicine, 164,* 1999–2004.

Ettinger, R. C. W. (1966). *The prospect of immortality.* New York: Mcfadden–Bartell.

Field, M. J., & Cassel, C. K. (Eds.). (1997). *Approaching death. Improving care at the end of life.* Washington, DC: National Academy Press.

Go, R. S., Hammes, B. A., Lee, J. A., & Mathiason, M. A. (2007). Advance directives among health care professionals at a community-based cancer center. *Mayo Clinic Proceedings, 82,* 1487–1490.

Golmakani, M. M., Niknam, M. H., & Hedayat, K. M. (2005). Transplantation ethics from the Islamic point of view. *Medical Science Monitor, 11,* RA105–109.

Gresham, S. D., & Gresham, G. E. (2005, June 1). Preparing for the end. www.highbeam.com/library/doc3.asp?DOCID5IG1:133007110&num3–5.

Gruman, G. J. (1966). *A history of ideas about the prolongation of life.* Philadelphia: The American Philosophical Society.

Hardin, S. B., & Yusufaly, Y. A. (2004). Difficult end-of-life treatment decisions. *Archives of Internal Medicine, 164,* 1531–1533.

Harris, J. (1994). The survival lottery. In B. Steinbock & A. Norcross (Eds.), *Killing and letting die* (pp. 257–265). New York: Fordham University Press.

Holloway, K. F. C. (2002). *Passed on, African American mourning stories.* Durham, NC: Duke University Press.

Joyce, K. A., & Williams, J. B. (2003). Body recycling. In C. D. Bryant (Ed.), *Handbook of death and dying:* Vol. 2 (pp. 775–783). Thousand Oaks, CA: Sage.

Karnik, A. A., Kamel, H. K., & Harper, D. (2002). Attitudes of college students toward end-of-life issues. *Internet Journal of Pain, Symptom Control, & Palliative Care, 2,* 1–7.

Kastenbaum, R. (1995). *Dorian, graying: Is youth the only thing worth having?* Amityville, New York: Baywood.

Lock, M. (2002). *Twice dead. Organ transplants and the reinvention of death.* Berkeley: University of California Press.

Lynch, T. (1997). *The undertaking. Life studies from the dismal trade.* New York: Penguin.

Mathisen, L. (2005, March 1). Use of physical restraint in adult critical care: A bicultural study. *American Journal of Critical Care.*

National Conference of Commissioners on Uniform State Laws. (2007). Revised Uniform Anatomical Gift Act (2006, revised 2007). www.nccusl.org

Overland, G. (2007). Survival lotteries reconsidered. *Bioethics, 21,* 355–363.

Sabatino, C. P. (2005, June 11). Ten legal myths about advance medical directives. www.abanet.org/aging/myths.html

Searight, H. R., & Gafford, J. (2005). Cultural diversity at the end of life: Issues and guidelines for family physicians. *American Family Physician, 71,* 515–522.

State of Arizona. (2007). Senate Bill 1099. Relating to the Revised Uniform Anatomical Gift Act. www.dnaz.org

Stein, R. (March 18, 2007). New trend in organ donation raises questions. *Arizona Republic,* p, A03.

Stein, R. (March 22, 2008). A third of patients on transplant list are not eligible. *Washington Post,* p. A01.

Taylor, J. (1651/1977). *The rules and exercises of holy dying.* New York: Arno. (Original work published 1651.)

Teno, J. M. Gruneir, A., Schwartz, Z., Nanda, A., & Wetle, T. (2007). Association between advance directives and quality of end-of-life care: A national study. *Journal of the American Geriatric Society,* 55, pp. 189–194.

Vermont Ethics Network (2006). Vermont Advance Directive for Health Care. www.vtethicsnetwork.org

United Network for Organ Sharing. (2004). www.unos.org

GLOSSARY

Advance directive: A legal document that specifies the type of health care an individual wishes to receive should that individual not be in a position to express his or her wishes in a critical situation.

Anatomical gift: A donation of all or part of a human body after the donor's death for the purpose of transplantation, therapy, education, or research.

Combined advanced health care directive: A single document in which the individual can address the full range of decision-making options

Cryonics: An approach that attempts to preserve a body at very low temperatures until medical advances have made it possible to cure the fatal condition.

Cryostasis: The condition of a body being maintained at a very low temperature.

Disinterested witness: A person who is not related to the individual making or revoking an organ donation decision and who would not be a recipient.

Durable power of attorney for health care: The transfer of legal authority to a person who would make health care decisions for a person who at that time is unable to make or communicate his or her own decisions.

Health care proxy: A person officially designated to make end-of-life and other health care decisions for an individual, should that individual be unable to make decisions because of illness or other incapacity.

Informed consent: The principle that patients should be provided with sufficient information to make decisions for or against accepting a treatment.

Living will: The first type of advance directive to be introduced, requesting that no aggressive treatments be attempted if the individual is in the end phase of life.

Patient self-determination act: A federal law that requires health care organizations to provide patients with the informed opportunity to establish an advance directive to limit medical treatment in specified situations.

Physical restraints. Devices such as mitts, bulky dressings, leather wrist straps, and restrictive vests that are sometimes used in hospitals to prevent patients from removing life support connections, falling out of bed, or otherwise injuring themselves.

ON FURTHER THOUGHT . . .

Useful online resources:

Access to End of Life Care.
    www.access2eolcare.org
Aging with Dignity.
    www.agingwithdignity.org
Careplanner.org
    www.careplanner.org
Death with Dignity
    www.deathwithdignity.org
Duke Institute on Care at End of Life
    www.iceol. duke.edu
Growthhouse
    www.growthhouse.org

National Alliance for Caregiving
www.caregiving.org
Organ donation regulations
www.organdonor.gov/
Promoting Excellence in End-of-Life Care
www.promotingexcellence.org
The Center for Practical Bioethics
www.practicalbioethics.org

Useful books:

Goldman, C. (2002). *The gifts of caregiving: Stories of hardship, hope, and healing* (with CD of radio program on same subject). Minneapolis, MN: Fairview Press.

Staton, J., Shuy, R., & Byock, I. (2001). *A few months to live: Different paths to life's end.* Washington, DC: Georgetown University Press.

Zaner, R. B. (2004). *Conversations on the edge: Narratives of ethics and illness.*Washington, DC: Georgetown University Press.

Organ donation: Knowledge, fears, values:

Go ahead. Stir up some trouble, or perhaps just some lively conversation with family and friends. Who would donate an organ: Why or why not? Who has already signed a directive to make organs available: Why or why not? What ideas, experiences, or feelings have encouraged each person to either accept or reject the option of organ donation? Check your facts with such publications as Lack's *Twice Dead* (see reference list), or visit an informative online site such as Living Bank International (www.livingbank.org).

Gamblers of either sex and all ages are at a higher risk for suicide.

chapter 7

SUICIDE

And if we can't remember who attended our son's funeral or forget the directions to our home or even our sister's name, we begin to understand that we are not suffering from a sudden onset of Alzheimer's—we are having memory lapses that are probably shielding us in some way from the full impact of our loved one's suicide. Or if we hear our loved ones speaking to us a couple of days after they have killed themselves or see them sitting on the living room couch, hey, we may not be truly insane but are instead suffering from "sensory disturbances."
—Michael F. Myers & Carla Fine (2007)

GLENDALE, Calif.: A suicidal man who allegedly parked his SUV in the path of a commuter train and triggered a horrific crash that killed 11 people was charged with murder, and could face the death penalty, authorities said today.
—Paul Chavez (2004)

133 B.C. The inhabitants of the Spanish city Numance, after being besieged for 8 years by the Romans, rather than surrender, chose to slit the throats of their women and children. Afterward they set fire to the city and challenged each other to death; the last survivor threw himself off the ramparts.
—Mancinelli, Comparelli, Girardi, & Tatarelli (2002)

U.S. soldiers in Iraq are killing themselves at a high rate despite the work of special teams sent to help troops deal with combat stress, the Pentagon's top doctor said Wednesday. . . . The Army also began offering more counseling to returning troops.
—Matt Kelley (2005, January 15)

Emmy, Susie, Tammy—My Dear Ones

Don't think badly of me. I am finally doing the right thing. I did so many things that were wrong or just plain stupid. Please remember one thing. That I love you and always have and always will. None of this was your fault. It was just time for me to get out of everybody's life so you can all have a life. Love you, love you, love you.

Mom

The bills are all paid.
—Suicide note of a 37-year-old woman

I remember sitting at this adding machine in this insurance office. These ladies were boss-ing me around and I'm adding numbers. . . . I decided right then: I already felt dead. Everything I did, I felt more dead. Nothing felt alive and nothing would help. I just felt it would be more congruent to be dead. Just not to have this body to keep being in.
—Karen, quoted by Richard A. Heckler (1994, p. 67)

His third try was to move out of the apartment that reminded him too much of Sadie and the life they had once shared. Max relocated to a sunbelt state, but he hated it. Surrounded by strangers and an alien environment, he felt more isolated and lonely than ever. He finally went out and bought a handgun and spent an evening staring at it.
—Kastenbaum (1994)

Family members alarmed by disturbed thoughts and unnerving experiences. An SUV abandoned on railroad tracks. An ancient city's resort to mass suicide with an enemy at its gates. An army charged with a dangerous and frustrating mission that is itself experiencing a high rate of suicide. A mother assuring her children that the bills have been paid before she takes her life. Another woman feeling that she is not really alive decides "it would be more congruent to be dead." An elderly widower feeling so lonely and adrift that life no longer seems worth living.

People who contemplate, attempt, and some-times complete suicide cannot be reduced to a simple stereotype: The facts say otherwise, as suggested by the opening examples. The notion that only a certain kind of person commits suicide is a distancing strategy. Nevertheless, there are general risk factors for suicide. It is our challenge to understand the relationships between the impulses of individuals and the forces operating within their worlds. In this chapter, we explore suicide in many of its individual and societal circumstances. We include statistical information and large-scale phenomena but will keep in mind that suicide is not an abstraction.

Suicide has both immediate and long-term effects on other people. Immediate responses can include anxiety and guilt: "Was there something I could have done to prevent this?" Survivors' grief after a suicide is often more complicated and disturbing than after a natural death (de Groot, de Keijser, & Neeleman, 2006). The family who experienced memory lapses and transient hallu-cinations was relieved to learn that this was not an uncommon response to traumatic bereave-ment by suicide (Myers & Fine, 2007). Long-term results of a suicide include a family's deprivation of a father, mother, husband, wife, or child. Survivors' attitudes toward their own lives can also be profoundly influenced. For example, a suicide in the family history is known to be a risk factor for additional suicides. The American Association of Suicidology estimates that more than 180,000 people are closely affected by a suicidal death each year, and that about 4.5 million people in the United States have lost a family member or friend to suicide.

The train wreck that killed eleven people and traumatized many others is a dramatic example of a suicide's impact on society—and this was an attempt, not a completed suicide. Few acts of self-destruction have such an obvious impact, but any suicide has the potential for clouding the lives of many other people. This tragedy also reveals something of society's mindset toward suicide. The local district attorney demanded the death penalty (Kelley, 2005):

> His despondency doesn't move me. The mere fact that he was a little upset or despondent doesn't mean he has a defense for anything. . . . Because this man was distressed, 11 people are dead from his selfishness (p. 18).

Juan Manual Alvarez was charged with eleven counts of murder, one for each person who died in the wreck. His appearance in court was delayed because "he was too weak from wounds he made to his wrists and chest before the wreck" (Kelley, 2005). This is an understandable response from the law enforcement perspective. Crimes should be punished: Mental health experts might offer a different perspective. A man who slashed his body to the point of disability was probably more than "a little upset or despondent." Alvarez's state of mind could be viewed as an example of the intense mental pain that has been found to be associated with suicidality (Orbach et al., 2003). Branding Alvarez as "selfish" suggests a rush to moral judgment without considering what has been learned about suicide in recent decades. An individual's desperate (and ambivalent) action can trigger conflicting responses from society. This apparently isolated act is not so isolated after all. (And is there perhaps something ironic about vowing to put a suicidal person to death?)

Suicide can be the outcome of an individual's stressful and frustrating experiences, often lubricated by the use of alcohol or other drugs. However, suicide has sometimes been a collective response to a situation experienced as unbearable. For example, mass suicide has occurred repeatedly in Jewish history, with the Masada episode (A.D. 73) the most often remembered but followed by others during persecution throughout Europe from the eleventh to the thirteenth centuries. In recent times, cult suicides such as those at Jonestown and Heaven's Gate have again demonstrated that a group of people can self-destruct for reasons that may or may not seem rational to others. Mass suicide also can include acts of homicide, as demonstrated by the beseiged people of Numance and members of the Jonestown community who were forced to drink poison.

Can a dead woman kill herself? Yes, and dead men, too; it happens many times every year. Karen became emotionally numb to protect herself from her sorrows and stresses. Few people, if any, seemed to notice. Feeling as though one were already dead may be protection from both life and death in the short term, but it can also be another step closer to a suicide attempt (Heckler, 1994).

The media paid no attention to Max during his more than 60 years of meeting his occupational, social, and family obligations. Little notice would have been taken had Max ended his life with his new handgun. He would have become just one more statistic: older white males have the highest suicide rate in the United States.

The woman who wrote a farewell note to her children had made two previous suicide attempts before taking a fatal overdose. She had been quiet and uncomplaining as she went about her responsibilities, so the family also went about its business and thought she would be all right. On the first anniversary of her death, the oldest daughter (age 13) made a serious but nonfatal suicide attempt. Individuals attempt and complete suicides, but self-destruction frequently is also a family matter.

Many deaths that are not recorded as suicides nevertheless were motivated by the intention to die. Unfortunately, some people also decide to take others with them. Motor vehicle accidents that are not entirely accidents and deliberate encounters with law enforcement officers ("suicide by cop") are among the ways in which a suicidal purpose is sometimes carried out. The September 11, 2001, terrorist attacks on the United States and campaigns of suicidal attacks in the Middle East made self-destruction a part of political/religious agendas.

Suicide occurs at every age from childhood onward. The victims are males and females, the affluent and the impoverished, the seeming failures and the apparently successful. People take their own lives in rural Vermont and urban San Francisco, and in crowded Tokyo and sparsely populated Lapland. The scope of the problem is worldwide and not limited to any particular class of person, although some groups are more at risk than others. Furthermore, the casualties of suicide include parents, children, spouses, lovers, and friends, all of whom are at risk for traumatic grief (Chapter 12).

We begin with a statistical profile of suicide attempts (also known as parasuicide) and completed suicides. More detailed attention will then be given to gender differences, suicide among youth, elders, Native Americans, Vietnam War veterans, and special circumstances in which there is a higher risk of self-destruction. We will then examine both cultural and individual meanings of suicide, with special attention to the descent into suicide and the attempt itself.

The "soup kitchen" became a fact of American life during the Great Depression that started in 1929. Unemployed men, unable to support their families and stressed by loss of occupation and self-esteem were vulnerable to thoughts of suicide, as were those who had made and lost fortunes.

This background will prepare us to consider the challenge of suicide prevention.

WHAT DO THE STATISTICS TELL US?

Suicide has been among the leading causes of death in the United States ever since fairly reliable statistics have been available. It is currently the 11th most common cause of death in the general population. In recent years there have been more than 30,000 certified suicides (almost 90 a day). Experts believe that the actual toll is even greater. It is not unusual for a death to be classified as accidental, natural, or indeterminate if the suicidal component has not been established beyond a doubt. Furthermore, many people still find it difficult to believe that a child might be capable of committing suicide, so the reported statistics among the very young could be underestimates. The suicides of ailing and socially isolated old men sometimes go into the records as arteriosclerosis or heart disease. Sympathetic medical examiners have also been known to shade the facts when there is any ambiguity as to cause of death at any age. The statistical profile, then, tends to under-represent the actual incidence of suicide.

The suicide rate is determined by the formula:

$$Suicide \ rate = \frac{Number \ of \ suicides}{Population} \times 100,000$$

It is easy to make a mistake here. We are more accustomed to thinking of percentages than of rates. The U.S. suicide rate of 11.0 would seem catastrophic if we mistreated the number as though a percentage. There would be close to 30 million suicides in the United States each year, instead of the 31,655 reported in the most recent data! The rate actually means that 11 people out of every *100,000* suicided during the year. The rate is also different from the *number* of total deaths by suicide. If, in fact, there were only 100,000 people in the United States, then only 10 or 11 would have committed suicide. The larger the population, the higher the number of deaths if the rate is held constant. It is possible, for example, to have more suicides per year as a population expands, even if the rate remains constant or even declines slightly. Now—on to the data themselves.

Suicide Patterns in the United States

North Americans are not among the most suicidal of people. The rate is about three times higher in the Russian Federation, Belarus, China, Estonia, Hungary, and Kazakhstan than in Canada and the United States. By contrast, Greece has a remarkably low rate (3.4) that is only about a third of the North American rate. Suicide rates tend to persist at about the same level for people with a common national or ethnic heritage; for example, Hungarians tend to have the same suicide patterns whether living in their country or in other nations. China is currently experiencing an alarming increase in suicides, estimated at approaching 500,000 per year.

Basic Facts

As indicated in Table 7-1, suicide does not occur equally across gender. There are other significant differences and patterns also to be considered:

1. *Completed suicides occur most often among white males. At every age, white males are at greater risk for suicide than females or black/ nonwhite males.* The difference is substantial: Four of five suicides are by males, and predominantly white males. Peck (2003) offers statistics from 100 years of history to support

his conclusion that suicide in the United States is mostly a white male problem.

2. *The white male suicide rate increases with age, but females and nonwhite males reach their peak vulnerability earlier in adult life.* Although the rate is highest among older white men, the actual number of suicidal deaths is higher for middle-aged men because there are more of them. Even a lower rate represents more fatalities.

3. *Suicide remains the third leading cause of death among youth (ages 15–24).* The impact of suicide is so powerful on adolescents and young adults because for the most part they are spared heart disease, cancer, stroke, and chronic respiratory diseases that are major contributors to death among people in their middle and later adult years.

4. *Bad economic times are usually associated with an increase in suicide rates.* The suicide peak in the United States occurred during the Great Depression of the 1930s, and a later period of recession produced another rise in suicide.

5. *The suicide rate is higher among people who: (a) suffer from depression or other psychiatric problems; (b) use alcohol while depressed; (c) suffer from physical, especially irreversible, illness; (d) deal with challenges and frustrations in an impulsive way; (e) are divorced; (f) have lost an important relationship through death or break-up; and (g) live in certain areas of the country.*

6. *Each suicide has an intimate affect on at least 6 other people.* This means that almost 200,000 people were added to the ranks of those bereaved by suicide in the most recent year for which complete data are available. All told, it is estimated that about 4.6 million Americans have had a suicide death among the people closest to them.

It is not surprising to find that such factors as depression, drinking, impulsivity, and illness are linked to suicide. Study after study confirms that depression and a sense of hopelessness often precede suicide attempts. Recent research adds that a sense of "emptiness" should be considered as an additional risk factor (Orbach et al., 2003). Suicide is often an impulsive act, especially

TABLE 7-1

Suicide, United States: Official Final Data (2005)

	Number	Per Day	Rate	% of All Deaths
Nation	32,637	89.4	11.0	1.3
Females	6,730	18.4	4.5	0.5
Males	25,527	71.0	17.7	2.1
Whites	29,527	80.9	12.3	1.4
Nonwhite	3,110	8.5	5.5	0.9
Blacks	1,992	5.5	5.1	0.7
Elderly (65+)	5,404	14.8	14.7	0.3
Young (15-24)	4,412	11.5	10.0	12.3

Source: American Association of Suicidology (2008).

Number of Suicide Deaths	32,439
Suicides per Day	89
Deaths per 100,000 population	11
Gender:	8th Leading Cause for Males
	16th Leading Cause for Females
Most Common Methods:	
Firearms	16,750
Suffocation	7,336
Poisoning	5,800
Tested Positive for Alcohol	33.3%

Source: Centers for Disease Control (2007). www.cdc.gov/nchs/fastats/suicide.htm

among young people, and alcohol is a contributing factor at all adult ages. Prolonged discomfort, increasing disability, and fear of further physical deterioration become more frequent situations in the later adult years and therefore contribute more to suicidality.

There is also a geography of suicide in the United States, and it takes what is perhaps a surprising form. Scenic and spacious Wyoming, Alaska, Montana, and Nevada have suicide rates about three times as high as competitive, crowded, fast-moving places such as Massachusetts, New Jersey, New York, and the District of Columbia (National Center for Health Care Statistics (2004). Lack of social support and connectedness seem to be a key factor in the nation's differential suicide rates within the same nation. The highest suicide rates in the United States are found in western states, especially in rural areas that offer relatively few opportunities for social interaction and support. The lowest rates occur in

high-density states where it is very difficult not to bump into people all the time.

But who chooses to live in Nevada and who in New Jersey? Are stresses greater in the "most suicidal" states, or are social support systems less available there? Clearly, we need studies that are more up close and personal. We also see that homicide and suicide rates do not necessarily keep company. For example, the District of Columbia is notorious for its consistently high murder rates but has a lower suicide rate than any of the 50 states.

What About Suicide Attempts?

Up to this point, we have focused on completed suicides. It is more difficult to estimate the frequency of suicide attempts, many of which never show up in official documents. The available data, however, do indicate that suicidal thoughts are not uncommon in the general population. The American Association of Suicidology estimates that about 5 million living citizens of the United States have made suicide attempts. There are two national studies, both of which could use updating. In just one year, 420,000 cases of self-inflicted injury were reported by hospital emergency departments (McCraig & Burt, 2001). Another national study (Ikeda et al., 2002) estimated a rate of 95.9 nonfatal self-inflicted injuries. The female rate was significantly higher than the male: 107.7/83.6. The actual number and rate is probably higher, since the reports include only those suicide attempters with injuries serious enough to require emergency treatment. In a survey of high school students in the United States more than one of six reported having seriously considered suicide in the past year—and almost one in twelve had actually made at least one attempt. We can see why mental health experts urge us to take suicidal thoughts seriously: Ideas can become plans, plans can become attempts, and attempts can become the loss of life. *Parasuicide* will be considered further as we explore self-destructive actions in various populations and contexts.

The Human Side

The impact of suicide cannot be gauged by numbers alone. Even attempts that do not result in death can have significant consequences. For example, family and friends are put on alert and may respond either by renewed efforts to help the individual or by further emotional isolation of the attempter because of their own heightened anxiety. The suicide attempt might win temporary attention and concessions—or it might make things worse by being interpreted as manipulative and thereby leading to further resentment and withdrawal by others.

, I have observed a tremendous range of responses to suicide attempts. In one instance, colleagues became more sensitive to the individual's sense of despair and were able to provide valuable help, both with emotional support and practical actions, to change a frustrating situation. In another instance, however, the parents refused to be "impressed" by their adolescent daughter's near-fatal attempt and in effect challenged her to "finish the job." She did.

The social cost of suicide is high, although impossible to calculate precisely. Occasionally one suicide seems to encourage another as some vulnerable people identify with the deceased and see self-destruction as an acceptable means of solving their problems. When the suicide of a young celebrity is reported vividly by the media, there may be a short-term increase in suicide attempts and completions by some people who have identified with the star and who have been having problems of their own. "Copycat suicide" has been shown to occur in many nations following the suicide of a person with whom some people closely identify, but these effects are usually limited and discontinue after a short time (Stack, 2000).

The human side of suicide also includes children left without parents and therefore made more vulnerable to stress and self-doubts that can haunt them throughout their lives. Children with family members who attempted or completed suicide are more likely to make suicide attempts themselves at some point in their lives. Suicide has a ripple effect of stress and distress that starts with the immediate family and friends and may continue to widen. Behind each number in the suicide statistics there are families, friends, and colleagues who will never be quite the same again.

FOUR PROBLEM AREAS

A more detailed look at suicide among youth, elderly persons, ethnic/racial minorities, and Vietnam War veterans will illustrate some of the many relationships between individual self-destruction and society.

Youth Suicide

Suicide is the third leading cause of death between the ages of 15 and 24. Only car crashes and homicide were responsible for more than 4,599 deaths by suicide in the most recent national data available (2004). The suicide rate among adolescents and young adults had nearly tripled between the mid 1960s and mid 1980s. It then decreased and become more stable—until "a dramatic and huge increase," according to the Centers for Disease Control (Bluestein, 2007, p. 1). Much of this unexpected increase occurred with preteen and teenage females, though males also had a higher rate. Another difficult to explain trend was evident: hanging and, to a lesser degree, suffocation had become the most common suicide methods for preteen and teen females. There are tentative theories, but not yet firm explanations for this recent increase in youth suicide and the shifting choice of method.

Consider these additional facts:

1. *Academic pressure seems related to suicide among college students but not in a simple way.* Many undergraduates who commit suicide had a higher grade point average than their peers. They had performed below their expectations—or what they took to be their parents' expectations. "I couldn't face Dad and that big scene there would be after all the money he had spent on my education and how he had wanted to be proud of me and blah, blah, blah!" This is how one student explained his near-fatal suicide attempt to a counselor, and many others have had similar experiences.

2. *Most of those who have gone on to commit suicide expressed their despondency to others and made explicit comments about their intentions.* Unfortunately, few youths who were at risk for suicide received mental health treatment or counseling (National Household Survey on Drug Abuse [NHSD], 2002). Clinicians have long held that many suicidal people do issue a cry for help. This seems to be true of many of the youths who see suicide as a possible solution to their problems. Every expression of suicidal intent provides an opportunity for a helpful intervention.

3. *Counseling is often effective in preventing youth suicide.* Many colleges and universities now offer counseling services for students experiencing loss, depression, and frustration. Suicidal thoughts, feelings, threats, and gestures can be recognized before impulsivity and depression turn into self-destructive action. There is evidence that an increasing number of college students are making use of this resource and finding their way back

to a more positive state of mind (Schwartz, 2006).

4. *Alcohol is a frequent contributor to suicide at all ages.* A sudden change in drinking habits may be a particularly important factor because the risk of suicide increases when a person goes on a "jag." Alcohol and drug abuse have been identified as especially important factors in youth suicide. Adolescent males who consume alcohol are estimated to be 17 times more likely to attempt suicide, and females three times more likely (Groves, Stanley, & Sher, 2007). It has also been found that many adolescent alcohol abusers are from families with the same problem (Sher, 2007). Furthermore, those who drink to excess also have more cognitive and language deficits. It is possible that neuropsychological dysfunction might have a role in the development of adolescent alcohol disorders as well as become an effect.

5. *The loss of a valued relationship is one of the most common triggering events for youth suicide.* This can involve the death of a parent, breaking up with a lover, having a quarrel with a close friend, being disappointed in a role model, or learning that one's favorite dog or cat has died. Many people experience these kinds of losses and stresses without becoming suicidal. However, past experiences of loss, rejection, and unworthiness make some youths more vulnerable to suicide when new interpersonal problems arise.

Risk is especially high when an emotionally needy young person seeks salvation through a relationship that is not likely to endure. Katie, a bright and articulate college student, was trying to make a life for herself after a stressful childhood in a dysfunctional family. Academic achievement provided one life-support line, but it was difficult for Katie to meet her own expectations for "that next A." More crucial was Katie's relationship with Mark, her sometimes attentive, sometimes elusive boy friend. On the first page of her first diary book, Katie wrote:

I am depressed and suicidal. My body feels restless and tired. I don't know who to turn to for help. I don't want to bother anyone with my battle. I've been acting out in all sorts of ways. I just feel like crying. . . . I love Mark so deeply, but I don't know if it's True love for him. . . . I really want to marry him so badly. . . . I really hate my life where it is, with everything I am. . . . God give me strength. Help me today. I feel so unbelievably lonely and battered (quoted in Pennebaker & Stone, 2004, pp. 61–62).

On the last page of the last of five diaries, she turned again to God:

Please, dear God, bring some wonderful, encouraging, unbiased, loving, respecting people in my life. . . . I want to feel whole inside, instead of being severed in hundreds of little pieces. . . . Please help me through this and next week . . . things are so hard now (Pennebaker & Stone, p. 73).

Soon after writing that entry, Katie committed suicide by hanging in her dormitory room. She had tried hard to escape from an anguished childhood and make a go of her life. The fear of being abandoned by Mark was literally a life-and-death matter for Katie. She did not experience herself as a whole person with intrinsic strength and value. Unfortunately, every day other youths also experience upsurges of suicidal thought when a relationship critical to their sense of self-worth has ended or become jeopardized.

6. *Heavy metal music attracts depressed and suicidal youth—it does not cause suicide.* Many heavy metal fans come from dysfunctional families, experience difficulties in coping with the world, and are low in self-esteem (Stack, 1994). The angry pounding rhythms resonate with their feelings, reducing their sense of aloneness, but have not been shown to contribute directly to suicide. An informal history of death metal and grind-core (Mudrian & Peel, 2004) discusses bands such as "Napalm Death, Death, Morbid Angel, Carcass, Obituary, Deicide, Entombed, and Cannibal Corpse" (p. 22). Many other groups could be added to this list. This intense identification with death probably has contributed to some youth suicides, but perhaps the opportunity for self-expression and the storm of violent sound has also provided a safety release for some young people. With or without heavy metal music, depression creates an elevated risk for suicide among both youth and adults.

7. *Teens and adolescents who frequently change their place of residence are at a higher risk for suicide.* This connection is also found with youth who expect to move soon. Geographical mobility weakens interpersonal support as well as the comfort of a familiar environment. A research team notes that "frequency of moving, distance moved, recency of move, and difficulty in staying in touch were all factors that appear to be associated with increasing odds of nearly lethal suicide attempts" (Potter et al., 2001, p. 47).

8. *Family patterns often have a role in youth suicide.* Leenaars and Wenckstern (1991) have found that families with rigid rules and poor communication ("Nobody ever listens to anybody") are more likely to be associated with youth suicidality. Father or mother absence, alcoholism, mental illness, and incest are other contributing factors. Suicidal youths, then, may represent distress calls on the part their entire families.

All of us may have the opportunity to help an adolescent or young adult find an alternative to suicide. This process begins with our willingness to take this measure of concern and responsibility. The next step is to become familiar with some of the most typical signs of suicide risk in this age group (Table 7-2). We will want to keep in mind that all young men and women have their own unique biographies and their own distinctive coping styles. We will also want to avoid a mechanical approach to detecting possible suicidality, considering instead this particular person in his or her particular situation.

I would add two other observations. First, many suicidal youths are misguided by vague and wishful thoughts about death. There is often the assumption that the person will be able to witness the response of survivors. "Look how upset they will be!" "They'll be sorry they treated me so bad." "They'll know I really meant it." I have also heard many expressions of the assumption that death is "just a trip," perhaps similar to a pleasant alcohol or drug high. They have not read Greyson's (1992–1993) study in which he found that people who reported near-death experiences also reported very strong antisuicide

The high decibel, pounding rhythms of heavy metal music do not cause suicide, but do attract angry, depressed, and suicidal youth.

TABLE 7-2

Youth Suicide: Factors Associated with Higher Risk

- There have been suicidal attempts by other members of the family.
- The person himself or herself has made a previous suicide attempt.
- There have been recent changes in this person's behavior, including level of social activity, sleeping, eating, choice of clothes, and use of alcohol or drugs. The behavior change can take either the direction of withdrawal from previous interests and activities, or a sudden burst of pleasure-seeking and risk-taking activities. The clue is that in either case this person is acting very much differently than usual.
- A sense of hopelessness, apathy, and/or dread is expressed. "What's the point of trying again?" "There's nothing I can do about nothing." "So, who cares anyway? I don't!"
- Explicit or implicit statements are made about ending his or her life. "I've had enough of this crap!" "You're going to see me on the ten o' clock news!" "I want to get it all over with, and I will!"
- The thought process has narrowed to the point that everything seems open or closed; there is little or no ability to acknowledge shades of meaning and only extreme courses of action are envisioned. "I'll kill her, or I'll kill myself." "I can never get anything right." "He was the only person who understood me and I can't live without him." "There's only one way out of this mess."
- Abrupt flashes of anger interfere with activities and interactions. He or she becomes touchy and unpredictable and seems to overreact to small frustrations or provocations. There may also be an increase in glowering resentment and uncooperativeness, even if this does not explode into overt displays of anger. Aggressive and antisocial behavior occurs more often among males than females as a forerunner of a suicide attempt.

attitudes. Another common presuicidal belief is that death is better than life (as compared with the alternative view that death refers to the absence of life). A tendency to envision death as more rewarding than life may contribute to the decision to take one's life.

Second, it is important to remember that suicidal impulses do not have free reign. People of all ages also have strong reasons not to take their lives, despite episodes of discouragement and frustration. One of the keys to suicide resistance among youth is the fact that they have powerful reasons for wanting to live, such as the desire to experience more of life, discovering their own special purpose in life, wanting to grow together with friends, and not wanting to hurt family.

Do Children Commit Suicide?

It has often been assumed that few if any children commit suicide. Unfortunately, this assumption is not true. Children do think about death (Chapter 11) and the uncertainties and frustrations of life. Third graders have a clear understanding of suicide and even some younger children realize that people can and do take their own lives. Mishara (2002) adds that although almost all children at second grade level and above have seen some form of suicide on television, these images are:

> different from the vast majority of suicides in the real world. Those who commit suicide on television almost never suffer from severe depression or mental health problems, they are almost never ambivalent about whether or not they should kill themselves, and it is rare that children see suicidal persons receiving help or any form of prevention (p. 836).

Israel Orbach and his colleagues have conducted a series of studies on "children who don't want to live." Orbach (1988) identified a typical progression toward a potentially lethal suicide attempt:

> The process starts with a harmless attempt, by which children can assess the effect it has on their surroundings. At the same time, this attempt represents a test of their ability to cope with their fear of death. A second attempt often follows the

first—especially if there is only a minimal response from the social environment. This second attempt is a little more bold and dangerous, and has more serious consequences (p. 27).

Children often give a number of verbal and nonverbal messages about their desperation and their intent prior to a lethal suicide attempt. All too often, adults simply do not believe the children mean what they say.

Recognition of suicidal thoughts and actions in childhood becomes even more important when we realize that this is also the foundation from which many suicides in adult life originate. For example, a young child who considers himself or herself unwanted and unloved may have thought of suicide repeatedly and even make one or more attempts that escape notice. In adolescence or young adulthood, this person may encounter new experiences of rejection and disappointment that resonate with the earlier anxiety and self-destructive tendencies. This child whose suicidal orientation was ignored years before may become part of the suicide statistics in adolescence or the early adult years.

A valuable study by Yang and Clum (2000) finds that stressful experiences in childhood can increase the risk of suicide in adult life by distorting the way the child thinks about self and world. The development of suicidal behavior in children and adults follows the same general pattern. The earlier phases of this pattern include a sense of intolerable pressure from the family, a depressed attitude, and various coping attempts that do not work very well and result in accumulated frustrations and loss of self-confidence. If this stressful situation is not altered, the idea of suicide appears and the child or adult now attempts to cope through some type of self-destructive behavior. If others still do not respond in a helpful and effective manner, the individual feels increasing pressure and a sense of failure that confirms the feeling that suicide is the only solution. Self-destructive behavior is often set into motion as early as childhood, but may claim its casualty at any later developmental level as well.

Do children commit suicide? In returning to this question, we must reply: Yes, sometimes, but it is just as important to recognize that suicidal orientations may develop early in childhood and have their fatal outcomes later in life. Having faced this harsh reality, we are in a better position to be helpful both to the children who are at particular risk for development of a suicidal orientation and to the troubled families whose own anxieties are represented in the child's distress. Lives can be saved by preventing the establishment of self-destructive thoughts and tendencies in childhood. As Orbach and others have observed, even those children who are experiencing high levels of stress still have a desire to grow, to flourish, to live.

Suicide Among Elderly Persons

We left Max staring at his newly purchased handgun. The elderly white man remains the person most vulnerable to suicide. Since 1990, the largest increase in the suicide rate has been among people 85 years of age and older. Combine the increasing suicide rate with age and the fact that more people are living into the later adult years and we can see that there is a powerful trend toward self-termination as the world population ages. Suicide rates among white men increase from middle age onward. Despite this elevated risk, suicide among the elderly often fails to receive sufficient attention. The victim may have been socially isolated for some time before death, or the community may be less disturbed by the act than when a young person is involved (Kastenbaum, 1995). Nevertheless, suicide in later life not only represents the premature death of a fellow citizen, but an implicit commentary on the place of the elderly person in society.

The male suicide risk increases significantly with advancing age. Social isolation and health concerns are among the contributing factors.

Physical illness and other sources of distress do not necessarily make self-destruction the plan of choice. My colleagues and I have worked with many older people who had reason to despair over the harsh realities of life. Often these people were able to draw upon their own personal resources and find the strength and will to live within a relatively short time. The key in some cases was a short reprieve from a stressful situation or objective changes to improve their quality of life; in other cases, it was a therapeutic alliance and counseling. Stress and despair can be experienced at any age—and the same is true of recovery. Several other findings about suicide in later life follow:

1. *The major demographic risk factors include being white, male, older than the age of 65, living alone, and residing either in a rural area or a transient inner-city zone* (Grek, 2007; Osgood, 1992).
2. *Social isolation is a theme that runs through most of the risk factors.* Living alone is associated with a higher risk of suicide. Elderly suicide rates tend to be higher in areas where divorce rates and interstate migration are also higher (Conwell, 2001).
3. *Depression increases the risk of suicide.* Mood disorders are the strongest predictors of suicide attempts in elderly people (Beautrais, 2002). This is not the same as concluding that depression "causes" suicide. People cope with depression in many ways and not all suicidal elders show an obvious picture of clinical depression.
4. *Physical illness is a major risk factor for suicide among elderly adults.* Again, it should be kept in mind that (a) many elders cope with physical problems without becoming depressed and (b) depression may occur without a basis in significant physical problems.
5. *Alcohol use increases the risk of suicide among elderly adults.* Alcohol abuse is approximately twice as frequent among suicidal adults as among the population in general. Increased use of alcohol is often intended to ward off depression and suicidal thoughts, but eventually, however, alcohol and/or drug abuse tends to increase the probability of suicide because of the impact on social isolation, health, and clarity of thought.
6. *Failure to cope with stress increases the risk of suicide among elderly adults.* Persistent stress syndromes (see also Chapter 12) can develop when individual's coping responses are overwhelmed by life changes and crises encountered in the later adult years. Lack of adequate social support systems intensifies the stress. Once it has started, the psychophysiological stress reaction is difficult to terminate and itself can become a major stressor, sapping individual's strength and producing anxiety.
7. *Loss of relationships increases the risk of suicide among elderly adults.* Bereavement and divorce are the most common types of relationship loss for elderly adults. Some older adults also experience a particularly harrowing kind of loss of relationship when the spouse is afflicted with Alzheimer's disease or a similar condition of dementia. The spouse is still there, but the familiar and mutually supportive relationship has altered radically.

The Lethality of Suicide Attempts in the Later Adult Years

In general, older adults are at even greater risk for death when they make a suicide attempt. The ratio of suicide attempts to deaths is much smaller for elders, especially males. Overall, elders have a 4:1 ratio of attempts to completions, as compared with the young adults' ratio of 20:1. Elderly males and females most often choose firearms as their mode of suicide. This is true for adults in general in the United States. However, the proportion of firearms use is even higher among elders: about three of every four elderly male suicides involve the use of firearms. Elderly males are less likely than younger adults to give clear warnings of their suicidal intent, especially if they live alone and have little participation in community activities. The lethality of the suicide attempts is also increased by the attention given to avoiding discovery or interference. Furthermore, elders are less likely to recover from suicide attempts that produce serious trauma but from which a younger person might survive. Older adults who are an elevated risk for suicide often show several of the characteristics identified in Table 7-3.

TABLE 7-3

Elderly Adults: Ten Indicators of Possible
Suicide Risk

1. Sad, dejected, or emotionally flat mood
2. Stooped, withdrawn, fatigued, lack of eye contact
3. Careless in grooming and dress
4. Restlessness, handwringing, constant motor activity
5. Inattention, lack of concentration, losing the thread of the conversation
6. Loss of appetite/weight
7. Sleep disturbance (insomnia or oversleeping)
8. Loss of interest in activities that previously were pleasurable
9. Loss of interest in other people
10. Preoccupied with vague and shifting physical complaints

Preventing Suicide in the Later Adult Years

Some people are so anxious about their own prospect of aging that they feel that depression, helplessness, and suicide are only to be expected. Our first priority, then, is to come to terms with our own "inner elder."

If the motivation is there, we can do much to detect high suicide risk in elders and to help provide alternatives. Physicians and other human service providers often have interactions with elders who are one step away from suicide. Studies have found that up to half of the people who commit suicide had seen a physician within a month of their death (Murphy,1995). It is probable that elders are overrepresented in this group because relatively few physicians are trained in detecting depression and suicidality. Fortunately, increased awareness of this risk on the part of service providers can result in timely and effective interventions, as Gerk (2007) has documented in a recent survey of the literature.

There is reason for optimism in the prevention of elder suicide. By and large, people do not reach their later adult years unless they have both resilience and skill. Max, for example, had demonstrated competence in school, work, and interpersonal relationships throughout his life. He had overcome many challenges, savored some successes, and adjusted to some disappointments. The death of his wife was a severe loss to him. Along with the sorrow there was the question of how—and why—he should go on with his life. After several coping attempts had failed, Max decided to try a solution that is deeply engrained in the tradition of this nation: When all else fails, kill somebody (see Chapter 8). However, after staring at that gun, Max realized that this was not his solution. Just as he was not a person who was made for sitting around in the sun, so he was not a person who dealt with problems in an explosive and violent manner. And so Max went on to find another solution. He returned to his old neighborhood and drifted naturally over to the library that had been his home away from home in childhood. Max soon became first an unofficial assistant to the librarian and, eventually, a person who the children and youth of the neighborhood sought out for advice and companionship. Max not only felt useful and connected again—he *was* useful and connected. He took the money he received from selling the gun and plunked it into the library's fund to help low-income children purchase their own books.

We have been focusing on elder male suicide because this is the subpopulation that is most at risk. As we have seen, though, elderly women also tend to use lethal means when they attempt suicide. It is also probable that a large but undocumented number of elderly women hasten their deaths by not looking after their health and gradually withdrawing from social contact. Deaths of this type are known as subintentional. They are not certified as suicides, but those who are familiar with the situation often believe that the person contributed to the death in a significant although indirect manner.

Baby Boomers at Risk?

On its way to elderdom, the baby boomer generation is showing some indications of stress and vulnerability to suicide. It is too early to draw conclusions, but there are alarming statistics. The Centers for Disease Control and Prevention have found a 20% increase in the suicide rate for 45-to-54 year olds in a recent five year period. This is an increase much greater than for any other age group. It is possible that this precipitate rise in suicide among middle-aged people—women substantially more than men—will turn out to be a statistical blip, but it is also possible that baby boomers are experiencing significant difficulty in adjusting to the challenges of life transition. As Patricia Cohen (2008) notes: "Just why thousands of men and women have crossed the line between enduring life's burdens and surrendering to them is a painful questions for their loved ones. But for officials, it is a surprising and baffling public health mystery."

Suicide Among Ethnic and Racial Minorities

The conditions of life—and, therefore, of death—differ greatly within a nation as large and diverse as the United States. We focus on the two groups for which the most information on suicidality has become available. There are actually many differences within these groups, including lifestyle, education, socioeconomic status, and all the usual demographics, so we would not want to fall into stereotyped thinking.

Native Americans

In Native Alaskan villages, a culture of sorrow. The older brother killed himself. The younger one used a gun. They died 38 days apart. . . . They've lost their culture, they don't have a way to support their family, and then what we see is a lot of alcohol use. There's such a feeling of hopelessness, particularly for young men (Yardley, 2007, p. 2)

Throughout much of the world, the people native to a region have given way to forces from other lands who were equipped with more advanced military and technological resources. Outsiders often call native people "indigenous populations." In recent years, they have often characterized themselves as "first people." By whatever name, they have often been deprived of their previous means of existence, been victimized by discrimination, and faced systematic campaigns to destroy their cultural heritage (Hunter & Harvey, 2002). Elevated suicide rates are often among the consequences, with the indigenous people of Australia, Canada, and New Zealand, as prime examples. The Royal Commission on Aboriginal Peoples (1995) left no doubt as to the basic cause: "collective despair or lack of hope" (p. 38).

The white man's conquest and development of the New World was also catastrophic to the ancestors of many of those who are now known as Native Americans. It is equally troubling to think that the present high suicide rate among Native Americans is a continuing part of that heritage.

Here are the basic facts about suicide among Native Americans:

1. *The rate is exceptionally high.* Native Americans as a total group have the highest suicide rate of any ethnic or racial subpopulation. The suicide rate of 19.3 is more than a third higher than that of the general population.
2. *Tribal differences in suicide rates are large and also vary over time.*
3. *Alcohol is a major factor in Native American suicide.* Although there is a strong association between alcohol and suicide for the general population, it is even more so with Native Americans. Heavy alcohol consumption has been found to be associated with about two thirds of the suicides among American Indians in New Mexico over a 10-year period (May et al., 2002). Alcohol abuse has been related to high unemployment, prejudice, cultural conflict, and the loss of heritage, among other factors. Suicide is clearly a symptom of social stress and disorganization as well as a tragic outcome for the individuals and their survivors.
4. *Unlike the general population, it is among the young Native Alaskans that depression, alcoholism, and suicide are at peak levels: caught between two cultures, neither of which are adequately supportive.* Women seem to have suicidal thoughts over a longer period of time but are also more likely to share these feelings with others (LeMaster et al., 2004).
5. *The average life expectancy remains relatively low for Native Americans.* Those who survive into their later adult years seem to be highly resistant to suicide—quite the opposite of the lifespan risk for suicide among whites.

Programs that provide realistic opportunities for youth to pursue their goals and dreams and that strengthen tribal values are likely to result in a sharp decrease in suicide.

African Americans

Deprivation, stress, and racial discrimination were visited upon African Americans from their earliest years as "property," and this was followed by more long years of seeking equality and justice. We might therefore expect that suicide rates would also be very high among African Americans. This is not the case, however. The suicide rate has actually been markedly lower than it is in the white majority, a consistent pattern ever since such data have been collected reliably. The most recent data are presented in Table 7-4.

TABLE 7-4
African American and White Suicide Rates*

Females	
African American	1.5
White	4.8

Males	
African American	9.1
White	19.9

*National Vital Statistics, 2004 [Report 53 (5)].

The very low suicide rate among African American women stands apart from all other large-scale population data. What accounts for this remarkable resistance to suicide? A plausible and significant answer is starting to emerge. Two sets of researchers have come up with findings that are essentially in agreement (Marion & Range, 2003; Willis et al., 2003). Religious belief and social support contribute to a problem-solving style of acting together that provides a strong buffer against suicidality. Suicide is often regarded as a failure of faith and an offense against God. Close emotional support from family, friends, neighborhood, and church help to prevent feelings of being alone, abandoned, and helpless in the midst of life's struggles.

Hispanic suicide has yet to be studied systematically. This shortcoming is related to difficulties in defining "Hispanic" clearly enough to classify health outcomes. At present, about 2,000 Hispanic suicides are reported each year, with a very low estimated rate of 5. There is not much that can be added at this time, given the limited information available. Even less is known systematically about suicide among people of Asian heritage, so again, reluctantly, it is better to say nothing further rather than to pass along possibly errant impressions and speculations.

Military Suicide

People who serve the nation in the armed forces are at heightened risk for suicide, both during and after their war experiences. This added threat to life became evident through the study of Vietnam War veterans. The stress of engaging in a confusing war in a remote land was often followed, upon returning home, by a sense of being shunned by a public that had become increasingly critical of the purpose and conduct of the conflict. Posttraumatic stress disorder was common. Many of the combatants could not help but take the war home with them, and it proved difficult to return to their previous relationships and life patterns. Years later, the Vietnam Memorial Wall would remind the nation of the sacrifices made by fellow Americans during the war and arouse more compassion (Chapter 12). In the meantime, there was often a sense of estrangement and depression—and, for some, suicide.

The actual number of suicides and attempts associated with the Vietnam War will probably never be determined. The prevalence of suicidal thought was described by Alexander Paul, himself a Vietnam veteran, in his fact-based novel, *Suicide Wall* (1996). Chuck Dean (1990), also a veteran, found that estimates of suicide by Vietnam veterans ranged from 20,000 to 200,000. The highest figures include indirect suicide through single-car accidents and other deaths that were not officially classified as suicides. Many veterans struggled with suicidal thoughts at some point during their reintegration into society. Perhaps many lives were saved by good friends, a loving family, and, not least, the returning veteran's own personality strengths. There is little doubt, however, that society's discomfort with the Vietnam War increased the stress upon men and women returning from the horrors of war.

More recently, there has been heightened concern about suicide among members of the U.S. armed forces in Iraq (Kelley, 2005):

Suicide has become such a pressing issue that the Army sent an assessment team to Iraq . . . to see if anything more could be done to prevent troops from killing themselves. The Army also began offering more counseling to returning troops (p. A18).

A recent major study has provided the most substantial information about suicide among male veterans, following 320,890 men over a 12-year period (Kaplan et al., 2007). The results are disturbing; the suicide risk of these veterans was twice as high as men who were not veterans. At highest risk were white and college-educated veterans, as well as those with activity limitations. Suicide risk was distinctive: other causes of death did not differentiate between veterans and non-veterans. The researchers called attention to the fact that veterans of deployment in Afghanistan and Iraq are also likely to be at high

risk. Severely wounded soldiers (Underwood, 2008) and members of the National Guard or Reserves who were on active duty (Associated Press, 2008) were at particularly high risk.

Suicides among military personnel on active duty have reached their highest level since records have been compiled. The number of attempted suicides has increased sixfold since the start of the Iraq War, with the army unprepared either for the markedly increased suicidality or number of posttraumatic stress disorders that contribute to depression, frustration, and difficulties in preserving interpersonal relationships and coping with everyday life (Priest, (2008).

Congress reacted quickly to public outrage over disclosure of the Veterans Administration's inadequate response to the needs of veterans

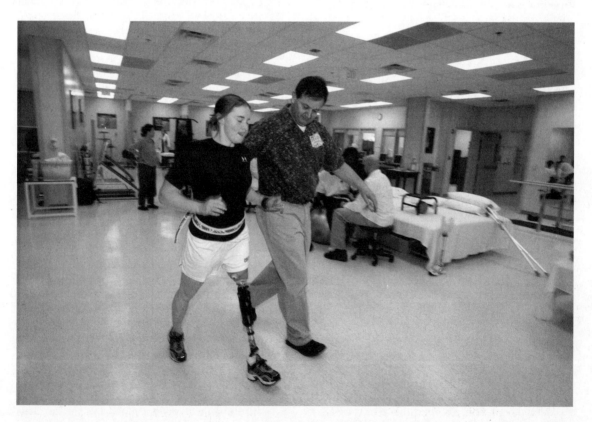

Attempted and completed suicides have become much more frequent among active military personnel and veterans. Physical rehabilitation can also help to restore confidence and hope for the future. Here, the assisteance is provided by Lt.Melissa Stockwell and physical therapist Bob Bahr who work together at the Walter Reed Army Medical Center.

returning with mental as well as physical disabilities. The Joshua Omvig Veterans Suicide Prevention Act (named for an Iraq War veteran who suffered from posttraumatic stress disorder and committed suicide) requires the Veterans Administration to upgrade its counseling and other services in an effort to reduce suicidality. It remains to be seen whether this measure will have the intended effect. Unfortunately, there have been charges of systematic misinformation on the part of the Veterans Administration regarding the frequency of military suicides and attempts. In 2007, the VA reported 800 attempts, while independent sources estimated the actual number as around 12,000 (McClatchy, 2008). A VA official later apologized saying he did not think there was a deliberate attempt to mislead Congress or the public.

High-Risk Situations for Suicide

The risk of suicide is increased in some situations other than war. Here are several important examples:

1. *Suicides often increase after a natural or man-made disaster.* This pattern has been found among victims of floods, earthquakes, and hurricanes in 377 nations (Krug et al., 2003). Suicidal and other self-injurious behaviors increased after the September 11, 2001, terrorist attacks, and these effects might still be continuing (Wouter de Lange & Needleman, 2004). Anxiety, depression, and suicidality are frequent responses to these traumatic losses. Mental health services, offered both immediately and over a period of time, could prevent many acts of self-destruction.

2. *People with HIV/AIDS are at a higher risk for suicide.* The American Foundation for Suicide Prevention estimates that the risk of suicide is up to 20 times greater for people with HIV/AIDS than for the general population. The feeling of being isolated and rejected can contribute more to suicidality than the disease itself. However, as with other life crises, people with HIV/AIDS often have come to terms with their situation and continued to live meaningful and useful lives. Furthermore, the improved survival outlook for people with HIV/AIDS in recent years is another protection against suicide.

3. *Gambling is associated with a higher risk of suicide.* "Las Vegas, the premier U.S. gambling setting, displays the highest levels of suicide in the nation, both for residents of Las Vegas and for visitors to that setting. In general, visitors to and residents of major gambling communities experience elevated suicide rates. In Atlantic City, abnormally high suicide levels for visitors and residents appeared only after gambling casinos were opened. The findings do not seem to result merely because gaming settings attract suicidal individuals" (Phillips, Welty, & Smith, 1997, p. 373).

4. *Schoolyard bullies and peer harassment increase suicidality.* Children and teens who have been pushed around, insulted, threatened, and mocked by classmates not only feel miserable as a result, but also are at a higher risk for depression and suicide (Rigby & Slee, 1999). This situation becomes even more dangerous when victims feel they have no social support from family, teachers, or friends. Bully and harassment victims report more suicide ideation. Homicidal thoughts may also occur. For example, the Columbine High School killers felt that they had been rejected and mocked by classmates and/or teachers. The mass killings on the Virginia Tech campus were also committed by a disturbed person who felt rejected by his peers.

5. *"Suicide by cop" has become an established term because so many incidents have occurred around the nation.* The term was introduced in 1983 by Dr. Karl B. Harris, Chief Medical Examiner for the County of Los Angeles. He identified many instances in which an armed suicidal person confronted a police officer in such a way as to force the officer to shoot in self-defense. In these cases, it was later discovered that the suicidal person's gun was unloaded or nonfunctioning: The idea all along had been to force the officer to engage in the police version of assisted suicide. This type of confrontation is very stressful for the officers, both at the time and afterward. A creative and effective alternative has been developed by some law enforcement units:

Cop suicide is a powerful reminder that we cannot deftly separate individual and societal responses, nor can we keep suicide and homicide in separate categories.

Gender and Suicide

In the United States and most other nations, women are less likely than men to commit suicide. How should we interpret this fact? First, we might remind ourselves that the death rate for males generally is higher at all age levels for all causes except those specific to females (e.g., pregnancy and birth). Sex differences in life expectancy have favored females ever since records have been kept (Stillion & McDowell, 2001/2002). Females born in 1850 had an average life expectancy of about 40 years—2 years more than males. A century later, this gap had expanded: Females born in 1950 had a life expectancy of 72 years, more than 5 years longer than their male peers. This differential in life expectancy continues to increase. Lower male life expectancies also occur in most other nations, including those in which fewer people survive into the middle and later adult years. Suicide might then be part of male's greater vulnerability to life-threatening conditions and stresses.

There is, however, a major exception to the rule. It has been estimated that China has 21% of the world's population but 44% of the suicides—and 56% of the world's female suicides (Canetto, 2002). Most of these suicides seem to be motivated by a sense of hopelessness. Painful and frustrating experiences have led many Chinese women to feel that they have little or no chance of a good life. The situation is especially desperate in rural areas where government policies, including limiting married couples to having one child, have disrupted traditional family patterns and increased the stress of life (Jianlin, 2000). Abortion and infanticide (Chapter 10) have also increased under the intolerable pressure. Again, we remind ourselves that a high suicide rate is not only alarming in and of itself, but that it also represents an even more widespread sense of anxiety and desperation because some sufferers stop short of suicide.

Most of the female suicides in China seem to be of the type that sociologist Emile Durkheim classified as fatalistic: death as a way to escape an oppressed and hopeless life. (We will be considering Durkheim's influential theory later in this chapter.) Another approach has been articulated recently by psychologist Silvia Sara Canetto. She notes that each society has its own models and rules for suicidal behavior. It is as though there were scripts to follow in the performance of self-destructive behavior. There is some evidence that suicide is one of the more culturally acceptable scripts for desperate Chinese women who have few other choices available. Canetto (2002) applies the same concept to the gender–suicide link in the United States:

> Nonfatal suicidal behavior is considered less masculine than fatal suicidal behavior. . . . Males are particularly critical of other males who survive a suicidal act. Studies also show that killing oneself is seen as a masculine and relatively strong act. . . . Men who kill themselves are viewed as better adjusted than women who kill themselves, independent of the reasons for the suicide (p. 817).

If the cultural script depicts completed suicide as masculine, then, females may have less inclination to perform this role. A suicidal threat or nonfatal attempt would be more in accord with cultural expectations. The gender– suicide connection is still a long way from being understood, however, and we would not want to apply any general theory to all individual situations.

Questions also prevail over answers in a recently emerged controversy regarding cosmetic breast augmentation and suicide. The basic facts seem to have been well established: six epidemiological studies have found that women who received cosmetic breast implants had approximately twice the expected suicide rate based on estimates of the general population (Sarwer, Brown, & Evans, 2007). There are limited data to suggest that low self-esteem, depression, and anxiety are more common among women who seek cosmetic breast implants, but thisis an hypothesis awaiting further confirmation.

Balancing Individual and Cultural Influences on Suicide

It would be useful to find a balance between individual and sociocultural factors. The realities of everyday life and prospects for the future differ appreciably for a white, Anglo-Saxon, Protestant undergraduate; an elderly African American widow; and a youth living on a poverty-stricken reservation. The same act of desperation can flow from many sources. Prevention and intervention efforts will be more effective in some circumstances if they are focused on the individual; in other circumstances, a broader social policy approach may be necessary. We now examine some major cultural and individual influences on suicide.

SOME CULTURAL MEANINGS OF SUICIDE

The act of suicide has been interpreted in many different ways throughout human history and tells us much about worldviews and values of societies that have come before us (Minois, 1999; Murray, 1998, 2000). Most of these earlier conceptions are still busy competing with each other. We are also faced with newer situations, such as persistent vegetative states and the intensified advocacy for "death on demand" and physician-assisted death (see Chapter 10). New interpretations of suicide may emerge from such new challenges.

Suicide as Sinful

The Catholic Church has condemned suicide since at least the fifth century. St. Augustine established the Catholic position with two fundamental objections: (1) suicide precludes the opportunity to repent of other sins, and (2) the Sixth Commandment tells us: "Thou shalt not kill." Self-murder is not exempt from this commandment, according to St. Augustine. He did, however, volunteer a few exceptions to his own rule (426/1971):

> Abraham indeed was not merely deemed guiltless of cruelty, but was even applauded for his piety, because he was ready to slay his son in obedience to God, not to his own passion. . . . Samson, too, who drew down the house on himself and his foes together, is justified only on this ground, that the Spirit who wrought wonders by him had given him secret instructions to do this (Book I, Chapter XXI).

St. Augustine, so hard on suicide, condoned Jephthah's execution of his daughter because he had promised God he would sacrifice "whatever

first met him as he returned victorious from the battle." This church father's pronouncement has troubled some believers through the centuries by ruling against suicide, yet justifying a father's killing of his daughter in order to keep his own reckless promise. St. Thomas Aquinas (1279/1971) added another objection to suicide: Only God has the power to grant life and death. The self-murderer is engaging in the sin of pride. This self-assertion brings shame on the whole family. Some regimes through the centuries seized upon this belief as an excuse for confiscating the property of families in which such a dishonorable death had occurred.

Condemnation of suicide as a violation of the Sixth Commandment is difficult to square with the warfare and violent death that has at times actively pursued by defenders of the faith. Religious wars and the persecution of heretics repeatedly have violated the edict, "Thou shalt not kill." As Jacques Choron (1972) observes, "during the Middle Ages, mass suicide was frequent among persecuted sects of Christian heretics and non-Christian minorities. . . . The category of non-Christians included Moslems and Jews, who refused to be converted to Christianity and preferred to commit suicide" (pp. 25–26). The persecuted victims were sinners for committing suicide, but their persecutors were lauded for inflicting torture and death in the name of their religion. Nevertheless, The Old and New Testaments do not directly prohibit suicide, nor do they even seem to find this action particularly remarkable. Some of the early Christian thinkers regarded the death of Jesus as suicide (Brown, 1998), as did deeply reflecting Christians of later times, such as John Donne (1646/1977).

Other influential voices within the Christian tradition have offered alternative interpretations. For example, philosopher David Hume (as quoted in Colt, 1991) reasoned along these lines:

> I am not obliged to do a small good to society at the expense of a great harm to myself; why then should I prolong a miserable existence . . .? If upon account of age and infirmities, I may lawfully resign any office, and employ my time altogether in fencing against these calamities, and alleviating as much as possible the miseries of my future life; why may I not cut short these

miseries at once by an action which is no more prejudicial to society? (p. 43).

Suicide as Criminal

The intertwining of church and state once made it easy to regard suicide as both criminal and sinful. Through the years, however, the civil and divine realms of authority have become more independent of each other. The word *suicide* itself seems first to have entered use in about the middle of the seventeenth century. *The Oxford English Dictionary* gives the earliest citation, attributing the following statement to Walter Charleton in 1651: "To vindicate ones self from . . . inevitable Calamity, by Suicide is not . . . a Crime." Suicide is more apt to be punished when it is interpreted as a crime as well as a sin. Suicide attempts have often brought severe punishment on top of the moral condemnation. This has included torture, defamation, and impoverishment.

The interpretation of suicide as crime is waning. Criminal laws have been erased from the books. It was once common for insurance companies to treat suicide as a crime intended to defraud the underwriters. It is now possible to have death benefits associated with suicide, although with limitations and restrictions built into the contract. Decriminalization of suicide is based upon the realization that penalties have not served as effective deterrents and that few people were willing to enforce the laws. Law enforcement agencies have become effective frontline resources for suicide prevention in some communities, liberated from the obligation of treating the attempter as a criminal.

Suicide as Weakness or Madness

Some people who commit suicide can be classified as psychotic or severely disturbed, but this is not true of all who attempt to take their own lives. Individuals with diagnosed psychiatric conditions have a higher suicide rate than the population at large. People diagnosed as depressive psychotics tend to have the highest rates of completed suicides. They are also more likely to have made one or more suicide attempts. Prevention of suicide does require diagnostic and therapeutic attention to people suffering from depression or other psychiatric disorders. However, psychiatric disorder does not by itself adequately explain or predict suicide. Many people go through disturbed periods without attempting suicide. It might be tempting to believe that a person has to be crazy to commit suicide, but this is simply not true.

What about the related belief that suicide is the outcome of weakness? This view became salient as a dubious spin-off of the survival-of-the-fittest doctrine (Darwin, 1859/1971). Suicide was regarded by some as one of nature's ways to preserve the species by weeding out the less fit, an interpretation not endorsed by Darwin himself. This position is not taken as prominent today as it was in the heyday of rugged individualism. Nevertheless, we can still see it in operation. "If you can't stand the heat, get out of the kitchen!" was one type of comment heard after an executive leaped to his death from offices high above Manhattan. Media coverage emphasized the length of time that his fallen body tied up traffic! Little attention was given then or later to his state of mind, the meaning of his suicide, or the impact upon survivors.

Suicide as "The Great Death"

The Buddhist tradition in China and Japan includes the image of *daishi,* which translates roughly as "The Great Death." Zen masters have demonstrated how a person might pass admirably from this life. The discipline of the master appealed to the warrior. The samurai would seek *daishi* on the battlefield. This influence remained strong enough through the centuries to enlist the self sacrifices of *kamikaze* pilots in World War II.

Suicide itself has been honored as a form of *daishi. Seppuku* was a traditional form of suicide in Japan, better known in the West as *hara-kiri.* The act itself consisted of disembowelment, usually with a sword. By opening his abdomen, the individual is showed the world that his center of being was pure. The sword was inserted into the *hara,* home of the breath that is a link to both life and divinity. The terminal act therefore involved a network of physiological, individual, social, and religious referents.

This form of death could serve as an honorable alternative to execution. People condemned to death would be given the privilege of becoming their own executioner. Voluntary *seppuku*, by contrast, might flow from a number of different motives on the part of the individual (e.g., to follow a master into the great beyond or to protest an injustice). Placing one's life at the disposal of an honorable motive was a much admired action. In our own time, the self-immolation of Buddhist monks in Southeast Asia to emphasize their religious and political protests has also made a deep impression on observers.

The ancient Greeks and Romans also considered suicide to be an honorable death (Colt, 1991):

> In Alexandria in the third century B.C. the philosopher Hegesias taught that life was so fleeting and full of cares that death was man's happiest lot. He lectured so eloquently that . . . many of his listeners committed suicide. Two centuries later, during the reign of Cleopatra, herself a suicide, there seems to have existed . . . a school that taught the best ways of committing suicide. Some "students" were rumored to have killed themselves during sumptuous banquets. Such excess anticipated the Roman Empire. For if the Greeks rationalized suicide, the Romans made it a fashion, even a sport (p. 148).

And so an action that later was considered a sin by some people and a crime by others was regarded by Romans of the classical period as perhaps, the most noble and glorious thing a person could do.

Suicide as a Rational Alternative

The belief that suicide can bring a glorious death has a more subdued echo in another cultural tradition that dates from ancient times: suicide as a rational alternative to continued existence. Individuals do not destroy themselves in hope of thereby achieving a noble postmortem reputation or a place among the eternally blessed. Instead, they wish to subtract themselves from a life whose quality seems a worse evil than death.

Stoicism, a philosophical position that was enunciated in ancient Athens and Rome, has since become virtually a synonym for rational control. Alvarez (1970) explains that stoicism was:

> a last defense against the murderous squalor of Rome itself. When those calm heroes looked around them they saw a life so unspeakable, cruel, wanton, corrupt, and apparently unvalued that they clung to their ideas of reason much as the Christian poor used to cling to their belief in Paradise and the goodness of God despite, or because of, this misery of their lives on this earth. Stoicism, in short, was a philosophy of despair; it was not a coincidence that Seneca, who was its most powerful and influential spokesman, was also the teacher of the most vicious of all Roman emperors, Nero (p. 66).

Renaissance thinkers often praised death as refuge from the cruelties and disappointments of life. Erasmus (1509) observed what a distance there is between our aspirations for the human race and the failings discovered on every side in daily life. The Renaissance spirit of hope and progress soon became shadowed by so profound a disappointment that it sometimes seemed it could be cured only by death.

There have been many times in human history when misery was so pervasive that it seemed natural to think seriously of suicide. However, other people, also thinking rationally, have devoted themselves to improving the conditions. Others have "irrationally" persisted with life, guide by faith, hope, and obligation to others.

A POWERFUL SOCIOLOGICAL THEORY OF SUICIDE

Theories of suicide have been challenging traditional attitudes. Foremost among the early theories was the comprehensive sociological model offered by Emile Durkheim in 1897. *Le Suicide* (1897/1951) became a cornerstone for the emerging science of sociology. Durkheim's ideas continue to command the attention of those who study and seek to prevent suicide. His approach was audacious for its time. Suicide was not a matter of the individual's relationship to God, nor were moral values the primary focus. Instead, suicide could be viewed most effectively as an outcome of interaction patterns between individuals and their societies.

The Importance of Social Integration

All individuals are more or less integrated into their societies. Society itself may be stable, consistent, and supportive, or it may be falling apart under stress—or even morphed into a destructive force. The individual, then, may be weakly or strongly integrated into a high- or low-solidarity culture, as shown in Table 7-5.

TABLE 7-5
Types of Connection Between Individual and Society

Individual's integration into society	Society's solidarity
High	High
High	Low
Low	High
Low	Low

The type of relationship between integration and solidarity is crucial for suicidal risk, according to Durkheim. How much does the culture control the individual? The weakly integrated person in a cohesive society (Low-High in Table 7-5) and the person trapped in a disorganized culture (High-Low) both are endangered because there is not enough group control. Inadequate group control increases the possibility of suicide, as individuals are left to their own impulses and resources. However, suicide can also result from too much control by society, as we will see. Durkheim's theory, then, invites attention both to the cohesiveness of society and the social integration of any particular individual.

All cultures also have *collective representations* that convey their spirit or personality. These are expressed through the guiding symbols, themes, and rituals. Unfortunately, this group spirit can turn morose and self-destructive. Individuals who are highly integrated into the culture are more likely to absorb the pessimistic mood of the larger society and may act it out with fatal results. The very forces that should hold a society together can take on the opposite character and lead to what we might call *sociocide*. The mass suicide and homicide in Jonestown, Guyana, that resulted in the eradication of a unique community and more than 900 lives, is one such example.

Four Types of Suicide

Durkheim identified four types of suicide. Each represents a distinctive relationship between individual and society. The *egoistic* suicide is committed by people who do not have enough involvement with society. They are not under sufficient cultural control. The executive who literally fell from on high is one probable example. Celebrities in the entertainment field, creative artists who follow their own stars, and people who make their own rules on the basis of their wealth and power can put themselves beyond the reach of cultural constraints. Intellectuals are also common within the category of egoistic suicide. Sensitive to underlying currents of melancholy and despair in the culture and drifting in their own thoughts, they have little outside themselves to grasp when the suicide impulse arises.

Very different indeed is the *altruistic* suicide. Already mentioned were such examples as the *seppuku* tradition and the *kamikaze* combat death. Altruistic suicide occurs when the individual has what might be considered an excessive concern for the community. This is usually the strongly integrated person in a high solidarity culture (High-High, Table 7-5). Altruistic suicides tend to be less common in Western societies but often are admired when they do occur. The soldier who volunteers for a "suicide mission" in order to protect comrades or achieve a military objective can be considered both a hero and an altruistic suicide. Durkheim does not mention physicians and medical researchers who voluntarily expose themselves to fatal illness in order to help others, nor rescue specialists who put their own lives at risk. The difference between acceptance of a high-risk and suicidal behavior has much to do with the individual's intention.

Durkheim's third type is called *anomic* suicide. Social breakdown is reflected most directly in the anomic suicide. People are cast adrift by the failure of social institutions. Unemployment is an important example. The person thrown out of work has lost a significant tie to society. Bad times, unemployment, suicide—a predictable sequence. Similarly, people who are forced to leave their occupation because of age may enter an anomic condition that leads to suicide. When the rupture between individual and society is sudden and unexpected, then the probability of suicide is thought to be especially high. This situation arises, for example, when the death of a spouse or other important person downgrades the survivor's place in society.

This set of three suicide types dominated the picture for many years. Recently, however, more attention has been given to a fourth type that Durkheim introduced but treated more as a curiosity. In *fatalistic* suicide a person is overcontrolled by society. The individual feels stifled and oppressed; all opportunities and prospects seem to be blocked. Durkheim spoke of slavery as a condition that engenders fatalistic suicide but thought that civilization had put this kind of oppression well into the past. Oppression and subjugation have not disappeared from the human condition, however, as tyrannical regimes persist into the twenty-first century.

Both the altruistic and the fatalistic suicide involve excessive control of the individual by society. In altruistic suicide, the individuals appear to share wholeheartedly in the collective representations. They die for their people. In fatalistic suicide, they die in despair of ever being able to actualize themselves in a culture that affords little opportunity for self-esteem and satisfaction.

We move now from a sociological approach to the individual's own thoughts, motives, and life style as factors in suicide.

SOME INDIVIDUAL MEANINGS OF SUICIDE

Just as the preceding discussion did not exhaust all the cultural and sociological meanings of suicide, so this section can only sample some of the individual meanings. The intent is to convey something of the various states of mind with which people approach a suicidal action.

Suicide for Reunion

The loss of a loved one can be experienced as so unbearable that the survivor is tempted to "join" the deceased. Recently bereaved people often experience the "presence" of the dead. This may be part of the normal response to the death of a loved person. But desperate longing may impel a person to follow the dead all the way to the other side if the relationship has been marked by extreme dependency. "I can't go on without him." "I am not complete without her." "What's to become of me?" "I can't manage by myself." Sometimes these feelings are accompanied by suicidal thoughts. Reunion fantasies may have some temporary value while bereaved individuals reconstruct their lives, but they can also lead to suicidal actions.

Children are particularly vulnerable to reunion fantasies. The child is still in the process of attempting to establish identity as an individual. The parent or older sibling who has "gone off to heaven" has left the survivor with painful feelings of incompleteness and yearning. Some adults remain relatively childlike in their dependency on others and feel very much the same way when separated by death. Suicide to achieve reunion seems most likely when the person lacks a fully developed sense of selfhood, whether because of developmental level or personality constellation; when death has removed a significant source of support; and when there are salient cultural messages that make death appear unreal and the afterlife inviting.

Suicide for Rest and Refuge

Worn down by tribulations, a person may long for a "good rest" or a "secure harbor." A vacation far away from the grinding routine may restore energy and confidence. Life may be experienced as too exhausting and burdensome. The miracle of an ordinary good night's sleep can seem out of reach as depression deepens. Under such circumstances, the fantasy of a prolonged, uninterrupted sleep can take on a heightened allure. The sleep–death analogy is readily available in America as in most other cultures (Chapter 3). It is tempting to take a few more pills than usual and just drift away.

This attitude toward suicide is also encouraged by cultural tendencies to blur the distinctions between life and death. Advertisements instruct us to solve problems by taking something into our mouths (puff on a cigarette; swallow pills for headaches, indigestion, or any form of distress). People with oral escapist tendencies dominant in their personalities might be especially vulnerable to these lures of suicide, but the risk is there for anybody who has sat in front of a television set since childhood. Why not make ourselves a little more comfortable, take that one more something that can help us sleep away all our troubles permanently?

Suicide for Revenge

The lover is rejected. The employee is passed over for promotion. Another child is preferred and pampered. Some people repeatedly feel that they are treated unfairly—and sometimes this is true. Their achievements never seem to be recognized. No matter how hard they try, love and appreciation are withheld. A college student had firsthand experience of this kind of situation:

> I felt crushed. Absolutely crushed. It was my first really good semester. No incompletes. No withdrawals. All A's and B's. And no "episodes." I kept myself going all semester. I really felt strong and independent. I knew I shouldn't expect too much when I went home, but I guess . . . I mean I know I expected a little appreciation. You know, like maybe Mother just smiling and saying, "Had a good semester, didn't you? I'm happy for you" or "I'm proud of you," though she would never say that.

This young woman felt that her achievement passed without notice: in fact, the family hardly noticed that she had come back home. If her family would not pay attention when she did something right, maybe they would when she did something dramatically wrong. "I wanted to hurt them—and hurt me—just enough." She slashed away at her wrist and arm. The self-wounding temporarily released some of her despair. She had not injured herself seriously, so she wrapped the wounded area in a bulky bandage. *Nobody seemed to notice.* A few days later she removed the bandage, exposing the patchwork of fresh scars. There still was no obvious response from the family. Instead, they were enthusiastically anticipating the graduation and upcoming marriage of one of her cousins.

She felt crushed again when she was passed over in the wedding arrangements:

> I couldn't even be part of somebody else's happiness. . . . I knew that revenge was stupid. But I felt like doing something stupid. Listen everybody: you're 100% right! I am a stupid person. And here is something really stupid to prove it!

She hurled herself from a rooftop.

> I wanted to kill myself then. I think I did. But I also wanted to see the look on their faces when they saw that bloody mess on the sidewalk. I could see myself standing alongside the rest of them, looking at that bloody mess of myself on the sidewalk, and looking at their shocked looks. . . . *I didn't think what it would be like if I half-killed myself and had to live with a crushed body. Maybe that was the really stupid part of it.*

This talented young woman survived a suicide attempt that might have been fatal or crippling. The pain and trauma relieved some of her emotional tension for awhile. Yet she felt that she might "have to" do it again, perhaps "next time for keeps." She did not need a psychologist to suggest that her suicide attempts were efforts to punish others by punishing herself. (At last report, this woman was alive, well, and somehow a stronger person for the ordeals she had undergone.)

The example given here illustrates several other characteristics often shown by the person who is on a self-destructive footing. This woman's fantasy included the virtual witnessing of her suicide. *She had divided herself into murderer and victim.* People who attempt suicide for any reason sometimes act upon the dubious assumption that they will somehow survive their deaths in order to observe the effects.

She also experienced some tension release through the self-destructive action itself. It is not unusual for the sight of one's own blood to relieve built-up emotional pressures, if only for a while. Another woman who had slashed her wrists on several occasions told me, "I felt as if I had done something finally. I wasn't paralyzed any more. I wasn't suffering helplessly. I took action into my own hands, and that felt good." Perhaps the experience of surviving this type of suicide attempt encourages the fantasy that one would still be around to feel better after a fatal attempt as well.

The low self-esteem of many suicide attempters is also evident in the instance given here as well as in Katie's troubled life and death. The combination of revenge fantasy and low self-esteem appears to be a particularly dangerous one.

Suicide as the Penalty for Failure

The victim of suicide may also be the victim of unfulfilled self-expectations. The person acts as accuser, jury, judge, and executioner. Some take the alternative of lowering expectations to close the gap. Some people find other ways to cope. However, for other people a critical moment arrives when the discrepancy feels too painful to be tolerated. If something has to be sacrificed, it must be themselves, not the rigid goals or excessively high standards.

A sense of failure is prominent among many people who take their own lives. The psychological autopsy technique (a special kind of case review) often finds that adult male suicides have occurred after the person was fired, demoted, or passed over for promotion. Female suicides are more often related to real or perceived failures in relationships. Young female suicides often had a history of persistent troubles with men. Those who married and had children had further difficulties in meeting the responsibilities of the maternal role. Older women who took their lives often seem to have lost or given up most of their social roles and obligations. For women younger than 50 years old, work failure does not seem to be nearly as salient a factor in suicide as it is for men. The suicidal person often has experienced repeated failure in both personal relationships and occupational success.

Fortunately, not every person who experiences failure commits suicide. This has led to Warren Breed's (1972) influential concept of a *basic suicidal syndrome*. The syndrome includes rigidity, shame, and isolation, as well as failure itself. There is only one goal, one level of expectation,and only one way to achieve it. A person who has come up short today might succeed tomorrow—but people with Breed's suicidal syndrome are shadowed by a sense of shame and cannot let themselves off so easily. "I am no good. Never will be. I am nothing." This syndrome has

been found by Breed and his colleagues most conspicuously in white, middle-class adults, both men and women. It does not seem to hold for lower-class black men who kill themselves.

It is going too far to speak of this as *the* basic suicidal syndrome. Breed readily acknowledges that there are also other patterns associated with suicide. But the high-aspiration, shame-of-failure dynamics revealed by his research do come close to the meaning of suicide for many in American society today. It does not tell us, however, why some people with a basic suicidal syndrome take their own lives while others find different solutions for their problems.

Suicide as a Mistake

People sometimes survive their potentially fatal suicide attempts. An unexpected rescuer appears on the scene, a determined self-mutilator misses a vital spot, an overdose induces vomiting instead of coma, a loaded gun fails to fire. Victims may also "betray" themselves, as in the case of bridge jumpers who survive the often deadly fall and then swim desperately for life.

However, there can be a discrepancy in the other direction as well. Some people kill themselves even though there is good reason to believe that they had not meant to do so. The victim had counted on being rescued. The wound or overdose were not supposed to be lethal. Precaution had been exercised to limit the effect, and yet the outcome was death. The person may have wanted very much to survive and enjoy a better life, but a mood, a desperate maneuver, and a misjudgment brought that life to a sudden close.

The individual contemplating a self-destructive act frequently is of two minds. This is the impression, for example, of volunteers who pick up the phone when a call is made to a suicide prevention hotline. The very fact that a person would reach out for human contact in this way suggests some continuing advocacy for life. Suicidality is often an ambivalent state of mind, as impulses toward life and death contest for supremacy. Ambivalence can reveal itself in the details of a life-threatening act. Why would she have taken the overdose just a few minutes before her husband was due home if she was entirely of a mind to take her life? And yet she did take the pills and has wagered her life

German artist Fran Masereel's woodcuts convey the impersonality and alienation that some individuals experience in big city life—despair and suicidality can breed in such circumstances. (Untitled picture from *The City*, 1925).

on the assumption that her husband will return home at the usual time.

Helping people to survive their mistakes is an important part not only of suicide prevention but of public health safety in general. Access to lethal means of self-destruction could be made more difficult, thereby placing some time and distance between a momentary intention and a permanent error. For example, suicide rates dropped significantly in England when coke gas was no longer widely available as a mode of suicide in the home and when its toxicity was reduced.

Mental health specialists persistently advocated the construction of a lower span sidewalk for the Golden Gate Bridge, a place that had become known widely as a "suicide shrine." Seiden (1977) followed up on more than 700 people who had approached either the Golden Gate Bridge or Bay Bridge with suicidal intentions and who were intercepted by alert citizens or police before completing the action. *Ninety-six percent of these people did not make subsequent fatal attempts, and all the survivors favored construction of a barrier,* Seiden found. "If there had been a barrier every one of them reports they would have reconsidered" (p. 274). The suicidal intention had been strong but ambivalent. The attempters had given society a chance to catch them before making a fatal mistake.

A Psychoanalytical Approach to Suicide

Since life seeks to preserve itself, how could any of us pursue self-destruction? Sigmund Freud first suggested (1917/1959) that suicidal individuals turn a murderous wish against themselves. What looks to the world like a suicide may be the symbolic murder of a person whose compelling image has remained lodged in the mind since childhood when the distinction between self and other was not fully developed. (There is actually some contemporary evidence for this hypothesis: suicidal adolescents had particular difficulty in differentiating between negative aspects of themselves and their parents, [Brunstein et al., 2007]).

Freud did not remain satisfied with this somewhat startling theory. Later (1923/1961) he offered a more philosophical concept. Each of us has a pair of instinctual drives that have different goals. There is a life instinct, *Eros*, and a death instinct, *Thanatos*. Eros is the force leading to expansion, growth, adventure, and pleasure. Thanatos is the biological force that tempts us to withdraw from the field of action, shut down our lives, and seek silence and death. These drives constantly interact. When Thanatos gains the upper hand, we are more likely to engage in a self-destructive action. Why *self*-destructive? Because much of our aggression has been forced inward as first our parents and then the world forbid and punish outward aggression. Everybody is vulnerable to suicide because there are

obstacles in our pathway to gratification (Eros) and much of our aggression is forced inward.

This twin-instinct theory still has something to offer (Kastenbaum, 2000) but has not earned much application to day-by-day interactions with people at suicidal risk, and researchers have yet to come up with convincing ways of testing the theory. However, the psychoanalytical approach does alert us to the long developmental career that precedes a self-destructive action. A young child, for example, may internalize the negative attitudes conveyed by parents. This burdens the child with a superego that is excessively oriented toward criticism and self-destructive action. Chaotic and inadequate parenting may also jeopardize children by leaving them with a brittle ego that fragments and shatters under pressure.

Many present-day clinicians and researchers take sociocultural factors more into account. As we have seen, for example, some Native Americans are at exceptionally high risk for suicide and other self-destructive actions. Their sense of low self-esteem comes from the deprivation and discrimination experienced in their contacts with mainstream U.S. society. Native American children are in danger of growing up with a severe lack of confidence in their identities and worth as well as with tendencies to keep aggressive impulses locked up under high pressure until efforts at control fail. This is in contrast with the pride and satisfaction children would have taken in being Cheyenne in preceding generations, for example, when the people were independent and possessed a favorable group self-image. These dynamics of low self-esteem and self-directed aggression can lead to fatal outcomes other than suicide, as witnessed by the high alcohol-related death rates on the same Native American reservation. The psychoanalytical approach, then, remains useful today, but its interpretation must be tested against experience, and other relevant factors should also be considered.

The Descent Toward Suicide

How do people move toward suicide? Richard A. Heckler (1994) offers a useful description of experiences that often occur along the way to a possible suicide attempt and its potentially fatal outcome:

- An experience of loss and/or trauma that deprives the person of emotional support and sensitizes the person to the possibility of further losses. These hurtful experiences often occur early in life when the person is most vulnerable and most in need of support and guidance. For example, the father may have abandoned the family, followed by the mother's depression and drug addiction, and then her death.
- The experience of losing hope for a satisfying life and losing the belief that the world is a coherent and rational place where good intentions and good actions have good consequences.
- The sense of descending, sinking, falling slowly into a subhuman kind of existence. This is accompanied by low self-esteem and a feeling of helplessness—like trying to run through quicksand.
- Withdrawal and communication breakdown increasingly isolate the individual from others. There is often a mutual withdrawal from significant emotional interactions as family members and friends also find themselves unable to cope with the situation of loss and trauma.
- The presuicidal person now constructs a facade as protection against further emotional pain. Karen, as quoted in the beginning of this chapter, built a robot-like facade around her doubts, fears, and vulnerabilities. She was just there, doing her work, trying to be socially invisible to avoid interactions. In a sense, though, she was not there at all. Within the facade of a competent but distant and uninviting person, she experienced the deadening effect of this protective strategy and "just felt it would be more congruent to be dead. Just not to have this body to keep being in."
- The descent continues, the person now enters what Heckler calls the *suicidal trance*. There is a greatly restricted range of thoughts and feelings. One is aware of one's suffering but of little else. There is a deepening conviction that the only options available are to continue suffering or to free one's self from suffering through death.
- The person now exists as though trapped in a tunnel. Death increasingly seems to be the only logical and possible exit.

- The movement toward suicide is likely to be accelerated by the impression that death is somehow beckoning to the individual, offering release, even commanding the act of self-destruction (for some people, this takes the form of hallucinatory voices, but others are aware that their own minds are making the decisions).
- A precipitating event can trigger the actual suicide attempt when the person is already primed toward death as release. Often this precipitating event is some form of rejection from another person.

The descent toward suicide can be halted at any of these points by understanding and helpful interactions, as well as by the individual's own resourceful efforts. The deeper the person has descended into the presuicidal sequence, however, the more difficult the challenge. Nevertheless, it is an encouraging fact that Heckler's case sample is drawn from people who did "wake up, alive." I was impressed by the courage and resourcefulness of many of the people Heckler described who fought uphill battles against despair before making suicide attempts. I have also known some people like this myself, and perhaps you have, too. The private hells they have had to survive often were not at all of their own making.

FACTS AND MYTHS ABOUT SUICIDE

Some of the major social and individual meanings of suicide have been considered. Now we consider myths that have grown around the subject over the years.

- *People who talk about suicide will not actually take their own lives.* This statement is not true. Approximately three out of every four people who eventually kill themselves give some detectable hint ahead of time, whether by less serious attempts or by verbal statements. (The latter are sometimes as direct as can be—e.g., "I'm going to blow my head off," "If things don't get better in a hurry, you'll be reading about me in the papers.") This is one of the most dangerous myths because it encourages us to ignore cries for help. The rejection of the communication can itself become the last straw for people contemplating suicide.

- *Only a specific class of people commit suicide.* It is sometimes held that suicide is a particular risk of either the poor or the rich. The poor are supposed to feel helpless and deprived, the rich to be bored and aimless. These simplifications fail to consider the complexity of people's relationships to society. People in all income brackets and social echelons commit suicide.
- *Suicide has simple causes that are easily established.* It would be closer to the truth to say that many of us are satisfied with simple and easy explanations. This chapter has emphasized meanings and situations rather than causes of suicide, which are often far from simple.
- *Asking people about suicide will put that thought in their minds and encourage suicide attempts.* This is one of the most common of the mistaken assumptions. Many lives have been saved by opening communication on the prospect of suicide.
- *Only depressed people commit suicide.* People with a diagnosis of depression do have a higher suicide rate than those with other psychiatric syndromes or those without known syndromes. But suicide may occur in any type of psychiatric disorder. People may not even seem to be especially unhappy immediately before fatal actions. It is dangerous, then, to overlook suicidal potential on the basis of the assumption that only depressed people take their lives.
- *Only crazy or insane people commit suicide.* This mistaken proposition is related to the one just described. Many suicides are associated with obvious mental disorder, but rational people can also feel overwhelmed by circumstances and without effective means of coping.
- *Suicidal tendencies are inherited.* Some families do have suicidal traditions that seem to perpetuate themselves. But there is little evidence for a hereditary basis, even in studies made of identical twins. The explanation for suicide must be sought elsewhere—with particular attention to family patterns of communication.
- *When suicidal people show improvement, the danger is over.* The period following apparent improvement is actually one of special danger. Sometimes this is because clients have improved enough to be discharged from mental hospitals

and therefore have more opportunity to commit suicide. It may also be related to a recovery of enough energy to take action. Sensitivity and interpersonal support are especially needed when people seem to be pulling out of suicidal crises.

- *People who are under a physician's care or who are hospitalized are not suicidal risks.* This is wishful thinking. Many people who commit suicide have received some form of medical or psychiatric attention within 6 months preceding the act. Suicides can and do occur in hospitals. Furthermore, the institutional situation itself can contribute to anxiety, low self-esteem, and other conditions conducive to suicide (Kastenbaum, 1995).
- *Suicide can be prevented only by a psychiatrist or mental hospital.* Some of the most successful suicide prevention efforts are being made by a variety of people in the community who bring concern, stamina, and sensitivity to the task. It is neither necessary nor realistic to pass all the responsibility to a few.

SUICIDE PREVENTION

We have already touched on suicide prevention in several ways. Improving our ability to observe signs of possible heightened suicidal risk in children, youth, and adults is a useful first step. Recognizing that a number of common assumptions about suicide are not supported by fact is another useful step. Now we will consider some other contributions that we can make to suicide prevention as individuals and as a society.

Individual Guidelines to Suicide Prevention

Many suicides can be prevented. Perhaps you have already played a role in preventing suicide without realizing it. The companionship you offered a person during a crucial period or the confidence you displayed in a friend after he or she suffered a failure experience might have provided just enough support to dissolve a self-destructive pattern in the making. Whenever we bring sensitivity and a genuinely caring attitude to our relationships with other people, we may be decisively strengthening their life-affirming spirit.

How we are to best proceed depends upon who the suicidal person is, who we are, and what kind of relationship we have to go on together. A few general guidelines can be offered, however:

- *Take the suicidal concern seriously.* This does not mean panic or an exaggerated, unnatural response. It does mean time, attention, and active listening.
- *Do not issue a provocation to suicide.* Strange though it may seem, people sometimes react to the suicidal person in such a way as to provoke or intensify the attempt. Do not be one of those "friends" who dares this person to carry out the threat make or who intimates that he or she is too "chicken" to do so. Do not belittle or joke away the suicidal state of mind—this might intensify the need to do something desperate so that others will appreciate how bad the individual really feels.
- *Go easy on value judgments.* "You can't do that—it's wrong!" This is seldom a useful response. It is not very helpful to inject value judgments when a troubled person is starting to confide self-destructive thoughts.
- *Do not get carried away by the "good reasons" a person has for suicide.* The response to a suicidal individual can involve much reading of our own thoughts and feelings into the other person's head. We may think, "If all of that were going wrong with my life, I'd want to kill myself too!" This conclusion might be attributed to the other person all too hastily. It is possible to respect the reality factors in the suicidal individual's situation without lining up on the side of self-murder. This respectful, nonevaluative approach is taken by many of the people who pick up the phone when a crisis hotline call is put through.
- *Know what resources are available in the community.* Who else can help this person? What kind of help might this person find most acceptable? What services are available through local schools, religious groups, mental health centers? Does your community have a crisis intervention service? How does it operate? Learn about, and if possible participate in, your community's efforts to help those who are in periods of special vulnerability.
- *Listen.* This is the advice you will hear again and again from people who have devoted themselves to suicide prevention. It is good advice. Effective listening is not passive. It is an intent, self-giving action that shows the troubled person that you are there and provides an opportunity for the person to start rebuilding trust and self-confidence.

Systematic Approaches to Suicide Prevention

Many communities have 24/7 crisis hotlines and other services that can be useful both to a suicidal person and to the individual's worried family, friends, and colleagues. Large metropolitan areas have centers specifically dedicated to suicide prevention. Mental health specialists in clinics or private practice are also available in many areas. Further information can be obtained through local human service directories and the American Association of Suicidology.

Suicide prevention centers usually offer 24-hour telephone counseling services. Some also provide walk-in clinics where people may receive crisis counseling. Many of those who use these services are able to work through their crises without resorting to suicide. However, there are also many people with high suicidality who do not contact a center. Younger adults and women are more likely to seek help through a suicide prevention center than are older adults and men. Suicide prevention centers often try various types of public information and outreach programs to encourage contacts from older adults and men. It is not easy to bring some of the people at greatest risk into the orbit of the suicide prevention center, so alternative ways of reducing suicide must also be pursued.

The community may decide to take other actions to reduce suicide risk. These programs range from making access to "jumping off places" more difficult to promoting both recreational and employment programs for youth. Reducing access to guns could be a particularly effective component of a community's suicide prevention efforts for elders because elders are less likely to shift to other modes of self-destruction. It has been found that restricting the availability of firearms is associated with a reduction in suicides (Maris, 2003).

One of the most promising systematic approaches to suicide prevention is through educational programs. School-based programs have been developed in the United States (Shaffer & Gould, 2000) and Europe (Mishara & Ystgaard, 2000). Educators and parents must first work through their own anxieties and become more familiar with the facts of suicide. Gatekeeper training is another approach that shows promise. Clergy, teachers, school staff members, police officers, bartenders, and physicians are among the people who often have contact with people who are in suicidal crises. Improving their ability to recognize and respond to the crises can save many lives.

Three Emerging Challenges

Suicide prevention efforts have increased over the years, but new challenges continue to arise, such as the following.

Antidepressants: Prevention or Added Risk?

Medication that reduces depression should also reduce self-destructive actions, given the well-established connection between the syndrome and suicidality. Suicide rates have indeed fallen since the use of antidepressants became more common in the 1980s. It is not clear how much of the credit should be attributed to antidepressants because much else has been happening in society (including some success in restricting availability of firearms). People with severe depression who take Prozac or other anti-depressants do seem to be at less risk for suicide than those who are unmedicated.

However, warning flags have been raised about possible adverse effects. The media have given substantial coverage to clinical trials that found an increase in suicide in children and adolescents who were taking antidepressants. There are now cautions on the labels of antidepressants regarding their use by minors. At present, there is such a surge in studies and position papers that it is difficult to evaluate in a balanced way the advantages and disadvantages of antidepressants in prevent of suicide. The pharmaceutical industry and many health care providers have come to the defense of antidepressants. For example, research psychiatrists have noted that most suicides are the result of untreated depression (Zarembo, 2005). Therefore, the beneficial effects of antidepressants should not be denied to people in need. It is generally agreed, though, that more research is needed, for example, on the question of whether antidepressants have different actions on the brains of children and adults (Frantz, 2004). There is an increasing call for the development of more effective antidepressants that will not have adverse reactions. Eventually, finding and disabling a possible "genetic trigger" for depression might be the answer that is sought; in the meantime, there are other promising avenues of research to explore.

Wong and Licinio (2004) note that "depression is one of the world's most lucrative drug targets" (p. 136). When big money as well as lives are at stake, perhaps we should keep careful watch. Furthermore, less attention has been given to a problem that medical and mental health practitioners have known for some time: People who receive antidepressants sometimes experience a feeling of panic—and this can set a self-destructive course in action. We face the larger issue, then, of balancing interventions based on medication with those that call upon enlightened and effective human contact.

Survivor Vulnerability

The stress that family members and friends experience after a suicide is now starting to receive the attention it deserves. Their suffering and risk has been confirmed by a comprehensive review of the literature. They are likely to become more vulnerable to

> heightened levels of guilt, shame, anger, family dysfunction, and social stigmatization. Survivors of any sudden, traumatic death of a loved one have an increased chance of developing disorders such as traumatic grief. . . . Perhaps most tragically, evidence suggests that suicide survivors may be at elevated risk for someday completing suicide themselves (Jordan & McMenamy, 2004, p. 337).

Mental health experts are now recommending that more assistance be made available to suicide survivors. It remains to be seen whether or not the nation's priorities can be expanded to include outreach services for bereaved survivors of suicide and other traumatic deaths.

Internet Suicide Pacts

Naoki is a 34-year-old Japanese bank employee who has been off work because of stress-related problems for 6 months. He explained to BBC correspondent Andrew Harding (2004) why he was considering joining a suicide group:

> Well, I'm depressed—and that's a disease. But to be honest, I think I've always been interested in killing myself. . . . then I visited a Web site and thought—ah, if I join this, I won't have to go through with it on my own. It's like crossing the road when the traffic light is red. . . . It's not so scary when you're with others (p. 2).

In the 2-week period before this interview, three groups of three people and two groups of four had been found dead by carbon monoxide poisoning in cars on remote mountain roads. They were among the increasing number of Japanese who were planning, and sometimes completing, suicide through the many Internet Web sites and chat rooms devoted to suicide. Another BBC report (2004) suggests that the continuing rise in youth suicide is related to economic problems and an increasing sense of isolation. (Durkheim's alienation form of suicidality seems applicable to the phenomenon Japanese call *hikomorei:* dropouts from society who stay in their rooms and interact mostly with the Internet.)

It is possible that Internet suicide ventures among young people will become a significant problem in the United States as well. Now is not too early to consider ways of reducing this risk. Consideration might be given to supporting Web sites that offer more constructive ways of approaching life crises. Naoki, in fact, has started his own Web site to help other people work through their difficulties without resorting to suicide.

Please note: Physician-assisted death, also known as physician-assisted suicide, is examined in Chapter 10.

Are Suicide Terrorists Suicidal?

Mass violence in the twenty-first century is as brutal as ever before (see also Chapter 8). People have been hacked to death by machetes or incinerated at a distance by computer-guided weapons. The suicide terrorist has entered this crowded field with still another way of dealing death. The societal, political, and military dimensions of these terrorist operations continue to be widely discussed. Here we focus on the question most relevant to this chapter: Are suicide terrorists actually suicidal?

No, they are not suicidal in any meaningful sense of the term. That seems to be the clear answer, based on a review of available worldwide information (Townsend, 2007). The available information indicates caution in speaking of a "typical" suicide terrorist. There are individual differences and circumstances, and it is probable that the act is prompted by several converging motivations. Nevertheless, most have been young men without deep relationship attachments who were part of an organization that holds strong religious beliefs. It is notable that these intensely religious people have engaged in violent self-destruction behavior despite the fact that Islam forbids suicide: It is not acceptable under any circumstances (Abdel-Khalek, 2004). Despite this ban by Islamic scriptures, so-called "suicide cells" have indoctrinated some members to believe that self-destruction is praiseworthy if it also kills enemies of the faith. Terrorists have angrily dismissed the assumption that they are suicidal. For example, one man whose mission was aborted told the interviewer, "This is not suicide. Suicide is selfish, it is weak. This is *istishad*" (Post, Sprinzar, & Denny, 2003). His mission, in other words, was to become a martyr.

Overall, the evidence suggests that the personality and circumstances of terrorists differ significantly from most people who complete or attempt suicide. In essence, suicide is usually prompted by the desperate impulse to end what is experienced as a failing, miserable, and hopeless life. By contrast, the terrorist acts in a jubilant frame of mind with two powerful motivations: (1) The intent of killing as many people as possible and thereby frightening others, and (2) enjoying immortal blessings by earning the status of martyr. Murder and access to immortal splendor are the primary objectives, not the taking of one's own life. There is much more to learn about the origins, functions, and implications of suicide terrorism, but at this point it appears to be something that cannot be readily explained within mainstream suicide theory and research.

SUMMARY

We have seen that suicide takes many forms and that both thoughts and attempts are more common than we might have supposed. Suicide is the eleventh most common cause of death in the general population of the United States, but even higher for adolescents and young adults. Male suicide rates are higher than female rates almost everywhere, but the pattern is reversed in China, where many women, especially in rural areas, suffer from oppression and hopelessness and where female suicide is more in accord with cultural values than in most other nations. Special attention was given to youth suicide, and particularly to risks experienced by college students. We saw that children can also be suicidal, indicating that their concerns need to be taken more seriously by adults. Suicide rates are highest among elderly people, especially white males. An unexplained increase in suicide among middle-aged adults suggests that the baby boomer generation might be experiencing significant difficulties in adjusting to life transitions. The risk factors are identified and discussed. Suicide rates are alarmingly high among young Native Americans and Alaskan Natives, as well as indigenous people throughout the world. African Americans, especially women, consistently have a lower suicide rate than whites, perhaps because of their social support network and active religiosity. Members of the armed forces and veterans are at much higher risk for suicide than others of their age. More attention is urgently needed for traumatized military personnel returning from deployment in Afghanistan and Iraq. Several situations were identified as holding increased risk of suicidality: having HIV/AIDS, gambling, victimization by bullies and other peers, and "suicide by cop."

Rival meanings of suicide have been promulgated in society: suicide as sinful, as criminal, as weakness or madness, as "The Great Death," and as a rational alternative. Sociobehavioral scientists and clinicians have offered their own explanations. Durkheim's pioneering sociological theory is reviewed, featuring his concepts of social integration, collective representations, and the altruistic, anomic, egoistic, and fatalistic types of suicide. Several individual meanings of suicide were then discussed: suicide as reunion, rest and refuge, revenge, penalty for failure, and mistake. Freud's first theory explained suicide as anger toward others that has been turned inward; his second theory proposed warring life (*Eros*) and death *(Thanatos)* instincts in which self-destructive tendencies may dominate because of problems experienced in early development. Richard Heckler's description of "the descent toward suicide" added to our understanding of the sequence of problems, losses, and failed attempts at coping that can lead first to suicidal thoughts, then to attempts and, finally, to death.

Common myths about suicide were identified and critiqued (e.g., that people who talk about suicide will not actually take their own lives). We then considered what we can do to prevent suicide as individuals and as citizens. Three emerging challenges were discussed: the benefits and risks of antidepressant medication, the vulnerability of suicide survivors, and the Internet as a staging ground for youths making suicide pacts. Finally, we examined a challenging question that has emerged from the bloodshed in the Middle East: Are suicide terrorists actually suicidal?

REFERENCES

Abel-Khalik, A. (2004). Neither altruistic suicide, nor terrorism but martyrdom. A Muslin perspective. *Archives of Suicide Research, 8,* 99–113.

Alvarez, A. (1970). *The savage god.* New York: Random House.

Associated Press. (2005, January 14). Suicide rate among soldiers up in Iraq. http://msnbc.msn.com/id/3956787

Associated Press. (2008, March 16). Most suicides in Guard, Reserves. *Arizona Republic,* p. B4.

Beautrais, A. L. (2002). A case control study of suicide and attempted suicide in older adults. *Suicide & Life-Threatening Behavior, 32,* 1–9.

BBC News. (2004, October 12). Nine die in Japan 'suicide pacts.' http://news.bbc.co.uk/asia-pacific/373572.stm

Blankenstein, A. (1998, August 24). Handling suspects who seek "suicide by cop." *Los Angeles Times.*

Bluestein, G. (2007, September 6). American girls' suicide rates rise. *Arizona Republic,* p. A7.

Breed, W. (1972). Five components of a basic suicide syndrome. *Life-Threatening Behavior, 3,* 3–18.

Brown, R. E. (1998). *The death of the messiah* (2 vols.). New York: Doubleday.

Brunstein, K. A., Zalsman, G., Apter, A., Meged, S., Har-Even, D., Diller, R., & Orbach, I. (2007). *Comprehensive Psychiatry, 48,* 8–13.

Canetto, S. S. (2002). Suicide influence and factors: Gender. In R. Kastenbaum (Ed.), *Macmillan encyclopedia of death and dying:* Vol. 2 (pp. 815–818). New York: Macmillan.

Chavez, P. (2005, January 28). Murder charges filed in train crash. *Arizona Republic,* p. A14.

Choron, J. (1972). *Suicide.* New York: Scribner.

Cohen, P. (2008, February 19). Midlife suicide rises, puzzling researchers. www.nytimes.com/2008/(02/19/us/9suicide.htm?_r=1&dsth=1%oref=slogin&em

Colt, G. H. (1991). *The enigma of suicide.* New York: Simon & Schuster.

Conwell, Y. (2001). Suicide in later life: A review and recommendation for prevention. *Suicide & Life-Threatening Behavior, 31* (Suppl.), 32–47.

Darwin, C. (1971). *Origin of the species.* Cambridge: Harvard University Press. (Original work published 1859.)

Dean, C. (1990). *Nam vet.* Portland, OR: Multnomah Press.

de Groot, M. H., de Keijser, J., & Neeleman, J. (2006). Grief shortly after suicide and natural death. *Suicide & Life-Threatening Behavior, 36,* 418–432.

Donne, J. (1977). *Biathanatos.* New York: Arno Press. (Original work published 1646.)

Durkheim, E. (1951). *Suicide.* (J. A. Spaulding & G. Simpson, Trans.). New York: Free Press. (Original work published 1897.)

Erasmus. (1994). *The praise of folly.* New York: Penguin. (Original work published 1509.)

Frantz, S. (2004). Hunt on to explain antidepressant risk. *Nature Reviews Drug Discovery, 3,* 1–2.

Freud, S. (1959*). Mourning and melancholia.* Collected papers: Vol. 4 (pp. 152–172). New York: Basic Books. (Original work published 1917.)

Freud, S. (1961). *The ego and the id.* New York: Norton. (Original work published 1923.)

Grek, A. (2007). Clinical management of suicidality in the elderly: An opportunity for involvement in the lives of older patients. *Canadian Journal of Psychiatry, 52, Supplement 1,* 1–14.

Greyson, B. (1992/1993). Near-death experiences and antisuicidal attitudes. *Omega, Journal of Death and Dying, 26,* 81–90.

Groves, S. A., Stanley, B. H., & Sher, L. (2007). Ethnicity and the relationship between adolescent alcohol use and suicidal behavior. *International Journal of Adolescent Medical Health, 19,* 19–25.

Harding, A. (2004, December 7). Japan's internet 'suicide clubs.' http://news.bbc.co.uk/hi/programmes/newsnight/4071805.stm

Heckler, R. A. (1994). *Waking up, alive.* New York: Ballantine.

Hendin, H. (1995). *Suicide in America* (Rev. Ed.). New York: Norton.

Hunter, E., & Harvey, D. (2002). Suicide influences and practices: Indigenous populations. In R. Kastenbaum (Ed.), *Macmillan encyclopedia of death and dying:* Vol. 2 (pp. 818–821). New York: Macmillan.

Ikeda, R. Mahendra, R., Saltzman, L., Crosby, A., Willis, L., Mercy, et al. (2002). Nonfatal self-inflicted injuries treated in hospital emergency departments—United States, 2000. www.cdc.gov/mmwrhtml/Mm5120a3.htm

Jianlin, J. (2000). Suicide rates and mental health services in modern China. *Crisis, 21,* 118–121.

Jordan, J. R., & McMenamy, J. (2004). Interventions for suicide survivors: A review of the literature. *Suicide & Life-Threatening Behavior, 34,* 337–349.

Kaplan, M. S., Huguet, N., McFarland, B. H., & Newsome, J. T. (2007). Suicide among male veterans: A prospective population-based study. *Journal of Epidemiology & Community Heath, 61,* 619–624.

Kastenbaum, R. (1994). Alternatives to suicide. In L. Tallmer & D. Lester (Eds.), *Now I lay me down. Suicide in the elderly* (pp. 196– 213). Philadelphia: The Charles Press.

Kastenbaum, R. (1995). The impact of suicide on society. In B. L. Mishara (Ed.), *The impact of suicide* (pp. 169–186). New York: Springer.

Kastenbaum, R. (2000). *The psychology of death* (3rd ed.). New York: Springer.

Kelley, M. (2005, January 15). Soldiers' suicide rate climbs. *Arizona Republic,* p. A18.

Krug, E. G., Kresnow, M. J., Peddicord, J. P., Dahlberg, L. L., Powell, K. E., Crosby, A. E., et al. (2003). Suicide after natural disasters. www. nejm. org

Leenaars, A. A., & Wenckstern, S. (1991). *Suicide prevention in schools.* New York: Hemisphere.

LeMaster. P. E., Beals, J., Novins, D. K., & Manson, S. P. (2004). The prevalence of suicidal behaviors among Northern Plains American Indians. *Suicide & Life-Threatening Behavior, 34,* 242–254.

Mancinelli, I., Comparelli, A., Girardi, P., & Tatarelli, R. (2002). Mass suicide: Historical and psychodynamic considerations. *Suicide & Life-Threatening Behavior, 32,* 91–100.

Marion, M.S., & Range, L. M. (2003). African American college women's suicide buffers. *Suicide & Life-Threatening Behavior, 33,* 33–43.

Maris, W. W. (2003). Understanding suicide in the 21st century. *Preventing Suicide, 2,* pp. 4–7.

May, P. A., Van Winkle, N. W., Williams, M. B., McFeeley, P. R., DeBruyn, L. M., & Serna, P. (2002). Alcohol and suicide death among American Indians of New Mexico: 1980–1998. *Suicide & Life-Threatening Behavior, 32,* 240–255.

McClatchy Newspapers. (2008, April 24). Senator: VA hid suicide tries. *Arizona Republic,* p. A1.

McCraig, L. F., & Burt, C. W. (2001). National Hospice Ambulatory Medical Care Survey: Advance data from vital and health statistics; no. 320. Hyattsville, MD: U.S. Department of Health and Human Services. CDC, National Center for Health Statistics.

Minois, G. (1999). *History of suicide. Voluntary death in Western culture.* Baltimore: Johns Hopkins University Press.

Mishara, B. L. (2002). Suicide over the life span: Adolescents and youths. In R. Kastenbaum (Ed.), *Macmillan encyclopedia of death and dying:* Vol. 2 (pp. 832–835). New York: Macmillan.

Mishara, B. L., & M. Ystgaard (2000). Exploring the potential of primary prevention: Evaluation of the Befrienders International Reaching Young Europe Pilot Programme in Denmark. *Crisis, 21,* 4–7.

Mudrian, A., & Peel, J. (2004). *Choosing death. The improbable history of death metal and grindcore.* Los Angeles: Feral House.

Murphy, G. E. (1995). 39 years of suicide research. *Suicide & Life-Threatening Behavior, 25,* 450–457.

Murray, A. (1998). *Suicide in the Middle Ages: Vol. 1. The violent against themselves.* New York: Oxford University Press.

Murray, A. (2000). *Suicide in the Middle Ages: Vol. 2. The curse on self-murder.* New York: Oxford University Press.

Myers, M. F., & Fine, C. (2007). Touched by suicide: Bridging the perspectives of survivors and clinicians. *Suicide & Life-Threatening Behavior, 37,* 119–126.

National Household Survey on Drug Abuse. (2002). Substance use and the risk of suicide among youths. www.samhsa.gov/oas/2k2/suicide/suicide/html

Orbach, I. (1988). *Children who don't want to live.* San Francisco: Jossey-Bass.

Orbach, I., Mikulinger, M., Gilboa-Schechtman, E., & Sirota, P. (2003). Mental pain and its relationship to suicidality and life meanings. *Suicide & Life-Threatening Behavior, 33,* 231–244.

Osgood, N. J. (1992). *Suicide in later life.* New York: Lexington.

Paul, A. (1996). *Suicide wall.* Portland, OR: PakDonald Publishing.

Peck, D. L. (2003). Suicide and suicide trends in the United States, 1900–1999. In C. Bryant (Ed.), *Handbook of death and dying:* Vol. 1 (pp. 319–338).

Pennybaker, J. S., & Stone, L. D. (2004). What was she trying to say? A linguistic analysis of Katie's diaries. In D. Lester (Ed.), *Katie's Diary* (pp. 55–80). New York: Brunner-Routledge.

Phillips, D. P., Welty, W. R., & Smith, M. M. (1997). Elevated suicide levels associated with legalized gambling. *Suicide & Life-Threatening Behavior, 27,* 373–378.

Post, J. M., Sprinzak, F., & Denny, L. M. (2003). The terrorists in their own words: Interviews with 35 incarcerated Middle Eastern terrorists. *Terrorism and Political Violence, 15,* 171–184.

Potter, L. B., Kesnow, M., Powell, K., Simon, T. R., Mercy, J. A., Lee, R. K., et al. (2001). The influence of geographic mobility on nearly lethal suicide attempts. *Suicide & Life-Threatening Behavior, 32* (Suppl.), 42–48.

Priest, D. (2008, January 31). Soldier suicides at record level. *Washington Post,* p. A01.

Rigby, K., & Slee, P. (1999). Suicidal ideation among adolescent school children, involvement in bully-victim problems, and perceived social support. *Suicide & Life-Threatening Behavior, 29,* 119–130.

Royal Commission on Aboriginal Peoples. (1995). *Choosing life: Special report on suicide among Aboriginal Peoples.* Ottawa: Royal Commission on Aboriginal Peoples.

Sarwer, D. B., Brown, G. T. K., & Evans, D. L. (2007). Cosmetic breast augmentation and suicide. *American Journal of Psychiatry, 164,* 1006–1013.

St. Augustine. (1971). *The city of God.* In R. M. Hutchins (Ed.), Great books of the Western world: Vol. 18 (pp. 129– 620). Chicago: Encyclopedia Britannica. (Original work published 426.)

St. Thomas Aquinas. (1971). *Summa theologica.* In R. M. Hutchins (Ed.), Great books of the Western world: Vol. 19. Chicago: Encyclopedia Britannica. (Original work published 1279.)

Schwartz, A. J. (2006). College student suicide in the United States: 1990–1991 through 2003–2004. *Journal of American College Health, 54,* 341–352.

Seiden, R. H. (1977). A tale of two bridges: Comparing suicide incidences on the Golden Gate and San Francisco-Oakland Bay bridges. *Crisis, 13,* 32–40.

Shaffer, D., & Gould, M. (2000). Suicide prevention in schools. In K. Hawton & K. V. Heeringe (Eds.), *Suicide and attempted suicide* (pp. 76–91). New York: Wiley.

Sher, L. (2007). Functional magnetic resonance imaging in studies of the neurobiology of suicidal behavior in adolescents with alcohol use disorders. *International Journal of Adolescence Medical Health, 19,* 11–18.

Stack, S. (2000). The heavy metal subculture and suicide. *Suicide & Life-Threatening Behavior, 24,* 15–23.

Stillion, J. M., & McDowell, E. E. (2001/2002). The early demise of the "stronger" sex: Gender-related causes of sex differences in longevity. *Omega, Journal of Death and Dying, 44,* 301–318.

Townsend, E. (2007). Suicide terrorists: Are they suicidal? *Suicide & Life-Threatening Behavior, 37,* 22–34.

Underwood, A. (2008, May 29). War on wounds. *Newsweek,* p. 44.

Willis, L. A., Coombs, D. W., Drentea, P., & Cockerham, W. C. (2003). Uncovering the mystery: Factors of African American suicide. *Suicide & Life-Threatening Behavior, 33,* 412–419.

Wong, M.-L. & Licinio, J. (2004). From monoamines to genomic targets: A paradigm shift for drug discovery in depression. *Nature Reviews Drug Discovery, 3,* 136–151.

Wouter de Lange, A., & Needleman, J. (2004). The effect of the September 11th terrorist attacks on suicide and deliberate self-harm: A time trend study. *Suicide & Life-Threatening Behavior, 34,* 439–447.

Yang, B., & Clum, G. A. (2000). Childhood stress leads to suicidality via its effects on cognitive functioning. *Suicide & Life-Threatening Behavior, 30,* 183–198.

Yardley, W. (2007, May 14). In Alaskan villages, a culture of sorrow. *The New York Times.* www.nytimes.com/2007/05/14/us/14Alaska.html?

Zarembo, A. (2005, February 3). Study links Prozac to lower suicide rate. *East Valley Tribune,* p. A12.

GLOSSARY

Altruistic suicide: Committed by people who have extremely high or excessive concern for society (Durkheim).

Anomic suicide: Committed by people who fail to receive support and meaning from society (Durkheim).

Collective representations: The symbols and themes that convey the spirit and mood of a culture.

Daishi: An ideal or "Great Death" in Buddhist tradition.

Egoistic suicide: Committed by people who are not under sufficient control by societal norms and obligations (Durkheim).

Fatalistic suicide: Committed by people who are stifled and oppressed by society (Durkheim).

Parasuicide: Attempted suicide.

Seppuku: Suicide by ritualistic disembowelment (in Japanese tradition). Also known in West as *hara-kiri.*

Stoicism: A philosophical tradition that emphasizes rationality and the ability to withstand despair, provocations, and temptations.

Suicidal trance: A state of mind in which a person sees death as the only way to relieve suffering and gives little attention to anything else.

Suicide: Self-murder.

Suicide rate: A measure that is computed by multiplying the number of suicides by 100,000 and dividing by the population number. The suicide rate is not to be mistaken for a percentage.

ON FURTHER THOUGHT . . .

Useful online resources:

American Association of Suicidology
www.suicidology.org
Canadian Association for Suicide Prevention
www.thesupportnetwork.com/CASP
International Association for Suicide Prevention
www.who.int/ina-ngo
Organization for Attempters and Survivors of Suicide in Interfaith Services
www.oasis.org/
Sibling Survivors
www.siblingsurvivors.com
Suicide Information & Education
www.siec.ca

Specialist journal:

Suicide and Life-Threatening Behavior
www.guilford. com

Danger zones:

There are times when people are at particular risk for suicide. At least two of these danger zones have been identified: (1) soon after learning that one has a progressive and life-threatening illness; (2) soon after the death (especially if unexpected) of a close family member. Most people who do not turn to suicide while in these danger zones find other ways to cope with their situations. Here is the challenge: How can people be helped or protected during these times without having their lives invaded or restricted by well-meaning family, friends, or professional caregivers? What should be the guiding principles? How should we go about it—or should we not go about it at all?

This peaceful scene might be only a step away from disaster. The children are playing near a recently built Buddhist shrine in Cambodia. Also nearby, perhaps, are undiscovered landmines that were planted in many locations during the violent Khymer Rouge regime.

chapter 8

VIOLENT DEATH: MURDER, TERRORISM, GENOCIDE, DISASTER, AND ACCIDENT

BERLIN. Death came for Hatun Surucu at a cold bus stop here three years ago. The 23-year-old was the sixth Muslim woman murdered by a relative in Berlin in as many months for being "too Western."
—Joanne Jowan (2008)

I found a man groaning under a tree. He had been shot in the neck and jaw and left for dead in a pile of corpses. Seeking shelter under the very next tree were a pair of widows whose husbands had both been shot to death. Under the next tree I found a 4-year-old orphan girl caring for her starving 1-year-old brother. And under the tree next to that was a woman whose husband had been killed, along with her 7- and 4-year-old sons, before she was gang-raped and mutilated.
—Nicholas D. Kristof (2004a, September 11, p. 1)

It is the leading cause of death in people ages 10 to 24 around the world. Most of these deaths could have been prevented.
—World Health Organization (2008)

On December 26th, I was down by the ocean, talking to a friend, and I saw that the water was shaking. I thought, there is some problem in the middle of the sea.
—Victor Desosa, quoted by William Herman (2005, p. A18)

MESA, ARIZONA: A 16-year-old Mesa student was arrested Wednesday night after police uncovered a list of 53 students he wanted to kill with a rifle he was saving money to buy, Mesa police said Thursday. The teen also detailed how he planned to make a mask and gloves from the skin of his first victim, and then go to the school and kill everybody on the list while he was disguised as the dead student.
—Kristina Davis (2004, p. A3)

Is this world a safe place? Not for those who fall victim to *murder, terrorism, genocide*, disaster, or accident. Some of these deaths challenge our worldview: How can people do such things to each other? In this chapter we consider deaths that stun and enrage, deaths that increase our fear of disorder and vulnerability. Every society's death system is stressed by sudden and disturbing deaths. Violent deaths of human origin traditionally are separated into such categories as murder, infanticide, war, genocide, and terrorism. Other catastrophic events are labeled as accident and disaster. The distinctions are not always that clear-cut, however. One person's terrorism, for example, might be another person's legitimate war. An accident might have been set up by negligence and disregard for safety.

It is painful to reflect on the tragedies encompassed by this chapter, but we would learn nothing by turning away. Consider, for example, just the events already mentioned.

Hatun Surucu was the victim of an *honor killing*. It is estimated by the United Nations that more than 5,000 such murders occur each year (Lederer, 2007). Who are the victims? Always females. Who are the killers? Always members of their own family. Why? Because the sister, daughter, wife or mother was accused or suspected of bringing shame on the family. These murders take place within cultural traditions that severely constrain the rights and opportunities of women. This practice is so deeply entrenched and widespread that United Nations Secretary-General Ban Ki-moon has urged that all nations end the pandemic of violence against girls and women. Most nations have passed laws against beatings and sexual attacks as well as honor killings, but often the crimes continue and are not prosecuted. According to the U. N. leader, violence against women is tolerated under the fallacious cover of cultural practices and norms, within the walls of the home. Or it is used as a weapon in armed conflict, condoned through tacit silence and passivity by the state and the law enforcement community (Lederer, op. cit., p. A18).

Constant surveillance, forced marriages, abduction, false imprisonment, and genital mutilation are often part of the pattern within which honor killings occur. Suicides are also part of the pattern. Shafiliea swallowed bleach after being kidnapped, forced to marry a chosen husband who, along with his entire family, exploited and abused her. It is possible that this was a combined suicide/murder because she dared complain about her treatment (Payton, 2008b). Torpekay, also pressed into forced marriage and a life of abuse, poured gasoline on herself and set herself on fire. She did survive that agonizing attempt (Payton, 2008b). Some of the most horrific in-family murders have more to do with money than with even a stretched concept of honor. Reports from India continue to describe "dowry killings" that are so common that there is even a commonly used term for the phenomenon, "bride burning," because many newly wed women die from being doused with kerosene and set on fire.

The husband's family then reports the death as a "kitchen accident" (Chu, 2007, p. A26).

Young women are also subject to beatings by the husband's family for not bringing in a large enough dowry. Women as property are exceptionally vulnerable to abuse, and abuse sometimes ends only with murder.

Hatun had won a divorce from her forced marriage at age 16. She stopped wearing a headscarf and was now training to become an electrician and dating German men. Her 18 year-old brother killed her for having a boyfriend and bragged to his girlfriend about what he'd done. (Because this crime occurred in a "too Western" nation, the brother was convicted and imprisoned.)

Honor killings and other abuses against women invoke long-standing questions about moral relativism. Should all cultural practices be tolerated and accepted? And, if so, who should be make the adjustment: the Western nation into which honor killing has been imported, or the female-as-property practitioners when they relocate themselves into an equalitarian country? Or are there basic human rights that should be protected in all cultures? This issue becomes more complex if we take to heart the observations of Secretary-General Ban Ki-Moon and others that violence against women is often used as a political and military weapon, and that *izzat* (honor) seems to be insulted by a woman's expression of her own interests, but not by gang rape or genital mutilation.

For many of us, *Darfur* was an unfamiliar name that we might have had difficulty locating on a map. Genocide might have been a more familiar term, but few of us might have felt connected with the realities it denotes. Kristof (2004a, September 11) challenged us to witness the horrendous results of genocide in a distant land. How many have died of violence, starvation, and untended disease in the Darfur area of Sudan? Nobody will ever know for sure. Available information indicates that the toll has been approaching 200,000, as many survivors of the most aggressive phase are struggling with stress, illness, and malnutrition. Genocide is a term introduced by Raphael Lemkin (1944) when he escaped from Nazi Germany. *Genos* is a Greek word signifying race or tribe. The Latin suffix-*cide* signifies killing. Genocide therefore refers to the deliberate and systematic destruction of an ethnic or racial group or a nation. The Darfur massacre fits this definition. Janjaweed mercenaries massacred the inhabitants of this fertile area of Sudan so they could appropriate their property. The invaders' merciless assault was intensified by their beliefs that the black African inhabitants could be destroyed with impunity because they were regarded both as an inferior race and as people who did not share their religious faith. Rape, disfiguration, and slaughter were commonplace. Violence against women was an especially merciless component of the onslaught. Astoundingly, in a return visit Kristof discovered that the two widows and their surviving children he had found under adjoining trees were still alive, had become close friends, and were recovering in a United Nations refugee camp (Kristof, 2004b, October 16). However we might try to explain it, spasms of genocide have replaced reason and compassion with brutality and slaughter.

Are road traffic crashes "accidents?" The World Health Organization believes otherwise. Their statistics indicate that traffic injuries are the leading cause of death for people between the ages of 10 and 24—worldwide! (Brown, 2007). These deaths are still classified as accidents in standard mortality reports. Nevertheless, WHO experts are among the many who hesitate of speak of "accident" when it is clear that the risk of injury and death has been heightened by environmental circumstance and/or public attitudes. Most of these fatal events are regarded as avoidable. The death toll among the young is especially high in developing countries in which many roads and vehicles are unsafe, and prosecution for speeders and drunken drivers minimal. Motorcyclists, operating often without helmets, are particularly vulnerable in both developed and developing nations. Improvements in public education—for pedestrians as well as motorists—

and a higher priority for road safety could sharply reduce the death toll. Nobody denies that real accidents happen. However, to dismiss injury or death as accidental is to ignore the conditions that present an avoidably high risk.

Sometimes it is nature that threatens peaceful lives with sudden and violent death. The *tsunami* that devastated coastal areas of southern Asia on December 26, 2004, is thought to have resulted in more than 175,000 deaths. The village of Galbokka was in an area of Sri Lanka that was engulfed by the massive wave. The people of Galbokka, however, escaped the fate of most other settlements. Victor Desosa, its headman, immediately noticed the strange behavior of the ocean and remembered having seen a similar situation many years previously while a merchant marine. He shouted to his people: "Go! Go!" The inhabitants of Galbokka and neighboring towns scrambled uphill—just before a 20-foot wall of water smashed into their village. Approximately 5,000 people were in danger, only one person died. In recent years, there has been progress in understanding natural disasters and developing ways to prevent, or at least reduce, death and destruction. Disaster preparedness is becoming a significant facet of the death system.

The nation was shocked in 1999 when fourteen students and a teacher were massacred by two students at Columbine High School in Littleton, Colorado. The students' plan could have resulted in a great many more deaths, including those of police officers and other rescuers (Meloy et al., 2001). Something about this violent episode lit a fuse on other high school campuses in various parts of the nation. The 16-year-old with a list of fifty-three fellow students he wanted to kill had to be taken very seriously by authorities. A few months later, another Arizona high school student was taken into custody after she had prepared a detailed plan to kill teachers and security guards. Rifles, semiautomatic pistols, and boxes of ammunition were found in her home. The girl had a history of self-mutilation and suicidal thought (Davis, 2005). Mass murder on campus erupted again on April 16, 2007, when a sophomore biology major at Virginia Tech University shot thirty-two students and teachers before killing himself. Cho Seung-Hui was later described as a loner with eccentric habits whose occasional statements were hard to understand. This explosion of violence was followed by grief for what had happened and fear of vulnerability to other such tragedies. Blame was quickly leveled (justified or not) at law enforcement, university authorities, the ready availability of guns for mentally disturbed people, and the mental health system.

We are ready now to consider death by violence more systematically. We begin with murder, then continue to war, genocide, terrorism, disaster, and accident. Along the way, we will learn not only about violent death, but also about some characteristics of the society in which we live.

MURDER

A person who takes the life of another has committed *homicide*. It becomes murder if a court rules the killing intentional and unlawful. All murders are homicides; some homicides are murders. You may have committed "justifiable homicide" if you used lethal force to protect your own life; or you may be guilty of "negligent homicide" if your carelessness resulted in the death of another person. "Manslaughter" is another distinction used in the criminal justice system when a person is accused of contributing to a death with out intending to have done so. For the purposes of this chapter, however, we will use the simplest and most direct word, murder.

Murder: The Statistical Picture

A college student from a Middle Eastern nation confided to me that on his first visit to the United States he had locked himself inside his Chicago hotel room. Why? "We loved American movies, but people were always getting shot or blown up. I wanted to come to America, but I didn't want to get killed." He soon discovered that the United States is not nearly as violent as some of its most popular movies. Nevertheless, he had chosen to study in the nation with the highest murder rate in the Western world. (Vital statistics are either unavailable or unreliable for some nations.) *Who are the killers in the United States? Who are the victims, and what are the trends?* Unless otherwise noted, our data are based on the most recent available comprehensive information provided by the Bureau of Justice Statistics of the U.S. Department of Justice (2005):

- In 1950 the murder rate was 4.0 per 100,000 in the population. By 1980 the rate had soared to 10.2, the all-time high. The rate started to dip in 1995. The rate declined even more sharply as we moved into the twenty-first century. By 2002 there was a remarkable further drop to 5.6 (although there were still more than 16,000 homicides at that level). This decline was variously attributed to a healthy economy, more efficient police work, and a slightly smaller percentage of young males in the population. Subsequent but incomplete data now suggest that the homicide rate might be increasing again (Lichtblau, 2004). Recent data from Baltimore, Boston, Jacksonville Newark, and Philadelphia indicate a surge of killings (Dale, 2007). Numerous explanations are being offered: rising unemployment, cutbacks in federal support for law enforcement agencies, a shift in emphasis to preventing terrorism instead of controlling street drug traffic and other street crime, and failure to reduce the availability of guns. It remains to be seen whether this most recent trend will continue. It is possible that the mix of factors contributing to surges in murder rate varies from one place to another.
- Firearms (especially handguns) are used in about two of every three homicides. Knives are the next most common. The pattern of weapon use has remained about the same in recent years. Teenage killers are particularly likely to use a gun.
- Southern states continue to have the highest homicide rates, the northeastern states the lowest. Metropolitan areas consistently have higher murder rates than smaller cities and rural counties. Drug and gang-related activities are more common in large cities and are responsible for many of the homicides. The risk of murder often varies markedly within the same state and even within the same community. People living in impoverished areas are more likely to be victims of crime, including murder.

- Men are most often both the killers and the victims. When a female is the victim, the murderer is male in nine of ten cases. When the victim is male, the killer is male in eight of ten cases. About three of every four murder victims are male.
- People are most at risk to become a murder victim between the ages of 25 and 44. Racial differences do exist; homicide victimization rates for blacks are six times higher than for whites, most overrepresented in drug-related deaths, though less often as victims of sexual assault or workplace killings.
- Murders most often are committed by killers who are of the same race as the victims. This fact is worth emphasizing because interracial murders often arouse more fear and anger.
- At least three of five murders are committed by people who are relatives, lovers, friends, neighbors, or colleagues of the victims. The media tends to spotlight killings by strangers. However, the killer and the victim were usually acquaintances, and relatives or intimate companions (most often spouses or ex-spouses).There is a striking geographical difference in the frequency of homicide between people who had a close relationship with each other. Homicides classified as "intimate," "family," "infanticide," and "eldercide" are much more common in large cities (Bureau of Justice Statistics, 2008).
- Murder has become the leading cause of death for women in the workplace. Men are usually the killers. Some observers believe that male insecurity and rage may be intensified by increasing competition from women, especially during a time of high unemployment. Another possibility is that the workplace has become more dangerous for everybody because of the overall social climate of violence and ready access to firearms. Both men and women can become frustrated and angry in a variety of workplace situations, but men are more likely to respond with a lethal outburst.

Patterns of Murder in the United States

A man with a long criminal record ambushes and executes another criminal; this was his day's work. Another man nervously attempts his first holdup. Something goes wrong and he fires his gun at the clerk, then flees in panic. After a bout of drinking, a rejected lover breaks in upon the woman, her children, and her new friend. He sprays the room with bullets from a semiautomatic rifle. A deranged woman strangles her child to obey the voices in her head. She then attempts to take her own life. One, all-encompassing explanation for murder would be difficult to establish. It is more useful to look at some of the specific patterns that murder takes in the United States. We will examine (1) violence and abuse in the home, involving spouse, children, or parents as victims; (2) young men's use of guns, including use in school shootings; (3) mass and serial killers; and (4) political murders (assassinations).

Domestic Violence

Law enforcement officers are well aware that they themselves are at peril when they respond to calls about a family disturbance. (Fortunately, fewer officers have been losing their lives since improvements in tactical and communicational training, and the use of bulletproof vests [Batton & Wilson, 2006].) The killer is usually a man, whether the murder grows out of a domestic or criminal situation. Wives are the most common victims of intrafamilial killings, followed by husbands, sons, daughters, fathers, brothers, mothers, and sisters.

Men and Women Who Kill Their Partners

Many women are subjected to repeated abuse and violence from their male partners (Gracia, 2004). More than a thousand such women a month are killed, even though they had previously sought help from the police or the courts. Often the police had been called to the home on previous occasions. Unfortunately, battered women who resist abuse or fight back are more likely to be killed than those who suffer in silence (Ewing, 1997). Ewing adds that:

control is the ultimate issue in most of these relationships. Batterers have an obsessive if not a pathological need to control the lives of the women with whom they share intimate relationships (p. 22).

Influential cultural traditions have given men enormous latitude for controlling the lives of their wives and children. In the past, wife beating was seldom treated as a criminal offense when women were required to abide by their husbands' decisions and denied the right to vote or own property. There are women today who remember when they were refused a credit card unless it was registered in the name of her husband or father even though they were themselves employed. The approximately 1.5 million physical assaults upon women by their male partners are part of a lingering tradition of male dominance with few consequences for abusive behavior.

Women may also kill, however, especially when they have suffered long-term humiliation, abuse, and injury at the hands of a man.

> "I'm going to kill you, you bitch. I'm going to kill you this night!" Bella ran from side to side in the room, but couldn't get to the door because Isaac had blocked it off. Isaac forced her into a corner, holding her up with a hand in her hair, and began hitting her repeatedly with his fist. Bella could hear the children screaming and kept crying to them to get help. She was sure Isaac would kill her if no one intervened. Then he began to bang her head against the wall. Bella was too dizzy to resist anymore, and just hung on. The attack ended a few minutes later when a relative stopped by and restrained him (Browne, 1987, pp. 61–62).

This violent episode is typical of many others experienced by the battered women in Angela Browne's pioneering study. The rages were often sudden, unprovoked, and savage. Many women described their husbands as having become entirely different people during the assaults (e.g., "He'd get a look in his eyes and start to breathe differently. . . ." "It was like dealing with a stranger." In Bella's case, she endured 20 years of severe abuse until one night Isaac threatened to kill their oldest daughter when she came home. Isaac fell asleep first, however, and Bella and another daughter shot him and then set the house on fire. Although permanently disabled as a result of the repeated attacks, Bella was found guilty of murder in the first degree and sentenced to life in prison.

Legal protection and social support for battered women is still a work in progress in the United States (Zink et al., 2004). There is more public awareness, peer support, and shelters, though often not enough to meet the need. A significant development in Israel offers a possible model for implementation in the U.S. and elsewhere. Murder is regarded as such a serious offense by the Israeli public that the killer's motivation is given little weight. However, the highly publicized case of a wife killing her husband after many years of physical and psychological abuse led to the passage of a law that differs from the standard pattern in Western countries (Herzog, 2006). Judges now have the right to impose a more lenient penalty when a person who suffers prolonged abuse by a domestic partner takes that partner's life. This consequential change in the justice system was strongly influenced by the society's condemnation of spousal abuse.

People Who Kill Children

A grade school teacher may have been speaking for many others when she told me:

> We don't want to notice. We don't want to suspect. We don't want to believe . . . But we have to notice, we have to suspect, and, more and more we have to believe that this child is being very badly mistreated and is at risk for . . . everything. Including death. Including death.

It is no longer unusual to find police officers on the pediatric unit of a hospital. They have been called by a physician or nurse who recognizes a young child's injuries as being the results of abuse (beating, shaking, burning, throwing against a wall or down a flight of stairs) or neglect (starvation, dehydration, lack of physical care). From a nurse on a unit devoted to the care of infants:

> The worst thing is that it happens at all. The next worst thing is that it is becoming almost routine. You see this incredibly beautiful baby. And you see what has happened to it. And you know that even though the baby makes it through this time, you know there very likely will be a next time. Some cases, as soon as we have our first look, we're on the phone to the police. Let me tell you, they hate it, too, maybe as much as we do.

Child abuse and neglect sometimes ends only with death, a pattern that has become all too familiar to social workers, and health care providers.

Most observers attribute the rising abuse and murder of children to dysfunctional families. The inability of families to care for their children is in turn attributed to such factors as unemployment, alcohol and drug use, and the abandonment of mothers and children by the father. Most infant/child homicides occur at home, using weapons of opportunity that include household objects. The killers are usually parents or other caregivers. As with adult homicides, African American children are at significantly higher risk (Bennett et al., 2006). There are at least three additional factors:

Lack of parenting skills. Many people who become threats to their own children have themselves had little opportunity to learn how to be caring and effective parents. Fortunately, these same people often are motivated to improve their parenting skills when given the opportunity through education and counseling.

Mental disorders. Postpartum psychosis is often involved in the murder of infants by their mothers. Male as well as female adults can have mood swings and impulse-control deficits that lead to violent acts against their children.

The replacement father syndrome. This is my name for a situation that is responsible for many instances of severe and repeated child abuse, all too often with a fatal outcome. A woman is left to cope alone with her children. She takes a new lover. For this man, the children are just in the way, unwanted distractions and responsibilities. In a surprisingly high number of instances, the man is set off by the infant's crying or young child's "disobedience." But there is something else here as well: There is an impulse to destroy the children of the previous husband or lover. During an episode of stress or alcohol- or drug-clouded thinking, the new lover attacks the child or children. These attacks may also be premeditated and carried out in a deliberate way—sometimes with the passive acceptance, or even the cooperation of, the woman who does not want to lose her new man.

Neonaticide (the killing of a newborn baby) requires special attention. Most women who commit this act are young, white, unmarried, uneducated, and poor. They have very little in the way of social support and are suffering from depression. Sometimes they conceal their pregnancy from others until the last moment. Usually they have made no plans for either the birth or the care of the child—they are simply overwhelmed and trying to make the problem go away, and do not expect anyone to help them. Most of these young women do not feel sufficiently connected to society to explore the alternative of adoption. Some young women in this predicament do leave the baby at a clinic or child care center. However, many of the unwanted infants are placed in a plastic bag and tossed in a trash or garbage bin to lessen the chance of a connection being made with the mother, and because the symbolism of trash and garbage resonates with the young woman's own feelings of worthlessness and horror.

Children Who Kill Parents

Each year about 300 parents are killed by their children in the United States. *Parricides* are much more often committed by sons than daughters (Moeller, 2001), and by adolescents rather than younger children. The overall pattern:

- Most of the murdered parents and stepparents are white and non-Hispanic.
- The victims are usually in their late 40s or 50s.
- Most of the killers are white, non-Hispanic males.
- Most of the juveniles who kill their parents had been victims of severe abuse by those parents.

Characteristics of adolescents who kill their parents are listed in Box 8-1.

It has often been observed that abuse and violence beget more abuse and violence. This proposition has been well documented in the study of parricide.

Young Men with Guns

The guns that kill are almost always in the hands of men, and most of the men are young. The role of the murderer has been passing to

---

BOX 8-1   ADOLESCENTS WHO KILL THEIR PARENTS

1. A pattern of family violence
2. Failed efforts by the adolescents to get help
3. Failed efforts by the adolescents to escape from the family situation
4. Isolation and few social outlets
5. A family situation that became increasingly intolerable
6. Increasing feelings of helplessness
7. Inability to cope with increasing stress, leading to a loss of self-control
8. Little or no previous involvement with the criminal justice system
9. Ready availability of a gun
10. Alcohol abuse and/or alcoholism in the home
11. Evidence that the adolescent may have been in a dissociative state at or near the time of the killing
12. Evidence that the adolescent offender and other family members felt relieved by the victim's death.

Source: Moeller (2001).

even younger men in recent years: those of ages 15–24 now have the highest rate of committing homicides—as well as the highest rate for becoming a victim of homicide. Nine out of 10 law enforcement officers who are killed in the line of duty are victims of guns in the hands of young men.

Many killings occur during drug-related transactions; others occur as part of gang rivalries. The general public tends to pay less attention to these deaths than to murders that seem to be casual, random, and unpredictable. The belief that such killings are becoming more common has led to the present state of anxiety in which schools, public offices, merchants, and private individuals feel the need for increased security—a need that has resulted in more purchases of guns for self-protection.

One of the most alarming developments has been the apparent increase in drive-by shootings. Law enforcement agencies generally have not tracked drive-by shootings as a special class of crime. Many of these episodes are gang-related, and not a few include the use of alcohol or other drugs. Substance-impaired judgment, however, is not enough to account for such attacks on people unknown to the men holding the guns. How, then, can we understand these incidents?

Consider the following hypotheses:

1. Young males who engage in drive-by and other forms of gun violence have not developed a sense of identification with the human race at large. There is little awareness of how others think and feel, or little empathy. In their own lives they might have been treated without understanding and compassion.
2. Peer acceptance, important for most young adults, is a dominating motivation when plans and prospects for the future seem bleak. "I had no idea of who I could really be," recalls a former member of a violent gang. "So I did for today and waited to get dead."
3. Guns—and automobiles—provide remote devices for dealing death. One can be a "man" by killing another human being as easily as one operates a remote control for the television set.

Every generation known to history has faced the challenge of socializing its young males and directing their spirit and energies into constructive uses. Our generation certainly has its work cut out for it.

School Shootings

In recent years there has been a marked increase in the fear of lethal violence on the campus from middle school to university. Security concerns now compete for attention and funding with the basic educational mission. Many students, parents, and educators sense that schools are losing their special place in the community. Threat and disorder seem to have less respect for the school zone. The protective response to this perceived threat also could have its effects. Chances are that your local school boards and law enforcement agencies have been considering ways of strengthening security. Some members of the community are resisting measures that might induce an atmosphere of excessive control. Here in Arizona there is a legislative proposal that would encourage teachers to carry guns—a good idea, or not? The school campus is becoming a microcosm of U.S. society at large since 9/11. What should be the priority of homeland security as compared with continuing to live as expected and desired?

There is a need to sort out realistic concern from excessive fear. David Altheide's *Creating Fear: News and the Construction of Crisis* (2002), and *Terrorism and the Politics of Fear* (2006) document the potential of the media to manipulate our emotions when a possible threat emerges. Fear, once unleashed and guided by mass media and political interest, can become self-sustaining and dominant. But there is also another side to the media coverage, which now is strongly abetted through Internet postings. Students who feel rejected, mistreated, and misunderstood have the temptation to make themselves "somebody" through an act of violence. Youths who might have found other ways to express and work through their dysphoric feelings could become obsessed with the grand plan of getting even with those who have put them down, and gaining a kind of salvation through their postmortem fame.

The ready availability of guns and recipes for bomb making has opened a dangerous avenue of expression for youth grievances. Furthermore, the victims are no longer limited to a particular person who is perceived as having mocked and rejected the killers. A pair of angry adolescents might choose an entire set of fellow students (e.g., athletes, people of a different race), or just let loose on anybody unfortunate enough to be on the scene. One "quiet kid, pretty much like the others" might bring a rifle and a backup pistol to school one day and fire at his classmates. But why?

- *Killing has gained more acceptance as a way of solving problems.* This belief flourishes in the media and popular culture, with particular attraction for young males. Killing of self or others has often been regarded as the "manly" response to insult and stress. Manhood and guns can have a powerful emotional linkage. The higher rate of male suicide is related to the lethality of the most frequently chosen method—guns. Students who plan or carry out school shootings often intend to complete the death work by turning their guns on themselves.
- *There is no other way to deal with rejection, frustration, and loss.* This belief is mistaken. Nevertheless, some teenagers become killers because they have not yet learned other way to deal with a threat to their relationship with their girlfriends, schoolmates, or teachers. The thought process is therefore likely to be truncated, even reduced to the fatal either/or: "Either she comes back to me or I have to kill—somebody, maybe everybody." A 15-year-old arrested for killing his parents and two classmates and wounding 20 others explained: "I had no other choice." Take frustration, inexperience, and oversimplified thought processes and add the availability of weapons—the potential for a lethal outcome is there.
- *The world is divided between Us and Them (or just Me and All of You).* Anybody who has survived adolescence is likely to remember the "in groups," the students who seemed to get all the attention and all the breaks. Even people who were among the most popular students later report that they often suffered from feelings of uncertainty, anxiety, and being left out. Furthermore, all the prejudices that have been nurtured in society have the opportunity to play themselves out in the high school years. The Columbine High School shootings, for example, had a racist component that has been associated with the influence of skinhead organizations. There are always others to blame and attack when things go wrong in one's own life.

A neglected question: why do so many students *not* turn to violence when they are angry, frustrated, and depressed? What in themselves, their families, the schools, and the communities serves as protection and alternative?

Mass and Serial Killers: Who Are They and Why Do They Do It?

The *mass killer* is alarming to society both because of the many lives destroyed and because his very existence confounds our expectations of human feeling and conduct. A mass killing is one in which several people die in a single episode. Typically, mass murders in the United States involve firearms and are the work of a lone killer (a male). Most often, the killer knows few if any of his victims. He may have wanted to get back at a particular person he thought had treated him badly, but had no compunction about slaying many others as well. As with the school shootings, mass murderers in general often have a strong suicidal streak, willing even to die at the scene of their crimes. This is in contrast to most *serial killers*, who intend to keep on killing as long as they can.

The public perception of the mass murderer has generally proved to be accurate—a person who feels rejected by society, angry at real or imagined mistreatment, and motivated to "get back" at all that has oppressed him, even though he has suffered no harm from the particular individuals he has killed. James Oliver Huberty personifies this description. He had lost his long-time job as a skilled worker when the plant had to downsize because of economic conditions. He moved to another state, found another job, but lost it. Over the years, he had often practiced shooting his rifles into the basement wall and occasionally frightened his neighbors by brandishing a weapon. One afternoon he told his wife he was going to "hunt humans." She assumed that James was just trying to get her upset again. He kissed her good-bye and walked back to the McDonald's where he and his family had lunched a few hours earlier. He opened fire, killing 21 and wounding another 19 before being felled by a police sharpshooter.

The available explanations about such killers remain inadequate, however, because only a very few people with a background of dysfunctional families, rejection, and hard times become mass murderers. Some mass murderers are psychotic, but again, not all psychotic people become mass murderers. In general, mass murderers (and serial killers) do not attract much attention until they are apprehended or shot. Others have little sense of their own identities and are willing to become disciples of a charismatic person—such was the situation with Charles Manson and several of his followers. Their mass killing episodes may also be compared with the hate group dynamics expressed by Nazis and emulated by others. Rarely is the mass murderer a hardened criminal, although a spotty history of property crime is common (Fox & Levin, 2001). The killings sometimes follow a period of frustration when a particular event triggers sudden rage; yet, in other cases, the killer is coolly pursuing some goal he cannot otherwise attain.

A mother comforts her daughter after one of the D.C.—area sniper killings that targeted people at random.

The mass murderer is typically a white male in his late 20s or 30s. However, media coverage through the years underestimated the frequency of African American serial killers. A study by Anthony Walsh (2005) requires a revision of this assumption. Walsh examined United States homicide data from 1945 to 2004. He found that 90 of the 413 serial killers were African American. This translates to a 2 to 1 overrepresentation of African Americans among serial killers. Fear of being accuses of racism is one possible reason for avoiding mention of African American serial killings, but Walsh suggests that the more significant factor is that the victims usually are African Americans as well—and, therefore, not as "newsworthy." A thorough reevaluation of the relationship between race and serial killing remains to be done.

Several additional facts about mass killers are worth keeping in mind:

1. Mass killers do not draw their violence from the Southern tradition of homicide, although murder is most common there. It is possible Southerners have continued to provide more support for each other through neighborhoods, churches, and other community organizations, thereby reducing the sense of alienation that can lead to violence against others.
2. Boom cities attract many people whose high hopes fail to be fulfilled. They become bitter, disillusioned, and ready to try something different to get rid of their frustrations and anger (as was the case with Huberty).
3. Most mass murderers are not psychotic but have an antisocial personality (also known as "sociopath" or "psychopath"). This type of killer does not hear voices that order him to kill. Basically, the antisocial personality does not feel affection or empathy for other people. This is the person who uses other people without remorse. The antisocial personality is likely to have a low tolerance for frustration and to explode in rage when things go wrong.

Nineteenth-century London's "Jack the Ripper" was a male who chose women for his victims. Prostitutes have long been at special risk for serial killing. Other serial killers, however, have attacked children or hospital patients, while others have selected almost any available target. Female serial killers come to attention less often because they use poison and other "quiet" methods and often have a financial motive (Hickey, 2005).

It is probable that the most lethal serial killer in U.S. history was an opportunistic physician who was active in Chicago just a few years after the depredations of Jack the Ripper in London. H. H. Holmes is described as a charismatic person who was skillful in attracting lonely or naïve women, gaining access to their sexual favors and funds, then making them disappear in the bustling chaos surrounding the 1893 Chicago World's Fair (Larson, 2004). His approach was cold blooded and methodical. When Holmes was through with a woman, he most often tricked her into entering a gas chamber he had constructed in his hotel. He would then dispose of the woman's remains in another unit not often found in hotels: a crematorium. He might have killed a hundred women—or twice or three times that number—before being apprehended. His persona as a charming and considerate physician concealed a person who believed that other people existed only to serve his needs.

Experts caution against reducing all serial killers to a single stereotype. Selerian (2002) notes that "serial killer" is not a medical diagnosis or scientific concept: it only refers to a person who murders repeatedly. Some serial killers are delusional, others are sexual predators, and still others experience periodic impulses to hunt and kill. There often are early warning signs, however. The child who takes pleasure in tormenting animals could be on the watch list for future serial killers.

Political Murder: Assassination in the United States

Abraham Lincoln, John F. Kennedy, Robert F. Kennedy, and Martin Luther King, Jr.—The *assassinations* of these four leaders have become a disturbing part of American history. The murder of a political leader has both its private and its public side. A child loses a father, and a wife her husband. Some people take comfort in the theory that a rational individual would not make an attempt on the life of a political figure. The mental illness theory does not account for all or even most of the *assassination* attempts. Some of the most prominent political assassinations and assassination attempts in the United States are listed in Table 8-1.

Four types of assassins have been identified: Type I—Political Extremists; Type II—Rejected and Misguided People; Type III—Antisocial Personalities; and Type IV—Psychotics. Social isolation or disturbances of interpersonal relationships were characteristic of most of the assassins. They differed, however, in their motives for their assassination attempts. This can be most clearly seen when comparing the Type I and the Type IV assassins.

The public stereotype of the crazed assassin is represented by the men who threatened the lives of Andrew Jackson, James Garfield, and Theodore Roosevelt. These people were delusional. Guiteau, for example, had a friendly attitude toward Garfield but convinced himself that the president must be killed to "save the Republic." He would later say that God had made him do it. By contrast, the Type I assassins were extremists motivated by political objectives. Booth, Collazo, Torresola, and Sirhan identified themselves with nationalistic causes. Czolgosz thought that by killing McKinley he would be striking a blow for "the good working people." None of these men were insane (within a legal framework) or psychotic (within a psychiatric framework).

Type III assassins were antisocial personalities. These men, such as Bremer, Byck, and Zangara, hated the society they felt had rejected them. Unable to express feelings other than helplessness or rage, they cast about for a symbolic target. They did not have personal animosity toward their intended victims. Like the mass murderers, the Type III assassins showed no remorse. Although neither the typical mass murderer nor the Type III assassin is "crazy," each has a fundamental character flaw in the ability to feel and express ordinary human feeling.

TABLE 8-1

Political Assassination Attempts, United States

Year	Intended Victim	Assassin	Outcome
1835	Andrew Jackson	Richard Lawrence	Unharmed
1865	Abraham Lincoln	John Wilkes Booth	Killed
1881	James Garfield	Charles Guiteau	Killed
1901	William McKinley	Leon Czolgosz	Killed
1912	Theodore Roosevelt	John Schrank	Unharmed
1933	Franklin Roosevelt	Giuseppe Zangara	Unharmed[a]
1935	Huey Long	Carl Weiss	Killed
1950	Harry S. Truman	Oscar Collazo & Griselio Torresola	Unharmed[b]
1963	John F. Kennedy	Lee Harvey Oswald	Killed
1968	Martin Luther King, Jr.	James Earl Ray	Killed
1968	Robert Kennedy	Sirhan Sirhan	Killed
1972	George Wallace	Arthur Bremer	Wounded
1974	Richard Nixon	Samuel Byck	Unharmed[c]
1975	Gerald Ford	Lynette Fromm	Unharmed
1975	Gerald Ford	Sara Moore	Unharmed
1981	Ronald Reagan	John W. Hinckley, Jr.	Wounded

Sources: Clarke (1982) and Crissman and Parkin (2002).

[a]Chicago Mayor Anton Cermak was killed and four others were wounded in the volley of shots fired at President Roosevelt.

[b]Security guards Leslie Coffelt and Josph Downs were wounded; Coffelt died as he returned fire and killed Torresola.

[c]Byck killed two Delta pilots and wounded a cabin attendant in a failed attempt to crash the plane into the White House.

TERRORISM

Terrorism did not begin with the attacks of September 11, 2001. What did begin was a mixed sense of vulnerability, anxiety, grief, and rage that continue to this day. Once a rather distant concept—terrorism was something that happened sometimes to other people in other places it now became salient in American life. A previous bombing of the New York's World Trade Center had killed 6 people and injured hundreds of others, but left the massive establishment intact. The explosion that killed 168 people and demolished the Alfred P. Murrah Federal Building in Oklahoma City on April 15, 1996, was an alarming event whose national impact was eventually reduced when it was learned that domestic, rather than foreign terrorists were to blame. Then came 9/11/01. Here, we will size up terrorism at large, and then discuss events and concerns in the United States.

Terrorism in History

Terrorism has a long and diverse history. The Assassins were members of an eleventh-century Middle Eastern religious sect devoted to bringing about a new millennium. The Assassins carried out expert terrorist operations for about 200 years. Disguising themselves and armed with hidden daggers, they killed powerful leaders and created a climate of terror. The Assassins expected to die as they completed their missions.

During this same period, Christian Crusaders fought for possession of the Holy Sepulchre (which actually no longer existed). The Crusaders were not terrorists, but they did abandon themselves to episodes of massacre and atrocity. For example, they slaughtered many of the inhabitants of Jerusalem, including women and children. The Jews of this city, who had played no particular role in the hostilities, were herded into a mosque and burned alive. The Inquisition, established in 1231, persecuted suspected heretics through much of Western Europe. Thousands were burned alive, and many others died under torture. The later Protestant version of religious persecution was no less cruel and deadly. Suspected Catholic priests and sympathizers were subjected to elaborate torture before execution. Many conquerors have used

terror tactics to undermine the will to resist. Tamerlane, for example, buried thousands of his victims alive, and a Transylvanian ruler was known as Vlad the Impaler for that reason. Terrorism often it has become an expression of brutal impulses under the banner of a rationalized purpose.

For the word *terrorism* itself, we must turn to the French Revolution. About 30,000 suspected "enemies of the people" were sent to the newly invented guillotine in 1793–1794. Robespierre had the curious belief that slicing off heads that had contained politically incorrect thoughts would engender an enlightened society in which everybody lived in love and harmony. Like most other terrorist actions, the "reign of terror" failed to achieve its objectives, and Robespierre himself went to the guillotine.

An enduring image of this reign of terror was created by the artist, Jacque-Louis David. The pale man drooping over the side of a wooden tub on the next page was a physician and the most influential French journalist of his time. He was also a fanatic who was not satisfied with the bloody work already in process: the beheading of members of the aristocracy. He insisted that all traitors be slaughtered—and Jean-Paul Marat would provide list after list. Panic ensued as anybody who was disliked by anybody else became at risk for the guillotine. Another keen advocate of the revolution was a young woman by the name of Charlotte Corday. She came to Paris, where she bought herself a green hat and a kitchen knife. Corday gained entrance to Marat on the pretext of having a fresh list of traitors for him. Marat assured her, "Don't worry, in a few days I will have them all guillotined." And then she stabbed him to death. It was Marat she considered the most vile traitor for turning the "Liberty, Equality, Fraternity" movement into a horror show. (And, yes, she was soon beheaded.) The great David had blood as well as paint on his hands: he himself had signed about 300 death warrants.

Terrorism then, and terrorism now: it has a way of escaping everybody's control, no matter what its supposed original purpose and scope.

Terrorism remained afoot throughout the nineteenth century. The Thugs (or Thuggees) of

India robbed and strangled travelers. The Thugs regarded these killings as acts of religious devotion. Like many other terrorists, they professed to hold death in contempt.

The Ku Klux Klan (KKK) and the Molly Maguires exemplify terrorist groups that formed in the United States shortly before and after the War Between the States. Started in 1867, at first the KKK attempted to protect Southern whites from threats to their accustomed way of life. Before long, however, the KKK had become a terrorist organization intended to keep the freed African Americans "in their place." The KKK engaged in property destructions, threats, beatings,

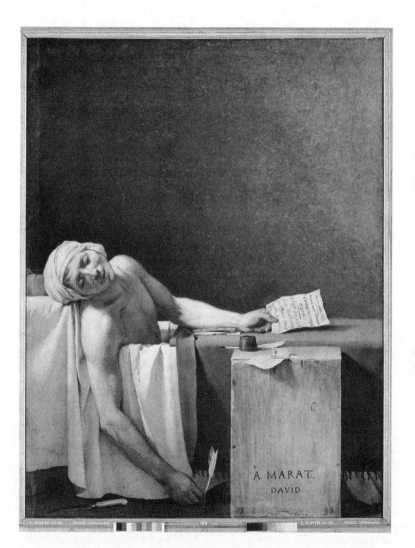

A distinguished physician and journalist, Jean-Paul Marat was also a fanatic who sent many of his French compatriots to the guillotine during the reign of terror. His own blood joined the flow when he was assassinated in his bathtub. The artist, Jacque-Louis David, also signed many execution warrants.

and lynchings. The KKK often had the support of the local establishment (or actually was the local establishment under its robes). Thousands of African Americans were lynched, but the actual number cannot be determined, in large part because these murders usually were covered up and no records were kept. Historian Philip Dray (2003) observes that:

Atrocities in isolated Southern backwaters often went completely unremarked upon, as did race-riot killings of blacks by mobs or police officers in cities. Almost every black American family has a story in its history of an ancestor who "come up missing," who vanished into that empty place—the rural crossroads or rail siding, the bayou or jail cell. It is a living memory to most black Americans that their forebears were lynched and routinely subjected to violence and intimidation, and that they lived in almost constant fear of seeing a loved one lynched or of being targeted themselves (p. xi).

Despair and anger inspired a protest song that has become a part of American culture. Billie Holiday introduced "Strange Fruit" in 1938. Despite the popularity of the song and the singer, Columbia Records refused to produce it—believing it too controversial. A smaller company did make a recording, and it has remained a haunting reminder of the violence that was condoned for many years in the United States as though it did not exist. The lyrics are given in Box 8-2.

The Molly Maguires first made themselves known in the 1860s as many Irish Americans faced oppressive and dangerous circumstances. Wakin (1984) describes one of these situations:

In Pennsylvania, the oppressors were mine owners who brutalized the miners and their families. The miners went down into the dangerous hell of the mines, often with their children along, digging up wealth for the owners and a marginal living for themselves. New waves of immigrants enabled the owners to keep wages low; workers were forced to live in company houses and buy at company stores. Even while working, many a miner received, instead of his monthly pay, a "bobtail check" showing that he owed the company money (p. 147).

BOX 8-2 STRANGE FRUIT

Southern trees bear strange fruit,
Blood on the leaves and blood at the root,
Black bodies swinging in the southern breeze,
Strange fruit hanging from the poplar trees.

Pastoral scene of the gallant South,
The bulging eyes and the twisted mouth,
Scent of magnolias, sweet and fresh,
Then the sudden smell of burning flesh.

Here is fruit for the crows to pluck,
For the rain to gather, for the wind to suck,
For the sun to rot, for the trees to drop,
Here is a strange and bitter crop.

Source: "Strange Fruit" By Lewis Allan. Copyright © 1939 (Renewed) by Music Sales Corporation (ASCAP). International Copyright Secured. All Rights Reserved. Reprinted by Permission.

The Molly Maguires were victims turned terrorists. They threatened and beat mine owners, then used bombs to create an atmosphere of terror, killing several people they considered to be oppressors. Like many other organizations that resorted to terror, it failed to achieve its basic objectives. Nineteen of its own members were executed, and it would be many hard years before conditions for miners would be somewhat improved.

Twentieth-Century Terrorism and Genocide

What will historians say about the recently elapsed twentieth century? One fact will be impossible to overlook: the infliction of deprivation, cruelty, and death upon millions of people. Never before were there so many victims of human violence. How many people died as a result of persecutions and massacres in the twentieth century? Twenty five million deaths would be a conservative estimate (and does not include direct war casualties). Fanatic Khmer Rouge battalions slaughtered more than a million Cambodians in their attempt to impose a Communist reign on a traditional society. Stalin became the most blood-stained mass killer of all time when he supervised the massacre and starvation of 11 million of his own citizens in 1929–1932 and then took another 600,000 lives in the purge of 1937–1938. During the partition of India in 1946, Hindus and Sikhs moving east were slaughtered by Muslims, and Muslims moving west were slaughtered by Hindus and Sikhs. As a result, about a million died.

The list goes on, each entry presenting its distinctive version of inhumanity. Japanese soldiers tortured, bayoneted, burned, and buried alive perhaps as many as 400,000 Chinese civilians in Nanking. Additionally, Japanese physicians and scientists conducted lethal experiments on Chinese civilians. *The Secret Genocide of Axis Japan's Germ Warfare Operation* is the subtitle of historian Daniel Barenblatt's (2003) disturbing book.

Japanese Unit 131 tested various methods of spreading man-made epidemics of anthrax, cholera, dysentery, and other pestilences. It is estimated that their biological warfare campaign killed about 600,000 people. Water supplies were contaminated and disease-bearing rats and fleas were released into the population. Survivors recall that smiling doctors also handed out contaminated food to hungry children.

In 1994 Hutu extremists in Rwanda conducted a systematic genocide campaign against their Tutsi countrymen. The two groups had already clashed in both war and terrorist activities, but now the Hutu were out to exterminate the Tutsi. Death squads killed about 50,000 Tutsi's in just a few days. Families were hacked to death with machetes or burned alive. It was estimated that about 300,000 died while the international community was "evaluating the situation." The most frequently cited programs

A Cambodian survivor prays for Khmer Rouge victims in front of a map made from their skulls.

The Holocaust took more than a million lives during World War II and left many others widowed and orphaned. Here are a few children who survived Nazi imprisonment in the Auschwitz (Poland) camp.

of mass terrorism do not even include government-sponsored massacres in Pakistan and North Korea that have seemed to vanish from collective memory.

Numbers can be numbing. We can grasp and respond to the death of one person, to the death of a family, perhaps to the death of all occupants

of a jet liner. It is much harder to grasp both the individual and the mass tragedy when the victims are numbered in the thousands or in the millions. Meet a survivor, though, and the reality starts to come through. For example, an aged woman in Arizona never forgot how her childhood and very nearly her life were destroyed when Turkey launched a campaign to eliminate its Armenian population. In her own neighborhood, the men were rounded up for "routine questioning" that turned out to be excruciating torture, followed by killing. She and her family barely managed to escape: about 800,000 other Armenian women, men, and children did not. Peter Balakian (2003) reminds us that most of the Armenian intellectual and cultural leaders were imprisoned, tortured, and killed in the capital city of Constantinople on one night (April 24, 1915). They could not believe such a thing could be happening to them.

A generation later, victims of the Nazi genocide also were stunned to find that their countrymen and neighbors had turned upon them with such brutality. As World War I raged, relatively little attention was given to the slaughter of civilians in Armenia. Unimpeded by international pressure or dissension in their own land, the Turks proceeded to massacre Syrians, Assyrian Christians, and Greeks as well. Adolph Hitler would later observe that the international community had barely seemed to acknowledge these massacres; perhaps they wouldn't much care if he did the same with Jews, Romani (Gypsies), and other people who did not deserve to live.

It is not within the scope of this book to examine these events in detail. However, we can offer a few observations that are based securely upon the available evidence:

1. Terror has often been unleashed against people who share the same land, but are *perceived as different*. Most German Jews, for example, were law-abiding and patriotic. However, when Hitler pushed the anti-Semitism button, Germans who also happened to be Jewish were first ostracized, then slaughtered. Hindus, Sikhs, and Muslims alike had shared the hardships of drought, famine, and colonial subjugation, but the mutual perception that their religious differences were all-important led to widespread atrocities and killings during the partition of India and creation of Pakistan—and hostilities have again resumed.

2. Killing is often preceded by *denying the other person's fundamental reality as a human being*. Those "others" are less than human. In this sense, the murder takes place first in the mind. In his penetrating analysis of genocidal terror, Eric Weitz (2003) documents the connection with fallacious beliefs in racial or ethnic "purity" and equally fallacious interpretations of the post-Darwinian "survival of the fittest" doctrine. One superior race is truly human; the others are to be exploited or eliminated because they are flawed subhumans. Declare that a threat or crisis exists, and one's logical course is to destroy or enslave those unworthy Others.

3. *Fear kills*. Reigns of terror have often been triggered because those in power have feared overthrow. The Stalinist purge of 1937–1938, for example, was directed almost exclusively at Soviet citizens suspected of harboring politically unreliable thoughts. These regime-sponsored murders had the effect of seriously weakening Soviet military capabilities in advance of the Nazi invasion. An alleged plot against the government of Indonesia aroused fear-driven hysteria of such magnitude that 600,000 fellow citizens were slaughtered in a short period of time, most of them innocent of any crime or criminal intention.

4. *Cold-blooded "rationalism" kills*. There have been many episodes of terrorism in which the attackers were frenzied by high passions. However, some of the most destructive terrorist operations have been systematically planned as "rational" ways to achieve political objectives. Stalin again comes to mind with the systematic starvation, as well as murder, of millions of peasants who supposedly were to be liberated by the Communist revolution.

5. *Religious intolerance instigates and justifies terrorism*. Many people live harmoniously with people of other faiths. Nevertheless, some of the bloodiest reigns of terror have been launched by people who were convinced both that they alone have the true religion and that they therefore must convert or destroy all others. There is no hesitation, no reflection, no compassion. True believers often appear on both sides of religious/ethnic issues. For example, the "ethnic cleansing" in Kosovo drew much of its virulence from religious intolerance. The actual differences

Thousands of people were massacred and thousands more succumbed to starvation and disease as they fled their homes in Darfur (Sudan). Here a boy infected with hepatitis E has reached a hospital in a safe zone and is being comforted by his mother.

in religious belief and practice might seem insignificant when compared with what is held in common, but to the people involved it can be sufficient cause for bloodshed.

I have known mental patients who heard voices urging them to kill another person. They suffered terribly because they did not want to kill and yet could not stand the pressure—so they sought help. I have yet to learn of a religious cult that asked for help to rid itself of murderous impulses.

6. *Terrorism fails*. Seldom has a terrorist organization or movement achieved its objectives. The Nazis' "final solution," for example, was not only brutal to the extreme, but also contributed significantly to Germany's defeat. *Germany without Jews* (Engelmann, 1984) was a weakened nation, having lost many of its leading scientists, physicians, and other professionals. Furthermore, Germany was left with a heritage of guilt and shame over the participation of many people who became *Hitler's Willing Executioners* (Goldhagen, 1996). In an earlier epoch, an arrogant Spanish monarch banished the Moors who had been contributing much to their culture for centuries. The harsh conditions of this banishment led to a great many deaths. This "purification" or "ethnic cleansing" plan, dealt Spain a self-inflicted blow from which it never recovered. Repeatedly, terrorism has failed to achieve lasting success; most often it has led to violent discord among the terrorists themselves, retaliation from others, and the loss of opportunities for improving one's conditions by positive efforts.

7. *Silence nurtures the expansion of terrorism and genocide*. Samantha Power has characterized genocide as "A Problem from Hell" (2002) in her disturbing examination of the American response to mass violence throughout the twentieth century. "Official knowledge, official silence" has been a recurrent theme. How much responsibility should one nation take for the horrors being inflicted in another land? How much responsibility, if any, should we have as individuals? What guidance should we draw from religious values? Ethical issues become matters of urgency whenever the specter of genocide arises.

9/11/01 AND ITS CONSEQUENCES

The transition to the twenty-first century brought no relief from terrorism and genocide. September 11, 2001, became a date that divides past and future in the United States. Commercial jets, hijacked by terrorists, crashed into the World Trade Center (WTC), the Pentagon, and a field in Shanksville, Pennsylvania. The death toll is given in Table 8-2.

TABLE 8-2

Deaths from the Terrorist Attacks of 9/11

	WTC	*Pentagon*	*Shanksville*
Jetliner	92	65	64
Ground	2,801	184	0
Total	2,893	249	64

The Day of the Attacks

The sense of immunity from mass violence came to an abrupt end on this date. Survivors, first responders, and witnesses quickly realized that things would never again be the same. The words of first responders to the World Trade Center attacks (Libaw & Goldman, 2002) vividly express the shock when all that was solid and familiar suddenly dissolved. New York City fire captain Dennis Tadia: "It did happen, right? It's not something I'm going to close my eyes and open again and I'm going to see the tower again? It's not there." Jose Casaliggii, another member of the fire department, reports:

> You have two 110-story buildings. You don't find a desk, a chair, a phone, a computer. The biggest piece of a phone I found was half a keypad. The buildings are dust. How are we supposed to find people? (p. 2)

Witnesses of the World Trade Center attack were appalled as they watched people leap to their deaths rather than perish in flame and smoke. Firefighters who had experienced many previous disasters were overwhelmed by the sight and sound of bodies hitting the pavement.

The Japanese surprise attack on Pearl Harbor on December 7, 1941, had a powerful and enduring impact on American attitudes. The events of 9/11 had an even more profound effect. The casualties were mostly civilians, the destruction occurred on the mainland, the skyline of a great city was altered, and millions of people could see the events on their television sets as they occurred. Smoke continued to rise from the World

Trade Center disaster site (Ground Zero) for another 6 months, and body recovery efforts persisted long after hope of rescuing live victims had vanished. The attack was also repeated in video reports on a daily basis, etching it into the consciousness of children as well as adults.

The valiant rescue effort earned worldwide respect and admiration. Nevertheless, chaos had won. Thousands had died. The towers had fallen. Death—raw, unpredictable, unfair death—could still break loose in a society that had established so many levels of physical, symbolic, and ritualistic protections against mortal danger. We were not supposed to die young, violently, and in public, especially in a place where international commerce flourished. Our society's apparent victories over death anxiety had been snatched away in one morning of terror, to be replaced by a long wave of grief and stress that continues to this day.

The two other terrorist attacks of 9/11 were just as deadly to jetliner passengers and crew—all died. The fate of United Airlines Flight 93 differed from the other hijacked airliners. Modern communication technology—telephones in the sky—made it possible for some passengers and crew to learn of the two earlier attacks. Assaulting the hijackers, they prevented the airliner from completing its mission of destroying another major target and killing many more people on the ground. This disaster will long be remembered for the poignancy of the last telephone conversations between several passengers and their family members and the quick thinking and resolve with which they responded against the hijackers.

Immediate Response to the Loss and Trauma

Doctors and nurses rushed to New York City hospitals and clinics, and the call went out for blood donations. The health care system demonstrated its ability to overcome bureaucratic tangles and make its resources quickly available during a crisis. But where were the patients? Gradually, the almost unbelievable situation became clear: Those directly affected by the attack were beyond medical assistance. The absence of survivors seemed to merge with the silence at Ground Zero. All those active, lively people had vanished in just a few minutes.

Firefighters and other first responders had also expected to save people. There would be much exhausting labor and frustration before the volunteers were forced to conclude that there were no lives to be saved. There was another important objective to achieve, however: recovering and identifying the victims. It was recognized that the affected families could not put their lives back together until they had a sense of closure, which included a funeral and memorial service for the persons they had lost. The firefighters also felt strongly for their comrades who had not returned from the WTC; together they also had been a kind of family. The men and women searching through the debris developed their own spontaneous rituals when a body was found. All in the vicinity would pause in their work, kneel, and observe a moment of silence. Then—back to work. Eventually, memorial services were held for families who were left without the physical remains of their loved ones.

Memorial services and media coverage were exceptional in their recognition of individuals who lost their lives at all of the attack sites. At first, the high number of fatalities dominated national response. Soon, though, attention became focused on the individuality of the victims. The care taken to remember individuals probably served as a significant step in the long process of healing. Compassion arose not only throughout the United States but also throughout many other nations. This sense of sharing in the sorrow was probably enhanced by the fact that many people elsewhere had visited New York or knew people who lived and worked there. The sorrow of bereaved family members resonated with the personal experiences of those who had experienced traumatic loss in their own lives.

Soon after the disaster, there was a perceptible increase in overt religiosity and patriotism. Churches reported higher attendance, and flags went on display throughout the nation. The search for understanding, strength, and protection as well as the comfort of being with other people contributed to this heightened expression of faith in God and devotion to country. This large-scale emotional response to a large-scale disaster brings to mind the terror management theory of death anxiety that we considered in Chapter 1. The arousal of individual death anxiety might prompt people to seek intensified support from the pillars of society.

The courage and determination of rescue workers impressed and inspired the public. First responders replaced "celebrities" as cultural heroes, recalling days past when volunteer firefighters were among the most admired people in society. A new generation now realized that there are "real-life" heroes among us.

The first phase of response was marked by sorrow and pain but also by a sense of national unity and compassion. It could also be described as a feeling-oriented and self-reflective phase. Many people experienced vicarious grief (Chapter 11), sorrowing for other people's sorrow. There was concern for the stress and trauma experienced by bereaved family members, especially the possible impact on children. And when NYC Mayor Rudolph Giuliani mentioned that these events had forced him to think about his own mortality, it is probable that many others agreed. Perhaps it

was time to reflect upon our own lives, with a renewed awareness of death in mind.

The Mood Changes

Compassion, altruism, and a sense of unity are often prominent in the early response to a disaster. This was certainly the case with 9/11, but, as in many other post-disaster situations, the early mood and response had limited staying power (Weaver, 2002).

Feeling-orientation and personal reflection soon gave way to military rhetoric and the call to arms against terrorism. It would be national policy to destroy the terrorist and improve protective measures against further attacks. Airport security would be tightened—and tightened again and again. Attempts would be made to seal the borders against terrorist infiltrators. Congress would vote to establish a new cabinet-level Department of Homeland

Sorrow, compassion, and a surge of heightened patriotism
united the nation after the September 11, 2001, terrorist attacks.

Security. Funding priorities would shift to deal with the terrorism issue. Government agencies would be granted additional powers of surveillance and investigations, detain suspects, and use lethal force when deemed necessary.

The military stance quickly took precedence over the feeling-orientation and self-reflection that had characterized much of the public and personal response. The national image was transformed from passive victim to aggressive crusader. Preparation for action turned attention away from the quest for meaning, reflection, and emotional recovery. People who had lost family members and friends in the terrorist attacks would continue to struggle with the emotional impact and the recovery process. The general public, though, was being instructed to set aside the inner challenge of feelings and reflections and dedicate itself instead to the external threat of terrorism (Kastenbaum, 2002).

Within a few months of the terrorist attacks. church attendance declined to its previous level (Rose, 2002). American flags were less frequently displayed. Baseball games were played without the singing of "God Bless America." An early proposal to establish 9/11 as an official national day of mourning was tabled for lack of support (CNN, 2002), and the public went back to ignoring news of the world (Tribune Wire Services, 2002). People were still affected by the attacks, some very much so. Life in the United States, however, was trying very hard to return to normal.

The national mood now allowed criticisms to be expressed. Bereaved families organized in protest against the bureaucracy that had been established to provide death benefits. Recovery workers disputed with the City of New York. Criticisms swirled around the design and construction of the new WTC and the possibility that federal law enforcement agencies had missed opportunities to prevent the attacks. These and other concerns were addressed in detail by *The National Commission on Terrorist Attacks Upon the United States* (2004). This remains one of the most forceful and instructive books to emerge from a governmental committee, and is recommended for all with an interest in learning what did and did not happen on 9/11, along with suggestions for avoiding future catastrophes.

Is 9/11 Still Happening?

The catastrophic day is still happening in altered memories and attitudes that affect the lives of many people. But research continues to indicate that 9/11 has ongoing effects in stress-related symptoms that influence individuals, families, and the workplace. The passage of time seems more to have revealed rather than to have attenuated the effects. We begin with a national survey that found a broad increase in stress-related symptoms among most Americans immediately after the terrorist attacks (Schuster et al., 2001). Its findings included:

- Nine of 10 adults reported at least one stress-related symptom.
- Nearly half the adults reported one or more "substantial" symptoms of stress, that is, a disorder that interfered significantly with their lives.
- Nearly half the children were worried about their own or their loved ones' safety, and one in three were experiencing stress symptoms.

Children who watched the most television had more stress symptoms. People with pre-existing psychiatric vulnerabilities were at heightened risk for a severe stress response after the attacks (Panda & Weiden, 2001). People without a previous psychiatric vulnerability became more at risk for post-traumatic stress disorder (Stephenson, 2001; see also Chapter 11) if they had witnessed the disaster first hand (e.g., seeing people leap from a tower, discovering a mutilated body).

Attention was given to increased risk for depression and suicidality (Salmon & Sun, 2001). The first known suicide occurred 3 months after the attack when the widow of a WTC victim shot herself. Experts fear that the number of suicides is substantial and not necessarily limited to the period immediately after the attack. Mental health experts and public and private agencies had cooperated following the Oklahoma City bombing to offer counseling and support to bereaved family members. There was a similar response in New York City, with the media informing people about the availability of grief support services and encouraging their utilization. Psychological and social support for traumatic grief was no longer to be regarded as a sign of weakness or mental illness. New York school-children were considered to be at "extreme risk" from anxiety-related disorders associated with the attacks (Bauder, 2002).

Did 9/11 also have effects on physical well-being? Yes, at least for people who were in the vicinity of the WTC. Six months after the attack, workers reported substantial rates of physical symptoms, especially problems with breathing and irritation of mucous membranes (Bernard et al., 2002). A new term came into existence: "World Trade Center cough" (Prezant et al., 2002). The cough was a symptom of severe respiratory symptoms that required medical leave of at least 4 weeks. Even a brief exposure to the smoke and dust at Ground Zero was enough to jeopardize the health and imperil the life expectancies of previously healthy people.

It is possible that stress and distress as a result of the 9/11 attacks could undermine both the quality and length of life for many people. For example, accident researchers report that since the attacks, more people have been driving while drowsy because they decided against air travel. More people driving while exhausted and stressed have, in turn, contributed to motor vehicle accidents (Brody, 2002). Those who have increased their use of alcohol as a result of the stress would also be at a higher risk for involvement in accidents.

More recent studies continue to find evidence of 9/11-related terror. Children who lost a family member in the 9/11 attacks remain at increased risk for emotional and stress-related problems (Chemtob et al., 2007). Reviewing the research literature, Comer and Kendall (2007) conclude that children exposed to terrorist events and media coverage experience elevated levels of separation anxiety along with other symptoms of disturbance. They note that we do not yet have firm evidence on the role played by media coverage as distinguished from the terrorist events themselves. Comer and Kendall introduce the term *secondhand terrorism* with respect to possible media excess in raising anxieties about future attacks (a conclusion reached independently by Altheide [2002, 2006]). Adult vulnerability was most severe among those who had direct exposure to the attacks, lived or worked near by, or consumed much of the media coverage. People with low income and educational levels, poor social supports, and prior psychotropic drug use have also been experiencing more stress. (Laughame, Janca, & Widiger, 2007). Several studies indicate that many people are showing a resilient response—getting on with their lives with energy and purpose—and yet, at the same time, still experiencing an alteration in their physiologic reactivity (Tucker et al., 2007). It is possible that our survival response systems have adapted to a more vigilant level out of concern for possible future dangers.

The terrorist attacks of 9/11 differed in almost every way from the everyday operation of our society's death system. Death came without warning; there was no time to prepare and little time to respond. There was no opportunity to provide care for the dying and, therefore, no opportunity to affirm relationships until the end. The horrific circumstances at Ground Zero deprived families of the opportunity to conduct funeral and memorial services in a timely and acceptable way. On the positive side, the family survivors were not alone in their grief as the nation mourned with them. Social consolidation after death similarly was a challenge for the entire nation. Making sense of death remains a continuing challenge because our assumption that a familiar world is a safe world was shown to be mistaken, and for other psychological, philosophical, and religious reasons. Killing, often an overlooked facet of the death system, claimed prominence. We were forcefully reminded of the potential for violence within both individuals and their societies.

The impact of 9/11 is also continuing in the form of widespread efforts to improve prevention, intervention, and postvention in the event of terrorist attacks. Many nations have been developing emergency plans and resources. In the United States it is no longer unusual for health professionals and other care providers to collaborate in training programs. "Planning Medical Care for High-Risk Mass Gatherings" (Leonard, Winslow, & Bozeman, 2007) is an example of the ongoing attention to minimizing casualties of a terrorist attack.

A death system summary is offered in Table 8-3.

Does Killing Beget Killing?

The idea that killing might "feed" on itself—that is, instigate motivations for further killing—is illustrated in instances of predominantly one-sided killing, such as genocide, in which initially limited killings escalate into progressively bigger massacres (Marten et al., 2007, p. 1251).

A research team has recently explored this idea in a set of social psychological experiments. Their methodology is a long way from the brutal reality of terrorism and genocide. The participants (introductory psychology students, of course) were asked a question that one does not encounter very often: "Please rate how similar/different you think you are to small insects." The participants were then told that the study was related to the role of exterminators who deal with bugs, and that they would be engaging in that activity themselves, if they wished to accept this mission. At this point, Marten et al., had participants who located themselves at various points of similarity to insects, and also had their consent to do some bug killing for science. The device was then produced. The "extermination machine" was a modified stainless steel coffee grinder from which protruded a tube and a funnel. A bug would be placed in the funnel, the participant would press a button, and sounds of whirling blades and grinding bugs would be heard. In actuality, no bugs were harmed during the study and the participants were later informed that they had not been killers after all.

Several experimental conditions were in effect throughout the three related studies, e.g., sometimes the participants only observed, sometimes they were instructed to press the button. What was learned? In Study 1, fewer bugs were killed by participants who perceived themselves as relatively more similar to the bugs. But wait—if high similarity participants were given a "practice period," they became rather enthusiastic killers when performing at their own discretion. In this sense, killing seemed to beget killing. The same finding was obtained in Study 2, which was a refined variation on Study 1. Study 3 was limited to participants who expressed some degree of similarity with the bugs; they were also asked to report their mood at the moment. The new finding was that participants who killed more bugs also reported a positive change in their mood. The researchers are working with a fairly complex theory about the mindset that leads to murder and

TABLE 8-3

Functions of the Death System and the 9/11 Attacks on America

Function	Comment
Warning and predicting	Warnings not evaluated, given priority, or followed up effectively; attacks come as surprise.
Preventing	Failed to prevent deaths on airliners; failed to prevent loss of life on ground, but design features of WTC towers and courageous actions by first responders reduced the number of casualties.
Caring for the dying	Victims either died on the scene or escaped without life-threatening injuries.
Disposing of the dead	Exceptionally long and arduous efforts to recover bodies of victims; identified remains not found for all believed to have died at WTC.
Social consolidation after death	Delay and stress in grief recovery for bereaved families because so many bodies not found or identified; the cities attacked and the nation as a whole responded strongly and compassionately.
Making sense of death	Major issue immediately after the unexpected trauma; temporary stimulus to personal reflections on life and death.
Killing	National shift to killing (war on terrorism) orientation after assault by an external death system.

genocide. The main point for us here is the evidence—limited though it is—for the proposition that violence feeds on itself. After the first abuse, assault, or killing, the others are easier. Martens et al., are well aware that their experimental model is far distant from real life atrocities, but their work can also make us aware of some of the dynamics that might impel good people to do astonishingly bad things.

ACCIDENT AND DISASTER

Accidents and disasters have in common the fact that the deaths they cause were not intentioned. Unfortunately, intentionality can be difficult to establish, as can be observed in many legal proceedings. Often, we cannot be sure of another person's state of mind, and sometimes we may not be clear about our own intentions. Furthermore, people may have a degree of responsibility for accident or disaster deaths, even if they had no intention of doing harm. Here is one of many examples in which a sequence of behaviors can lead to an "accidental" death:

An 8-year-old girl became trapped by fire in her second-floor bedroom. Firefighters rushed to the scene but:

> could not make the turn onto the girl's narrow street because of illegally parked cars. So they knocked down fences and plowed cars out of the way in a frantic effort to reach the dwelling. Officials say the delay in reaching the girl almost certainly contributed to her death, "When we say seconds count, it sounds cornball, but it's true," Fire Lt. William Dewan said yesterday at the station (Farmer, 2002, p. B1).

Illegally parked vehicles are commonplace in Boston and are a chronic source of traffic congestion and driver stress. It is probable that many other lives have been put at heightened risk over the years because of illegally parked vehicles. Those who had made Bowen Street nearly impassable did not foresee or intend the death of Katie Orr, but it might be said that they had some responsibility for this outcome.

There was even more to this situation. The fire was started by the young girl's father in the early morning hours. He was in bed, using an oxygen tank and smoking a cigarette. It is almost certain that he had been repeatedly warned against smoking while using oxygen. It is also probable that his respiratory illness had been caused by smoking. Chances are that the agonized death of his daughter was not intentional, but the "accident" certainly was set up by his nonresponsible behavior as well as that of the drivers who illegally congested the street. Many other accidents result from a sequence of decisions and behaviors that have a share of the responsibility even if not intentioned to result in injury or death.

Despite these difficulties, the concept of unintended death provides a useful pathway through the kinds of death that are customarily called accidents or disasters.

Accidents

We begin with a statistical overview of accidents. We will then look more closely at the contexts and dynamics that are often associated with accidental deaths.

The Statistical Picture

Accidents have always been a major cause of death. What might be surprising is the fact that the rate of accidental deaths has declined through the years. The number of unintentional-injury deaths has stayed fairly constant, though, because the population has continued to increase while the rate decreased.

National Center for Health Statistics data reveal that more than 100,000 accidental deaths occur in the United States annually. The National Safety Council estimates that an injury accident occurs every 2 seconds and a death every 6 minutes. Motor vehicular injury accidents, the most common type, occur every 16 seconds, and a motor vehicular death every 13 minutes. Alcohol intoxication remains a major factor in motor vehicular fatalities, being involved in about two of every five deaths. Motor vehicular fatalities are the most common type of accidental death from age 1 to 75 and, as we have seen, are the number-one cause of all deaths between the ages of 10 and 24. Infants are most vulnerable to suffocation, elders to life-threatening falls. The vulnerability of elderly men and women often is increased by preexisting health factors. They may also have more limited powers of recuperation from trauma and stress.

Therefore, an accident from which a younger person might recover is more likely to prove fatal to an elderly person.

The National Safety Council (2005) has given us something to think about in its calculation of the odds of death by accident in the United States (using the most recent available data, 2002). Table 8-4 presents excerpts from a longer list that includes disasters as well as accidents. Two types of information are provided: the odds of becoming an accidental death victim in one year, and the lifetime odds.

TABLE 8-4
The Odds of Accidental Death in the United States

Type of Accident	One-Year Odds	Lifetime Odds
Air	440,951	5,704
Boating	697,194	9,019
Bus occupant	6,696,307	86,628
Car occupant	17,625	228
Cave-in, falling earth	5,505,600	55,551
Contact with machinery	441,628	5,713
Contact with sharp objects	2,742,297	35,476
Drowning	83,534	1,081
Earthquake	9,288,426	120,161
Electric current	634,232	8,205
Excessive cold	445,729	5,776
Excessive heat	822,689	10,643
Falls	17,712	229
Firearms (accidental)	377,876	4,888
Fireworks display	57,588,244	744,997
Flood	31,993,469	413,887
Lightning	4,362,746	56,439
Motorcycle rider	89,562	1,159
Off-road motor vehicle	371,058	4,800
Overexertion & privation	2,617,647	29,102
Pedestrian	47,273	612
Poisoning	16,407	212
Smoke, fire, flames	91,149	1,179
Streetcar occupant	71,985,305	931,246
Venomous animal	3,788,700	40,013

Source: National Center for Health Statistics.
www.cdc.gov/nchs/fastats/acc-inj.html

The odds of dying from any kind of injury were 1 in 1,755. The odds of a person born in 2000 ending his or her life by accident at some point is 1 in 23. There is an impressive difference between one-year and lifetime odds of a fatal accident throughout the listings.

We have placed "occupant of streetcar" in a conspicuous place to remind us that many factors go into determining risk of death. The low streetcar risk has something to do with the fact that there are very few streetcars still in operation (even at that, the number of fatalities quadrupled from one in 1999 to four in 2002). When they were numerous and shared the road with horsedrawn vehicles and automobiles, streetcars were sometimes a high risk, as memorialized by the baseball team known as the Los Angeles (formerly Brooklyn) Dodgers. The odds are shaped by the frequency of the events as well as the risk per event.

The Human Side of Accident Fatalities

The automobile passenger who is killed when broadsided by another vehicle was in a much different situation than the elderly pedestrian who slipped on an icy sidewalk or the young child who drowned in the family pool when, for one tragic moment, nobody was standing watch. There also can be important differences within the same general type of fatal accident. For example, reckless driving is often responsible for fatal motor vehicle accidents in which a young person is behind the wheel—poor maintenance of the vehicle is often a contributing cause as well. By contrast, failure to take sufficient note of traffic conditions and slow reaction times are more often associated with fatal accidents for which elderly drivers are responsible. Additionally, the single-car accident is often associated with use of alcohol or drugs and sometimes also with a self-destructive intention (in which case the "accident" is not entirely an accident).

The victim's contribution to a fatal accident has long been recognized. People of a certain age will remember the verses posted on a series of roadside signs around the country. There were hundreds of verses, with not a few intended to keep the sponsor's customers alive, as in the following example:

SPRING
HAS SPRUNG
THE GRASS HAS RIZ
WHERE LAST YEAR'S
CARELESS DRIVER IS . . .
BURMA-SHAVE

A recent study supports and extends earlier research about the risky driver: this is most likely to be an angry person with the impulse to seek arousing sensations (Schwebel, Severson, Ball, & Rizzo, 2006, p. 809). The authors draw implications for prevention:

Most current interventions to reduce motor vehicle crashes target engineering of the road environment or the motor vehicle. Prevention programs designed to change driver behavior are less common; when they are implemented, they tend to focus broadly on all drivers. Results from this study indicate interventions targeting sensation-seeking, unconscientious, and angry drivers might be more theoretically and economically sensible.

Some of the most devastating accidents have been primed by human error, indifference, or greed. In these instances, it is more accurate to speak of the lethal episode not as an accident but as a probable outcome.

Consider one of the most tragic examples in U.S. history. On April 27, 1865 the steamship *Sultana* started its voyage north from Vicksburg. Almost all the passengers were Union soldiers, including hundreds who had been incarcerated in prison camps under conditions of extreme stress and deprivation. They were all exhausted survivors of a long and bitter conflict, finally on their way home. Early the next morning, the steam boilers exploded, the ship splintered, and passengers and crew were hurled into the cold waters of the Mississippi River. Of the 2,200 people aboard, 1,700 died almost immediately, and another 200 died of exposure and injuries later. This was then, and still is, the largest loss of life on an American ship, the casualties exceeding even those of the Titanic.

An accident? The *Sultana* was built to accommodate 376 people. About six times as many people were crowded aboard. Furthermore, there had been clear indications that the boilers were failing (Salecker, 1996). Greed and indifference to the safety of human lives had created a situation that markedly increased the probability of catastrophe. The tragic outcome is classified officially as an "accident," but this was far from an unpredictable event. The death toll was also increased by the fact that few of the passengers knew how to swim—largely because relatively few people in the United States at that time were proficient swimmers. There have been numerous other examples throughout the world in which ships have gone down with a heavy loss of life because of overcrowding and neglect of safety measures. It is a dangerous misrepresentation to classify fatal events that were shaped by human error and greed as accidents. "Accident" implies that nothing could have been done to prevent the loss of life—thereby contributing to lack of prevention in the future.

The failure to learn from experience has haunted many other types of accident-prone situations. In 1942 the nation was shocked when a very avoidable fire in Boston's Cocoanut Grove nightclub killed 492 people. The circumstances and practices that led to this holocaust were analyzed and condemned. From this point on, it was vowed, fire safety in night clubs and other gathering places would be much improved. But in 1977 it did happen again, and in almost the same way, as 165 people perished in a fire at the swank Beverly Hills Supper Club in Southgate, Kentucky. So stricken was the local community that to this day it has refused to allow any new building on the site—except for a memorial cross (Kurtzman & Wartman, 2007). Safety inspectors today will routinely find violations of the rules that have been put in place to prevent the next fire.

Airline catastrophes provide many examples in which human error has contributed significantly. For example:

The captain of an American Airlines jet that crashed in Colombia last December entered an incorrect one-letter computer command that sent the plane into a mountain, the airline said Friday. The crash killed all but four of the 163 people aboard (Associated Press, August 24, 1996).

The pilot had not made a careless error. He thought he was entering the coordinates for Cali, the intended destination:

But, on most South American aeronautical charts, the one-letter code for Cali is the same as the one for Bogotá, 132 miles in the opposite direction. The coordinates for Bogotá directed the plane toward the mountain.

The ambiguity and confusion in the communication system included the fact that most computer databases used different codes for Bogotá and Cali. The lack of standardization among computer databases led the captain to make one fatal keystroke. For all the efficiency and potential of computerized processes, there is also the risk of fatal error.

Cushing (1994) found dozens of other instances in which inadequate communication resulted either in fatal accidents or near misses. Improved awareness of the communication process and its hazards could sharply reduce the possibility of accidents in aviation and other transportation situations. The automatic assumption that we have understood what the other person meant and that the other person has understood what we meant can produce what Cushing has aptly titled, *Fatal Words* (1994).

We reduce the probabilities of a fatal accident happening to others or ourselves every time we check out our assumptions, monitor our communications, and resist the temptation to rush full speed ahead without charting the waters.

Laws of Accident Causation?

There is general agreement that accidents are often the outcome of multiple causes. Nevertheless, it might be possible to identify common factors. Elvik (2006) has made a case for a set of four laws of accident causation within the realm of traffic injuries and deaths. He draws on a large range of statistical data. The universal law of learning states that detection and control of traffic hazards increases with the driver's experience. The law of rare events takes surprise into account. We are more likely to become involved in a type of accident that we did not happen to have in our cautionary expectations. An example

would be suddenly encountering an icy slick on the road at an unexpected time and place. The law of complexity is closely related to a driver's tendency to allow only a small margin for safety. This minimal hedge against disaster can combine with other factors, such as road design and traffic, to develop a situation whose many elements can be too difficult to sort out and control. Finally, the law of cognitive capacity focuses on the driver's "surplus" attention: the ability to think and talk about other things while operating the vehicle. A driver's mental capacity can become overtaxed by physical or psychological impairment, and/or excessive attention to other matters. Alcohol is one of the common contributors to a critical decline in cognitive capacity while operating a motor vehicle.

Natural Disasters

Seventeen minutes before noon, the ground started to roll gently . . . people froze and marveled at the feeling of the earth turning oceanlike, but they were not panicked; the town had suffered these rollings ever since the English had been on Jamaica . . . "It is an earthquake. Don't be afraid; it will soon be over" (Talty, 2007, p. 291).

It was Port Royal that was soon over. The remarkably flourishing city (home to some of the world's most illustrious pirates as well as merchants and planters) was essentially liquefied within a few minutes of its 1692 disaster. The church steeple slammed into the crowd, a "hollow rumbling Noise" sounded from all directions, and earth became water, streets rising and falling, and citizens swept along like corks on a wave. Some people were trapped in rapidly hardening sand until suffocated or swarmed upon by wild dogs. Notorious and flamboyant Port Royal had become a lost city.

This catastrophe was certainly a natural disaster. However, it also bore the mark of human motivation and quirk. Many people knew it was an unstable and dangerous location, but also one that was terrific for business opportunity and indulgence in one's pleasures of choice. Warnings of catastrophic disaster were shrugged off as the party went on. Today in the United States and elsewhere, locations at high risk for natural disaster are more popular than ever. These are not pirate hang-outs, but they are among the most attractive places to live—as long as one sets aside nature's warnings. Disaster experts routinely warn the public about settling into high risk locations, but there is little indication that these spoilsport messages have had much effect.

Not all unintentional lethal events can be classified simply as man-made or natural. Occasionally the term *hybrid disaster* is used to make this point. The changes we make in our physical environment can either increase or decrease the probability of a disaster. Soil erosion as a result of poor farming practices is among the historical examples; global warming as a partial result of technology and consumerism is a current and future example.

"Natural disaster" customarily refers to an episode that occurs within a limited period of time. Earthquakes, storms, floods, and fires are the most common types, although the less common volcanic eruptions can also be deadly.

Through the centuries, earthquakes have been responsible for some of the most devastating disasters. In all likelihood, the most lethal earthquake occurred in 1556 when an estimated 830,000 died in Shaanxi, China. Tangshan, China also suffered a quake that claimed 242,000 lives in 1976. The Chinese earthquake of 2008 near Chengdu was responsible for more than 60,000 deaths. Japan and India have had quakes with more than 200,000 fatalities. The tsunami that struck coastal areas of Southeast Asia in 2004 might have been generated by an underwater quake, if not a volcanic eruption.

There is now a significant literature on prevention of natural disasters, enhanced by growing attention to postvention: care for bereaved survivors who need material and emotional support. Much can be learned from the human dysfunctions that contributed to such disasters as The Great Chicago Fire of 1871 and the historic flood experienced by Johnstown, Pennsylvania, in 1889, as a result of a dam break. Measures that can be taken include design, construction, and maintenance of disaster-resistant buildings and preparation for effective response by a broad spectrum of agencies that can provide immediate and continued assistance (Wallace, & Webber; 2004; Weaver, 2002). Increased attention is also advocated to communication processes before, during, and after a disaster. Health care professionals and other community organizations have become more aware of the need to develop a clear chain of command and an efficient emergency management system to make best uses of their combined resources (Shover, 2007).

SUMMARY

Sudden and violent deaths take the forms of murder, war, terrorism, disaster, and accident. We have seen that the boundaries between these forms of violent death are not always firm and stable. When is armed attack war, and when is it terrorism? When is an accident actually homicide? We have also observed connections between individual actions that result in death and societal beliefs and practices.

We first acquainted ourselves with characteristics of the people who are most likely to be killers and victims. For example, most murders are committed by people who are of the same race as the victims, and in most cases the victims and the killers had previously been known to each other. We then explored several types of murder. Domestic violence includes abusive men who kill their partners and women who kill the men who have been abusing them. The tragedy of adults who kill children—even newborn babies—was also examined, including the rising incidence of child abuse and neglect, the lack of parenting skills, and the replacement father syndrome. Domestic violence includes parricide as well: children who kill their parents; often these murders were preceded by years of abuse at the hands of the parents. Young men with guns account for the largest number of murders, and school shootings have added another dimension to youth violence.

A mass killing is one in which several people die in a single episode. The killer is typically a white male, and his weapon a firearm. There is often a suicidal component, the killer motivated to die at the scene of his crimes. Mass killers tend to be people who feel rejected and mistreated by society. They often fit the profile of an antisocial personality, also known as a sociopath. Serial killers take the lives of three or more people over a period of time. Almost all identified serial killers are male, although some

Massive rescue efforts were organized after a devastating earthquake in China in May 2008. By contrast, victims of the preceding storm and flooding in Sri Lanka were given very little assistance from their totalitarian regime.

experts believe female serial killers have also operated, using poison and other "quiet" methods that are less likely to be detected. Political assassins have included some people who were delusional and incoherent, but others resemble mass killers in their frustration and anger against society. Still another type of political assassin is the person who hopes to redeem a life of failure and misery with an act of violence that will make him "famous."

Terrorism and genocide were rampant throughout the twentieth century, and have crossed over into the twenty-first without missing a beat. The 9/11/2001 terrorist attacks on the United States and the genocidal massacres in the Darfur region of the Sudan are the most prominent but not the only examples of mass killing that have already challenged the wisdom

and resources of the world in the third millennium. We also pondered a study that suggests killing begets killing.

Finally, we learned about disasters and accidents as the causes of violent death. The accident rate in the United States has decreased over the years but could be sharply reduced if fewer intoxicated drivers were at the wheel.

REFERENCES

Altheide, D. L. (2002) *Creating fear. News and the construction of crisis.* Hawthorne, NY: Aldine de Gruyter.

Altheide, D. L. (2006). *Terrorism and the politics of fear.* New York: Rowman & Littlefield.

Associated Press. (1996, August 24). *Columbia crash linked to pilot error.*

Balakian, P. (2003). *The burning Tigris. The Armenian genocide and America's response.* New York: HarperCollins.

Barenblatt, D. (2003). *A plague upon humanity. The secret genocide of Axis Japan's germ warfare operation.* New York: HarperCollins.

Batton, C., & Wilson, S. (2006). An examination of historical trends in the killing of law enforcement officers in the United States, 1947–1998. *Homicide Studies, 10,* 79–97.

Bauder, D. (2002, August 20). *NBC seeks psychiatric help on 9/ll coverage.* New York: Associated Press.

Bennett, M. D., Hall, J., Frazier, L., Patel, N., Barker, L., & Shaw, K. (2006). Homicide of children aged 0–4 years, 2003–04: Results from the National Violent Death Reporting System. www.safetylit.org/citations/index.php?fuseaction=citations.viewdetails&citation1ds%5b%5d=citjournalarticle_57943?23

Bernard, B. P., Baron, S. L., Mueller, C. A., Driscoll, R. J., Tapp, L. C., Wallingford, K. M., & Tepper, A. L. (2002). Impact of September 11 attacks on workers in the vicinity of the World Trade Center. [Special issue]. *Monthly Mortality & Morbidity Report, 51,* 8–10.

Brody, J. E. (2002, January 17). Driving while drowsy on rise. Traffic experts struggle to find solutions, *Arizona Republic, B 1.*

Browne, A. (1987). *When battered women kill.* New York: The Free Press.

Bureau of Justice Statistics. (2005). Homicide data. www.ojp.usdoj.gov/bjs

Bureau of Justice Studies. (2008). Homicide trends in the U.S. http://ojp.usdoj.Gov/bjs/homicide/race.htm.

Chemtob, C. M., Conroy, D. L., Hochauser, C. J., & Laraque, D. (2007). Children who lost a parent as a result of the terrorist attacks of September 11, 2001: Registry construction and population description. *Death Studies, 31,* 87–100.

Chu, H. (2007, November 22). Indian brides terrorized by in-laws over dowries. *Arizona Republic,* p. A26.

Clarke, J. W. (1982). *American assassins.* Princeton, NJ: Princeton University Press.

CNN news.com (2002, September 2) Poll: Support for 9/11 holiday/IPS

Comer, J. S., & Kendall, P. C. (2007). Terrorism: The psychological impact on Youth. *Clinical Psychology: Science and Practice, 14,* 179–212.

Crissman, J. K., & Parkin, J. (2002). Homicide. In R. Kastenbaum (Ed.), *Macmillan encyclopedia of death and dying:* Vol. 1 (pp. 423–426). New York: Macmillan.

Cushing, S. (1994). *Fatal words.* Chicago: University of Chicago Press.

Dale, M. (June 30, 2007). East Coast cities see homicides soar. *East Valley Tribune,* p. A22.

Davis, K. (2004, April 9). Police arrest teen after 'kill list' found. *Arizona Republic,* p. 3.

Davis, K. (2005, May 5). E. V. girl had script for school rampage. *East Valley Tribune,* p. A1–2.

Dray, P. (2003). *At the hands of persons unknown. The lynching of black America.* New York: Modern Library.

Elvik, R. (2006). Laws of accident causation. *Accident Analysis and Prevention, 38,* 742–747.

Enders, W., & Sandler, T. (2006). *The political economy of terrorism.* New York: Cambridge University Press.

Engelmann, B. (1984). *Germany without Jews.* New York: Bantam.

Evans, T. (2007, April 30). Making of a massacre. *Newsweek,* pp. 22–31.

Ewing, C. P. (1997). *Fatal families. The dynamics of intra familial homicide.* Thousand Oaks, CA: Sage.

Farmer, T. (2002, November 12). Clear out: Menino launches parking crackdown after fatal fire. *Boston Herald,* p. B1.

Fox, J. A., & Levin, J. (2001). *The will to kill.* Boston: Allyn & Bacon.

Goldhagen, D. J. (1996). *Hitler's willing executioners.* New York: Knopf.

Gracia, E. (2004). Unreported cases of domestic violence against women: Towards an epidemiology of social science, toleration, and inhibition. *Journal of Epidemiological Community Health, 58,* 536–537.

Herman, W. (2005, January 14). The man who saved his village. *Arizona Republic,* pp. A2, A18.

Herzog, S. (2006). Battered women who kill. An empirical analysis of public perceptions of seriousness in Israel from a consensus theoretical perspective. *Homicide Studies, 10,* 293–319.

Jowan, J. (2008, January 18). Caught in the clash of civilizations. http://stophonourkillings.com

Kastenbaum, R. (2002). Terrorist attacks on America. In R. Kastenbaum (Ed.), *Macmillan encyclopedia of death and dying:* Vol. 2 (881–885). New York: Macmillan.

Kristof, N. D. (2004a, September 11). Reign of terror. *The New York Times.* www.nytimes.com/2004/09/11/opinion/11kristof.html

Kristof, N. D. (2004b, October 16). The dead walk. *The New York Times.* www.nytimes.com/2004/10/16/opinion/16kristof.html

Kurtzman, L., & Wartman, S. (2007, May 27). Survivors relieve the horrors of fatal nightclub fire in '77. *Arizona Republic,* p. A22.

Larson, E. (2004). *The devil in the White City: Murder, magic, and madness at the fair that changed America.* New York: Vintage.

Laughame, J., Janca, A., & Widiger, B. (2007). Posttraumatic stress disorder and terrorism: 5 years after 9/11. Personality disorders and neuroses. *Current Opinion in Psychiatry, 20,* 36–41.

Lederer, D. M. (2007, March 9). U. N. chief urges end to violence against women. *East Valley Tribune,* p. A18.

Lemkin, R. (1944). *Axis rule in occupied Europe: Laws of occupation, analysis of government, proposals for redress.* Washington, DC: Carnegie Endowment for International Peace, Division of International Law.

Leonard, R. B., Winslow, J. E., & Bozeman, W. P. (2007). Planning medical care for high-risk mass gatherings. *The Internet Journal of Rescue and Disaster Medicine, 6*, 1–12.

Libaw, L., & Goldman, M. C. (2002, September 12). Unspeakable horror. Eyewitness accounts of N. Y. attacks. ABC.NEWS.com

Lichtblau, E. (2004, October 26). Violent crime dipped in '03; murder rose. *The New York Times.* www.nytimes.com/2004/10/26/national26crime.html

Martens, A., Kosloff, S., Greenberg, J., Landau, M. J., & Schmader, T. (2007). Killing begets killing: Evidence from a bug-killing paradigm that initial killing fuels subsequent killing. *Personality and Social Psychology Bulletin, 33*, 1251–1264.

Meloy, J. R., Hempel, A. G., Mohandie, K., Shiva, A. A., & Gray, B. T. (2001). Offender and offense characteristics of a nonrandom sample of adolescent mass murderers. *Journal of the American Academy of Child and Adolescent Mass Murderers, 40*, 719–728.

Moeller, T. G. (2001). *Youth aggression and violence.* Mahwah, NJ: Lawrence Erlbaum Associates.

National Commission on Terrorist Attacks Upon the United States. (2004). *The 9/11 commission report.* New York: Norton.

National Safety Council. (2005). What are the odds of dying? www.nsc.org/1rs/statinfo/odds.htm

Panda, A. U., & Weiden, M. (2001). Trauma and disaster in psychiatrically vulnerable populations. *Journal of Psychiatric Practice, 7*, 426–431.

Payton, J. (January 10, 2008a). "Picket the homes of honour killings." http://stophonourkillings.com

Payton, J. (January 16, 2008b). Marriage practice victimizes young girls. http://stophonourkillings.com

Power, S. (2002). "A problem from hell." *America and the age of genocide.* New York: Basic Books.

Prezant, D. J., Weiden, M., Banauch, G. I., McGuinness, G., Rom, W. D., Aldrich, T. K., & Kelly, K. J. (2002). Cough and bronchial responsiveness in firefighters at the World Trade Center site. *New England Journal of Medicine, 347*, 806–815.

Rose, J. (2002, September 4). From fear to reality. A year after 9/11, a look at America's predictions of change. *Arizona Republic,* B1.

Salecker, G. E. (1996). *Disaster on the Mississippi.* Annapolis, MD: Naval Institute Press.

Salerian, A. J. (2002, October 24). What makes a serial killer tick? United Press International. www.upi.com

Salmon, J. L., & Sun, L. H. (2001, December 19). Victims at risk again. Counselors scramble to avert depression, suicides after Sept. 11. *The Washington Post,* p. A01.

Schustus, M. Z., Stein, B. D., Jancov, L. H., Collins, R. L., Marshall, G. N., Elliot, M. N., Zhnye, A. J., Kanoose, D. E., Morrison, J. L., & Bern, S. H. (2001). A national survey of stress reactions after the September 11 attack. *New England Journal of Medicine, 345*, 1507–1512.

Schwebel, D. C., Severson, J., Ball, K. K., & Rizzo, M. (2006). Individual differences in risky driving: The roles of anger/hostility, conscientiousness, and sensation-seeking. *Accident Analysis and Prevention, 38*, 801–810.

Shover, H. (2007). Understanding the chain of communication during a disaster. *Perspectives on Psychiatric Care, 43*, 4–14.

Stephenson, J. (2001). Medical, mental health communities mobilize to cope with terror's psychological aftermath. *Journal of the American Medical Association, 286*, 1823–1825.

Talty, S. (2007). *Empire of blue water.* New York: Crown.

Tribune Wire Services. (2002, June 10) Foreign news still foreign to U.S. after September 11.

Tucker, P. M., Pfefferbam, B., North, C. S., Kent, A., Burgih, C. E., Parker, D.E., & Hossain, A. (2007). Physiologic reactivity despite emotional resilience several years after direct exposure to terrorism. *American Journal of Psychiatry, 164*, 230–235.

Wakin, E. (1984). *Enter the Irish-American.* New York: Thomas V. Crowell.

Wallace, M., & Webber, L. (2004). *Disaster recovery handbook: A step-by-step plan to ensure business continuity and protect vital operations, facilities, and assets.* New York: AMACOM.

Walsh, A. (2005). African Americans and serial killing in the media. *Homicide Studies, 9*, 271–291.

Walsh, J. (1996, September 9). Killings down but 'crime storm' looms. *Arizona Republic,* pp. A 1, A 24.

Weaver, J. D. (2002). Disasters. In R. Kastenbaum (Ed.), *Macmillan encyclopedia of death and dying:* Vol. 1, (pp. 231–240). New York: Macmillan.

Weitz, E. D. (2003). *A century of genocide. Utopias of race and nation.* Princeton, NJ: Princeton University Press.

Zink, T., Elder, N., Jacobson, J., & Klosterman, B. (2004). Medical management of intimate partner violence considering the stages of change: Precontemplation and contemplation. *Annals of Family Medicine, 2*, 231–239.

GLOSSARY

Assassination: The murder of a public official or other political figure.

Genocide: Mass killing intended to destroy an ethnic, religious, or racial group.

Homicide: The act of killing a human being.

Honor Killing Honor Killing Murder of a female by other members of the family because she was suspected of bringing shame to them.

Mass killer: A person who murders a large (but not fixed) number of people in a single episode.

Murder: The criminal act of killing a human being.

Parricide: Murder of a parent.

Replacement father syndrome: When a new husband or lover engages in abusive and life-threatening actions against the children of the wife's previous mate.

Serial killer: A person who commits murders on repeated occasions.

Terrorism: Violence or threat of violence in which civilians are the targets.

Tsunami: A series of extremely long waves generated by earthquake, landslide, or underwater volcanic eruption. Previously known erroneously as "tidal waves."

ON FURTHER THOUGHT . . .

Learn more about the effects of mass violence on children:

Nancy Boyd Webb (Ed.). (2003). *Mass trauma and violence: Helping children cope.* New York: Guilford Press.

Learn more about the eruption of suicide terrorism:

Pape, R. A. (2005). *Dying to win.* New York: Random House.

Genocide, up close:

Does genocide still feel like something distant and abstract? It is difficult to realize the raw reality of genocide if we have not been victim or witness. Or *perpetrator*. For an intense, illuminating account from interviews with people who massacred their neighbors in Rwanda:

Hatzfeld, J. (2005). *Machete season.* New York: Farrar, Straus and Giroux.

For another informed perspective, read the harrowing report from the commanding officer of the U.S. assistance mission to Rwanda:

Dallaire, R. (2005). *Shake hands with the devil.* New York: Carrol & Graf.

Useful online resources:

Assassination Archives and Resource Center
　　http://aarclibrary.org/
Murder Victims.com.
　　www.murdervictims.com
National Hazard Center
　　http://Colorado.edu/hazards/resource/
National Organization for Victims Assistance
　　www.try-nova.org
The History Place
　　http://historyplace.com/genocide

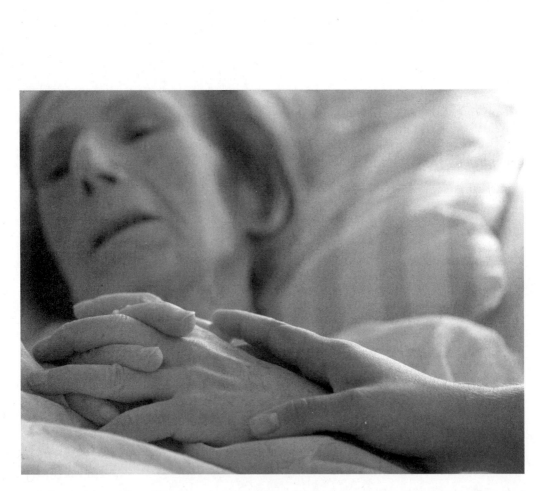

Not alone, the comfort of human companionship and touch is welcome throughout the end of life passage.

EUTHANASIA, ASSISTED DEATH, ABORTION, AND THE RIGHT TO DIE

Chantel Sebire, 52, was diagnosed nearly eight years ago with esthesioneuroblastoma, a rare form of cancer. The illness left her blind, and with no sense of smell or taste, her lawyer said.She could not use morphine to ease the intense eye pain because of the side effects.
—Associated Press (March 20, 2008)

Theresa suffered a cardiac arrest. During the several minutes it took for paramedics to arrive, Theresa [Schiavo] experienced loss of oxygen to the brain, or anoxia, for a period sufficiently long to cause permanent loss of brain function. Despite heroic efforts to resuscitate, Theresa remained unconscious and slipped into a coma. She was intubated, ventilated and trached, meaning that she was given life saving medical technological interventions, without which she surely would have died that day
—Wolfson (2003, p. 4)

We heard screaming coming from another crater a bit away. . . . He kept begging us to shoot him. But we couldn't shoot him. Who could shoot him? We stayed with him, watching him go down in the mud. And he died. He wasn't the only one. There must have been thousands up there who died in the mud. Or almost worse, suffered in it, wounded.
—Quoted by Winston Groom (2002, p. 215)

I swear by Apollo the physician, and Aesculapius, Hygeia and Panacea and all the gods and goddesses, that, according to my ability and judgment, I will keep this oath and this covenant. I will give no deadly medicine to anyone if asked, nor suggest any such counsel, and in like manner I will not give to a woman an abortive remedy. With purity and with holiness I will pass my life and practice my Art.
—The *Hippocratic Oath* (fifth century, B.C.)

DEATH COUNSELING

IS SOMEONE IN YOUR FAMILY TERMINALLY ILL?

Does he or she wish to die—and with dignity?

Call Physician Consultant [Telephone No.]
—Classified newspaper advertisement (June 1987)

Tell me about a time when a patient asked you for help in dying.
—Judith Kennedy Schwarz (2005)

The woman said the baby's naked body, spotted alongside a road in a small town in Hunan province, was still warm—she had been dumped and had just died. Many passers-by on their way to work ignored the child. . . while some stopped to look, then walked on, until an elderly man eventually put the tiny body into a box and carried it away
—CNSNews (2001)

Euthanasia is still one of the important things we do.
—Veterinarian Nick Trout (2008a)

You could find Nature in the South Bronx if you had legs enough to walk to a park where they kept grass and trees, and even squirrels. But you could also find Nature on the very sidewalks of New York as a single blade of grass succeeded in reaching for the sun between cracks in the pavement. Nature is famously insistent about filling earth, water, and sky with life forms, and these life forms are famously insistent about staying alive. Humans are an especially puzzling life form. Sometimes we are vigorous and resourceful about staying alive. Sometimes, though, we terminate life by suicide (Chapter 7) or violence against others (Chapter 8). In this chapter, we look at *euthanasia*, assisted suicide, and abortion. These endings differ in significant ways, but all involve decision making under stressful conditions. Here is a brief sampling of situations:

• The lives of Chantel Sebire and Theresa Schiavo were devastated by personal catastrophes that became the core of national controversy. Schiavo remained on life support for 15 years, never regaining consciousness. Sebire was acutely aware of her disfiguring facial tumor, loss of function, and intense pain. Schiavo's situation came to general attention only when her husband requested removal of the feeding tube. Similar requests are not unusual when brain death (Chapter 2) is involved. However, in this instance it led to a controversy in which political power plays crowned the fire of a medical, legal, ethical, and religious controversy. One woman's personal tragedy became a nation's concern (as discussed later in this chapter). Sebire's ordeal is more recent, but has already had an impact on French law, medical practice, and public opinion. There

was enormous compassion for the former school teacher, but French law, although permitting withdrawal of treatment, did not countenance *active euthanasia*: the direct termination of a patient's life. Sebire was found dead in her home a few days after a court had rejected her doctor's request to provide euthanasia. Her death was ruled "not natural," but the legal system declined to investigate further and prosecute. Every case in which the question of euthanasia arises has its unique aspects, and the local attitude and practice can also differ. Had Sebire been a citizen of The Netherlands, her wish to have her life ended would most probably have been granted. In other places there might or might not be a physician who will quietly carry out this action and a community that will look the other way.

• *"Mercy death"* is probably the earliest and purest form of euthanasia. A dying person or animal is spared further suffering by a blow or shot that ends its life quickly. This kind of action has been known and respected on battlefields and accident sites for longer than anybody can remember. War memoirs are filled with instances in which a soldier provided mercy death for either a fallen comrade or enemy. In the example given previously, the British infantryman was not dying, but he would soon be dead. He was one of many soldiers on both sides of the war who would be slowly pulled into the depths of a bomb crater whose mud acted like quicksand. His comrades had tried hard to save him, but there was no way. As horrifying as it was to watch him slowly sink into the mud, none of the young men could bring themselves to shoot him. That same day—and the next day for years to come—British, French, German, and other

Hippocrates is often considered the father of medicine and the Hippocratic Oath has long been regarded as a fundamental statement of the physician's mission. An unknown artist in the Middle East offered this depiction in the third century B.C.

soldiers would be slowly dying in the zone accurately known as "no-man's land." The fatally wounded called out for relief while they still had breath. A comrade who responded to these pleas would most likely be cut to pieces by machine gun fire or blasted apart by a mortar round. Mercy death was almost a luxury in the trench warfare that relentlessly claimed the lives of the young men of Europe and, near the end, of the United States. Euthanasia, however, is not always such a straightforward proposition, as we will continue to see.

- The Hippocratic Oath is based on the writings of a physician who practiced on the Greek island of Cos 2,500 years ago (Edelstein, 1943). This ancient document is still very much at issue today: Can a physician violate the injunction to give no deadly medicine and still be a physician? Dr. Jack Kevorkian is not the only physician who intentionally contributed to the death of his patients, but his words and actions have had a powerful influence on the right-to-die controversy. Furthermore, the shadow of involuntary euthanasia has been cast over the movement to provide assisted death. People who know their twentieth century history have understandable concerns about any movement that would encourage the taking of a life under the name of euthanasia.

The role of nurses in euthanasia and assisted death often is not given the attention it deserves. Medical tradition and regulations place most decision-making responsibility in the hands of physicians. Nurses might or might not agree with these decisions. Furthermore, patients and families sometimes will confide their feelings to nurses more openly. A study by Judith Kennedy Schwarz (2005) explored the ways in which nurses respond to patients' requests for assistance in dying. This is one of an increasing number of studies that reveal the stress and ambivalence that can be experienced by health care professionals when patients express the wish to have their lives terminated.

- Seeing the dead and discarded baby alongside a road must have been profoundly painful, even to the passersby who could not bring themselves to deal with it. Babies and children are considered precious in Chinese culture. Nevertheless, the people of China have been confronted with a combination of forced abortion and infanticide ever since the regime decided upon a drastic policy of population control. Abortion issues, like euthanasia, take many forms. Seeing the more familiar form of the abortion controversy within a larger perspective could be helpful.

- Many of us have been faced with a euthanasia decision close to home and heart—an animal companion who is a distinctive part of the family. Veterinarian Nick Trout was providing an update on the improved care and longevity of animal companions ("Age 15 is the new 11 for dogs!") when the issue of euthanasia came

up. His thoughtful observations (Trout, 2008a; 2008b) are worth consulting when and if the situation arises in our own lives. Accurate information is certainly helpful in reaching and coming to terms with the decision.

In this chapter, we consider the related topics of euthanasia, physician-assisted suicide, abortion, and the right to die. The Black Stork (Pernick, 1996) phenomenon reminds us of the connection between eugenics, euthanasia, and assisted death. We have prepared ourselves for this challenge by studying end-of-life decisions (Chapter 6), suicide (Chapter 7), and killing (Chapter 8). We begin here with the Hippocratic Oath, then acquaint ourselves with key terms and concepts. This is followed by attention to public attitudes toward the set of right-to-die issues, and a review of some of the major cases that have influenced the right-to-die controversy. We will then be ready to look at the assisted death issue in some detail, with particular attention to Oregon, the only state in which assisted termination is legal. The emotionally and politically divisive issue of abortion will conclude our exploration. Can we keep open minds through it all?

"I SWEAR BY APOLLO THE PHYSICIAN": WHAT HAPPENED TO THE HIPPOCRATIC OATH?

Kevorkian's classified advertisement that was quoted earlier in this chapter was a signal that "death with dignity" was becoming more than a rallying cry. Here was a physician who offered to perform a service that most of his colleagues did not even want to talk about. It was a service, in fact, that seems to be specifically banned by the Hippocratic Oath.

We often assume that (a) all physicians have sworn allegiance to this oath right up to the present day and that (b) this covenant does, in fact, represent the core belief system for physicians from antiquity forward. Neither assumption is correct. Many physicians graduate from medical school without being asked to take the Hippocratic Oath. Kevorkian (1991) characterizes the oath as irrelevant. Furthermore, the Hippocratic Oath has encountered opposition since its inception. Many in the ancient world considered it reasonable and even honorable to seek release from the rigors, pains, and disappointments of life. The prohibition against giving "deadly medicine" probably had become a widespread practice. The concurrent prohibition against abortion was also contested, with Aristotle as one of the leading dissenters.

Today some physicians continue to rely on the Hippocratic Oath, but many have never entered into this covenant, and all are confronted with new and complex problems that Hippocrates never had to deal with. Even physicians who accept the Hippocratic Oath must find a way to reconcile these precepts with the decisions they make day by day. Physicians in the United States generally work within the system. They must find ways to help their terminally ill patients without violating either their own moral code or the law of the land. Abandoning the patient or offering to provide assisted death are extremes that most physicians would not choose. Whatever one's position on physician-assisted death, though, one cannot simply invoke the Hippocratic Oath as the unquestionable authority. We must work things out for ourselves.

KEY TERMS AND CONCEPTS

We will be better prepared to understand controversies about life-and-death issues when we become more familiar with key terms and concepts.

A literal translation of the term *euthanasia* would be good or happy *(eu)* death *(thanasia)*. It would be more accurate to understand this original usage as "dying without pain and suffering." At first, euthanasia referred to the individual's state of being (e.g., "She died peacefully"). Later, euthanasia came to signify actions performed to hasten death. Today, the term euthanasia retains something of its original meaning: a peaceful, painless exit from life. But it has taken on another meaning as well: the intentional foreshortening of a person's life to spare that person from further suffering.

Many people distinguish sharply between a life that is foreshortened by doing something and a life that is foreshortened by deciding not to do something. *Active euthanasia* applies to actions that are intended to end the life of a person or animal that is suffering greatly and has no chance of recovery. A lethal injection would be a clear example of active euthanasia. *Passive euthanasia* refers to the intentional withholding of treatment that might have prolonged life. Deciding not to place a person with massive brain trauma on a life-support system would be an example of passive euthanasia, as would the decision not to treat pneumonia or an opportunistic infection in an immobilized and cognitively impaired long-term patient.

A health care provider or family member who feels that it is acceptable to "let him/her go" (passive euthanasia) might be deeply troubled by the prospect of giving direct assistance to death (active euthanasia). The legal system and society in general have been more tolerant of the "letting go" approach. Few are inclined to make trouble when health care providers and family members agree that it would be pointless to introduce further procedures that would only prolong suffering or a vegetative state. Advance directives (Chapter 6) now provide legalized opportunities to request end-of-life management that is consistent with the passive euthanasia approach. There is still substantial opposition to active euthanasia. Many physicians strenuously object to placing their services at the disposal of death. "Doctors are supposed to keep people alive. If doctors also kill people, then who can trust them?!" Some physicians and other health care providers are also strongly opposed on personal religious/moral grounds. Furthermore, a person who engages in active euthanasia could be accused of manslaughter or homicide.

We will still hear about active and passive euthanasia because these were the original terms of the controversy. Today, however, most physicians and bioethicists speak instead of withdrawing or withholding life supports. Instead of dealing with the somewhat abstract and unwieldy concept of euthanasia, we can focus on whether or not certain practical actions should be introduced, continued, done, or discontinued.

A challenging question continues to be asked: How much does it really matter whether the life is terminated by passive or active means? The outcome is the same, but discontinuing life support and administering a lethal injection seem very different. There are people of conscience who hold opposite views. What do you think—and why? Perhaps considering the ventilator and the slippery slope argument (which follow) will help.

There is also a fairly new term to consider: *terminal sedation*. This alternative is selected by some physicians who are committed to relieving a dying patient's distress without resorting to active euthanasia (Rietjens et al., 2004). Drugs and dosage are selected for their ability to keep the patient in deep sedation or coma until death. What family and caregivers see is a person who appears to be sleeping peacefully but never wakes up. Terminal sedation seems to be used most often when the patient is suffering severe pain, agitation, or dyspnea (breathing difficulties). Physicians conversing among themselves sometimes refer to this practice as "slow euthanasia." This is an apt term because the terminal sedation regimen is also understood as an unobtrusive way of hastening death. It is assumed that terminal sedation is introduced with the knowledge and approval of patient and family. Research on terminal sedation is limited at this point, so there is much to learn. Do you see terminal sedation as significantly different from traditional medical management at the end of life? As significantly different from the more recognized forms of passive and active euthanasia?

Three other concepts are keys to our understanding of the controversies that swirl around euthanasia, assisted death, and the right to die. The foundation is built on a principle that goes by several names: liberty, privacy, autonomy, and self-determination. (Experts in law can distinguish among these terms, but the basic idea is what matters to us here.) The *liberty principle* affirms that individuals are free to make their own decisions and exercise their own rights except in ways that have been specifically reserved for the state. We can do anything that has not been forbidden by law. The state reserves for itself the right to protect public security and safety, and this obligation can take precedence over individual choice. The balance between the liberty principle and the rights of the state pervades all spheres of society and has shifted back and forth over time. It is only in recent years, however, that the liberty principle has become salient in

health care decisions. A series of court rulings held that "the State's interest in preserving an individual's life was not sufficient by itself to outweigh the individual's interest in the exercise of free choice" (Veatch, 1998, pp. 155–156).

These judicial rulings helped to pave the way for the eventual legalization of advance directives (Chapter 6). Nevertheless, the courts were also aware that not all individuals were in a position to exercise a right-to-die decision. This is where the other two concepts become important. What does it take to be in a position to choose death over life? It takes *informed consent*, and it takes *competence*. Medical authorities must give full disclosure to patients before proceeding with treatments. What risks as well as benefits might occur? Only when armed with adequate information would a person be in a position to make an informed decision. This right to informed consent became federal law as a result of scandals involving medical experimentation with patients who did not realize they were participating in a research project that could have critical effects on their health and survival. The most notorious of these studies had been conducted by the government itself when the U.S. Public Health Service:

> examined the effects of untreated syphilis among rural black men in Tuskegee, Alabama. Thousands of men were kept in total ignorance of the experiment, their infection, and the seriousness of syphilis. They were consistently steered away from receiving effective treatment so the United States government could monitor how the disease progressed, its many serious side effects, and its rate of fatality (Lens, 2002, p. 475).

Physicians are now required to explain the procedures, benefits, and risks in such a way that patients clearly understand what is involved. That brings us to the other key concept. Competence to understand the information, make a rational decision, and express that decision cannot be assumed. The person might be profoundly mentally retarded, suffering from severe brain damage, or unable to communicate in speech or writing. I have known instances in which "competence" seemed to be an interaction effect as physician and patient lacked a shared language with which to communicate effectively.

We shall note in Chapter 10 that children tend to be excluded from participation in decision making about their own care. The child is not considered competent to give or withhold informed consent for medical procedures in general. Does this mean that every possible treatment must be given (imposed) on a child? And who should decide?

I would not want to underestimate the practical difficulties in assuring that the liberty right is respected, adequate information given, and patient competence expertly assessed. There is this level of protection and due process to work with, however. In many of the examples that follow in this chapter, we will see how difficult it can be when patients cannot participate fully in decision making and when, therefore, it is not clear what choices they would have made if given the opportunities.

Nazi "Euthanasia"

There is another really hard question to consider: *Can we—and should we— detach ourselves from the memory of horrors that have been perpetrated in the name of euthanasia?* There are still many people among us who remember how the political, medical, economic, and military forces of a modern nation all collaborated in the murder of millions of people. The holocaust that eventually claimed millions of lives was preceded by Hitler's policy of *Vernichtun lebensunwerten Lebens*. Nazi doctors participated in the "extermination of valueless life." The victims were fellow German citizens, non-Jewish, who were invalids, infirm, unable to care for themselves—a large proportion of the institutionalized population (Lifton, 1986). Killing these helpless people required the cooperation of physicians and other people who had been entrusted with their care.

German society might have rejected this brutal program had it been exposed for what it was. However, the murders were disguised as euthanasia. The Nazi leadership declared that these people were being put out of their misery for their own good. And, yes, it would also save the cost of feeding and housing them. Enough physicians believed (or pretended to believe) this explanation in order to make the program a success.

What the Nazis did to their helpless citizens had nothing at all to do with euthanasia. These people were not terminally ill. They were not suffering intractable pain. They did not ask to be killed. They were simply murdered, one by one, through a process that had a bureaucrat at one end and a physician at the other. Discovering that he could induce physicians, lawyers, and other responsible people to engage in "mercy killing," Hitler moved on to his genocidal assaults against Jews and Gypsies (Friedlander, 1995).

The Black Stork

An almost forgotten episode in U.S. history brings the euthanasia issue even closer to us. A keen interest in both eugenics and euthanasia developed early in the twentieth century. Preventive medicine was starting to reduce mortality rates and increase life expectancies. Why not go all the way? Why not keep "defective" people out of the population in the first place? Eugenicists proposed sterilization of people thought to have defective genes. And why not also let defective newborn infants die? And, while we are at it, why not end the lives of patients as soon as it is clear that they are incurable? A crusade was born! Euthanasia was favored by those who did not think eugenics went far enough. A prominent Chicago surgeon by the name of Harry J. Haiselden combined eugenics with euthanasia. He boasted of having allowed the deaths of at least six "defective" infants. Then he urged other physicians to help him weed out those unfit for the new and improved version of society.

Physicians who did save defective infants came under attack by eugenicists (Pernick, 1996). At first the public was divided in its response to the eugenics and euthanasia movements. By the 1920s the public had pretty much rejected the euthanasia component—but not before it had attracted the enthusiasm of some German physicians and political thinkers:

> By the 1930s racial hygiene, eugenics, and euthanasia played a complex but central role in the evolution of Nazi ideology and in the legitimization of Nazi genocide. Depicting their intended victims as carriers of racial "diseases" constituted

An influential movement in the United States urged death for babies with birth defects and for others who were considered to be burdens on society. The Black Stork was a symbol used by critics of this movement.

a key feature of Nazi propaganda . . . . Programs for killing incurably ill institutional patients, such as the operation code-named "T-4" that secretly gassed over 100,000 disabled Germans, pioneered the machinery and trained the medical personnel who were then transferred to run the death camps for the "racially diseased" (p. 164).

Can there be any wonder that the terms *euthanasia* and *mercy killing* still trigger suspicion and anger on the part of those who know how they have been so cruelly misused? The Native American woman who told me of the forced sterilization of many women in her tribe was not being paranoid: she was simply reporting facts.

The Ventilator and the Slippery Slope

The distinction between withholding or withdrawing treatment is meaningful. Even so, thoughtful people might disagree on what course of action should be taken. Consider, for example, the *ventilator* (Iserson, 2002). This is a familiar piece of equipment in the intensive care unit. It is frequently used for relatively short-term situations, as when a patient who is likely to recover from illness or trauma needs some respiratory assistance. It is also frequently used in potentially long-term life-support situations. Suppose that a patient has been attached to a ventilator for weeks or even months. Families and hospital staff now agree that this person has no chance for recovery and is receiving no quality-of-life benefit from the life-support system. Somebody pulls the plug. The patient dies (or, sometimes, not). This would be an example of withdrawing treatment. But suppose instead that a person has just been brought to the hospital after a massive stroke or with severe brain trauma from an accident. It is obvious to the medical team that the higher brain centers have been destroyed. Death will soon occur unless the unresponsive body is hooked up to a life-support system. The decision is made against using a ventilator. The patient is soon certified as dead.

The patient dies in both of these scenarios. The "instrument" of death in both scenarios is the ventilator. How much importance should we attach to the difference between withdrawing and withholding treatment? Are both methods equally moral and acceptable (or equally immoral and unacceptable?)? And what if it was up to you? Would pulling the plug be no more difficult than deciding not to connect the plug in the first place? Whatever your judgment and your decision, you are sure to find some experts agreeing and others disagreeing.

Euthanasia, assisted suicide, physician-assisted death, medicide, and other such terms all differ from suicide by involving the actions of another person. Suicidal people carry out their own intentions. Assisted death, by definition, requires another person to contribute actively to the outcome. How much importance should be attached to this distinction? If a person really wants to have his or her life ended, do the details matter? "Yes," you might argue, "because it places a heavy responsibility on another person." "No," you might argue, "because it is the intention and the outcome that count, not the particular method." Attempts to legalize assisted deaths in the United States have often involved these counterarguments.

We use the *slippery slope argument* when we oppose a particular instance of assisted death because it might contribute to widespread abuse in other instances. "I can understand and sympathize with a person's request to be put out of his or her suffering," we might say. "But if society consents to 'mercy killing' in this instance, then tomorrow we will be asked to consent in a case where the right to die is not quite so clear. And so it will go, until we slide all the way down the slope." The recent ordeal of Chantal Sebire has been such an example.

Perhaps too many people would give up too soon when confronted not only with a terminal illness, but with other crises as well. Perhaps death would become too easy an out. Perhaps euthanasia would even become the normative way of ending our lives. And perhaps that option would be seized on by the bean-counters as a nifty way to control the costs of health care in a graying society? Depending on our anxieties and imagination, we could visualize a very slippery slope indeed. There are sharp disagreements today regarding the applicability of the slippery slope argument to a particular life-and-death decision, and these disagreements are likely to continue for some time.

It is important to keep in mind that the *living will* and other advance directives do not include provisions for assisted death. Many people who support the living will as an expression of the individual's preferences do not support assisted death. However, one sentence in the standard living will does walk the boundary: "I do, however, ask that medication be mercifully administered to me to alleviate suffering even though this may shorten my remaining life."

Suppose that you are a physician. The patient you are attending has entrusted you with a signed and witnessed copy of her living will. She is dying. She is also in physical and emotional distress. "I want to die," she tells you. It had been your intention to control her pain with morphine. A heavier dose would not only relieve her pain but also hasten an easy death. Would you feel justified in prescribing a lethal dose because it is consistent with the *advance directive* (". . . even though this may shorten my remaining life")? Or would you feel that you were dishonoring your profession or even committing murder?

OUR CHANGING ATTITUDES TOWARD A RIGHT TO DIE

In recent years, the public has had more opportunity to learn about right-to-die issues. As we have already seen (Chapter 6), the doctrine of informed consent has made a difference, and the public soon proved supportive of natural death acts that support advance directives such as the living will. A national survey was conducted while open discussion of right to die issues was still in its early phases (*Times Mirror*, 1983). Most Americans already believed that there were circumstances in which a person should be allowed to die and that terminally ill people do have the right to accept or reject treatment options. More personally, most people said they would ask their doctors to stop treatment if they were in great physical pain and unable to function in daily activities because of an incurable disease. Yet there was also a consensus that medical personnel were not paying much attention to the patients' wishes (i.e., trying to resuscitate patients who had asked that this procedure not be done). Most

respondents had heard about the living will and thought it a good idea, but few had actually completed such a document for themselves.

But what about the possible next step—euthanasia or assisted death? Perhaps surprisingly, seven of ten people felt it was justified to terminate a life if a person was suffering terrible pain from a terminal disease. The survey question was specific to married couples: if the pain was severe and could not be relieved, would it be an act of mercy to end the life of one's dying spouse (with the consent of the spouse, of course)? At this point, the role of the physician as terminator was not yet salient. The attitudinal picture was not as clear-cut as it might seem from the findings already mentioned. Do people have the moral right to end their own lives if afflicted with incurable disease? The public was divided on this question. There was a slight edge for those who agreed there is a moral right to suicide under this circumstance—but firm disapproval for ending one's life simply because it has become burdensome either to one's self or family. Americans were also about equally divided about whether they would want to have everything done to save their lives or to choose comfort management instead.

Much has happened since the 1980s. The establishment of hospice care programs to provide comfort, pain relief, and family support has alleviated the prospect of suffering for many people and, therefore, the desperate impulse to hasten the end of life. However, the opposite extreme has also become offered as an option: physician-assisted death (discussed later in this chapter). How has public opinion responded to these and other recent developments?

The results of subsequent national polls have been summarized by the Death with Dignity National Center (2002) and the Pew Research Center (2006). The public has become much more aware of the living will and, to a lesser extent, other types of advance directives. There is also a marked increase in willingness of family members to discuss end-of-life medical care issues with each other. Most respondents believe that people should be able to exercise the right to make their own decisions in seeking or rejecting medical procedures, or choosing the hospice action. The public remains divided, though, about physician-assisted suicide. Withholding or withdrawing medical treatment is often regarded as an acceptable choice, but taking direct action to end a life is most often regarded as an immoral or criminal intervention. And the public remains about equally divided between its own end-of-life preferences. The next person you talk to is about as likely to say, "I want them to do everything they can to keep me going," as "I don't want to linger in pain and dependency. When the time comes, I want to go peacefully."

Changes in attitudes toward death in the United States have been documented by Bert Hayslip, Jr., and Cynthia A. Peveto (2005). Findings of their own recent study were compared with the pioneering research of Richard A. Kalish and David K. Reynolds (1976). Respondents now believe that physicians should tell terminally ill patients the truth about their conditions and that funerals and memorial services should reflect the personalities and values of the deceased individuals and their families. The public has become more active in participating in its own end-of-life decisions. Interestingly, there was also a higher priority given to spending time with loved ones and remaining in the interpersonal flow, as compared with the earlier tendency to withdraw when terminally ill.

Professional organizations such as the American College of Physicians have continued to oppose assisted death. According to physicians Timothy E. Quill and Christine K. Cassel (2003), these organizations:

> rightly emphasize that palliative care should be the standard of care for the dying, and that the inadequacies that exist in its delivery should be remedied. But such position statements generally understate the limitations of palliative care to alleviate some end-of-life suffering, and they do not provide adequate guidance about how physicians should approach patients with intractable suffering who are prepared to die (p. 208).

Individual physicians and nurses have their own opinions on this difficult and controversial subject. There continue to be situations in which responsible and well-informed health care providers might disagree on what should—and should not—be done.

THE RIGHT-TO-DIE DILEMMA: CASE EXAMPLES

We have examined some of the key concepts and learned how the public views them. Now we consider some of the specific human experiences that have influenced the present status of the right-to-die issue and that will also play a role in future developments. Details are important, so we will go beyond the headlines. You will probably notice a pattern here. The most discussed and consequential cases have been those of Karen Ann Quinlan, "Debbie" (a pseudonym), Nancy Cruzan, and Terri Schiavo. All women. All young. All white. A coincidence?

The Ethics of Withdrawing Treatment: The Landmark Quinlan Case

Karen Ann Quinlan became the center of national attention when she lapsed into a coma after a party on the night of April 14, 1975. One friend applied mouth-to-mouth resuscitation while another called the police, who also attempted resuscitation and took her to a hospital. She started to breathe again, but did not return to consciousness. Traces of valium and quinine were found in her blood. Drug-induced coma was the preliminary diagnosis. Later this diagnosis was disputed, and it has never been fully clarified. Whatever the cause, Quinlan suffered severe and irreversible brain damage as a result of oxygen deprivation.

Weeks and then months passed. Quinlan remained in the hospital. Her vegetative functions were maintained on a ventilator, with intravenous tubes providing fluids and nutrition. Her body gradually wasted away. After a few months, the once vital and attractive young woman had become a 60-pound shriveled form, curled into a fetal position. Talk of recovery and a miraculous return to life became less frequent as time went by. The hospital expenses continued to mount day by day.

Karen Ann was the adopted child of deeply religious parents. Joseph Quinlan maintained hope for nearly half a year. Finally his priest persuaded him that morality does not require that extraordinary means be used to prolong life. The Quinlans asked two physicians to turn off the ventilator. They declined to do so. The physicians were not sure of the moral implications of such an action. Their professional training had not prepared them for this kind of situation. They were also concerned about the possibility of facing malpractice or even felony charges. For those physicians at that time, the request to "pull the plug" was almost equivalent to the first astronauts' walk in space.

What were the Quinlans to do? They pursued their request through the courts. This time-consuming legal process provided the opportunity for many to air opinions in the media and in professional circles as well as in the courts. Confusion was also generated. For example, there was a tendency to speak of Karen Ann as though she were already dead, even though EEG tracings still showed weak electrical activity in the brain. A neurologist described her condition as a "persistent vegetative state." This phrase would be repeated many times about many other nonresponsive persons in the years to come. An attorney for New Jersey described a brief visit to her room:

> Her face is all distorted and she is sweating. Her eyes are open and blinking about twice a minute. She's sort of gasping. I've never seen anything like that. . . . I was there for seven minutes and it seemed like seven hours (Kron, 1975, p. 22).

Medical testimony was given that Karen Ann would die within a short time if removed from the ventilator.

The court ruled against the Quinlans' request. The judge specifically rejected the argument that religious freedom should be the basis for approving the removal of the life-support system. This decision was appealed to the New Jersey Supreme Court. Here, for the first time, a court ruled that a ventilator could be turned off. However, the court imposed a condition: Physicians must first agree that Karen Ann had no reasonable chance of regaining consciousness. The New Jersey attorney general decided not to challenge this decision. The United States Supreme Court's turn would come later in the Nancy Cruzan case.

Finally, 14 months after she had lapsed into a nonresponsive state, Karen Ann was disconnected from the ventilator. She was expected to die quickly. However, her persistent vegetative state proved persistent indeed. Karen Ann remained alive (in some sense of the word) for more than 10 years until she succumbed to pneumonia in 1985. Many an observer drew the inference that expert opinion is not always respected by the forces that govern life and death.

Karen Ann's predicament was not the first of its kind but became the starting place for efforts to develop due process in right-to-die issues. It was recognized that medical technology now made it possible for many people to be maintained in a persistent vegetative state, but that it perhaps should not be employed beyond a point of no return. Guidelines were needed, and a system of checks and balances established.

There was been a long and winding road from the Karen Ann Quinlan dilemma to the present day. It has been estimated that 10,000 to 35,000 Americans exist in persistent vegetative states and as many as another 150,000 have minimal consciousness syndrome (Maitland, 2005). Nobody knows for sure how many people are in such a condition. Some could remain unresponsive and "brain dead" (Chapter 2) yet alive for years. Families and caregivers must deal with this difficult situation day after day. Court decisions have sometimes clouded and sometimes clarified our understanding. Meanwhile, physicians and other health care providers responded in various ways to their new challenges. One of these responses became the subject of a continuing controversy. The principals in this drama were a young physician and a young woman who became known as Debbie.

"It's over, Debbie": Compassion or Murder?

The Quinlan case was characterized by a long period of consultations, discussions, and legal proceedings. Many people participated, and many facts were brought forward for public, as well as family and professional, scrutiny. A very different case was reported in a leading medical journal. No author's name was attributed to "It's over, Debbie," when this brief report was published in the *Journal of the American Medical Association* (Anonymous, 1988). The article was offered

There is an emerging consensus that physicians should tell the truth to terminally ill people. Perhaps more challenging is the art of listening to the patients' response.

as a personal experience and consisted of only three paragraphs. This is the story:

A presumably young physician, a resident in gynecology, was called in the middle of the night by a nurse on the gynecologic–oncology (cancer) unit. This was not the physician's usual duty station. The doctor "trudged along, bumping sleepily against walls and corners and not believing I was up again." Upon reaching the unit, he picked up the patient's chart and was given some "hurried details" by the nurse. A 20-year-old patient was dying of ovarian cancer. An attempt had been made to sedate her by using an alcohol drip, but this had led her to vomit "unrelentingly."

Entering the patient's room, the resident saw that the patient was emaciated and looked much older than her actual age. "She was receiving nasal oxygen, had an IV, and was sitting in bed suffering from what was obviously severe air hunger, the physician reported." There was another woman in the room who stood by the bed, holding the patient's hand. The physician had the impression that "The room seemed filled with the patient's desperate effort to survive." The physician also observed that the patient was breathing with great difficulty. The article states that the patient had not eaten or slept in 2 days nor had she responded to chemotherapy. Presumably this information had been gleaned from the doctor's quick glance through the patient's chart.

Trying to take in the whole situation, the resident felt that it was a "gallows scene, a cruel mockery of her youth and unfulfilled potential. Her only words to me were, 'Let's get this over with.'" The physician returned to the nurses' station to think things over. There the physician decided that he would "give her rest." The nurse was asked to draw morphine sulfate into a syringe. " 'Enough,' I thought, 'to do the job.'" The physician returned to the patient's room and told the two women that he was going to give Debbie "something that would let her rest and to say good-bye." Within seconds of the intravenous injection, the patient's breathing slowed, her eyes closed, and her distress seemed to be at an end. The other woman stroked Debbie's hair as she slept.

The doctor "waited for the inevitable next effect of depressing the respiratory drive." Four minutes later, the breathing slowed further, sputtered, and came to an end. The dark-haired woman stood erect and seemed relieved. "It's all over, Debbie," (p. 272).

This brief report raised a furor among the readers of this widely read and respected medical journal. The media picked it up, and the public was immediately drawn into the controversy as well. The response was divided, but critical reactions dominated.

Here are what I see as the most salient questions raised by this incident:

- The physician had no prior acquaintance with the patient or her companion. This means that a stranger made and carried out the life-and-death decision. Should a physician assist the death of a patient with whom he or she has no previous relationship and no background of knowledge?
- The decision was made very quickly and without consultation. Did the decision have to be made that quickly? Do physicians have the responsibility to get a second opinion before taking a life? The physician was fatigued. Should physicians be able to take their own states of mind and body into account when on the verge of making important decisions?
- The physician's anxiety was heightened by the fact that the patient was also young. It was difficult to establish a protective sense of emotional distance: This terrible thing could also happen to the physician.
- The physician seems to have projected his or her own thoughts and feelings on the patient. The "gallows" and "cruel mockery" images emerged from the physician's own mind

and might or might not have resonated with Debbie's own thoughts. Should physicians be required to demonstrate competency in dealing with their own emotions before being entrusted with other people's lives?
- At first the physician felt that "The room seemed filled with the patient's desperate effort to survive." Just a few minutes later, the physician ended Debbie's life. There was no indication in the published report that the physician ever tried to reconcile the impression with the action. Should physicians be required to demonstrate the ability to monitor their own thoughts in an alert and critical manner before being entrusted with other people's lives?
- The nurse was ordered to prepare a lethal injection. Is it morally defensible to order another person to participate in an assisted death? Should the nurse have been given the opportunity to express her feelings and philosophy? Did the nurse have the responsibility to refuse this order and inform the physician that she is reporting this incident immediately?
- The physician ordered a lethal dose of medication instead of a dose that might have provided relief without ending the patient's life. This alternative does not seem to have been considered. Does a physician have the right to end a life before attempting to relieve pain and other symptoms by nonlethal means? Was the physician adequately trained in symptom alleviation?
- The patient's distress had been intensified by a procedure (the alcohol drip) that had produced new symptoms without alleviating the existing symptoms. Did this hospital routinely fail to provide adequate pain relief because of ignorance, indifference, or the fear of making an addict out of a terminally ill patient? Was it the failure of the hospital's overall symptom relief program that placed both the young resident and the young woman in this extremely stressful situation?
- Debbie spoke only one sentence to the doctor. Did the doctor try to converse with her or her companion? Did the physician hold her hand, establish eye contact, and attempt to have at least a little more guidance from her before making the decision to end her life? Should

doctors be required to demonstrate communication competence in critical care situations before being entrusted with other people's lives?

- The doctor told the two women that he was giving Debbie (a) something that "would let her rest" and (b) and to say good-bye. What actually happened, according to the report, was that Debbie closed her eyes and died shortly thereafter without having the chance to say good-bye or anything else. Was the physician actually concerned with enabling leave-taking communication between Debbie and her companion? Did the physician really believe that death and "rest" are identical outcomes? Or did the physician misrepresent what he or she was actually doing in order to reduce his or her own anxiety level? What responsibility to truth and open communication should be expected of the physician in critical care situations?

Karen Ann Quinlan never regained consciousness after her 1975 accident. The question of whether she should be disconnected from life support became the focus of the first major public controversy about the legal, medical, moral, and religious aspects of a "right to die."

An Arrow Through the Physician's Armor

One of the painful lessons in this episode involves the physician's own physical, mental, and spiritual state and the nature of the health care system. A tired and probably overworked physician found himself in a stressful situation that neither medical training nor personal experience had equipped him to master. His own insulation from dying and death was pierced momentarily by seeing another young person in such a painful and vulnerable condition. The physician felt an urgent need to relieve Debbie's anguish as well as his own sense of personal vulnerability and inability to restore her health.

The physician had several options. These included taking other measures to relieve the patient's distress and discontinuing those that were adding to her distress. The physician could have consulted with others—the nurses who had been caring for Debbie as well as more experienced physicians. The physician could have made more effort to learn who Debbie was and what she wanted. It is not unusual for people to wish themselves dead when experiencing acute distress—but to be grateful later that another alternative had been found.

All these options required time and patience—and time was not what this tired, poorly prepared, overmatched, and anxious physician could afford. The decision to end Debbie's life was influenced by the physician's urgent need to terminate a situation in which he or she felt powerless, vulnerable, and depressed. The needs and feelings of other people were barely considered, nor the philosophical, religious, sociopsychological, and legal factors that might lead one to hesitate before taking another person's life.

Much of the critical response called attention to the physician's disregard of standards and due procedure. Other doctors were aware that their own images and reputations were endangered by such episodes. The ease with which one young physician disposed of Debbie's problems by disposing of Debbie in the middle of the night seems to be a prime example of how slippery the slope can be.

We should keep in mind, however, that the anxieties of doctors (or hospital administrators) can lead to the opposite outcome as well: bodies being maintained on life-support systems despite the obvious futility of this procedure and despite the family's and even the patient's own expressed wishes. The legal justice system in our society, for all its flaws, does at least allow time and does require evidence. Decisions hastily made in the middle of the night by doctors who are poorly trained in self-monitoring and interpersonal communication afford few, if any, safeguards.

A Supreme Court Ruling: The Nancy Cruzan Case

The Supreme Court of the United States issued its first direct ruling on the subject 15 years after the Quinlan case brought the right-to-die issue to public attention. Nancy Cruzan, 26, had been critically injured in an automobile accident on January 11, 1983. When discovered by paramedics, Cruzan was lying face down in a ditch—no respiration, no heartbeat. The paramedics were able to revive her respiration and cardiac functions, but the young woman remained unresponsive. Physicians judged that she had suffered trauma to the brain and oxygen deprivation.

Three weeks later she could grimace, display motor reflexes, and take a little nourishment by mouth. There may have been slight responsivity to pain and sound. Nevertheless, Nancy Cruzan did not respond to conversation, express thoughts and needs, or engage in either verbal or nonverbal communication. Surgeons implanted a feeding tube with the permission of her husband. It was not necessary to use a ventilator because she continued to breathe on her own. Rehabilitation efforts failed. No improvement was noted or expected, but she remained alive and the state of Missouri continued to pay for her care. Nancy Cruzan's parents asked hospital personnel to discontinue the tube feeding and hydration. It was understood by everybody involved that this action would result in the young woman's death. The hospital declined to do so without court authorization. This request would go all the way to the U.S. Supreme Court (1989). This is a summary of what happened:

1. The trial court ruled that Nancy Cruzan had a fundamental right to refuse or accept the

withdrawal of what it termed "death-prolonging procedures."

2. It was also ruled that she had expressed her general intent in a conversation with a close friend a year previously. Nancy had told her friend that if very ill or seriously injured she would not want to continue her life unless she could live "at least halfway normally."

3. The Missouri attorney general appealed this ruling to his state's supreme court. By a four-to-three margin, the lower court's ruling was overturned. The life-support procedures would have to be continued. A key point in this decision was the fact that Nancy had not prepared a living will or any other document that established her intent beyond a reasonable doubt.

4. The U.S. Supreme Court recognized the principle that "a competent person has a constitutionally protected . . . interest in refusing unwanted medical treatment" (p. 183). Nevertheless, by a five-to-four margin, the nation's highest court refused to overturn the decision. Nancy Cruzan had the right to refuse "death-prolongation" procedures, but the state of Missouri had the right to require what it considered to be clear and convincing evidence that this would really have been Ms. Cruzan's intentions if she could now express herself.

5. The Supreme Court, however, had created a way out of the dilemma. The state itself could reconsider the evidence and approve withdrawal of life-support activities. And that is just what happened. Nancy Cruzan's physician had opposed withdrawal of life support. But now, after 6 years, he had seen enough. A court-appointed guardian asked the physician if he still thought it was within the patient's interest to continue the tube feeding and hydration. "No, sir. I think it would be personally a living hell!" A Jasper County judge ruled that the parents' request could be honored. There were no further legal challenges this time, although a throng of protesters (not people who had known Nancy Cruzan personally) voiced their disapproval. The young woman died quietly 12 days after the tubes were removed.

What was learned from this ordeal? The U.S. Supreme Court did affirm the principle that a competent person has the right to refuse treatment that would only prolong suffering and that local jurisdictions could require due process. The Cruzan vs. Missouri decision, however, did not address all the issues that can arise in right-to-die cases; it did not even address all the salient issues in the Cruzan case.

What lessons can we draw? We can see it would be useful to establish our wishes in the form of a written advance directive. Nancy Cruzan's situation would have been resolved sooner and with less stress for everybody concerned had she executed a living will—but how many 23-year-olds (or 46-year-olds, for that matter) do you know who have actually done this? We can also see that the decision to withdraw life support is a difficult one when respiratory, cardiac function, and motor reflexes persist without external aids. The Missouri State Supreme Court emphasized that "Nancy is diagnosed as in a persistent vegetative state. She is not dead. She is not terminally ill. Medical experts testified that she could live another thirty years" (1989, p.180). We need to be well informed and secure in our understanding about what it means to be alive and a person.

Finally, we are left with the question of perceived social value. Both Karen Ann Quinlan and Nancy Cruzan were young people who seemed to have full lives ahead of them. What about elderly people who find themselves in similar predicaments? Hemlock Society author Donald W. Cox (1993) notes:

> On November 30, two weeks prior to Judge Teel's order to remove Nancy's feeding tube from her stomach, the Court of Common Pleas in Lackawanna County (Scranton), Pennsylvania held that a sixty-four-year-old incompetent woman in a persistent vegetative state was entitled to have a naso-gastric tube withdrawn. The hospital removed the tube and the woman died peacefully and quietly, in sharp contrast to the front-page publicity that enveloped Cruzan's death a few weeks later (p. 86).

Many elderly men and women have died in this manner. Others have died when health care personnel have decided against starting life-support procedures. As a nation, we seem to place less value on the lives of older adults. We assume that old people are supposed to be depressed and therefore seldom intervene. When older people seem ready to die—well, that's what they're supposed to do, right?

TERRI SCHIAVO: WHO DECIDES?

There is a sequence of events to be considered before we come to the "Schiavo case" as it emerged in the media spotlight. Our basic source is Jay Wolfson's (2003) official report to Florida Governor Jeb Bush, a balanced, detailed, and humane account of a complex situation, and to the succinct account Daniel Eisenberg published in *Time* (2005). Other sources are cited as appropriate.

The Ordeal Begins

The Theresa (Terri) Schiavo known to her family and friends vanished in the early morning of February 25, 1990, when she was felled by a heart attack. A decade later she remained on life support in a skilled nursing facility, her condition not brought to the attention of the general public. She continued to receive physical, occupational, recreational, and speech therapies, but showed only reflexive movements, random eye opening, and no communication ability (Wolfson, 2003). At first, husband Michael and her parents the Schindlers had worked together closely in caring for and hoping to rehabilitate Terri. However, Terri's husband and parents eventually came to different opinions about her possibility for recovery. Furthermore, a court judgment had found a fertility clinic guilty of malpractice in overseeing Terri's attempts to become pregnant. The award was in the million-dollar range. Money started to matter.

> This fund was meticulously managed and accounted for and Michael Schiavo had no control over its use. There is no evidence in the trust of any mismanagement of Theresa's estate, and the records on this matter are excellently maintained (Wolfson, p. 5).

Following this court judgment, the Schindlers petitioned the court to remove Michael as guardian, alleging that he was not caring for Terri. The court ruled against this petition, noting that Michael had taken a forceful role in assuring that Terri consistently received the best care possible. This conflict between husband and parents would continue through the years.

Terri contracted a urinary tract infection in 1994. Michael Schiavo and the physician agreed there was no longer even a remote chance for her recovery. They decided not to treat the infection. Additionally, a DNR (do not resuscitate) order was posted so that no resuscitation would be attempted if she should have another cardiac arrest. Until this time, he had held on to hope for her possible recovery. After waiting another 3 years, Michael petitioned to discontinue life support. Clinical review confirmed that Terri's condition was that of "a diagnosed persistent vegetative state with no chance of improvement." Mrs. Schindler stated that Terri displayed special responses, mostly to her, but these were not observed or documented by others.

The Schindlers continued their efforts to revoke the decision to remove Terri's feeding tube. There were repeated court considerations of this request, in which the Schindlers were given opportunity to produce testimony and offer evidence. These legal proceedings were still continuing more than a decade after Terri's collapse, but had not yet become the subject of general public attention. In a significant development, the court gave credibility to testimony that when still in good health Terri had mentioned that she would never want to be put on life support if something happened to her. The decision once again found the request to discontinue life support in order. Much more was yet to happen, but it will be useful to pause for comment before describing the next phase.

Comments I

The situation that enveloped Terri Schiavo, her husband, parents, and caregivers had many significant elements.

When it started: Paramedics and emergency medical technicians, emergency rooms, and life-support technology are fairly recent additions to the health care system. There was a 911 telephone number for Michael to call, and an effective response system that brought skilled personnel to Terri's assistance, although even that prompt response was not rapid enough to prevent the anoxia. All that would follow—the years of persistent vegetative functioning, the family disputes, the national controversy—would not have happened in an earlier generation when fewer emergency options were available. By 1990, there was more that could be done to try to save a life, and so these things were done. These efforts added Terri to the lengthening list of people existing on the life/death borderline.

Who decides? The ordeal of the Schiavo and Schindler families occurred at a time when the living will and the right to exercise informed consent had been affirmed. Much had been discussed and learned from earlier cases, particularly those of Quinlan, Debbie, and Cruzan. An advance directive in which Terri expressed the wish to have resuscitation and life-support efforts withheld would very likely have been respected. However, it was unusual at that time for a young person to make a living will, and it is still uncommon today. The courts sifted through reports of conversations in which Terri might or might not have clearly communicated her views. Unfortunately, Terri was in no condition to express her wishes once she had become incapacitated. She might have designated a person to speak in her behalf if such a situation should arise, a health care proxy. However, this would also have been an unusual action for a young person. From this lack of definitive knowledge of Terri's own wishes there developed a long, complex, and adversarial process to determine who should make the decision about Terri's fate and on what basis.

Michele Mathis (2005) explains that:

> when a patient is no longer able to make medical treatment decisions for herself, care providers and those who know the patient well should try to effectuate the treatment choices she would have made. This is the *substituted judgment* standard of surrogate decision-making. Substituted judgment is regarded with approval as a way of carrying the value of patient self-determination forward into a time when the patient is incapable of autonomy. This is now referred to as the best interests standard for medical decision-making, and is relied upon when there is no information about what the patient might have wanted (p. 3).

But—whose judgment should be substituted for the incapacitated Terri Schiavo's?

Whose fault? Relationships among the people close to Terri were also strained by uncertainty regarding the cause of her collapse. Had the fertility clinic failed to safeguard her health? Had Terri seriously harmed her body by a previous weight loss program? Or was it something else? The medical facts do not allow for a firm conclusion even now. The lack of closure kept uncertainty and anxiety at a high pitch. (Later the Schindlers would charge that Michael had physically abused Terri, a claim that earned little support and was dismissed after the autopsy.)

Do the doctors really know? What would Terri have wanted? Who should decide? Who, if anybody, was at fault? These uncertainties were augmented by distrust of medical judgment by the Schindlers and, later, by some politicians and media professionals. Terri was seen by numerous physicians, and her records were reviewed by outside experts, including those that were court-appointed. The finding kept coming up: persistence (or permanent) vegetative state. Nevertheless, the Schindlers insisted that Terri continued to have thoughts and experiences and might yet recover. As time went on, the disconnect would become increasingly evident between medical judgment and the perceptions and wishes of some members of the family and the public. This pattern would become accompanied by increasing concern about the public's limited understanding of conditions such as the persistent vegetative state.

The Public Controversy

The Schiavo case moved into public awareness when Michael petitioned a court for removal of Terri's feeding tube. The court ruled that Terri would not have wanted to be kept alive but stayed the order to give the Schindlers time to appeal. The Florida Supreme Court denied the appeal and the U.S. Supreme Court refused to consider a further appeal. The Schindlers continued to pursue other courses of action in the legal system, all of which received serious consideration. Judges were giving both sides ample opportunity to present evidence and arguments. A medical panel was appointed with five doctors, one chosen by the court, and two by each side in the controversy. These proceedings carried forward into 2002, when the judge ruled that there was no substantial possibility that Terri's condition could be improved. For the second time, an order was issued to withdraw the feeding tube, and for the second time, its application was postponed to give the Schindlers opportunity for further appeal. Florida governor Jeb Bush filed a brief on their behalf and Terri Schiavo's 13-year ordeal was now in the national political, religious, medical, and ethical spotlight.

The next medical procedure was followed by an unprecedented political action. The feeding tube was disconnected, but Governor Bush asked the state legislature to pass "Terri's Law," which, quickly enacted, provided the opportunity to have the tube reinserted. President George W. Bush praised this action, thereby further rallying pro-life support. Politics now towered over the medical and legal systems.

Headlines and talk shows blazed with opinions and expert (or not so expert) commentary. Federal and state government had chosen to oppose medical opinion and the judgment of several courts. The courts did not give in. A Florida judge ruled that Terri's Law was unconstitutional, and the Florida Supreme Court agreed. The U.S. Supreme Court was again petitioned to hear the case, and again declined. As Mathis (2005) notes, Terri Schiavo had become the central figure in one of the most adjudicated cases in the nation's history. There was still more to come (Eisenberg, 2005). The Florida legislature came up with a new law to prevent removal of

Court and medical findings were challenged by demonstrations against the decision to remove Terri Schiavo's feeding tube.

the feeding tube, but this one was also rejected in court. Just a few weeks later, it was the U.S. House and Senate that agreed on a federal bill to counter the court ruling to take Terri off life support. These fast-moving proceedings were unprecedented in American history—the executive and legislative branches of the government putting other issues aside (e.g., post 9/11 terrorism) to overturn the judicial branch and the medical opinion on which it had relied. The bill was quickly passed and quickly signed by the president, but not before the feeding tube was disconnected. Repeated appeals to state and federal courts were made by the Schindlers. All were denied. The courts were firm in their judgment that Terri Schiavo was in a persistent vegetative state and had no hope of recovery.

Terri Schiavo died of dehydration on March 31 after 7 years of heated public controversy surrounding her condition. The Schindlers had never given up their efforts to keep her alive. According to medical experts, Terri had been unconscious since the loss of oxygen to her brain 15 years previously. Repeated assessments had never discovered any electrical activity in her brain. Autopsy found that her brain had shrunk to half its size and had suffered severe and irreversible damage. The medical examiner concluded that "no amount of therapy or treatment would have regenerated the massive loss of neurons" (Stacy, 2005).

Surveys made it clear that the public disapproved of Congress's attempt to intervene and thought that the opposition to removal of life support had more to do with politics than ethical principles and values (Eisenberg, 2005). There was particular scorn for Senate Majority Leader Bill Frist, a heart surgeon. He had stated that Terri Schiavo was "not somebody in persistent vegetative state," although he had not examined her nor reviewed her case. His later denial of that statement undermined his credibility, and might have contributed to his loss of the Senate leadership position (Babington, 2005).

Comments II

Consider considering: The anguish and tensions experienced by Terri's husband and parents might have been intensified by the way our judicial system works. The system is basically adversarial. People are pitted against each other, and the interactions can become nasty and intimidating. By contrast, a system with the purpose of coming to the best possible outcome would encourage examination of perspectives, sharing, and mediation. Family courts have had some success in offering a less confrontational approach. Ethics committees have also worked in a sensitive and informed manner to resolve right-to-die issues without resorting to the pressurized court situation. Perhaps more opportunity should be provided for respectful consideration of values and viewpoints, and less reign should be given to the impulse to literally make a federal case out of a tough situation.

The knowledge gap: A brief videotape of Terri Schiavo was shown repeatedly on television. I saw what you saw. She was alive and moving. Perhaps there was purpose. Perhaps she was responding to a relationship. Looking at the tape, it was not difficult to suppose that the diagnosis of persistent vegetative state was too extreme. Nevertheless, I trust the medical experts on this one. The diagnosis of severe brain impairment has gone well beyond guesswork. The medical experts who examined Terri Schiavo and analyzed the findings knew what they were doing, as court after court agreed. For the most part, however, the media did not come up to that level. The videotape was routinely presented without reference to the date it had been recorded and without competent discussion of what we were seeing. Furthermore, it was later revealed that the videotape reviewed by lawmakers had been edited to make the best possible case for Schiavo's status. A continuing problem is the gap between general public conceptions of brain damage and the specialized knowledge that is continuing to develop in clinical practice and neuroscience. Finding a way to reduce that gap would make for fewer misunderstandings and unnecessary confrontations. It might also avoid the distress we feel when we assume that thirst and hunger can be experienced when a person is locked into a persistent vegetative state.

Prime people: A disturbing headline flashed across the newspaper page in my hands 2 months after Terri Schiavo's death: "MISSING: News Coverage on the Disappearance of Anyone Who's Not an Attractive, White Female" (Texeira, 2005). The article was all too accurate, however. It was focused not on Terri, but on what was at that time the latest example of an attractive white female (Natalee Holloway) whose disappearance was a top story. The author points out that most of the missing adults tracked by the FBI are men, and that many of those abducted or kidnapped are black. News editors believe, however, that the public is more interested in "prime people," especially attractive white females. This bias certainly exists in the right-to-die realm. The most reported, studied, and influential cases have had the same demographics as the prime people who have gone missing. I am not suggesting that we should have ignored the disappearance of Natalee Holloway or the ordeal of Terri Shiavo. I wonder, though, about the spectacular lack of attention to the many people in life-challenged conditions who are aged or otherwise not perceived as valuable or "interesting" enough. The death system takes its priorities from the values and caprices of society at large.

DR. KEVORKIAN AND THE ASSISTED-SUICIDE MOVEMENT

The assisted suicide controversy in the United States is closely associated with the opinions and practices of a retired pathologist by the name of Dr. Jack Kevorkian. His activities dominated the media spotlight until they reached a crescendo when the television program "60 Minutes" featured a video that showed him giving a lethal injection to Thomas Youk. Kevorkian challenged prosecutors to try him for murder. They did so—successfully—and Kevorkian was subsequently convicted of second-degree murder and imprisoned in a Michigan penal facility. He served 8 years of his sentence and, at the age of 79, was released from prison with his promise to refrain from any further assisted death activities.

Kevorkian often described his services as assisted suicide. This term locks in a particular interpretation (suicide), with which not all proponents of assisted death agree and with

which most suicidologists disagree. We will use the more neutral term, *assisted death*, which provides maneuvering room for a variety of interpretations. The most common term now in use is physician-assisted death. This term is unnecessarily limiting: family members and friends have also been known to assist in bringing about death.

Assisted Death in the Kevorkian Manner

Consider first the principle objections of the mainstream medical establishment to any form of assisted death:

- Taking a life is inconsistent with the responsibilities and values of a physician, a healer.
- Some physicians could not even begin to consider the possibility of assisting death because of their deeply held religious convictions.
- The life might be "mis-taken." Nature often surprises even the most adroit physician. The impulse to relieve suffering might therefore result in ending a life that had potential for recovery.
- Serious legal consequences might befall any physician who engaged in assisted death.

When Kevorkian started his campaign in 1990, he had practically no support from either medical organizations or court rulings. He hoped to arouse the public and thereby force the medical profession to change its position. This plan required Kevorkian to reveal rather than conceal his actions. He was eminently successful in arousing public opinion on this subject through media attention and controversy.

People who have known Kevorkian over the years characterize him as a very intelligent man with a keen grasp of medical history (Nicol and Wylie, 2006). Families who have sought his services often speak of him as a compassionate and understanding person. On the other hand, critics resent Kevorkian's verbal attacks on those who do not agree with him, his apparent delight in publicity, and his "lone wolf" approach. Not just what Kevorkian did, but how he did it has had a continuing influence on attitudes toward assisted death.

Kevorkian's Agenda

Kevorkian hoped to add planned death to the list of shattered taboos, now that legal sanctions against abortion and suicide have weakened. The agenda he presented included the establishment of centers in communities across the nation in which people could not only have assisted deaths upon their request, but also in which biomedical research could be done on dying and death. These *orbitoria* would go much further than previously has been possible to investigate the nature of death. We should not be squeamish about pursuing research across the borders from dying to death. Kevorkian was also a strong advocate for organ donation and attempted to establish a program through which condemned prisoners could donate their body parts. He was angered and disappointed when prisoners as well as officials declined this opportunity.

Kevorkian's Method

People turned to Kevorkian when there did not seem to be either hope for improvement or relief from suffering. He would discuss the situation with the patient and family members. Some of these sessions were recorded on videotape, others are excerpted in a biography co-authored by two of his close friends (Nicol & Wylie, 2006). Kevorkian repeatedly emphasized that he did not pressure patients to make the final decision quickly or to make that decision in the direction of assisted death. Carol Loving (1995/1996) describes the final scene in which her son Nick was to be terminated by Kevorkian:

> Dr. Kevorkian kept telling him, "If you don't want to go through with this, you don't have to. You don't have to worry about hurting our feelings. If you want to postpone for a week, a month, a year, don't even hesitate." My son kept saying, "No, No, let's do it. I want to go. I want to go. So I helped him with his mask to get it all adjusted . . . ." Dr. Kevorkian told him, "Now anytime you feel comfortable and ready you just go ahead and pull it. The gas will start." (p. 175).

The death of Nick Loving was accomplished through an apparatus constructed by Kevorkian he sometimes referred to as the "Merciton" but which is better known in the media as "the suicide machine." Whether Kevorkian used this or some other procedure for a particular patient, it was intended to be the patient who took the decisive action. It is for this reason that Kevorkian could speak of having "assisted" at a death. The fact that Kevorkian did not himself take the final action also was intended as protection against possible charges of murder. He forfeited this protection and crossed the line he himself had specified when he gave Thomas Youk a lethal injection.

Evaluating Kevorkian's Approach

Physician-assisted death as advocated and practiced by Kevorkian has been subjected to many criticisms. There is the religious–moral objection that a physician is playing God. Only God can give and only God should take life. This objection is potent for those who hold a religious belief of this type, and also influential for others who think that, for whatever reason, Kevorkian has stepped across a line that should be respected. There is also the objection, already noted, that the physician must always be on the side of life.

Additional problems demand attention when we look at the data for the deaths that Kevorkian has acknowledged facilitating. A detailed presentation of these data has been provided in two articles written by Kalman J. Kaplan, director of a suicide research center in Chicago, and his research team (Kaplan et al., 2000; Kaplan et al., 2000). The most important data come from medical examiners who personally investigated the cases. Information of this kind was available for 93 cases.

1. *Most of the people whose deaths have been assisted by Kevorkian were not terminally ill.* Only 28.3% were terminally ill. Since the majority (69.9%) were not terminally ill, significant questions must be raised: (a) How adequate was Kevorkian's medical assessment of the patients? (b) How valid is his claim for relieving the suffering of dying people if most were

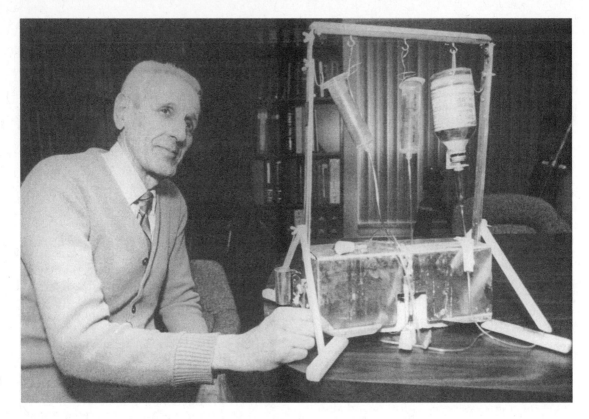

Jack Kevorkian with his suicide machine. Kevorkian was "present" at the deaths of more than a hundred people before being found guilty, imprisoned, and eventually released on his promise not to resume this practice.

not dying? and (c) Do these data confirm the fears of a very slippery slope? In other words, did the availability of "death on demand" lead to premature death?

2. *The gender bias in Kevorkian's clientele suggests that his practice encouraged increased suicidality among women.* All of Kevorkian's assisted deaths had been women before the Michigan law against assisted suicide was signed by the governor. During the period that Kevorkian was dealing with legal proceedings against him, he participated in the deaths of eleven men and nine women. As soon as he was acquitted on charges of assisted suicide, Kevorkian returned to the original pattern in which by far the greater number of assisted suicides were women. In the general population, women are much

less likely than men to commit suicide. The reverse is true among Kevorkian's assisted-death patients.

3. *Those assisted to death by Kevorkian fit the general profile of suicide attempters rather than terminally ill people.* For example, they had a high incidence of depression and dependency and a low incidence of the conditions that are the most common causes of death in the United States. The implication is that Kevorkian either stimulated or was the receptive target for unhappy people who might otherwise have either attempted nonfatal suicide attempts or found other ways to deal with their situations.

4. *Another disturbing element was Kevorkian's failure to diagnose or treat their depression.* Many people with depressive episodes or tendencies

are effectively treated every day. Some of these people do express the desire to end their lives in order to end their miseries. Competent medical help has often contributed to a restoration of their spirits—but competent medical help with their lives is not what they received from Kevorkian.

5. *Kevorkian functioned without adequate medical information and consultation.* He seldom asked for a second opinion—and did so less and less as he continued his practice. This was especially unfortunate because Kevorkian did not have expertise in many of the specific medical conditions that affected his patients, nor in psychiatric evaluation or palliative care. Part of the problem came from the unwillingness of other physicians to cooperate with him. He could have done much more, however, to make sure his patients had the advantage of medical and psychiatric expertise before assisting them to death.

6. *Death is much too extreme a solution to the relief of suffering.* For those people who are in severe pain (most of his patients were not) there were alternatives. It is interesting to take an international example here. There was a sharp negative response by the public after an eminent Japanese physician administered a lethal drug to his patient. The director of a hospice wrote:

Even if there is so much pain that it cannot be eliminated through the use of painkilling drugs

like morphine, it is possible to enable the patient to sleep without feeling the pain by using large doses of tranquilizers or anesthetics. Physical pain is not a reason for permitting euthanasia (Kato, 1996).

Japanese philosopher Histake Kato (1996) reported an incident in which a friend of his was in excruciating pain during an attack of pancreatitis. The first doctor he saw did not take painkilling measures. His friend switched to another hospital where the pain was removed. "In other words, both doctors who have the best know-how about eliminating pain and doctors who have no know-how at all exist side by side in the Japanese medical system." Kevorkian did not establish his credentials for the up-to-date and effective relief of pain, and he has shown little familiarity or interest in the hospice movement. He did not offer an alternative other than death.

7. *Despite his disclaimers, Kevorkian rushed some people into assisted death without adequate safeguards and consideration.* His very first case, Janet Adkins, was in good health, suffering no pain, and, in fact, had been playing tennis with her teenage son. Kevorkian seemed to become her instrument of destruction on the promptings of her husband. There are other cases in which Kevorkian seems to have strayed from his own criteria (see Box 9-1). Data show that as time went on,

---

BOX 9-1 KEVORKIAN'S STANDARDS AND KEVORKIAN'S ACTIONS

Kevorkian's Standards	**Kevorkian's Actions**
Call for psychiatric consultation	Rarely called for consultation
Call for pain specialist consultation	Rarely called for pain specialist
24-hour waiting period after final request	Many deaths in less than 1 day
Extensive patient counseling	Brief conversations; no professional counseling
Stop the process if any sign that patient is ambivalent	Some patients were clearly ambivalent but assisted death was carried out

Kevorkian moved more rapidly from first meeting with the patient to the death. He increasingly violated the criteria he had himself insisted upon in his public statements. Kaplan reported on one of these cases (1998):

Gale, a 72 year old former merchant marine, was suffering from emphysema. There is no question that he asked to die, but there is evidence that Gale had a great deal of ambivalence after the gas mask was put on his face, asking twice that it be removed. Kevorkian's original record of the incident. . . found in a garbage bag outside his assistant's house, indicated that Kevorkian removed the mask in response to Gale's first request, but did not remove it in response to the second (p. 173).

8. *Kevorkian used "silencing" techniques to defend his actions.* This pattern is clear in his book and in many of his presentations through the media. It is only the physician who should assist deaths. It is only the physician who understands. This attitude dismisses the experiences, values, knowledge, and feelings of a great many other people, including clergy, nurses, social workers, attorneys, sociologists, anthropologists, and philosophers. Kevorkian is open to the charge of excessively medicalizing dying and death.

Oakland County (Michigan) Judge Jessica Cooper offered her own evaluation of Kevorkian's activities in sentencing him to a term of 10 to 25 years when he was found guilty of second-degree murder: Kevorkian had been convicted on charges of second-degree murder after he invited *60 Minutes* to show a videotape in which he administered a lethal injection (a departure from only "assisting" in a death).

This trial was not about the political or moral correctness of euthanasia. It was all about you, sir. It was about lawlessness. It was about disrespect for a society that exists and flourishes because of the strength of the legal system. No one, sir, is above the law. No one. You were on bond to another judge when you committed this offense; you were not licensed to practice medicine when you committed this offense, and you hadn't been licensed for eight years. And you had the audacity to go on national television, show the world what you did and dare the legal system to stop you. Well, sir, consider yourself stopped. (www.catholic.org/euthanasia/kevsen.html)

The Netherlands: A Social Experiment Watched Closely by the World

When Kevorkian first advertised his services, he was aware that physician-assisted death had already gained a foothold in The Netherlands. This enterprising and often surprising nation was the first to accept the option of assisted death. Belgium followed suit in 2002 (Gastmans, Van Neste, & Schotsmans, 2004), but there the trend has stalled. Dutch courts established a tradition of sanctioning cases of medically assisted death brought before them during the 1980s (Gomez, 1991). These were interpretations of the existing laws in individual situations. These decisions drew a mixed reaction from legal experts, health care professionals, and the general public. Euthanasia was not officially made legal, but a new law passed in 1993 spared doctors from prosecution if they followed an established set of rules. This was followed in 2000 by a law that more clearly decriminalized assistance in dying. It was opposed strenuously by several religious groups, but was passed by a large margin (Religious Tolerance, 2008). Since that time, public opinion has been strongly favorable to this policy, though with occasional expressions of concern about the way it has been carried out by some physicians. You will notice in Box 9-2 that there is a provision that goes beyond the more limited conception of euthanasia as acceptable only for terminally ill people.

The issue is not so easily resolved, however. Some Dutch health care providers are opposed to assisted death for personal and/or moral reasons. Others are worried about the adequacy of the decision-making process: Do the people involved always communicate adequately with each other and have full knowledge of the available options? Still others accepted the legalization of assisted death in its present form, but harbored concerns about the possibility of their nation taking more dangerous steps down that slippery slope. This fear was intensified on

---

> ### BOX 9-2   RULES FOR ASSISTED DYING IN THE NETHERLANDS
>
> - The patient must be suffering unbearably. However, they need not be terminally ill.
>
> - The patient must make a request on a voluntary, well considered, and sustained basis.
>
> - The doctor and patient must have had a long-term relationship.
>
> - There must be no reasonable alternative to relieve the patient's suffering.
>
> - The doctor must consult at least one other independent physician.
>
> - Due medical care must be followed.

April 29, 1995, when an infant born in terrible pain with a spinal column defect was injected with a muscular relaxant that stopped her breathing. The baby girl's parents had authorized the procedure. The Dutch Ministry of Justice prosecuted the physician on the charge of premeditated murder. The physician was found guilty but not convicted. The trial was intended not to punish this physician but to establish new guidelines for assisted death (or, as some still prefer, euthanasia) for newborns with severe disabilities.

This case was important not only because it involved a newborn person, but also because (a) the decision was in the form of substituted judgment and (b) despite the infant's serious physical defect and pain, she was not terminally ill. The little girl could not speak for herself. Is it reasonable and moral for anybody, even her parents, to make the decision to end her life? Or is the acceptance of this act of assisted death a dangerous slide further down the slippery slope that could result in widespread killing of newborns and perhaps others who do not meet somebody's criteria for being an acceptable person? Opponents were concerned that the slope had now become much too slippery—one person could make the decision to end the life of another person. Euthanasia had become involuntary, and therefore verged on homicide. However, proponents pointed out that the parents had loved their baby and accepted her disabilities. What they could not bear was the fact that the baby was suffering pain and that the pain could not be relieved. From this perspective, the parents and the sanctioning government were approving a compassionate end to a life that would have been dominated by suffering.

Another difficult issue arose in 2002 when a former senator requested assistance in dying because he was "tired of life." He suffered from immobility, incontinence, and dizziness, conditions that did not respond to medical treatment. The court ruled that this circumstance had not been addressed in the decriminalization law, so physicians were left to their own discretion and risk when people want to end a life that has come to feel unbearable.

The Netherlands' experiences with assisted death perhaps offer more problems than answers. And the answers, when forthcoming, sometimes are unexpected. For example, an institutionalized Dutch woman requested assisted death. The request was denied, but she was told that the institution could not force her to eat. She took no food and only a little water for several days and continued to express her wish to die. The institution then respected her decision and stopped offering her food. Well, they did give her some apple juice.

> To the surprise of those who attended to her needs, her physical situation had not really deteriorated after three weeks. It was discovered that the contents of apple juice can keep people alive well over a hundred days and that, if she kept drinking apple juice, she would probably not die from starvation at all. A week later the nurses happened to serve the residents a hot meal with french fried chicken. At the smell of this dish the woman all of a sudden asked whether she could have some, too. Ever since she has been eating her

meals again and for many months afterward she happily participated in all different kinds of activities the nursing home had to offer (Meijburg, 1995/1996, p. 192).

Gradually the woman's physical condition deteriorated and "she died a natural death." This is one of many vignettes suggesting that there may be a lot of unknowns and a good deal of ambiguity in the interaction between a person requesting assisted death and those who must respond to this request in some way. Perhaps it is not surprising that physician-assisted death remains a deeply divisive issue in the nation that has been most receptive to the idea.

Criticisms of euthanasia practice in The Netherlands continue to accumulate. There are charges that the lives of newborns who are regarded as severely and incurably impaired are terminated much more often than reported—but that the same practice almost certainly occurs quietly in other countries (Johnson, 2005). Substantial research reports indicate that consultations with patients and families are sometimes bypassed and that other safe practice guidelines are also frequently disregarded (Cohen-Almagor, 2003, 2004). Interviewed physicians have defended their decisions, citing the particular situations involved.

The Netherlands' experience suggests that any movement toward legalization of assisted death or other forms of euthanasia should be accompanied by thorough discussion, clarification, and enforceable regulations.

Australia: Yes, and Then No

Australia provides another instructive example of the difficulties that accompany attempts to introduce legalized physician-assisted death. The Northern Territory Parliament enacted a law in 1996 that specifically legalized euthanasia and assisted suicide. Less than 1 year later, the Australian National Senate overturned this law and forbid any of its territories from passing measures that would make assisted suicide legal. As in other nations, the case for assisted death was made on the behalf of terminally ill people whose suffering had not been relieved. And again, as in other nations, the controversy alarmed and educated the public. Should this person be granted her wish for assisted death to avoid further suffering, or should physicians be more conscientious and effective in providing relief for pain and other symptoms?

Two very practical questions soon came into focus: What physician would agree to terminate a life, and what physician would be qualified to do so? Only one Australian physician, Dr. Philip Nitschke, agreed to take on this responsibility, and only after discovering that none of his colleagues would step forth. (Like Kevorkian, he also constructed a "death machine," but his was computerized and asked the patient—three times—whether he really wanted to die before delivering an injection that produced sleep, followed by death. The only use found for the device was as a science museum display.) Obviously, passage of assisted-death legislation does not ensure a readiness in the medical community to participate. The several terminally ill people seeking assisted death under the new law and the one physician willing to respond to their wishes became the center of heated controversy (Nitschke, 2000; Street & Kissane, 2000). Some people advocated vigorously for assisted death when there was no relief for suffering, but the nation, as a whole, was not ready for this option. The issue of physician qualifications for assisting death remained unsettled.

ASSISTED DEATH IN THE UNITED STATES

Many people in the right-to-die movement were opposed to Kevorkian's approach. They did not want to rely on the judgment of one physician operating outside the legal and medical system. There was particular concern that some (perhaps most) of the people whose lives were being terminated by Kevorkian might have found another way to cope with their situations, given adequate counseling and support. The nation as a whole was moving toward the enactment of natural death acts (successors to the living will) that affirmed the right of individuals to control their end-of-life care through informed consent and advance directives. Performing an action with the intent of terminating a life seemed to go far beyond the emerging consensus that people have the right to have treatment withheld or withdrawn.

The Oregon Death with Dignity Act

The voters of Oregon did take that one long step further by supporting a measure legalizing assisted death in 1994 and reaffirming it in 1997. The act applies only to terminally ill adults in Oregon. This obviously would have excluded most of the people in whose deaths Dr. Kevorkian assisted. Eligibility for assisted death in Oregon requires that the person be older than 18 years and have an incurable and irreversible disease that will probably produce death within 6 months. This rules out people who have progressively deteriorating conditions but who are not at a high risk for death at the present time. "Tired of living" also does not qualify. The requirements are more comprehensive and detailed than those of The Netherlands. There is another, even more significant difference: the lethal medications are to be self-administered. A physician supplies the medication, but the patient is the one who ends his or her own life. Euthanasia as such is specifically prohibited.

Whether one approves or opposes assisted death, it is important to know the actual requirements of the Death with Dignity Act (DWDA) rather than rely on second-hand sources (Box 9-3). These provisions were worked out after several years of consultation among health care providers, legal experts, and specialists in bioethics.

What has happened since the DWDA became operative in 1998? About 30,000 people die in Oregon each year, about 300,000 over the 10-year period through 2007. People who self-terminated under DWDA rules were a small fraction of this total. In 2007, 85 terminally ill people received prescriptions for lethal medication, but a smaller number, 46, actually took the drug. A total of 341 patients have self-terminated through the decade. The DWDA was responsible for about 16 deaths out of 10,000. (http://oregon.gov/DHS/ph/pas/index.shtml) The practicing physicians who participated had an average of 20 years of experience and were mostly in the specialties of internal medicine, oncology, and family medicine. The prescribing physician or other health care providers were present at the time of all the deaths. Most of the patients were in their late 60s, and cancer was by far the most common primary illness.

Why did these terminally ill people express the wish for assisted death? Their physicians reported that the most frequent was the loss of ability to participate in actions that make life enjoyable, and the feeling of a progressive loss of dignity. Unbearable pain was not among the most frequently mentioned reasons. Although it might seem surprising that pain is not necessarily the most common reason for requesting assisted death, this finding has also been observed in other studies (e. g., Arnold, 2004).

There have been interesting side effects of the Oregon program. Most (90%) of the patients died at home and were enrolled in hospice care. Physicians report that they have been improving their knowledge of pain medications for the terminally ill as well as their skill in recognizing depression; they were also referring patients to hospice more frequently (Ganzini et al., 2001). The effect of this program on physicians has been perhaps stronger than anticipated (Dobscha et al., 2004):

> Requests for assisted suicide had a powerful impact on physicians and their practices. Physicians often felt unprepared, and experienced apprehension and discomfort before and after receiving requests. Prominent sources of discomfort included concerns about adequately managing symptoms and suffering, not wanting to abandon patients, and incomplete understanding of patients' preferences, especially when physicians did not know patients well . . . . Regardless of whether they prescribed or not, physicians did not express major regrets about their decisions. Requests often facilitated discussion of important issues, and many physicians felt that the process increased their confidence (p. 451).

Nurses have reported that they try to explore what patients really mean when they ask to have their lives terminated (Schwarz, 2005). As one hospice nurse observed: "Things are often not as they seem. It takes detective work to find out what they mean by 'help me die,'" (p. A8).

BOX 9-3   OREGON DEATH WITH DIGNITY REQUIREMENTS

Basic Provisions
- The DWDA allows terminally ill Oregon residents to obtain and use prescriptions from their physicians for self-administered, lethal medications.
- Ending one's life in accordance with the law does not constitute suicide.
- The DWDA specifically prohibits euthanasia, where a physician or other person directly administers a medication to end another's life.

Eligibility
- 18 years of age or older
- A resident of Oregon
- Capable of making and communicating health care decisions
- Diagnosed with a terminal illness that will lead to death within 6 months

Procedure
- Patient must make two oral requests to his or her physician, separated by at least 15 days.
- Patient must provide a written request to his or her physician, signed in the presence of two witnesses.
- The prescribing physician and a consulting physician must confirm the diagnosis and prognosis.
- The prescribing physician and a consulting physician must determine whether the patient is competent to make and communicate the decision.
- If either physician believes the patient's judgment is impaired by a psychiatric or psychological disorder, the patient must be referred for a psychological examination.
- The prescribing physician must inform the patient of feasible alternatives to DWDA, including comfort care, hospice care, and pain control.
- The prescribing physician must request, but may not require, the patient to notify his or her next-of-kin of the prescription request.

Additional Physician Responsibilities
- Physicians must report to the Department of Human Services all prescriptions for lethal medications. Reporting is not required if patients begin the request process but never receive a prescription.
- Pharmacists must be informed of the prescribed medication's intended use.

Protections From Criminal Prosecution
- Physicians and patients who adhere to the requirements of the Act are protected from criminal prosecution.
- The choice of DWDA cannot affect the status of a patient's health or insurance policies.
- Physicians, pharmacists, and health care systems are under no obligation to participate in the DWDA.
- Action taken in accordance with the DWDA does not constitute suicide, mercy killing, or homicide under the law.

Adapted from Oregon Revised Statutes as found at http://oregon.govDHS/ph/pas/ors.shtml

---

When nurses listened actively to the wishes of dying patients, they often discovered that the patients had specific needs in mind, for example, reassurance that they would not be connected to machines or that they would be given adequate pain relief medication. In many instances, the nurses could help arrange the situation so the patients did not feel desperate and overwhelmed—and the wish for assisted suicide was withdrawn.

Apprehension that the DWDA would lead to an explosion of deaths-on-demand have not materialized. Two other fears—that women would be exceptionally vulnerable to this option, and that palliative care would be ignored—have also failed to occur. It seems clear that Kevorkian's idiosyncratic approach to assisted death has influenced many people to resist even the markedly different approach established in Oregon.

The Oregon DWDA has faced repeated challenges from the start to the present time. The Catholic Church has been a consistent and often effective adversary, whose opposition has much to do with the fact that Oregon remains the only state with such an act on the books. Dowbiggen (2005) observes that disagreements among the several right-to-die groups advocating such legislation has created additional difficulties. The U.S. Department of Justice has repeatedly challenged the law, but was rejected by a federal appeals court. The majority of the Ninth Circuit Court ruled that then-Attorney General John Ashcroft had overstepped his authority. Judge Richard C. Tallman wrote that:

> The attorney general's unilateral attempt to regulate general medical practices historically entrusted to state lawmakers interferes with the Democratic debate about physician-assisted suicide and far exceeds the scope of his authority under federal law (Liptak, 2004, p. 1).

The failure of this effort to revoke the Oregon Death with Dignity Act has led to other attempts, for example, the prohibition of federal funding for medical assistance, which would have the most impact on low income people. Oregon's program is likely to receive continued scrutiny and opposition, with its future status uncertain at this time. Also uncertain at this time is the possible adoption of an Oregon-type program in other states. Public opinion remains divisive, and there are vigorous forces on both the pro and con sides. Initiatives have failed in California, Hawaii, Maine, Michigan, and New Hampshire.

INDUCED ABORTION

Assisted death presented us with the challenge taking into account the medical, legal, ethical, and political dimensions that make it difficult to form a clear and coherent picture. Abortion also confronts us with a complex challenge, but with obvious differences. A competent adult can decline medical treatment and a limited precedent has been set for requesting assisted death. Courts, legislators, and ethics committees have tried to make sure that the decision represents the individual's own intentions, not the guesses, beliefs, or wishes of others.

The fetus, however, cannot participate in the decision-making process. Who, then, has the right to decide? The woman? Her partner? A doctor? A judge? A religious establishment? Society at large? Everybody? Nobody? The debate about whose decision should stand often brings the rights of the individual and the rights of societal institutions into sharp conflict. The tension crackles among institutions as well. For example, which interpretation of which set of religious teachings should be taken as the will of God? The abortion controversy has its rational arguments pro and con, but powerful emotions often dominate and can lead to actions as extreme as the murder of physicians. It makes sense, then, to begin with some basic facts about abortion.

Basic Facts about Induced Abortion

Some pregnancies do not result in the birth of a live and viable infant. These spontaneous abortions are usually classified as miscarriages, although statisticians sometimes use the term *fetal loss*. Unintended abortions are not unusual. It is estimated that in the U.S. about one pregnancy in five ends in abortion. Family Planning Clinics funded by the federal Public Health Service Act are credited with having prevented about 20 million unintended pregnancies over a period of 2 decades. It is estimated that nine million of these pregnancies would have ended in abortion (Guttmacher Institute, 2000). "Strictly defined, abortion is the expulsion or removal of an embryo or fetus from the uterus before it has developed sufficiently to survive outside the mother (before viability)" (DeFrain, 2002, p. 1). We will focus here on induced abortion, an intentioned action.

Most abortions are performed in the first 12 weeks of pregnancy. The earlier the abortion, the simpler the procedure, and the less risk to the woman. In recent years, a combination of two drugs (mifepristone and misoprostol) has become frequently used to halt development and expel the embryo. Few serious medical complications have been reported with this procedure. About 9 out of 10 abortions in the United States occur in the first trimester and therefore require the less invasive procedures.

This pharmaceutical innovation is having implications for the abortion debate, as DeFrain (2002) notes:

> Clinics that perform abortions are regularly picketed by antiabortion protesters in the United States, making the experience of obtaining a legal abortion difficult for many women. If use of this method spreads in spite of opposition from antiabortion groups, abortion will become an almost invisible, personal, and relatively private act (p. 2).

Most radical and controversial are late-term abortions, conducted 4 or 5 months into the pregnancy. Now also known as a partial-birth abortion, this procedure destroys the brain of the infant and delivers the body. This type of abortion has been banned by laws in many states. An exception is usually made for late term abortions that are considered necessary to save the woman's life. This type of regulation has been contested intensely by many physicians as well as women rights activists. It is argued that there is a right to protect one's health, and that this should be based on the judgment of a physician involved with the case, not a remote and prohibitive law. For example, Dr. Nada Stotland (2007), president of the American Psychiatric Association, is one of the many who have pointed out that federal legislation on this issue was based on lack of attention to research findings: induced abortion does not result in the mental and physical trauma claimed by its opponents and now enshrined in law.

Abortion was neither a crime nor a major issue in the United States until newspapers started to advertise abortion-inducing preparations. Moralists quickly rallied against abortion as a way of concealing extramarital affairs and thereby corrupting the nation's values. Antiabortion measures were signed into law

throughout most of the nation by the early 1900s. Women had no enfranchised voice in this development, as almost all politicians were men and women had not yet been given the constitutional right to vote. It is unknown how many potential abortions were prevented by the criminalization of abortion. However, it soon became clear that abortions were still taking place but under more unsanitary and dangerous conditions, too often at the hands of careless or unskilled practitioners. The rules changed again in 1973 in the historic *Roe vs. Wade* case when the U.S. Supreme Court concluded that states did not have the right to regulate early term abortions: That decision must be left to the woman and her physician. This did not really settle the issue, however.

The continuing opposition to abortion expresses itself in campaigns to overturn the *Roe vs. Wade* decision. Meanwhile, public opinion has taken a "permit-but-discourage" attitude, favoring the continued legality and availability of abortion but suggesting that more efforts be made to reduce the number of abortions (Alan Guttmacher Institute, 1999a; 1999b, & Web site: www.agi-usa-org).

Difficult Issues and Questions

Many thoughtful people are tormented by abortion-related issues. People on both sides of the issue would prefer that the situation never arises in which a woman feels unable or unwilling to see a pregnancy through. The same person can feel compassion for a woman in a stressful, even overwhelming situation, but also pain for the child who never will be. Unfortunately, mutual respect and effective communication has sometimes been blocked by the strong feelings that are understandably associated with the abortion controversy.

Here are three of the issues that remain challenges to our hearts and minds:

1. *State policy vs. individual and family needs.* International human rights organizations have severely criticized the Chinese government for its policy of limiting married couples to one child and one child only. The policy started with the good intentions

of controlling population growth and therefore extricating China from its long-standing cycle of poverty and making it a more technologically advanced nation. China has made significant strides toward both goals. The government claims it has prevented 250 million births. But the stress and pain suffered by the Chinese people, especially in the vast rural regions, has been enormous. The pleasures and supports of family life have been denied to many people—children have been growing up without brothers and sisters. More to the point—the systematic abortion and infanticide of girls has become a national horror and disgrace. An estimated 500,000 to 750,000 female fetuses are aborted every year after (illegal) ultrasound screening (CNSNews, 2001). That number does not include the many other babies who are delivered live but then are killed or abandoned out of parental desperation. In Chinese tradition, boys have been crucial for supporting the parents in their later years and keeping the family going. The punishment for disobeying the law is harsh, and many abortions are forced upon women who want desperately to have the child (Livingstone, 2005). The government has been trying to make its policy more humane, but reports of oppression, reprisal, and forced abortion are still being heard. How far can or should a government go to regulate birth and pressure for the death of the unborn? What rule or guide would you establish?

2. *General principle or particular situation?* The Catholic Church's rejection of abortion is a prominent example of applying a general rule to individual situations. The opposite extreme would be the position that a woman has the right to do whatever she chooses with her body, including its contents. Other positions could also be identified or imagined. But are any two circumstances identical? Should the realities of a particular situation be considered with an open mind, or is it best to deal with all cases on the basis of a firm and simple rule? (This is not a new dilemma for the Catholic Church. For centuries, "case books" have been prepared to help priests bridge the gap between general rules and the many unique situations they are likely to encounter.) How would you have it? One rule for all situations, reliance on good judgment in particular situations, or some way of integrating both approaches?

3. *When do life and personhood begin?* The question of when or under what circumstances life ends (Chapter 3) has its counterpart here. A moment's reflection teaches us that the beginning of a life and the beginning of a human life are not necessarily the same. Sperm and ova are life forms even if they never meet. The embryo is a different proposition from either sperm or ova. The developing fetus has significant new attributes. It would be difficult to deny the existence of life before birth. But when does this become a human life, a person? We can choose to approach this question by reading theological discourses on when in the course of development the soul is created, implanted, or transformed. Instead we might prefer to rely upon developmental psychobiology and judge on the basis of the functions available to a fetus or infant. Then again, we might feel that the anthropologists hold the key to this question as they describe the ways in which a society either bestows or denies personhood even to adults. It has not been all that unusual for one group of people to consider other groups less than human and, therefore, not equal, not deserving, and not exempt from enslavement and killing. What is the most realistic, sensible, and humane way to regard the life and personhood of the unborn?

SUMMARY

There was a time when a few people discussed the right to die from a theoretical perspective. Today many people are intensely involved on a personal level. Should terminally ill people have the right to ask a physician to end their suffering by ending their lives? This question has become complicated by factors such as: (1) memories of the abuse of eugenics and so-called euthanasia through the last century; (2) differing interpretations of the power of the Hippocratic Oath; (3) concerns about the adequacy of care that physicians offer to terminally ill people; but also (4) concerns about the failure to take advantage of the palliative care (hospice) options that now are available; (5) the attempt to broaden physician-assisted suicide to include any person who wants to die, terminally ill or not; and (6) the gap between theory and practice in carrying out physician-assisted death. Moral and religious considerations play a significant role in all these issues. While defining our key terms, we explored the unsavory side of some past euthanasia programs, then looked at current attitudes toward a right to die. We next acquainted ourselves with some of the most important individual cases that brought the right-to-die issue to national attention and led to the first round of rulings and decision making. Although each case was unique, all revealed the complexities and ambiguities that often confront us in life-and-death situations. Particular attention was given to the ordeal of Terri Schiavo and her family. It eventually became a national issue in which federal and state governments, the judicial and medical systems, and many private individuals became deeply involved. Possible lessons to be learned from this experience are offered.

We then devoted sustained attention to physician-assisted suicide, starting with brief looks at developments in The Netherlands and Australia and then focusing on the approach taken by Jack Kevorkian, M. D. We learned that there are many troubling questions about the practice of physician-assisted death as carried out by Dr. Kevorkian. Next, we looked at continuing developments concerning the Death with Dignity Act in Oregon, the only state in which assisted death has legal status. Finally, we explored the key issues surrounding the abortion controversy.

REFERENCES

Alan Guttmacher Institute. (1999a). *Induced abortion worldwide*. New York: Alan Guttmacher Institute.

Alan Guttmacher Institute. (1999b). *Sharing responsibility: Women, society, and abortion worldwide*. New York: Alan Guttmacher Institute.

Alan Guttmacher Institute. (2000). *Fulfilling the promise: Public policy and U.S. family planning clinics*. New York: AGI.

Anonymous. (1988). It's over Debbie. *Journal of the American Medical Association, 259,* 272.

Arnold, E. M. (2004). Factors that influence hastening death among people with life-threatening illness. *Health and Social Work, 29,* 27–35.

Associated Press. (2008, March 20). French woman who sought euthanasia dies. http://topics.nytimes.com/topnews/health/diseasesconditionsandhealthtopics/deathanddying/index.html=nyt-classifier

Babington, C. (2005, June 17). Frist defends Schiavo case remarks. *Arizona Republic,* p. A21.

BBC News. (2008, March 19). French euthanasia-row woman dies. www.bbc.co.uk Navigation

CNSNews.com. (2001, February 15). China uses abortion as female genocide. www.newsmax.com/cgi-bin

Cohen-Almagor, R. (2003). Non-voluntary and voluntary euthanasia in The Netherlands: Dutch perspectives. www.highbeam.com/library/doc3asp?

Cohen-Almagor, R. (2004). *Euthanasia in The Netherlands: The policy and practice of mercy killing*. Boston: Kluwer.

Cox, D. W. (1993). *Hemlock's cup*. Buffalo, NY: Prometheus.

Death with Dignity Center. (2002). www.deathwithdignity.org

DeFrain, J. (2002). Abortion. In R. Kastenbaum (Ed.), *Macmillan encyclopedia of death and dying:* Vol. 1 (pp. 1–5). New York: Macmillan.

Dobscha, S. K., Heintz, R., Press., N., & Gazini, L. (2004). Oregon physicians' responses to requests for assisted suicide: A qualitative study. *Journal of Palliative Medicine, 7,* 451–462.

Edelstein, L. (1943). *The Hippocratic Oath: Text, translation, and interpretation*. Baltimore: Johns Hopkins University Press.

Eisenberg, D. (2005, April 4). Lessons of the Schiavo battle. *Time,* pp. 24–30.

Friedlander, H. (1995). *The origins of Nazi genocide*. Chapel Hill: The University of North Carolina Press.

Gastmans, C., Van Neste, F., & Schotsmans, P. (2004). Facing requests for Euthanasia: A clinical practice guideline. *Journal of Medical Ethics, 30,* 212–217.

Gazini, L., Nelson, H. D., Schmidt, T. A., Kraemer, D. F., Delorit, M. A., & Lee, M. A. (2001). Physicians' experiences with the Oregon Death with Dignity Act. *New England Journal of Medicine, 342,* 557–563.

Gomez, C. R. (1991). *Regulating death.* New York: Free Press.

Groom, W. (2002). *A storm in Flanders. Tragedy and triumph on the western front.* New York: Atlantic Monthly Press.

Hayslip, B., Jr. & Peveto, C. A. (2005). *Cultural changes in attitudes toward death, dying, and bereavement.* New York: Springer.

Hoffman, K. B. (2007, May 26). Kevorkian's cause founders as he's freed. http://myeartylink.net/article/top?guid-20070526b0co_3ca6–15526

Iserson, K. V. (2002). Persistent vegetative state. In R. Kastenbaum (Ed.), *Macmillan encyclopedia of death and dying:* Vol. 2 (pp. 668–669). New York: Macmillan.

Johnson, L. A. (2005, March 9). Study: Newborn euthanasia often goes unreported in Netherlands—and probably other countries. AP Worldstream.

Kaldjian, L. C., Jekel, J. F., Bernene, J. L., Rosenthal, G. E., Vaughan-Sarrazin, M., & Duffy, T. P. (2004). Internists' attitudes toward terminal sedation in end of life care. *Journal of Medical Ethics, 30,* 499–503.

Kalish, R. A., & Reynolds, D. K. (1976). *Death and ethnicity: A psychocultural study.* Los Angeles, CA: University of Southern California Press.

Kaplan, K. J. (1998). The case of Dr. Kevorkian and Mr. Gale: A brief historical note. *Omega, Journal of Death and Dying, 36,* 169–176.

Kaplan, K. J., Lachenmeier, F., Harrow, M., O'Dell, J. C., Uziel, O., Schneiderhan, M., & Cheyfitz, K. (2000). Psychosocial versus biomedical risk factors in Kevorkian's first 47 physician-assisted deaths. *Omega, Journal of Death and Dying. 40,* 109–164.

Kaplan, K. J., O'Dell, J., Dragovic, L. J., McKeon, C., Bentley, E., & Telmet, K. J. (2000). An update on Kevorkian-Reding 93 physician-assisted deaths in Michigan: Is Kevorkian a savior, serial-killer or suicidal martyr? *Omega, Journal of Death and Dying, 40,* 209–230.

Kastenbaum, R. (1994/1995). Ralph Mero: An Omega interview. *Omega, Journal of Death and Dying, 29,* 1–16.

Kato, H. (1995/1996, June 25). Doctors need re-educating. Sankei Shimbun.

Kevorkian, J. (1991). *Prescription: Medicide.* Buffalo, NY: Prometheus.

Kron, J. (1975, October 6). The girl in the coma. *New York Magazine,* pp. 17–24.

Lens, V. (2002). Informed consent. In R. Kastenbaum (Ed.), *Macmillan encyclopedia of death:* Vol. 1 (pp. 473– 476). New York: Macmillan.

Lifton, R. J. (1986). *The Nazi doctors.* New York: Basic Books.

Liptak, A. (2004, May 17). Ruling upholds Oregon law authorizing assisted suicide. *The New York Times.* www.nties.com/2004/05/27/national/27SUIC.html7h

Livingstone, J. (2005, November 29). Forced abortions: First minister's chinese guest oversaw horrendous abuses. *The Daily Mail,* London.

Loving, C. (1995/1996). Nick Loving and Dr. Jack Kevorkian: An Omega interview with Carol Loving. *Omega, Journal of Death and Dying, 32,* 165–178.

Maitland, L. (2005, April 8). *Talk of the Nation Science Friday* [Radio broadcast]. National Public Radio.

Mathis, M. (2005, June 1). Terri Schiavo and end-of-life decisions: Can law help us out? *Medical and Surgical Nursing,* pp. 1–4.

Meijburg, H. H. V. D. K. (1995/1996). How health care institutions in The Netherlands approach physician-assisted death. *Omega, Journal of Death and Dying, 32,* 179–196.

Nicol, N., & Wylie, H. (2006). *Between the dying and the dead. Dr. Jack Kevorkian's life and the battle to legalize euthanasia.* Madison: University of Wisconsin Press.

Nitschke, P. (2000). "Desiring death, dispensing death" by Annette Street and David Kissane: A commentary. *Omega, Journal of Death and Dying, 40,* 249–254.

Pernick, M. S. (1996). *The black stork.* New York: Oxford University Press.

Quill, T. E., & Cassel, C. K. (2003). Professional organizations' position statements on physician-assisted suicide: A case for studied neutrality. *Annals of Internal Medicine, 138,* 208–211.

Rietjens, J. A. C., van de Heide, A., Vrakking, A.M. Onwuteaka-Phillipsen, B. D., Van der Maas, P. J., & van der Wal, G. (2004). Physician reports of terminal sedation without hydration or nutrition for patients nearing death in the Netherlands. *Annals of Internal Medicine, 141,* 178–185.

Schwarz, J. (2005, April 1). Before the storm, there was Terri. *East Valley Tribune,* p. A8.

Stacy, M. (2005, June 16). Schiavo autopsy backs husband. *East Valley Tribune,* pp. 1, 11.

Stotland, N. (2007, July 20). The myth of abortion trauma syndrome: Update, 2007. *Psychiatric News, 42,* p, 28.

Street, A., & Kissane, D. (2000). Desiring death, dispensing death. *Omega, Journal of Death and Dying, 40,* 231–248.

Texeira, E. (2005, June 16). Missing: News coverage on the disappearance of anyone who's not an attractive, white female. *East Valley Tribune,* p. 10.

Times Mirror Center for the People and the Press. (1983). *Reflections of the times: The right to die.* Washington, DC: Times Mirror Center for the People and the Press.

Trout, N. (2008a, March 22). Animal medicine from a vet's-eye view. National Public Radio: *Fresh Air.*

Trout, N. (2008b). *Tell me where it hurts.* New York: Broadway Books.

Veatch, R. M. (1998) The ethics of death and dying, In A. R. Jonsen, R. M. Veatch, & L. Walters (Eds.), *Source book in bioethics* (pp. 113–252). Washington, DC: Georgetown University Press.

United States Supreme Court. (1989). Missouri vs. Cruzan. In R. M. Baird & S. E. Rosenbaum (Eds.), *Euthanasia. The moral issues.* Buffalo, New York: Prometheus (pp. 179–212).

Wolfson, J. (2003). *A report to Governor Jeb Bush and the 6th Judicial Circuit in the Matter of Theresa Marie Schiavo.* http://.jb-williams.com/ts-report-12-03.htm

GLOSSARY

Advance directive: A document that specifies the type of health care individuals wish to receive should they not be in a position to express their wishes in a critical situation.

Assisted death: An action taken by one person to end the life of another person, at that other person's request.

Black Stork: A movement to "weed out" defective infants to keep "defective people" out of the population.

Competence: The mental ability to make a rational decision about important matters in one's life (a law concept).

EEG tracings: Electrical activity of the brain as displayed on a moving scroll or computer monitor, using an electroencephalogram.

Euthanasia: Originally, an easy death, one without suffering. Later applied also to actions taken to end a life. "Active" euthanasia involves an action that ends the life; "passive" euthanasia refers to withdrawal or withholding of actions that might prolong life.

Hippocratic Oath: A code offering ethical principles for the practice of medicine, attributed to a Greek physician of the fifth century B.C.

Informed consent: The principle that patients should be provided with sufficient information to make decisions for or against accepting a treatment.

Living will: The first type of advance directive to be introduced, requesting that no aggressive treatments be attempted if the individual is in the end phase of life.

Mercy killing: At one time, the more common term for what is now referred to as assisted death.

Orbitoria: Clinics or centers at which assisted death would be provided at patients' request and in which biomedical studies would be conducted.

Slippery slope argument: Holds that accepting assisted death for any person will increase the demand and approval of death for many other people.

Terminal sedation: Administering drugs to dying patients with severe pain or other stressful symptoms with the purpose of keeping them in a deep sedative or comatose state until death. Also known informally as "slow euthanasia."

Ventilator: A machine that provides respiration for people who are unable to breathe adequately on their own.

ON FURTHER THOUGHT . . .

The Double Effect

Many people experience mixed feelings when euthanasia or assisted death situations arise. One strong impulse is to approve a course of action that will prevent or relieve suffering. Another strong impulse is to refrain from actions that are likely to foreshorten a person's life. The double-effect principle is sometimes seen as a way of resolving this conflict. A distinction is made between intent and consequence. One intends to relieve suffering: this justifies the action. If the patient's death is hastened by this action, it is an unfortunate, but not an ethically negligent consequence. Suppose you find yourself as part of the decision-making process. Would you accept the double-effect principle? Why or why not? Is this a sound, logical, and ethical way of making the decision or an unconvincing way to cope with an uncomfortable situation? If you reject the double-effect principle, what alternative would you choose, and why?

Useful online resources:

Access to End of Life Care
    www.access2eolcare.org
American Society for Bioethics and Humanities
    www.asbh.org
American Society of Law, Medicine, and Ethics
    www.aslme.org
Center for Death Education and Bioethics
    www.uwlx.edu/sociology/cde&b
Hastings Center
    www.thehastingscenter.org
National Institutes of Health Bioethics on the Web
    www.nih.gov/sigs/bioethics/
University of Miami Ethics Program
    www.ethics.miami.edu

Learn more about euthanasia and ethics:

Battin, M. B. (1994). *Least worth death. Essays in bioethics on the end of life.* New York: Oxford University Press.

Dowbiggin, I. (2003). *A merciful end. The euthanasia movement in modern America.* New York: Oxford University Press.

Smith, W. J. (1997). *Forced exit. The slippery slope from assisted suicide to legalized murder.* New York: Random House.

Learn more about the quest to live long without exactly growing old:

Boia, L. (2004). *Forever young: A cultural history of longevity.* London: Reaktion.

Gruman, G. J. (2003). *A history of ideas about the prolongation of life.* New York: Springer.

Kastenbaum, R. (1995). *Dorian, Graying: Is youth the only thing worth having?* Amityville, NY: Baywood.

BOX 9-4 CHAPTER UPDATE

State of Washington voters in the November 4, 2008 elections approved a physician-assisted suicide measure closely modeled on Oregon's law (http://seattletimes.awsource.com/html/local news/2008.335265_apwassistedsuicide2ndldwritethru.html.) Google for updated developments.

Children's curiosity encompasses life and death. They come to realize that it is difficult to understand the one without also understanding the other.

chapter 10

DEATH IN THE WORLD OF CHILDHOOD

I was dead. Then I wasn't. In my dream I was dead, then I knew it was a dream, and that's how I knew I wasn't dead, only dreaming that I was. And then I woke up . . . [OK. You said you had a question.] I do. I was sleeping and I dreamed I was dead. Do dead people—sometimes—dream they are sleeping and not really dead? [That's a great question. I don't know the answer.]
—8 year-old boy, conversing with author

My father doesn't feel good. He doesn't actually say anything, but you can see it in his eyes. (Girl, aged 8)

I think that he was very sad and upset. He didn't say it directly, but in the way he talked. He was so stressed and he shouted. (Girl, aged 9)

I think that he is sad, but he's good at hiding it. He's strong, he helps mother a lot. (Girl, aged 13)
—Quoted by Mikael Thastum et al. (2008)

Carlos asked whether hearts stop beating and then start again, and what happens to your heart when you die. "Does it go on vacation then?" he asked.
—Elizabeth Rider (2004, p. 328)

It was proof that his father had died on Sept. 11, 2001. But for Brendan, who is 5, the news that a piece of Thomas Fitzpatrick's humerus had been recovered was vexing. "Can we get all the pieces and put them together?" he recently asked his mother at their home in Tuckahoe, N. Y. "So he could be alive."
—Andrea Elliott (2004)

The mother died in the hospital, where the children were not allowed to see her. I came to the funeral with the children, where they saw their mother's body in the open casket. The two older children seemed satisfied with just touching their mother and giving her a kiss, but the youngest one wanted to do more. He was about three years old, and he wanted to see if he could wake her up.
—Margarita M. Saurez and Susan J. McFeaters (2000, p. 58)

One night, after visiting the cemetery, Coleen asked her father how deep her Mother was buried. She seemed relieved when Joseph explained that it was very deep—six feet. Coleen was consoled because she had stepped on the mound and was worried that she had stepped on her Mother.
—Grace Hyslop Christ (2000, p. 103)

How was the frog? The frog was dead, dead, dead. What else could it be? We buried it a whole summer ago!
—3-year-old Cynthia's report after she and her older brothers checked out the place where they had held the funeral and burial for a frog briefly known the previous summer

Children are more observant of death-related phenomena than many adults have supposed. The ability to enter the child's world of life and death can be immensely valuable in responding to the needs of children as illness, death, and grief enter their minds and lives.

RESPECTING THE CHILD'S CONCERN AND CURIOSITY

What does it mean to be dead? Why does a person get dead, and what can we do about it? Who else might get dead? These are among the questions that arise as children experience absence, loss, separation, and change. Each of the children mentioned in the preceding text was attempting to comprehend something important about death—and life. The 8-year-old was testing out the distinction between sleep and death, dream and reality. The three girls were keen observers of what they were not supposed to notice: their fathers' struggles with terminal cancer.

It was his yearly check up. Carlos, "a quiet 7-year-old with light brown tousled hair and big brown eyes, sat on the examination table, swinging his legs back and forth" (Rider, 2004, p. 1). His question about hearts that stop beating did not seem related to any recent deaths or other losses. The doctor explained that "It's a natural curiosity. Children are curious about death at all ages. Younger children see death as transient, yet around Carlos's age they begin to understand . . . that death is permanent." Carlos still wanted his question answered. "When do people die?" The answer: they usually do not die until they are very old with white hair and wrinkles. Carlos

considered this deeply, then said that he could make his hair white and paint wrinkles on his face. "Would I die then?" "No," the doctor replied, "You would still be 7 years old." Carlos relaxed. The doctor was right: It does not take a death in their own lives to prompt children to wonder about mortality. Curiosity about life almost certainly leads to curiosity about death. Carlos was attempting to assimilate death into his comprehension of the world (e.g., the heart going on vacation). He was also trying to quell a new kind of anxiety: What if that heart he feels in his chest should stop beating? Fortunately, his mother had not dismissed his concern and the doctor had said something reassuring. That Carlos leaned back and relaxed suggests that he, like many other normal children, can experience the physical discomfort associated with death anxiety—but also that adults have the ability to alleviate this distress.

Brendan's father had been a victim of the 9/11 terrorist attack on the World Trade Center. The anguish of many bereaved adults was intensified by the absence of an intact body that could be honored in funeral and memorial services. How, then, could a 5-year-old comprehend what had happened? Brendan's wish to assemble the remains and return his father to life might be dismissed as naïve and magical thinking. The longing for renewal and resurrection, though, has been a resilient theme for untold centuries. The boy was urgently seeking some way to return his world to the way it should be. The death of a loved one in childhood can be a spur to creative and critical thinking with the underlying intention of making things right again and escaping further loss. But as unresolved grief, this death can also haunt a person throughout the adult life course.

The youngest of the three children at the funeral wanted to see if he could awaken his mother.

> I let him try, and he did it as little ones do. First he tried to open her eyelids, and then he touched her face. Finally he called her name. After several attempts he turned to me and said, "I cannot wake her up." He wanted to try again, and I let him try one more time, because through my own Latina cultural filters, there was nothing wrong or disrespectful in touching a dead body (Saurez & McFeaters, 2000, p. 58).

This 3-year-old also hoped to bring a parent back to life. He had the courage to put his hands on this strangely unresponsive form. And what about the courage and perspective shown by the adult companion who permitted him to try, even though it would be painful to watch?

The young child's conception of death and the dead is not the same as the adult's. Coleen did not yet fully comprehend the difference between alive and dead. She knew that her mother was buried, but she might be disturbed if somebody stepped on the grave. This attribution of life qualities to the dead was associated with Coleen's level of mental development, limited experience with death situations, and the cultural milieu from which she was drawing her language, concepts, and attitudes. We will be looking at these factors in more detail later.

Children often learn of death through the loss of a pet. Here a father helps his daughter with a funeral for her goldfish.

Cynthia and her older brothers had taken an experimental approach to the same issue: What is the difference between alive and dead? Many conduct their own little experiments, often without their parents' knowledge. Burying the frog in the first place (please note that it was dead at the time!) was also a way of acquiring a sense of partial control over the mysterious disappearance into nonbeing. Perhaps—just perhaps—the frog would be ready to hop back to its nearby pond. Already sensitive to the fragility of life, the young experimentalists were vicariously burying and attempting to restore a little of themselves through the fate of the bog dweller. Cynthia seized the spokesperson role, proudly announcing their discovery that dead is dead. Had she comprehended the permanence of death at such an early age? Yes, and no. This seeming contradiction will be addressed later in the research section.

It is understandable that adults would want to protect children from the anxiety and sorrow associated with the death of a loved person and from intimations of their own mortality. However, no child is spared the possibility of losing loved ones. No child is exempt from life-threatening risks. No child grows up without noticing that sometimes what is here today is gone tomorrow. Whether we are ready to accept it or not, death is a part of the child's world.

Our exploration begins with the adult's conception of the child's conception of death. Next we explore the child's understanding of death as observed in both research and natural settings. This is followed by learning how children cope with the death of others, and how we can be helpful to them in their grief experiences. Some children also must cope with their own life-threatening conditions. We will learn much from what these children themselves have said. We then examine our society's tradition of excluding children from participating in life-and-death decisions that are of personal concern to them. The chapter concludes with an exploration of bedtime rituals as practices for death, and guidelines for sharing and responding to the child's death concerns.

ADULT ASSUMPTIONS ABOUT CHILDREN AND DEATH

How was the subject of death treated in your home when you were a child? This is the first of several questions that are raised in Box 10-1: Exploring Your Experiences with Death in Childhood. Please turn to these questions now. These questions will help you to bring your childhood experiences forward into the present moment. The activity of writing down your memories will also help you to compare your experiences with those of other people and to think about how these experiences may have influenced your life.

Here are examples of some of the most frequent responses to the first question:

- They sat in dark rooms and became quiet.
- Very hushed and away from us as children. There were 2 deaths and 3 near deaths, from when I was 7 to when I was 10. I felt like I was left out of all of them. No one ever explained anything to me.
- I don't remember any conversations about death with my parents. My Mom went back East for my uncle's funeral and my grandparents' funerals, but I did not go.
- Death was not something that was discussed with children. When my grandfather died, though, it was chaotic. The adults talked to each other about how the death took place. Everyone offered opinions of how the wake and funeral should be carried out. There were arguments and disagreements. All of us kids were completely left out.
- Since I am and come from a Christian home, death was addressed often as a concept and limited to an afterlife. When someone actually did die it was put in perspective with God at the center. "He or she is in a better place. . . ." At times I found this very comforting; at other moments I felt put off by their rehearsed responses.
- After the cat died, we were told about death in that the life is gone. No more movement, no more breath, etc. It seemed to make sense.

BOX 10-1 EXPLORING YOUR EXPERIENCES WITH DEATH IN CHILDHOOD

Write your answers on a separate sheet of paper.

1. How was the subject of death treated in your home when you were a child? What questions did you ask of your parents? What answers did you receive?

2. What most interested or puzzled you about death when you were a young child?

3. Do you remember the death of a pet or other animal at some time in your childhood? What were the circumstances? How did you feel about it? How did other people respond to your feelings?

4. Do you remember the death of a person at some time in your childhood? What were the circumstances? How did you feel about it? How did other people respond to your feelings?

5. Can you identify any ways in which childhood experiences with death may have influenced you to this day?

6. What do you now think is the best thing a parent could say to or do with a child in a death situation and why?

7. What do you now think is the worst thing a person could say or do with a child in a death situation and why?

Some people remember being given straightforward, naturalistic information. Most often, however, families seemed to have followed a family rule of silence (Book, 1996). Why do adults often have such difficulty in communicating with children about death? The answer has much to do with the adults' own fears, doubts, and conflicts. Perhaps Sigmund Freud (1914) was on the mark when he suggested that, having lost their own childhood innocence, adults want very much to believe that their children live in a fairy-tale world, safe from the stings of reality.

CHILDREN DO THINK ABOUT DEATH

The most basic fact has been well established: Children, even young children, do think about death. Evidence comes from many sources.

Early Experiences with Death in Childhood

One of America's first distinguished psychologists, G. Stanley Hall (1922) and his student, Colin Scott, asked adults to recall their earliest

experiences with death. These childhood experiences were recalled in vivid detail:

> The child's exquisite temperature sense feels a chill where it formerly felt heat. Then comes the immobility of face and body where it used to find prompt movements of response. There is no answering kiss, pat, or smile. . . . Often the half-opened eyes are noticed with awe. The silence and tearfulness of friends are also impressive to the child, who often weeps reflexly or sympathetically (p. 440).

Funeral and burial scenes often were the very earliest of all memories. More recent studies also find death experiences to be common among adults' earliest memories. For example, an Italian-American butcher shared his earliest memory with me:

> I was still in the old country. We all lived in a big old house, me, my family and all kinds of relatives. It was just a few days after my fourth birthday, and there was grandmother laid out on a table in the front room. The room was full of women crying their eyes out. Hey, I didn't want any part of it, but somebody said grandmother

was just sleeping. I doubted that very much. Grandmother never slept on a table in the front room with everybody crying their eyes out before. But what I really remember most is what I want to forget most. "Kiss your grandmother!" Yeah, that's right. They made me walk right up and kiss grandmother. I can still see her face. And I can still feel her face. Is that crazy? I mean, after all these years, I can still feel her cold dead face and my lips against it.

Although this man was the owner and chief butcher of a specialty meat shop, he experienced panic when he was in the presence of a human corpse. The early childhood experience with death had somehow become part of his adult personality. Another compelling example was reported by a college student to another researcher who was inquiring into earliest memories:

As a young child, I would receive ducks and chickens as an Easter present. One of these chicks was able to survive the playing and was able to grow into a nice white hen. She was my pride and joy, following me and coming when I called. The hen stayed at my Grandmother's. One Sunday dinner the main course was "fried chicken." It took me several minutes to realize just what had happened. To say the least, I was devastated and do not eat chicken to this day (Dickinson, 1992, p. 83).

In a follow-up study, Dickinson (1992) found that college students still had intense memories of their early childhood experiences with death. It was startling to learn how anger, "outright hatred at times," continued to be felt toward "a parent who had killed the (pet) animal, whether it was a parent who had accidentally run over the animal or the vet who 'put the animal to sleep'" (p. 172). These students often felt that the explanations their parents gave them in childhood were unsatisfactory. Most often the children had been told that a deceased person had gone to heaven. Some had been reassured because heaven was said to be a happy place. One 4-year-old girl, however, became upset when her father told her that her kitten "went to heaven to be with God." She responded: "Why does God want a dead kitten?" A 3-year-old also became angry when told her grandmother had gone to heaven:

"I don't want her in heaven. I want her here!" Not only are young children affected by death-related events, but they may recall these experiences with intense emotions many years later.

The childhood loss and death theme was evident again in research interviews several students and I conducted with residents of Sun City and Sun City West, Arizona. These people were asked for their earliest memories of any kind. The respondents went back at least 60 years and sometimes more than 80 for their memories. Many incidents were pleasant to recall; others were odd and hard to explain. However, more than one person in three reported an earliest memory that conveyed some encounter with death, loss, or separation:

- "The green chair nobody sat in any more. I remember going into the room and out of the room and back into the room time after time. Maybe Grandfather would be sitting in his chair the next time I entered the room. I know I was 4 because I just had a birthday with 4 candles on the cake."
- "There were lots of people in the street, and there had been some kind of accident. I wanted to see what. A horse was on the ground and there was a twisted up, tipped over cart behind it. Somebody, a man, was saying they ought to shoot it. I got one look and then somebody pushed me away or led me away. I don't know what I thought about it at the time, but I can still see that horse."

Some previous readers of this book have taken their early memories as the starting point for their personal research. One young woman, for example, recalled having felt alone and frightened, "and there was something about the ocean and the beach in it." No other details came to mind from this memory that seemed to have taken place just before her kindergarten days. She decided to ask her parents what had actually happened. They were reluctant, but:

then we had one of our best talks ever! Mom had had a miscarriage and the doctor had said she couldn't have any more babies or she might die herself. It never occurred to them to say any of this to a little kid like me. But while we were talking I suddenly remembered them getting rid of baby things, a crib and all, giving them away, and my mother looking real strange and distant. And that was when they sent me to live with a family I didn't like much so they could also get away a few days, together, and try to feel normal again. I can understand that perfectly now. But then, it was like they were going to get rid of me, too! And in my little kid's mind, the beach and the ocean were part of it all. Maybe they were going to leave me all by myself on the beach, or maybe a big wave was going to come and get me!

This student had developed a pattern of avoiding beaches and large bodies of water, although she was also attracted to these places. The frank conversation with her family not only helped her understand the unpleasant and unaccountable early memory, but also dissipated her anxieties

about going to the beach. Other students have also found that it was possible to gain a better understanding of their own quirks and fears by recalling early memories of loss. It would be going much too far to say that a particular childhood experience "causes" us to behave or feel in a particular way in adult life. Nevertheless, childhood experiences tinged with death, loss, or separation can become significant influences on the way we see life and cope with death.

Death in the Songs and Games of Childhood

The "innocent" songs and games of childhood through the centuries have often been performances of death themes. The familiar ring-around-the-rosie song and round dance achieved

Run and hide! "It" has been a proxy for death in many versions of this childhood game.

popularity during the peak years of the *plague* in fourteenth-century Europe. The "rosies" referred both to a symptom of the disease and the flower petals that people hoped would protect them; the "all fall down" is self-explanatory. The children who enacted this little drama knew their danger. We can imagine the security they sought by joining hands. The ritual impersonated the trauma and separation death. Helpless passivity and fear were transformed into a group effort to master the threat. The children who had fallen to the earth would leap to their feet with joyful shouts after completing the ring-around-the-rosie dance. For the moment, at least, they were still very much alive.

The death theme is explicit in many hide-and-seek and tag games, such as "Dead Man Arise!" This type of game has many names and local variations. In Sicily, for example, children played "A Morsi Sanzuni" (Opie & Opie, 1969).

> One child lay down pretending to be dead while his companions sang a dirge, occasionally going up to the body and lifting an arm or a leg to make sure the player was dead, and nearly stifling the child with parting kisses. Suddenly he would jump up, chase his mourners, and try to mount the back of one of them. . . . In Czechoslovakia . . . the recumbent player was covered with leaves, or had her frock held over her face. The players then made a circle and counted the chimes of the clock, but each time replied, "I must still sleep." This continued until the clock struck twelve when, as in some other European games, the sleeping player sprung to life, and tried to catch someone (p. 107).

In tag games, the person who is "It" must not peek or move while the other players conceal themselves. The scary thrill is experienced both by the victim and the monstrous "It" who has discovered the hiding place. Every participant gets to be both slayer and slain. Even the slightest touch has grave significance: The victim instantly is transformed from lively participant to death personified ("It"). Further resemblances to death are suggested in those variations in which the victim must freeze (enter suspended animation?) until rescued by one who is still free (alive).

Concern with death has been a common theme in children's play through the centuries. This tradition continues today with computer-mediated destruction games that compete with each other for violent special effects. As a child in the streets of New York, my friends and I played a variation of cops-and-robbers, mostly sporting wooden guns (some armed with rubber bands). Medieval children brandished their "swords" as they replayed Crusader–Saracen battles. Today ready-made computer games feature multiple killings in which there is no personal relationship between killer and slain and in which the objective often is to rack up an imposing score. There is concern that the encouragement and practice of violence in the games children play might have a disturbing effect on their cognitive and emotional development (Wass, 2002; see also "killing begets killing" in Chapter 8). It is also possible that children's attitudes toward death can be distorted by emphasis on the act rather than the consequences of killing. I wonder also about the increasing frequency of solitary children playing pre-programmed games instead of improvising their own rules in adventures with other children. Does this practice reduce the opportunity to grow through shared experiences, including death-related concerns? No answer, at present.

Research and Clinical Evidence

Formal research consistently finds a pattern of development in the child's understanding of death. A very young child does not and cannot, comprehend the essential facts of death. However, sometimes they do! These discoveries occur not when scheduled by research but when child and situation come together. We offer first three examples of spontaneous discoveries, followed by a review of formal research findings:

• A boy, aged 16 months, was enjoying one of his regular visits to a public garden, accompanied by his father, an eminent biomedical scientist. The boy's attention was captured by a fuzzy caterpillar creeping along the sidewalk. Suddenly, large adult feet came into view, and the caterpillar was crushed (unwittingly). Immediately the boy showed an alarmed expression. He then bent over the remains, studying them intently. After a long

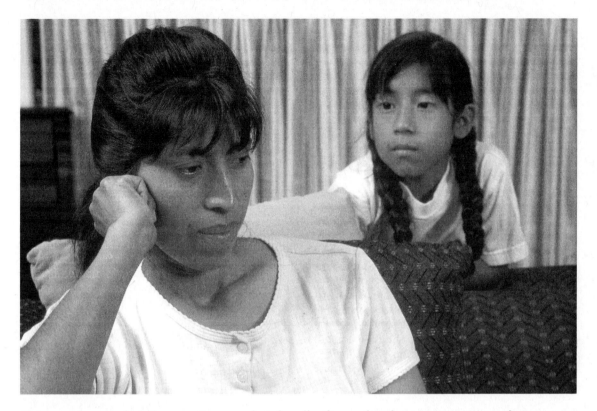

Children can not only feel a parent's sorrow but also offer the comfort that was once given to them.

moment, he stood up and informed his father, in a sad and resigned voice, "No more!" "No more!" Can there be a more direct and concise comment? From that moment the boy became reluctant to stay in the garden. He looked with distress at fallen blossoms that he had not previously seemed to notice. It took several comforting attempts from his father before he would again visit this place of beauty and, now, of death.

- An 18-month-old discovered a dead bird as he and his father walked through the woods. The boy crouched over the bird, his face taking on the expression of the classic Greek mask of tragedy. "Bird!" he said. "Yes," his father replied, "A bird; a dead bird." For the next several days the boy insisted on visiting the dead bird, looking at it very carefully but not saying anything. One day there was a crisp autumn breeze, and leaves floated down from the trees. The boy picked up a leaf and handed it to his father—insisting that his father place the leaf back on the tree. The father said this could not be done, but, with the boy's insistence, he tried. The leaf would not stay put. The father tried again and again. The boy then looked sad and turned away. He never asked again to have a leaf restored to its tree nor did he look again at the dead bird.

There was no doubt in the minds of these very young children that death was something special. Older children explored ways of expressing and overcoming the sorrow of loss:

- An 8-year-old boy was improvising loudly at the piano. He was in a mood of deep contemplation, not just idly banging away. "What are you playing?" his father asked. "A funeral song for Lovey" (the family cat, recently killed on the highway). As the boy continued his improvisations, he explained the meaning of each passage, "This is Lovey sharpening her claws on a tree . . . This is Lovey when she has just heard the can opener . . . This is Lovey curled up and purring. . . ."

This child understood something of death's significance and, furthermore, felt the need and obligation to perform some ritual in honor of the deceased. The toddler's "No more!" in his encounter with the crushed caterpillar is a flash of insight into mortality that is occasionally heard even from very young children. How, then, can researchers conclude that young children do not comprehend death? There is a reason: the flash of insight usually disappears, replaced by more age-appropriate ways of thinking. I suggest that this is a hurried retreat from an alarming discovery, facilitated by the lack of a mature system of thought in which the mortality insight can be integrated. As adults, we are often situational in our responses—perhaps operating mostly on logic in one situation, emotion in another. Children are even more inclined to respond according to the feeling of a particular situation. Children's comprehension of death seems to vary from situation to situation, and mood to mood, although this phenomenon has seldom been studied.

Research Case Histories

Three brief case histories drawn from my research will provide a glimpse of individual and family patterns. A general review of research findings will follow. This section presents narrative data from structured interviews with the mothers of schoolchildren.

Teresa

Teresa is a 7-year-old described by her mother as a quiet girl who enjoys her own company: "She's just a very nice girl, not afraid to express any emotions at all." Teresa is especially interested in plants and how they grow and is much involved in her family.

INTERVIEWER: Has death come into Teresa's life?
MOTHER: My mother died, her grandmother, in January of this year. . . . We all knew she was dying. I told Teresa and I told June [her sister] that she was dying. They wanted to know, "What is dying, where is she going to go, why is she going, why is she leaving me? She's my Grandma! I don't want her to die!" . . . And she was just very curious about the whole business of the wake and the funeral and "Why do we have to do this, why do we have to do that." The big thing was, "I don't want to see other people sad, because it makes me sad."

INTERVIEWER: How did Teresa respond to the death when it actually came?
MOTHER: She comforted me. She would cry when I cried. She would put her arms around me and she would say, "Please don't cry; everything will be all right. Grandma isn't suffering anymore. Grandma is happy now."

INTERVIEWER: What did Teresa understand about Grandma's death?
MOTHER: She understands that she was put in the ground in that cold outer casket, but Teresa realizes that she is not there. She's in spirit, beside her, watching and loving her always. And Teresa sees a bird—my mother was a bird freak—and she said, "I wonder if Grandma can see that bird?"

INTERVIEWER: What did Teresa not understand about this death?
MOTHER: She still doesn't understand why. You know, why take her from us now, she wasn't old; Grandma was a young woman [age 54]. Why was she so sick, you know. Did she do something bad?

INTERVIEWER: Does Teresa have any death concerns or fears?
MOTHER: I think she'd be very much afraid of losing me at this point because since my mother has died she's becoming extremely touchy with me; she gets a little bit upset when I have to go

out, you know. "Please come back soon!"

INTERVIEWER: How have you answered her questions about death?

MOTHER: I don't want to get into hell and heaven and that, because I don't want them to get hung up on it. . . . I really don't think we discussed it, you know, before it actually hit us; we never really discussed it with the children. . . .

INTERVIEWER: Has it been difficult to discuss death with Teresa?

MOTHER: Not with Teresa, not at all. With June, yes, but not with Teresa.

INTERVIEWER: How do you feel in general about the way Teresa thinks about death?

MOTHER: I think she's got her head pretty well together. She's really probably done better than I have. . . . Two or three months after my mother died, I was sitting by myself, having my crying jag and getting it all out, and Teresa got up out of bed. You know, I was sitting in the dark. I just knew it was coming. I had put them to bed. So she got up, and she came beside me and she said, "Mama, I know why you're crying." And I said, "Why, Teresa?" And she said, "Because you miss your mother." And I said, "You're right." And Teresa said, "But you always have to remember, how good she was to us, remember she used to take us uptown and buy us ice cream and she used to sing us songs and remember when she bought me this bracelet." And within a matter of, say 3 minutes, I felt so relieved, like, you know, tons had been lifted off me; from this 7-year-old child, you know, really laying it on me and telling me, come on, you know, you got to go on living. . . . And the oldest one [June] will not discuss it at all. You know, it's too bad.

INTERVIEWER: Do you have any questions of your own about what to do with a child in things related to death?

MOTHER: There are things I don't know, and so I wouldn't know how to explain it to them. I don't know how to make it easier for them . . . Everybody dies—why do you grieve then? Why is there a wake, why is there a funeral? There are things I don't understand, so I'm sure they don't understand, you know, why the pain?

INTERVIEWER: Should parents and children discuss death together?

MOTHER: It's so very important! I can remember my own first experience with death and how frightened I was of it. I think it's something that should be talked about in a family and . . . I'm having a hard time expressing myself, but I really think that when people die, that we love, we shouldn't have to grieve. . . . Why do they put us through the wakes, the funeral? This is what we saw when we were children; we saw grieving after death—and my children will grieve over death.

INTERVIEWER: What is the worst thing a parent could say or do with a child in a death situation?

MOTHER: I would hate to stifle emotions. I would hate to say, "Stop all that crying!" Or, the other thing is, "He's gone away for a vacation. He's left us, but he'll come back." That's a bunch of lies, and children see through these things.

INTERVIEWER: What is the best thing a parent could say or do with a child in a death situation?

MOTHER: Let the children see what goes on. Let them be totally involved with the family, to be able to express with the family their own emotions and to be totally included in what goes on instead of shifted off to a friend's house.

INTERVIEWER: How curious about death were you when you were Teresa's age?

MOTHER: I wasn't at all . . . until I was about 10 years old. . . . I lost my cat, and, I remember, I cried all day upstairs in my room because I thought: This is death. I'm going to lose my mother. And I cried and cried, and I was so scared and I had nightmares.

INTERVIEWER: How was death handled in your home when you were growing up?

MOTHER: It wasn't. I said to my mother once, "I'm so afraid that you were going to die." And she just said, "I'm not going to die." And . . . she died. [These words were spoken very softly and sadly.]

INTERVIEWER: Was that the way she should have handled it, or what do you think she should have done instead?

MOTHER: I think that she should have drawn more out of me and really given me time that I needed, and maybe have said—well, I don't know what you can say to a child to make it any easier when there is a threat, a scare of losing a parent, but just be able to sit down and discuss it. . . .

INTERVIEWER: What are your thoughts and feelings about death now?

MOTHER: Since my first death was my mother, I think it was very hard . . . . I just accept the fact that she is dead and I will no longer see her, but I just hang on to the thought that she's not suffering and that she knew she was dying even though nobody told her. . . . She said more with her eyes, more than anything else in the world. I feel very . . . I feel peace within myself.

INTERVIEWER: Did she tell you her thoughts or feelings at all?

MOTHER: No, she was aphasic . . . and paralyzed. She couldn't talk. The only thing she could do was move one arm and one hand and the night before she died, we went in there and they took her out of the special care unit and just took off the respirator and let her die and she just kept pointing up to heaven. She knew she was dying and she just . . . made us feel at ease. Because I was glad she knew, and she knew that I knew, so we wouldn't have to play the game: "Okay, Ma, we'll get you out of here in a couple of weeks." It was kind of peace, you know, that we shared.

INTERVIEWER: Is there anything you would like to add?

MOTHER: I think we should teach children about death in schools. I don't mean we shouldn't teach them at home, but in school, too. Let people know what often happens in grief, so they won't be so surprised. . . . Should start early because it's like sex education, you know, you almost don't talk about it until it happens, until there is a problem.

Stanley

Stanley is another 7-year-old who is described by his mother as "just the nicest boy a mother could ever want. Does what you tell him to—most of the time. . . . His life is pretty much centered around the family and his dog."

INTERVIEWER: What does Stanley understand about death?

MOTHER: That whoever would die they're not going to see again and that's about all. As far as feeling for the person, he hasn't come to that stage yet. . . . We have a dog, and if he died I wouldn't know what he would feel. I really don't. I would say he would be too little to think much about it.

INTERVIEWER: What does Stanley not understand about death?

MOTHER: What the purpose of death is. Why we were put on the earth for a reason and why we're going to die. Stanley is definitely too little to understand why somebody's laying in a casket. Especially if it is somebody young. You try to explain to him that God put him on this earth but He called him back. He wanted him back. I don't think he can comprehend that at all.

INTERVIEWER: How have you answered Stanley's questions about death?

MOTHER: Sometimes I tell him that the person was very old and very sick. If it was a little boy, that the little boy was very sick and God wanted him back. . . . God put us here but He isn't going to let us stay here. We're all here temporarily and even though you boys are little doesn't mean you couldn't die tomorrow. Even Stanley, I told him, you could die tomorrow. I could die tomorrow. We don't know when. God doesn't tell us. It doesn't mean that just sick people die. Anybody can die—people get hit by cars.

INTERVIEWER: What is the worst thing a parent could say or do with a child in a death situation?

MOTHER: To hide it from them. If you want to cry, cry. That's the best thing. Make him experience it with you. Why not? They've got to be exposed to it the way it is.

INTERVIEWER: How was death handled in your home when you were growing up?

MOTHER: My parents shielded us from all of that. . . . We never got the answers we really wanted, so as a result we stopped asking. That was about anything, even about death. . . . But death can bring people together, it's just that in our family it didn't. Would have been nice if our parents had let us join in, instead of getting our relatives to babysit us while they went and did it all . . . going to the funerals and all of that. . . . I would have liked to have been at their side.

INTERVIEWER: What are your thoughts and feelings about death now?

MOTHER: I'm very conscious about death now. It panics me, truthfully, it really panics me. I know we can't live forever. If I knew I was dying, I just wouldn't want to wake up in the morning, that's all. I'm not too happy about other people dying either. . . . Dead people are supposed to be with God. We're supposed to be happy but we still can't. Part of us says we are—part of us says we're not!

Brian

Brian is 8 years old and "a bright boy with lots of curiosity. He's especially interested in rocks and minerals, gems, animals, underwater stories. He reads about them all the time, and talks about anything. But not death."

INTERVIEWER: What does Brian understand about death?

MOTHER: Oh, he understands it . . . I think. But he doesn't really like to talk about it. He doesn't like the idea that any of us will die. Like he said to me, "You'll never, never die, Mom." I tried to explain to him, well, that's not true, that I will die and so will Daddy, and when that time comes he must accept it because that's part of living. He understands what I'm saying. You can see that from the look in his eyes. But it makes him very, very sad, and he'll go, "I don't want to talk about that, I'd rather not—please, Mom!"

INTERVIEWER: What does Brian not understand about death?

MOTHER: Only one thing I can think of. His Daddy likes to hunt. He goes deer hunting and he killed, you know, a young deer. Brian couldn't quite understand that. He thought the deer was so beautiful and to kill him. . . . Well, we had to tell him why he killed the deer, and the deer hurt, and if he wasn't killed, if so many deer weren't killed a year, the balance of nature would be off.

INTERVIEWER: Does Brian have any death concerns or fears?

MOTHER: Losing one of us that he loves. He's very, very close to Cris [his sister] so, of course, he doesn't want her to leave the house. He's often said this. If she doesn't come home when she said she's supposed to come home he'll call me and say, "I'm awfully worried because she's out in the car, if she has an accident and gets killed, Mom, I don't know what I'll do." And I mean upset. I've seen him cry and tears going down his face and he'll say, "I would just die if my Crissy dies."

INTERVIEWER: What is the worst thing a parent could say or do with a child in a death situation?

MOTHER: Well, I'm going to say this from experience. I think the worst thing to do is not let the child grieve. To tell them they can't cry . . . bottling up these emotions does something to that person and carries on into their adult life. It does irreparable damage if you ask me, and I guess you did.

INTERVIEWER: How was death handled in your home when you were growing up?

MOTHER: Nobody prepared me for it, nobody answered my questions, nobody told me one thing or the other. "I don't want to talk about it," would be the answer, or "I don't know why you ask me such foolish questions."

INTERVIEWER: What are your thoughts and feelings about death now?

MOTHER: Now, it's much different. I feel the more I think of it, the more at peace I feel with the fact that death is going to come. When I was younger I was hoping, oh, I'd never die, and now I know that I am, and the time comes I don't think I'll be afraid to die. . . . I have more acceptance of the fact of death now than I did when I was— even ten years ago or even five years ago. . . . I think it comes with time. Even so, having children makes death more important in a way, too, your responsibility to them.

Reflections and Questions

Young as they are, Teresa, Stanley, and Brian already differ in their experiences and concerns. Following are a few reflections and questions on their research case history excerpts:

1. It is often the death of particular people or animals that arouses the child's concern: Grandma for Teresa, Crissy and the deer for Brian. The possibility (Crissy) as well as the actuality (Grandma) of death can stimulate thought and feeling. Stanley is confronted with specific death concerns by his mother ("you could die tomorrow. I could die tomorrow"). Children do not have to comprehend death in its most abstract aspects to recognize that it threatens their relationships with the people who are important to them.

2. Experiences, attitudes, and ways of coping with death are part of the intimate flow of life between children and their parents. The influence operates in both directions. Brian's questions about the slain deer, for example, and his intense fear for Crissy's well-being present challenges for the parents' own attitudes toward death.

3. People within the same household can have different orientations toward death. Teresa and June, for example, differ in their openness to discussion of death. The same death also may have varying effects on the children, depending upon their developmental phase, personality, and position in the family. It is useful to become well acquainted with

the entire family constellation if we want to understand the implications of one particular child's view of death. From other data, it was clear that Brian, as the only boy in the family, wanted very much to be like his father—but does this mean he, too, will have to go deer hunting?

4. Teresa's mother favors an open communication process and reflects thoughtfully on her own behavior as well as her children's. She has unresolved questions in some areas, such as the value of funerals and the grief process. Despite these unresolved concerns, Teresa's mother shows flexibility and the ability to learn from experience. By contrast, Stanley's mother does not seem to have sorted out her own assumptions about life and death. When Stanley notices a death-related incident, she passes along a received dogma that has been familiar to her since her own childhood—but that she has never much thought about. The abstraction level and tone of her explanation was of doubtful help to Stanley. Parents who are not able to cope with a child's death-related curiosity on a simple, naturalistic level because of their own discomfort may be perpetuating the anxieties for still another generation. Imagine Stanley's thoughts after his mother's explanation: "God does not want healthy people? Is it wrong to want people to live? Is God the enemy who takes my friends away? Do I have to get very sick and die to be loved by God?" I have, in fact, heard reflections of

this type from children whose curiosity about death was answered by verbose patter that placed the blame on a loving but inscrutable God.

5. Although Teresa's mother had a warm and loving childhood, her parents had glossed over the topic of death. This made it more difficult to cope both with the death of her mother—who had promised she was not going to die—and the feelings of her own daughters. Brian's and Stanley's mothers also grew up in homes where death was not to be discussed with the children. This background of death avoidance in the childhood home was typical for the mothers in our study. Today's young mothers seem to be more aware of the value of discussing death with their children as part of their general preparation for life. However, most often they have not benefited from such good examples in their own homes while growing up. We now have a transitional generation of parents who are trying to relate to their children in an area that was off-limits when they themselves were young. This leads to second guessing of their own responses: "Did I say the right thing?" Eventually, however, the new openness should make death a less divisive topic between parent and child in generations to come.

It is not by accident that the research case histories sampled here are based on the mothers' reports. The fathers declined to discuss this subject. Family death education seems to be viewed as something for "the women" to handle.

BOX 10-2   LESSONS FROM THE RESEARCH CASE HISTORIES

- It is the death of particular people or animals that enlists the child's concern.

- Death-related experiences, attitudes, and behaviors are part of the intimate flow of life between children and their parents.

- There may be several different orientations toward death within the same household.

- Parents whose own discomfort interferes with their response to their children's death-related curiosity are likely to perpetuate these anxieties for another generation.

- There is now a transitional generation of parents who are trying to communicate in an open manner with their children, although their own experience was of family silence about death.

CONCEPTS AND FEARS: DEVELOPING THROUGH EXPERIENCE

It is clear that death has a place in the thoughts of children. But just what do children make of death? How do their ideas develop from early childhood onward? And what is the relationship between how children think about death and their fears? Early studies emphasized maturation. Children's understanding of death was found to improve along with the general development of their mental abilities. Later studies indicated that life experiences also play a significant role. A 13-year-old, for example, generally will show an understanding of death that is more accurate and complete than that of a 4-year-old. Is this because the older child has developed more advanced cognitive structures? Or is it simply because the older child has had another 9 years of life experience from which to learn? The evidence suggests that the child's understanding of death is influenced by both maturation level and life experience, although much remains to be learned about the interaction of these factors.

"Auntie Death's" Pioneering Study

Our understanding of the way children think about death has been greatly influenced by a pioneering study that is worth reviewing in detail. Hungarian psychologist Maria Nagy (1948/1969) invited 378 children, ranging in age from 3 to 10 years, to express their death-related thoughts and feelings. The children came from a variety of social and religious backgrounds. The older children were asked to draw pictures and to "write down everything that comes to your mind about death." Children of all ages were engaged in conversation. As Nagy reviewed the children's words and pictures, she found that three age-related stages could be established (Table 10-1).

Stage 1

Stage 1 includes the youngest children, from about the third until the fifth year. The dead are simply less alive. They cannot see and hear—

TABLE 10-1
Stages of Death Comprehension in Childhood (Nagy)

Stage	Age Range	Interpretation of Death
1	3–5	Death is separation.
		The dead are less alive.
		Very curious about death.
2	5–9	Death is final—but one might escape it!
		Death is seen as a person.
3	9–adult	Death is personal, universal, final, and inevitable.

well, maybe they can, but not very well. They are not as hungry as the living. They don't do much. Being dead and being asleep are pretty much the same, but not exactly. The youngest children also thought of death as temporary. The dead might return, just as the sleeping might awaken. Uppermost in the minds of many children was the theme of death as departure and separation. What has actually become of the dead person is a matter of guesswork, imagination, and wishful thinking. However, it is the absence of that person that is most obvious and most compelling.

Nagy's preschoolers were full of questions about details of the funeral, the coffin, the cemetery, and so on. The child's active engagement with the challenge of comprehending death was also observed by Sylvia Anthony (1940/1972) with young British children. Respondents in both studies believed that death was not much fun, having to lie around in a coffin all day, and all night, too. The dead might be scared and lonely, too, away from all their friends. Even very young children knew what it was like to feel scared or lonely, so these states of mind could readily be attributed to the dead.

The combination of what the young child knows and does not know about death can arouse anxiety. "He would like to come out, but the coffin is nailed down," one 5-year-old told "Auntie Death," the name bestowed on the psychologist by the children. People are being cruel by nailing down the coffin. There are many possibilities for misinterpretations based on the young child's limited conception of death, especially if the available adults fail to understand how the child is likely to interpret death-related phenomena.

Stage 2

The next stage begins at age 5 or 6 and lasts until about the ninth year. The child now recognizes that death is final. The older the child within this age range, the more firm the conclusion. The dead do not return. Another new theme also emerged during this stage. Many of the children represented death as a person. Interestingly, *personification* is one of humankind's most ancient modes of expressing the relationship with death. One 9-year-old confided:

> Death is very dangerous. You never know what minute he is going to carry you off with him. Death is invisible, something nobody has ever seen in all the world. But at night he comes to everybody and carries them off with him. Death is like a skeleton. All the parts are made of bone. But then when it begins to be light, when it's morning, there's not a trace of him. It's that dangerous, death (p. 11).

The association of death with darkness is an ancient habit of mind, expressed by people in the earliest civilizations that have left us records. Light is equated with life. It is not unusual for the child's conception of death to include elements that once were the common property of adults.

The personification of death as a skeleton was fairly common in Nagy's sample of 5- to 9-year-olds. These personifications often were frightening, representing enormous if mysterious power. "Kill the death-man so we will not die" was a frequent comment. Some children also depicted death as a circus clown—supposedly the embodiment of mirth. Other children saw dead people as representing death, while still others personified death in the form of angels. Even angelic death, however, did not remove the sting of fear. "The death angels are great enemies of people," declared a 7-year-old. "Death is the king of the angels. The angels work for death."

There is one more significant characteristic of Nagy's Stage 2. *The realization of death's finality is accompanied by the belief that this fate might still be eluded.* The clever or fortunate person might not be caught by the "death-man." A child might be killed crossing the street, for example. But if children are very careful in crossing the street, they will not be run over, and therefore they will not die. Children in this age range tend to see death as an outside force or personified agent. "It's that dangerous, death." However, the saving grace is that we do not absolutely have to die. Death is not yet recognized as universal and personal.

Stage 3

The final stage Nagy identified begins at about age 9 or 10 and is assumed to continue thereafter. The child now understands that *death is personal, universal, and inevitable as well as final.* All that lives must die, including oneself.

Discussion of death at this age has an adult quality: "Death is the termination of life. Death is destiny. We finish our earthly life. Death is the end of life on earth," declared one 9-year-old boy. A 10-year-old girl added a moral and poetic dimension: "It means the passing of the body. Death is a great squaring of accounts in our lives. It is a thing from which our bodies cannot be resurrected. It is like the withering of flowers."

This new awareness is compatible with belief in some form of afterlife, as with the 9-year-old boy who said, "Everyone has to die once, but the soul lives on." In fact, it might be argued that the child does not really have a grasp of afterlife concepts until death itself is appreciated as final and inevitable.

What Has Been Learned Since "Auntie Death"?

Nagy's findings remain useful today, although the tendency to personify death between ages 5 and 9 seems to have diminished greatly, according to most follow-up studies. Perhaps this is a change wrought by the new childhood with its exposure to mass media and high technology. There also seems to be a tendency for children in America today to move through the stages at an earlier age than what was found by Nagy.

Five-year-old Michael gives us an example of the way some young children today are integrating technological developments into their dawning conceptions of dying and death. Researcher E. J. Deveau (1995) comments on Michael's drawing (Figure 10-1):

Michael . . . is concerned with burial, fantasy, and the world beyond. He integrates modern technology into his account of how God converts the dead into angels after hauling them up to heaven. His description of how people die is very concrete and practical, in keeping with what might be expected at this age (p. 86).

In the picture, according to Michael, "God uses a machine that turns them into an angel." People die "when they eat bad food, the bad food

FIGURE 10-1
Michael's God Machine. Reprinted with permission from D. W. Adams & E. J. Deveau (Eds.), *Beyond the Innocence of Childhood*, Vol. 1: "Perceptions of Death Through the Eyes of Children and Adolescents. Amityville, NY: Baywood, 1995.

sticks to their heart and the blood can't get in the heart and then you have a heart attack . . . or something like that."

It is also probable, as Deveau has suggested, that the stages are not absolute and fixed, but, rather, represent temporary "resting places" in the child's continuing attempt to come to terms with death both cognitively and emotionally.

There is general agreement that basic understanding of death is usually achieved by about age 9 or 10. Nagy had identified the basic components as inevitability, nonreversibility, universality, and personal inclusion ("I will die, too"). Later studies added *cessation* and *causation*. Children come to understand that in death the body no longer can perform its functions (cessation), and that it is this loss of function that results in death (causation). Studies reviewed by Kenyon (2001) find that children with superior intellectual and verbal skills demonstrate more advanced concepts of death than other children of the same age. Boys are more likely than girls to depict violent causes of death.

Developing a mature comprehension of death is but part of the child's project to understand what the whole world is about. There are many stimulating contributions to the study of children as fledgling philosophers and scientists (e.g., Rosenberg, Johnson, and Harris (2000). Of particular interest here are those studies finding that preschool children already have the knack of distinguishing between living creatures (e.g., a starfish), and nonliving objects (e.g., a robodog). Many 3- and most 4 year-olds realize that living creatures eat, grow, and die, while toys and stuffed animals do not (Jepson & Gelman, 2007). This does not mean that these very young children have firmly grasped the more abstract meanings of death. It is possible to confuse children—and adults—if presented with sophisticated robotic devices that are designed to simulate speech, memory, and conversational characteristics. Nevertheless, children seem to get off to a fast start in distinguishing between alive and not-alive. "Dead" would have little or no meaning if one did not recognize the basic alive/not-alive distinction. Preschool children are also

working on their ability to distinguish sleep from death. This remains a fuzzy issue throughout adult life because "sleeping" and "resting" are often used as euphemisms for "dead." Cross-cultural research indicates that many children are able to make this distinction by age 4 (Barrett & Behne, 2004). Studies also find that children often rely on what they hear from adults, as well as on their own observations (Harris & Koenig, 2006). This is not always a good thing. Adult language sometimes baffles children ("Argggh! The battery's dead!").

Does Anxiety Influence Children's Thoughts About Death?

Some studies focus on thoughts, some on fears. In everyday life, these processes jumble along together. A recent study brings them together. The researchers conclude that awareness of the biological basis of death reduces uncertainty and restrains disturbing fantasies. They encourage adults to discuss death and dying with children in biological terms. Fears are most common in the nighttime, as expressed by younger children, and by girls, though very common for both genders (Gordon et al., 2007). The specific fears are numerous, and often vague. What they have in common is anxiety about personal safety. Most of the children find somebody with whom to share their fears. The researchers note that death-related fears show up early in childhood and continue thereafter. They propose an explanation: survival is an urgent issue right from the beginning of life, so one should be ever vigilant.

Does *death anxiety* take on different characteristics from early to later childhood? Lonetto (1980) found that younger children expressed more separation anxiety, while older children expressed more sadness about death itself. "The happy smiles of the dead depicted by the younger children have all but faded away in the representations given by ten-year-olds, who show the dead with closed mouths and eyes" (p. 146). The older children were more likely to depict death as scary and horrible, and they also focus more on their own possible death as compared with others.

By age 11 there was more use of abstract symbols in the drawings, indicating a new way of coping with death. At this age children could hint at death and represent its meanings (e.g., a valentine with tears pouring down its face) without having to draw all the unpleasant details. The use of black as the only color became dominant among the older children. Jenny put it into words:

> Death is blackness . . . like when you close your eyes. It's cold and when you die your body is cold. Frightening, I don't want to die . . . I wonder then, how I'm going to die . . . I feel scared and I try to forget it. (p. 154)

Cultural Influences on Children's Concepts of Death

Children's thoughts about death are influenced by cultural belief systems and patterns of communication. In the United States, Christian beliefs have been the most pervasive, and adults have mostly tried to avoid death-talk with children, a situation that has been moderating in recent years. Chinese children in Taiwan perhaps have more to deal with in constructing their own views (Yang & Chen, 2007). They are exposed to a lively mix of religious traditions that have varying interpretations of dying, death, mourning, and afterlife. There is, however, a prevailingly negative climate of feeling regarding death—even more intense for those who have abandoned all religions. As compared with the United States, Taiwanese children are more likely to have been influenced by the belief that death is death: if anything happens thereafter it is strange and hardly worth thinking about. Many children try to discuss death with their parents, who turn out to be even more avoidant than their American counterparts. Like American children, the Taiwanese draw images from the media with its emphasis on violent deaths. Unlike American children, they also have ghosts to deal with, an enduring part of the Chinese legacy.

Japanese culture presents similar challenges to the child's development of death concepts and attitudes.

The negative view of death is so deeply embedded in Japanese society that even professionally trained personnel tend to think that the mention of death could hurt and shock children, a taboo almost unavoidable in Japanese culture. Children symbolize hope and the future, and as such, are to be kept as far as possible from death. Consequently, very little is known about Japanese children's perceptions of death (Sagara-Rosemeyer & Davies, 2007, p. 204.)

Japanese children today are exposed not only to the death communication taboo, but also to the sharp edges of a fragmenting traditional culture. Violent crimes by youth and suicide rates are among the signs and alarms of this accelerating shift from "the old ways" to whatever new situation will emerge. Sagara-Rosemeyer and Davies sampled children's responses through interviews, drawings, and discussion of the drawings. One of the most interesting findings was the children's conceptions of life, death, and afterlife as a totality, a flow that begins with God's gift of *Inochi* (life) to the embryo. This conception seems to differ from the attitude most often observed in the United States and other Western nations, namely, that life and death should keep their places in separate categories. There is at least the hint that Japanese children tend to view the course of life and death within the frame of a larger picture. Nevertheless, like the Chinese children, they also encounter the challenge of integrating Eastern religious tradition with Christianity and its images of heaven and hell.

The possible effects of exposure to violence becomes an issue wherever children's death concepts are studied. For example, children in Sweden and the U.S. had similar concepts of death at the same age. However, United States children more often depicted violent causes of death, while Swedish children more often depicted chapels in cemeteries, tombstones, crosses on church steeples, caskets, and other cultural symbols of loss and grief. It is possible that the much greater frequency of violence and death on U.S. television as compared with Swedish television may have a strong bearing on these differences in children's representations of death (Wass, 2002). Children who grow up as witnesses to violent death are likely to have different outlooks than those who have experienced a more protective environment. There is also growing evidence that witnessing sudden and violent death, as in a disaster, can have a powerfully disturbing effect on children, including severe posttraumatic stress syndrome (Eksi et al., 2007). Such a traumatic experience, especially if not ameliorated by supportive interventions, can have an enduring effect on the individual's basic conception of life, death, and self.

The role of religious beliefs and expectations is suggested by a study of Muslim girls, ages 6 through 10, in South Africa (Anthony & Bhana, 1988/1989). The realization that death is universal and inevitable seemed to be grasped at an earlier age by Muslim children—but this did not mean that they also accepted the irreversibility of death. "They believe that the dead come alive again under certain circumstances, such as when angels question them in the grave. It can, thus, be seen that the responses of the children are characteristic of their cultural and religious environments" (p. 225). The Muslim children were also more likely to believe in the importance of praying for the dead. No doubt there are many other variations in children's thinking about death as they respond to their culture's belief systems and expectations. It has become all too common to see newsreel footage of children playing at being soldiers in cities where many continue to die of actual violence.

Children born before and after the conquest of fatal childhood diseases and the introduction of television differ in their experiences. Children who view Disney movies could come across more than 20 death scenes. They will notice that all the justified deaths are those of "the bad guys" (Cox, Garrett, & Graham, 2004/2005). This suggests:

the trend in Disney films to vilify the antagonists to a point where they are seen as deserving their

death. . . . All unjustified deaths were those of protagonists, showing that good characters never deserve to die (p. 278).

Parents seem to have their work cut out for them in helping children interpret deaths seen in movies or television. Is it helpful to think of death as something one either does or does not deserve? Even more difficult questions might be raised by the violent and gritty deaths that are now common in video entertainment. Before movies and television took hold, children were more likely to learn about death from real life events. My father would occasionally speak of his brothers who died of diphtheria in childhood. Many other long-lived adults have memories of family members dying from contagions and infections that are seldom encountered today. On the other hand, school shootings that have traumatized many children were practically unknown in past generations. Every new generation of children brings distinctive experiences to its understanding of death-related issues. It would be questionable to assume that tomorrow's children, growing up in tomorrow's world, will have precisely the same ways of thinking and feeling about death as the children of today and yesterday.

Do Imaginary Friends Die?

Some children have very good friends who live only in their imagination. These companions can play many roles in a child's life and are most often associated with a normal course of development. The impressive and often diverting variety of *imaginary companions* has been well described (Gleason, 2004). Although known in the literature as "companions," almost all our respondents preferred to speak of them as "friends," so both terms will be used here. Could these imaginary friends (IFs) help us learn more about the child's understanding of loss, change, and death? Taylor (1999) shares one of the few reports in the literature of an imaginary friend's death. A 4-year-old boy had played regularly with Tippy, an imaginary girl, and Tompy, an imaginary boy, both a year older than himself. A few months later, though, his great friends were no longer part of his life.

Her imaginary friend is a special part of her life. But what will become of this friend later?

ADULT: Do you have a pretend friend named Tompy?

CHILD: Oh, Tompy, Tompy. They were dead. They got dead today. Oh . . . the day before the day. They just got dead.

ADULT: So how old is Tompy?

CHILD: Well, he's 7,200 years old . . . . But Tompy's real defective. He has a sore knee. . . . We're really good friends (nodding). The other one's a girl.

ADULT: They're good friends?

CHILD: Yeah, they were.

ADULT: They were? So, are they still alive?

CHILD: Oh, they're still alive but . . . (makes sound effect and falls back as though hit). . . .

ADULT: Do you play with Tompy sometimes?

CHILD: (In critical tone of voice) Did you forget what I told you? (pp. 123–124).

This interaction was more complicated than the summary given above. In the middle of the discussion, the child was distracted by Gadget—his latest imaginary friend, a small and frisky mouse. The child was inconsistent—perhaps capricious—in shifting Tompy back and forth between alive and dead. Furthermore:

The child's words and his tone of voice suggested that Tompy was remembered with some fondness, but no profound sense of loss. Gadget had clearly taken over (p. 124).

Dr. Lynn Fox, one of my non-imaginary friends, and I decided to explore this facet of the child's world. Retrospective interviews were conducted with university students and staff. Two children who were still acquainted with their IFs also were scooped into the study (Kastenbaum & Fox, 2007). The general findings were consistent with previous studies. Most of the IFs had entered their lives during the preschool years and exited around the time they entered kindergarten; a few stayed in the picture much longer. The IF usually looked like anybody else, although only visible to the lucky child. Most were obedient and adoring companions. Some were a more daring version of one's own self. The IFs were most often regarded as being as real as "regular" people. However, there was also a floating quality: the IF could be more or less real, depending on circumstances (at its "most realist" when nobody else was around).

So—did imaginary friends die? Yes, but that was not the most common outcome. The relationship usually ended with the IF fading away as school days began with a host of new friends and activities. These partings were uneventful and unmourned. It had been time for the IF to go. However, about one IF in five did perish. Their deaths were the result of accident, error, disaster, or bad luck or sometimes because of something the child either did or failed to do. In most cases, the children had believed their IF would never—and should never die. "She was *mine*, and should always be there when I wanted her!"

The circumstances of death offer illuminating glimpses of the young child's developing and rather experimental worldview. An IF could be killed in an event that the child actually experienced. For example:

> "I was wearing my green coat that I wore all the time. I was naughty, I climbed the credenza. It fell on us both. And that's how he died. . . . I remember it was 2 P.M. and sunny outside. I looked at the wallpaper as the light shone on it, and saw the gold flecks, and said, 'Oh, that looks pretty.' Then the shelves fell over us. . . . I didn't talk to him. I just knew he was gone. No tears, no sadness."

Another type of death involved the impulsive use of word magic. IF Todd was so well accepted by (real) family that the boy's father asked what

kind of pizza he would like when they went out that night. The boy replied:

> "Todd's not coming. He got run over. By a fire engine. Run over dead. He just ran out into the street to see what was happening and the fire engine got him. I don't know why I said that. It just came into my head and that's the way it was. . . . I don't know if I felt sad at all. Just something that happened."

There was more context for the unexpected death of IF Barneybus. The girl's mother had been pregnant but "lost" the baby: a disturbing and mystifying event. When a neighbor girl demanded a turn at playing with Barneybus, "I told her that he had gone to the hospital because he was dead. That wasn't true, but that's what popped out of me. But after I said that, that seemed to be it. He must have been dead because that's what I said!"

If words could kill, so loving, even desperate, attention could keep either an IF or a "regular" person alive:

> "If I think hard about people, they won't die. I was worried about the school work and if the kids would like me, I noticed [IF] Emmy wasn't there any more. She just stopped breathing, dead. *I had stopped thinking about that much about her*, so that's what happened."

Mother, having made a batch of her delicious ice cream, told IF Bobby there was not enough for him to have a share this time:

> "He died. Bobby was very upset that he could not be part of the family any more, and he died. That was the end of Bobby."

Many of the children were not ready to accept the adult insistence on a firm distinction between categories. An IF, then, did not have to be always either alive or dead. There was an easygoing fluidity in the children's way of thinking. For example, Graham had not said much about the imaginary friend he had wanted to keep to himself. He surprised his family one day by saying that Jeff Green was dead: no further information forthcoming. Come Halloween, though, and Jeff Green was brought back to life "this one more time, so he could go trick and treating." Jeff would replace Graham for this occasion. The next day, Jeff was dead again, which did not disturb Graham. "Jeff was like me, only more cool. We thought he should have a good time." Nevertheless, Graham was adamant that alive and dead were absolutely different conditions—and that Fred Green, alive or dead, would be with him for the rest of his life.

The overall picture is of lively young minds that move between fantasy and reality without the constraints that are expected of adults. Ideas of life and death flow and float as part of this sea of adventuring. Identity is also subject to whatever transformations the child can come up with. For example, the essence of an IF can be shape-shifted to a frisky little mouse, and friends can be created, multiplied, and dismissed as need or whim dictates.

Deaths of imaginary friends are recognized as significant but do not appear to have deep and enduring impact. This could be a way of developing a sense of mastery over loss, change, and death. One can experience a kind of real loss and yet also a kind of not real loss, and so build up confidence. Furthermore, the older child and adult often report a sense of having survived their imaginary friends, even if those friends have just faded away into the mists of time rather than died. The creation and loss of imaginary childhood friends could be regarded as a rite of passage to the adult world, with its harsh separation of reality and fantasy.

I love the juice, but the sun goes up; I see
the stars
and the moonstar goes up,
And there always goes today. And the sun
Love people. But one always dies.
Dogs will die very sooner
Than mummies and daddies and sisters
and
brothers because
They'll not die til a hundred and
Because I love them dearly
—Hilary-Anne Farley, age 5 (in Lewis, 1966, p. 143)

Hilary-Anne Farley, a Canadian girl only 5 years of age at the time, was bursting with love but also acutely aware that time and loss are inevitable: "there always goes today;" "but one always die." Does this sound like a child who has no clue about the reality and universality of death? She even recognizes differential longevity and the ambiguity of time. Here is time as the enemy that takes people away, but here also is time as insulation between now and death ("They'll not die til a hundred"). Young Ms. Farley calls upon the force of her love and need to protect her family from death. They will live a long life "Because I love them dearly."

For Better or for Worse

Wish fulfillment? Of course. But the poem as a whole resolutely faces the reality of death and loss. Children who relinquish their IFs one way or another are also testing and practicing for the more profound losses that time and circumstance will bring.

HOW DO CHILDREN COPE WITH BEREAVEMENT?

For some children, death has already become a reality. They have lost a person who had been very important in their lives. We look now at the effects of *bereavement* on children and the ways in which they attempt to cope. We will see that an increasing number of American children may be at risk for prolonged and disturbing grief reactions as a result of a traumatic bereavement.

A Death in the Family: Effects on the Child

A death in the family can draw attention away from the needs of the children. When a parent dies, for example, the surviving parent's grief can interfere temporarily with the ability to care for the emotional, or even the physical, needs of the children. Sometimes it is a *sibling* who dies. The parents may have become so involved in the plight of the dying child that other children are neglected. The surviving children may feel isolated if the adults fail to recognize their distress signals. Sensitive adults take into account both the child's developmental level and the role that the deceased person had played in the child's life. What does this child understand about separation and death? Does the child understand that death is final and universal? Was the deceased person an older sibling whom the child had looked up to? Was the deceased a younger sibling whom the child had resented as a competitor for parental attention? Does the surviving child believe that she could join the lost sibling if she managed to get herself killed?

Attention should be given to the quality of the child's personal and family situation prior to the bereavement. Had this been a tightly knit family in which the child enjoyed a strong sense of love and security? Was it a broken or bent family characterized by anxiety and insecurity? The impact of bereavement is influenced by the child's developmental level, the specific loss that has been experienced, and the previous pattern of family security and affection.

Bereaved children may express their distress in ways that do not seem closely associated with the loss. For example, serious problems in school may appear for the first time. Children may turn on playmates with sudden anger. Fear of the dark or of being alone may reappear. The child's behavior pattern can show the effect of bereavement without an obvious show of sorrow. They may be further inhibited from direct expression if commanded by the surviving parent to be "brave." Tears are then stigmatized as signs of weakness and disobedience.

Young children often express their memories of a lost parent through specific activities that had linked them together. An adult can preserve a valued relationship by replaying memories in private or sharing them with others. But a 2-year-old boy who loses his father is more likely to express his longing and sadness through actions:

> For weeks he spent much of his time repeating the daily play activities that had constituted the essence of his relationship with his father. He also insisted, over and over, on taking the walks he had taken with his father, stopping at the stores where his father had shopped and recalled specific items (Furman, 1974, p. 55).

The toddler's need added to the mother's emotional pain, but she recognized that it was the best way he had to adjust to the loss. Young children are likely to focus on a few strong memory images, in contrast to the bereaved spouse who has many recollections from all the years of marriage, and more skill in verbalization. The young child carries much of the remembrance of the lost parent in the form of scenes and activities shared with the lost person. Many years later, there might be an episode of unexpected overwhelming sadness when a situation touches off a precious memory. The mental image of the lost parent often remains with children long after the death. The silent sadness of the bereaved child can be painful for the adult to acknowledge. But how are we to support and comfort unless we can accept the reality of the child's suffering?

It can be even more difficult to accept the child's response when it includes anger. The surviving parent may be horrified to hear criticisms of the deceased parent coming from the children. This can happen precisely at the time that the widowed spouse is at the peak of idealizing the lost husband or wife. Yet the expression of anger may be a necessary part of the child's adaptation to the loss. One of the reasons some adults find it very painful to accept the child's expression of mixed feelings toward the deceased is that these feelings are within them as well. Whoever helps a bereaved spouse express grief openly and begins the long process of recovery is also helping the children by returning the strength and sensitivity of their remaining parent.

Several consistent differences have been found in the behavior of children who have suffered parental bereavement as compared with children who have both parents living.

Children with parental bereavement:

- Tend to be more submissive, dependent, and introverted;
- Show a higher frequency of maladjustment and emotional disturbance, including suicidality (Chapter 8);
- Show a higher frequency of delinquent and criminal behavior;
- Perform less adequately in school and on tests of cognitive functioning;
- Experience more physical symptoms;
- Become more concerned that the family will fall apart.

Coleen, the girl who was afraid she had hurt her mother by stepping on her grave, experienced several of these difficulties. Within a month of the death, she reported headaches and stomachaches and became extremely worried about her father's increased drinking and grouchiness. To make it even worse, her father and her sister were giving each other a hard

time. "Mother used to make it better and stop them, but she isn't here anymore" (Christ, 2000, p. 103). It is useful to note that (1) many of Coleen's concerns were linked with specific situations and (2) she was already exploring ways of dealing with these problems. For example, she would soon be a junior bridesmaid for her cousin, even though Mom wouldn't be there with her, "but I'll pretend she is watching me from heaven." *Pretend!* She had the mental flexibility to find comfort in the idea of her mother watching her from heaven while not necessarily taking this to be an objective fact. Coleen was also anxious about the way her friends would treat her when she returned to school—would they be asking a lot of uncomfortable questions, or what?

As it turned out, the friends were supportive and understanding, sending her many condolence and encouragement cards even before she came back to school. And it was that much better when she was chosen to dance in a show at school. Coleen was fortunate in having a supportive family and the opportunity to meet with a school counselor, but she also demonstrated her own resourcefulness in coping with her situation. We see bereaved children's realistic concerns and strenuous efforts to deal with them repeatedly in case histories such as those described by Grace Hyslop Christ (2000). Although children may have incomplete conceptions of death, their ability to recognize and deal with the realities should not be underestimated. The more fully we can enter into the child's private world of hurt and fear, the better position we are in to provide understanding and comfort.

Posttraumatic Stress Disorder (PTSD) Following a Violent Death

Sudden, unexpected death has a more severe impact on the survivors, whether children or adults (see Chapter 11). This impact can be further intensified by threatening features of the death—for example, a drive-by shooting, a suicide, or mutilation of the corpse in an accident

There is now more professional and public awareness of the syndrome known as *post-traumatic stress disorder* (PTSD). This condition was officially recognized as a diagnostic entity in 1980. It became salient during the Vietnam War, and again currently in people serving in Afghanistan or Iraq. A person comes through extremely stressful situations and at a later time, suffers "flashbacks" of the experience. During these episodes, the individual behaves in seemingly irrational, bizarre, and perhaps dangerous ways—not at all in keeping with his or her previous personality. These episodes often are frightening to family, friends, and the individual experiencing them.

Recognition of PTSD in children who have experienced *traumatic* bereavements or other encounters with death is now starting to receive some of the attention it deserves (e.g., Doka, 2000). Some teachers and school systems have already developed programs and techniques for reaching out to children who have been exposed to traumatic death.

Children with PTSD are more likely than others to have difficulty paying attention, concentrating, and making and keeping friends. Such a dysfunctional pattern is especially harmful in childhood, when so many basic personal and interpersonal skills are being developed (Weaver & Festa, 2003). The child with PTSD is also likely to be frightened, as shown by the following excerpt from a psychotherapy session with Nancy Boyd Webb (2002) in which Susan, age 9, shares her reaction to the automobile death of a school mate.

SUSAN: I'm having bad dreams that wake me up every night. Then in the morning I don't want to get up. I'm tired all the time, even when I go to bed at 8 o'clock.

WEBB: That sounds pretty bad! Can you tell me what the dreams are like?

SUSAN: I dream that there is a gorilla in my closet and that he is going to sneak up to my bed and grab me and then take me away and roast me on a barbecue.

WEBB: That must be pretty scary! Does the dream wake you up?

SUSAN: Yes, and then I run into my mom's bed (p. 196).

Children can be helped to overcome PTSD, but first we must be observant enough to recognize their distress and its possible connection to a disturbing death-related experience. In recent years, it has become evident that children are vulnerable to PTSD as a result of terrorist attacks. Children who had lost a friend or acquaintance in the 1995 Oklahoma City bombing of a federal office building had PTSD symptoms and also watched more television coverage of the disaster. Even children who did not know any of the victims experienced distress and disturbance, though not to the same extent (Pfefferbaum et al., 2000).

The 9/11 attack at the World Trade Center affected many children in the New York City area. Nearly one child in five suffered a severe or very severe reaction (Fairbrother et al., 2003). Parental bereavement through terrorist attack has been found to have physiological as well as psychological effects that persist for years afterward (Pfeffer et al., 2006). Their severe stress reaction includes dysfunction of the endocrine system that undermines influence, personality, balance, and coping skills. Anxiety and depression continue in body as well as mind. Family counseling and therapy has proven useful for some of these suffering children.

Long-Term Effects of Childhood Bereavement

The effects of childhood bereavement are not limited to childhood. Loss of a significant person in childhood can have an important effect on subsequent development. Major physical and mental illnesses occur more often in the adult lives of those who were bereaved as children. For example, some children take on the identity of their dead sibling. This is most likely to happen when the family had given preference to the child who is now deceased and then responds with approval to the impersonation. The borrowed identity is likely to generate significant problems in adult life.

Nevertheless, people bereaved in childhood often demonstrate resilience. For example, mothers whose own mothers had died in childhood showed symptoms of depression, worried about their own deaths, were overprotective, and perfectionists (Zall, 1994). Despite these problems, however, many proved to be effective mothers themselves. They responded to the challenge of their own parental role by completing their unfinished grieving over the deaths of their mothers.

> For many years I didn't want children. I decided to take the risk, with my husband's encouragement, and the experience of motherhood has been the most challenging and even more delightful than I ever dreamed. Because of my early loss and fear of dying and leaving my children, I have been extremely conscientious about teaching the children to separate from me very early in their lives. I tend to spend a great deal of time with them.

Parental bereavement can be found in the childhood of many people who made exceptional achievements in adulthood. Consider, for example, the great naturalist, Charles Darwin. All through his life Darwin retained the memory of his mother's deathbed, her black velvet gown, and the work table. Curiously, though, he remembered hardly anything of her appearance or his conversations with her. He remembered being sent for, going into her room, being greeted by his father, and crying afterward. Even stranger, Darwin had much more detailed recollections of the funeral of a soldier that he attended a few weeks later.

Biographer Ralph Colp, Jr. (1975) was struck by Darwin's apparent repression of many of his memories of his mother and her death while details of the soldier's death remained fresh in his mind. Colp finds that death-related themes were closely interwoven with Darwin's work throughout his life. These themes showed up even in the notes he made in the margins of books, as well as in his dreams. One of the major themes disclosed was a "keen instinct against death." Colp and others believe there is a connection between Darwin's ardent advocacy of life and his fascination with the evolution of new life forms. Darwin's growing awareness of a process of natural selection in which entire species die off resonated with the feelings he still carried from the time of his mother's death. In his middle adult years,

Darwin expressed fear of sudden death and regarded his theory as an indirect form of continued personal survival.

Near the end of his life, Darwin returned to the first creatures that interested him as a young boy—worms. He had enjoyed fishing and had mixed feelings about sacrificing worms to this cause. As an elderly and ailing man, Darwin did little studies of worms. In Colp's words, "Thus, the old man, who as a boy had killed worms, now, night after night, observed how he would soon be eaten by worms" (1975, p. 200). This line of thinking was not as morbid as it might sound. Scientist Darwin respected worms as coinhabitants of planet Earth, who have a key role in maintaining the living ecology by literally passing the earth through themselves. That he, too, Charles Darwin, would become part of the worm and part of the earth again was not a cliché or a horror story but an acceptable aspect of our natural history.

Ten thousand examples would provide 10,000 different stories of the direct and indirect ways in which childhood bereavement influences the entire life course. How each story turns out years later is likely to depend much on the kind of attention and support the child receives. We look now at some approaches that have proved useful.

Helping Children Cope with Bereavement

1. *Develop and maintain an open communication pattern with children.* It is unrealistic to wait until a crisis situation develops. The child who is shunted aside whenever there are "important things" to discuss is deprived of opportunity to learn communication skills that are useful in difficult situations. The family in which children feel that they can receive a careful and sympathetic hearing is a family that will be able to cope more resourcefully together when faced with bereavement or other stressful life events.

2. *Give children the opportunity to decide about attending the funeral.* Adults often assume that children would either not understand funerals or be harmed by the experience.

However, many children appreciate the opportunity to make their own decisions. It can be helpful to describe what the funeral will be like in words the child can understand, and answer questions that might arise at that time. Some families also encourage children to make suggestions about details of the funeral. By being included in the family drama, children felt acknowledged and thereby supported by their families, thus setting the stage for legitimizing their roles as mourners and to say goodbye, to feel close to their parent for one last time, and for the community to join them in doing this. Nevertheless, Silverman (2000) and other experts suggest that the child who has decided against attending the funeral should not be forced to do so against his or her wishes.

3. *Check out what the child is thinking and feeling—do not assume that we know what the death means to him or her.* Griffith (2003) observes that the youngest are many times the unseen, unknown, and invisible grievers (p. 217). Children as young as 3 years of age have been helped with the expression of their grief through art therapy, but first we must be willing to enter their worlds of experience rather than make assumptions:

"With children never interpret a head nod when you are explaining something to them as you would with an adult. They have learned the gesture from adults, but frequently it is for the child simply the easiest way to get the 'helping' adult to leave them alone. . . . Always gently ask the child to tell you what they have just heard and to explain it to you in their own words" (Hersh, 1995, p. 91).

4. *Encourage the expression of feelings.* This point was made by many of the mothers in our case history study. Mental health professionals agree. Young children can express themselves through play and drawings, often enhanced by storytelling. Feelings can also be expressed through vigorous games that allow the discharge of tension and anger. An especially valuable way for children to express their feelings is to help comfort others. For example, a child attending a funeral later reported that "At the end while I was crying, my little cousin came up to me and gave me a hug and said it was okay. She was only three" (Silverman & Worden, 1992, p. 329). Comforting and altruistic behavior can begin early in life.

5. *Provide convincing assurance that there will always be somebody to love and look after the child.* The death of a parent arouses fears that the surviving parent and other important people may also abandon the child. Verbal assurances are useful, but not always sufficient. Bereaved children may become anxious when the surviving parent is out of sight or has not come home at the expected time. Sending the children away for a while often intensifies the feeling of abandonment. Adult relatives and friends who spend time with the children after their bereavement are helping the surviving parent to provide reassurance that there will always be somebody there for them.

6. *Professional counseling deserves consideration if the bereaved children are at special risk.* The death of both parents, for example, constitutes a special risk, as does a death for which the children might feel that they are somehow at blame. There is one special risk that each year arises for thousands of children:

Mom told us to sit down and she said, "Girls, your Dad died." We both cried right away. We went down to the garage where everybody was. People began holding us and trying to make us feel better. No one knew what to say. We felt like everyone was just staring at us. It was like a big, bad dream. And to make matters worse, we found out from our Mom that Dad had killed himself. . . . It still is hard for us to understand. We were only five and nine years old (Carolyn and Kristin as quoted in Dahlke, 1994, pp. 116–117).

The two girls had to contend—suddenly—both with the death of their father and the puzzle and possible stigma of his suicide. Their consuming question was: "If Daddy loved me, why did he leave me?" This became the title of a little book that the girls wrote together over a period of time with the encouragement of a professional counselor, David Dahlke. Every page of the girls' book reflects their personal growth experience as they explored their thoughts, feelings, values, and choices with the counselor's assistance. We learn, for example, that the children became afraid that if mother married again her new husband would also commit suicide. Carolyn reported, "I felt Dad threatened suicide a lot. I asked him, 'What if you kill yourself?' and he said, 'I won't do that!' . . . But he did. He lied to us. . . . Dad was mixed up" (p. 117).

Carolyn and Kristin showed insight and resilience as they dealt with their loss and the questions it raised. Other children who suffer parental bereavement under traumatic and stressful conditions can also receive valuable assistance from qualified counselors.

7. *Select an age-appropriate book or two that speaks to a child's sense of loss after a death.* Fortunately, there are now many sensitive and helpful books available written for this purpose. Somebody in your circle of friends may have such a book to recommend, or you can consult the valuable survey on death-related literature for children edited by Charles A. Corr (2003/2004).

THE DYING CHILD

Children sometimes think about death, loss, and separation even when there has been no obvious event to arouse their concern. Writing about his own childhood, Spalding Gray (1986) recalls:

the time when I woke up in the middle of the night and saw my brother Rocky standing on his bed, blue in the face and gasping for air, crying out that he was dying. My mother and father were standing beside the bed trying to quiet him, and Mom said, "Calm down, dear, it's all in your mind." And after he calmed down, my father went back to bed, and my mother turned out the light and sat on the edge of Rocky's bed in the dark. . . . We were all there, very quiet, in the dark, and then Rocky would start in, "Mom, when I die, is it forever?" And she said, "Yes, dear." And then Rocky said, "Mom, when I die, is it forever, and ever, and ever?" and she said, "Uh-huh, dear." And he said, "Mom, when I die is it forever and ever and ever . . . ?" I just went right off to this (p. 14).

It should not be surprising, then, to learn that children who actually are afflicted with life-threatening illnesses are keenly aware of their predicaments. Shira Putter, who died at the age of 9 from a rare form of diabetes, has left a diary that includes this sadly perceptive entry: "Daddy doesn't care about me. I know he comes to visit me practically every day, but once he comes he always seems so far away. It's like he can't wait to leave again." (Grollman, 1988, p. 12). She was reluctant to share this concern with her mother because "I didn't want her to get upset." But she did tell her mother who then explained "that Daddy does love me and that was part of the problem. He loves me so much that it hurts him to see me sick and in pain. She asked me to please try to understand." This little episode put everybody more at ease, including Daddy, and restored the usual family pattern of warm and caring interactions.

Dying children may hesitate to share their concerns because of the fear that this would make their parents feel even worse. On other occasions, Shira did remain silent when she could see that her parents were upset by new complications in her condition. Far from being unaware of the perils they face, children may take a kind of parental role themselves and try to protect adults from anxiety and sorrow.

Each day can bring some new threat or challenge. Shira, for example, had to cope with the fact that her favorite doctor took himself off her case because he was so upset by her continued physical decline. The fear of abandonment by the most important people in their lives is often a major concern of the dying child—and too often based upon the way that some adults do distance themselves from the child. The adult's personal anxiety is an other type of response. Neonatologists with intense personal fear of dying were more likely to approve of hastening the death of terminally ill infants by sedation or withdrawal of treatment (Barr, 2007).

Shira and her family were able to maintain mutual support until the very end. In one of her last diary entries, Shira writes of their Passover celebration:

> In a way, it seemed like any other Passover. We said all the prayers. We sang all the songs. But when we were reciting the blessing, thanking God for letting us celebrate this special occasion, everyone started crying. Then, for about a minute, we all stood together quietly, holding hands. It was as if, without saying anything, I was telling everyone what was in my heart. That I loved them and wanted to be with them, but I couldn't make it much longer. That I wasn't afraid of dying anymore, so they had to let me go. They just had to (p. 70).

Anthropologist Myra Bluebond-Langner (1977, 1988) spent many hours listening to hospitalized children and observing their interactions with parents and staff. The children were keenly aware of their situations. One morning, for example, Jeffrey asked Bluebond-Langner to read to him from the classic children's book, *Charlotte's Web* (White, 1952) "the part where Charlotte dies." This chapter, "Last Day," offers a combination of humor, drama, and consolation. "Nothing can harm you now" is one of its thoughts. Another is: "No one was with her when she died." When Bluebond-Langner completed her reading of the chapter, Jeffrey dozed off. He died that afternoon.

Many of the terminally ill children that Bluebond-Langner observed passed through five stages in the acquisition of information:

1. I have a serious illness.
2. I know what drugs I am receiving and what they are supposed to do.
3. I know the relationship between my symptoms and the kind of treatment I am getting.
4. I realize now that I am going through a cycle of feeling worse, getting better, then getting worse again. The medicines don't work all the time.
5. I know that this won't go on forever. There's an end to the remissions and the relapses and to the kind of medicine they have for me. When the drugs stop working, I will die pretty soon.

The children soon became sophisticated about hospital routines. They learned the names of all their drugs and how to tell one kind of staff member from another. Little escaped them. Staff members would have been astonished had they realized how much the children picked up. Most of all, perhaps, the children learned from each other. They would notice that they were now on the last drug that another child had received before his or her death or that people were now starting to treat them differently, meaning that something important had changed in their conditions. Seriously ill children work hard at understanding what is happening to them. The adult who assumes that a sick child is too young to understand anything is probably making a serious mistake. Consider this sequence reported by Sourkes (1996):

A 3-year-old boy played the same game with a stuffed duck and a toy ambulance each time he was hospitalized. The duck would be sick and need to go to the hospital by ambulance. The boy would move the ambulance, making siren noises.

THERAPIST: How is the duck?
CHILD: Sick.
THERAPIST: Where is he going?
CHILD: To the hospital.
THERAPIST: What are they going to do?
CHILD: Make him better . . .

During what turned out to be the boy's terminal admission, he played the same game with the duck. However, the outcome of the ritual changed dramatically:

THERAPIST: How is the duck?
CHILD: Sick.
THERAPIST: Is he going to get better?
CHILD: (Shaking his head slowly) Ducky not get better. Ducky die (pp. 157–158).

Two days later, the boy drew a picture of "a vibrant firefly, smiling broadly as it emerges from the blackness into the . . . light." He explained: "Fireflies glow in the dark and show others the way" (p. 158). He died that evening.

Care of the Dying Child

Along with emotional support and sensitive communication, dying children need medical, nursing, and other support services. In recent years, the hospice approach to terminal care has been extended to include children. The basic philosophy is the same as with hospice care in general: to help the dying person experience the highest quality of life possible under the circumstances. This is accomplished by skillfully controlling pain and other symptoms and by working with the family to support their own caregiving efforts.

Although a hospital stay is sometimes necessary, the focus is usually on home care. Children as well as adults often feel most secure within their own homes. Because there can be situations in which neither the hospital nor the home seems to be the best place to care for the dying child, some hospice organizations have also established respite care facilities. These are usually small, home-like centers in which the child can receive care for a few days or weeks while the family copes with other problems. Levetown (2002) points out that the children's own views of their situations are more likely to be understood and respected if the care team includes a child psychologist or child life therapist. The American Academy of Pediatrics has endorsed the inclusion of a child therapist, but this has not yet become a standard practice.

Whether the children are at home, in a respite care center, or in a hospital-based hospice service, the overall philosophy remains the same: give comfort, relieve distress, and help the patients and family preserve their most basic values of life during this difficult time. A growing number of pediatric caregivers are applying hospice principles and techniques. Up-to-date information can be obtained from Children's Hospice International (www.chionline.org). Another useful source of information is the Initiative for Pediatric Palliative Care (www.ippcweb.org). There are encouraging trends. The comfort care needs of terminally ill infants and children were not generally given high priority in the past. Recent reports demonstrate advances both in compassionate (MellixhMP, 2007) and technologically sophisticated care (Hooke et al., 2007).

The care of dying children has much in common with the situation of bereaved children:

1. The opportunity to express their concerns through conversation, play, drawing, writing, shared reading—whatever modality is most effective and natural for the particular child. Modeling clay figures or drawing pictures of the family may help to transform inner feelings into a tangible communication that can be shared with others. Resentment and anger may be expressed on occasion in the children's play or art; this is usually a natural response to overwhelming circumstances, and the opportunity to "get it out" often proves valuable.

2. Confirmation that they are still normal and valuable people, despite the impairments and limitations imposed by illness. Sensitive parents and other caregivers will find ways to affirm and strengthen children's basic sense of self. They will not allow "dyingness" to overshadow every interaction, every plan, every project. Instead, opportunities will be found for children to do things that are still within their sphere of competence and to stay involved with roles and activities that have brought pleasure. One 10-year-old boy, for example, taught his younger siblings how to play chess while he was dying of *leukemia;* a girl, also 10, kept the statistics and figured the batting averages for her softball team after she herself could no longer play. With the availability of home computers, it is now also possible for children to enjoy computer-assisted learning programs, drawing, writing, and games with relatively little expenditure of energy.

3. Assurance that family members and other important people will not abandon children, no matter what happens. Nonverbal behavior is a vital component of interaction

that can either affirm or undermine the family's words of reassurance. As illustrated by Shira's diary, children are quite aware of discomfort, tension, and conflict on the part of the adults in their lives. By their everyday actions as well as their words, parents and other caregivers must continue to convey their dedication to being with—to staying with—dying children, come what may.

4. Reassurance that they will not be forgotten. Often dying children fear they will not be a part of what will happen in the family when they are no longer there. They may also fear that they will be replaced in the family constellation by another child, instead of remembered and valued for their uniqueness. In some situations, it may be useful to use mental imagery exercises to help children prepare for impending separation and to participate in the future through imagination. Children may also come up with their own ways of feeling a part of the future, requiring of the adults only their sympathetic attention and cooperation. For example, a child may wish to give some favorite toys to a sibling or friend, or to make a video that can be watched on birthdays or other special occasions.

In addition to these common needs and themes, each child with a life-threatening illness is almost certain to have distinctive ideas, hopes, and apprehensions. What special wish or secret fear is on the mind of this particular child? There is no substitute for careful listening and observation and for respecting the individuality of each child.

Siblings of the Dying Child

He's been sick a lot this year. . . . But I kind of get used to him being sick. . . . I really want to know what it's like to stay home and watch and take care of my brother for a whole day when he's sick. And I know what to do. Every night you (a person with *cystic fibrosis*) have to get on this machine. And it's because you get all this mucus in your lungs and it's hard to breathe. And when you get sick, you really get sick. . . . And sometimes you die at an early age. But I

don't think that will happen to Jason, because he's in pretty good shape. That's about it (Bluebond-Langner, 1996, pp. 78–79).

Eleven-year-old Regan and her family lived every day with 9-year-old Jason's illness and with the prospect of his early death. She adjusted to this situation as did everybody else in the family: Life has to go on, and people have to do what they have to do. She was well informed about her brother's condition and had personal knowledge of somebody who had died young of the same medical condition, cystic fibrosis. But nobody in her family had died—yet. Nobody was dying—yet. Nevertheless, Regan's own childhood experiences were shadowed by the possibility of her brother's death and by the family's daily efforts to carry on "normally" despite their burden of anxiety.

Anxiety and sorrow about the dying child can lead to neglect of other family needs. Parents may not give adequate attention to their own health, for example. The continuing stress can lead to a narrowing of attention, a concentration on "just what most needs to be done," and increased irritability and distraction even on the part of the most devoted parents. And, as recent findings suggest, the brothers and sisters of dying children may be at particular risk during this difficult period.

Bluebond-Langner observes that

The well siblings of terminally ill children live in houses of chronic sorrow. The signs of sorrow, illness, and death are everywhere, whether or not they are spoken of. The signs are written on parents' faces: 'My mother always looks tired now,' and 'Even my Dad's crying a lot.' The signs are there in hushed conversations: 'You learn everything by listening in on the (phone) extension . . .' (1988, p. 9).

The following problems were observed in well siblings in the course of Bluebond-Langner's pioneering research (1977; 1988):

1. Confusion about what role they are supposed to play in the family. Should they try to be like the sick child? Should they try to become "assistant parents"? Or should they become invisible, "just blend into the woodwork and get out of the way"?

2. A feeling of being deceived or rejected by their parents: "They don't tell me the truth. . . . Nobody really cares about me any more. . . ."

3. Uncertainty about the future. "What's to become of all of us?. . . Does it do any good to have plans any more?"

4. Changes in the relationships among the siblings. For example, the illness and hospitalization of the sick child deprives the others of a companion:

> Siblings often find that they cannot reciprocally to one another. . . . For example, while Jake lay dying, complaining of his back hurting him and not being able to breathe, his brothers offered to rub his back. He pushed them away saying, "no, no, not you. Only Mommy now." The ill child's alliances shift from a closeness to both the parent and the sibling to a closeness with the parent divorced from that of the sibling (Bluebond-Langner, 1988, p. 13).

5. Feelings of guilt and ambivalence. The well siblings are distressed by the suffering of the sick child, but may also feel relieved—and feel guilty about feeling relieved—that they are not the ones who are dying.

6. Frustration in not being able to express their feelings and fears to their parents, who are so preoccupied with the dying child and with their own feelings.

Not all well siblings had all these reactions, nor did these feelings occur all the time. In some families, few obvious problems developed until the sick child had become extremely frail and disabled. Until that time, the parents had managed to find some time and energy for the other children and keep a semblance of normal family life going. But the well siblings themselves often took account of changes in the sick child's condition and needs. They recognized that the sick child now required a great deal of attention from the parents and they were less likely to feel rejected or in competition.

Compassionate relatives, friends, neighbors, and teachers can lighten the burden by giving attention to the well siblings during and after the terminal process and by unobtrusively helping the parents in coping with the responsibilities of everyday life. The family with a dying child certainly needs and deserves sensitive, understanding, and mature companionship from all the community.

The Stress of Working with Dying Children

"I can't make good things happen or prevent bad things from happening, no matter how hard I work, no matter what I try. So I just can't keep doing this, I just can't!" *Burnout* has become a familiar term in the workplace. It is used most often in reference to a sense of exhaustion, frustration, and futility. All who provide care for dying children are vulnerable to anxiety and sorrow—sometimes a sense of guilt as well because they are unable to save the child. Papadatou (2006) has identified a condition she calls "the wounded healer." Her research has found that many nurses and physicians become grief-stricken while working with terminally ill children. This is a form of disenfranchised grief (Doka, 2002): Professional caregivers are not supposed to experience and express their patient-related sorrows and anxieties. Unfortunately, health care professionals are not always well prepared for this challenging kind of work. Papadatou believes that the medical profession's traditional emphasis on diagnosis and treatment of the disease has contributed to neglect of the dying child as a person—and neglect as well of the feelings of those who work closely with the dying child (2006).

She describes an innovative educational program for pediatric nurses at Children's Hospital (Athens, Greece). Pediatric nurses are provided with close and supportive supervision as they work with dying children and their families. They are given the opportunity to discuss their cases with a psychologist and work with a supportive professional team. A sensitivity group experience is also included and group members keep a journal of their experiences, providing another outlet for personal reflection. These and other techniques now being evaluated in Athens might well provide a new model that will help to prepare nurses throughout the world to provide care for dying children while also reducing their own stress.

SHARING THE CHILD'S DEATH CONCERNS: A FEW GUIDELINES

It is in the child's own interests to identify threats to his or her well-being, even within the harbor of a loving family. Our children will encounter death in many forms—close and distant, imaginary and realistic. Many parents today received little guidance in death-related matters when they were young. And so may face inner struggles when called upon to respond to a child's questions.

This is not a "how-to" book, but there are several guidelines that have proven helpful.

1. *Be a good observer.* Notice how the child is behaving. Listen to what he or she is really saying. Do not rush in with explanations, reassurances, or diversions unless there is some overriding necessity to do so. You will be more helpful to the child if you are relaxed, patient, and attentive enough to learn what needs the child actually is expressing rather than those you might assume to be there. For example, the child who suddenly asks a parent, "Are you going to be dead?" might have been thinking about something Grandmother said last week or any number of other happenings that aroused this concern. Taking a moment to learn how this question arose in the child's mind could also help to provide an appropriate response.

2. *Do not wait or plan for "one big tell-all."* Maintain a continuing dialogue with the children in your life as occasions present themselves. The death of pets, scenes in movies, newspaper articles, or television programs—whatever brushes with mortality the children have—all can offer the opportunity for discussion. This does not mean, of course, that parents should remain poised to jump on a death dialogue opportunity. But it is more natural and effective to include death as one of the many topics that adults and children can discuss together. And we are more likely to be helpful when we are not ourselves caught up in the midst of a death situation. Combine a child who has been kept ignorant about death with an adult who is grief stricken or uptight and well have something less than the most desirable situation.

3. *Do not expect all of the child's responses to be obvious and immediate.* When a death has occurred or is impending, the child's total response is likely to unfold over time and to express itself in many ways. Changes in sleeping habits, mood, relationships with other children, and demands on adults may reflect part of the child's reaction to the death, even though the connection may not be obvious. Be patient; be available.

4. *Help the child remain secure as part of the family.* Sometimes adults have the panicked impulse to remove children from the scene when death has come too close (e.g., sending them off to a relative or neighbor). Examine such impulses before acting on them. Consider what the children might learn from the opportunity to participate in the family's response and what lingering questions, misinterpretations, and fears might remain if they are excluded.

5. *Use simple and direct language.* Too often what adults say to children becomes a sermon, peppered with words and concepts that mean little to them. Provide children with accurate information. See if they understand what you have said (e.g., by having them explain it back to you) and make sure that you have responded to what they really wanted to know in the first place. At the same time, do not overwhelm the child with a barrage of information that could confuse rather than instruct.

6. *Be accessible.* The child's sense of comfort will be strengthened by the very fact that you are available to talk about death when the need arises. Your expression of feelings that are natural to the situation (worry, sorrow,

perhaps even anger) are not likely to harm the child but rather will provide a basis for sorting out and expressing his or her own feelings.

7. *Be aware of all the children in the family.* It is natural to concentrate the family's resources and attentions on the seriously ill child. Other children in the family continue to need love and reassurance, however, and need to participate somehow in the total process.

8. *Keep the relationship going.* How a life-threatened child responds at a particular moment might be disturbing to parents and other adults. We do not want to see or hear certain responses. Losing the closeness and support of important adults is a great danger to the child. This, in fact, is one of the reasons why children may not share their thoughts and feelings with us. We do not have to approve or agree with everything the child tells us about death, but we do have to maintain a supportive relationship.

THE "RIGHT" TO DECIDE: SHOULD THE CHILD'S VOICE BE HEARD?

The controversial "right to die" issue (Chapter 9) usually focuses on adults but also can arise with children. Consider Marie, for example. Marie was a patient for most of her young life; she had little opportunity to experience a normal childhood because of severe kidney disease and the effects of treatment.

During Marie's short life, she experienced numerous hospitalizations and separations from her family, who eventually abandoned her. Massive nosebleeds . . . terrified her mother and led to seven emergency hospitalizations and transfusions. Marie's lonely, monotonous hospital days were interrupted only by traumatic episodes which affected her both physically and emotionally (Meagher & Leff, 1989/1990, p. 178).

Marie was especially fearful of the kidney dialysis sessions. She was put in restraints for this procedure, producing long periods of unrelenting stress. "Marie's mother would not be waiting for her after the ordeal had ended. Sedatives would not be used to ease the passage of time" (p. 179). Marie did not receive medication for her pain whether in or out of dialysis. A dialysis nurse stated that giving her sedatives would only "spoil" Marie—she must learn to cope with pain. When Marie cried out for relief from pain, her pediatricians went through an elaborate placebo procedure, attempting to deceive the girl rather than offering actual medications. The placebo stunt did not relieve Marie's pain, and no other relief was offered. Marie's agony, her anger, and her fear all intensified until she became comatose and died.

How could this little girl have been allowed to suffer so long and so greatly? Did this pattern of "care" represent a violation of her rights? Do children have the right to participate in decisions regarding the quality of their own lives and the prospect of their own deaths? Meagher and Leff are firm in their own opinion: "Marie has the absolute right to expect that any procedure or course of treatment be in her best interest" (p. 283). She has the right to be spared the pain and stress of undergoing procedures that offer no reasonable probability of extending her life for a sustained period. She would seem to have the right "at least to participate in the decision to refuse treatment or to withhold further interventions" (p. 185). However, as Meagher and Leff are quick to point out, the law does not necessarily agree with this conclusion. A person must be competent in the eyes of the law in order to make decisions, and "competent" is invariably part of the phrase, "competent adult." The competency of adults is determined on a case-by-case basis: Some adults are competent, others are not, and this status may change with time and circumstance. By contrast, children are considered not competent as a class. The legal decision maker is either a parent or a person who has been entrusted with the responsibility of acting in place of the parent (*loco parentis*, in legal parlance).

Marie's predicament is part of a larger pattern described by Klugman (2005):

> Many people are reluctant to write a document that suggests withholding or withdrawing life-sustaining treatment from a child. . . . Parents often feel responsible for their child's illness and have difficulty dealing with their emotions. Such turmoil does not create an environment for well-informed, well-reasoned decision-making (p. 230).

Klugman urges that children capable of understanding their situation be allowed the opportunity to participate in the decision-making process by expressing their own preferences. A child's assent to the withholding or withdrawal of medical interventions still does not have legal standing, but deserves careful consideration.

There is a growing movement toward giving children more of a say in the management of their conditions. The American Academy of Pediatrics has recommended that children be included in medical decision making and the National Commission for Protection of Human Subjects of Biomedical and Behavioral Research has proposed that by age 7 a child should be given the opportunity to accept or reject participation in a research project (Hinds et al., 2002).

SUMMARY

Adults often believe—or want to believe—that children do not understand death and should be protected from all death-related situations. The facts are quite different. Children are naturally curious about loss, disappearance, and death. Furthermore, no child is too young to experience the anxiety associated with separation experiences. Most studies indicate that children do not have a firm grasp of death's finality, irreversibility, and universality until about age 10. Nevertheless, even very young children can have moments of sudden discovery (e.g., the frog was "dead, dead, dead. What else could it be?"), and the mystery of death is very much in their minds throughout their developmental process. Many of today's parents grew up in homes in which death was never to be discussed, especially in the presence of children. This increases their difficulties in communicating about death with their own children. We learned something about the interaction between parents and children on the subject of death through a sampling of research case histories. It was clear that experiences, attitudes, and ways of coping with death are part of the intimate flow of life between children and their parents, and it is also clear that it is the death of particular people or animals that evoke children's concern.

Studies indicate that young children's experiences of death and loss often become life long memories that last through adulthood. Psychologist Maria Nagy ("Auntie Death") found three stages of progressive understanding of death in her pioneering research. The youngest children thought of death as a continuation of life in a diminished form. The realization that death is final occurs in the next stage, about age 5, but there is still hope that one can be smart or lucky enough to elude death. By age 10 (Stage 3), most children understand that death is personal, universal, and inevitable as well as final. More recent studies emphasize the relationship between separation anxiety and children's thoughts of death. For children as well as adults, our thoughts about death are often, if not always, tinged with anxiety. There are basic similarities in death conceptions among children in various cultures, but also some culture-specific characteristics, as exemplified in Japan and Taiwan.

The ongoing study of imaginary friends (IFs) in childhood has added another perspective. Floating conceptions of "living" and "dead," and "real" and "pretend" contribute to a creative exploration of life's mysteries. The deaths of imaginary friends generally are educational rather than devastating.

The death of a parent or other family member is highly stressful to children. We have seen that children's responses to this stress may be deeper and more intense than what appears on the surface. Posttraumatic stress disorder (PTSD) is a particularly disturbing response to a death that has occurred in a sudden and violent manner, as in terrorist attacks. PTSD has not often been recognized in children, but research and clinical experience has been directing more attention to this problem. Suggestions are made for helping children cope with bereavement.

Dying children often understand more about their conditions than adults realize—but also often have little voice in how their conditions are managed, as we discovered in Marie's situation. Nurses and others who work closely with dying children also experience high levels of stress. Fortunately, there is now some attention being given to helping nurses prepare themselves for serving the needs of dying children while reducing their own stress.

The family with open and supportive communication patterns can offer much to children as they discover death and loss in its many forms. Many of us, though, must first overcome our own reluctance to accept the fact that death does touch children and that children are very much attuned to loss and separation experiences.

REFERENCES

Anthony, S. (1972). *The discovery of death in childhood and after.* New York: Basic Books, Inc. (Revision of *The child's discovery of death.* New York: Harcourt Brace and World, 1940).

Anthony, Z., & Bhana, K. (1988/1989). An exploratory study of Muslim girls' understanding of death. *Omega, Journal of Death and Dying, 19,* 215–228.

Barr, P. (2007) Relationship of neonatologists' end-of-life decisions to their personal fear of death. *Archives of Disease in Childhood, 2,* F 104–107.

Barrett, H. C., & Behme, T. (2004). Children's understanding of death as the cessation of agency: A test using sleep versus death. www.sciencedirect.com

Bluebond-Langner, M. (1977). Meanings of death to children. In H. Feifel (Ed.), *New meanings of death* (pp. 47–66). New York: McGraw-Hill.

Bluebond-Langner, M. (1988). Worlds of dying children and their well siblings. *Death Studies, 13,* 1–16.

Bluebond-Langner, M. (1996). *In the shadow of illness.* Princeton, NJ: Princeton University Press.

Book, P. (1996). How does the family narrative influence the individual's ability to communicate about death? *Omega, Journal of Death and dying, 33,* 323–342.

Christ, G. H. (2000). *Healing children's grief.* New York: Oxford University Press.

Colp, R. J. (1975) The evolution of Charles Darwin's thoughts about death. *Journal of Thanatology, 3,* 191–206.

Corr, C. A. (Guest Ed.). (2003/2004). Special issue: Death-related literature for children. *Omega, Journal of Death and Dying, 48,* whole issue.

Corr, C. A., & Corr, D. M. (Eds.). (1996). *Handbook of childhood death and bereavement.* New York: Springer.

Corr, C. A., & Corr, D. M. (2002). Children. In R. Kastenbaum (Ed.), *Macmillan encyclopedia of death and dying*: Vol. 1 (pp. 123–130). New York: Macmillan.

Cox, M., Garrett, E., & Graham, J. A. (2004/2005). Death in Disney films: Implications for children's understanding of death. *Omega, Journal of Death and Dying, 50,* 267–280.

Dahlke, D. (1994). Therapy-assisted growth after parental suicide: From a personal and professional perspective. *Omega, Journal of Death and Dying, 23,* 113–152.

Deveau, E. J. (1995). Perceptions of death through the eyes of children and adolescents. In D. W. Adams & E. J. Deveau (Eds.), *Beyond the innocence of childhood:* Vol. 1 (pp. 55–92). New York: Baywood.

Dickinson, G. (1992). First childhood death experiences. *Omega, Journal of Death and Dying, 25,* 169–182.

Doka, K. J. (2000) Using ritual with children and adolescents. In K. J. Doka (Ed.), *Living with grief. Children, adolescents, and loss* (pp. 153–160). New York: Brunner/Mazel.

Doka, K. J. (2002). Disenfranchised grief. In R. Kastenbaum (Ed.), *Macmillan encyclopedia of death and dying*: Vol. 1 (pp. 359–362). New York: Macmillan.

Eksi, A., Braun, K. L., Ertem-Vehid, H., Peykerli, G., Saydam, R., Topariak, D., & Alyanak, B. (2007). Risk factors for the development of PTSD and depression among child and adolescent victims following a 7.4 magnitude earthquake. *International Journal of Psychiatry in Clinical Practice, 11,* 190–199.

Elliott, A. (2004, September 11). Growing up grieving, with constant reminders of 9/11. www.nytimes.com/2004/09/22/nyregion/11kids.html?7th

Fairbrother, G., Stuber, J., Galea, S., Fleischman, A. R., & Pfefferbaum, B. (2003). Posttraumatic stress reactions in New York City children after the September 11, 2001 terrorist attacks. *Ambulatory Pediatrics, 6,* 304–311.

Farley, H.-A. (1966). Sun goes up. In R. Lewis (Ed.), *Miracles.* New York: Simon & Schuster.

Freud, S. (1914). On narcissism: An introduction. In *Collective Works:* Vol. 4 (pp. 30–59). London: Hogarth.

Furman, E. F. (1974). *A child's parent dies: Studies in childhood bereavement.* New Haven, CT: Yale University Press.

Gleason, T. R. (2004). Imaginary companions and peer acceptance. *International Journal of Behavioral Development, 28,* 1–6.

Gordon, J., King, N., Gullone, E., Muris, P., & Ollendick, T. H. (2007). Nighttime fears of children and adolescents: Frequency, content, severity, harm expectations, disclosure, and coping behaviors. *Behaviour Research; and Therapy, 45,* 2464–2472.

Gray, S. (1986). *Sex and death to the age of 14.* New York: Vintage Books.

Griffith, T. (2003). Assisting with the "big hurts, little tears" of the youngest grievers: Working with three-, four-, and five-year-olds who have experienced loss and grief because of death. *Illness, Crisis & Loss, 11,* 217–225.

Grollman, S. Shira. (1988). *A legacy of courage.* New York: Doubleday & Co.

Hall, G. S. (1992). *Senescense: The last half of life.* New York: Appleton.

Harris, P. L., & Koenig, M. A. (2006). Trust in testimony: How children learn about science and religion. *Child Development, 77,* 505–524.

Hersh, S. P. (1995). How can we help? In K. J. Doka (Ed.), *Children mourning; Mourning children* (pp. 93–96). Washington, DC: Hospice Foundation of America.

Hinds, P. S., Bradshaw, G., Oakes, L. L., & Pritchard, M. (2002). Children and their rights in life and death situations. In R. Kastenbaum (Ed.), *Macmillan encyclopedia of death and dying:* Vol. 1 (pp. 139–147). New York: Macmillan.

Hooke, M. C., Grund, E., Quammen, H., Miller, B., McCormick, P., & Bostrom, B. (2007). Propofol use in pediatric patients with severe cancer pain at the end of life. *Journal of Pediatric Oncology Nursing, 1,* 29–34.

Jipson, J. L., & Gelman, S. A. (2007). Robots and rodents: Children's inferences about living and nonliving kinds. *Child Development, 78,* 1675–1678.

Kastenbaum, R., & Fox, L. (2007). Do imaginary companions die? *Omega, Journal of Death and Dying, 56,* 123–152.

Kenyon, B. L. (2001). Current research in children's conceptions of death: A critical review. *Omega, Journal of Death and Dying, 43,* 63–91.

Klugman, C. M. (2005). A life cut short: When children die. In K. J. Doka, B. Jennings, & C. A. Corr (Eds.), *Ethical dilemmas at the end of life.* Washington, DC: Hospice Foundation of America.

Levetown, M. (2002). Children: Caring for when life-threatened or dying. In R. Kastenbaum (Ed.), *Macmillan encyclopedia of death and dying:* Vol. 1 (pp. 147–154). New York: Macmillan.

Lonetto, R. (1980). *Children's conceptions of death.* New York: Springer.

Meagher, D. K., & Leff, P. T. (1989/1990). In Marie's memory: The rights of the child with life-threatening or terminal illness. *Omega, Journal of Death and Dying, 20,* 177–191.

Nagy, M. H. (1969). The child's theories concerning death. In H. Feifel (Ed.), *The meaning of death.* New York: McGraw-Hill. (Reprinted from *Journal of Genetic Psychology,* 1948, *73,* 3–27).

Opie, I., & Opie, R. (1969). *Children's games in street and playground.* London: Oxford University Press.

Papadatou, D. (2006). Care provider responses to the death of a child. In *Oxford textbook on pediatric palliative care.* New York: Oxford University Press.

Pfeffer, C. R., Altemus, M., Heo, M., & Jiang, H. (2007). Salivary cortisol and psychopathology in children bereaved by the September 11, 2001 attacks. *Biological Psychiatry, 61,* 957–965.

Pfefferbaum, B., Gurwitch, R. H., McDonald, N. B., Leftwich, M. J. T., Sconzo, G. M., Messenbaugh, A. K., & Schultz, R. A. (2000). Posttraumatic stress among young children after the death of a friend or acquaintance in a terrorist bombing. *Psychiatric Services, 51,* 386–389.

Rider, E. (2004). Does your heart go on vacation? *BMJ Public Health Journals.* Bmjjournals.com/cgi/content/full/328/7444/890?maxtoshow

Rosenberg, K. S., Johnson, C. N., & Harris, P. L. (Eds.). (2000). *Imagining the impossible. Magical, scientific, and religious thinking in children.* Cambridge, UK: Cambridge University Press.

Sagara-Rosemeyer, M., & Davies, B. (2007). The integration of religious traditions in Japanese children's views of death and afterlife. *Death Studies, 31,* 223–247.

Saurez, M. M., & McFeaters, S. J. (2000). Culture and class: The different worlds of children and adolescents. In K. J. Doka (Ed.), *Living with grief. Children, adolescents, and loss* (pp. 55–70). New York: Brunner/Mazel.

Silverman, P. R. (2000). When parents die. In K. J. Doka (Ed.), *Living with grief. Children, adolescents, and loss* (pp. 215–228). New York: Brunner/Mazel.

Silverman, P. R., & Worden, J. W. (1992). Children's understanding of funeral ritual. *Omega, Journal of Death and Dying, 25,* 319–332.

Sourkes, B. M. (1996). *Armfuls of time. The psychological experience of the child with a life-threatening disease.* Pittsburgh: University of Pittsburgh Press.

Taylor, M. (1999). *Imaginary companions and the children who create them.* New York: Oxford Press.

Thastrum, M., Johansen, M. B., Gubba, L., Oleson, L. B., & Romer, G. (2008). Coping, social relations, and communication: A qualitative exploratory study of children of parents with cancer. *Clinical Child Psychology and Psychiatry 6, 13,* 123–138.

Wass, H. (2002). Children and media violence. In R. Kastenbaum (Ed.), *Macmillan encyclopedia of death and dying:* Vol. 1. (pp. 133–139). New York: Macmillan.

Weaver, R., & Festa, D. K. (2003). Developmental effects on children suffering disruption from paternal loss in infancy. *Illness, Crisis & Loss, 11,* 271–281.

Webb, N. B. (2002). Traumatic death of friend/peers: Case of Suan, age 9. In N. B. Webb (Ed.), *Helping bereaved children* (2nd ed., pp. 189–211). New York: Guilford.

White, E. B. (1952). *Charlotte's web.* New York: Harper & Row.

Yang, S. C., & Chen, S.-F. (2007). Content analysis of free-responses to personal meanings of death among Chinese children and adolescents. *Death Studies, 30,* 217–241.

Zall, D. S. (1994). The long term effects of childhood bereavement: Impact on roles as mothers. *Omega, Journal of Death and Dying, 29,* 219–230.

GLOSSARY

Bereavement: The loss of a loved one through death.

Cystic fibrosis: A hereditary disorder in which lungs and other organ systems are blocked by abnormal mucous secretions. A life-threatening condition.

Death anxiety: Emotional distress and insecurity aroused by encounters with dead bodies, grieving people, or other reminders of mortality, including one's own thoughts.

Imaginary companion: A "pretend friend" that is real to the child but does not exist in objective reality.

Inache (Japanese): Life, as a gift from God to the embryo.

Leukemia: A progressive disease that produces distorted and dysfunctional white blood cells, increasing susceptibility to infection, bleeding, and anemia. Sometimes a life-threatening condition.

Neontologist: Health care professional who works with newborn infants.

Personification: Representing an idea or feeling as a human or humanlike form.

Plague: A virulent contagion that resulted in the deaths of at least one fourth of the population in the late fourteenth century and that is generally considered to have been bubonic disease, carried by rats and fleas as well as stricken humans. Also known as "The Black Death."

Posttraumatic stress disorder: A delayed response to a death that has occurred under highly stressful conditions. The traumatic event is reexperienced repeatedly, and other disturbances of feeling, thought, and behavior are also likely to occur.

Sibling: A brother or sister.

Trauma: A wound, injury, or emotional shock that produces injury.

ON FURTHER THOUGHT . . .

Useful Internet resources:

Candlelighters Childhood Cancer Foundation
www.candlelighters.org
Children's Hospice International
chiorg@aol.com
Dougy Center for Grieving Children
www.grievingchild.org
National Alliance for Children with Life-Threatening Conditions
www.chionline.org

Books for children or adults, or for children and adults to read together:

Many deal with loss of animals and include sad moments but have been praised for helping children to understand and express grief.

Coburn, J. B. (1964). *Anne and the Sand Dobbies: A story about death for children and their parents.* New York: Seabury.

Gipson, F. (1990). *Old Yeller.* New York: HarperTrophy.

Goldman, L. (2005). *Children also grieve: Talking about death and healing.* London: Jessica Kingsley.

Hurd, E. T. (1980). *The black dog who went into the woods.* New York: Harper & Row.

Krasny, L., & Brown, M. (1998). *When dinosaurs die: A guide to understanding death.* New York: Little Brown.

Lewis, P. G., & Lippman, J. (2004). *Helping children cope with the death of a parent: A guide for the first year.* New York: Praeger.

Rawlings, M. K. (1939). *The yearling.* New York: Scribner's.

Stoll, E. G. (1964). *My turtle died today.* New York: Holt, Rinehart & Winston.

Viorst, J. (1971). *The tenth good thing about Barney.* New York: Atheneum.

White, E. B. (1952). *Charlotte's web.* New York: Harper.

See also: a series of activity workbooks for young bereaved children by K. L. Carney, published by Dragonfly (Wethersfield, CT); and two workbooks by M. Heegaard: *When someone very special dies: Children can learn to cope with grief* (1988, Minneapolis: Woodland Press); and *Saying goodbye to your pet: Children can learn to cope with pet loss* (2001, Minneapolis: Fairview Press).

Books to help adults help children understand death and grief:

Dougy Center. (1997). *Helping children cope with death.* Portland, OR: The Dougy Center.

Nadeau, J. (1998). *Families making sense of death.* Thousand Oaks, CA: Sage.

Silverman, P. R. (2000). *Never too young to know: Death in children's lives.* New York: Oxford University Press.

Worden, J. W. (1996). *Children and grief: When a parent dies.* New York: Guilford.

Concerned that the public would fail to support military action in Afghanistan and Iraq, the White House tried to prevent publication of photographs of corpses or bodies returned in coffins. Law suits and protests eventually resulted in the availability of photographs such as the one shown here. Grief counselors believe that responding to a loss is much more difficult when the fact and circumstances of death are not brought out in the open.

chapter 11

BEREAVEMENT, GRIEF, AND MOURNING

Though a stranger to you I cannot remain silent when so terrible a calamity has fallen upon you and your country. . . . No one can better appreciate than I can, who am myself utterly brokenhearted by the loss of my own beloved Husband, who was the Light of my Life, my Stay—my All, What your sufferings must be; and I earnestly pray that you may be supported by Him to whom alone the sorely stricken can look for comfort, in this hour of heavy affliction.
—A widow, quoted by Susan Stamberg (2008, p. 3)

It may make us uncomfortable, or even anger us, but we must realize that it's never our place to force someone to grieve in a way we find acceptable. When someone dies, the bereaved family members must be forgiven if they are pleased to be getting their lives back, even if they can't say it out loud.
—Jennifer Elison (2008, p. 18)

The first time I met a close colleague after the death of my child he was sitting right across the table but turned away from me and conversed intensely with the guy next to him. Then he left the room without even saying goodbye to me—that had never happened before.
—Kai Dyregrov (2003/2004, p. 31)

Maria cried almost constantly; Mario stood by her and also cried. But a strange thing happened to him just before they were to leave the hospital. He experienced what is known in the Latino community as an ataque de nervios. He felt light headed, and he fell to the ground and suffered a series of convulsive bodily movements.
—Beder (2004, p. 96)

I've seen my father, literally seen him standing in the lane with his hand out to me. I talk to him all the time. I talk to my mother. I saw my son standing by the road waiting to be picked up a couple of times. And then it wouldn't be anybody there, or it would be a post, or it would be somebody who looked like him.
—Terkel (2001, p. 273)

A fleet of unlicensed vehicles would close off a street, heavily armed men in plainclothes would storm an apartment or house, terrify the family, break in and pillage possessions, then assault and kidnap one or more family members, usually a young adult. The victims were taken to centers hidden around Buenos Aires and the rest of the country where they would be brutally tortured for hours to days to months before being killed.
—Thornton (2000, p. 281)

Many of us can remember the moment that we learned a treasured life was taken away from us. Perhaps it was a telephone call or a knock on the door. Perhaps we had been there to witness the passing for ourselves. Some of us continue to live with or within that moment even many years later. And almost all of us discover that the loss has remained an ongoing part of our lives even when the moment of separation has long passed. We are the bereaved. We are the grieving. We are the mourning. And, as will be seen, we are also the vulnerable. This chapter examines one of most profound links with the whole procession of the human race: the capacity to suffer deeply and yet to renew our commitment to life when separated by death from a beloved person.

SOME RESPONSES TO LOSS

We have already stepped briefly into the lives of people who responded to a death in their distinctive ways. The widow who wrote that compassionate letter based on her own loss was Queen Victoria. The widow who received the letter was Mary Todd Lincoln. Today many people continue to feel that solace and understanding is best conveyed by a person who has experienced a similar devastating loss. "The Stage of Grief No One Admits to: Relief" is the challenging title of Elison's reflection on the death of her husband in a motor vehicle accident. There was the shock of the sudden death, the sorrow—but also a sense of relief that she was no longer caught in what she felt to be a failed and unhappy marriage. Elison later became a counselor and encountered other bereaved people "whose predominant emotion was relief." These included parents of a baby who would have required 24-7 care without hope of having anything resembling a normal life, and the family of a person who, as a drug addict, had turned into a monster. Knowing that a person has become bereaved, then, does not necessarily tell us what that loss means and how it is being experienced.

The grieving mother abandoned by her colleagues was one of many people who shared such experiences with sociologist Kari Dyregrov. People would cross the street or just look away—and probably thought that this avoidance behavior wasn't noticed! Studies often find that our society does not offer effective support for the bereaved. Why do we withdraw when a person most needs support, and what kind of support is experienced as most helpful?

Maria and Mario were thrilled about the impending birth of their first child. Unfortunately, Maria suffered a miscarriage that required hospitalization and a surgical procedure. Both took this loss hard. Although there is a stereotype that men "bear up better" in bereavement, Mario had a very difficult time, including another "attack of nerves" during which he lost consciousness. What was the influence of cultural expectations on Mario's distress and—more importantly—could grief counseling help?

Folk singer Rosalie Sorrels had known many deaths during her long life, starting with her childhood on a farm. "You know, I never thought of death as unfriendly" (Terkel, 2001, p. 266). Furthermore, she did not find it alarming that she still met some of her favorite dead people from time to time. In her interview with Studs Terkel, the distinguished oral historian, Sorrels described a continuing bond with the dead. Is this unusual? Is it "pathological" or "healthy"?

Death squads terrorized the citizens of Argentina during the oppressive (1976–1983) military regime. This was terrorism carried out not by outsiders but as government policy. People were afraid to protest or even ask questions because of the threat that one might be the next to disappear without notice. *Los Madres de la Plaza de Mayo* was an improbable response to this intolerable situation. One by one, women whose children had been kidnapped by the regime reached out to each other for support. Many had already tried to contact the authorities to learn what had happened but were rudely dismissed. The slow process of healing could not really begin while the fate of their children remained unknown.

That the women should bond together to protest against the terrorist regime was almost unbelievable. Women were supposed to restrict themselves to their duties at home and not meddle in public affairs, even when these affairs touched them deeply (Thornton, 2000).

When ordered to move on by the police, they . . . started *la ronda,* the walk around and around the Plaza, which was to become a trademark of their peaceful protest. . . . The women were threatened with weapons and dogs, sometimes had cocked guns put to their heads, and sprayed with water cannons or tear gas . . . (p. 282).

Despite intimidation, ridicule, and some "disappearances" within their ranks, the mothers persevered. Hebe de Bonafini, mother of two missing sons, explains why:

If they cannot be here, then I have had to take their place, to shout for them. . . . I feel them present in my banners, in my unending fatigue, in my mind and body, in everything I do I think that their absence has left me pregnant forever (de Bonafini, 1991, p. 287).

The Mothers of the Plaza experienced an inner transformation through which they realized that they were rebelling not only against the constricted role of women in their society, but also against a militaristic regime in which force and violence were systematically employed against the public at large. And the public eventually responded to their example, contributing to the downfall of the militaristic government. They were discovering a new self—one of courage, dignity, and worth. Their grief was being transformed into action for the good of all (Thornton, 2000, p. 283).

In this chapter, we will look carefully at the grief and recovery process. The term "recovery" does not necessarily mean that life goes on just as it was before the bereavement; this is an unlikely outcome, as Balk (2004) has observed. "Recovery" as used here refers to the ability to continue with a life that is meaningful to the individual and with the ability to cope with obligations and challenges. We consider parents who have lost children and children who have lost parents, husbands who have lost wives and wives who have lost husbands, and siblings who have lost siblings. Sometimes, though we do not seem to have the right to grieve—we were not family, yet the pain is there. Accordingly, we will also look at hidden or disenfranchised grief. There are also circumstances in which none of

us are "supposed" to grieve because the person who died was not considered to be really a person in the full sense of the word (for example, developmentally disabled children, Milo, 1997). We must also look carefully at the concepts of "normal" and "complicated" grief and evaluate the effectiveness of counseling.

We begin by clarifying basic concepts and becoming acquainted with major theories of grief. How people actually cope with loss will then be examined in some detail. This will include attention to the impact of grief on the survival of the survivors: Is grief hazardous to our health? Although we will discover common patterns and themes, we will also become aware of great individual differences and of the role played by sociocultural expectations. Finally, we will build upon these observations to improve our ability to recognize and respond helpfully to the grief experience, whether in ourselves or others.

DEFINING OUR TERMS: BEREAVEMENT, GRIEF, MOURNING

Bereavement, grief, mourning—these words cannot convey the impact a death can bring upon the survivors. However, a clear understanding of these words will help us to find our way through these challenging experiences.

Bereavement: An Objective Fact

Bereavement is an objective fact. We are bereaved when a person close to us dies. There is no hard and fast rule about how far this term should be extended. The death of a coworker, for example, might or might not be considered a bereavement, depending on the relationship that had existed. Bereavement conveys the idea of a tearing apart, a forcible separation that results in the loss of something we once had. That "something" is a vital and perhaps sustaining relationship.

Bereavement is also a change in status. A child becomes an orphan, a wife a widow, a husband a widower. It is an objective fact that serves as a clue to possible psychological, social, and physical distress.

Bereavement is also an outcome of large-scale social phenomena. Widowhood and orphanhood are major consequences of epidemics, natural disaster, terrorism, and war. Thousands of families had their lives shattered by deaths in the terrorist attacks of September 11, 2001, and the Myanmar cyclone of May 2008. The lethal events were swift; the consequences will be enduring. Perhaps we can spare a thought for the millions who were bereaved by the killing fields and trenches of World War I ("The War to End All Wars"). Thousands of men died each day (Groom, 2002). World War I slaughter and bereavement has had a profound and continuing effect on society. As the acid smoke of battle started to clear, millions died worldwide from a savage variety of influenza that was especially lethal for youth and left family survivors in shock and grief.

Bereavement can also occur less conspicuously even though on a large scale. Although more people now live longer, there are also more widows than ever. Social isolation and loneliness have become recognized as a major source of stress and vulnerability. Although bereavement by itself is only a bare objective fact, it is also a fact that tends to generate increased vulnerability and stress.

Grief: A Painful Response

Grief is a response to bereavement; it is how the survivor feels. It is also how the survivor thinks, eats, sleeps, and makes it through the day. The term itself does not explain anything. Grief requires careful understanding on a person-by-person basis; it is not a word that can be taken as a simple explanation of what is being experienced and why.

Furthermore, grief is not the only possible response to bereavement. There may be anger or indifference, for example. Some individuals show what psychiatrists term a dissociative flight from the impact of death—a pattern of extreme, even psychotic denial. Other people recognize their loss but delay their emotional response, as when a person has critical responsibilities to perform and does not have the "luxury" of dealing with personal feelings. Nevertheless, the grief response is so frequent and so painful that it is of primary importance

for those who wish to understand and comfort the bereaved.

A useful distinction is often made between the grief experienced at the first recognition of the loss and the grief that continues long afterward. Here is the classic description of acute grief (Lindemann, 1944):

> The picture shown by people in acute grief is remarkably uniform. Common to all is the following syndrome: sensations of somatic distress occurring in waves lasting from 20 minutes to an hour at a time, a feeling of tightness in the throat, choking with shortness of breath, need for sighing, an empty feeling in the abdomen, lack of muscular power, and an intensive subjective distress described as tension or pain (p. 145).

Other symptoms also commonly seen are insomnia, failures of memory, absentmindedness, problems in concentrating, and the tendency to do the same things over and over again.

Erich Lindemann was working with people who had been stunned by the sudden death of loved ones in the Cocoanut Grove fire (Boston, 1942), in which 400 people perished in less than 15 minutes and others died later of burns and smoke inhalation. It has since been learned that the total symptom picture seen by Lindemann may not be expressed by every person who has an acute grief reaction. Nevertheless, Lindemann's description still conveys a vivid sense of what it is like to be overwhelmed by grief.

Grief affects all spheres of life. The grieving person's body doesn't work very well. George Engel (1963) was among the first to suggest that an intense and prolonged grief reaction can precipitate a life-threatening condition in bereaved people with underlying physical problems. Current theory and research continues to provide support for considering grief to be a physical disorder as well as a personal crisis. It is the whole person who grieves, and this person is part of a network of interpersonal relationships. Grieving, then, takes place both within and between people and shows its effects in all spheres. Consider, for example, a few of the major changes in the way our bodies function and how the way in which we grieve can influence our thoughts and relationships.

Neuroendocrine Changes in Grief

The grief experience operates as a stressor. The particular type of somatic reaction often depends on whatever physical weaknesses preexisted in the bereaved person (Hall & Irwin, 2001). Individual differences in cognitive, behavioral, and relational responses also influence the neuroendocrine system's response to the stress of grief. The response to loss can itself contribute to further distress. For example, if we become withdrawn and inactive, we also increase our vulnerability to opportunistic infections because of lowered muscle tone. Furthermore, new problems continue to arise as the survivor attempts to adjust to an altered life situation. The homeostatic mechanisms of the body try to moderate the stress as the first shock of the loss is followed by a period of active grieving. Unfortunately, this adaptation to chronic stress itself can be a source of further problems. Some grief responses become increasingly difficult to "get over" because our central nervous system has dedicated itself so effectively to moderating the effect of the stress. In other words, we may have to deal with our physiological response to stress as well as the stress itself.

Studies indicate that the stress of grief intensifies wear and tear on the body, along with increased risk of cardiovascular, infectious, and inflammatory disorders. Stress-related hormones become more active. Hall and Irwin (2001) report that the higher levels of cortisol, epinephrine, and norephrine are signs that grieving people are undergoing a destabilization of their physiological systems that place their health and survival at higher risk.

The immune system, our primary defense against pathogens, appears to be especially vulnerable to the stress of grief (Genevo, 2003). The "killer cells" that destroy threatening invaders have been shown to become fewer and less active in women who have either experienced a death or are living with the anxious expectation of a death. Unfortunately, there are also some indications that this heightened vulnerability may persist over an extended period of time.

Infant monkeys show significant immunological and other physiological changes when they are separated from their mothers for even a short time (Laudenslager, Boccia, & Reitre, 1993). The infant monkeys who were most agitated, slouching, and withdrawn were also those whose immune systems were most affected by the stress of separation. However, when the mother and infant are reunited, the young monkey's immune system returns to normal. (It would be interesting to know what is happening to the mother's immune system during this time as well!) Behavioral and physiological stress was reduced during maternal separation when the monkeys were kept in a familiar environment and could see their peers. Familiar surroundings seem to have some value in buffering the effects of the loss experience. Monkeys as well as humans experience both behavioral and physiological stress when separated from their "significant others"—and monkeys as well as humans can cope with this stress more successfully when provided with social support before and during the grief process. Physical aspects of distress can be intensified by how we respond to the loss. Going without proper nutrition and rest and neglecting self-care is a dysfunctional pattern—add alcohol and indiscriminate use of medications and it gets worse.

Personal and Interpersonal Responses to the Stress of Grief

The mind of the grieving person may not work as well as usual. Problems with attention, concentration, and memory increase the person's risk to self and others. A person who usually is alert and responsible becomes an inattentive driver, a parent who fails to notice household hazards, or a worker who becomes careless on the job. It is the emotional side of grief that often besets the survivor with the greatest distress, however. Glick, Weiss, and Parkes (1974) report examples such as the following from their pioneering study of spousal bereavement:

> When I got home from the morgue, I was just out for the rest of the day. I just couldn't help myself. I thought I would have a nervous breakdown, and my heart was going so fast. The man at the morgue said, "Well, if you don't stop crying, you're going to have a nervous breakdown." But all I could do was cry. That's all I could do. And I told him, "If I don't cry, God, my heart will burst." I had to cry, because he wasn't going to be back no more (p. 17).

This woman had just found herself transformed from wife to widow. She first experienced shock and could not feel or think at all. Then she could not stop herself from overwhelming feelings. People in acute grief sometimes feel that they are "going crazy," that they will keep "getting worse and worse and then just fall all apart." Those who have made it through such intense grief themselves can be very helpful to those who are in the midst of such experiences. Distress does not end with the first wave of shock and grief. It is not enough to realize that a loved one is dead. One now faces the further realization that life is supposed to go on. There may be further waves of confusion, anxiety, rage, and other painful inner states. The sense of numbness can also return, sometimes to linger as though it would never go away.

That grief can return in wave after wave of distress was discovered in an important study of nineteenth century American diaries. Paul C. Rosenblatt (1983) found that recurring experiences of grief were common. People who felt they had recovered completely from the pangs of grief might be engulfed in a wave of distress months or years later. Some of the diary entries expressed a more profound sense of grief years after the loss than they had at the time of the death:

"I think of Ma so much, & the horror of her taking never leaves me. Why should that condition come to her. Why should she keep it secret so long. What would have prevented it" (p. 23).

This entry was written two and one-half years after the death of this man's wife. He had expressed no sense of grief for her in some time.

Many occasions could renew the sense of grief: "I think of Henry every time I sit at table and see his place is vacant. [Sitting again] in our old pew, I could not help thinking of my dear parents and before I could stop myself was crying bitterly . . ." (p. 27).

Anniversaries, places that rekindle a memory, and people who remind us of the lost person have the power to start a new wave of grief long after the death. Grief may return again and again, long after the bereavement. Most people seem to recover well from their first intense grief episode. The vulnerability often remains, although subsequent episodes are likely to be much briefer—an image, a sudden pang, a catch of the breath, a readiness to weep . . . and then, after a pause, a going on with life.

Mourning: A Signal of Distress

Mourning is the culturally patterned expression of the bereaved person's thoughts and feelings. Bereavement is a universal experience. No society has been spared the loss of people it valued, loved, and depended on. How people express their loss is not universal, however. These expressions vary from culture to culture and also change over time, as we will see. Dennis Klass (2002) observes that even the basic concepts of grief and mourning differ appreciably across cultures:

Grief as a real subjective state grows from a culture that prizes and cultivates individual experience. There is no equivalent to the term grief in some other languages; indeed, in some cultures, as in Japan, the concept of emotions that are only in the individual seems foreign (p. 373).

Perhaps, then, the connection between inner state (grief) and outer expression (mourning) is so close in some societies that we should not try to separate them. But since most of us do live within a society that emphasizes individual experience, the distinction between mourning and grief remains helpful. You might have already observed a real-life distinction between grief and mourning. For example, people who have no close friends available sometimes keep their grief to themselves rather than burden acquaintances with whom there has been no prior history of mutual sharing.

There are exceptions in which a particular sign of mourning is recognized throughout much of the world. It is believed that the first influential example of a flag being displayed at half-mast occurred in 1612 when *Heart's Ease*, a ship returning from a discovery expedition, came into view (Prothero, 1997). A member of the crew had been killed during an altercation with Eskimos. Two possible symbolic reasons have been suggested for the half-masting: (1) the sea-going equivalent to bereaved people neglecting their appearance as a signal of their distress; and (2) the lowered flag leaves a space above for the to-be-imagined emblem of

Death. Half-masting became an established maritime practice, and then came ashore with the observance of a recent death by lowering the flag at public places. When war ships took to the air, a related practice developed: the missing man formation.

Too Many Deaths to Mourn?

Geoffrey Gorer (1977) observed striking changes in mourning behavior within a few years in his own culture. When his father died aboard the *Lusitania*, capsized by a torpedo in 1915, his mother became "a tragic, almost a frightening figure in the full panoply of widow's weeds and unrelieved black, a crepe veil shrouding her . . . so that she was visibly withdrawn from the world." But within a few months, there had been so many deaths from World War I that "Widows in mourning became increasingly frequent in the streets, so that Mother no longer stood out in the crowd." Too many people were being touched too closely by death. The functioning of society as a whole would have been impaired had every bereaved person pursued every step of the traditional mourning ritual.

The gold star in the window of many a home in the United States during World War II indicated that an unique life had been lost. Each gold star mother experienced her personal bereavement, but collectively they signified a loss felt by the entire nation. This public empathy and support did not develop for families grieving for loved ones killed in Vietnam, a war that divided rather than unified the country. It would take the long-delayed creation of the Vietnam Memorial Wall (Chapter 12) to link individual with public loss.

The Gulf War produced still a different type of public mourning response. Death was notably absent from the messages about the Gulf War that reached viewers and readers in the United States (Umberson & Henderson, 1992). Smart bombs "serviced" their targets, while not-so-smart bombs resulted in "collateral damage." The attempt to eliminate images of death from Gulf War reports may have contributed to the public's difficulty in mourning those who died on all sides of the conflict. The Oklahoma City bombing aroused sorrow and anger throughout the general public. The

community and its leadership worked together in a sense of sustained purpose that not only resulted in an innovative memorial (see Chapter 12) for the victims but also made it evident that healing was everybody's endeavor.

Mourning for the September 11, 2001 victims had even larger dimensions. There were numerous memorial services, some informal and limited to the people most closely concerned, and some replete with prominent officials, celebrities, and national television coverage. Strenuous efforts were made to identify and recover remains so that family mourning could begin. Two other facets of the mourning for terrorist attack victims also stand out: (1) the individuality of each victim was recognized at every opportunity (e.g., reading of the names, displaying their photographs), and (2) New York City itself was treated as victim (e.g., sorrow for loss of the WTC towers, and, indirectly, for the blow to the image and stature of a city that had been the first destination of many immigrants and the long time symbol of American power). Some catastrophes strike so severely at the core of a people that intensive mourning seems to be essential for recovery even to begin.

The ongoing military actions in Afghanistan and Iraq have generated two discordant types of public response. The government restricted viewings of the flag-draped coffins, fearing that they might increase criticism of the war effort. Local news programs, however, have reported casualties, honored their service, and voiced support for family. Some Web sites have also persisted in reporting and discussing each individual death. Where there is acknowledgment of the deaths, it is with compassion untainted by the stigma that haunted those who served in the Vietnam War.

Culturally Varied Patterns of Mourning

Within the United States there are varied patterns of mourning—compare those of Americans who are of African, Chinese, Korean, Japanese, Italian, or Central European–Jewish heritage, for example. Furthermore, mourning traditions are subject to change. Many people have been uprooted from their native lands or have chosen to move elsewhere in search of opportunities for an improved quality of life. Their

A flag lowered to half-mast can be a temporary public memorial for one person or for many who have recently died. This lowered flag, however, is an enduring sign of mourning for the thousands of Holocaust victims at the Buchenwald camp, seen below.

practices can encounter difficulties in their new surroundings. Consider, for example, the challenges faced by the Hmong when relocated to the United States.

Hmong Mourning Practices in Laos and in the United States

The Hmong people have been known to history for almost 5,000 years. Those who selected Laos as their home became victims of that nation's violent political upheavals during the 1960s. Many fled in fear for their lives in the mid-1970s, and of these refugees about 120,000 relocated in the United States.

Mourning in Hmong Homelands

Hmong mourning practices are closely related to their religious beliefs: a spiritual world that coexists with the physical. The newborn infant is under the care of spirit-parents before its birth and must be inducted into the world of the living through an appropriate ritual. Ancestor-spirits interact with the world of living people. These spirits can either help or harm the living, so it is important to show them all possible respect.

Bliatout (1993) has identified the following types of helpers who must be available for the mourning rituals to provide safe conduct for the dead and comfort for the survivors:

• *Guide to the spirit world:* This person will recite the *Qhuab Ke* verses from memory, with mention of every place in which the deceased lived. Unless this recitation is offered, the deceased will neither know that he or she has died nor find his or her way back to the place of birth. It is crucial to return to one's birth place because the placenta has been buried there and is needed if the soul is to make its return to the spirit world.

- *Reed pipe player and drummer*: Their music provides safe passage for the soul of the deceased. The performance makes great demands on the stamina of the musicians, and the instruments themselves are sacred. Mourning cannot start without this music.
- *Counselor to the family*: An elder is selected to sing comforting traditional songs to the family on the evening before the funeral.
- *Counselor to the dead*: Only deceased elders receive this special attention in which texts are recited to guide the soul on its journey between the world of the living and the world of ancestral spirits. Funeral, safe passage, and mourning rituals are more elaborate for elders.
- *Funeral director and assistant*: They make sure that all tasks are being carried out properly.
- *Shoemaker:* "These special shoes turn up at the toe; without them, the souls will be unable to cross the big river, walk the treacherous paths, step over valleys of snakes . . . and arrive at the spirit world" (p. 87).
- *Stretcher-maker*: This person creates a symbolic horse from bamboo thatch and two long wooden poles. The deceased will lie on this pallet for several days until the burial.
- *Geomancer* (a kind of shaman): This person determines the best time for the burial.
- *Food server*: This person is specially trained to communicate with the souls of the deceased.
- *Warrior*: This person shoots arrows or fires his gun in the air and engages in other rituals to help protect the deceased on his or her journey.
- *Coffin makers*: This individual must also locate just the right tree to cut down and use. There must be no metal in the coffin or any material other than the specific wood that is required.
- *Sacrificial ox slayers*: They must choose the right ox or oxen for this purpose. A whole day may be devoted to rituals associated with the sacrifices.

The funeral and mourning processes blend into each other all along the way. For example, the 13th Day End ritual must be performed after that amount of time has passed since the burial. It is on this occasion that the soul is finally released

from its body and is free to journey to the spirit world. In the meantime, nobody works at their normal tasks other than preparation of food and other basic life-support activities.

Hmong Mourning in the United States

What happens when Hmong relocate to the United States? Here is a sampling of the problems that Bliatout (1993) has identified:

- *The American medical system urges or requires autopsies in some cases.* "This is considered one of the most horrible things that can happen to a Hmong person, as it is believed that the person will be born mutilated in the next life" (p. 96).
- *Often there is no opportunity for the Hmong to wash, dress, lay out the body themselves, or provide the symbolic (stretcher) horse.* This can interfere significantly with the grieving and mourning process.
- *The reed pipes and funeral drum may not be allowed because they might disturb the neighbors!* Again, mourners may fear that they are jeopardizing the safety of the deceased soul as well as their own lives because of this failure to honor and protect their dead. The sacrifice of oxen, the firing of guns, and other traditional rituals are also likely to be banned or to become impractical in their new environment.
- *Some Hmongs convert to Christianity and adopt lifestyles associated with our industrial–technical, mass media culture.* This can lead to a rift within and between Hmong families which, in turn, is likely to interfere with their established patterns of communal mourning.

The Hmong story—still in the process of transition—has many other parallels in our pluralistic society. Long-established traditions of mourning are not immune from challenge, whether by culture conflicts or catastrophic events, as the following examples illustrate.

Appreciating Universality and Diversity in the Response to Bereavement: Three Examples

People living within one culture sometimes misinterpret the bereavement responses of people within another culture. The mistaken assumption that life is cheap in Asia, for example, has been fostered by outsider ignorance of culturally expressed modes of mourning. Even within the "same" culture, there can be a lack of understanding about what the bereaved person goes through.

Racism and Grief: Dying was his Specialty

Pulitzer Prize–winning poet and novelist Alice Walker has described personal experiences that illuminate both what is universal and what is distinctive about a particular culture's response to grief. In a book written primarily for children—*To Hell with Dying* (1988)—Walker tells of her love for an old man by the name of Mr. Sweet. He was not the usual type of elderly person who is found in a children's story: "Mr. Sweet was a diabetic and an alcoholic and a guitar player and lived down the road from us on a neglected cotton farm" (p. 1). Nevertheless, he was a continual source of delight and instruction for Walker and her older brothers and sisters. Dying was one of Mr. Sweet's specialties. He seemed very close to death on several occasions but was rescued by the Walker children who, on a signal from their father, would:

> Come crowding around the bed and throw themselves on the covers, and whoever was the smallest at the time would kiss him all over his wrinkled brown face and begin to tickle him so that he would laugh all down in his stomach, and his mustache, which was long and sort of straggly, would shake like Spanish moss and was also that color (p. 3).

Mr. Sweet had long ago discovered that the careers he wanted for himself—doctor, lawyer, or sailor—were out of reach for a poor black boy. He might have lived in grief all his life, having lost his childhood vision of an exciting and rewarding career. Instead, he excelled in bringing joy to the children in his rural neighborhood. Alice Walker, belonging to a new generation, achieved the college education that contributed to her brilliant writing career. Using these skills, she has given us a portrait of love and grief during a period of time in American history when many people of African heritage were denied equal access to opportunity.

The smiles and tears of *To Hell with Dying* have universal resonance—but the particulars reflect the unique patterns of life in a rural black community during a recent period of our own society. An outsider, for example, would have no way of knowing that the old guitar in a young black woman's hands was a tangible expression of both loss and continuity, grief and love.

Yoruba Compassion

How do Africans cope with grief and mourning in their homelands? There are as many answers as there are varied heritages, but an instructive example comes from the Yoruba of Western Nigeria (Adamolekun, 1999). There is a strong tradition of support for people in mourning. Every person in mourning is greeted daily by other members of the community with expressions of concern, support, and encouragement. These expressions are specific to the kind of bereavement that was experienced (e.g., a spouse, parent, or child); how the death occurred (e.g., long illness or sudden accident); and to the age, gender, and situation of the mourning person. This careful differentiation of message makes it clear that the society is aware of the distinctive loss. All of the salutations acknowledge the pain of the loss and many congratulate the mourner for having the courage to bear up to this sorrow. The bereaved person is reminded to take good care of one's self in order to meet obligations for the family:

The Yoruba response clearly shows that the community is aware of the grieving person's loss, recognizes the sorrow and stress, and encourages the person to go on with life. This supportive, community-wide support is less evident in the United States and other urbanized, technologically driven nations where there is little patience with the mourning process.

AIDS, Multiple Deaths, and Grief

Somebody dies. Family and friends grieve. The community comes forward with practical and symbolic support in accord with its traditions. The long process of healing begins.

What happens, though, when there are just too many deaths within too short a time? When all the community survivors are in grief and many in jeopardy of losing their own lives? Traditional ways of grieving and mourning can be overwhelmed, leading to catastrophic individual and societal consequences (Kastenbaum, 2004a; 2004b). In our own times, the AIDS pandemic continues to be responsible for such stressful situations, although less pervasive in the news media. Jennifer Hunt (2004) observes that:

> Multiple deaths in one extended family over a short time have become the norm in many parts of sub-Saharan Africa. In Zimbabwe, deaths due to AIDS are common, and the traditional grief models do not account for the ability of families to survive in the face of consecutive and concurrent deaths (p. 285).

The staggering number of AIDS-related deaths occur within an already unsettled nation that became independent as recently as 1980 and is experiencing a rapid shift of population from the countryside to increasingly overcrowded and dysfunctional urban areas. Furthermore, the gender roles are also in transition. For example, it is difficult for a professional woman to balance the obligations and restrictions placed on her by tradition with her own accomplishments and needs. The traditional Zimbabwe way of life is difficult to sustain in this situation, and such is also the case with the traditional way of coping with death. Many people are practicing Christians, yet with continuing influence from earlier folk and religious traditions. The mourning rituals differ in many details from those of the Hmong but are comparable in the intensity, time, and effort required. Our usual ideas about grief and mourning do not seem adequate to comprehend the challenge of respecting the dead and moving ahead with life in such challenging circumstances.

A grieving person in one society probably has much in common with grieving people in other societies. However, tradition and ongoing circumstances can exercise powerful influence over the nature and effectiveness of the mourning process.

WHAT KIND OF GRIEF?

It is clear that the grieving process is not identical for all people in all circumstances. There is an ongoing effort by clinicians and researchers to make useful distinctions among types of grief. We will look at several of the terms that have been proposed to describe different forms of grief: *normal, pathological, complicated, traumatic, resolved, unresolved, and anticipatory.*

Normal and Complicated Grief

Mental health experts now agree with the poets that grief is a human, and not necessarily a weak or pathological response to loss. This is a departure from the once-common opinion that people should just take the loss of a loved one in stride and get on with their lives without making a fuss. Nevertheless, there are situations in which grief is so extreme, so debilitating, and so enduring that the individual seems heading for catastrophe. The difference between a "normal" and a potentially endangering grief response has therefore become a focus of interest.

I don't much care for the term "normal" because the grieving person often feels anything but that. The term becomes more useful if we accept the suggestion of distinguished researcher Margaret S. Stroebe (2001) who proposes that *grief is normal when it stays within the bounds of a particular cultural tradition.* What, then, of grief that escapes these bounds? What about abnormal or pathological grief? Stroebe rejects the terms "abnormal" and "pathological grief because they neglect the interpersonal side of the situation and unnecessarily stigmatize the distraught person. She prefers the less-value-laden term, *complicated grief.* The grief response can be complicated in several ways. The common feature is that the bereaved person does not move from the shock and pain of loss toward a substantial return to an active and fulfilling life.

Traumatic grief is another term that is worth considering. (Jacobs, 1999; Range, 2002). It refers to a severe and disabling response to sudden, unexpected, and, often violent death. Family and friends of terrorist attack victims are especially vulnerable to traumatic grief. The survivor's whole world seems to have collapsed, and it is difficult to restore a sense of meaning and purpose. Such continues to be the experience of those who are barely surviving genocide in Darfur. Helping people who are experiencing the traumatic form of grief often seems to

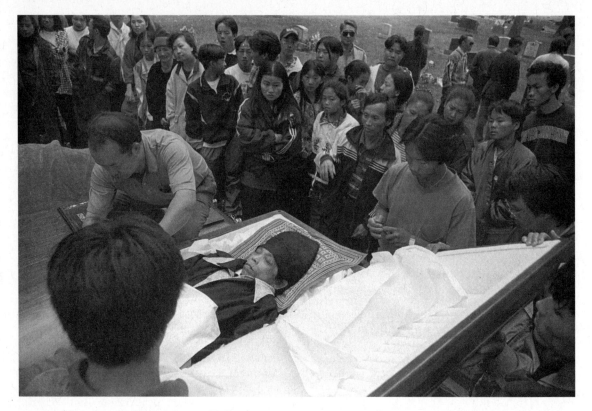

Hmong funerals include complex rituals for the passage of the deceased person to the next life and the safety of the family. Here the body is being checked for metal or other foreign objects that might leave a curse on the family.

require professional counseling or therapy and special attention to the circumstances surrounding the death. It remains to be learned, however, whether traditional methods of counseling would be sufficient to help people who have lost their entire world of relationships and meanings. The re-establishment of belief systems, rituals, and dependable relationship patterns would seem to be a major priority.

Anticipatory Grief

Grieving sometimes begins before a death occurs. Some counselors believed that *anticipatory grief* has become increasingly common in recent years as people live longer with life-threatening conditions (Beder, 2002). There is more time to worry, more time to plan, more time to experi-

ence stress, but also more time to make decisions, clarify values, and strengthen relationships. The concept of anticipatory grief has directed attention to the state of mind of people prior to bereavement. It has often been assumed that people who have the opportunity to prepare themselves for the loss will experience less distress when it does occur and also throughout the grieving process. This assumption has been critiqued by pioneering thanatologist Robert Fulton (2003) who does not find the evidence persuasive. Joan Beder (2003) notes that anticipatory grief does not seem beneficial in situations such as Alzheimer's disease where death is expected, but not imminent. The possible benefits of anticipatory grief might best be regarded as a working hypothesis in need of further study. Nevertheless, we would do well to improve our understanding of the individual and the situation prior to an expected death.

Resolved and Unresolved Grief

There are competing points of view on recovery from grief. Some experts believe that grief can and should be resolved within a reasonable (but not standard and fixed) period of time. Others believe that the loss of a crucial relationship is never completely resolved: We move on with our lives, but we will never again be the same. This controversy is significant because it can influence the way we respond to grieving people. What should we expect? For what it's worth, I doubt that it's useful to push people toward resolution on any imposed time schedule, and I also share the doubt that the effects of a profound bereavement will dissolve simply with the passage of time. From the practical standpoint, though, we can be helpful by attending to signs of movement or lack of movement toward recovery from the most debilitating effects of grief. Resolved and unresolved grief can be useful concepts, but only when linked to careful observations and not subject to arbitrary expectations.

Hidden and Disenfranchised Grief

Grief may be intensified and its resolution delayed when the bereaved are denied the opportunity to express their feelings. This is the concern with hidden or *disenfranchised grief*. A person's grief is hidden when it is not recognized by others because the individual has not expressed either the loss or feelings about the loss. For example, Gail, a school teacher, did not believe she had the right to express her grief in the presence of her students (Rowling, 1995):

> I knew I was heading towards a class in an hour's time. I knew that even within an hour I would not have myself pulled together enough to face the class. I mean, if you went and sat in front of a class and cried for forty minutes they would riot, because they haven't got the rapport with what is happening with you at the moment (p. 323).

Grief may be hidden because the individual is not considered "entitled" to these feelings. In such a case, it can be said that the grief is disenfranchised.

I have observed many examples of hidden and disenfranchised grief among nurses and other caregivers. For example, staff members of a long-term-care facility often become attached to the people in their care. An aged woman with no living relatives would be "adopted" by a nurse who had lost her own grandparents. The caregiver would then experience grief when this resident died. However, our society often does not acknowledge the right of a caregiver to grieve and mourn. The health care system in particular has had a history of being intolerant of professionals who become "too involved" with their patients and "too upset" at their deaths. This tendency is still strong, although the emergence of the hospice movement and peer support groups offer an alternative approach. My colleagues and I in a geriatric hospital noticed that staff members who had been emotionally close to recently deceased patients were more likely to be involved in single-car accidents and to experience a variety of illnesses requiring sick days. These negative outcomes were sharply reduced after the staff organized peer support groups and gave each other permission to love and mourn their patients.

AIDS has brought many additional examples of disenfranchised grief. The lover–companion of a person with AIDS may not be considered "family" and therefore may be denied the right to mourn. In fact, lovers in general have often been excluded from supportive interactions because their relationships to the deceased were not that of spouses, parents, children, or siblings. Societal attitudes do change, however, and there is increasing recognition that lovers have both the need and the right to mourn.

Parents of stillborn babies often have been forced to keep their grief to themselves. We have seen (Chapter 3) how difficult it was to persuade the health care system to regard the loss of a stillborn infant as the real death of a real person, and, therefore, "acceptable" for grieving. Validating the reality of a death is an essential first step in providing support to women experiencing stillbirth (Cacciatore,

2007). The sorrow of losing a companion animal has also been excluded from serious consideration by society in many instances, though many families know better. Grief counselor Michelle Linn-Gust (2007) and veterinarian Nick Trout (2008) are among the experts who recognize how much animal companions can mean to a family and how much their deaths can be mourned.

Lavin (1989) brings another neglected kind of hidden grief to our attention in discussing the bereaved person who is developmentally disabled:

> If they have been sheltered all their lives, they may face the death of a loved one unprepared. Often parents shield their normal children from death and are reluctant to include them in the rites of mourning, keeping them away from wakes and funerals. There is a greater tendency for the parents of the developmentally disabled to continue the shielding process longer. Thus the disabled . . . may be denied access to mourning rituals . . . and therefore are not exposed to role models who show them how to cope effectively with loss (p. 231).

Similarly, experiences have been reported by foster parents who look after children with severe disabilities and are therefore at higher risk for death (Schormans, 2004). The foster parents feel grief comparable with the loss of a birth child: "We don't feel like foster parents . . . Mom and Dad, we consider ourselves as mother and father" (p. 357).

THEORIES OF GRIEF

Grief itself is not theoretical. However, there are questions that invite theory and research. Here we consider several approaches to understanding the meaning of grief in human experience. Theories of grief try to explain not only the general or "normal" process, but also why this experience sometimes overwhelms the bereaved person and what might be done to help. We will see that a key issue is at dispute: Is it better to detach ourselves from strong attachment to the deceased loved one, or somehow to integrate this lost relationship into our ongoing life?

The *Grief-Work Theory*

Sigmund Freud (1919/1959) introduced the first influential theory following World War I. He was shaken to discover that supposedly civilized nations could behave so brutally toward each other. Freud offered the following propositions from his personal sorrows as well as his observation of widespread grief and mourning:

1. *Grief is an adaptive response to loss.* It is not just an expression of emotional pain. Grief is also a kind of work that must be performed. Our "pay" for this work is the restoration of our peace of mind and social competence.
2. *The work of grief is difficult and time-consuming.* It goes on day after day, night after night. We increase the stress and make grief work more difficult if we demand that the bereaved person quickly snap back to "normal."
3. *The purpose of grief work is to accept the reality of the death and thereby become liberated from the strong attachment one had to the "lost object."* We must recover the emotional investment—he used the Greek word, *cathexis*—we made in the deceased person so that we can reinvest it in other relationships. The detachment (*decathexis*) process requires accepting the fact that the loved one is really and truly lost to us. This acceptance must occur on a deep emotional level; it is not enough to have only an intellectual acknowledgment of the loss.
4. *Grief work is carried out through a long series of confrontations with the reality of the loss.* Survivors must deal with all the feelings and memories that bring to mind their attachment to the deceased person. Often one must confront the same point of attachment over and over again. For example, the survivor might have to listen repeatedly to a particular song that was a favorite of the deceased person before this song loses its power to overwhelm one with anxiety and sorrow.
5. *The process is complicated by our resistance to letting go of the attachment.* We want to stay in touch with the "lost object" in any way we can. This need can sabotage our efforts to accept the loss and return to normal life.

6. *The failure of grief work results in continued misery and dysfunction.* Time itself does not heal. In fact, we do not reenter the mainstream of time until we have liberated ourselves from attachment to the deceased person. Survivors who remain intensely attached to the deceased person over a prolonged period of time are considered to be suffering from pathological grief. (We would now call it complicated grief and not expect resolution neatly within the first year of bereavement.)

Despite its limitations, grief-work theory deserves much credit for acknowledging grief as a core aspect of the human experience and encouraging sensitive attention to the bereaved person.

From Grief-Work to Attachment

Freud's original theory emphasized the intrapsychic response to loss—how we attempt to deal with our own thoughts and feelings. Later contributors have called more attention to the interpersonal context of grief work: how a loss affects our relationships. The current interest in *attachment behavior* and bonding owes much to British psychiatrist John Bowlby's investigations. Bowlby (1969, 1973, 1980) connects the biological need for survival with grief and mourning. The vulnerable young of many species exhibit distress and attempt to draw their absent mother to their sides by whatever sounds and other communication signals they have in their repertoire. The mothers also seek their missing young by calling or signaling to them. Neither the young nor the mothers can relax until they have rejoined each other.

Adults also show the need for attachment when there is danger afoot. For example, citing a study of baboons, Bowlby (1969) notes that

Not only infants but adults also when under stress are strongly disposed to cling to a companion. Thus an adult female, when alarmed, clings to the back of her husband or is embraced by him. Conversely, when he is under stress during a fight, a male is likely to embrace one of his wives (p. 42).

Adult grief resonates with our early experiences of separation. Every dog has been a frightened puppy, every cat a stressed kitten, and every adult human an anxious baby. We have all had the anxiety of separation experiences, even if these were but fleeting episodes. The depressive state of a bereaved spouse has its precedent in the infant who felt himself or herself to be abandoned and vulnerable. The feeling that "I can't live without you" may have its roots in the sense of vulnerability that also accompanies separation between parent and young and between mates in many other species.

Why, then, is grief work so difficult? The goal of attachment behavior is to maintain the security provided by a significant interpersonal relationship. Any situation that threatens this bond will call forth:

action designed to preserve it; and the greater the danger of loss appears to be, the more intense and varied are the actions elicited to prevent it. In such circumstances all the most powerful forms of attachment behaviour become activated— clinging, crying and perhaps angry coercion. This is the phase of protest and one of acute physiological stress and emotional distress. *When these actions are successful the bond is restored, the activities cease, and the states of stress and distress are alleviated* (Bowlby, 1980, p. 42).

I have added italics to the last sentence because here Bowlby provides a valuable insight for understanding the intensity and persistence of grief responses. We respond effectively to a threatened loss of relationship by communicating our concern and putting ourselves on full alert. This response does not work, though, when it is death that separates us from a loved person. We can whisper, shout, and ready ourselves for heroic efforts, and yet the other person does not return. This persistent absence may be accompanied by persistent stress. What is the survivor to do when efforts to restore the relationship by yearning, remembering, crying, praying, and raging have failed? The survivor may keep trying and trying (Bowlby, 1980):

This means that the person's attachment behaviour is remaining constantly primed. . . . The condition of the organism is then one of chronic stress and is experienced as one of chronic distress. At intervals, moreover, both stress and distress are likely again to become acute (p. 42).

Bowlby's description is consistent with ongoing research into the physiological stress of bereavement. Our response to the stress of loss can itself become the source of continuing stress: we can't get what we want and we can't stop trying and, in the meantime, not much else gets done. Grief work is so difficult because it must overcome our desperate yearning to restore the lost love object through fantasies and emotions. We need patience and we need persistence—and some help from our understanding friends.

Another British researcher, Colin M. Parkes, conducted some of the most important studies of the psychosocial transitions involved in coping with the loss of a loved person. How do people attempt to get on with their lives after bereavement? Under what conditions does grief work fail, leaving the survivor in a state of prolonged social and personal dysfunction? These are examples of the questions that Parkes has been trying to answer. Parkes (2001; 2006) has identified three basic components of grief work:

- *Preoccupation with thoughts of the deceased person.* This represents a continuing search process (reminding us of the attachment-seeking signals and behaviors Bowlby describes in many species).
- *Repeatedly going over the loss experience in one's mind.* This is a painful process in which the survivor seems to be testing out the reality of the loss (Did this terrible thing really happen?).
- *Attempts to explain the loss.* It is somewhat easier to accept the reality of a death if the loss somehow makes sense, had a reason behind it. During this part of the grief-work process, the survivor is asking self and others "Why, why, why?"

How Useful is Grief-Work Theory?

Our understanding of grief has been enriched by the contributions of Freud, Bowlby, Parkes, and others who have cultivated the grief-work approach. Nevertheless, this theory has its limits. Margaret Stroebe (2001) is among those who have suggested that grief-work theory was accepted before sufficient research had been done. Her own findings indicate that some bereaved persons had not devoted themselves to grief work yet were functioning well and free of depression—while some who were hard at grief work were making only a limited recovery. These outcomes do not support the proposition that we must detach ourselves from emotional bonding to the deceased person through a long, difficult, and painful process. Nevertheless, the absence of grief work was related to adjustment problems for some individuals—mostly on the part of widowers who attempted to distract themselves from the loss.

In light of these findings, it would be useful to give more attention to individual differences in personality and coping styles. Reviews of the research literature have affirmed that not all bereaved persons need to express themselves in the same way or to share the same experiences in order to make their way through the stress of grief (Geneva, 2003; Lund & Caserta, 1997/1998). Camille B. Wortman and Roxanne Cohen Silver (1989; 1992) also conclude there is no evidence that people who attempt to confront the loss do better than those who do not. The lesson, they believe, is that we must look more closely at the relationship that has been lost (e.g., mother–child or husband–wife) and all the circumstances involved.

Although Freud was fascinated by cultural differences, he did not take them into account in his grief-work theory. Many thanatologists today recognize the importance of cultural influences on the ways people cope with grief. For example, bereaved persons in Bali are expected to distract themselves and participate in cheerful interactions, whereas those in Egypt are encouraged to share their pain and sorrow with others. Quite possibly there is more than one way to cope effectively with the loss and stress of bereavement, with both personality style and sociocultural expectations having their influences.

From Attachment to Continuing Bonds

Attachment theory soon bonded itself to the original grief-work formulation. There was a logical next development and it was advanced by

Dennis Klass, Phyllis R. Silverman, and Steven L. Nickman, along with their contributors to the book, *Continuing Bonds* (1996, p. 3). Examples from many cultures and situations were provided of grief that kept the lost loved one somehow alive to the survivor over the years. The authors directly challenged "the idea that the purpose of grief is to sever the bonds with the deceased in order to free the survivor to make new attachments. We offer an alternative model based on the mourner's continuing bonds with the deceased." In this theoretical model, it is no longer to be considered pathological if a person keeps an attachment with the deceased over a long period of time. The continuing bonds approach raised opposition to counseling and therapy assumptions that led to a relentless assault on the bereaved person's attachment to the person who was somehow present as well as absent.

The continuing bonds approach does not deny all facets of grief-work theory, but it has become an influential alternative to the desirability of removing the emotional attachment to the deceased person. Advocates of continuing bond theory point out that the bereaved person does not necessarily become trapped in time, condemned to repeating and recycling the lost relationship. Silverman (2003, p. 187), for example, observes that:

> A continuing bond does not mean, however, that people live In the past. . . . The way the bereaved relate to the deceased changes as they develop over the life cycle, whether they be young or old mourners. People need to stop thinking of grief as being entirely present or absent. People rarely just "get over it," nor do they ever really find closure.

But are continuing bonds always or even usually helpful? This question is proving rather difficult to study for a variety of reasons, e.g., how accurately can "continuing bonds" be disentangled from "grief" (Schut et al., 2006)? A review of the research literature (Field, 2006) offers two conclusions: (1) continuing bonds are often an adaptive part of adjustment to loss, but (2) can also contribute to difficulties in adjustment in certain circumstances. Researchers and counselors are now attempting to identify the situations in which continuing bonds are most

likely to have positive or negative effects on the grieving person's adaptation. It could be a while before the larger picture emerges. In the meantime, we might refrain from drawing hasty conclusions about whether a bereaved person "should" or "should not" maintain a strong emotional attachment to the deceased. Compassionate support serves well whether one is more attached to grief-work or continuing bonds theory. Recent studies discussed by Mikulinger and Shaver (2008) point the way to a more detailed and versatile application of attachment theory and its relationship to continuing bonds.

Other Theoretical Approaches to Understanding Grief

There are now other alternatives or supplements to grief-work theory. Each offers something useful to think about.

Stage Theory

The Kübler-Ross (1969) stage theory of dying has also been applied to grieving. Stage theorists usually specify that the first response to bereavement is shock, numbness, and disbelief. The final phase is the reestablishment of physical and mental balance. Descriptions of the middle phases of the grief process and the total number of phases are points that differ from one stage theorist to another. Many grieving people do experience some of the feelings, and attempt some of the coping strategies, that are listed in the various stage theories. It is not clear, however, that everybody in fact does go through all these stages.

Both applications of Kübler-Ross stage theory—to dying (Chapter 4) and to grieving—were quickly and widely accepted despite the lack of supportive research. Perhaps curiously, many writers, counselors, and educators did not seem troubled by the continued absence of research confirmation, or by clinical reports that also raised questions about the validity of this model. Now there are findings from an actual study. Maciejewski et al. (2007a, p. 716) base their findings on the Yale Bereavement Study that followed more than 200 people for 3 years following their loss. It was found that counter to stage theory, disbelief was not the initial, dominant grief indicator. Acceptance was the most commonly endorsed item.

In a follow-up article, Maciejewski et al (2007b, p. 297) add that:

> The stage theory of grief has captured the imagination of clinicians and the public. Despite its recognized limitations (e.g., that it will not predict exactly how every bereaved person will grieve), it remains taught in medical schools, posted on authoritative Web sites (e.g., National Cancer Institute), and continues to guide thinking about bereavement for many clinicians, educators, and researchers.

The Dual-Process Model

Stroebe and Schut (2001) have been impressed by the marked differences in grief responses that they have found in years of research. The dual-process model acknowledges this variability and suggests that a "normal" response can take many different forms. Key to this model are two processes: (1) emotional working through of grief and (2) adapting to new roles and situations in the altered world. A bereaved person might deal effectively with one of these processes while experiencing significant problems with the other. Recovery is in trouble if a person focuses on only one of these areas of concern. In robust recovery, a bereaved person tends to oscillate between emotional recovery and coping with the external realities of life. The person who is quickly back at work might seem to be making a strong recovery, but it is at the expense of avoiding the emotional issues. It is often thought that men and women grieve differently. The facts, however, suggest that there are two general styles of grieving, and both of these can be found in each gender. Masculine-style grieving puts the emphasis on keeping busy and getting things done. Feminine-style grieving gives more attention to emotions, but the person who is immersed in thoughts and feelings might drift away from obligations and interactions. The dual-process model is particularly useful for those interested in exploring both grief-work and continued bonding approaches.

Cultural traditions and pressures tend to lead bereaved people toward either the internal or the external mode of coping with grief. Hunt (2004) uses the dual-process model in her enlightening case example of "what it means to be a grieving black Zimbabwean woman today" (p. 288). The dual-process model can be recommended for consideration by both counselors and researchers.

An Evolutionary Biology Model of Grief

Is grief *adaptive?* Does this distressing condition actually have a positive function? Yes, according to the evolutionary biology model proposed by John Archer (2001). He suggests that grief is not only a human universal, but that a grief-like reaction also occurs in social birds and mammals when they lose a significant other either through death or separation. This conclusion had already been reached by John Bowlby and, before that, by Charles Darwin (1872). Archer has refined this principle: The grief expressed by birds and mammals is similar to that of young children rather than to that of adult humans. Their distress is acute but less complicated.

Archer's (2001) second conclusion is that grief is maladaptive: It has detrimental effects on the survival of the bereaved animal or person. This is a puzzle from the evolutionary perspective: Why would humans and other animals have such a strong response pattern that jeopardizes survival?

> Why were individuals who grieved not replaced by those who greeted the death of a mate or offspring with emotional indifference? Such individuals would, it seems, be better able to carry on with essential maintenance activities and be more motivated and able to find a mate and raise offspring (pp. 268–269).

Archer answers this question in a fascinating way. The grief itself is not adaptive—but social bonds are very much advantageous for survival. Grief is an unavoidable byproduct of a bird, mammal, or human determination to build and maintain strong emotional bonds with others. A journey to the evolutionary biology realm, then, offers a renewed appreciation for the significance of intimate relationships. The pain of separation is a risk that comes with attachment to another person (or dog, cat, horse, or macaw). By implication, when we decide against having any close relationships, we may be reducing the sorrow and anxiety of bereavement but also the benefits of social support.

HOW DO PEOPLE RECOVER FROM GRIEF?

We have already seen that there are more ways than one to cope with bereavement. In this section, we explore these patterns in more detail. First, we consider what has been learned about the death of a spouse. This will include a harrowing visit with Third World widows. Next, we will turn to responses to the death of children, to the grief and death of elderly adults, and then to survivors of traumatic or stigmatized death. Finally, we will complete our examination of the impact of grief by looking at the most extreme outcome: death of the bereaved person.

When a Husband or Wife Dies

"Until death us do part." This traditional phrase in marriage vows continues to be meaningful. Death as the event that ends a marriage occurs ever more frequently in the later adult years. Consider the situation at age 65 and older: The U.S. Census Bureau estimates that about 45% of women and 14% of men who had been married were now widows or widowers. At age 85 and older, spousal bereavement rises to 80% for women and 43% for men (2003). These numbers would be even higher were it not for the increase in divorces. Coping with the loss of a marital partner and somehow going on with life are challenges that many people will be facing at some point. Fortunately, spousal bereavement has been the subject of many careful studies that have included interviews as well as background information. We will draw first on findings from major studies conducted in the United States and England by Colin Murray Parkes and his colleagues (Glick, Weiss, & Parkes, 1974; Parkes, 2001; Parkes & Weiss, 1983).

The Immediate Impact of Spousal Bereavement

Most of the women had been experiencing anticipatory grief. However, the impact of the actual death was still felt deeply. But those who found themselves suddenly transformed into widows suffered even more intensely. They felt overwhelmed, anguished, as though there were no limits to the catastrophe that had befallen them. The suddenly bereaved woman might feel so numb that she feared she would never again move, act, or think, or she might cry as though she would never be able to stop.

The husband who became a widower usually responded to the impact of the death very much as the widow did. The men differed, however, in how they interpreted their feelings. Although the women often emphasized a sense of abandonment, the men reported feeling a sort of dismemberment. The women would speak of being left alone, deprived of a comforting and protecting person. The men were more likely to feel "like both my arms were being cut off." These differences seemed related to what marriage had meant for widow and widower. Marriage had sustained the man's capacity to work. For the woman, marriage had provided a sphere of interpersonal engagement.

Emotional and Physical Reactions Soon After Bereavement

Bewilderment and despair often continued beyond the first impact of loss. There were still periods of weeping, especially for the women. Physical symptoms appeared and sometimes lingered for weeks or months. Many women reported aches and pains, poor appetite, sleep disturbances, loss of stamina, headaches, dizziness, and menstrual irregularities. Often a widow would wake up in the middle of the night and remain tormented by grief and the reality of her partner's absence. Some women tried to wear themselves out by working hard and staying up late. Others turned to sleeping medications. The dread and emptiness of facing the night alone were relieved for some of the bereaved by having close friends or relatives who kept them company until sleep finally took over. Each woman had to find her own balance between the desire to receive help and the fear of becoming dependent on others.

The typical widower attempted to maintain control over his feelings because he considered it unmanly to let go. Such statements as "It's not fair!" were seldom made by men. Although less troubled by anger than the widow, the widower did have difficulty with guilt. He was more likely to blame himself: "I wasn't sensitive enough to her." "I should have made things easier." The widower's guilt reaction tended to subside fairly soon, although the need for rational control over all responses to the death persisted.

Leave-Taking Ceremonies

Leave-taking ceremonies went well for most of the bereaved in this study. It was helpful to hear from others that they had done their part to ensure a proper farewell. This bolstered their sense of confidence in managing difficult affairs despite their shock and suffering. The widow was seen by all as the final authority on what should be done, regardless of different wishes that, for example, the husband's family might have. In this way, the widow began to gain public acceptance as the new head of the family. The widows often felt that in arranging the ceremonies they were able to continue the expression of their love, devotion, and attachment.

The funeral directors usually were seen as supportive and caring persons. Nevertheless, there were painful moments. Some widows suddenly felt the full pangs of a late husband's death at a particular point during the funeral process, such as the last viewing of the body. The complete realization of the death, however, did not seem to dawn upon the bereaved at any one moment in time, although some of the moments were critical steps toward this realization. Most widows seemed to be operating on very limited emotional energy. They neither sought out nor took in what the clergy might have had to say. Understandably, the widows tended to be absorbed in their own feelings. Many of the widows were religious, however, and seemed to find some comfort in clergy's repetitions of traditional beliefs about the continuation of soul or spirit after death.

The leave-taking ceremonies did not seem to be quite as important to most of the widowers in this study. They gave less attention to the details and did not express as much gratitude toward the funeral directors. They were also more likely to feel that the cost of the funeral was too high. The emotional significance of the funeral itself may have been relatively less important for the men because they were primarily concerned with how they would manage in the months to come. The funeral and all that it involved was something that they had to "get through" rather than the milestone it represented for many widows.

Grief and Recovery: The First Year

The long months after the funeral often were the most difficult for both widow and widower. For a short time, there had been concentrated attention upon the needs of the bereaved. But the deceased spouse remains dead and the bereaved person's emotional and pragmatic problems continue day after day. The widows realized that they had to reorganize their lives, but now they lacked the clustering of help that had been available to them in the first days after bereavement. They often felt that they should not burden others with their sorrow. A "decent" amount of time had to pass before they could reenter ordinary life and yet did not feel comfortable with a full-blown expression of mourning such as is customary in some societies.

Sorrow and anxiety remained intense even though the widows now seldom spoke of their grief. Many engaged in obsessional reviews. Events surrounding the husband's death were relived over and over. Mulling over the death is a component of grief work that, as Stroebe has found, seems helpful to some, although not necessarily all, survivors.

The obsessional reviews often were concerned with what might have happened instead of what actually did happen. How could the accident have been avoided? How might it all have turned out differently? The widows frequently searched for meaning through these reviews. Why had their husband been taken away? It was not the name of the disease or the technical reason for the accident that concerned the widow so much as the need to make sense of the death. If "Why me?" is the question some people ask when they learn of their own terminal illness, then "Why him?" seems to be the survivor's parallel question. These questions often lost some of their intensity over time, but the search for meaning continued to linger. Convincing answers proved hard to find.

Children who have lost a mother or father through death often have a need to revisit the places they had seen with their deceased parent.

Although it remained painful to review the events leading up to the death, memories of the husband himself and of shared experiences generally were positive. This was especially true in the early weeks and months. A tendency to idealize the lost spouse was observed. The deceased husband was the best man who ever lived, a wonderful husband, a marvelous father—he had no faults whatsoever. Later, a more balanced view usually emerged. The widow would still think about him frequently and positively, but now some of his quirks and imperfections gained recognition as well. The widow might also find herself suddenly angry at the husband for leaving her with the children to raise by herself. These episodes of negative feelings seemed to be part of the long process of developing a realistic attitude that the widow could live with through the years.

Often the widow's feelings about her husband went beyond vivid memories. She might have a strong sense that he was still there with her. This impression would make itself felt soon after the death and remain with her off and on for a long time. The sense of presence was especially persistent for women who had experienced the sudden loss of their spouses. More extensive haunting experiences were reported by women who had had no opportunity to prepare themselves for their losses. For most of the widows, it was comforting to feel that their husbands were still there somehow. Even when the sense of presence was vivid, the widows knew that their husbands were really dead. It was neither unusual nor crazy for widows to feel this sense of presence.

Widows with children at home usually recognized their responsibilities clearly and felt that the need to provide parental care helped to keep them from becoming lost in their own grief. Often there was a new resolve to be a better good mother. The widows felt the need to be straightforward and realistic with the children yet also to shelter and protect them and keep their spirits up. The widows were in a difficult position in trying to provide answers to their children while still searching for answers themselves.

The Widowers' Response

Although the bereaved man was almost as likely to feel the presence of his wife soon after the bereavement, as time went by this phenomenon became much less common. The men also tended to cut off the obsessional review after just a few weeks. The widower did not seem as tolerant of his impulse to dwell upon the past; he pushed himself right back to immediate realities, although, like the widow, he too felt a desire to replay the circumstances of the death. The widowers were also less likely

to speak openly about their feelings. They did not usually seek out the opportunity to share either the events themselves or their personal reactions.

The typical widower gave no outward sign of his grief. Yet a close look at the quality of the widower's personal life, including the occupational sphere, indicated a decrease in energy, competence, and satisfaction. The widower usually made a more rapid social recovery but a slower emotional recovery than the widow. A year after his wife's death, the widower was much more likely than the widow to feel lonely and depressed.

Other studies have found that for both women and men, the lost spouse might occasionally return as a dream–visitor over many years—perhaps even throughout the survivor's lifetime. These dream visitations do not proceed through stages or tasks. Instead, many different themes are expressed in the dreams (Belicki et al., 2003), including:

- Dreamer and deceased encounter one another, greeting each other enthusiastically.
- Dream of romantic or sexual encounter with deceased.
- Deceased appears to dreamer's surprise. Often the apparent death seen as a mistake.
- Dreamer is physically separated from the deceased, for example, by some physical barrier (pp. 100–101).

Dreams of the deceased spouse seem to have more staying power than most other dreams; they linger in the waking memory and become a part of the mental and emotional fabric of ongoing life.

Types of Recovery from the Impact of Marital Bereavement

People who did not have the opportunity to prepare for the spouse's death suffered more distress, not only immediately, but for some time afterward. More than a year later, the spouse who had experienced sudden, unexpected bereavement was more socially withdrawn, remained more preoccupied with the details of the death, had more difficulty in accepting the reality of the loss, and in general was experiencing more disorganization in daily life.

This suggests that we cannot rely upon the passage of time by itself to facilitate recuperation from the trauma. Social support is needed both in the early period of acute bereavement and over the many months and even years required to adjust to the devastating loss.

The response to early bereavement provides useful clues as to how the individual will respond as the months go by. Those who were most disturbed a few weeks after the death usually were the ones who continued to be disturbed a year later. The person who had strong feelings that the death was unreal and who tried to behave as though the spouse were still alive also was likely to have more difficulty than others over an extended time.

The quality of the marital relationship influences the grief and recovery process. When the partners had very mixed feelings toward each other, the experiences associated with bereavement often were more disturbing. Similarly, it was harder for the survivor to adjust if the relationship had been based on a clinging dependence. If soon after bereavement the surviving spouse felt cast adrift, empty, and helpless, then difficulties in adjustment were likely to be more prolonged. More recent studies also indicate that the kind of attachment bond that existed between the couple has a strong relationship to the way in which grief and recovery occur (Waskowic & Chartier, 2003).

Unresolved Grief

All of the newly bereaved people studied had to face the question of who they were now, having lost part of their identities with the loss of their spouses. Two years later, some had made substantial recoveries from grief. Those still in despair had not formed a coherent and acceptable conception of the death, nor were they able to modify their self-images in preparation for new lives without a spouse. Furthermore, they were more likely to use tranquilizers, drink and/or smoke heavily, and to wonder whether anything in life was worthwhile. Why did some people experience such complications in the grief and recovery process? Why do some people fall into one pattern and some into the other?

Careful study of individual case histories distinguished among three types of concepts of *unresolved grief:*

- *The unexpected grief syndrome* occurs in some people when the spouse dies without warning; therefore they do not have the opportunity to prepare themselves for the overwhelming loss. Disbelief and intense anxiety often became not only the first but also the continued responses.
- *The conflicted grief syndrome* can occur when death ends a troubled relationship, often one in which separation or divorce had been contemplated. Some of the marriages in the study had been to alcoholic men whose behavior had created a climate of fear and disorder. Other marriages had been marked by depression and withdrawal. The unresolved grief experienced by survivors of troubled marriages appears in a sense to be continuations of the frustrations and disappointments that had characterized the relationships while the spouses were alive.
- *The chronic grief syndrome* is marked by the survivors' strong feelings of dependency. Yearning for the deceased is often a part of any grief experience, but for people with this syndrome it becomes predominant. The survivors have unusually powerful dependence on the deceased spouses and do not feel personally capable of taking on the responsibilities of life with their partners gone.

The type marriage relationship and the circumstances of the death itself (sudden or anticipated) can help to identify those who are at particular risk for intense and prolonged distress. Suicide attempts and severe depressive reactions requiring psychiatric treatment are among the risks. Most bereaved men and women make their way through without reaching extremes of despair or self-destructiveness. Nevertheless, we should not lose sight of the fact that some people do remain locked in their grief and mourning for an extended period of time to the extent that they cannot derive satisfaction from their own lives or meet the needs of others. Adult children are especially valued as sources of help by older widows and widowers. This help includes practical assistance, such as home maintenance, shopping,

In Edvard Munch's (1896) *Death in the Sick Room,* some family members turn away and sink into their private grief while others offer comfort.

and coping with insurance and other financial transactions.

The Psychosocial Transition

Parkes (2001) calls attention to the *psychosocial transition*, the change from who we were to who we are now after a death has altered our lives:

All of us, from the moment of our birth, have been building inside ourselves a model of the world, a set of assumptions on the basis of which we recognize the world that we meet and plan our behaviour accordingly. . . . Not only does a major psychosocial transition require us to revise a great number of assumptions about the world, but most of these assumptions have become habits of thought and behaviour that are now virtually automatic. A widow will come down for breakfast in the morning and find that she has laid the table for two when there is now only one person to eat it (p. 91).

This challenging situation could be regarded as an example of what anthropologists have described as *rites of passage* (Gennep, 1960; Turner, 1969, 1992). Whether through physical or symbolic space, a person might need to move from "here" to "there" and in so doing shed an existing status for a new one. This happens, for example, when a youth is initiated into adulthood through traditional rituals or two single people go through a wedding ceremony. People are most vulnerable when they are between "here" and "there." This is what is meant by being in limbo, sometimes a lengthy period during which one is not quite who one used to be and not yet who one will become. That is clearly the situation for a person in the midst of psychosocial transition after bereavement—and it suggests that appropriate social rituals could be helpful in guiding and protecting the individual during this precarious time.

The Family That Has Lost a Child

Losing a child to death is one of the most painful of all human experiences. Anguish is immediate. Unfortunately, the impact of the loss on the surviving family members can also be long lasting, though seldom obvious to outsiders.

Shadow Grief: Perinatal Death

The sorrow of a child's death often seems to follow a family like a shadow. After observing the reactions of mothers who had lost a baby before or soon after birth, Peppers and Knapp (1980) introduced the term, *shadow grief*. Years after the death, many of the mothers were still feeling the anguish. In a later study, Knapp (1986) found the same phenomenon among parents who had lost older children to death. They were no longer completely dominated by grief, but the shadow or cloud had a way of making itself known as they moved through life:

> On the surface most observers would say that the "grief work" has been accomplished. But this is not the case. Shadow grief reveals itself more in the form of an emotional "dullness," where the person is unable to respond fully and completely to outer stimulation and where normal activity is moderately inhibited. . . . Under certain circumstances and on certain occasions, [it] comes bubbling to the surface, sometimes in the form of tears, sometimes not, but always accompanied by a feeling of sadness and a mild sense of anxiety . . . (pp. 40–41).

Knapp's findings are consistent with observations that many others have made. Parents who have lost a child often feel that their own lives also changed at that moment. Furthermore, they may not want to relinquish the grief. The pain is part of the memory—and the memory is precious.

The death of so young a child has often been given relatively little attention by society. The lack of communal recognition and support tends to isolate the parents in their grief. Some newspapers have even prohibited publication of newborn death notices, and it is difficult to find sympathy cards on the market for *perinatal death*. This term refers to infants who die at any point from the 20th week after conception through the first month after birth. Premature birth is still the most common cause of perinatal death, although advances in medical and nursing techniques have saved some neonates who otherwise would have died. Deaths also occur for a variety of other reasons (e.g., a genetic defect or a prenatal infection) and sometimes for reasons that are never clearly determined. We cannot exclude socioeconomic causes, either. Even in the United States, many pregnant women still do not have access to or are not aware of perinatal health services.

Complications of Perinatal Grief

Grief over a perinatal death is similar in many respects to grief over any loss. There are some special circumstances, however. For example, the mother may still be sedated or exhausted at the time she learns of her child's death. She is also ready to mother her baby, both physically and emotionally. This total readiness, including lactation to provide breast milk, now has no opportunity to express itself. Parents may have to listen to such unhelpful comments as "Well, you still have other children," and they may also find it difficult to explain the loss and provide comfort to the other children while they are troubled by their own grief.

Sensitive caregivers have learned that their first step is to recognize that a significant loss has occurred (or is about to occur, if the infant is still alive but not expected to survive). We can be more helpful to the parents and siblings when we ourselves comprehend the meaning of this loss. The family that has experienced perinatal death often feels misunderstood and abandoned by others:

> Most bereaved parents tell us that the support they received from others at the time of the baby's death did not continue very long. They

think that others do not continue to "live" their grief as they do. Others expect them to recover within a few short weeks (Cordell & Thomas, 1997, p. 299).

The health care system is becoming more responsive to the emotional needs of family members. In some hospital settings, the family is encouraged to interact with the newborn in a natural and loving way. Photographs may be taken of parents holding the baby, and various memorabilia (such as the child's first footprints or a lock of hair) may be given to them. Reynolds (2003/2004) suggests that parents be informed of the option to see and hold their stillborn infant but that they not are pressured to do so; whether or not this practice is helpful is a matter of controversy at present. "Bereavement protocols" that help prepare hospital staff to provide emotional support for family members are becoming more common, and group counseling has also proved helpful (Cordell & Thomas, 1997). Cacciatore (2007) has made a breakthrough contribution toward expression of grief and mourning by persuading officials to issue birth certificates for stillborn infants.

Effects of a Child's Death on the Parents' Worldview

The loss and sorrow that follows the death of the child may be intensified by a crisis of belief or faith. This response appears to be especially strong when the child's life was taken by murder (Mathews & Marwit, 2003/2004) and is thought to occur in other sudden and traumatic types of death as well. The parents may feel that the world no longer makes sense, that one can count upon neither upon God nor community.

There is some evidence that preserving an emotional connection with the deceased child helps to prevent the destruction of the parents' worldview. Klass (1992/1993) found that the "inner representation" of the dead child continues to be experienced by the parents for many years, if not throughout all their lives. He defines inner representations "as characterizations or thematic memories of the deceased, and the emotional states connected with these characterizations and memories" (p. 383). Parents can interact with their inner representations of the child through such means as:

- *Memory:* bringing the child to mind often.
- *A sense of presence:* the feeling that the child is still there with them in some way.
- *Hallucinations:* the experience of seeing or hearing the child.
- *Incorporation:* taking the characteristics or virtues of the child into their own personalities (e.g., rescuing lost animals as the child had often done).

Staying in contact with the inner representation of the dead child makes it easier for the survivors to keep their worldviews intact. The sorrow and sense of loss are still there, but the feeling that something of the child still lives with or within them seems to reduce doubts about their worldviews. These symbolic interactions with the deceased are not signs of pathology—for example, it is not "crazy" to sense the child's presence or even to catch fleeting glimpses of the child.

Talbot (1998/1999) has found that the hardiness of some mothers:

seems to have been forged in the fire of agonizing grief—grief which has been consciously confronted and transformed into the gift of compassion. . . . They have lit a pathway to survival and personal growth: By identifying and incorporating a loved one's best characteristics, it is possible to find ways to honor the past while building a future. By understanding what has been learned from loss and grief, it is possible to reach out and help make the world a better place for self and others (p. 184).

The Future of the Marital Relationship After the Death of a Child

The loss of a child creates stress and strain for the family unit as a whole (Rubin & Malkinson, 2001). For example, sexual intimacy can diminish, even though many couples report an increased need for physical contact and comfort. The parents often report feeling more irritable and more likely to direct anger at each other. This can become particularly destructive when one parent blames the other either for the death or for past actions related to the lost child. Furthermore, communication tends to break down for bereaved couples. The parents may withdraw into their own grief and therefore away from each other. There may also be a reduction in self-disclosure and emotional exchange—an avoidance of the core issues. Nevertheless, most couples do not divorce or even seriously consider this possibility after the death of a child. Instead, there will be many years of trying to integrate the continuing absence of the child with the challenges and opportunities of their ongoing lives. Recent studies indicate that most parents achieve what Barrera et al. (2007, p. 152) call *integrated grief*.

> This is a difficult process that does not overcome the sense of devastation and loss, but enables the parents to experience a sense of control over their expression of grief and a relatively effective style of navigating life without the deceased child. . . . They also expressed a positive outlook on life and described having learned from their experience.

Like many other researchers, Barrera et al. observe that people do not all respond the same to bereavement, and that social support can make a significant difference.

Shirley A. Murphy's (2008) ongoing studies have identified two very different situations in which parents are most at risk for extreme distress when a child dies. Sudden, violent death, as in accident, disaster, or homicide can have a severe impact on the parents lives, and so can the experience of enduring a child's extended illness that results in death. Support for bereaved parents is likely to be more effective when there is understanding of the specific experiences they have been through.

The Grief of Grandparents

Grandparents and parents experience many of the same feelings of loss. In addition, grandparents also are likely to experience vicarious grief for the parents (Kastenbaum, 1987; Rando, 2002) as well as their own direct grief over the death of the child. It hurts them to realize how much their adult children are sorrowing for the death of the grandchild. Furthermore, it is even more unexpected for people to outlive their grandchildren. Such an unexpected and "untimely" death can generate a worldview crisis just as in the case of the parents.

White (1999) has found that the death of a grandchild causes extreme anguish, regardless of the child's age. Most of the bereaved grandparents had a strong need to talk about their grandchildren. This need could be frustrated if the family has responded with withdrawal and silence or if communication patterns between the grandparents and their adult children had previously been inadequate. Some grandparents felt helpless because they could not protect their adult children from the pain of loss—similar perhaps to the frequent desire of parents to shield their young children from awareness of death and dying. Nevertheless, grandparents often did provide valuable support to the bereaved parents just by being there with them, as well as by helping with chores and expenses. The overall message is clear: Grandparents often are much affected by the death of a child and have a significant role to play in the family's response.

Today, grandparents often remain overlooked when counseling and other forms of social support are provided. Nehari, Grebler, and Toren (2007) found that many grandparents were struggling with their perceived "right to grief" and for a sense of isolation from their bereaved children: "They won't talk with us about the pain." The researchers set up meetings between parents and grandparents of the deceased child. The sessions were highly emotional and intense, resulting in improved communication among all the grieving family members.

BEREAVEMENT IN LATER LIFE

We are vulnerable to bereavement at any age. In the later adult years, there is an increased vulnerability, but loss is often met with a vitality and resilience that exceeds what one might have expected.

Sorrow upon Sorrow, Loss upon Loss

Life satisfaction does not necessarily decline with age. Gerontologists have discredited the assumption that usefulness and the enjoyment of life end at a certain age. Nevertheless, it is also true that the longer a person lives and forms loving attachments, the more there is to lose. Loss may follow upon loss, taxing the individual's ability to cope. This is the concept of bereavement overload (Kastenbaum, 1969). Long-lived people usually have survived many people that they were deeply attached to. Furthermore, loss of physical abilities, employment, social respect, and familiar environments are all life changes that can trigger responses similar to what occurs when an interpersonal relationship is terminated by death. We accumulate these losses just by staying alive over an extended period of time.

What changes would be expected in people of any age who have been forced to cope with too many losses in too short a period of time? They might try to reconstitute their personal world by replacing the losses, or they might lose themselves in work or other engrossing activities. These alternatives, however, are often closed to elders. What now? One might become increasingly preoccupied with bodily functions and experience less free energy to invest in new activities or relationships. Furthermore, the experience of multiple losses may lead to a sense of extreme caution. "I had better not care about anybody or anything else. Sooner or later I will lose these people and things as well. And I just cannot bear to lose and mourn again."

The whole constellation of "old behaviors," then, can develop from multiple, unbearable bereavement. Suicide attempts also can be generated from such a psychological state. The individual may give up when stricken by a relatively minor ailment and allow the condition to worsen or reduce his or her activities so drastically that both body and mind are in poor tone to respond to any kind of stress. Such considerations suggest that bereavement in old age is a condition deserving careful and systematic attention.

The older person is vulnerable to deaths of many kinds. Most common is the death of siblings (Moss, Moss, & Hansson, 2001). But elderly adults also lose a spouse, adult children, grandchildren, and even parents. I have stood at the side of a 74-year-old man as tears ran down his cheeks because his 97-year-old father was dead. The outsider might rush to the conclusion that the death of a very old parent should not mean so much to a child also advanced in years. Consider, however, how long this relationship had to develop and flourish and what a blow it now was to go on without the father he had known for three quarters of a century.

It is not only the death of a human member of the family that can prove devastating. On several occasions I have discovered that an elderly patient with whom I was working first sank into a depressed, no-point-in-living state following the death of an animal companion. What might seem to be "the depression that comes with age" can turn out to be a grief reaction to the death of an animal companion, as well as to the death of a human companion.

However, the overall picture is more positive than it has usually been assumed. Older widowed persons often have effective coping abilities that help them to get on with their lives, even though they regard the death of their spouses as having been the most stressful event they have ever experienced. After months of high stress after the death of their spouses, many elderly persons are able to restore order and hope to their lives. Resiliency does not mean that words such as "recovery" or "renewal" describe their situation, however, nor does it mean that bereaved elders go through a standard set of stages. For example, the elderly widows studied by Bennett and Bennett (2000/2001) experienced the feelings described by stage theories but not in any particular order (no fixed sequence > no stages!). They also explained that life goes on for them but that it is not really the same life. As one widow put it:

There's always this great hole inside that hurts, and . . . I was building a pattern, a life round it. I couldn't—you can't ever fill it, but you build a life round (p. 244).

Studies continue to find that elderly people often maintain their physical health and remaining interpersonal relationships after the death of a loved one (D'Epinay, Cavalli, & Spini, 2003). They sorrow for the loss and are more likely to experience loneliness but still find meaning and satisfaction in life. As a woman a week shy of her 100th birthday told me, "There is life, dear, and there is death. What else can anyone expect?"

Elderly bereaved people often have a wealth of experience and skills that not only can be applied to reintegrating their own lives but also to enriching the lives of others. Often these people need only positive human companionship and a little help with some of the details of everyday life in order to continue as resourceful and well-integrated members of society.

ARE BEREAVED PEOPLE AT HIGHER RISK FOR DEATH?

Yes, in general the risk of illness and death does increase following the loss of a person who has been very important to us. Most grieving people experience some physical distress, and most make strong recoveries. "A broken heart," though, is not just a picturesque phrase. Research supports folk knowledge here. We should not underestimate the physical effects of sorrow and anxiety.

Differential Mortality Risk: The Statistical Pattern

Almost all studies have found excessive mortality rates for bereaved persons (Goodkin et al., 2001). (The exceptions are a few studies with small samples.) This pattern holds true in Europe and Japan as well as in North America and has been consistent throughout the twentieth century.

Who Is Most at Risk?

Some people are more at risk than others. Widows and widowers are at higher risk than married men and women. This risk is even greater for widowers. The mortality rate is higher for men than women at every adult age

level, and bereavement further increases the differential.

The relationship with age is not what one might have expected. Younger adults have a relatively higher excessive mortality rate after bereavement. The death of a spouse is followed by a sudden rise in the mortality risk of bereaved young adults. Most at risk is the young man whose wife has recently died. This risk is further intensified if the death was sudden and unexpected. Bereavement-related deaths most often occur within the first 6 months. These findings suggest that more attention should be given to the vulnerability of bereaved young men in the period of time immediately following the death. Lichtenberg (1990) remembers having felt "out of control: one moment I was torn apart, and the next moment I was calm. It was frightening to hurt, to be numb, to feel panic, and I worried that I would collapse . . ." (p. 86). We never want to forget that there is always a human story behind the statistics.

What Are the Leading Causes of Death Among the Bereaved?

Heart disease and cancer are the leading causes of death among bereaved people just as they are for the population in general. However, there is another type of death that increases greatly after bereavement—violent deaths, especially suicide. Stroebe and Stroebe (1993) report that within the first week after bereavement, the suicide rate for men was 66 times greater than would have been expected. The suicide rate for women was more than 9 times greater than expected. Suicide shows the greatest increase among all causes of death, although heart disease accounts for most of the fatalities. This heightened risk of suicide soon after the death of a spouse has not yet received the attention it deserves.

As noted earlier, the body's ability to resist infection through the immune system can also be impaired during the turmoil of grief, as it is in other types of stressful situations (Goodkin et al., 2001). We do not have to be medical experts to offer companionship and support to bereaved people—and by so doing, perhaps to reduce stress levels, protect immune functioning, and even save a life.

Although emotionally painful as a reminder of the loss, a cemetery visit can also be a consoling way of affirming one's love.

HOW WELL DO WE SUPPORT THE BEREAVED?

The widower is reducing his colleagues' anxieties when he goes right back to work and gives no indication that he expects special concern. "I am okay," he is saying, in effect, "I am not mourning." The widow releases others from obligation by refraining from displays of mourning. "She's a strong woman," her friends say with admiration. Many other cultures have expected and respected a sometimes extended period of mourning—not so with our rather impatient mainstream society today. However, the absence of mourning behaviors too easily gives the illusion that the person is "over" the loss. This may be one of the reasons why some bereaved people have fears of going crazy. All of the anxiety and confusion, all the depths of feeling, seem to be on the inside. The rest of the world continues to move along in its usual way. With little social recognition or tolerance for grieving, the bereaved can be made to feel as though their sorrow and stress are signs of pathology or weakness.

American Society's Discomfort with Grief and Mourning

How well a culture's death system is functioning can be estimated by examining the support it provides for the bereaved. Mourning gets in the way of a society oriented toward time and efficiency. Mourning does not seem to serve any real purpose in such a setting. Pressures have been increasing against the expression of personal loss, with the exception of unusual circumstances such as the 9/11 terrorist attacks. There are still places in the United States where people

A New Orleans tradition: the band plays a solemn procession on the way to the funeral, then celebrates life on the way back with the boisterous, "When the Saints Go Marching In!"

will pause in respectful silence when a funeral procession goes by, whether or not they know the identity of the deceased. But the funeral procession has become a target of efficiency practitioners in most urban areas: "Traffic is bad enough as it is!" Similarly, there are pressures against the use of land for cemeteries. Why should the dead stand in the way of progress?

Memorialization of the dead and support for the bereaved have fallen relatively low on the list of priorities of the mainstream American death system. People still gather around for the funeral—often with reluctance—and for a short period of ritual and visiting. After that, however, the bereaved is frequently left alone. How long do colleagues sympathize with somebody who has suffered a significant loss? How long are relatives and neighbors prepared to be sensitive and supportive? I have noticed an increasing impatience with grief. The mourner is supposed to

shape up after a short time and let others get on with their lives. In this cultural context, it is not surprising to come across a doctoral dissertation (DiMeo, 1978) featuring a "prescribed degriefing intervention method (DIM)" that requires but a single treatment session! DIM, indeed! Quicker is cheaper, better, more cost-effective. But are we really prepared to line up for "degriefing" when overcome by profound sorrow and loss? There are still powerful local customs, though, in which the living offer their companionship unstintingly to the dead and the grieving. James K. Crissman (1994) describes such practices in *Living and Dying in Central Appalachia*.

Perhaps our impatience with grief is one of the reasons why so much attention is given to the question of how long grief is supposed to endure. It is one of the questions most frequently raised by the public and bruited about by professionals. The sense of chronic time urgency that characterizes the type A personality also seems to characterize much of American society. We are reluctant to pause for death, and thinking about the dead is regarded as a waste of time.

American society's withdrawal of support from the bereaved represents a break from most historical traditions. In some religious and ethnic groups, there remains a sense of closeness, of reconfirming bonds with each other. This may even include a legitimized relationship with the dead (as in the Hmong). The survivors may have prayers to say, offerings to make, vigils to keep. There is time and opportunity for personal grief to find expression in a socially approved form. The newly dead can remain as an important person during a critical period of psychological adjustment to the loss. The bereaved need not pretend that the funeral marks the end of the relationship with the parent, spouse, sibling, child, or friend. It is possible to have thoughts and feelings about the deceased, even to sense the presence vividly, without violating social norms. In this sense, societies that have functioned with less technological sophistication often have embodied more insights into the psychological needs of the bereaved. As a society, Americans may be uncomfortable with the seeming irrationality or inefficiency of grief. If so, this says rather more about dominant values in the United States than about the realities of core human experience.

The need to feel connected with those who have passed from our lives might, however, now be finding new avenues of expression. "Expressions of Grief on the World Wide Web" (De Vries & Roberts, 2004) documents the increasing use of online communication as an innovative means of mourning. Deaths are even finding their way into Second Life. Not long ago, mental health experts and researchers Klass, Silverman, and Nickman (1996) urged that we give ourselves permission to establish continuing bonds with the dead, rather than trying to free ourselves of all attachments to the "lost object." This reconsideration now seems to be in progress.

MEANINGFUL HELP FOR BEREAVED PEOPLE

Society is coming to realize that we can help each other through our times of grief. Phyllis Silverman (Kastenbaum, 1993/1994), founder

of the Widow-to-Widow Program, reviews the issues that had to be resolved in establishing this pioneering peer-support program.

Widow-to-Widow: The Phyllis Silverman Interview

There were no peer-support programs to deal with bereavement, grief, and mourning when Silverman was completing her doctoral studies at Harvard. It was thought that grief was a kind of illness that had to run its course. Did Silverman accept this medical model?

> When we talk of grief as illness, we make it sound like a foreign or alien object that has invaded our bodies and which we must in some way expunge, as, for example, a wound that heals after the scab falls off, or a cold that must run its course. With the "proper treatment" we can make it go away. With this model we maintain a sense of ourselves as machines. . . . We get no sense of context, of the complexity of an experience, and of its fullness (p. 251).

Silverman observed grief to be a central fact of human existence, not simply an illness from which we hope to recover.

> People, living or dead, are part of who and what we are. . . . We don't "get over" people. We live in a web of relationships. We are still connected to the dead. . . . Because my father died, I haven't stopped being his daughter. When someone important dies we are changed by this loss. Our lives will never be the same. . . . The self we knew with that other person is gone. We need to re organize, find a place for this relationship, and develop other selves (p. 252).

One of her first research findings was that grief did not simply fade away after a brief period of crisis. Public health specialists at the time were endorsing a crisis theory of mental health and illness. With skillful professional intervention, the crisis should be resolved within about 2 weeks (well in keeping with our society's expectations for a "quick fix" to grief and anything else that ails us).

> When I first offered this view to widowed women—they laughed at me! They said that if you had your act together in two years—so that your head felt screwed on, so you could look

ahead—you were lucky! The more I talked with the widowed, the more I realized that our models of grief were not correct (p. 253).

Silverman came up with a different model and a different approach to helping bereaved people. This model includes the following principles:

- *Grief does not have a final outcome.* Bereavement leads to a series of changes over many years. "People grow, gain new perspective on who they are, and learn how to deal more resourcefully with their own feelings and with other people."
- *Grief can most usefully be regarded as a life transition.* Although bereavement does produce a crisis and does have significant physiological aspects, it is basically a human experience that alters one's relationship to self and others. Life does go on, but it goes on somewhat differently.
- *People can help each other.* One does not necessarily have to turn to professional assistance, although this may be indicated in some circumstances. Peer support—such as widows comforting each other—can be effective. Furthermore, when people with similar problems help each other, they do not thereby become "patients" who are dependent on the medical system. A network of social support is needed:

There are usually several mourners in the death of a spouse, and they need each other to share their feelings about the deceased, to remember together, and to support each other as they acknowledge their pain and loss. They need friends to help with the concrete tasks of living and managing their family from the time before the funeral to the establishment of a lifestyle appropriate to their new situation.

Silverman introduced the Widow-to-Widow Program at a time when neither professional grief counselors nor other peer-support groups had yet appeared. The program was very successful and soon became replicated throughout much of the nation. Many other peer-support groups have since emerged (e.g., The Compassionate Friends who help parents who have lost a child through death). Silverman thinks of peer support as "the first line of defense. Most of us get through major crises in our lives with help from our friends." When people with similar

problems help each other, all discover that they are not alone and all are in a position to learn valuable coping skills from each other.

Although many people have found comfort in peer-support groups of various types, there are hazards here as well. Julie Wambach (1983) conducted a series of participant–observer contacts with self-help bereavement groups. She reported an inflexible philosophy that assumed widows should go through a sequence of stages of mourning in a prescribed time-period. This rigid timetable and the concept of stages had no basis in fact. Many widows felt pressured by the timetable and rigid expectations. Discrimination against the older widows was also observed. As Wambach also notes, there are probably many important differences in the nature and functioning of self-help bereavement groups so that a reasonable degree of caution is recommended. Even the best of ideas can go wrong.

Helpful and Unhelpful Responses to the Bereaved Person

Not everything that we communicate to bereaved people is helpful. Range, Walston, and Polles (1992) obtained ratings (from "most helpful to "least helpful" on a 5-point scale) for a number of statements that are often made to bereaved people. The statements rated most and least helpful are shown in Table 11-1.

TABLE 11-1
Five Most and Least Helpful Statements to Bereaved People

Most Helpful	Least Helpful
"I'm here if you need somebody to talk to."	"Didn't the funeral home do a good job?"
"If there is anything I can do, please let me know."	"Did you know this was going to happen?"
"Put your faith in God."	"Was he/she in much pain?"
"Tell me how you are feeling."	"It's okay to be angry at God."
"He/she will always be in your memories."	"It was so sudden!"

Source: Range et al. (1992).

As we can see from Table 11-1, the most appreciated statements were those that expressed the individual's commitment to being there for the bereaved. (The first two statements were by far the most favorably rated.) Asking specific questions or reminding them of specific sources of distress (e.g., "It was so sudden!") were not felt to be helpful comments. This study implies that we should raise and answer a question of our own: "Is my intention to comfort the bereaved person or control my own anxiety?"

"No response" can be at least as painful as saying something unhelpful. The participants in Dyregrove's study (2003/2004) often felt abandoned when family, friends, and colleagues did not offer the support the bereaved had expected:

> According to the survivors, it hurt even more when network members tried to excuse their absence by claiming to have been "so busy," "having to work so much lately," etc. . . . . Survivors gave a lot of examples in which network members had avoided talking about anything associated with death, or did not refer to the deceased by name. . . . Some frenetically talked about anything but what had happened and the situation of the survivor (pp. 31–32).

Emotional honesty would seem to be the basic requirement for helpful interactions with the bereaved.

Professional Help: When Is It Needed?

"Grief counseling" as such was almost unknown until recent years. It has now become an accepted mental health service, especially when practiced by people with adequate training and experience (Wolfe, 2002). It is no longer unusual for grief counseling to be recommended to people whose response to bereavement is especially traumatic, painful, debilitating, or prolonged. There have been many reports that counseling can be very helpful when grief is overwhelming and the bereaved person is unable to cope. However, there has also been a growing controversy about the necessity and usefulness of counseling for all people who have recently experienced bereavement. This controversy is too significant to ignore—and new findings are having an effect that is little short of explosive. What is it all about?

Some counselors believe that the distress and dysfunction associated with "normal" grief should not really be considered "normal"—it would be better to help people move more swiftly and securely through this ordeal. Others have taken a more cautious attitude. They note that most people do cope with their grief and move on with their lives; therefore, professional intervention does not seem necessary. There is also a more alarmist view that has been expressed in the phrase, "grief police." The concern is that interventions might be imposed by overzealous people with more enthusiasm than understanding. Not long ago simplistic interpretations of Kübler-Ross's (1969) presentations had led to ill-advised attempts at hustling people through "the five stages of dying." The more severe critics of grief counseling believe the same thing may be happening again. Fortunately, this issue does not have to be contested solely on the basis of enthusiasms and suspicions. There have been studies of bereavement interventions, so perhaps some facts would help.

The Project on Death in America sponsored an intensive analysis of all recent research on bereavement interventions. This work was carried out by the Center for the Advancement of Health, which recruited a scientific advisory committee to review and evaluate the studies. The report (Genevo, 2003) has commanded attention and stimulated animated discussion. Whether the conclusions will also influence practice and generate additional research remains to be seen.

The report offers several broad conclusions:

- Grief is a universal human experience, not a pathology.
- There is no one "normal" way of experiencing and responding to grief. Instead, there are such tremendous individual differences that it would not be wise to apply a judgmental attitude or insist that every bereaved person should follow a "standard" procedure.
- Normal grief does not usually lead to long-term problems, and the ways in which people

come to terms with loss can be positive for emotional health.

- Health problems often result from prolonged and intense grief.
- Counseling and medical interventions can be helpful for people who are overwhelmed by what is currently called "complicated" grief.
- Research findings and clinical experience suggest that many bereaved people do not need professional counseling: they get by with the help of their friends. But is counseling likely to do harm to a grieving person? Recently there has been a short but lively controversy. Neimeyer (2000) contended that grief therapy is usually ineffective and perhaps even harmful for persons experiencing a normal bereavement. This statement was widely reported in the media as though an established fact. Larson and Hoyt (2007) point out that this conclusion was based on a dissertation (Fortner, 1999) that used a flawed methodology and which does not seem to have received peer review or publication. At present there is still a cloud of misinformation floating above the evaluation of grief counseling, as the earlier negative statements continue to recycle despite informed critical response from Larson and Hoyt and others who are familiar with the growing research literature. It is clear that there is much still to learn about the effectiveness of grief counseling in a variety of situations, but it is also clear there is no clear reason for dismissing its value.

WIDOWS IN THIRD WORLD NATIONS

We have been considering bereavement, grief, and mourning with some attention to world cultures, but mostly to our own experiences in the United States and other developed countries. There are cultures, though, in which both life and death are harder for most people. There are many ways to interpret the world and live our lives, and certainly there is danger of criticizing somebody else's customs without really comprehending them. However, there are also practices that are difficult if not impossible to condone. And this brings us to the plight of widows in Third World nations. Begin with the universal facts of spousal bereavement: the permanent loss

of a person who was of great importance in one's life. Recall the stresses and challenges that are encountered even when the widow has significant support from the community. Imagine what it would be like if she had to deal not only with what most widows have to deal with, but also faced the absolute devastation of her life from that point forward. This is the fate even today of many widows in developing or Third World countries.

It has been shown that widows in Third World countries often are deprived of the most basic human rights. Margaret Owen (1996; 2002) reports that spousal bereavement is a kind of death for the woman as well, a social death. Widowhood deprives them almost completely of status (Owen, 2002):

> and consigns them to the very margins of society where they suffer the most extreme forms of discrimination and stigma. Widows in these regions are generally the poorest of the poor and least protected by the law because their lives are likely to be determined by local, patriarchal interpretations of tradition, custom, and religion. Unmarried women are the property and under the control of their fathers; married women belong to their husbands. Women are in limbo and no longer have any protector. The misery inflected upon Third World widows is not a matter of chance or particular circumstance: It is rooted in cultural values and practices, and not restricted to just a few countries. Across cultures they become outcasts and are often vulnerable to physical, sexual, and mental abuse. It as if they are in some way responsible for their husband's death and must be made to suffer for this calamity for the remainder of their lives (p. 947).

The AIDS pandemic is creating more widows who are at increased risk for this disease as they become sexually available to male relatives of the deceased husband and to other men as they become impoverished and unprotected. In Nigeria and some other places, there is even the expectation that widows will submit to "ritual cleansing by sex" through taking on strangers or other men designated by her husband's family. Far from "cleansing," of course, this practice further increases the risk of contracting a sexually transmitted disease. Many other women have also been widowed and subject to rape as a consequence of violence and war in such nations as Afghanistan, Angola, Cambodia, Rwanda, Sierra Leone, and Uganda.

Fortunately, this large-scale abuse of widows has started to attract international attention. A nongovernmental organization known as Empowering Widows in Development (EWD) has been established as an umbrella group for more than fifty grass-roots organizations of widows in East Asia, South Asia, Africa, and Eastern Europe as well, where similar same conditions have been observed. Operating with limited funds and not much cooperation from some world governments, advocates for Third World widows are hoping to educate the public about this mostly neglected tragedy and encourage corrective efforts.

ON THE FUTURE OF GRIEVING AND MOURNING

How we grieve and mourn are processes rooted in whatever might be universal in human nature, but also in society's currents and crosscurrents. Here we call attention to several significant changes that could become more pervasive in the years ahead.

- *Who will mourn for the mourners?* A death has occurred among people who preserve a way of life that has spanned many centuries. There is an intense and moving response in, for example, a Bulgarian mountain village and an Israeli desert settlement (Gamliel, 2007). Central to the ritual is a passionate lament expressed by an elderly woman. She explains, sorrows, and rages for the whole community. Less and less is this traditional event taking place. There are few if any to replace the woman who it might be said conveys the soul of the people at the time of parting. Soon there may be nobody to mourn in the old way, and in this silence something of the people's tradition might be forever gone.
- *Imitating the dead? Dazing through oblivion.* Perhaps the dead are the lucky ones. And when a person one has counted on has been taken away from us, perhaps life is bearable only if deadened. It turns out that heroin addiction

often originates in grief (Allen, 2007). People already stressed and depressed in their deprived urban surroundings are particularly vulnerable to a drugged escape from the pain of life after a traumatic bereavement. Deaths that occur to the wrong person—say, a child—or the wrong way—violence or unrelieved suffering—can be overwhelming, especially if social support is lacking.

SUMMARY

A person important to us dies. This loss is known as bereavement. We experience a shifting mix of feelings including anxiety, anger, and confusion. This condition is known as grief. We express our bereavement and loss to others in ways that are culturally patterned. This is known as mourning. In this chapter, we have seen that grief does not necessarily run its course in a year or any other fixed period of time. Instead, each individual and family has its own pattern of response and recovery that depends much on the nature of the death and the survivor's own general patterns of coping with stress and loss. Grief is more than an emotional state: It also is accompanied by the body's response to stress, especially in the neuroendocrine system. The health and even the survival of the survivors can be endangered by a severe or prolonged stress reaction.

There are marked cultural differences in the way people have learned to respond to a death, and these differences are represented within the diverse U.S. population as well as in other societies, as we have seen through numerous examples. Freud's influential grief-work theory emphasizes that it is a long and arduous process to accept the reality of the death and liberate one's self from the emotional pull of the deceased. Many counselors and researchers now believe that it is not necessary to cast off the lost loved one; instead one can reconstruct the relationship and keep the continuing bonds going in a revised and more adaptive way.

We have also seen that people differ considerably in how they recover—or fail to recover—from bereavement. Gender differences and the way in which the person died (e.g., suddenly or with time to prepare for the loss) are among the important influencing factors, but so is the nature of the relationship between the deceased person and the survivor. Particular attention was given to grief and recovery when the deceased person is a child or spouse, as well as bereavement among grandparents and other elderly people. The limited support given to bereaved people in the United States remains a subject of concern, and suggestions were offered for providing support to the bereaved people in our own lives. There is now evidence that counseling can be effective for people with intense and prolonged grief responses, but that it is seldom useful and can even be harmful for people experiencing normal grief who are coping with loss in their own distinctive ways. There is now a growing consensus that counseling is most effective when requested by the grieving person.

REFERENCES

Adamolekun, K. (1999). Bereavement salutations among the Yorubas of Western Nigeria. *Omega, Journal of Death and Dying, 39,* 277–286.

Allen, C. (2007). The poverty of death: Social class, urban deprivation, and the criminological consequences of sequestration of death. *Mortality, 12,* 80–94.

Archer, J. (2001). Grief from an evolutionary perspective. In M. S. Stroebe, R. O. Hansson, W. Stroebe, & H. Schut (Eds.), *Handbook of bereavement research* (pp. 263–284). Washington, DC: American Psychological Association.

Balk, D. (2004). Recovery following bereavement: An examination of the concept. *Death Studies, 28,* 361–374.

Barrera, M., D'Augustino, N. M., Schneiderman, G., Tallett, S., Spencer, L., & Jovcevska, V. (2007). Patterns of parental bereavement following the loss of a child and related factors. *Omega, Journal of Death & Dying, 55,* 145–167.

Beder, J. (2002). Grief: Anticipatory. In R. Kastenbaum (Ed.), *Macmillan encyclopedia of death and dying: Vol. 1* (pp. 353–355). New York: Macmillan.

Beder, J. (2004). *Voices of bereavement. A casebook for grief counselors.* New York: Brunner-Routledge.

Belicki, K., Gulko, N., Ruzycki, K., & Aristotle, J. (2003). Sixteen years of dreams following spousal bereavement. *Omega, Journal of Death and Dying, 47,* 93–106.

Bennett, K. M., & Bennett, G. (2000/2001). "And there's always this great hole inside that hurts": An empirical study of bereavement in later life. *Omega, Journal of Death and Dying, 42,* 237–252.

Bliatout, B. T. (1993). Hmong death customs: Traditional and acculturated. In D. P. Irish, K. F. Lundquist, & V. J. Nelsen (Eds.), *Ethnic variations in dying, death, and grief* (pp. 79–100). Washington, DC: Taylor & Francis.

Bowlby, J. (1969). *Attachment.* New York: Basic Books.

Bowlby, J. (1973). *Separation.* New York: Basic Books.

Bowlby, J. (1980). *Loss.* New York: Basic Books.

Bozeman, J. C. (1999). A journey through grief: An analysis of an adult child's grief in the loss of a mother. *Illness, Crisis, and Loss, 7,* 91–99.

Cacciatore, J. (2007). Effects of support groups on post traumatic stress responses in women experiencing stillbirth. *Omega, Journal of Death and Dying, 55,* 71–90.

Cordell, A. S., & Thomas, N. (1997). Perinatal loss: Intensity and duration of emotional recovery. *Omega, Journal of Death and Dying, 35,* 297–308.

Crissmann, J. K. (1994). *Death and dying in Central Appalachia.* Urbana, IL: University of Illinois Press.

Darwin, C. (1872). *The expression of the emotions in man and animals.* London: Murrey.

De Bonafini (1991). Life stories. In S. Castro-Klarén, S. Molloy, and B. Sarlo (Eds.), *Women's writing in Latin America: An anthology* (pp. 280–284). Boulder, CO: Westview.

D'Epinay, C. J. L., Cavalli, S., & Spini, D. (2003). The death of a loved one: Impact on health and relationships in very old age. *Omega, Journal of Death and Dying, 47,* 265–284.

De Vries, B., & Roberts, P. (Eds.). (2004). Expressions of grief on the World Wide Web. Special issue of *Omega, Journal of Death and Dying, 49*(1).

DiMeo, V. V. (1978). Mourning and melancholia: A prescribed degriefing intervention method (DIM) for the reduction of depression and/or belated grief. Unpublished doctoral dissertation. United States International University, San Diego.

Dyregrov, K. (2003/2004). Micro-sociological analysis of social support following traumatic bereavement: Unhelpful and avoidant responses from the community. *Omega, Journal of Death and Dying, 48,* 23–44.

Elison, J. (2007, January 29). The stage of grief no one admits to: Relief. *Newsweek,* p. 19.

Engel, G. L. (1963). A unified theory of health and disease. In D. Ingele (Ed.), *Life and disease* (pp. 7–24). New York: Basic Books.

Field, N. P. (2006). Continuing bonds in adaptation to bereavement. Introduction. *Death Studies, 30,* 709–714.

Freed, P. J., & Mann, J. J. (2007). Sadness and loss: Toward a neurobiopsychosocial model. *American Journal of Psychiatry, 164,* 28–34.

Freud, S. (1959). Mourning and melancholia. *Collected papers: Vol. 4.* New York: Basic Books. (Original work published 1919.)

Fulton, R. (2003). Anticipatory mourning: A critique of the concept. *Mortality, 8,* 342–351.

Furman, E. F. (1974). *A child's parent dies.* New Haven: Yale University Press.

Gamliel, T. (2007). "Wailing lore" in a Yeminite-Israeli community: Bereavement, expertise, and therapy. *Social Science & Medicine, 65,* 1501–1511.

Genevo, J. L. (2003). *Report on bereavement and grief research.* Washington, DC: Center for the Advancement of Health.

Gennep, A. V. (1960). *The rites of passage.* Chicago: University of Chicago Press. (Original work published 1909.)

Glick, L. O., Weiss, R. S., & Parkes, C. M. (1974). *The first year of bereavement.* New York: Wiley.

Goodkin, K., Baldewitz, T. T., Blaney, N. T., Asthana, D., Kumar, M., & Zheng, W. L. (2001). Physiological effects of bereavement and bereavement support group interventions. In M. S. Stroebe, R. O. Hansson, W. Stroebe, and H. Schut (Eds.), *Handbook of bereavement research* (pp. 671–704). Washington, DC: American Psychological Association.

Gorer, G. D. (1977). *Grief and mourning.* New York: Arno Press.

Groom, W. (2002). *A storm in Flanders. Tragedy and triumph on the Western Front.* New York: Atlantic Monthly Press.

Hall, M., & Irwin, M. (2001). Physiological indices of functioning in bereavement. In M. S. Stroebe, R. O. Hansson, W. Stroebe, & H. Schut (Eds.), *Handbook of bereavement research* (pp. 473–492). Washington, DC: American Psychological Association.

Hogan, N. S., Worden, J. W., & Schmidt, L. A. (2003/2004). An empirical study of the proposed complicated grief disorder criteria. *Omega, Journal of Death and Dying, 48,* 263–278.

Hunt, J. (2004). Sole survivor: A case study to evaluate the dual-process model of grief in multiple loss. *Illness, Crisis, & Loss, 12,* 284–298.

Jacobs, S. (1999). *Traumatic grief.* New York: Brunner/Mazel.

Kastenbaum, R. (1969). Death and bereavement in later life. In A. H. Kutscher (Ed.), *Death and bereavement* (pp. 27–54). Springfield, IL: Charles C. Thomas.

Kastenbaum, R. (1987). Vicarious grief: An intergenerational phenomenon? *Death Studies, 11,* 447–454.

Kastenbaum, R. (1993/1994) Phyllis R. Silverman: An Omega interview. *Omega, Journal of Death and Dying, 28,* 251–260.

Kastenbaum, R. (2004a). *On our way. The final passage through life and death.* Berkeley: University of California Press.

Kastenbaum, R. (2004b) Death writ large. *Death Studies, 28,* 375–392.

Kastenbaum, R. (2008). Grieving in contemporary society. M. S. Stroebe, W. Stroebe, R. O. Hansson, and H. Schut (Eds.), *Handbook of bereavement research and practice. Advances in theory and intervention* (pp. 67–85). Washington, DC: American Psychological Association.

Klass, D. (1988). *Parental grief. Solace and resolution.* New York: Springer.

Klass, D. (1992/1993). The inner representation of the dead child and the worldviews of bereaved parents. *Omega, Journal of Death and Dying, 26,* 255–273.

Klass, D. (2002). Grief and mourning in cross-cultural perspective. In R. Kastenbaum (Ed.), *Macmillan encyclopedia of death and dying:* Vol. 1 (pp. 382–389). New York: Macmillan.

Klass, D., Silverman, P. R., & Nickman, S. L. (Eds.). (1996). *Continuing bonds: New understandings of grief.* Bristol, PA: Taylor & Francis.

Knapp, R. J. (1986). *Beyond endurance.* New York: Schocken Books.

Kübler-Ross, E. (1969). *On death and dying.* New York: Prentice-Hall.

Larson, D. G., & Hoyt, W. T. (2007). What has become of grief counseling? An evaluation of the empirical foundation of the new pessimism. *Professional Psychology: Research and Practice, 38,* 347–355.

Laudenslager, M. K., Boccia M. L., and Reitre, M. L. (1993). Consequences of loss in nonhuman primates, individual differences. In M. S. Stroebe, W. Stroebe, and R. G. Hansson (Eds.), *Handbook of bereavement* (pp. 129–142). Cambridge, UK: Cambridge University Press.

Lavin, C. (1989). Disenfranchised grief and the developmentally disabled. In K. J. Doka (Ed.), *Disenfranchised grief* (pp. 229–238). Lexington, MA: Lexington Books.

Lichtenberg, P. A. (1990). Remembering Becky. *Omega, Journal of Death and Dying, 21,* 83–89.

Lindemann, E. (1944). The symptomatology and management of acute grief. *American Journal of Psychiatry, 101,* 141–148.

Linn-Gust, M. (2007, April). From the backyard to the pet bed: The changing role of animals in society. *The Forum* (Association for Death Education and Counseling), *33,* 1, 3.

Lund, D. A., & Caserta, M. S. (1997/1998). Future directions in adult bereavement research. *Omega, Journal of Death and Dying, 36,* 287–304.

Maciejewski, P. K., Zhang, B., Block, S. D., & Prigerson, H. G. (2007a). An empirical examination of the stage theory of grief. *Journal of the American Medical Association, 297,* 716–723.

Maciejewski, P. K., Zhang, B., Block, S. D., & Prigerson, H. G. (2007b). The stage theory of grief—reply. *Journal of the American Medical Association, 297,* 761–765.

Mathews, L. T., & Marwit, S. J. (2003/2004). Examining the assumptive world views of parents bereaved by accident, murder, and illness. *Omega, Journal of Death and Dying, 48,* 115–136.

Mikulinger, M., & Shaver, P. R. (2008). An attachment perspective on bereavement. In M. S. Stroebe, R. O. Hansson, H. Schut, & W. Stroebe (Eds.), *Handbook of bereavement research and practice: Advances in theory and intervention* (pp. 87–112). Washington, DC: American Psychological Association.

Milo, E. M. (1997). Maternal responses to the life and death of a child with a developmental disability. *Death Studies, 21,* 443–476.

Moss, M. S., Moss, S. Z., & Hansson, R. O. (2001). Bereavement and old age. In M. S. Stroebe, R. O. Hansson, W. Stroebe, & H. Schut (Eds.), *Handbook of bereavement research* (pp. 241–260). Washington, DC: American Psychological Association.

Murphy, S. A. (2008). The loss of a child: Sudden death and extended illness perspectives. In M. S. Stroebe, R. O. Hansson, H. Schut, & W. Stroebe (Eds.). *Handbook of bereavement research and practice: Advances in theory and intervention* (pp. 375–396). Washington, DC: American Psychological Association.

Nehari, M., Grebler, D., & Toren, A. (2007). A voice unheard: Grandparents' grief over children who died of cancer. *Mortality, 12,* 71–80.

Niemeyer, R. A. (2000). Searching for the meaning of meaning: Grief therapy and the process of reconstruction. *Death Studies, 24,* 541–558.

Owen, M. (1996). *A world of widows.* London: ZED Books.

Owen, M. (2002). Widows in third world nations. In R. Kastenbaum (Ed.), *Macmillan encyclopedia of death:* Vol. 2 (pp. 947–952). New York: Macmillan.

Parkes, C. M. (2001). *Bereavement* (3rd ed.). New York: International Universities Press.

Parkes, C. M. (2006). *Love & loss: The roots of grief and its complications.* New York: Taylor & Francis.

Parkes, C. M., & Weiss, R. S. (1983). *Recovery from bereavement.* New York: Basic Books.

Peppers, L. G., & Knapp, R. J. (1980). *Motherhood and mourning. Perinatal death.* New York: Praeger.

Prothero, D. (1997) Origin of the term "Half Mast" or Half Staff." http://flagspot.net/flags/xf-half.html#origin

Rando, T. A. (2002). Bereavement: Vicarious. In R. Kastenbaum (Ed.), *Macmillan encyclopedia of death and dying:* Vol. 1 (pp. 59–60). New York: Macmillan.

Range, L. (2002). Grief: Traumatic. In R. Kastenbaum (Ed.), *Macmillan encyclopedia of death and dying:* Vol. 1 (pp. 379–382). New York: Macmillan.

Range, L. M., Walston, A., & Polles, P. M. (1992). Helpful and unhelpful comments after suicide, homicide, accident, or natural death. *Omega, Journal of Death and Dying, 25,* 25–32.

Reynolds, J. J. (2003/2004). Stillbirth: To hold or not to hold. *Omega, Journal of Death and Dying, 48,* 85–88.

Rosenblatt, P. C. (1983). *Bitter, bitter tears.* Minneapolis: University of Minnesota Press.

Rowling, L. (1995). The disenfranchising grief of teachers. *Omega, Journal of Death and Dying, 31,* 317–330.

Rubin, S. S., and Malkinson, R. (2001). Parental response to child loss across the life cycle. In M. S. Stroebe, W. Stroebe, and R. O. Hansson (Eds.), *Handbook of bereavement research* (pp. 219–240). Cambridge, UK: Cambridge University Press.

Schormans, A. F. (2004). Experiences following the deaths of disabled foster children: "We don't feel like 'foster' parents." *Omega, Journal of Death and Dying, 49,* 347–370.

Schut, H. A. W., Stroebe, M. S., Boelen, P. A., & Zijerveld, A. M. (2006). Continuing relationships with the deceased: Disentangling bonds and grief. *Death Studies, 30,* 757–766.

Silverman, P. (2003). Continuing bonds. In R. Kastenbaum (Ed.), *Macmillan encyclopedia of death and dying:* Vol. 1 (pp. 184–188). New York: Macmillan.

Stamberg, S. (2008, April 18). "Dear first lady": Letters offer glimpse of history. www.npr.org/templates/story.php?storyId=89723829

Stroebe, M. S. (2001). Introduction: Concerns and issues in contemporary research on bereavement. In M. S. Stroebe, W. Stroebe, R. O. Hansson, and H. Schut (Eds.), *Handbook of bereavement research* (pp. 3–22). Cambridge, UK: Cambridge University Press.

Stroebe, M. S., & Schut, H. (2001). Models of coping with bereavement: A review. In M. Stroebe, W. Stroebe, & R. O Hansson (Eds.), *Handbook of bereavement research* (pp. 375–404). Cambridge UK: Cambridge University Press.

Stroebe, M. S., and Stroebe, W. (1993). The mentality of bereavement: A review. In M. S. Stroebe, W. Stroebe, and R. O. Hansson (Eds.), *Handbook of bereavement research* (pp. 175–195). Cambridge, UK: Cambridge University Press.

Stroebe, M. S., & Stroebe, W. (2001). The mortality of bereavement: A review. In M. S. Stroebe, W. Stroebe, & R. O. Hansson (Eds.), *Handbook of bereavement research* (pp. 175–195). Cambridge, UK: Cambridge University Press.

Talbot, K. (1998/1999). Mothers now childless: Personal transformation after the death of an only child. *Omega, Journal of Death and Dying, 38,* 167–186.

Terkel, S. (2001). Will the circle be unbroken? *Reflections on death, rebirth, and human hunger for a faith.* New York: New Press.

Thornton, S. W. (2000). Grief transformed: The mothers of Plaza de Mayo. *Omega, Journal of Death and Dying, 41,* 279–290.

Trout, N. (2008). *A day of humor, healing, and hope in my life as an animal surgeon.* New York: Broadway.

Turner, V. (1969). *The ritual process: Structure and anti-structure.* Chicago: Aldine.

Turner, V. (1992). Death and the dead in the pilgrimage process. In E. Turner (Ed.), *Blazing the trail. Way marks in the exploration of symbols.* Tucson: University of Arizona Press.

Umberson, D., & Henderson, K. (1992). The social construction of death in the Gulf War. *Omega, Journal of Death and Dying, 25,* 1–16.

Walker, A. (1988). *To hell with dying.* San Diego: Harcourt Brace Jovanovich.

Wambach, J. A. (1983). *Timetables for grief and mourning with and without support groups.* Unpublished doctoral dissertation, Arizona State University, Tempe.

Waskowic, T. D., & Chartier, B. M. (2003). Attachment and the experience of grief following the loss of a spouse. *Omega, Journal of Death and Dying, 47,* 77–91.

White, D. L. (1999). Grandparent participation in times of family bereavement. In B. de Vries (Ed.), *End of life issues* (pp. 145–166). New York: Springer.

Wolfe, B. (2002). Grief counseling and therapy. In R. Kastenbaum (Ed.), *Macmillan encyclopedia of death and dying:* Vol. 1 (pp. 389–393). New York: Macmillan.

Wortman, C. B., & Silver, R. C. (1989). The myths of coping with loss. *Journal of Counseling and Clinical Psychology, 57,* 349–357.

Wortman, C. B., & Silver, R. C. (1992). Reconsidering assumptions about coping with loss: An overview of current research. In S. H. Filipp, L. Montada, & M. Lerner (Eds.), *Life crises and experiences of loss in adulthood* (pp. 341–365). London: Cambridge University Press.

GLOSSARY

Anticipatory grief: Anxiety and sorrow experienced prior to an expected death.

Attachment behavior: Originally, the communications and actions by which a mother and her young seek to preserve their proximity and security. Now, the same in relation to any individuals.

Bereavement: The status of having lost a family member, friend, colleague, or other significant person through death.

Continuing bonds: A meaningful relationship with a deceased loved one that enhances rather than interferes with ongoing life.

Disenfranchised grief: A response to a death in which the individual is not regarded as having the right to grieve and must keep the sorrow hidden.

Dissociative flight: An extreme avoidant or denial response to a death.

Grief: The complex emotional, mental, social, and physical response to the death of a loved one.

Grief-work theory: The process of gradually accepting the reality of the loss and liberating oneself from attachment to the deceased (Freud).

Mourning: The expression of the sorrow of loss and grief in a manner understood and approved by the culture.

Shadow grief: A cloud of sorrow that follows a parent for many years after the death of a child.

Traumatic grief: The intense response to a death that has occurred in a sudden and violent manner.

ON FURTHER THOUGHT . . .

What is the future of grieving and mourning?

Consider what has already happened. Once infants and children were at greatest risk for death. Families grieved intensely, but there was also a powerful theme of fatalism: So many children die; that's the way it is. Today in developed nations many people reach or exceed the Biblical allotment of three score and ten. If their deaths are to be grieved and their lives celebrated, it will seldom be by their parents. Who will be grieving and mourning and how when long lives fade into death?

Consider also the passionate mourners, the people who express the heritage and values of a traditional culture when one of its members passes. The elderly woman in a Bulgarian mountain village or Yeminite-Israeli desert settlement (Gamliel, 2007) who knows every phrase and nuance of the traditional lament is herself on the endangered list. It is often the woman deeply rooted in tradition who is expected to stand between the community and death and, in so doing, affirm the group's value and viability. These valuable people are themselves passing away, and with few replacements in sight. What then?

There's more (Kastenbaum, 2008): throughout much of human history people lived patterned lives consisting of a continuity of kin, places, activities, and beliefs. The United States and many other societies are now much more mobile, with discontinuities and fragmentation of life patterns that have been replaced by mass media illusions of unity and belonging. What is becoming of grieving and mourning as people die less often from a coherent, patterned way of life that will mean what to whom? And what of the challenge to faith, justice, and meaning in a world where many become victims to devastation and violence? How—and again, who—will grieve and mourn?

And, yes, there is even more: but it is your turn to observe and reflect. What is the future of grief and mourning, and how would we prefer to see it take shape?

Useful online sources:

Bereaved Parents of the USA
   www.bereavedparentsusa.org
Bereavement Resources
   www.nmha.org/infoctr/factsheets/42cfm
Compassionate Friends
   www.compassionatefriends.org

Concerns of Police Survivors (COPS)
  www.nationalcops.org
Dougy Center for Grieving Children
  www.grievingchild.org
GriefNet
  www.rivendell.org
Mothers Against Drunk Driving (MADD)
  www.madd.org
National Center for Posttraumatic Disorder
  www.dartmouth.edu/dms/ptsd/index.html
National Organization of Parents of Murdered Children
  www.pomc.com

Pet Grief Support Page
  www.petloss.com
SHARE: Pregnancy and Infant Loss Support
  www.nationalshareoffice.com
SIDS Alliance
  www.SIDSalliance.org
Society of Military Widows
  www.militarywidows.org
WidowNet
  www.widownet.org

"The mystery of Stonehenge has apparently been solved. The mysterious circle of large stones in southern England was primarily a burial ground for almost five centuries, and the site probably holds the remains of a family that long ruled the area, new research concludes" (Kaufman, 2008).

chapter 12

THE FUNERAL PROCESS

Win a pre-paid cremation. Complete all of the reply slip information and you will be eligible for a drawing each month.
—Advertisement received by author (2008)

Pre-prepared funeral tributes. Solve funeral eulogy problems for ONLY $15. These funeral tributes come in sets of three all of which are about one minute long. They are especially written to enable you to mix and match them. . . . Send us your credit card details.
—A commercial Web site (2008)

In America, the first world war remains a largely forgotten conflict. It has no national monument on the Washington Mall, no blockbuster film, no iconic image equivalent to soldiers' raising the flag on Iwo Jima.
—Tony Dokouph (February 18, 2007, p. 50)

NEW YORK-Dancers and singers helped dedicate a memorial Friday at the site of the African Burial Ground, where free blacks and slaves were buried more than two centuries ago and then forgotten as Manhattan expanded above their heads.
—Samantha Gross (October 5, 2007).

Ohio: Every citizen may freely speak, write, and publish the person's sentiments on all subjects. . . . but no person shall picket or engage in other protest activities . . . within three hundred feet of . . . or within one hour before or one hour after the conducting of an actual funeral or burial service at that place. No person shall picket or engage in other protest activities, nor shall any association or corporation cause picketing or other protest activities to occur, within three hundred feet of any funeral process.
—Quoted from Ohio statutes by Nieri Mathis Rutledge (2008)

To look at a skeleton as the missing relative of a person I might pass on the street was dangerous: it would challenge my stamina for the work we had to do. . . . The bones were almost shouting at me, and it was the stress-based fatigue I was working under that made this shouting so painful.
—Clea Koff (2004, p. 154)

"Our Father, who art in heaven," the 17 year-old said, shackled to four other teen-age inmates, "hallowed be thy name. Thy kingdom come. Thy will be done." The 51-year-old woman in the casket had died alone, of heart disease, the deacon told the 10 pallbearers, all convicted criminals. No one had claimed her body.
—Judi Villa (2004)

The wind blew the head down one night in 1685. A sentry secreted it beneath his cloak and took it home. Then began its long wandering, passing from hand to hand and indignity to indignity before obtaining a decent burial almost two centuries later.
—Edwin Murphy (1995, p. 20)

The parent who brought her child to see a body followed a passed-on narrative tradition for the African American community. "I came to bring my son," said one father. Another explained that he planned to bring his children back to the funeral home to let them understand "you're not too young to die."
—Karla FC Holloway (2002, p. 136)

I have no weddings or baptisms in the funeral home and the folks that pay me have maybe lost sight of the obvious connections between the life and the death of us.
—Thomas Lynch (1997, p. 36)

There are powerful reasons for respecting the dead and their physical remains. The most powerful reason might be the most personal, as upon the death of a person we have loved and respected. However, there are also reasons that extend beyond our personal relationships.

I respect the dead because:

- This also shows respect to the people who were close to them;
- It would violate social expectations if I did not show respect;
- We can't go on with our individual and communal lives until feelings and issues aroused by the death have been settled amicably;
- I am troubled by death, so this is a way to do something positive;
- The dead have moved into a spirit realm whose god or gods I must respect;
- The spirits of the dead might take revenge on me if I did not show respect;
- I hope that my physical remains will be treated with respect when the time comes.

You might not agree with all of these statements, but you probably don't disagree with all of them, either. Furthermore, as a decent person you probably don't have to think twice about treating the dead and their remains with respect.

It's all the more striking, then, that there have been so many exceptions. And, as usual, we can learn from the exceptions as well as the more common practices. We will also see that the dead are often caught up in societal change and conflict.

A SAMPLER OF RESPONSES TO THE DEAD

I was dead in the sights of two funeral enterprises when one invited me to participate in a drawing for a pre-paid *cremation,* and other to purchase a pre-paid one minute long funeral tribute. Perhaps this was treating "Occupant's" future corpse with respect. Who wouldn't want to "solve funeral *eulogy* problems," and "mix and match" the wonderful things that will be said about us? Or perhaps these solicitations are simply making it clear that death, not long ago taboo in U.S. culture, has now been embraced as a source of marketing opportunities? Death is, alas, tragic, but not so tragic when there is money to be made from the pre- and as well the post-dead. Funeral-related transactions have been with us for a long time, but have reached new proportions as corporate enterprises.

Respect and Remembering

Respect for the dead requires remembering the dead. Some historically-minded people are trying to raise awareness today of those who fell in World War I as we approach a century's distance from the last artillery barrage and poison gas dispersion. We might join them in wondering about our cultural amnesia for the suffering endured by combatants and civilian populations. Dokouph (2007, p. 50) observes that

> WWI was the last war fought without modern methods of bearing witness. There are virtually no film reels, few battle photographs, only a smattering of reliable frontline news reports, and much of what exists was either produced under suffocating censorship or made as propaganda . . . Nobody filmed a single battle.

It should be noted, though, that the Civil War, fought half a century before, has not been forgotten. The events and experiences persist in still photography, diaries, military records, histories, novels, and re-enactments. By contrast, the nation is perceived as having nearly forgotten its men and women who lost their lives in "The Great War." The increasing call for appropriate memorialization is intended to express recognition for the family survivors as well as the fallen, and to close a gap in national consciousness (Bertman, 2000).

The African Burial Ground in Manhattan was among the many historical sites that were overtaken by rapid urban expansion. New construction often included new destruction, often without a thought for what would be lost. Perhaps ironically, it was during another new construction project in 1991 that the burial ground was rediscovered with more than 400 sets of remains. In this case, the public was ready to respect and remember. The site was quickly designated as a national historic landmark, and more recently as a national monument. A memorial

In recent years funerals have been disturbed by protestors with hate messages. In this scene (June 27, 2005), members of the Westboro Baptist Church in Kansas hold signs over the head of mourners for a special services soldier who had been killed by a roadside bomb in Afghanistan. Members of this church believe that the terrorist attacks on the United States and the casualties in Iraq and Afghanistan are the result of tolerance for homosexuality.

was constructed, and a museum planned to honor the freed slaves who lived, worked, and died in the formative early years of New York City. The dead might be respected, or not: but first they have to survive the turbulence of change in both landscape and mindscape.

The dead and their mourners are not always safe from ongoing societal conflict. It is no longer unusual to hear reports of funeral services being attacked and mourners massacred as part of Middle East violence. In the United States there have been so many disturbances of the *funeral process* that most states have enacted laws that criminalize such behavior (Ohio taken as one example among many). Rutledge (2008) notes that:

> Funeral picketing . . . has resulted in a frenzy of legislation in a short period of time. The group responsible . . . Westboro Baptist Church, has targeted soldiers killed in Iraq and Afghanistan, homosexuals, political figures, and even children. Some may want to dismiss Westboro as a fringe group that should not be taken seriously, but they have been taken seriously by at least twenty-seven states, the federal government, and mourners who have been eyewitnesses to the group's tactics.

Do the dead and their mourners have more right to privacy than protesters have to their demonstrations? Should the newly-dead be exempt from conflicts among the living?

The Bones Start Screaming

Forensic anthropologist? That would be a person who studies prehistoric skeletons in a university museum, perhaps living her own good life in Berkeley, California. Clea Koff, however, accepted the challenge of working with the United Nations Criminal Tribunal in Bosnia, Croatia, and again in Rwanda. She was still in her early 20s when the bones started screaming at her. Koff was part of an international team trying to identify the thousands of genocide victims. One mass grave in Rwanda was found to hold almost 500 men, women, and children who had been brutally massacred. She did her best to keep her objective, professional attitude in place. There were careful, detailed observations to record, skull after skull. One day in Bosnia, it was too much for her.

While inspecting the skeletal remains of a teenager, Koff:

> lost an element of self-control. I felt so awful, so full of hurt and emotion, and mixed in with that was a knee-buckling sense of privilege that I was touching the bones of someone whose family was out there and wanted more than anything to have him back, no matter what condition he was in, and yet I was the only one holding him. I felt sorry for him and for everyone in the world (Koff, 2004, p. 153–154).

Koff's older colleagues recognized her distress as well. They had been through that flood of grief themselves. Soon she was back at her work: there were so many more bodies and so many more relatives waiting for closure, waiting to memorialize their loved ones, waiting to start the painful process of getting on with their own lives. Identifying and respecting the dead could not come close to making up the loss, but it could restore an intangible sense of rightness to the bereaved families and communities. Koff would bring this sense of mission to her work in Rwanda where she became known as "the bone woman" and, along with her colleagues, helped a devastated nation move toward rebuilding itself.

"These People Got Nobody"

Compassion and respect were also foremost when a chain gang of juvenile criminals completed another of its assignments at the White Tanks Cemetery for indigents in the Phoenix, Arizona area. The bodies lowered into earth were not victims of genocide, although some had been murdered or shot while committing crimes. Most had lived and died alone. All seemed to be without family or friends to acknowledge the deaths and accompany them to the grave. The young convicts surprised themselves by feeling sorrow for the people they had never met. They also could see themselves unloved and abandoned at the end of their lives. "God be with you," one of the teenagers prayed, as he scooped up a handful of dirt and tossed it on the casket. "These people got nobody," another said. Another reflected: "Some of them probably took our paths. This is where I could end up. Not only dead but in this place. You're never going to forget" (Villa, 2004).

Postmortem Abuse

The toppled head in question had suffered six axe wounds on the neck because the executioner was having a bad day. Perhaps he was nervous about the assignment. Oliver Cromwell had been until recently The Lord Protector of England. He was the most formidable person in the kingdom until his adversaries gained the upper hand. His head had been impaled on a spike so that all could see what becomes of traitors (Murphy, 1995). This postmortem abuse was a political action to intimidate anybody else who might be of a mind to threaten the Crown. Preventing dignified burial is another way of disrespecting both the dead and their mourners. Tatanka Yotanka was such a victim. The leader (better known as Sitting Bull) of the Hunkpapa Teton Sioux was assassinated in 1890 while in federal custody. The government refused to release his body for traditional Sioux funeral rituals, rejecting family requests, religious protests, and court proceedings. At first there was a misguided fear that returning Sitting Bull's remains would incite an uprising. It was not until 1953 that a raiding party comprising his descendants and the town mortician succeeded in "kidnapping" the remains and providing a burial on Sioux land. At last word, the government had not yet officially released his remains to the Sioux community.

Funerals have often been deeply significant events in African American life (Holloway, 2002). African Americans had to live with and sometimes die from the consequences of racial discrimination. It was therefore not realistic to bring up children as though life would always be safe and sweet. Funerals were occasions to educate the young and to express the strong emotions of the adults within a positive and supportive framework. Cromwell and Tatanka Yotanka had exceptional lives but were flagrantly disrespected in death by mainstream society. Many African Americans have had to cope with disrespect from mainstream society from cradle to grave.

"Laid Out"

The funeral director of Milford, Michigan, was reflecting on fundamental changes in the American way of life throughout the twentieth century. In the past, home was where most people were born and died:

> There were households in which, just as babies were being birthed, grandparents were aging upstairs with chicken soup and doctors' home visits until, alas, they died and were taken downstairs to the same room the babies were christened in to get what was then called "laid out." Between the births and deaths were the courtships—sparkings and spoonings between boys and girls just barely out of their teens, overseen by a maiden aunt. . . . The smitten young people would sit on a "love seat"—large enough to look into each other's eyes and hold hands, small enough to prevent them getting horizontal (Lynch, 1997, p. 35)

As time went on, though, more of life's activities took place outside the home, although the professional establishment that prepares the dead for final disposition became known as funeral home. Lynch's observations make it clear that we cannot understand how a society cares for its dead without also understanding how that society lives. More specifically, death in the United States became increasingly removed from intimate family life, although there are signs of a reversal, as we will see in the home and green funeral movements.

It is one thing to witness funeral and memorial services, and another thing to be a participant. Many people feel uncomfortable and unsure about what to do. For example, some people feel overwhelmed by the challenge of speaking at a funeral. "What should I say? What if I say the wrong thing?" This anxiety has created a potential consumer market that has not gone unnoticed by opportunistic salespeople. Purchase "pre-prepared funeral tributes" and we will not have to think for ourselves, not have to work through our own personal experiences, thoughts, and feelings. The real cost, though, is not the fee but the lost opportunity to say what is really in our hearts rather than take a generic tribute package off somebody's shelf (somebody who doesn't know either ourselves or the deceased).

Today there are more options than ever about our own participation in funeral and memorial observances, and each decision either affirms or weakens our sense of meaningful involvement. It would be useful, then, to reflect on our understanding of the funeral process.

WHAT DO FUNERALS MEAN TO US?

Why go to a funeral? In fact, why have funerals at all? Perhaps we should replace the expensive and inconvenient funeral service with the click-click of the computer keyboard as we visit the departed at their cyberspace addresses. But perhaps there is something so fundamental in the human response to death that we need the physicality, the companionship of the funeral.

I believe the funeral is part of a deeper and more complex process in which we both separate ourselves from the dead and try to establish a new relationship with the dead and with each other. This chapter, therefore, examines not only the funeral but the total process through which society responds to the death of one of its members. We will look both at what is happening today as well as the cultural traditions from which our own needs, beliefs, and practices have emerged.

British sociologist Tony Walter (1992) asks us to confront the possibility that investing in the dead was often a dominant cultural value:

> It is one thing today to have a simple Georgian headstone or a well-constructed table tomb gently weathering in a country churchyard. It is something else to have a municipal cemetery stuffed with tottering Victorian sentimentality in which the once so affected heirs have long since lost interest (Walter, 1992, p.106).

In the Old Testament we learn that:

> David went and took the bones of Saul and the bones of his son Jonathan from the men of Jabesh-gilead, who had stolen them from the public square of Beth-shan. . . . And they buried the bones of Saul and his son Jonathan in the land of Benjamin in Zela, in the tomb of Kish his father (Old Testament, Sam. 21:12, 14).

King David's enemies valued these remains as negotiable symbols. Those who possessed these bones also possessed power. A great many other people, before and after King David, have also felt that a proper funeral and secure disposition of the body are essential for the family's peace of mind. The powerful need to possess and respect the physical remains of the dead asserted itself immediately after the terrorist attacks of September 11, 2001. Emphasis at first was on rescue efforts and hope. Later the emphasis shifted to recovery and identification of the remains. A respectful funeral would not heal the grief, but it would help to begin the process of healing.

Nevertheless, there is also resistance to the funeral process as it has been commonly practiced in mainstream society. It has been variously criticized as too costly, time-consuming, depressing, and artificial. As a teenager, I was appalled by the perfunctory funeral services held for a neighbor, "the old man who lived around the corner." It was a standard issue performance by a major funeral service corporation, with the "master of ceremonies" showing no knowledge or interest in the person who had died. I still get angry thinking about this! It is not difficult to understand why people who have had alienating experiences at a funeral service would have some reservations about the whole process.

What are *your* thoughts and feelings about the funeral process? Please answer the questions presented for your consideration in Box 12-1.

Respondents to these questions tend to sort themselves out into two major types: *rationalist* and *romantic*. A thoroughgoing rationalist would agree that funerals are expensive wastes of time that make people too emotional. Cemeteries should be phased out so the land can be used more productively. By contrast, a romanticist would observe that funerals are a comfort to the next of kin and that they are not all that expensive when one considers their meaning. Funerals are decisive and memorable events. Furthermore, people should show more, not less, emotion at funerals, and not begrudge the dead a peaceful place to rest their bones. *Recognize yourself?*

BOX 12-1 THE FUNERAL PROCESS: A SELF-EXAMINATION OF ATTITUDES, FEELINGS, AND KNOWLEDGE

---

1. Funerals are a waste of time.

   Agree ___   Tend to agree ___
   Tend to disagree ___   Disagree ___

2. Bodies should be donated for scientific use.

   Agree ___   Tend to agree ___
   Tend to disagree ___   Disagree ___

3. Funerals are a comfort to the next of kin.

   Agree ___   Tend to agree ___
   Tend to disagree ___   Disagree ___

4. People often are too emotional at funerals.

   Agree ___   Tend to agree ___
   Tend to disagree ___   Disagree ___

5. The death of a family member should be published in the newspaper.

   Agree ___   Tend to agree ___
   Tend to disagree ___   Disagree ___

6. All things considered, most funerals are not excessively costly.

   Agree ___   Tend to agree ___
   Tend to disagree ___   Disagree ___

7. People often do not show enough emotion at funerals.

   Agree ___   Tend to agree ___
   Tend to disagree ___   Disagree ___

8. The size, length, and expense of a funeral should depend on the importance of the deceased person.

   Agree ___   Tend to agree ___
   Tend to disagree ___   Disagree ___

9. Allowing for some exceptions, cemeteries waste valuable space and should be diverted to other uses.

   Agree ___   Tend to agree ___
   Tend to disagree ___   Disagree ___

10. It would be preferable to be cremated.

    Agree ___   Tend to agree ___
    Tend to disagree ___   Disagree ___

11. It would be preferable to be buried in a cemetery.

    Agree ___   Tend to agree ___
    Tend to disagree ___   Disagree ___

12. A funeral director should be required to give a summary of laws stating what is and what is not required before the bereaved purchase a funeral.

    Agree ___   Tend to agree ___
    Tend to disagree ___   Disagree ___

13. The average cost of a funeral in the United States is between $ ___ and $ ___.

14. Embalming the body is required:

    Always ___
    Under certain specified circumstances ___
    Never ___

15. An open-casket funeral can be held after body organs are donated:

    Always ___
    Seldom ___

16. My idea of the perfect funeral process is the following:

    _____
    _____
    _____
    _____

17. For me, the best or most useful aspects of a funeral are:

    _____
    _____
    _____
    _____

18. For me, the worst or most distressing aspects of a funeral are:

    _____
    _____
    _____
    _____

Not all the questions bear on the rationalist/romantic attitude split, however. We will return to these questions after we have surveyed the funeral process.

FROM DEAD BODY TO LIVING MEMORY: A PROCESS APPROACH

How do we transform our relationship to a living person into our acknowledgment of this person's death and a lasting memory integrated into our ongoing lives? This process has many dimensions, ranging from the legal, technical, and financial to the personal and the symbolic. Sometimes the survivors succeed in converting what has become a dead body into a living memory. Sometimes the process fails, and the survivors must shoulder a burden of unresolved feelings and unanswered questions.

Common Elements of the Funeral Process

We have already reflected on the passage from life to death (Chapters 2, 4, and 6). It is a biological process, a societal rite of passage, and, perhaps most of all, a mystery. The funeral process has a significant role in the symbolic transformation of a person into a corpse and the corpse into—what? Cultures differ in their beliefs about the new status taken on by the dead, and these differences show up in funeral and mourning practices. Although specific customs differ tremendously, certain basic elements often can be found.

Premortem Preparations

The law recognizes that actions taken in contemplation of death are unique. Gifts made under the shadow of death, for example, often are taxed more severely. Transfers of property and obligations between the dead and the living are of

The long and loving marriage of Paris industrialist N. Pigeon and his wife is commemorated in the Cimetiere de Montparnasse.

concern to all societies and usually are regulated by formal or common law (Miller, Rosenfeld, & McNamee, 2003). The community demands assurance that debts will be paid and that its rules of inheritance are enforced.

Either the dying person or a family member takes the initiative, giving instructions for cremation or burial and disposal of personal property. Colleagues might have to prepare for replacing the coworker who will not be coming back to the job. The physician may be interested in removing an organ for transplantation or in conducting an *autopsy* to determine the precise cause of death; therefore, the physician must decide how best to obtain permission. A funeral director may have already been consulted and carried out preliminary arrangements to see that the wishes of the family are respected. Often there is considerable anticipatory activity so that the right things are done when the death does occur. An unexpected death creates quite a different and more disturbing situation because there has been no opportunity for emotional or organizational preparation.

Immediate Postdeath Activities

The death becomes official when it is certified by a physician. The revised U.S. standard *death certificate* is shown in Figure 12-1. One immediate postdeath activity, then, is to convert the person into a statistic or, more accurately, to complete the record keeping that started with the certificate of birth. Another immediate action is to contact next of kin, should they not already be on the scene. It is common these days for the body to be cleaned and wrapped in a plastic sheet. If the death occurred in a hospital, the body will either be kept in the same room or transferred to an available nearby room pending the arrival of the next of kin. If a hospital is pressed for space, the body may be removed to the morgue after a short time.

Preparations for Burial or Cremation

The interval between death and the final disposal of the body is important in its own right. Often there are both practical and symbolic reasons for placing a space of time between death and final disposition. One of the most common is to allow time for distant friends and relatives to gather for the funeral. Disposition of the body may also have to await financial arrangements.

Did the deceased have an insurance policy with funeral benefits? Precisely who is prepared to spend how much on the funeral? Problems arise in less bureaucratic societies as well. Was there sorcery at work in this death? And, if so, was it a personal enemy within the tribe who must confess and make amends, or was it caused by another tribe; therefore, demanding lethal retribution?

Some deaths also raise questions that require action in the public interest. Was this death caused by negligence, suicide, or murder? Was the deceased the victim of a disease that poses a hazard to the general population? When such questions exist, it is usually the *medical examiner* (or coroner) who must decide whether or not a full investigation is needed. Perhaps most common is the case in which the cause of death is equivocal. Relatives may want to prove that a suicide is a murder because at stake is a considerable inheritance from an insurance contract that prohibits suicide. Insurance investigators may suspect fraud. A police department may feel that an intradepartmental investigation of a death is insufficient. Often, the bereaved family members may feel that they cannot start to get on again with their lives until they are convinced the cause and circumstances have been firmly established.

Send for the Medical Examiner

A medical examiner may order an autopsy when there is the possibility of a danger to public health. This happened when swine flu and Legionnaire's disease became problems in the 1970s, for example. Suspected cases of West Nile virus have often been investigated in recent years to protect against the spread of the disease. A source of additional information is *Death's Acre* (Bass & Jefferson, 2003), offering an inside view of forensic laboratory work at "the body farm." Medical examiners are also called upon when murder or criminal negligence are possible causes of death. *CSI: Crime Scene Investigation,* the popular television series, dramatizes the work of both field and laboratory specialists who augment the traditional work of the medical examiner. Other television programs also regularly feature *postmortem* detective work, usually featuring an eccentric but endearing pathologist. (Who is your favorite?)

TYPE/PRINT IN PERMANENT BLACK INK FOR INSTRUCTIONS SEE OTHER SIDE AND HANDBOOK

LOCAL FILE NUMBER

U.S. STANDARD
CERTIFICATE OF DEATH

STATE FILE NUMBER

DECEDENT

1. DECEDENT'S NAME *(First, Middle, Last)*
2. SEX
3. DATE OF DEATH *(Month, Day, Year)*
4. SOCIAL SECURITY NUMBER
5a. AGE–Last Birthday *(Years)*
5b. UNDER 1 YEAR — Months | Days
5c. UNDER 1 DAY — Hours | Minutes
6. DATE OF BIRTH *(Month, Day, Year)*
7. BIRTHPLACE *(City and State or Foreign Country)*
8. WAS DECEDENT EVER IN U.S. ARMED FORCES? *(Yes or no)*
9a. PLACE OF DEATH *(Check only one; see instructions on other side)*
HOSPITAL: ☐ Inpatient ☐ ER/Outpatient ☐ DOA
OTHER: ☐ Nursing Home ☐ Residence ☐ Other *(Specify)*
9b. FACILITY NAME *(If not institution, give street and number)*
9c. CITY, TOWN, OR LOCATION OF DEATH
9d. COUNTY OF DEATH
10. MARITAL STATUS – Married, Never Married, Widowed, Divorced *(Specify)*
11. SURVIVING SPOUSE *(If wife, give maiden name)*
12a. DECEDENT'S USUAL OCCUPATION *(Give kind of work done during most of working life. Do not use retired.)*
12b. KIND OF BUSINESS/INDUSTRY

SEE INSTRUCTIONS ON OTHER SIDE →

13a. RESIDENCE – STATE
13b. COUNTY
13c. CITY, TOWN, OR LOCATION
13d. STREET AND NUMBER
13e. INSIDE CITY LIMITS? *(Yes or no)*
13f. ZIP CODE
14. WAS DECEDENT OF HISPANIC ORIGIN? (Specify No or Yes – If yes, specify Cuban, Mexican, Puerto Rican, etc.) ☐ No ☐ Yes *Specify:*
15. RACE – American Indian, Black, White, etc. *(Specify)*
16. DECEDENT'S EDUCATION *(Specify only highest grade completed)* Elementary/Secondary (0-12) | College (1-4 or 5+)

NAME OF DECEDENT: ______ For use by physician or institution

PARENTS

17. FATHER'S NAME *(First, Middle, Last)*
18. MOTHER'S NAME *(First, Middle, Maiden Surname)*

INFORMANT

19a. INFORMANT'S NAME *(Type/Print)*
19b. MAILING ADDRESS *(Street and Number or Rural Route Number, City or Town, State, Zip Code)*

DISPOSITION

20a. METHOD OF DISPOSITION
☐ Burial ☐ Cremation ☐ Removal from State
☐ Donation ☐ Other *(Specify)* ______
20b. PLACE OF DISPOSITION *(Name of cemetery, crematory, or other place)*
20c. LOCATION – City or Town, State
21a. SIGNATURE OF FUNERAL SERVICE LICENSEE OR PERSON ACTING AS SUCH ▶
21b. LICENSE NUMBER *(of Licensee)*
22. NAME AND ADDRESS OF FACILITY

SEE DEFINITION ON OTHER SIDE

PRONOUNCING PHYSICIAN ONLY

Complete items 23a-c only when certifying physician is not available at time of death to certify cause of death.
23a. **To the best of my knowledge, death occurred at the time, date, and place stated.** *Signature and Title* ▶
23b. LICENSE NUMBER
23c. DATE SIGNED *(Month, Day, Year)*

ITEMS 24-26 MUST BE COMPLETED BY PERSON WHO PRONOUNCES DEATH →

24. TIME OF DEATH M
25. DATE PRONOUNCED DEAD *(Month, Day, Year)*
26. WAS CASE REFERRED TO MEDICAL EXAMINER/CORONER? *(Yes or no)*

CAUSE OF DEATH

SEE INSTRUCTIONS ON OTHER SIDE

27. **PART I.** Enter the diseases, injuries, or complications that caused the death. Do not enter the mode of dying, such as cardiac or respiratory arrest, shock, or heart failure. List only one cause on each line.

Approximate Interval Between Onset and Death

IMMEDIATE CAUSE (Final disease or condition resulting in death) → a. ______
DUE TO (OR AS A CONSEQUENCE OF):
b. ______
DUE TO (OR AS A CONSEQUENCE OF):
c. ______
DUE TO (OR AS A CONSEQUENCE OF):
d. ______

Sequentially list conditions, if any, leading to immediate cause. Enter **UNDERLYING CAUSE** (Disease or injury that initiated events resulting in death) **LAST**

PART II. Other significant conditions contributing to death but not resulting in the underlying cause given in Part I.
28a. WAS AN AUTOPSY PERFORMED? *(Yes or no)*
28b. WERE AUTOPSY FINDINGS AVAILABLE PRIOR TO COMPLETION OF CAUSE OF DEATH? *(Yes or no)*
29. MANNER OF DEATH
☐ Natural ☐ Pending Investigation
☐ Accident
☐ Suicide ☐ Could not be Determined
☐ Homicide
30a. DATE OF INJURY *(Month, Day, Year)*
30b. TIME OF INJURY M
30c. INJURY AT WORK? *(Yes or no)*
30d. DESCRIBE HOW INJURY OCCURRED
30e. PLACE OF INJURY – At home, farm, street, factory, office building, etc. *(Specify)*
30f. LOCATION (Street and Number or Rural Route Number, City or Town, State)

SEE DEFINITION ON OTHER SIDE

CERTIFIER

31a. CERTIFIER *(Check only one)*
☐ CERTIFYING PHYSICIAN *(Physician certifying cause of death when another physician has pronounced death and completed Item 23)*
To the best of my knowledge, death occurred due to the cause(s) and manner as stated.
☐ PRONOUNCING AND CERTIFYING PHYSICIAN *(Physician both pronouncing death and certifying to cause of death)*
To the best of my knowledge, death occurred at the time, date, and place, and due to the cause(s) and manner as stated.
☐ MEDICAL EXAMINER/CORONER
On the basis of examination and/or investigation, in my opinion, death occurred at the time, date, and place, and due to the cause(s) and manner as stated.
31b. SIGNATURE AND TITLE OF CERTIFIER ▶
31c. LICENSE NUMBER
31d. DATE SIGNED *(Month, Day, Year)*
32. NAME AND ADDRESS OF PERSON WHO COMPLETED CAUSE OF DEATH (ITEM 27) *(Type/Print)*

REGISTRAR

33. REGISTRAR'S SIGNATURE ▶
34. DATE FILED *(Month, Day, Year)*

DEPARTMENT OF HEALTH AND HUMAN SERVICES – PUBLIC HEALTH SERVICE – NATIONAL CENTER FOR HEALTH STATISTICS – 1989 REVISION

PHS-T-003

FIGURE 12–1

Books based on the investigation of real life deaths have achieved best-seller status (e.g., Ubelaker & Scammell, 1992). Public appetite for slab scenes does not yet seem to have reached its satiation point—a startling turnabout from the former attitude of "see no, hear no, speak no" death that prevailed not so long ago.

The examination itself can vary. In some instances, it may be sufficient to look for one or two telltale signs (e.g., the trace of certain substances in the lungs or intestines, the presence or absence of cerebral hemorrhage). However, dissection and examination of the body may be considered necessary, along with bacteriological and toxicological laboratory tests. Removing a corpse from its burial site is a serious matter that requires careful thought and good judgment. Courts may order *exhumation* to obtain bullets, hair fragments, or other physical evidence that could bear on the cause of death in criminal cases, including malpractice. Corpses are also sometimes exhumed by accident, as when a graveyard is disturbed by flood or construction activities.

The time interval also allows symbolic and psychological needs to be met. Among some ethnic and religious groups, the survivors have specific tasks to perform after death. These tasks help survivors express their affection for the deceased and support each other during the period of acute grief. Carrying out these responsibilities is also felt to be an act of piety. Society and its gods expect selected individuals to prepare special foods or create special objects to be placed in the grave. The symbolic meaning is often more important than the length of the interval. The Cheyenne, for example, buried their dead quickly so that the ghosts would swiftly take their departure. By contrast, societies as distant as Egypt and Greenland (Hansen et al., 1991) mummified their dead as a way of keeping them part of the community, calling upon their symbolic powers, or enhancing their chances for a brilliant afterlife.

The recently deceased person has occupied a transitional status in many cultures: no longer a live member of the community but not yet all the way dead. There was still the need to complete a rite of passage from the world of the living to the realm of the dead (Kastenbaum,

2004a, 2004b). It is a vulnerable situation for the spirit detained between both worlds and a dangerous time for the community. Observe for yourself the way this belief continues to express itself today when we respond to the newly dead with more compassion and more trepidation than we do to those who have long established themselves in the realm of the dead.

The process of preparing the body varies greatly from society to society. For example, *embalming* is far from universal and was seldom practiced in the United States until thousands of soldiers died far from home during the Civil War. It should be kept in mind that embalming does not confer lasting protection. In fact, the funeral industry quickly withdrew its claims that embalming preserved bodies permanently as lawsuits were filed and judges and penalties assessed for deceptive advertising (Roach, 2003). Embalming is now a widespread practice in the United States, although not required by law unless the body is to be transported out of state or for some other clearly specified reason. Embalming can serve emotional and symbolic needs. For example, each year Arizona ships more than 3,000 embalmed bodies back to the hometowns of those people who had left to spend their retirement in Arizona. "Postmortem emigration" also occurs in other Sun Belt states so that a body may be brought to a family plot in the hometown cemetery.

In some societies, considerable effort, expense, and artistic skill have been devoted to the embellishment as well as to the preservation of the body. The ancient Egyptians' creation of mummies (see Box 12-2) is the most famous example but not the only one. Some rich and powerful people in Western nations have also demanded and received extensive postmortem treatment before burial. The wife of Louis XVl's minister "ordered her body to be preserved in alcohol, like an embryo" so that her widowed spouse could spend the rest of his life gazing at her beautiful face (Aries, 1981, p. 386). Less is known about the circumstances that led to mummifications (known as "the Bog People") in northern Europe about 2000 years ago, although ritualized killing is suspected for at least some of the cases. Societies around the world have pursued methods for achieving some form

The art and science of mummification took many years to develop before reaching its pinnacle in ancient Egypt.

of preserving remains. We will look at our own society after reviewing the Egyptian approach.

Plastination: The Dead as Instructors

And now we have *plastination.* This is a process that converts organic material into durable objects. Dr. Roy Glover of the University of Michigan Medical School explains that

water and tissue are replaced with silicone in a process which, for most specimens, takes about one month. Preserved tissue is first dissected and then dehydrated with acetone. It is immersed in a silicone bath under vacuum until the replacement of acetone is completed.

Why?

The resulting tissue is safe to handle, the tissue has no odor and it is extremely durable. Thus, the anatomical specimens are safer to use, more pleasant to use, and are much more durable and have a much longer shelf life (Glover, 2002, p. 1).

Plastination is currently used to prepare anatomical specimens for biomedical education. It has also taken a spectacular form with the human action figures created by Dr. Gunther von Hagen (Chapter 2), and widely exhibited throughout the world. Not surprisingly, it has also been widely praised and criticized for recycling human remains and confronting us with possibly more than some of us want to see.

Settling into Earth

So familiar is the practice of embalming a deceased person, placing that person horizontally in a coffin, and placing that coffin horizontally in a cemetery gravesite that we might consider this to be a natural and universal tradition. Not

BOX 12-2   THE SACRED ART OF MUMMIFICATION: HOW AND WHY?

How were mummies made in ancient Egypt?

- The family selects the grade and price level of mummification, choosing from several wooden models. Royal mummification is, of course, the highest quality, whatever the expense. It is a first-class mummification that is described here.

- The internal organs are removed—the brain first, caught on an iron hook and fished out through the (slit) nostrils. The abdominal organs are then removed through an incision.

- In royal mummifications, the heart is replaced by the carved replica of a *scarab* (a dung beetle), symbolizing the perpetual cycle of life into death and death into life. The internal organs are transferred to canopic jars (stone vessels).

- The body cavity is thoroughly rinsed with palm wine.

- The face and body may be reshaped to restore blemishes and disfigurations that occurred during the final illness or the mummification procedure. This could include reshaping the breasts to provide a more natural appearance for a woman.

- Spices and many other aromatic substances are placed inside the body, which is then sewn up.

- The body is then covered by "divine salts" to foster drying and preservation. The standard period of time for the drying phase is 40 days, followed by another 30 days for final preparations.

- The salted and dried body is washed and wrapped in linen strips that are undercoated with gum. Features such as eyes and eyebrows are drawn in ink on the linen to recreate the face.

- The mummy of a powerful person is placed in a tapered coffin, and the coffin itself is lodged within a sarcophagus (stone chamber), which itself is sealed into a tomb.

- It should be emphasized that this is mummification on the grand scale. The procedure was simplified and less expensive measures were used for people who lacked regal or other high-power status.

But why?

- The practical aim was to preserve the body by emptying it of its fluids and the parts most subject to rapid decay, producing a dehydrated but otherwise faithful—almost lifelike—version of the deceased person. When conducted by skillful embalmers and not desecrated by tomb robbers, the results could be very impressive. There are pharaohs who look as though they are ready to reclaim their thrones more than 3,000 years after they drew their last breath. The high art of mummification was itself achieved only after many years of trial and error, with frequent failures.

- The more crucial aim was to guide a spirit that departed from the body at death—the *ba*—back to its former physical home where its companion spirit—the *ka*—awaited its nightly visits. The preserved body made it easier for the winged *ba* to locate its companion spirit, *ka*. Some archaeologists believe that the great pyramids were constructed not only to honor the sacred dead and protect their bodies, but also as a sort of astral communications center that provided a stronger signal for the communion of the spirits.

Principle sources: Ikram & Dodson (1998); Harris (1973).

so. For example, many tribal societies have believed that one's afterlife is critically affected by the precise way in which that person's corpse is managed. One common practice has been to place the body in a fetal position. The body is then wrapped or bound so that it will maintain this position and then placed on its side. Is this position intended to resemble sleep and keep the spirit comfortable until it is ready to depart with the feeling of having been well served by the community? Some anthropologists think so; we really don't know. The fetal position might also be seen as an attempt to return the deceased to the womb of earth, possibly to be reborn. There have also been societies in which people have been buried in a seated position, or even upside down. Occasionally members of a tribal society have shared their reasons, as when Solomon Islanders around the turn of the twentieth century reported that they bound their dead in seated positions so they wouldn't come back to annoy them. Cynical observers in Western societies have claimed that gravestones are intended to accomplish the same purpose.

Up in Flames: The Cremation Alternative

Cremation is an ancient practice whose beginnings are lost in the mist of prehistory (Davies & Mates, 2006). Some of the earliest writings have referred to cremation (e.g., the works attributed to Homer, Ovid, and Virgil, as well as Buddhist, Hindu, and Jewish scriptures). Historians believe that most ancient peoples (the Egyptians are one of the exceptions) chose cremation (Prothero, 2001). Some cultures have regarded assignment to the flames as a form of purification that helped to free the soul for its new form of existence. The Vikings, for example, would build a spectacular long boat to set afire with the corpse of their chief aboard. The flaming vessel would then cross to the spirit domain, taking along not only their chief but his selected sacrificial companions. Practical considerations influenced a society's method: Cremation was not a realistic option for people who lived where trees were scarce. Some cultures had multiple ways of dealing with the dead. In former days, for example, Adaman Islanders would bury those

who died very young or very old in a shallow hole, but those who perished in their prime received the prestigious treatment of having their bodies placed on a tree platform. Dead strangers would be cut into pieces and consumed by fire without ceremony because their ghosts immediately left for their homeland and therefore posed no local danger.

Cremation was generally opposed by Christianity from the later Middle Ages until the Reformation. Martin Luther shifted attention away from the body to spiritual salvation. Cremation gradually became less of a threat to one's fate in the afterlife. Several events prepared Europe to at least consider the cremation alternative. One of the most influential was the death of English poet Percy Bysshe Shelley in 1822. He died when overtaken by a storm while boating on a Swiss lake. Shelley's body was cremated on a pyre by his fellow poet and friend, Lord Byron—who then reached into the flames to rescue Shelley's heart. (Years later Shelley's heart was buried with his widow, Mary Wollstonecraft Shelley, who, still in her teens, had written a novel called *Frankenstein*.) Cremation had started to take on images and resonances of its own. By the middle of the nineteenth century, an international movement composed of medical experts was criticizing burial as a breeding ground for disease and recommending its replacement with cremation. Not long after, Queen Victoria's personal physician wrote a procremation work that started a spark in the United States (Prothero, 2001). Concern for public health has remained a significant theme in the advocacy of cremation.

But—times change! There is now rising concern about gases produced during the combustion process. In England this has already "resulted in the introduction of increasingly stringent laws governing the output of gases from cremator chimneys" (Davies, 2003, p. 768). The cost of preventing the release of mercury and other toxic products is also of concern. We cannot help but think again of the folk societies that for centuries have feared assault from spirits of the dead. In the twenty-first century, public health officials are troubled about breathing in the toxic fumes of crematory ovens.

Cremation in the United States

There were two "first" cremations of Euro-Americans. The "official" first cremation occurred on December 6, 1876, in Washington, Pennsylvania. Baron Joseph Henry Louis Charles De Palm's cremation was hailed by some as a significant achievement in transforming society from sentimentality to science, and denounced by others as Satanic blasphemy. The debate was on—and has continued to this day. The actual first cremation had occurred much earlier. Henry Laurens, a former president of the Continental Congress, was given the open-air cremation he desired, though over the misgivings of practically everybody else. Why did he make so unusual and so unpopular a choice? Because he was afraid of being buried alive (see also Chapter 1). And why was he afraid of that? Because his daughter, pronounced dead of smallpox, was close to being placed in the grave when she suddenly revived just in time. But even Laurens' cremation was not the first to have taken place in North America. Cremation had been practiced by some Native American peoples (such as the Tolkotin of Oregon) before the first Europeans came ashore.

Today in the United States, cremation is selected by about 1 person in 4, as compared with about only 1 in 14 in the 1970s. There are significant differences by state. Cremations are still uncommon (10% or less) in Alabama, Kentucky, Louisiana, Mississippi, Tennessee, and West Virginia. By contrast, upwards of 60% of the dead are cremated in Alaska, Arizona, Colorado, Florida, Idaho, Kansas, Montana, Nevada, New Hampshire, New Jersey, New Mexico, Oregon, and Washington. Obviously, local circumstances and traditions have their influence. Estimates of cremation rates in other nations place Japan clearly at the top (95%). Cremation has also become the most common practice throughout Europe in general (63%), as well as, with similar rates, Australia/New Zealand, Britain, China, and India. Religious customs and other influences have made cremation rare, however, in sub-Saharan Africa, Islamic countries, and Israel. Kearl (2004) links the increase in cremations to the decrease in attachment to a particular place in nations with mobile populations.

The Funeral Service

Both whole-body burial and cremation offer the possibility of conducting a funeral service. Two major purposes of the funeral service are: final placement of the remains, and society's public recognition that one of its members has made the transition from life to death. Perhaps the most familiar form is the church funeral service, in which respects are paid to the deceased in a church or funeral home; then mourners gather in the cemetery to hear eulogies and witness the casket being placed in the grave. Most often the arrangements are carried out by the funeral director—ordering flowers, providing the hearse and possibly other vehicles, and so on. A member of the clergy usually presides over the commemorative services. In "small town America" the clergyperson often knew the family well; this seems to be somewhat less common today.

Some rural areas still continue a more family- and neighbor-oriented process in which the funeral director has a less significant role. James Crissman (1994) describes a traditional approach that is being affected by changing times in *Death and Dying in Central Appalachia.* He speaks of "the code of the mountains," under which independence and loyalty help people to survive hard times. Not much is expected—or wanted—from outsiders.

The funeral service can be disturbed by unsettling events from within the family as well as external forces as previously mentioned. An elaborate funeral can attract so much attention to itself that it is difficult to keep a focus on the deceased. A lack of consensus among the mourners can also be a distraction. One common example is the decision to have either an open or closed casket. These two options are of almost equal popularity—almost a guarantee that some participants will be displeased with whatever choice is made. Even those who prefer an open casket may disagree on the way it is handled. Should Louise's visage be restored into a semblance of the robust person she was most of her life or be shown with the lines of exhaustion that developed during her last illness? Should Harry be displayed in his favorite old sloppy clothes or an elegant dark suit that he would literally never have been caught dead in? Nevertheless, the underlying purposes remain: to make a final disposition of the body and to use this occasion as a way of acknowledging that a life has passed from among us.

Memorializing the Deceased

Most societies attempt to fix the deceased in memory. In the United States a death notice is often (but not always) published in a local newspaper. An *obituary* may also appear, especially if requested by the family. Today many newspapers require a fee to print an obituary unless the individual is considered especially "newsworthy." Furthermore, metropolitan newspapers have been reducing the number of obituaries published because of space and economical pressures. Is this trend weakening the ability of our death system to meet the need of survivors? Do people feel alienated because the deaths of their loved ones are not acknowledged in the state's major newspaper? We do not yet know the answers to these questions, but traditional acknowledgments and responses to death are vulnerable to general social trends.

Traditional burial is almost always accompanied by a grave marker, whether simple or elaborate. Survivors often experience severe stress when war, terrorist attack, or natural catastrophe make it impossible to know precisely which grave is that of a relative or dear friend. Tens of thousands of unidentified soldiers lie buried in foreign lands, their graves usually marked by simple crosses. Many American families visited World War I burial grounds such as Flanders Field so they could at least be close to the place where their loved ones had fallen. In our own time, there are families who have experienced emotional pain for years because a member is still listed as "missing in action" in Vietnam. The despair of people who have lost family members in the tsunami disaster often is intensified by the lack of identified remains. The increasing use of DNA testing may assist in the identification of people who have died in war or catastrophe and thereby ease some of the survivors' grief. There was some success in identifying the victims of the September 11, 2001, terrorist attacks. Whether it takes the form of lighting a candle on the deceased's birthday, saying prayers, or making sacrifices or gifts in the name of the deceased, memorialization appears to be one of humankind's deepest needs when separated from a loved one by death.

Getting on with Life

The funeral process is devoted both to completing society's obligations to the deceased and supporting the survivors in their grief. The "life must go on" motif has often taken the form of a festive occasion. Family, neighbors, and best friends gather to eat, drink, and share lively conversation. In former generations, the food was usually prepared by family members, representing a gift in the service of life. It was a mark of pride to offer the delicacies and beverages in abundance. The guests were now expected to enjoy themselves, to be vital and frisky. There might be dancing and, as the feasting proceeded, even some romancing. Death had been given its due, now it was time for life to show what it was all about.

This type of festivity started to give way as society became more impersonal, mobile, and technologically oriented, and as efforts were made to banish death from public awareness. A cup of coffee with a few family members and friends has sometimes replaced the elaborate proceedings of earlier generations. Although the size and splendor of the postfuneral gathering may differ greatly, the underlying function is usually the same—to help people redirect their attention to the continuation and renewal of life. This is why conversation may seem unnaturally lively and why people may seem to eat, drink, and laugh too much considering the recent death of an intimate. If you happen to walk in while a risqué story is being told, it is easy to be offended and think that insensitivity and disrespect are afoot. However, lively and lusty behaviors after a funeral can represent a partial release from tension and the compelling need to show each other that life can and should go on—"Harry (or Louise) would have wanted it that way!"

MAKING DEATH "LEGAL"

Society's claim on the individual is demonstrated clearly at the points of entry and exit. Births and deaths have been recorded at the neighborhood church since medieval times.

Demands of the faith required that each soul be entered into the books and therefore subject to the expectations of God and the state. A written notice was also required as the soul was released to join its maker—proof that clergy was watching carefully over the flock. These records would be consulted if questions arose about kinship rights and obligations. Now, centuries later, the surviving records continue to be valuable. Historians seeking to understand the effects of a harsh winter in rural England in the seventeenth century or migration patterns in northern Italy 100 years later are almost certain to consult entries preserved at the local parish.

Certificates of death (Figure 12-1) and birth continue to serve similar functions in today's more secular society. The newborn and the deceased are affirmed as citizens beginning or ending their active roles in society. Church records now provide supplementary rather than official documentation. Despite all the changes that have occurred through the years, governing authorities still insist on "keeping the book" on the individual. Society presumes that none of us belong entirely to ourselves but are subject to "legalizations" both coming and going.

We now examine in more detail some of the major features of making death legal as part of the contemporary funeral process.

Establishing the Facts of Death

A death is real but not official until certified. It is the responsibility of the physician to establish the principal facts of the death and initiate an investigation if questions arise. Cause of death often requires the physician to identify several contributing factors. The following are examples:

- "Cardiovascular accident, secondary to hypertension"
- "Pneumonia, secondary to lung cancer"
- "Hemorrhage, secondary to cancer of the larynx"
- "Septicemia, secondary to extensive third degree burns"

The actual situation may be more complicated than death certificate can express. A woman in her 80s suffers from heart and urinary tract disorders in addition to a loss of bone mass and resiliency (osteoporosis). One day while she is simply ascending a staircase, the brittle bones give way. She falls. Both hips are broken. Her already impaired cardiovascular system is subjected to further stress. Internal bleeding proves difficult to control. Confined to bed and fitted with a catheter, she develops an infection that further saps her strength. Medical and nursing management becomes very difficult because treatments that might improve one condition can worsen another. Her lungs fill with fluid, and she dies. But what is the cause? Or what is the precise relationship among the many interacting factors that lead to death? The physician may or may not be able to give a definite answer but often can specify the major contributing causes.

The death certificate has its limits as a source of research data. Even so, it can provide useful information. For example, the information about this elderly woman's death adds to a growing body of data that emphasizes the need for better understanding and clinical and environmental management to prevent falls. Relatively few death certificates specify the underlying cause. Many death certificates also omit other information that would be needed to understand the circumstances of the individual's death. It is hard to escape the inference that some physicians are not giving much priority to completing thorough and accurate death certificates (Iserson, 2003).

The cause of death is often the most salient item of information required on the certificate, but the other entries are also of potential significance. Who is the next of kin? Was the death related to occupational hazard or stress? Has there been an unusually high rate of death from the same cause in this geographical area in the past few years? Questions such as these can have many implications for the well-being of surviving individuals.

WHAT DOES THE FUNERAL PROCESS ACCOMPLISH?

The funeral process would not have become so important to so many societies unless it served significant needs and values. In this section we gain additional perspective by observing how society responds to the death of its most powerful members. Every life and therefore every death should perhaps be considered of equal importance. In practice, however, societies consider some people more important than others.

When Great People Die

The loss of a great person often triggers a massive response. In fact, the question, "Who does this society consider really important?" can be answered by observing the funeral process. But it can be observed from another perspective as well: Given that a great person has died, what is it that society feels it must accomplish through the funeral and memorialization process? Here are a few examples that will illustrate the dynamics and principles involved.

The Silent Army of Ch'in Shih-huang-ti

Ch'in Shih-huang-ti was one of the most powerful of monarchs. He unified the people of an enormous and diversified region into nationhood and stimulated the development of a vigorous and distinctive culture. It was Ch'in, as the first emperor of China, who built the Great Wall more than two centuries before the birth of Christ.

His tomb was discovered in 1974. It had been effectively concealed within a large mound whose location was selected through the occult (and now fairly well known) art of *feng-shui,* which deterred evil spirits from disturbing either the deceased or the living. To call the site a tomb is an understatement—it answers better to the name of palace. Ch'in's tomb was built near the graves of earlier rulers and designed to surpass them all.

Several of the huge underground chambers have been excavated. Pit number one, for example, is a rectangle approximately 700 by 200 feet. It is divided into 11 parallel corridors, with the entire structure skillfully constructed by a combination of rammed earth, bricks, and timber crossbeams. In this pit, excavators found an entire army! Arthur Cotterell (1981) describes the scene:

The chambers are arranged in the battle order of an infantry regiment . . . 3,210 terracotta foot soldiers. They do not wear helmets; only Ch'in officers have these. But most of the infantry soldiers wear armour. These armoured men are divided into forty files; they stand four abreast in the nine wide corridors, and form two files in each of the narrow ones. The head of the regiment in the eastern gallery comprises a vanguard of nearly 200 sharpshooters, the ancient equivalent of artillery. They would have fired their arrows from a distance, once contact was made with the enemy. Between these sharpshooters and the armoured infantry are six chariots and three unarmoured infantry squads. Each chariot is pulled by four terracotta horses and manned by a charioteer and one or two soldiers. The guards would have wielded long flexible lances, measuring as much as six metres (20 feet), in order to stop enemy soldiers from cutting off the heads of the horses (pp. 22–23).

The artistic craftsmanship devoted to the creation of this subterranean army and the enormous economic resources poured into the enterprise are truly staggering. But why? What purpose was served by such a vast expenditure of labor and resources?

Ch'in's motivation probably included the following components:

- To support his claims as the greatest of all monarchs.
- To impress the deities and ensure his place among the immortals.
- To confound his enemies and secure a continuation of his royal succession.

Ch'in made history, but he also made enemies. His military adventures severely strained the economy. He was also not the most tolerant of men. Scholars who displeased him were buried alive, and any person who displeased him was thereby in mortal danger. The impressive tomb served to display his ability to defend his regime even from the grave, but it had another purpose as well. Like many other rulers, the first emperor of China craved immortality. Just as he literally required his subjects to sing his praises throughout his life, so he established a mute army to protect his afterlife from both earthly and spiritual foe. The plan didn't work, though. A fierce peasant revolution soon toppled the regime, and it is only in our own time that China has been able to recover detailed knowledge about its first emperor.

Death Makes a Hero

Dynamics of a very different sort produced one of the most elaborate funeral processes of the nineteenth century. England's Prince

The funeral for a Viking chief involved an elaborate ritual that was consummated when the long boat constructed for this purpose was set afire as it moved toward its destination with the gods. Valued goods accompanied the deceased chief, and, at times, so did a consort of women who were sacrificed to the gods as the journey began.

Consort died unexpectedly. This man, Prince Albert of Saxe Coburg-Gotha, had been married to the illustrious Queen Victoria. The public had disliked Albert because he was not an Englishman. Unexpectedly, after his death, a national cult developed around the late Prince Consort.

Much of the evidence remains available for inspection today. Examine the monuments and portraits throughout the British Isles—Balmoral, Aberdeen, Edinburgh, Nottinghamshire, South Kensington, Whippingham, Frogmore, Manchester, and so on. Among the physical tributes in London alone there is a memorial chapel in Windsor Castle and the Albert Memorial, which itself is only part of the impressive Victoria and Albert Museum. Parks were renamed in Albert's memory. Small statues of the dashing prince were sold as memorabilia. One could purchase Prince Albert belt clasps, lamps, pencil cases, and stationery. Eventually his handsome likeness would be put on packages and cans of tobacco (my father's favorite brand three generations later). Alfred Lord Tennyson wrote one of his most famous poems to honor him ("Idylls of the King"). Upon his death, the late Prince Consort became the most popular image and also something of an industry.

The widowed Queen of England demonstrated a worshipful attitude toward her late husband and would not allow people to speak of him in the past tense. His private rooms at three favorite residences were preserved just as they had been during his life. A visiting nobleman observed (Darby & Smith, 1983):

> She . . . referred to the sayings and doings of the Prince as if he was in the next room. It was difficult to believe that he was not, but in his own room where she received me everything was set out on his table and the pen and his blotting-book, his handkerchief on the sofa, his watch going, fresh flowers in the glass . . . as if he might come in at any moment (p. 4).

The observant Lord Clarendon noted a subtle contradiction in the arrangements. On the one hand, there were the fresh clothes, jug of hot water, and clean towels laid out for the use of the Prince, yet a tinted photograph of his corpse hung by the side of his bed. Obviously, the Queen was having difficulty in reconciling her conflicting needs to acknowledge reality and to preserve the illusion that her beloved was still with her.

What purposes did the funeral and memorialization process for Prince Albert achieve? I suggest the following:

1. *The elaborate memorialization process served the function of symbolically incorporating Albert into the British Empire.* In effect, he became an Englishman after his death. This was both a gesture of support for the queen and a way of grafting Albert's attributes onto the national self-image. His noble figure would always stand at alert attention or gracefully sit astride a beautiful horse. The memorialization also tried to make up for the citizens' cool attitude toward the foreigner while he was alive.

2. *Albert's death provided an excellent opportunity to express current sentiment and belief.* Victorian England had developed increasingly elaborate mourning practices. There was even competition to see who could express bereavement most impressively through dark clothing ("widow's weeds"), withdrawal from customary social activities and responsibilities, and idealization of the deceased. Cemetery architecture prospered, impressive statuary art aggrandized the departed and, therefore, the affluent mourners as well. These customs affirmed the prevailing belief in the certainty and blessings of immortal life, although there were critics of such ostentatious mourning. It was the Victorian age, after all, that provided Sigmund Freud with the raw material for his exploration of hidden motives and thwarted impulses (Gay, 1984). Albert's death, then, provided an opportunity to soothe personal fears and doubts through displays of confidence in divine justice and mercy.

The postmortem cult of the Prince Consort became an ideal representation of the virtues his generation cherished. He had been just the way they wished they could be. Further, once the man was dead, his memory could be polished and fixed for posterity without the danger of competition from his ongoing life. It is easier to admire dead heroes. They are less likely to turn around and do something that would force us to alter our judgment.

Many more examples could be given of elaborate memorialization processes. A common feature is the slow, stately tempo favored for the funeral procession itself. This provides more time for the realization of the death and its meanings to sink in. In contrast, the final arrangements for a person without fame or influence is likely to be simple, routine, and brisk. At Vienna's Central Cemetery, for example, most funeral services are run by the clock, with every element determined by the status of the deceased and family. How many shiny medals would you like to have displayed on how lengthy a carpet? How much money are you prepared to spend? The disassembly line I witnessed one cloudy day was more efficient than many a factory assembly line and so ever more depressing.

Great Britain was a nation swathed in tradition and decorated by the trappings and figures of royalty. What would happen when a new regime has taken hold—forcibly—in a not especially unified nation, and then loses its founder? Consider, the public afterlife of Vladimir Ilyich Ulyanov.

From Revolutionary to Relic

I'm standing beside Lenin. The man himself.

Can it be true he died ten years ago? I really feel like I'm looking at a man sleeping. You find yourself walking on tiptoe so as not to wake him. In preserving the body of its historic leader the USSR has achieved the seemingly impossible. The embalming of Lenin is the most perfect example I've ever seen of the art— better even than the mummies of ancient Egypt. Don't the Russian scientists say Vladimir Ilyich's body may be preserved for all eternity, without ever suffering the ravages of time? (An American visitor, quoted by Zbarsky & Hutchinson, 1997, p. 91)

Lenin led a failed revolution in czarist Russia in 1905 and fled the country. In 1917, Russia was at war and in crisis at home. Czar Nicholas II was overthrown, and the provisional government was beset with problems on all sides. At this moment in history, a mysterious sealed train entered Russia from neutral Switzerland. Lenin was its most important passenger. His ruthless leadership soon brought the Bolshevik Party to power. Germany, Russia's adversary, had financed this venture in order to knock Russia out of the war. Lenin became the founding father of a new nation, and the Communist experiment was up and running.

Seven years later, Lenin was dead. Wounded and then partially debilitated by strokes, Lenin became more of a symbol than an active leader during the last year of his life. Few shed tears. Lenin was known as an ice-cold person, obsessed by his plans and merciless in their execution. Presumably a liberator of the people, he showed little compassion or even interest in them. His death sparked a national crisis; those hoping to take his place were engaged in savage infighting. (The genocidal Josef Stalin came out the winner, and millions of Russian people were thereby doomed to suffering and death.)

The newly formed Soviet Union could not afford to lose its father figure. What if Lenin's corpse could be preserved indefinitely in a lifelike condition? And what if this corpse were installed within a grand mausoleum that would dominate Red Square, the spiritual heart of the nation? And what if people see for themselves that their founding father, their peerless leader, was still with them?

The irony here was obvious to all who dared take notice. Lenin's Soviet Union had no use for religion, the grandeur of the abolished czarist regime, or for "the cult of personality." Nevertheless, a shrine was created for Lenin so he could be revered as a de facto patron saint. However, the task of preserving Lenin's body for the ages had been bungled. The first efforts were primitive, leading to serious deterioration of the body (Zbarsky, 1997). The face and hands still looked presentable and were regularly touched up with ointment to prevent drying and cracking. Burial would have been a national scandal, the admission that Soviet science had failed. Zbarsky and his colleagues had to come up with innovative techniques to preserve the already deteriorated body. The restoration process included cosmetic repair of the face and substitution of false for real eyes to prevent the sockets from further shrinking.

How has Lenin fared as a relic? Very well, and not so well. Millions of people have visited his tomb, which became one of the most visible symbols both of Russia and of communism. But statues of Lenin were pulled down in countries that had been subservient to Moscow soon after the Soviet Union ceased to exist. The Russian people have increasingly expressed themselves in favor of burying Lenin's body. Rumors were regularly heard that Lenin's mummified corpse will be stolen some night and buried before the police can react (or perhaps even with police involvement). It is possible that now, years later, a few are still passionately concerned about the fate of Lenin's remains.

Strange, strange, strange—but then, not so strange after all. Many societies have not only venerated but used their powerful dead. The skulls of past chiefs may be consulted for advice, and the shrines of saints visited in hope of miraculous healing and other mercies. What we see in the memorial process for Lenin is an instructive reminder that a core of ancient belief and feeling can retain its potency into modern times. This emotional core was strong enough to entice a materialistic antireligious regime to devote itself to enshrining a corpse with so much determination that it might have earned grudging praise from the ancient Egyptians, but for intent more than craftsmanship.

Balancing the Claims of the Living and the Dead

Another major function of the funeral process is to achieve a balance between the competing claims of the living and the dead. This may sound like a strange idea. We often hear it said that funerals are for the living. However, the need to honor the claims of the dead is also well-entrenched in most death systems. Some of these traditions have been eroded by changing social conditions. Nevertheless, even today the need to balance the claims of the dead and the living can still be discovered if we look beneath the surface. First, consider how this process expresses itself in three traditional contexts: rural Greece, the Kotas of southern India, and Orthodox Judaism.

In the Shadow of Mount Olympus

Potamia is a village in northern Greece not far from Mount Olympus. The 600 people who live there remain in close physical and symbolic contact with the dead. The small cemetery is crowded with 20 or more grave markers that memorialize villagers who have died in the past few years. Anthropologist Alexander Tsiarias (1982) entered a building in the corner of the cemetery:

Although I knew what I would find inside, I was still not fully prepared for the sight that confronted me when I opened the door. Beyond a small floor space a ladder led down to a dark, musty-smelling area filled with the bones of many generations of villagers. Near the top of the huge pile the remains of each person were bound up separately in a white cloth. Toward the bottom of the pile the bones—skulls, pelvises, ribs, the long bones of countless arms, and legs—lay in tangled disarray, having lost all trace of belonging to distinct individuals with the disintegration of the cloth wrappings. Stacked in one corner of the building were metal boxes and small suitcases with names, dates, and photographs identifying the people whose bones lay securely within (pp. 10–11).

Bodies remain in the graveyard for 5 years and then are removed to the bone house. During this temporary burial, the survivors have ample time to visit their lost loved ones. The survivors' feelings often become expressed with great intensity as the time nears to exhume and transfer the body. Tsiarias recorded a mother's lament:

Eleni, Eleni, you died far from home with no one near you. I've shouted and cried for five years, Eleni, my unlucky one, but you haven't heard me. I don't have the courage to shout any more. Eleni, Eleni, my lost soul. You were a young plant, but they didn't let you blossom. You've been here for five years. Soon you'll leave. Then where will I go? What will I do? Five years ago I put a beautiful bird into the ground, a beautiful partridge. But now what will I take out? What will I find? (p. 15)

The small graveyard in Potamia is often filled with mourners, usually women. They come not only to express their sorrows through song, speech, and prayer but also to tend the graves. Candles are kept burning at the foot of each grave, and the grounds are tended with scrupulous care. Then they sit and talk to their dead and to each other. The village's communal life is strengthened through their role as survivors of the dead. For the women especially, the graveyard provides an opportunity to express their *ponos* (the pain of grief). The men find a variety of outlets, but the women are usually expected to be at home and to keep their feelings to themselves. "A woman performs the necessary rites of passage and cares for the graves of the dead 'in order to get everything out of her system'" (p. 144).

Queen Victoria of England gave her name to an entire age. She remained in mourning long after the death of her beloved husband, Prince Albert, and maintained his rooms as though he were about to return any day. One of her most comforting companions also is seen here: Sharp, who had a natural gift for looking mournful.

Through their graveside laments and rituals, the women try for a balance between the dead and the living. The custom of temporary burial is helpful in this process. The recently deceased is still treated as an individual and as a member of the community. In effect, there is a second and final death when the physical remains are deposited among the bones of the anonymous dead. It is easier to cope with the symbolic claims of the dead when a definite time limit has been set—in this case, 5 years. The memory of the deceased will continue to be honored, but removal of the remains to the bone house releases the survivors to devote themselves to their own life-oriented needs.

The survivors are obliged to tend the graves. As Tsiarias points out, this process involves a symbolic interaction and continuation between the living and the dead. The dead have the right to expect it, just as those who are now among the living can expect their survivors to honor their postmortem rights when the time comes. In Potamia and in some other communities where traditional value systems remain in place, the obligations of the living to the dead are clear, specific, and well known.

Kotas and Orthodox Jews

Peoples as different as the Kotas of Southern India and Orthodox Jews dispersed throughout the world continue to carry out extensive rituals to ensure that both the dead and the living receive their due. Their observations differ greatly in detail. The Kotas, who cremate their dead (Goldberg, 1981/1982):

> believe that death is contaminating and all who come into contact with death are defiled. Through the rituals of two funerals, the *Green Funeral* and the Dry Funeral, the spirit of the deceased is assisted in departing to the "Motherland" and the survivors are thereby cleansed so that they might resume their normal life within the society. Since the concept of an afterlife is not clear to most Kotas, the adherence to ritual is seen more as a cleansing process for the survivors, than for the attainment of existence in another world for the deceased (p. 119).

Orthodox Jews obey strict laws that reject embalming and cremation and require that funeral arrangements be simple and standard no matter what the family's financial status. The interval between death and burial is regarded as quite apart from usual time and custom. This period is known as *Aninut*—a time in which time stands still (Schindler, 1996). During Aninut, the grieving survivors are exempted from all social and religious obligations, other than arranging for the funeral. One should be devoted to honoring the dead and reflecting on the loss. Aninut therefore helps the survivors to begin the long process of recovery from grief by providing a little time to focus on the death in their own private ways without other distractions. The *Kaddish* prayer affirms faith in God; Shiva, the 7 days of mourning, unites the family in grief.

The ritual action of washing hands before sitting at Shiva has its parallel in the more elaborate purification rites of the Kotas. The Kota, the Orthodox Jew, the rural Greek villager, and many others with long ethnic traditions must fulfill obligations to the dead. When these obligations have been faithfully performed, it is time for the living to again turn their full attention to life.

MEMORIES OF OUR PEOPLE: CEMETERIES IN THE UNITED STATES

At first a nation of farmers who visited small towns with their artisans and shops, the United States soon became a coast-to-coast industrial power with humming factories, crowded cities, opportunistic ventures in every direction, and a large and mobile population. The history of cemeteries has faithfully moved in concert with our changing ways of life. In colonial times, most of the dead were buried in a church graveyard. This practice continued into the early years of the republic. As the population increased, however, these early burial grounds often proved inadequate. The dead as well as the living were becoming crowded.

The New Haven Burying Ground is a surviving example of the response to this emerging need. The city had established a cemetery in 1639 in what is now the center of New Haven (Plunkett, 1999). Graves were dug by friends and relatives, who placed them wherever it seemed suitable and also marked and tended the graves as they saw fit. Just 20 years later, there was already concern that the burial ground had become too crowded, but nothing was done about it. The poorly tended and helter-skelter burial ground had the virtue of being adjacent to a church but was otherwise becoming an increasing eyesore in the growing community. The closely packed grave sites did not speak well for dignity and respect. Moreover, the seasonal death toll from diseases such as malaria and tuberculosis further strained the resources of the graveyard. Some people worried about that the burial ground itself might be a source of infection.

The community finally responded in 1796 with the establishment of the New Haven Burying Ground (also known as The Grove Street Cemetery). Care was taken to select land that was accessible and yet would not block further community development. Furthermore, each grave lot became the property of a purchasing family—here was one of the first cemeteries in which "the family plot" became established. Unfortunately, even thoughtfully planned cemeteries are vulnerable to conflict and change. Some citizens advocated and some opposed new church constructions that would create problems for the again-overcrowded burying ground. Many grave sites were neglected. Animals and vandals invaded at night, the former digging up graves, the latter desecrating memorial stones and littering. The people of New Haven again rallied to protect their cemetery. This basic story has been repeated in many cemeteries as communities try to cope with urban change and years of neglect.

Major changes in cemeteries occurred throughout the nineteenth century. One of the most important was the introduction of "memorial parks," also known as "garden parks" and "landscapes of memory" (Linden-Ward, 1989; Morris, 2002). The first of these was Mount Auburn Cemetery (Cambridge, Massachusetts), whose spacious and inviting grounds became the inspiration for similar developments throughout the nation. The other major development was the establishment of national cemeteries to honor those who had fallen in war. Lincoln's Gettysburg Address on November 11, 1863, was given to dedicate the first national cemetery. By the end of the Civil War,

there were 14 national cemeteries for both Union and Confederate dead. The National Cemetery System today tends to the graves of more than 2 million veterans in more than 100 sites throughout the country. In history's odd way of doing things, the United States became that much more of a nation when the dead of the Blue and the dead of the Gray were placed to rest in the same meadows.

The Neighborhood Cemetery

There are still pockets of traditional symbolic interaction with the dead in American cities. While interviewing older people in small industrial cities, I often heard reference to the neighborhood cemetery. The cemetery remained the focal point of continuity, even if it was surrounded by abandoned factories and urban debris. One octogenarian confided:

> I know I should get out of this neighborhood. Hell, it isn't even a neighborhood any more. But how can I sell this house? It's where my mother and father lived and died. And who'd look after them? . . . Oh, sure, I'm out there every Sunday to keep things as nice as I can. It's not their [his parents'] fault what's happened to this neighborhood. Me and a few others still meet there; we keep up the graves. And it's not just my parents. Just about everybody else is there, too, I mean, six feet under. I keep them company. They keep me company.

This man was a forthright and independent person who was surviving in hard times by his courage and wits. His self-esteem was reinforced by the knowledge that he was continuing to fulfill his obligations to the dead.

Even in bustling, urban America, survivors often select images, materials, and objects connected with the deceased to somehow keep the beloved alive as part of themselves (Schwab, 2004). Cherished aspects of the deceased's personality can become part of the survivor's lifestyle, continuing the memorialization process well beyond the funeral itself. (The widow of the "old man around the corner" memorialized her husband by retelling the same well-worn jokes that she had always frowned at while he was alive. "Now, William, nobody wants to hear that awful story!")

Ethnic Cemeteries in the United States

The shores of the United States have attracted millions of people who sought to make new lives for themselves and their children. Others were brought here involuntarily, wrenched from their homelands and sold into slavery. Still other people lived freely in forests and plains until they encountered the aggressive newcomers who would eventually transform a wilderness into a powerful industrial nation. Memories of this incredible variety of people remain with us in many forms. Poet Stephen Vincent Benet (1942) reflects on this heritage:

> I have fallen in love with American names,
> The sharp names that never get fat,
> The snakeskin-titles of mining-claims,
> The plumed war-bonnet of Medicine Hat,
> Tucson and Deadwood and Lost Mule flat. . . .
> And the bullet-towns of Calamity Jane.
> I will remember Skunktown Plain. . . .
> You may bury my body in Sussex grass,
> You may bury my tongue at Champmedy.
> I shall not be there. I shall rise and pass.
> Bury my heart at Wounded Knee.

The land also remembers. Ethnic cemeteries affirm that "our people" contributed to the nation's history. Here are a few examples of cemeteries whose responsibility it is to preserve not physical remains, but memories and symbols of those who have gone before us.

1. *African American section, The Common Burying Ground, Newport, Rhode Island.* This colonial cemetery dates from 1650. More than 8,000 people were buried here until it became an historical site. Ann Tashjian and her husband, Dickran Tashjian (1989), photographed the gravestones and researched the history. Many of the grave markers described the deceased as "servant," which is thought to have been a New England euphemism for "slave." Some of the gravestones are elaborate in design and execution, suggesting that the deceased had been held in high regard by the white families they served.

   Do the gravestones or burial sites show any trace of the cultures and belief systems that the African Americans brought with them to the American colonies? *Not a trace.* The dominant white American culture of the time prevailed. If you visit this cemetery, make your way to the northern edge and you will see those African American grave markers that have survived the vicissitudes of time. You will see that they are similar to the other grave markers of the same time periods. Cherubs, for example, were popular adornments, and these appear on white and African American grave markers alike.

   The cemetery registers the subordinate place of African Americans in colonial New England; in death as in life, their own culture was denied expression. Death would bring freedom from servitude, but in public memory the African American would still be under the control of the dominant society.

2. *Navajo and Mormon companions, Ramah Cemetery, Ramah, New Mexico.* Members of The Church of the Latter-day Saints (often referred to as Mormons) started a community in Ramah, New Mexico, in 1876. The Ramah people of the Navajo Nation already lived there. The same graveyard serves families of both cultures, although their beliefs and practices differ markedly. There are no large memorial statues, and the ground is covered by native grasses and weeds.

   The Navajo section includes 71 graves that could be positively identified. Most are undecorated. Cunningham (1984) noted:

   > There is no indication of any attempt to bury family members side by side or close together. All the graves are approximately the same distance apart and are laid out in what is basically a straight line. The headstone or other marker and the grave are placed so that the main side of the marker and the head of the deceased point toward the West, and the deceased would face East if sitting or standing (p. 204).

   Navajo culture expresses itself through valued objects placed with the dead. In burying turquoise jewelry with the deceased, the family speeds the deceased's spirit on its journey to the afterlife and confuses and thwarts any *ch'iidii* (evil ghosts) that might covet these powerful objects.

The village cemetery can be a place for comforting socialization as people gather to look after their family graves.

The Mormon section (209 graves) has numerous markers, some of them homemade by family members. These markers display a large variety of style and materials, in contrast with the simple metal markers that identify the Navajo graves. The Mormon markers include examples of folk art revival (e.g., in red sandstone carvings) and such others as "an actual picture of the deceased as a part of their design and contemporary sand-blasted stones which allow very intricate and exact representations of floral motifs and even recognizable representations of Mormon temples at Mesa, Arizona, and Salt Lake City, Utah" (Cunningham, 1989, p. 204). The Mormon graves further differ from those of the Navajo in spatial arrangement: They are usually grouped according to family relationships, including some joint stones for husband and wife. The memorial stones also provide more information about the deceased.

The Navajo and Mormon dead in New Mexico appear to be more companionable than the African Americans and colonial whites in Newport. The New Mexico cemetery itself blends easily into its surroundings, the "landscaping" for both Navajo and Mormon being left up to nature. The family-oriented Mormons preserved this orientation in the arrangement of graves and markers, but did not impose their beliefs and practices on their Native American neighbors nor object to the jewelry burials. For their part, some Navajos have chosen to become Mormon—or "semi-Mormon"—and have expressed the thought that the worst of the evil spirits have departed from the burial grounds because of the Mormons' presence.

3. *Mexican-Americans in San Antonio's San Fernando Cemetery.* Many urban cemeteries look like many other urban cemeteries. Lynn Gosnell and Suzanne Gott (1989) describe the activity at a cemetery that has retained its special character:

> Throughout the year, but especially during religious and secular holidays, including Halloween, All Souls' Day, Christmas, Valentine's Day, Easter, Mother's Day, and Father's Day, the visitor to San Femando takes part in an energetic practice of grave decoration and visual display. During these days, cars and trucks jam the narrow traffic lanes which provide access to each block of this ninety-three acre cemetery. Relatives crowd the burial grounds, bringing with them gardening tools, flowers, and other decorative materials. . . . Some people busily tend to a gravesite, while others take time to chat and remark on a particularly well-decorated grave site. Still others stand quietly, singly or in groups, near the grave of a loved one. Grave decorating days within San Fernando Cemetery are therefore marked by a lively social interaction between the living and a heightened interaction between families and their deceased loved ones (p. 218).

Each family could remember and honor its own dead privately. But having a cemetery to share with other people who hold similar beliefs and values enhances the memorial process. Furthermore, at the gravesite, there are things to do for the loved ones, reminiscent of what living family members do for each other. No less important is the vista: "We are not the only people to have lost a loved one. It is the human condition. We are, all of us, together in our respect for the dead and our celebration of life." Finally, after the trip, the decorating, the interaction, the family returns home and is able to separate, for a while, from the dead. Some outsiders might be puzzled or even annoyed by all this activity at a cemetery: Have they never felt isolated by a loss, and never carried a death around with them, unable to set it down even for a moment?

These are but three examples of the ethnic cemetery in the United States today. What examples are in your own area? And what stories do they tell?

THE PLACE OF THE DEAD IN SOCIETY: YESTERDAY AND TODAY

Society today places a strong emphasis on curing illness and preventing death. By contrast, most death systems in the past emphasized relationships with the dead. Here is a brief comparison of the place of the dead in the past that will prepare us to consider the meaning and impact of the Vietnam Veterans Memorial, the World War II Veterans Memorial, and the World Trade Center Memorial that is still! yet to come.

When Are the Dead Important to the Living?

1. *The dead are more secure in past-oriented societies.* They maintain a role in the symbolic continuity of people with shared language and cultural values who have lived in the same place for many generations, perhaps for centuries. For example, the Penang Gang people of central Borneo give new names or titles to their family members when they die. This practice conveys their continuing affection for deceased people they loved and also provides them with powerful words (the death-names) that can be called upon in vows and curses (Brosius, 1995/1996). By contrast, in future-oriented societies, the past, habitat of the dead, is often seen as something to be set aside and improved upon.
2. *Geographical detachment is more likely to cause distress to the living in past-oriented societies.* Vietnamese families who were relocated by the American military during "pacification" efforts experienced great anguish in having to depart from the land where the spirits of their ancestors held sway. The world today is filled with people from traditional backgrounds who have been forced to leave their homeland and, therefore, their ancestors.

Perhaps when we have all become ancestors, there will be less concern for the dead because fewer people will have formed deep, long-term attachments to particular places (Scheidt, 1993).

3. *The dead will be remembered and "used" more often in societies in which children are highly valued as continuing the family soul over the gap created by death.* The only available study (Kastenbaum, 1974) suggested that young couples do not regard children as important for generational continuity. It is every generation, every family for itself. Should one generation feel responsibility for projecting the "family soul" across the death line to the next generation? More discussion and research on this topic would be welcome.

4. *Longer life expectancy and low vested power of the elderly make the dead less important.* In earlier times, many people died at an age we would now consider premature. The unfinished lives are therefore more likely to be carried forth in memory, an example of psychology's well-known Zeigarnik (1927) effect. Today more people live to an advanced age, and the survivors are less likely to experience a sense of incompleteness that needs to be compensated for by memorialization. Furthermore, in today's youth-oriented world, the older person does not as often control property and wealth and therefore is less likely to command obedience. And now there are so many long-lived people around that we have lost the

This funeral procession is traditional among the Balinese, but the occasion bears the mark of contemporary worldwide violence. Nearly 200 people were killed in a terrorist attack on a nightclub in Bali, Indonesia on Oct. 22, 2002.

status reserved for rarities. Older people also seem to be losing some of the special status once enjoyed when they were thought of as close to the gods and ancestral spirits.

5. *A society lacking unifying and transcending themes will assimilate the funeral and memorialization process into its utilitarian motives.* Without unifying beliefs, societies are more apt to doubt and quibble about funerals. For example, the cost of the funeral may become the most salient concern. If the dead are not very important, then why spend a lot of time and money on their disposal? (Even in the slower paced, rural South I have heard mourners complain that a funeral was "dragged on too long. One flower girl wasn't enough! They had to have three, and all of them took their own sweet time!") For the dead to be useful they will have to be functional, just like everybody else, and earn their place. If public recognition of the dead continues to diminish, organ donation may be one of the few ways in which the dead can remain a part of society if they no longer are considered to have intrinsic value.

6. *Societies that live close to nature need the assistance of the dead to promote fertility and regeneration.* The Merina of Madagascar, for example, made sure that the female element (the body) had thoroughly decomposed so that the male element (the bleached bones) would emerge purified and ensure that both the people and their harvests are fertile (Bloch, 1982). As in many other traditional cultures, the decomposition process is considered both dangerous and vital. It is from decay that the miracle of regeneration is wrought. Bloch sees one of the major functions of the Merina funeral process as transforming death into life. The dead are crucial to the cycle of life because it is literally from their breath and bones that the species regenerates itself. We might remind ourselves that "Hail to thee, dung beetle!" was a celebration of this phenomenon among the dynastic Egyptians. Furthermore, the ambivalence toward our neighborhood vampire (Chapter 13) reveals our fascination as well as our revulsion about the mysterious transactions between the living and the dead.

American Memory and the Casualties of War and Terrorism

With the rise of technology and industrialization, the dead have been losing status. There are signs, however, that many people are longing to reintegrate the dead into their lives.

Vietnam Veterans Memorial

What would persuade a nation so often described as death denying to be so moved by a memorial to a war that we wanted to forget as quickly as possible? And why would so many people not only make a pilgrimage to the memorial, but also bring objects of personal and symbolic meaning to leave by the wall?

Kristin Ann Hass (1998) recounts the fierce objections to Maya Lin's design for the memorial wall. It was too abstract, too intellectual. The black stone suggested mourning rather than heroism. The response to the design clearly revealed the nation's divided response to the war itself: Had we won a noble victory, or had the war been a human disaster, a senseless killing field? One of the decisive factors in the go-ahead was the support given by many veterans of the conflict who felt that making war should be not celebrated, but that the names of their buddies deserved to be honored and remembered.

The innovative design of the memorial wall proved to be ideally suited for its purpose. Everything about the wall invites reflection and personal involvement. The reflection is literal as well as symbolic: Visitors see themselves mirrored by the wall at the same time that they read the names. We all become part of the wall and its memories, if only for the moment. Furthermore, how the names are *not* arranged makes its own point. The conventional and arbitrary was set aside when it was decided not to present the names in alphabetical order. Rank, military unit, and home state were also ignored. Instead, with unassailable logic, the names are placed in the order of their deaths. This was a compelling way to make it clear that men and

The Vietnam Memorial Wall initially faced a wall of criticism, but since has been recognized as a compelling remembrance of the men and women who did not return from the war.

women died as individuals and should be remembered as such.

That so many people continue to bring something of their own to leave at the wall also suggests that this memorial still has much work to do.

> The things left at the wall make a lot of noise. They constitute a remarkable conversation. It is a conversation about the shape of the nation, the status of the citizen, and the problem of patriotism. It is a conversation about the impossibility of loss, the deaths of sons, and the births of granddaughters. . . . It is impassioned and unfinished, and it gives us a tremendous opportunity to witness the process of ordinary Americans struggling to make meanings of, to make sense of, the Vietnam War and all of its difficult and complicated legacies.

child's painting	red panties	Zippo lighter
eagle feather	cornhusk	cookie
stuffed dog	poem	key chain
tissue with lipstick	(Hass, 1998, pp. 123–124).	

World War I Memorial: Still Missing in Action

World War II Memorial

More than half a century passed before a national memorial was created to honor those who served and those who died (about 400,000) while in the armed forces in World War II. It took years of advocacy and private fundraising. Many of the veterans felt that the war had been almost forgotten—and with this neglect, the neglect of comrades who did not return. Creation of the Vietnam Veterans Memorial led to recognition that World War II veterans and their families were also deserving of this recognition. (A national monument for World War I veterans has yet to be created as a kind of cultural amnesia still persists.)

The World War II memorial was dedicated on May 29, 2004, with an estimated 150,000 people in attendance. It can be visited 24/7 in Washington, D.C., flanked by the memorials to Washington and Lincoln.

World Trade Center Memorial

While the smoke was still rising from Ground Zero, there were already calls for creating a memorial to the World Trade Center victims. Attention was focused on this largest site of death and destruction, although memorialization would later be created for the Pentagon and rural Pennsylvania sites as well. Many plans were offered, and many critics had their say. The nation itself had not yet decided how best to fix the disaster in its collective memory. What should the memorial express and accomplish? Should it be designed primarily to honor the dead? To comfort the bereaved? To restore a sense of national security? To tell the world that American business is still in business? To discourage other possible terrorists? To demonstrate the skill and creativity of the memorial planners? To become a prime tourist attraction? The project was soon entangled in competing emotional, political, and economic interests. It remains to be seen how the nation and the world will respond to the restoration of Ground Zero and its memorial tribute. The sense of national unity immediately following the disaster did not endure long enough to inspire a memorial consensus.

Oklahoma City Memorial

Another city, victimized by a domestic terrorist attack, developed an innovative memorial that has been very well received. The lives of 168 were lost when the Murrah Building, a federal facility, was destroyed on April 19, 1995. The people of Oklahoma City realized that clearing away the debris was not enough: A memorial should be erected on the site. They invited designs from around the world, but the decision was made by a committee that included family members, survivors, and rescuers as well as design professionals. The result was the Oklahoma City National Memorial and Memorial Center Museum. The museum includes an institute for the prevention of terrorism as well as an education and outreach service.

A compelling feature is a room-to-room procession that illuminates the course of events, from the chaos of the explosion, through the rescue and recovery efforts, and culminating in a tribute to hope in the form of a "water wall" that flows over a dark stone background. For many visitors, the most moving experience occurs in the "Gallery of Honor." Here there is a photograph or other image of each person who was killed in the bombing. The images are accompanied by a personal object that was selected by a family member. This memorial demonstrates the individuality of the victims and the caring response of family and community. The human tragedy is not distanced by a monumental and impersonal structure. By practically all accounts, this memorial and the process that created it was ideal for the people of Oklahoma City.

Who "Owns" Human Remains?

Human relationships often have their difficulties and conflicts. The same can be said of relationships between the living and the dead. Rival claims for "ownership" of human remains are more frequent than we might have supposed, and tell us something about varying perspectives and motives in society. A significant example is the custody and treatment of human remains and artifacts found in Native American grave sites.

Indigenous people throughout the world have protested the desecration of their grave sites by individuals eager to sell or possess remains and artifacts as curiosities. Scientists and museum curators have also been criticized for studying and displaying ancestral objects that should be with their own people. There was a long and painful history behind this protest movement: Looting Native American graves started with the Pilgrims. It was readily agreed that grave looting was unethical, although difficult to prevent. More difficult to resolve was the scientist's and historian's claim for the right to correct and advance knowledge. It is to the credit of all parties involved that an accord was reached after many years of controversy and frustration. An agreement was achieved through an international conference with face-to-face discussions between representatives of native peoples and those involved in studying or displaying human remains and artifacts. The document generated by this conference is known as The *Vermillion Accord* (the meetings having been held in Vermillion, South Dakota).

The main points of the Vermillion Accord (Davidson, 1990) are:

- Universal respect shall be given to the mortal remains of the dead.
- Disposition of human remains will be made in accordance with the wishes of the dead themselves whenever this is known or can be reasonably inferred.
- The wishes of the local community will be respected "whenever possible, reasonable, and lawful."
- The scientific value of studying human remains will be respected whenever such value can be demonstrated to exist.
- Negotiations with an attitude of mutual respect shall be conducted to accommodate both the legitimate concerns of communities for the proper disposition of their ancestors and the legitimate concerns of science and education (p. 641).

The Native American Graves Protection and Repatriation Act (NAGPRA) has since established criminal penalties for the sale, purchase, or transport of Native American human remains or cultural artifacts without an established legal right of possession. Notification and consent procedures were introduced to affirm the rights of Native American organizations to participate in all relevant decisions. In recent years, there has been a significant transfer of human remains and cultural artifacts from schools and museums to tribal organizations. Scientists and Native American organizations

have been learning how to work together in mutual respect. Many practical difficulties persist, not least of which is the complexity involved in determining the tribal identity of the deceased and the existing tribal organization that is the most appropriate custodian.

Does the availability of new technologies justify "disturbing" human remains to satisfy curiosity, make an interesting documentary, advance careers, or test the claim that a particular set of famous bones are in residence in a particular location? Or is it also in the interests of the dead to learn more about them and dispel assumptions that have clouded their reputation? For example, the powerful Medici family of sixteenth century Florence has been absolved of infamous murders by a team of forensic experts (Lorenzi, 2005). This controversy is likely to be with us for a long time.

"You Were the Best Dog Ever": The Pet Cemetery

I have turned over the rocky ground of Massachusetts and the dry sands of Arizona to bury several very important cats. When the first dog of the family died quietly in his basket bed, none of us could regard Toby's body as only the corpse of an animal. The same was true when Honey, the second dog, asked to go outside and moved with a purpose and stride we no longer expected in her enfeebled condition. A few minutes later, she was still beautiful, but dead. Millions of other people have had close attachments to their pets—or to animals they have worked with: the horse who drew the milkman's wagon, the dog who guided its visually impaired owner, and the elephant who hauled lumber. Attachment does not end at the moment of death, whether the loss is that of another human or of an animal companion.

The modern version of the pet cemetery seems to have started in France around the turn of the twentieth century. Not only dogs and cats, but also horses, monkeys, rabbits, birds (and a lioness) have been buried there. Perhaps the most famous "resident" is Rin-Tin-Tin, once the reigning animal star of Hollywood. However, the impulse to honor the memory of an animal companion through a funeral and burial process has been expressed throughout history. There are examples among the ancient Greeks and in the early years of our own nation. It is estimated that there are about 400 pet cemeteries in the United States.

Pet cemeteries express some of the same mixed and changing attitudes toward death that characterize society in general. For example, ritual has long played a significant role in Japanese culture. In recent years, memorial services have been developed for animal companions; their services are simplified versions of those performed for the passing of humans. They may be held at a pet cemetery or on family property. Smaller animals are returned to their elements, for example, a pet fish to the sea (but never flushed down a toilet, which would be regarded as desecration) (Kenney, 2004). Owners often continue their relationship with the animal companion through post-mortem rituals and visitations. Beloved dogs and cats were "family" and are honored and mourned as such.

For a U.S. example, consider Pet Rest Memorial Mortuary and Cemetery. Once located just up the road from Arizona State University (Tempe), Pet Rest provided the opportunity for a study by Vivian Spiegelman and myself (1990). At the time of our visits, Pet Rest resembled many another small cemetery—a fenced-in, park-like space with grave markers designed to individual specifications. Some markers displayed a photographic or sculptured representation of the deceased. Ceramic cats played inside a white picket fence. However, some monuments had already toppled into the weedy grass, and there was a general impression of neglect. What has happened?

Pet Rest had already become a "dead cemetery"—that is, no more burials were allowed, nor had anybody accepted responsibility for maintenance. The continuing influx of people into Arizona, the change from an agricultural to a residential community, the transformation of a small college into one of the nation's largest universities—these are among the factors that contributed to the decline and eventual destruction of Pet Rest. The land had become too

valuable, and officials were uncomfortable with having death on display while attempting to upscale commercial properties. The "final resting place" had proven vulnerable to the economic pressure and social change that also affect many "people cemeteries" across the nation. And now, Pet Rest no longer exists, its "eternal memory" replaced by a nationally franchised restaurant.

Some people choose to conduct their own memorial services and to satisfy themselves with photographs or personal videos. After a while, a trip to the local animal shelter might not erase memories of the lost animal companion but bring a new and lively life into the home. (This most recent time, we came home with Angel, The Incredible Leaping Dog, and now dutiful servant to the resident cats.)

Pet cemeteries have invited parody and mockery. Nevertheless, those who understand and value the bonds of affection that can form between one creature and another may judge that giving "too much" love is not the worst thing that might be said of a person.

THE FUNERAL DIRECTOR'S PERSPECTIVE

Funeral and memorialization practices are very much part of the world of the living and, therefore, subject to change. An interview with funeral director Tom Carrick proved helpful in identifying some of the major challenges and developments.

- *The impact of AIDS?*
  "Everybody in the funeral industry overreacted at first. Now we realize that we can do our part in dealing with AIDS and cannot behave in a discriminatory manner. We do give more attention to personal safety. Precautions are used in handling all cases now because one can never be certain about AIDS. For example, we wear gloves every time we touch a cadaver. Instead of smocks, we now use rubber aprons and complete protective clothing, including eye wear. All 'sharps' go into specified and controlled waste containers. Funeral personnel are doing the same things that

health care providers are doing—being more careful."

- *Are there changes in the way that funeral directors do business?*

"Enormous changes. Laws have changed and regulations have increased. For example, we are now mandated to provide full price disclosures to the public. Written consents are required for embalming. Employees must be given time off for continuing education sessions. Fair employment practices have increased access by women who are entering this field in larger numbers than ever before. These changes provide benefits to the public."

- *Have these regulations affected your cost of operations?*

"Yes, considerably so. Every funeral home has had to remodel to provide access for handicapped individuals and to meet other health and safety standards. Chemicals must be stored in sealed compartments with security locks, so that people do not become exposed to any risk from them. Most of these changes are worthwhile, but they are costly."

- *You mentioned that more women have become funeral directors in recent years. How has this change been received?*

"The public has had a favorable response. Many client families feel more comfortable in dealing with women. Frequently it is a widow who is making the arrangements. She may perceive a woman funeral director as more understanding and sympathetic. In the past, there was a reluctance to hire women and only a few women were qualified. Part of this reluctance came from the enormous amount of lifting that is involved. But now women work in construction; women drive trucks; women work successfully in many occupations that were thought to be for men only. It's not that the conditions of work have changed so much, it's the attitudes that have changed about what women can and should do. Funeral directing is a very conservative business that tends to be slow in adapting to change."

- *What does a person have to know to become a funeral director?*

"A person needs to become proficient in anatomy, chemistry, restorative art, pathology, business, accounting, and some law. These subjects are included in the licensure exams. Once a person is licensed, it is important to keep up with new developments through continued education, for example, handling situations in which contagious diseases might be involved. Unfortunately, there has been a tendency for continued education sessions to be oriented toward sales rather than consumer services. Our field could benefit by increasing the quantity and quality of continued education—and, fortunately, the trend is in this direction."

- *Can you take us through a typical funeral?*

"The funeral itself will typically begin with a musical prelude, followed by an opening prayer. About half the people we deal with are 'churched.' This leaves the other half in need of a presiding clergyperson, so we frequently recommend one. Some families give a high priority to the choice of a particular clergyperson. Others say, 'I don't care who you get for my Mom's funeral. I want it brief!' This illustrates the larger differences in how families approach funeral planning. Some are concerned about every detail; some could care less."

"After the opening prayer, there are often introductory remarks by a person who represents the family. In recent years, there has been more participation by family and friends. In particular, more teens are stepping up to contribute to the memorialization. Any number of family and friends may give scripture readings, recite poetry, eulogize the deceased, or play music, either live or recorded. Words of comfort are usually offered by the clergyperson, but others may also express themselves in their own words."

- *What is the usual length of a funeral these days?*

"The typical funeral lasts between 20 and 40 minutes. The public seems to prefer brief services. I don't really know why this is the case."

- *And what about the question of open or closed casket?*

"Most people still prefer the casket open for a portion of the time. Today it is most common for the deceased to wear their own clothing. It is usually a suit, shirt, and tie for a man, a dress for a woman. There are regional differences, however. Yesterday we had a funeral in which the man wore a western shirt and jeans. This might seem unusual in New York City, but not here Arizona or in Aspen. If somebody never wore a suit or necktie, why should they be forced to change their habits now? If a lady was always seen in a pink dress, they're probably going to bury her in a pink dress, and get pink flowers. . . ."

- *How much is the typical funeral likely to cost?*
"The national average is between $6,000 and $8,000 for a complete traditional funeral. This includes both mortuary and cemetery expenses, such as the burial plot, flowers, clergy, musicians, and limousine. The cost differs somewhat from one place to another. It tends to be higher in the eastern than in the western states."

- *There are different opinions about the appropriateness of including children in the funeral process. How do you see this?*
"I'm all for it. Death is part of life. Children should be exposed to it as often as it occurs. Parents may be poorly prepared to educate our kids about death and dying, but the best way to do that is to attend funerals when opportunity presents itself. We shouldn't be running and hiding from death. The ideal funeral should be an uplifting experience, reinforcing all the values this person stood for and why we loved this person and are here today."

- *What is your worst-case scenario about what might go wrong in performing a funeral?*
"I worry most about breakdown of equipment. What if the hearse breaks down or the air conditioning fails in the summer months either in the building or the limousine?

"In some 30,000 funerals only one stands out as a total embarrassment to me personally. I call it 'The Funeral from Hell.' Every conceivable thing went wrong—from equipment failures right down to the cemetery digging the wrong grave! Mom's name was even on the headstone, but they dug 25 feet away on a 115-degree day. To make it even worse, the death was a sudden and tragic one. Oh, yes, and the sound system at the church picked that day to quit working; actually, it exploded!

A key family member was late, one limo didn't show up, and another broke down. There was a mix-up with the flowers as well. Fortunately, this was the memorable exception, and I don't feel the need to have another funeral memorable in this way, ever!"

- *Looking back over more than 30 years as a funeral director, what stands out as most important to you personally?*
"I've walked in the shoes they're walking in, and I think people appreciate that. I identify with their loss, so it is natural for me to offer all the time they need and all the understanding I can bring to the situation. I remind myself each time that I am a total stranger who has been invited into a family's life at a time of loss and sorrow. My challenge is to put them at ease. This is not easy: 'How can I relax—my mother just died!' I derive my satisfaction from helping people through these stressful situations."

"I would like the readers of this book to know that we, as a society in general, need to understand how much death is part of life. As parents and teachers, we don't do a particularly good job of it. We are still a death-denying society. We don't talk about funerals unless we just came from one!"

For more about funeral planning and expenses, please see Chapter 7, End-of-Life Issues and Decisions.

IMPROVING THE FUNERAL PROCESS

Turn the calendar back to the middle of the twentieth century and we find the physician and the funeral director bearing major responsibility for society's confrontations with death. Few families felt prepared to take end-of-life decisions into their own hands: It was more usual and less anxiety-provoking to depend on the experts and their standard ways of managing terminal illness and the funeral process. A more independent-minded and participatory orientation has since been evident as, for example, in the vigorous development of hospice and palliative care programs and the swirling controversies about the right to die and physician-assisted death. Funeral practices have not escaped criticism in this reevaluation of tradition. There is a fairly broad consensus that a standard funeral "taken off the shelf" is not likely be the most appropriate choice for all families. It is time, then, to consider some of the emerging options.

Alternative Funerals

Some families and funeral directors have stayed within the traditional approach, but with distinctive variations that make it more personal and comforting. There are also alternatives that depart somewhat from tradition. In becoming more popular they are starting to become traditions of their own. Our examples here are the memorial society and green funeral options, and a "new" proposal from the funeral industry that might not be unanimously welcomed—but who knows? We also explore virtual memorials, though these do not encompass the physical remains.

The Memorial Society Option

Funerals can be simple, inexpensive, and responsive to the needs and values of particular individuals and families. This is the essence of the memorial society option. First coming to general attention in the early years of the twentieth century, this type of funeral arrangement has become favored by an increasing number of people who dislike what they consider the ostentation and outworn rhetoric of traditional funerals. It has also been appreciated as a cost-saving measure and as a way of avoiding the sales tactics of some commercial funeral services. Local nonprofit memorial societies were created by farm grange organizations and churches. Each of these organizations defined its own mission, but had in common the purpose of assisting families to retain control and make their own choices rather than turning all the details over to a commercial funeral service (Bergonzi, 2004).

A new level of coordination and influence was achieved with the establishment of the Funeral and Memorial Societies of America (operating in Canada as well as the United States). This coalition was responsible for a major improvement in consumer rights. In 1984, The Federal Trade Commission (kind of reluctantly) affirmed the right of consumers to receive information about the cost of particular funeral services and supplies, as well as their right to be informed of the applicable state regulations. Consumers are now in a better position to evaluate and compare services and costs. There are now also more funeral directors who welcome the opportunity to arrange funerals that are in keeping with the family's wishes, rather than to impose a "standard issue" service. The coalition has since changed its title to Funeral Consumers Alliance (FCA) to distinguish itself from numerous other organizations that have since described themselves as "societies." A useful Web site is the Funeral Ethics Organization (www.funeralethics.org).

I remember a wintry New England morning during which no music was performed, no prayers voiced, no ceremonies enacted. The coffined body of a neighbor's friend was lowered into the earth. Heads did bow and a few moments elapsed in spontaneous silence. There was not much to see, hear, or think about—except death. Then people started to breathe again, and walk back to their cars.

Green Funerals

Never mind embalming. Never mind solid coffins. Sooner or later, earth will claim the remains of humans as well as other land-based creatures. Why not accept and respect natural processes? Why not plan a green funeral?

People who agree with these propositions now have another possibility to consider. No longer uncommon in Great Britain, the green funeral movement has also been introduced in the United States. Burials take place in woodlands or meadows, with the intention of allowing the remains to return to earth in a natural form. The bodies are wrapped or placed in containers (such as willow) that do not resist biodegrading. One advocate writes that this process produces

> Wildlife habitats and forests from green burial sites, where native trees, wildflowers and protected animals are encouraged and meadow brown butterfly colonies, grasshoppers, insects, bats, voles, and owls multiply . . . where the

mechanical mower does not prey on a regular basis and a self-supporting ecosystem can evolve (Holmes, n. d.).

The green funeral can also serve as protest against cultural traditions that are perceived as outworn, impersonal, and oppressive:

> Mum chose a wonderful spot in a private area overlooking the hills and under a large, shady oak tree. . . . There was no rent-a-frock religious representative spouting unfelt platitudes and thinly veiled threats to those who might not sign up to his particular big truth. . . . During periods of silence the speeches were made by the birds and the wind in the trees. Strong words were spoken by the people who knew and cared for my mum and what she believed in (Ross-Bains, n. d.).

Some environmentalists advocate green funerals for their potential to conserve resources and reduce pollution. For example, it has been estimated that more than 800,000 gallons of embalming fluid and 30 million feet of increasingly scarce hardwood are buried in the United States each year (Smith, 2003).

Not everybody agrees with this rejection of tradition. There may also be inherent limitations. Two that come readily to mind: (a) situations in which embalming could be a necessity for public health reasons, and (b) availability of appropriate natural spaces. At present there are start-up organizations in North America that plan to assist people with green funerals, and both local and national units of the FCA might have useful suggestions to offer.

Flushing the Dead: Alkaline Hydrolysis

Through the centuries, the dead have been buried or cremated. Norma Love (2008) introduces us to a possible new option:

> Dissolving bodies in lye and flushing the brownish, syrupy residue down the drain. The process called alkaline hydrolysis, was developed in this country 16 years ago to get rid of animal carcasses. It uses lye, 300-degree heat and 60 pounds of pressure per square inch to destroy bodies in stainless-steel cylinders that are similar to pressure cookers.

Love quotes a funeral industry newsletter as enthusing that "It's not often that a truly game-changing technology comes along in the funeral service, but we might have gotten a hold of one."

This "game-changing" technology has been quickly opposed by clergy, and, although legal in two states (Minnesota and New Hampshire), it has not yet received regulatory approval anywhere in the U.S.

Advocates claim environmental advantages for *alkaline hydrolysis*. Most of the body is dissolved into a coffee-colored liquid "with the consistency of motor oil and a strong ammonia smell. If all goes well, it can be poured safely down the drain. The reduced solid remains take the form of a dry bone residue that resemble cremains, but without having produced crematorium emissions that can include mercury from silver dental fillings. The remains can be buried (taking up less of the limited cemetery space) or preserved in an urn. Presumably, funeral and memorial services could be arranged to suit family values, even though the process of body disposition is not traditional.

Dissolving corpses is not such a new idea, although technology seems to have become more efficient. Criminals have been known to dispose of awkward evidence in that manner, and communities faced with the threat of epidemics have done the same with possibly contagious corpses. Furthermore, it is estimated that about fifty facilities currently produce liquid medical waste from humans, animals, or both. An industrial waste manager observes that the public might be more troubled if it knew how much blood and embalming fluid already flows into sewage plants.

Are we today radically different from those who have had to deal with the physicality of death in the past without the mediation of advanced technology? Or are just as squeamish when faced with this raw side of nature? No need to answer that question—let's move on quickly to a more comfortable realm.

Virtual Memorials

Stone has long been a valued material for marking grave sites. It seems so solid, so enduring. It presides over a particular location and stands as a beacon to draw visitors near. Now, however, a nearly dimensionless form of memorialization is becoming increasingly popular. An Internet memorial occupies no fixed space. It is everywhere and nowhere. We cannot touch it or observe the changes that time and weather have wrought. The Internet is opening new possibilities for honoring the dead and sharing our personal thoughts and feelings. Bereaved persons have their choice of creating a new memorial Web page or placing a memorial in one of the existing Web cemeteries. Virtual Memorial Gardens (http://catless.ncl.ac.uk/vmg), Dearly Departed (www.dearlydeparted.net), and Worldwide Cemetery (www.cemetery.org) were among the first Web cemeteries to be established and all three offer free services. Establishing a personal Web page requires computer expertise and upkeep effort that not all bereaved people can manage. "Web rings" make it possible for virtual visitors to explore a broad spectrum of memorials.

Virtual memorials devoted to deceased children seem to be the most common. Many of these Web sites offer the story of the child's life and death, photographs and other images, and a guestbook or e-mail link for visitors. Older adults make less use of the Internet and therefore seem less likely to be constructing and visiting memorial Web sites. It is likely that as more computer-savvy people grow older, they will make more use of the potentials of bereavement support and memorial sites. An exploratory study (DeVries & Rutherford, 2004) has found missing the deceased is the most common theme in virtual cemetery memorials. Seldom was either the cause of death mentioned and, perhaps surprisingly, there were relatively few references to God or religion. Most online memorials were written in the form of a communication to the deceased rather than as a statement about the deceased.

Roberts (2004) identifies several distinctive advantages:

> Web memorialization provides unique, supplemental postdeath rituals for the bereaved. Web memorials, unlike most postdeath rituals, can be created at one's pace . . . and can be created by friends and others who were not included in standard mourning rituals. . . . Memorials can be changed and updated . . . and visited at any time and from any location. . . . The opportunity to visit a web memorial may be especially valuable to elders with limited mobility, for whom visiting an internment site is difficult. . . . Many of our survey respondents report sitting in front of the computer screen with others, visiting the memorial together (p. 43).

At present, Web-based memorials seem to be supplementing rather than replacing traditional practices. It remains to be seen whether distinctive Web sites created by individuals and families will continue to flourish or give way to sites sponsored by mortuaries and other organizations.

SPONTANEOUS MEMORIALIZATION IN RESPONSE TO VIOLENT DEATH

We turn now to an alternative response to violent death, one that has become increasingly common in recent years. *Spontaneous memorialization* has been defined as a public response to violent and unexpected deaths (Haney, Leimer, & Lowery, 1997). It provides the opportunity for members of the community to express their personal sorrow and compassion. Not all violent deaths elicit this response: The public must feel a sense of connection or identification with the victims and bereaved family. The widespread public response to the attacks of September 11, 2001, included many examples of spontaneous memorialization.

Spontaneous memorialization usually takes place at the site of the death or some other place that is associated with the deceased. It differs in this respect from traditional services that take place at a funeral home, church, or cemetery. Mementoes are left at the site of the death. These may include a wide variety of objects—flowers, teddy bears, bibles, even beer cans. (Some of the objects that have been left at the Vietnam Memorial Wall have already been mentioned.) These objects usually have meaning to the individual mourners and have some connection to the victim's life. The mourners often raise funds to assist survivors of the victim and may also become advocates for improved public safety measures.

People who did not know the deceased person may be touched by the death and decide to participate. As Haney, Leimer, and Lowery (1997) stated: "Spontaneous memorialization extends the boundaries of who is allowed or expected to participate in the mourning process." There is no formal organization of the response to the death, at least at first. People respond out of their shock, sorrow, or anger, and find a way of expressing their feelings. Haney, Leimer, and Lowery also found that there are no set time limits:

> Spontaneous memorialization ebbs and flows as individual mourners make their pilgrimages and contribute their offerings either immediately after the death, or during the weeks or months that follow. . . . Individual mourners may visit the site once or return again and again, either alone or accompanied by others (p. 162).

Here we see individuals coming together of their own volition to demonstrate community solidarity and concern in the face of deaths that should not have happened. Violent deaths shatter our expectations that people should be able to enjoy a long life before succumbing to "natural causes." Society's death system has not proved capable of preventing violent deaths and often cannot even explain them very well. The emergence of spontaneous memorialization, however, reveals that in opening our hearts to victims of violent death and their survivors we are affirming values that are at the core of our existence as a society.

Not everybody favors spontaneous memorialization. There have been protests based on concerns as varied as the public expression of religious beliefs and the possible depressing influence of witnessing so many reminders that life can end so quickly. Collins and Rhine (2003), among the first to identify the resistance to spontaneous memorialization, ask: "Which is the greater right; to grieve and mourn, or to be spared reminders of our mortality?" (p. 241).

INTEGRITY AND ABUSE IN THE FUNERAL AND MEMORIAL PROCESS

The corpse reminds us of the life that was and the life that is no more. It occupies a symbolic space between presence and absence, and between the mundane and the sacred. A society that neglects or abuses its dead has been driven to the edge of destruction by catastrophe (Kastenbaum, 2004b). Doing right by the dead remains a core value for most societies today. We have seen the strength of this motivation in the survivors of the tsunami and the September 11, 2001, terror attacks, but it can also be observed in the smaller circle of a family-oriented memorial society or green funeral. The funeral industry realizes that it is expected to provide its services not only with professional competence, but also with sensitivity to the feelings and beliefs of the survivors. It is all the more disturbing, then, when the public trust is betrayed. Sometimes it is not the funeral industry but other organizations that violate society's expectations for respectful treatment of human remains. There are appalling historical examples of neglecting and abusing corpses (e. g., Richardson, 1987). Unfortunately, there are also enough examples in our own time to warrant concern.

These examples include:

- Tri-State Crematory of northwest Georgia was discovered to have dumped corpses in a shed and scattered others throughout its property. Eventually 334 bodies were discovered, many in advanced stages of decomposition. Relatives were given "ashes of the loved ones" that were actually cement dust. Ray Brent Marsh pleaded guilty to theft, corpse abuse, burial service fraud, and making false statements and received a 12-year prison sentence (Poovey, 2004). He offered no explanation for his abuse and fraud. From time to time there have been allegations that other crematories or funeral homes have not properly conducted their operations or failed to return remains to the right families. The number of such incidents is difficult to estimate. Even if we assume this to be an uncommon occurrence, it is enough to become another source of anxiety for bereaved families.

- Tulane University's School of Medicine admitted to having sold its oversupply of donated bodies to the Army—which then blew up the bodies while conducting experiments to reduce land mine fatalities (Yerton, 2004a).
- UCLA Medical School admitted having sold cadaver body parts to a broker who in turn sold them to commercial biomedical corporations. The brokers involved in these medical school cases denied they had done anything wrong in arranging the deals. However, Yerton (2004b) confirmed that "Donor's families grieve all over again."
- Cadavers have also been used in some impact studies to test and develop improved vehicle safety (Roach, 2003). Crash dummies, despite their starring role in television commercials, provide less information than actual bodies.
- A series of investigative articles (Flatten, 2004a, b, c, d) found evidence that "Harvesting bodies and tissues is big business in Arizona—but families often are left out of the process" (2004b, A1). Brokers were also active in these arrangements. There is reason to believe that body harvesting for profit occurs on a national and international as well as local level, sometimes legally, sometimes illegally, and sometimes in that gray area in between.
- The burial insurance industry has been found guilty of overcharging and otherwise defrauding black Americans (Donn, 2004). Black families have been the target of persistent marketing for purchase of burial insurance and then sometimes have been denied payment of the benefit after having paid inflated premiums for many years.

We might feel that some of the motivations involved were laudable (e.g., reducing motor vehicle and military-related casualties) and others were without merit (defrauding and exploiting customers, disrespecting human remains). There are larger issues to consider as well. Have major social institutions (e.g., armed forces, universities) distanced themselves from the cultural values inherent in respect for the dead? Have religious and spiritual beliefs become so marginalized that turning a profit can so easily take precedence? Is our society strengthened or weakened when special interests commandeer the dead? It should be noted that the universities and various organizations in the funeral and insurance fields have condemned the abuses mentioned here, but these questions are far from being resolved.

SUMMARY

The funeral is part of a complex process in which we both separate ourselves from the dead and try to establish a new relationship with them that we can carry forward in our lives. We have examined the meaning of the funeral process in many places and times, including our own. How a society cares for its dead tells us much about the beliefs and lifestyles of that society in general. We noticed that society sometimes does forget even those dead who would seem deserving of special respect (e.g., World War I casualties, African-American pioneers in colonial New York). You were invited to reflect on your own attitudes, feelings, and knowledge about the funeral process, considering whether you are more the rationalist or more the romantic. Attention was given to the process of transforming a dead body to a living memory.

We identified basic elements of the funeral process, such as establishing the facts of death, the autopsy, the death investigator, legal issues, organ donation, *premortem* preparations, immediate postdeath activities, preparations for burial or cremation, the funeral service itself, and the longer process of memorializing the deceased. We gave particular attention to the sacred art of mummification, brought to a high level by the ancient Egyptians. We gained further insight through the case histories of three influential people whose deaths were the occasion for extraordinary memorialization: Ch'in shih-huang-ti, the first emperor of China; Prince Albert, husband of Queen Victoria; and Lenin, founder of the Soviet Union. Another major function of the funeral and memorialization process is to achieve a balance between the competing claims of the living and the dead. We learned how the dead have been regarded within three traditional contexts: rural Greece, the Kotas of southern India, and Orthodox Judaism. Next, we came back home to see how cemeteries in the United States have been shaping memories from colonial times to the present and how the nature and upkeep of these cemeteries has been closely related to powerful events such as the Civil War and sociotechnological change such as population pressures.

We also visited several ethnic cemeteries to see how the challenges of diverse people living together is reflected in the way their deaths are memorialized. We wondered under what circumstances the dead are most important to the living and learned that the dead are more secure in past-oriented societies (and under several other conditions that were identified). How public tributes to those casualties of war and victims of catastrophe can contribute to national healing was illustrated through the memorials to World War II and Vietnam War veterans and to the Oklahoma City and September 11, 2001, victims of terrorist attacks. We also noted progress in respecting the human remains and artifacts taken from the graves of Native American ancestors and returned to their people whenever possible.

Memorialization of our animal companions was also considered through a visit to Pet Rest Memorial Mortuary and Cemetery (itself a recent casualty of urban development). Our curiosity about the current status of funeral practice led us to an interview with a funeral director who provided frank and engaging answers to many of our questions. We then reminded ourselves that there are a variety of alternative funeral and memorialization possibilities, including the ever more common phenomenon of public spontaneous response to a particularly disturbing death or deaths. Virtual memorials are now offering a new way for bereaved to honor and remember those they have lost. Results from early studies of Web-based memorials are reported. The memorial society movement developed around the theme of simple, inexpensive, and participatory funerals. Green funerals take this approach further and could become increasingly favored in the United States. The funeral industry's own new proposal for disposal by liquidification was also taken into account. We concluded with a brief inquiry into deceptive and abusive practices that can threaten the integrity of the funeral and memorial practice and do emotional harm to the bereaved.

REFERENCES

Aries, P. (1981). *The hour of our death.* New York: Knopf.

Bagchi, I. (2005, February 9). Grave error? Singapore erases history for future. www.taphophilia.com/modules.php?name—News&file5article&sid51976

Bass, B., & Jefferson, J. (2003). *Death's acre. Inside the legendary forensic lab.* New York: Putnam.

Bertman, S. (2000). *Cultural amnesia: American future and the crisis of memory.* New York: Praeger.

Benet, S. V. (1942). American names. In *Poetry of Stephen Vincent Benet* (pp. 367–368). New York: Farrar & Rinehart.

Bergonzi, J. A. (2004). The memorial society option. *Generations, 28,* 57–58.

Bloch, M. (1982). Death, women, and power. In M. Bloch & J. Parry (Eds.), *Death and the regeneration of life* (pp. 1–44). Cambridge, UK: Cambridge University Press.

Cotterell, A. (1981). *The first emperor of China.* New York: Holt, Rinehart & Winston.

Crissman, J. K. (1994). *Death and dying in central Appalachia.* Urbana: University of Illinois Press.

Cunningham, K. (l989). Navajo, Mormon, Zuni graves: Navajo, Mormon, Zuni ways. In R. E. Meyer (Ed.), *Cemeteries and gravemarkers* (pp. 197–216). Ann Arbor: University of Michigan Research Press.

Darby, E., & Smith, N. (1983). *The cult of the Prince Consort.* New Haven, CT: Yale University Press.

Davidson, G. W. (1990). Human remains: Contemporary issues. *Death Studies, 14,* 491–502.

Davies, D. J. (2003) Cremation. In C. Bryant (Ed.), *Handbook of death and dying:* Vol. 1 (pp. 767–774). Thousand Oaks: Sage.

Davies, D. J., & Mates, L. H. (2006). *Encyclopedia of cremation*. London: Ashgate.

Day, M. H. (1990). The Vermillion Accord. *Death Studies, 14,* 641.

DeVries, B., & Rutherford, J. (2004). Memorializing loved ones on the World Wide Web. *Omega, Journal of Death and Dying, 49,* 5–26.

Dokouph, T. (2008, February 18). The war we forgot. *Newsweek,* p. 50.

Gay, P. (1984). *Education of the senses.* New York: Oxford University Press.

Glover, R. (2001). *Plastination laboratory.* www.med. umich.edu/anatomy/plastinate

Goldberg, H. S. (1981/1982). Funeral and bereavement rituals of Kota Indians and Orthodox Jews. *Omega, Journal of Death & Dying, 12,* 117–128.

Gosnell, L., & Gott, S. (1989). San Fernando Cemetery: Decorations of loss in a Mexican-American community. In R. E. Meyer (Ed.), *Cemeteries and gravemarkers* (pp. 217–236). Ann Arbor: University of Michigan Research Press.

Gross, S. (2007, October 5). African burial ground in Manhattan opens to public after dedication ceremony. Associated Press. http://myeartlik.net/asrticle/nat? guid=20071005/4705

Haney, C. A., Leimer, C., & Lowery, J. (1997). Spontaneous memorialization: Violent death and emerging mourning ritual. *Omega, Journal of Death and Dying, 35,* 159–172.

Harris, J. E. (1973). *X-raying the pharaohs.* New York: Scribner.

Hass, K. A. (1998). *Carried to the wall.* Berkeley: University of California Press.

Holloway, K. F. C. (2002). *Passed on: African American mourning stories.* Durham, NC: Duke University Press.

Holmes, A. (n.d.). Willow coffins. www.druidnetwork.org/ qwrites/passing

Ikram, S., & Dodson, A. (1998). *The mummy in ancient Egypt.* London: Thames & Hudson.

Iserson, K. (2003). Death certificate. In R. Kastenbaum (Ed.), *Macmillan encyclopedia of death and dying:* Vol. 1 (pp. 211–213). New York: Macmillan.

Kastenbaum, R. (1974). Fertility and the fear of death. *Journal of Social Issues, 30,* 63–78.

Kastenbaum, R. (1994). R. C. W. Ettinger: An Omega interview. *Omega, Journal of Death and Dying, 30,* 159–172.

Kastenbaum, R. (2004a). Why funerals? *Generations, 28,* 5–10.

Kastenbaum, R. (2004b). *On our way. The final passage through life and death.* Berkeley: University of California Press.

Kearl, M. (2004). Cremation: desecration, purification, or convenience? *Generations, 28,* 15–20.

Kenney, E. (2004). Pet funerals and animal graves in Japan. *Mortality, 9,* 42–60.

Koff, C. (2004). *The bone woman.* New York: Random House.

Linden-Ward, B. (1989) *Silent city on a hill: Landscapes of memory and Boston's Mount Auburn Cemetery.* Columbus: Ohio State University Press.

Lorenzi, R. (2005, February 9). Medici family murders debunked in Italy. www.taphophilia.com/mdules.pp? name5News&file5article&siddd51968

Love, N. (2008, May 9). Funeral industry explores use of lye to dissolve bodies. *Arizona Republic,* p. A14.

Lynch, T. (1997). *The undertaking. Life studies from the dismal trade.* New York: Penguin.

Miller, R. K., Jr., Rosenfeld, J. P., & McNamee, S. J. (2003). The disposition of property: Transfers between the dead and the living. In C. Bryant (Ed.), *Handbook of death and dying:* Vol. 1 (pp. 917–925). Thousand Oaks: Sage.

Morris, R. (2002). Lawn garden cemeteries. In R. Kastenbaum (Ed.), *Macmillan encyclopedia of death and dying:* Vol. 2 (pp. 518–520). New York: Macmillan.

Murphy, E. (1995). *After the funeral. The posthumous adventures of famous corpses.* New York: Barnes & Noble.

Plunkett, T. (1999). The New Haven burying ground. A brief history and discussion of the Grove Street Cemetery. www.archnet.asu.edu/ archnet/ uconn_extras/ historic/grove_street.html

Poovey, B. (1994, January 21). Ex-crematory operator gets 12 years in prison. *East Valley Tribune, p. B1.*

Prothero, S. (2001). *Purified by fire. A history of cremation in America.* Berkeley: University of California Press.

Redden, E. (2007, August 13). Rooted in tradition on very hallowed ground. *Washington Post,* p. C01.

Richardson, R. (1987). *Death, dissection, and the destitute.* London: Routledge & Kegan Paul.

Roach, M. (2003). *Stiff. The curious lives of human cadavers.* New York: Norton.

Roberts, P. (2004). Here today and cyberspace tomorrow: Memorials and bereavement support on the Web. *Generations, 28,* 41–46.

Rodman, G. B. (1996). *Elvis after Elvis.* Florence, KY: Routledge.

Ross-Bains, I. (n.d.). Perception of a green funeral. www.gloabideasbank.org/showidea.php?idea55040

Rutledge, N. M. (2008). A time to mourn: Balancing the right of free speech against the right of privacy in funeral picketing. *Maryland Law Review, 67,* 295–311.

Scheidt, R. J. (1993). Place and personality in adult development. In R. Kastenbaum (Ed.), *The encyclopedia of adult development* (pp. 370–376.) Phoenix: The Oryx Press.

Schindler, R. (1996). Mourning and bereavement among Jewish religious families: A time for reflection and recovery. *Omega, Journal of Death and Dying, 33,* 121–130.

Schwab, R. (2004). Acts of remembrance, cherished possessions, and living memorials. *Generations, 28*, 62–64.

Smith, N. (2003). Green burials and home funerals. *Mother Earth News*, April–May, 26–32.

Spiegelman, V., & Kastenbaum, R. (1990). Pet Rest Cemetery: Is eternity running out of time? *Omega, Journal of Death and Dying, 21*, 1–13.

Tashjian, A., & Tashjian, D. (1989). The Afro-American section of Newport, Rhode Island's common burying ground. In R. E. Meyer (Ed.), *Cemeteries and gravemarkers* (pp. 163–196). Ann Arbor: University of Michigan Research Press.

Tsiarias, A. (1982). *The death rituals of rural Greece.* Princeton, NJ: Princeton University Press.

Ubelaker, D., & Scammell, H. (1992). *Bones. A forensic detective's casebook.* New York: M. Evans.

Villa, Judi. (2004, April 23). Burial chain gang gets to juveniles. *Arizona Republic* p. B6.

Walter, T. (1992). *Funerals and how to improve them.* North Pomfret, VT: Hodder & Stoughton.

Yerton, S. (2004a, March 10). Donated bodies blown up by Army. *The Times-Picayune.* www.nola.com/search/index.ssf?base/library-39/107891295476540.xml?nola

Yerton, S. (2004b, March 12). Donors' families grieve all over again. Use of bodies by Army prompts sadness, anger. *The Times-Picayune.* www.nola.com/news/t-p/frontpage/index.ssf?/base/news-1/107907860840.xml

Zbarsky, I., & Hutchinson, S. (1997). *Lenin's embalmers.* London: The Harvill Press.

Zeigarnik, B. (1927). Untersuchungen zur Handlungs und Affektpsycholigie,. Das Behalten erledigter und underledigter Handlungen. *Psychologisches Forschung, 9*, 1–85.

GLOSSARY

Alkaline hydrolysis: The controversial process of dissolving a corpse into a liquid residual.

Aninut: The interval between death and burial in which "time stands still" and family members are given the opportunity to grieve in private (Jewish).

Autopsy: Medical examination performed on a corpse.

Ba: In ancient Egypt, a spirit that departs from the body at death.

Ch'iidii: Evil ghosts who rob graves (Navajo).

Cremation: Reduction of a corpse to ashes in a burning chamber.

Death certificate: Required legal form that is completed or verified by a physician, including basic information on the deceased person and cause(s) of death.

Embalming: A procedure that retards physical deterioration of a corpse by use of a preservative fluid.

Eulogy: Words said or written to honor a deceased person.

Exhumation: Also known as disinterment, this is the removal of a corpse from its place of burial.

Funeral process: The rituals, observances, and procedures that accompany the burial or other disposition of the body of a deceased person.

Green funeral: Burial without embalmment in forest or field with intention of returning remains to nature simply and directly.

Kaddish: Prayer on behalf of a deceased person (Jewish).

Medical examiner: Physician who examines autopsy findings and other evidence when there are questions about circumstances and cause of death. (Also known as medical examiner.)

Obituary: A (usually brief) published report that provides information on a person's life after his or her death.

Ponos: The pain of grief (Greek).

Postmortem: After death.

Premortem: Before death.

Scarab: A stone carved in the shape of a dung beetle; used to replace the heart in mummification (ancient Egypt).

Spontaneous memorialization: Voluntary public response to the death of a person by violence; characterized by expression of personal feelings and bringing mementoes to the site of the death.

Vermillion accord: A position statement on the ethical principles that should govern our treatment of human remains (based on a conference in Vermillion, South Dakota).

ON FURTHER THOUGHT . . .

Useful online resources:

Cremation Society of North America
   www.cremationassociation.org
Death Rituals & Funeral Customs
   www.encarta.msn.co
Funeral Consumers Alliance
   www.funerals.org
Funeral and Memorial Societies of America
   www://ubiweb.c.champlain.edu/famsa.directory.htm
International Association of Pet Cemeteries
   www.iaopc.com

Internet Cremation Society
  www.cremation.org
National Funeral Directors and Morticians Association
  www.nfdma.com
World Wide Cemetery
  www.interlog.com/cemetery

You have a decision to make:

They are three of your best friends. One is a contractor who finally has the opportunity to build an upscale residential development on choice land that has recently become available. Another is that brainiac who, to nobody's surprise, has become a rising star in science. The other person has the most interesting background, a Native American who has introduced you to a world you would not have otherwise known. What's the problem, then? The burial ground. The building project came to a halt. Lawyers now are the only people able to do anything. The developer wants to dig and build. The scientist wants to patiently excavate all the remains and artifacts as a contribution to knowledge. The Native American wants the remains to be respected and undisturbed. It happens that you are the person in the position to make the call. What do you decide—and on what basis? How can the rival claims be fairly evaluated? What is the best, and what is the worst, possible outcome? That's it! Have a nice day!

Young lovers who died before they could experience the fulfillment of their union might find themselves in the Elysian Fields for an eternity of pleasure, or so a Roman poet suggested.

chapter **13**

DO WE SURVIVE DEATH?

What one believes happens after death dictates much of what one believes about life, and this is why faith-based religion, in pressing to fill in the blanks in our knowledge of the hereafter, does such heavy lifting for those who fall under its power, A single proposition—you will not die—once believed, determines a response to life that would otherwise be unthinkable.
—Sam Harris (2004, p. 38)

I once asked a young Hezbollah *fighter how he knew there was a life after death. "I can prove it to you," he replied. "Do you believe that justice exists? Yes? Well, since there is no justice in this life, it must mean there is justice in the next life—so there is life after death."*
—Robert Fisk (2005, p. 1)

I looked over Jordan and what did I see,

Comin' for to carry me home!

A band of angels comin' after me,

Comin' for to carry me home!

Swing low, sweet chariot,

Comin' for to carry me home!
—Traditional American spiritual (arranged by Harry Thacker Burleigh)

Tasty vegetables of every kind

Grow in heaven's garden:

Good asparagus, beans . . .

Whole dishfuls are ready for us.

Good apples, pears and grapes;

The gardeners let us have anything.
—Traditional Austrian-German folk lyric (musical setting by Gustav Mahler)

As Lord Krishna said to his disciple:

Who thinks that he can be a slayer,

Who thinks that he is slain,

Both these lack knowledge:

He slays not, is not slain.

Never is he born nor dies; Unborn, eternal, everlasting be . . .
—Kramer (1988, p. 32)

Chinese police have arrested three men for killing two young women and selling their corpses as "ghost brides" for dead, single men. The women were victims of a belief dating back to before the Han dynasty in the highlands of western China that young men and women who die unmarried should go to their graves accompanied by a recently deceased partner to be their spouse in the afterlife.
—Jan Brea (2007)

Behold, I show you a mystery; We shall not all sleep, but we shall all be changed, In a moment, in the twinkling of an eye . . . for the trumpet shall sound, and the dead shall be raised incorruptible, and we shall be changed. . . . O death, where is thy sting? O grave, where is thy victory?
—I Corinthians, 15

The skeleton he will cause to be put together in such a manner that the whole figure may be seated in a chair usually occupied by me when living, in the attitude in which I am sitting when engaged in thought. . . .He will cause the skeleton to be clad in one of the suits of black occasionally worn by me.
—Jeremy Bentham (1832)

"I'd like backup copies of myself," one told me at a transhumanist conference, "something more durable than a carbon-based system."
—Brian Alexander (2003, p. 51)

The four men were sitting at a table outside a trailer park after their night on the town and entered into an argument about religion. The talk became heated when the subject turned to who would go to heaven and who would go to hell. Stoker said he would settle the argument and went into a house and returned with a shotgun, which he loaded and placed in his mouth. . . .
—Reuters, 2002

The prospect of an afterlife has stimulated faith and hope, but also dread and violence, through the centuries. In *The End of Faith* (2004), Sam Harris emphasizes the bloodshed that has all too frequently accompanied beliefs in an afterlife. It is a one-sided but not inaccurate reading of history—and of current events, reports that the terrorists of September 11, 2001, expected to be rewarded with admission to paradise were a sharp reminder that belief in survival continues to have powerful consequences. However, I have been with people whose long lives were about to end but who were comforted by the belief that they were going to a better place. Dying was a tribulation, but death would be both relief and arrival.

Before examining the present scene, we will examine some of the ways in which other people have tried to come to terms with the certainty of death and the uncertainty of what happens next. We begin with an historical perspective and consider the question of whether or not survival is something that needs to be proved.

CONCEPT OF SURVIVAL IN HISTORICAL PERSPECTIVE

The opening quotations immediately remind us that survival of death has taken on a wide variety of meanings and associations. Let's revisit them:

1. The soldiers in a sandbagged bunker during the Iran–Iraq war ranged in age from 14 to 21. Several had already been killed in combat, and all expected their turn would come soon. The young leader was concerned about the interviewer's inability to comprehend the true faith:

   It is impossible for you in the West to understand. Martyrdom brings us closer to God. We do not seek death—but we regard death as a journey from one form of life to another. . . . Our first duty is to kill the enemy forces so that God's order will be everywhere (Fisk, p. 2).

2. "Swing Low, Sweet Chariot" is one of many spirituals that originated during the long years of slavery and the troubled aftermath of emancipation. There was a double meaning: death would liberate the oppressed people from their sorrows. This prospect of delivery enabled them to deal with the harshness of their present lives. The hidden message was escape from their slave masters. For example, the popular spiritual "Wade in the Water" also conveyed useful advice: Walk through streams so the hounds of pursuit would have a more difficult time finding you.

3. Heaven was food in abundance! The musical setting of these verses in the finale of Mahler's Fourth Symphony is all charm and innocence—but ironically so. "Tasty vegetables of every kind . . ." is a starving child's vision of heaven. In real life through the centuries, many children did starve. "Give me some bread, or I'll die," pleads the boy in another of Mahler's songs. That boy does not get his bread, and he dies. We must— we must! have an afterlife because there's no justice on Earth, or there's no freedom, or there is not even enough to eat. The Iranian soldier, the American slave, and the Austrian child rely upon the next life for what is so painfully missing in this life.

But what of death itself? Consider several of the most influential religious perspectives:

4. Hindu tradition regards birth and death as illusions. The spirit or soul is always in process. *There is no death that one must survive.* It is in our nature to be "everlasting," even though we may not have a conscious memory of who we were in previous incarnations. Similarly, in Buddhist tradition we are always dying and undergoing rebirth through the course of our lives. This process continues after "death." What survives is the pattern of consciousness that has been shaped through many previous births, lives, and deaths.

5. China and Taiwan are impressively modernizing realms. Nevertheless, there are hardy survivals of ancient superstitions. These include the belief that the unmarried dead can invade the dreams of the living and make them thoroughly miserable. A constructive solution is to find a spouse to accompany the unmarried young to the grave. Ordinarily, the ghost bride would be a person recently deceased of natural cause. Murdering young women with the purpose of selling them as ghost brides was threatening to become an attractive moneymaking scheme when corpses started to fetch a high price. The authorities are now on the alert. Although ghost brides may seem to be far out, they are still part of a society's death system. A major social dynamic here is China's one-child policy that has resulted in an acute shortage of women and an oversupply of bachelors (Chen, 2007). Digging up a bride or murdering a woman unsuitable for marriage in order to market her corpse trades under the banner of supply and demand.

6. The passage from I Corinthians has been subjected to several interpretations over the years. For example: Does this transformation occur for all or only some people? Does it occur on a person-by-person basis or for all eligible humans in one ultimate "twinkling?"

The message of Christianity's victory over death was enhanced by reports that Jesus had brought a dead man back to life, as depicted in Rembrandt's (1630) *The Raising of Lazarus*.

There is a striking difference between the New Testament vision and those associated with the Hindu and Buddhist traditions. Death had been the enemy, the relentless adversary against which no human strength or strategy could prevail. Now it is death that has been defeated, its sting made harmless, and consigned to its own grave ("swallowed up in victory"). This electrifying message from the early years of Christianity did much to attract disciples and disseminate the faith throughout much of the world.

7. The academic skeleton in the closet was an attempt to devise a nonspiritual form of survival. Jeremy Bentham was as cool, collected, and sober as always when he drew up his last will and testament in London. Eminent during his life, he also has had a lasting influence on social philosophy with his theory that advocated the greatest amount of happiness to the largest number of people. As for Bentham's post-death agenda, he intended to look like himself as much as possible, keep his trusty walking stick, and attend

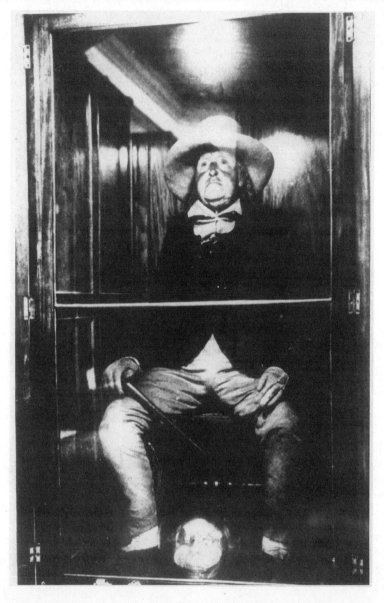

British philosopher Jeremy Bentham decided that the afterlife should include occasional appearances at faculty meetings, complete with a sturdy walking stick to maintain discipline.

occasional faculty meetings. (There are un-verified reports that Benthams have multi-plied, attending faculty meetings in many universities with glazed eyes and mummified heads. Sorry, no list available.)

8. Technological substitutions for spiritual survival have come a long way since Bentham—at least, in theory. The quest to add years to life was already a prime moti-vating force during the era of myths and

legends and became a spur to the development of science and technology, ever accompanied by superstition and humbug. The man who demanded a "back-up copy" of himself has now arrived on the scene. Should his desire to overcome the limits of a "carbon-based life form" be fulfilled? Would we feel the need for heaven, if we could stay right here for a long, long, long time?

9. Inquiring minds want to know. There have been countless arguments about heaven and hell through the centuries, but on a July evening in Godley, Texas, two young men concluded their discussion by putting the matter to a test. Clayton Frank Stoker swallowed as much of the shotgun as he could to discover whether he would go to heaven or hell. Johnny Joslin snatched the gun out of his friend's mouth, saying, "If you have to shoot somebody, shoot me." The shotgun fired (circumstances unclear), and it was Joslin who would be first to discover whether he was going to heaven or hell. (Yes, both had been drinking some that night.)

The gentlemen of Godley have made their inquiry into heaven and hell. It is our turn now. We begin with a self-quiz that provides an opportunity to express our personal views of some survival-of-death issues. It's okay to respond to all the questions whether or not you firmly believe in an afterlife (e.g., a person can have an image of heaven or hell even if not convinced of their existence).

BOX 13-1 SURVIVAL OF DEATH? A SELF-QUIZ

Part I. Beliefs

1. I believe in some form of life after death.

    Yes ____   No ____   Uncertain ____

2. I believe that a spirit or soul is separable from the body.

    Yes ____   No ____   Uncertain ____

3. I think of Heaven as a

    ____ Place in a divine sphere of being
    ____ A joyful state of mind or spirit, not an actual place

4. I think of Hell as

    ____ An actual place of torment and punishment
    ____ An anguished state of mind or spirit

5. Heaven is for people who

    ____ Believe in a particular religious faith, but not others
    ____ Believe in any religious faith
    ____ Perform exceptional and heroic acts
    ____ Live virtuous lives
    ____ End their lives with rituals and blessings
    ____ Are judged worthy by God

6. It is possible for living and dead people to communicate with each other.

    Agree ____   Disagree ____

7. We are reincarnated in a cycle of births, deaths, and rebirths.

    Agree ____   Disagree ____

8. It will be possible to overcome death someday by medical and technological advances.

    Agree ____   Disagree ____

9. It is morally acceptable to seek alternative forms of survival such as cloning, cryonics, and digital transformations.

    Agree ____   Disagree ____

continued on next page

BOX 13-1   SURVIVAL OF DEATH? A SELF-QUIZ *(continued)*

10. My dog and cat will go to heaven if they are very, very good.

    Agree ____   Disagree ____

Part II: Persuasion and Imagination

11. Suppose that you really wanted to persuade somebody that there is not life after death. What evidence, experiences, or line of reasoning would you use? Be as specific as possible and put your heart into it, as though you wanted very much to convince a person that there is no afterlife and had to call upon the strongest objections to this belief.

12. Suppose now that you wanted to persuade somebody that there is life after death. What evidence, experiences, or line of reasoning would you use? Again, be specific and put your best efforts into it.

13. You have already stated your own ideas and beliefs. What kind of experience, evidence, or logic could persuade you to change your mind? It does not matter if you consider the contrary evidence or experience to be very unlikely. What might lead you to change your mind if it did happen or were true?

14. Suppose that you actually have changed your mind. You have discovered that your present belief is mistaken. What difference would it make in your life? In what ways and to what extent would your life be different if you had to accept the opposite of your present belief about life after death?

15. What influence has your actual belief or disbelief had upon the way you live? What decisions has it influenced and in what way?

16. What do you think would be the best thing about life after death (whether or not you are a believer)?

17. What could be the worst thing about life after death?

18. How did you come to your present belief or disbelief about life after death?

19. What would you tell a child who asks what happens when a person dies?

Key Points

We will see how other people of our own time respond to survival of death questions. Several key points are worth emphasis at this time, however:

• *People differ in their interpretations of the afterlife as either literal or metaphorical.* For example, Pope John Paul II explained to a Vatican audience that:

> rather than a place, hell indicates the state of those who freely and definitely separate themselves from God. The Bible uses a symbolic language that figuratively portrays in a 'pool of fire' those who exclude themselves from the book of life, thus meeting with a 'second death' (Sheler, 2000).

By contrast, many other Christians continue to believe in an actual hell with actual flames and torments. Islamic paradise is also interpreted variously as an actual garden of comfort and pleasure and as a state of being that can only be hinted at by poetical descriptions (Wasilewska, 2002).

• *A dualistic philosophy is associated with most afterlife beliefs.* Body and soul are temporary companions with different purposes and fates. This idea has been influential from earliest known history to the present time.

- *What we might call the conservation theme has often been a powerful influence on survival beliefs.* People mighty in life also should be mighty in the afterlife. Status and privilege should be preserved. This theme was already salient with the dynastic Egyptians. The ordinary mortal need not apply for immortal privileges. The democracy of the dead eventually made significant inroads, although never completely overcoming the conservation impulse.
- *The final exam theme is common but not universal.* Death brings us to the moment of judgment: salvation or damnation. The final exam theme is salient in Christianity and Islam, though somewhat muted in early Judaism, where all souls enter the same pit (*sheol*).

We are ready now to look at the afterlife from the perspective of several belief systems. The journey of the dead is a good place to start, and then on to the destinations themselves.

The Journey of the Dead

Souls undertake a perilous journey after death. That has been the belief of many world cultures. "Undertake" is the right word here, because there are dark passages under the earth and dangerous arrivals. Most societies have performed rituals to acknowledge the death of a member and reduce the hazards in transitioning between the worlds of the living and the dead. On arrival, often one must pass through trials and judgments. Mythology tells us of a few living people who made voluntary journeys to the Land of the Dead. Their experiences are instructive.

Consider first *Gilgamesh*, the mythical king who ruled the Mesopotamian city-state of Uruk perhaps 5,000 years ago (Westwood, 2002). He is desired by Ishtar, but rejects her advances, knowing that her ex-lovers had very short lives. The spurned goddess of love sends her "hit man," the Bull of Heaven, but he is slain by Gilgamesh and his best friend, Enkidu. Offended, the gods kill Enkidu. Here is where it gets interesting: Gilgamesh starts to reflect on his own mortality. Even though his parents are gods, the young king faces the same fate as other mortals. Gilgamesh risks a journey to the underworld in hope of persuading the one immortal man to

grant him immortality as well. Adventures and misadventures ensue. At the end, Gilgamesh fails in his quest. He will not be an immortal. No human will ever escape death. This hard lesson has been passed on for thousands of years: If the great Gilgamesh with his god connections could not escape death, who can? We mortals had best adjust our attitudes and expectations.

Orpheus grieves for his beloved wife, *Eurydice*. She was murdered by the gods who commanded a serpent to bite her. Like Gilgamesh, Orpheus has a connection in high places as son of a divine muse and a mortal king, He boldly ventures into the underworld, where his music charms even Cerberus, the vicious three-headed watchdog. Orpheus persuades the gods of Hades to allow Eurydice to return with him. There is a condition, however: He must not look back at her until they cross the border. Orpheus cannot restrain himself quite that long, though—and Eurydice is gone forever. Cultural history again decrees that the dead must remain so.

The journey to the land of the dead has taken many forms. In Greek mythology, a cranky fellow by the name of *Charon* ferried the dead across the river Styx to Hades. The poet Virgil suggested that the entrance to this realm can be found near the volcanic Mount Vesuvius, where vapors and weird sounds issue from the mysterious realm below. The Hades welcoming committee was not especially encouraging: The souls of the dead moaned horribly and displayed their disfiguring wounds. The worst of the new arrivals were assigned to the most hellish regions for their crimes. The fate of Tantalus has given us the word *tantalize*. He was suspended from a tree, condemned to perpetual hunger while fruit remained just beyond his reach. Ordinary mortals who had not offered the gods a stew from their own children were abandoned to the ordinary miseries of Hades.

Arriving in the underworld was only the opening act in a complex and hazardous journey for ancient Egyptians. Fearsome demons would need to be convinced that the soul had not stolen, uttered evil words, judged others too quickly, killed a person—or fouled water. This was the preliminary test. The final exam involved weighing the deceased's heart against a feather that represented truth, order, and justice. If the heart was heavier (with wrongdoings), it would be fed to The Devourer, and the spirit would be cast into the darkness (Kastenbaum, 2004).

The vision of a dark passage to a dangerous or dreary place contrasts with another type of journey that is reserved for the elite, heroic, or especially lovable. These fortunate ones travel over great waters to a land of perpetual sunshine where fruit ripens for the picking, pure water flows, and every day is a vacation. Taylor (2000) notes that the *blest isles* were almost always in the far west or far east, depending on the location of the nearest great body of water. The Aztecs, living between two oceans, had two islands of the blest, one in either direction. The Blest Isles were considered to be real, though distant, places on Earth. Centuries later, travel brochures and Hollywood movies would tout tropical island paradises that were prefigured by the happy lands reserved for the few most deserving Aztecs, Scandinavians, Greeks, Celtics, and others.

The Roman poet Tibullus offered one of the most appealing versions of an island destination. The fortunate enter a paradise garden where lovers enjoy each other's company forevermore. Tibullus asserted that in times gone by (the so-called Golden Age), people enjoyed free and uninhibited lovemaking. Alas, this pleasure was no longer available in the modern world of the first century B.C. Paradise island, though, still awaited young lovers who had been taken by death before consummating their desires (McDannel & Lang, 1988).

The Buddhist journey as detailed in *The Tibetan Book of the Dead* (Evans-Wenz, 2000; Agha, 2003) differs from both a dread underground passage or a cruise to everlasting delights. In effect, we are birds of passage. To death we bring the selves we have been and the level of spiritual enlightenment we have achieved—and then we go on from there. A glimpse of this process was given in the description of Buddhist stages of dying (Chapter 4). Like the other great world religions, Buddhism has been interpreted in many ways, ranging from the literal to the abstract.

HEAVENS AND HELLS

Most people in most societies took survival as a fact. Sometimes the dead were buried with tools and other objects useful in the next life. The dead continued their interest in the living, either as guides and guardian angels or as vengeful spirits. Ideas about the afterlife eventually became elaborated and woven into theology, philosophy, poetry, song, and drama. Although belief was the norm, the words of a few dissenters have survived. Titus Lucretius Carus (54 B.C.) made the argument that "nothing can be produced from nothing," and, further, that "A thing . . . never returns to nothing, but all things after disruption go back into the first bodies of matter" (p. 3). Nature continually shapes, destroys, and reshapes her basic materials. Although there is no complete annihilation, there is also no imperishable soul that is immune from the general principle of transformation.

Love, death, and the brevity of life have been the doleful obsession of poets since ancient times:

> All who come into being as flesh
>   Pass on—and all men rest in the grave.
> So, seize the day! Hold holiday!
>   Be unwearied, unceasingly alive,
> You and your own true love.

This excerpt is from a poem written more than 3,000 years ago somewhere in Mesopotamia (Washburn & Majors, 1998, p. 22). The poet is not comforting us with a vision of paradise: Here is life today—enjoy the moment with those we love, for all who have become before us have passed on, and the same will be true of us.

THE DESERT RELIGIONS AND THEIR ONE GOD

In time, the deserts of Mesopotamia gave the world three enduring religions. All agreed that there is one supreme being. Another religion anticipated some of the doctrines and images of Judaism, Christianity, and Islam, but *Zoroastrianism* (Boyce, 1979; Mehr, 2003) lost its Persian homeland and has fewer followers today. Within each faith, there are believers in a literal heaven and hell and others who take these descriptions as allusions to peaceful and stressful states of being.

Jewish Survival Belief in the Ancient World

The Christian message emerged from competing sets of beliefs within Judaism. McDannel and Lang (1988) have identified three currents within Jewish survival belief:

1. *Yahweh is the God of life—and this life is all that we have*. We should therefore live for this one life in this one world that God has given to us. The Sadducee sect contended that the holy scriptures offer no promise of an afterlife. One can experience the presence of God in everyday life, so there is no need to ask for more.
2. *The faithful among the dead will arise to participate in a new and improved society*. This concept, associated with the Pharisees, shared the Sadducee's primary interest in life on Earth. Bad things happen to good people, especially when under oppressive foreign rule. This dilemma will be resolved when "the dry bones of a conquered Israel rise up and claim their place on a renewed earth" (p. 21). Only the right kind of person will live again, however, and the main point of this return is to create a more perfect society on Earth.
3. *There is a spiritual rather than a physical afterlife, in which the individual soul contemplates God*. This concept, associated with the Essenes,

shifted the emphasis from materialistic life on earth to a purified existence on another plane. The Essene conception was the last to emerge within the Judaic tradition and had moved closer to what would become the Christian interpretation.

Heaven and Hell for Christians

The boundary between the dead and the living can be crossed from either side. Ghosts do it, and so do *necromancers* who interrogate the dead. Jesus became part of this tradition when he raised Lazarus. He added an astonishing new dimension through his own resurrection. Jesus was hailed as a person who had died and resurrected for everybody's salvation, a proposition endorsed by St. Augustine, a founding father of Christian theology. The Israelites longed to be masters of their own nation on Earth. The new cult turned eyes toward heaven. Earthly life paled by comparison. Nevertheless, it was difficult to imagine heaven's realm of glory. The challenge of "picturing heaven" (Zaleski, 2003) remains with us. It seems easier to imagine the absence of fear and suffering than the bliss of heaven.

Hell was more vivid. The wicked suffered terribly. Fire in the darkness, the stench of sulfur, chains, cages, impalement—the torments seemed all too palpable. Such would be the fate of misguided Christians. Worse, still, were the agonies awaiting those "who had rejected the gospel,

©2005 Grimmy, Inc. Dist. by King Features Syndicate, Inc. grimmy.com 7/20

spurned baptism, or for other reasons remained independent of the new revelation" (Bernstein, 1993, p. 340). Hell did change over the centuries. The baroque era, for example, reveled in flash and festivity. "Good old-fashioned hell" was becoming an entertainment for an increasingly literate and worldly population. The Jesuits acted decisively to empower the horrors of hell for a new kind of Christian (Turner, 1993):

> They eliminated all tortures except fire, and all monsters except possibly "the worm that never sleepeth." What they added was unnervingly apt for the times—urban squalor. The Jesuit Hell was unbearably, suffocatingly, repulsively crowded. . . . In a dank claustrophobic amalgam of dungeon and cesspool, dainty aristocrats and prosperous merchants jostled . . . with coarse, foul-smelling, verminous peasants, lepers, and slum dwellers. . . . The infernal stench was disgusting and everlasting and composed of filth and feces and pestilence and running sores and bad breath . . . (p. 173).

Hell was no longer a cartoon, an amusement for sophisticates. All that the rising tide of individualism cherished would evaporate in the everlasting flames and unbearable stench. The Jesuit version was highly influential, and some Protestant sects also adopted the "sulfur and brimstone" approach.

Islamic Paradise and Jahannam

Islam emerged as a religious movement in seventh-century Arabia, inspired by the prophet Muhammad. The word *Islam* is often translated as *submission* but could also be known as *conversion* (Segal, 2004). Abraham and Jesus were both regarded as prophets who had preceded Muhammad. A person who accepted The One God was tolerated even if the worship took a Jewish or Christian form. Islam soon divided itself into rival power bases when none of the founder's sons survived into adulthood. It remains a less centralized religion than Christianity, the followers united by scripture and belief rather than organizational hierarchy.

In Islam, life is regarded as a spiritual struggle between good and evil. *Jihad* refers to the constant struggle between one's own lower and higher impulses, as well as to conflict with enemies of the faith. Muslims are expected to resist temptations and devote themselves to a moral life. Death and the Day of Judgment are brought to mind repeatedly through prayer, practice, and instruction. One should live in preparation for the "appointed hour" (Hanson, 2003). In this respect, Islamic doctrine has much in common with the European *Ars moriendi* tradition that was most dominant in the fifteenth century.

The Day of Judgment can come at any time. All souls will then meet their Creator. There will be paradise for the virtuous, Jahannam for the failed. A Book of Deeds is kept for every person. There is an inherent ambiguity in specifying a "day" of judgment or, as often described, the "hour" in which the judged mortals begin their spiritual existence. The day could be 50,000 years or a fleeting instant because Allah is not constrained by human notions of time. Furthermore, there is no assurance that the afterlife assignment will be permanent. At the end of time, there will be a final triumph of Islam (perhaps at the Day of Resurrection). There are hints in Qur'an that this eschatological event will be accompanied by the catastrophic destruction of the material universe. The heavens will storm, the mountains will vanish, and the earth will be shaken (Qur'an 52: 9–10). There is more than a passing similarity here to Native American religions that also predict that all of the world, not excepting the apparently everlasting mountains, will become as nothing.

Death itself is described by the Qur'an as a deep, dreaming sleep that Allah concludes either by making it permanent or sending the person back for another go at life (Wasilewska, 2002). (There is an obvious similarity to many contemporary near-death experience reports, as will be discussed here.) The faithful Muslim will be ready to face the Creator at any time. Forget about erasing a life of indolence and immorality by a deathbed conversion or a special favor from God.

> According to the early Christians, all sins were to be forgiven upon conversion. This was true even if the acceptance of Christ took place in the deathbed. . . . In Islam, repentance is a change in the course of life. . . . It is not for those who

go on doing evil deeds, until when death comes to one of them, he says: "Now I repent." (Wasli-weska, 2002, p. 2).

The Muslin version of heaven is a garden with rivers of pure water, milk, wine, and honey. Fruit is plentiful. The garden of paradise offers much to please. (Although alcoholic beverages are forbidden by the Qur'an, the wine of paradise does not intoxicate and can be enjoyed with no sin attached.)

The Qur'an does not support the type of paradise reportedly imagined by the September 11th terrorists. The male fantasy of 72 virgins seems to have originated in folk tales that were elaborated by numerologists There is, in fact, no specific number of "virgins" mentioned in the Qur'an, nor is it described as an arrangement for male use of females. In the Qur'an (13:23; 36:56), women and children are equally eligible for paradise if they have shined in the Book of Deeds. Both men and women enjoy the companionship of "those modest in gaze, having beautiful eyes, carefully protected, pure and beautiful ones . . . reclining on green cushions and beautiful carpets." The women dwelling in paradise are pure of character, carrying forward the Islamic emphasis on female virtue in earthly life. Paradise is a garden of delights for people who have reached an advanced level of spiritual development and who have the potential to continue their advancement in this favored setting.

Furthermore, it is by no means required that one becomes a martyr to win admission to paradise. People with blood on their hands and lust in their hearts might indeed be better candidates for *Jahannam,* the Muslim version of hell. Molten brass, boiling water, and infernal flames are in evidence here, as they were in the earlier hells conceived by Zoroastrians and Christians. The fiery torments have a therapeutic as well as punitive purpose: The fallen eventually might be purified of their sinful inclinations. It is not clear what benefits they might derive from encounters with:

> Scorpions and snakes as big as camels and stinking rivers fully of slimy creatures who cause them to vomit . . . The dwellers in Jahannam will wish to die but continue to exist in torment (Taylor, p. 199).

Consigned to hell are not only the obvious sinners but also those who refuse to help the needy, cheat in commerce, abandon themselves to luxuries, or commit adultery. The most severe punishments await those who worship idols or multiple deities instead of accepting the oneness of God—or those who deny Allah's resurrection and judgment of the dead.

We have already expressed our beliefs in a self-quiz (Box 13-1). The American people have also been asked to share their views on survival on several occasions. What have they been saying??

WHAT OTHER PEOPLE BELIEVE TODAY

Every now and then the public is asked to express its views about death and afterlife. A fairly consistent pattern has emerged, but it should be kept in mind that the surveys ask different questions of different population samples at somewhat different times. That being said, the findings are well worth our attention.

Baby Boomers Scan the Afterlife

The girls and boys born on and after January 1, 1946, would have no idea they had become pioneers of the baby boomer generation. Much has been said about this supersized cohort that emerged at the end of World War II. That each generation has its own general profile had not been a secret to social scientists, but the boomers were the first to be named famously and analyzed endlessly. Our focus here is on how boomers think of last things as they observe more wrinkles in the mirror, fill more prescriptions, and attend more funerals.

A study conducted by the American Association of Retired People (Newcott, 2008) harvested the thoughts of people 50 and over. Most (about 7 of 10) believed in an afterlife, the women more so (8 of 10). The boomer's afterlife belief was prevailingly optimistic: there is a Heaven (capitalization preferred by the respondents), and they will be there. However, the boomers judge that a great many other people will not make it. About 4 of 10 respondents believed there is a literal Hell awaiting future consignments of sinners.

Although citizens of the information age, many boomers find a place for the occult. Ghosts are real to most of the boomers, and many have had something that felt like an experience with a disembodied spirit. As citizens of the modern information age, reincarnation belief had been rarely reported in the United States in the past, perhaps 1 person in 100, as estimated by Russell (1998). It is not an uncommon belief among boomers (23%), however.

One might or might not be surprised that a substantial number of boomers (about 1 in 4) believe that death is the end-all—but continue to cherish their religion and attempt to live up to its moral code. Some, like Tom, operate with a conditional premise:

> You just gotta make up your own mind about things. I go to Mass. I live my life like there's life after death. But I don't believe there is. If it's true, well, hey, it's a plus. But if it ain't, I didn't lose anything (p. 2).

Unfortunately, these findings cannot tell us how much of the boomers' views have been shaped by their distinctive childhoods (e.g., the first fully "televisionated" generation) and how much by their experiences as they continue to move through the life course.

United States: A Nation of Believers?

Belief in life after death has been increasing in the United States since the 1980s, according to most studies (Gallup Poll, 1999; Greeley & Hout, 1999; Hayslip & Peveto, 2005; Lester et al., 2000/2001; Morin, 2000). There are more believers than nonbelievers in all the major studies, usually by a decisive margin. This finding encompasses both genders and all the ethnic and racial groups that have been surveyed.

Morin notes that even people who say they have no religious preference are more likely (63%) to believe in an afterlife, as compared with 44% who believed in an afterlife in the 1970s. Most respondents expect the afterlife to be comforting, and many believe it includes reunion with family and friends. There was also

consensus that any physical problems they have in this life would not be carried over to the next. Most (71%) respondents to the Morin's Fox News Survey were sure that hell is a real place—but even more (88%) said the same of heaven. Nevertheless, there was a sense of risk and foreboding as well. For example, most Gallup Poll (1999) respondents believed that there will be a day of judgment to determine who belongs among the blessed, but they were about evenly divided on whether a good person can go to heaven without a belief in God.

There was consensus that we need faith in God and *immortality* to make it through the tribulations of life. Beliefs were formed early in childhood, according to almost all respondents, but the nonbelievers were more likely to have reconsidered this topic in recent years. What to tell a child proved to be most difficult for those who were not very sure of their positions on survival, whether believers or nonbelievers. Nonbelievers more frequently expressed some conflict or uncertainty in what to say, but wavering believers also had their difficulties.

The apparent increase in afterlife belief could be a little misleading. A major survey (Pew Research Center, 2008) finds that more than a quarter of the American people have left the faith in which they were raised "in favor of another religion—or no religion at all" (p. 2). The percentage of people who how consider themselves unaffiliated has risen sharply, and is even higher among younger adults where 1 in 4 report no current association. Many Americans seem to be "shopping around" for a religious affiliation that meets their needs. This raises questions about the certainty with which core beliefs—such as the afterlife—are held. The Pew survey makes a contribution toward answering this question: most of the immigrants moving into the United States bring a strong religious faith with them, including belief in an afterlife. Overall, the Pew survey depicts a diversity and fluidity of religious belief in the U.S.

A Southern Perspective

Further insights were gleaned from a study focusing on the afterlife beliefs of residents of 13 Southern states (Miller, 2001). The longtime

Southerners are most likely to participate in evangelical forms of Christianity. Charles Reagan Wilson, director of the University of Mississippi's Center for the Southern Culture, explains that

> Southerners have a very literal understanding of heaven and hell. Death is not abstract. . . . . It's something you think about. Ministers talk about it, preach about it. 'Are you ready to meet the Lord?' You drive down the road in the rural South, you see these signs, 'Get right with the Lord' (Miller, p. 1).

The abiding role of religion in Southern life is expressed in the respondents' concerns about dying. "Not having a chance to say goodbye to someone" is the most frequently stated concern and one that is shared by many other people throughout the nation. The next two most common concerns, though, seem to be more salient in the South than in the nation in general: "Dying when out of touch with God or a higher power;" "Not being forgiven by God."

Belief in resurrection of the body has slowed the acceptance of cremation, which has been becoming a more frequent choice in other regions. In Alabama, for example, cremation is selected in only 1 of 20 funerals, the lowest percentage in the nation.

Southerners, especially in rural areas, seem to be carrying forward religious and social support traditions that once were more widespread. These include laying out deceased loved ones at home for visitations, and preparing tables full of dumplings, ham, deviled eggs, and many other dishes for friends and family after the funeral.

What Do Belief-Oriented People Believe about the Afterlife?

Some people give more attention to belief issues than others. These include the membership of Beliefnet, a major internet site. What views do they hold? Beliefnet conducted a survey of 10,567 members. The respondents included self-described wiccans, agnostics, atheists, and "spiritual not religious" as well as those within a major traditional religion. The complete findings can be found at www.beliefnet.com/story/162_16237.html. A briefer report on "Who's Going to Hell?" can be accessed at www.beliefnet.com/features/hellchart.html. Most respondents (4 out of 5) believed in an afterlife and 3 out of 4 of those respondents also believed in hell. About half the sample knew somebody whom they considered to be hell-bound; considerably fewer expected that to be their own fate. Born-again Christians were by far the most likely to answer that there was not a chance of hell in their destiny.

Ask a few questions of the data and we learn that:

- Christians are the most likely to believe that (a) at death the soul or spirit moves on to an eternal afterlife, and (b) the souls of the dead protect the living as angels or spirit guides, and can hear our prayers.
- Muslims are most likely to believe there is an in-between stage between death and the afterlife.
- As expected, Buddhists, Hindus, and wiccans were the most likely to believe in reincarnation—but, less expectedly, more than half of the respondents within these faith categories did *not* affirm reincarnation. Why? We don't know.
- Wiccans have most often dreamed about and felt the presence of a dead person. For the sample as a whole, it was very common to have a dream visitation from a dead person.
- Jews and atheist/agnostics are most likely to say "I don't know what happens after death."
- Some respondents in all the belief categories (including agnostics) report that they have had an experience with the dead—and this experience has almost always been positive.

The Afterlife: A Mirror of Society?

Observers with a sociological perspective have been puzzled by the hardiness of afterlife belief in the United States. Zuckerman (2004), for example, notes that religiosity and belief in an afterlife have been declining sharply in Europe for many years. Americans are much more likely to report belief in god and afterlife than citizens of Belgium, France, Iceland, Italy, Germany, the Scandinavian countries, the United Kingdom, and so on. One possible explanation is that the vigor of fundamentalist religious traditions provides a sense of community and social support that is difficult to find elsewhere in a mass, technological society.

Historian Alan Segal (2004) offers an in-depth review of afterlife beliefs throughout history. He concludes that:

> the afterlife is not a single eternal truth that is an unchanging reward of the righteous or faithful. It is, instead, a mirror of the values of the society that produced it. Watching the afterlife change is watching a society's hopes and fears change. . . . Heaven is the best we can think of for ourselves at any historical time and hell is the worst we can imagine (p. 698).

Segal is talking about the long sweep of history, but he is also talking about us. Our ideas, experiences, hopes, and concerns have not only been influenced by society and circumstance but will also influence beliefs and practice to come.

One of the few questions not examined by Segal proved of interest to many of us: the best-selling book, *Do All Pets Go to Heaven?* (Wohlberg, 2002). Wohlberg does not claim to have a definitive answer but raises the possibility that a merciful god might decide to open the gates of heaven to Angel, Pumpkin, Serena, Snowflake, and your animal companions as well. (I hope they all will get along.)

CAN SURVIVAL BE PROVED?

Some form of afterlife has been assumed by most societies. Nevertheless, there has also been doubt along the way. The ancient civilizations of Mesopotamia, for example, were thoroughly aware of the sands of time that erased rulers, dynasties, and the memory of great events and achievements. A few elite royal souls might be immortal, but the common person's prospects were grim. The Christian victory over death was a source of jubilation in the faith's early years, but that great day failed to arrive, and miseries and loss continued as before. Belief in afterlife would eventually face daunting challenges from science. Today not everybody agrees that survival needs to be proved or that science is equipped to answer

the question. However, even confident believers often seek affirmation and support, if not from science, then from custom and personal experience. In this section we consider some of the major ways in which people have been persuaded—or not—that there is life after death. We begin just about where the human mind did: with the dead and their ghosts. Next stop is the attempt to find evidence for the durable ancient belief in *reincarnation.* It will then be time to dim the lights but keep our eyes open as curiosity, hope, greed, and powerful cultural forces collide around the possibility of spirit visitors. Next, we consider the more recent upsurge of interest in reports of near-death experiences (*NDE*s) as possible evidence for survival. We then venture into the less charted waters of symbolic immortality and assisted survival.

Ghosts

It is not easy to take ghosts seriously today—not even if we substitute the more respectable-sounding term, *apparitions.* Ghosts have been for so long the stuff of campfire stories, parodies, and late-night movies that they might seem to be the least-promising source of evidence for survival. But ghosts deserve better than that. For one thing, ghosts have had a firm social reality in many cultures. A partial list of societies with strong traditions of interaction with the dead would include the Asian Indian, Celtic, Chinese, Japanese, Mexican, Scottish, and Welsh (Bryant, 2003; Freed & Freed, 1993). For example, villagers in the Delhi region of India must be cautious in their dealing with each other, because an aggrieved neighbor could become a troublesome ghost. Ghost Month in China (including Taiwan) encourages families to express their love and respect for those who have passed on (Emmons, 1982). By the end of the festivities, the spirits are ready to return to the other side, now with a fresh supply of ghost money to pay for special favors.

For some unfortunate people, ghosts still are nightmare stuff. Cambodians by the thousands were murdered during the brutal regime of Pol Pot. One common method of execution was to place a bag over the head. People forced to witness these executions often developed breath anxiety. Some Cambodian refugees have found sanctuary in the United States, but not within their troubled dreams. They experience sleep paralysis during which a shadowy figure is felt to be approaching them—the mournful ghost of a murdered person they had known well. Traumatized sleepers report "The ghost pushes you down" (Hinton et al, 2005). This anxiety provoking experience is interpreted as a flashback intensified by survivor guilt.

How did the belief in ghosts arise, and what keeps it going? Nobody truly knows the answers. Anthropologists have reported the widespread belief that a spirit version of one's self wanders off from the sleeper during dreams and perhaps on other occasions. It follows that the spirit would also exit from the dead, and perhaps mingle with the living from time to time. Ghosts would be among the usual suspects when something strange or alarming happens. A ghost might be visible but we could also infer its presence by mischief it produces. What keeps ghosts in circulation might well be exposure to stories and expectations from childhood, the power of suggestion, and their functionality in customs and rituals. Furthermore, one can never be quite sure that there is not a ghost around, even if one chooses not to believe in them.

In more modern times, Catherine Crowe's collection, *Night Side of Nature or Ghosts and Ghost Seers* (1848/2008) created widespread excitement and strengthened many people's belief in spirit survival. This book has been raided fiercely by other writers ever since, and some of the tales have been taken as proof of survival, despite the author's cautions.

In our own society, everyday people still report encountering everyday-type ghosts. These are not the stereotypes associated with haunted houses. They are an entire family downstairs in the rented house, making their breakfast, the aroma of freshly brewed coffee rising to the visitor's bedroom. The ghost is an old man who sits quietly reading a newspaper at the same hour each early evening. The ghost is a cat who visits so often that he is considered a part of the family (even by the dog) and whose habits have become as familiar to them as their own. The quite down-to-earth and sensible woman who told me about the ghost cat had not at first thought it was even worth mentioning because "it was just part of our life; it was just there when it wanted to be." Myers (1903/1975) was more impressed with such innocuous ghosts than with the reports he collected of exotic apparitions with their mysterious purposes and profound messages. Who would have invented such useless ghosts, and why would they have bothered? Apparitions that did not fit into cultural belief systems and did not seem to have any particular agenda or message seemed more credible to Myers than those who have been featured in ghost stories.

Nevertheless, it is the consequential spirit who has attracted the most attention and who has most often been taken as proof of survival. Perhaps most common is the ghost who visits to provide comfort during a time of crisis:

> My mother died in June. One Sunday morning early, we had a terrible thunderstorm. My husband was working away at the time, and as I have always been very nervous of storms, I went downstairs, taking the baby with me, and my eldest daughter also came down with me. She could see how I was shaking with fright. Suddenly I felt a very slight pressure on my shoulders, and heard my Mother's voice say, "don't be afraid Winnie dear, nothing will harm you." I immediately stopped shaking, and felt quite calm, and my daughter noticed the change in me, and said, "What's happened, Mum, you don't look frightened any more" (Green & McCreery, 1989, p. 201).

Another popular ghost figure is the one who warns us of danger: There is a problem with the electrical system in the new house; the bridge is unsafe to cross, and so on. How should a person respond to episodes in which one seems to have been comforted or warned by a ghost? Most of the people who have related such experiences to me were not quite sure just what had happened. Was that really a ghost? Is there really such a thing as a ghost? They had no way of knowing for certain. On the other hand, though, it was nice to be comforted, and there was no harm in taking the warning seriously enough to check it out.

Another type of ghost is reported to seek us out when it is the one in danger. We will meet the *crisis apparition* when we visit prime time spiritism.

The Ghost Dance: A Peaceful Vision Becomes a Tragedy

Sometimes ghosts have become innocent bystanders in a tragedy for the living. Consider an example in which a belief in ghosts and survival contributed to one of the most shameful pages in U.S. history. By the 1880s life had changed radically for the Native American peoples. The whites were in control almost everywhere. Meanwhile, Jack Wilson, a Paiute orphan, was being raised by a white family. It was thought that he was the son of Tavibo, who had prophesied that the whites would literally be swallowed up by the earth, and all the dead Native Americans would then return to life as part of the great celebration.

Jack Wilson was chopping wood one day when he heard a great noise and fainted. He awakened with a spiritual vision. Wovoka (the new name he had taken) had been to heaven, met his mother and other deceased people, and conversed with God (Hittman, 1990). He now dedicated himself to teaching his people that they must not drink whiskey or fight. Instead, they must love one another and live in peace with the whites.

The Lakota Sioux (shown here in 1892) and other Native American tribes performed exhausting rituals to invoke their ancestors to rescue them from the invaders who had taken over their lands and threatened their survival.

Wovoka encouraged his followers to renew their traditional circle dance while singing religious songs. There was nothing warlike about this ceremony, but nervous settlers became disturbed by a ritual they did not understand. Eventually, a militant spirit did arise around some campfires (Mooney, 1996). The earlier prophecy about the destruction of the whites and the raising of the dead became associated with the new movement. Some of the tribes recently defeated in combat with the U.S. Army came to believe that the dead could protect them. The ghost dance was created in the depths of their desperation.

Fasting and dancing to the point of exhaustion brought the warriors into contact with the powerful spirits of the dead who were also longing for liberation. From these rituals came the idea of a sacred article of clothing that could protect them from the white man's bullets. They would be safe in their ghost shirts. Accordingly, they did not give much attention to defensive precaution, and were in no position to defend themselves when attacked in their encampment at Wounded Knee—an attack that was more slaughter than military operation. Belief in ghosts and their powers had contributed to the massacre, though the savagery of the attack upon women and children became the shame of the U.S. Army.

Deathbed Escorts: Safe Conduct to the Other World

Mythology and folklore provide many examples of a guide who escorts the living across the border to death. (If the guide is an angel or other spirit deity, it is sometimes referred to as a *psychopomp*.) The guide often resembles the "gentle comforter" personification of death that was discussed in Chapter 2. A famous example from the nineteenth century features a "gray lady" who appeared to dying patients in a London hospital. When a modern physician decided to examine this legend, he discovered that some dying patients still insisted that the gray lady visited them often and even filled their water jugs. The reports were always of a gray uniform, but the staff nurses actually wore blue. These patients had not known that gray was the color of the nurses' uniforms in the earlier

years of the hospital. For other examples, Sir William Barrett's interesting, if perhaps not entirely reliable, *Deathbed Visions* (1926/1986) might be consulted.

Karlis Osis and his colleagues (Osis, 1961; Osis & Haraldsson, 1977) collected observations from more than 2,000 physicians and nurses in India and the United States. What did they find?

1. Patients at times were observed interacting with a visitor that others could not see. These patients were clear of mind, not drugged, confused, or delusional.
2. The visitations usually came to people who were known to be dying, but there were also instances in which the escort appeared to a person who was not thought to be gravely ill—and that person did pass away soon afterward.
3. The visitations were not always welcome. Sometimes the escort had to convince the patient that the time was near.
4. The escorts were varied: a parent, an angel, a messenger of God.
5. On rare occasions, something happened that physicians or nurses could witness:

   There was a staircase leading to the second floor. Suddenly he exclaimed "See, the angels are coming down the stairs. The glass has fallen and broken." All of us in the room looked toward the staircase where a drinking glass had been placed on one of the steps. As we looked, we saw the glass break into a thousand pieces. It did not fall; it simply exploded. The angels, of course, we did not see. A happy and peaceful expression came over the patient's face and the next moment he expired. Even after his death the serene, peaceful expression remained on his face (p. 42).

The deathbed visions had similar features in the United States and India. The visions could be distinguished easily from ordinary hallucinations, and many experiencing them had received no sedation.

Do these reports provide evidence for survival? The data were retrospective, and therefore, memory dependent. It is possible that the visitors were wish-fulfilling fantasies, perhaps released by physiological changes such as decreased oxygen uptake in the brain. The escorts might have been created by the dying person's own unconscious and projected into the outer world, where it would then be experienced as "real." One part of the dying person's self might have communicated with another part through the hallucination.

I have witnessed perhaps a dozen incidents in which a person near death seemed to be interacting with a companion that we could not see, and I have been told of others, but most people near death do not show evidence of having such experiences. Perhaps deathbed escorts are highly selective in their visitations, or perhaps they reside exclusively in the mind of the dying person.

Reincarnation

The ancient belief in reincarnation has itself come back to life in recent years in Europe, Australia, and North America, having remained influential in Asia and Africa through the centuries. Although Hindu and Buddhist versions of the reincarnation doctrine are the most widely known, other religions have also featured this idea. Judeo-Christian religious authorities generally have opposed reincarnation beliefs, but with only partial success. The idea of living more than one life seems to thrive even when it does not fit well into a particular religious dogma. Many in the United States today who believe in reincarnation were raised in the Christian tradition. The popularity of this belief was stimulated by so-called past life regressions (as with Bridey Murphy) and by heightened interest in survival of death as near-death experience reports made the rounds.

Believers in reincarnation have more than one interpretation of precisely what happens after physical death (Dillon, 2003). Some think the soul is born (or reborn) until its desires draw it toward the next incarnation. Others view the state between death and rebirth as a deep, restful sleep. A striking feature of most reincarnation beliefs is that the state of consciousness at the moment of death persists into the next station of the journey.

Is there evidence for reincarnation that would be persuasive to people who are not easy to persuade? One researcher stands out for his many years of careful investigation. Ian Stevenson's *Twenty Cases Suggestive of Reincarnation* (1974) did much to establish the credibility of reincarnation research and was followed by many subsequent contributions. His detailed case histories are models of their kind.

A typical case "suggestive of reincarnation" starts early in childhood, usually between ages 2 and 4:

> The child often begins talking about this previous life as soon as he gains any ability to speak, and sometimes before his capacity for verbal expression matches his need to communicate. Some children make only three or four different statements about a previous life, but others may be credited with 60 or 70 separate items pertaining to different details in the life remembered. . . . In most cases the volume and clarity of the child's statements increase until at the age of between five and six he usually starts to forget the memories. Or he talks about them less. Unexpected behavior . . . nearly always accompanies the statements the child makes about the previous life he claims to remember. . . . This behavior is unusual for a child of the subject's family, but concordant with what he says concerning the previous life, and in most instances it is found to correspond with what other informants say concerning the behavior of the deceased person about whom the subject has been talking, if such a person is traced (p. 324).

I asked Stevenson about the difficulties involved in his research (Kastenbaum, 1993b).

> The effort to exclude the normal transmission of information exists even in cases in which the two families are completely unknown to each other and perhaps live many miles apart. I have often had to content myself with saying that normal communication was improbable; only rarely can I say it was impossible (p. 169).

Stevenson investigated cases from Burma, India, Sri Lanka, Turkey, Lebanon, and in Native Americans. Smaller sets of cases have come from Brazil, Nigeria, Finland, Thailand, the United Kingdom, and the United States. Cases come to attention more readily in cultures that favor belief in reincarnation. Whether belief somehow generates the experiences or whether the experiences simply are easier to share within a sympathetic cultural milieu is difficult to determine. The specific elements in each case would have to be explained in any event.

Stevenson (1997a) crowned his long research career with a mammoth collection of case studies that are accompanied by medical records and photographs bearing on the validity of children's statements about a past life. He selected cases that had all the following characteristics:

1. The child described the way he or she died in a past life.
2. The child had a birthmark or birth defect that is consistent with that form of death (e.g., two bullet wounds in the chest or a knife wound on the neck).
3. A deceased person whose life and death matches the past life story given by the child is identified.
4. Medical records documenting the specific cause of death and condition of the body are obtained.
5. There is a very close match between the fatal wounds suffered by the deceased person and the marks or defects found on the child at birth.

Stevenson offers these physical evidence matches as the best evidence available that is "suggestive of reincarnation." Readers who wish to examine these cases in depth can consult his *Reincarnation and Biology* (1997a), a two-volume set of more than 2,000 pages with many photographs. Stevenson presents a summary and discussion of these findings in *Where Reincarnation and Biology* intersect (1997b). (The response from the bioscience establishment? Silence.)

Stevenson's cases raise two questions that are worth mentioning here. First, why were so many of the reported past lives ended by sudden and violent death? The number of murders and other violent deaths in Stevenson's sample goes well beyond expectations. Secondly, how could anybody be reincarnated unless everybody is reincarnated? What do you think?

There is an even more radical possibility I cannot resist sharing with you: Perhaps death is not the same for everybody. The possibility of *pluralistic death* would challenge our basic assumptions about the nature of life and the universe. There is survival of death, or there is not survival—or so it is generally believed. Either of these alternatives seems more rational than the possibility that death might be different at different times to different people in different situations. Nevertheless, as I have suggested elsewhere, this bizarre-seeming idea appears consistent with some basic precepts of the philosophy of science (Kastenbaum, 1993). The idea that death might be relative to life and its variable context opens the possibility that there might be both survival and nonsurvival!

WHEN SPIRITISM WAS IN FLOWER

Would you like to be part of history? The year is 1848. With other neighbors in this upstate New York village, we crowd into the home of the Fox family. Young daughters Margaret and Katie put on a show for us. They ask questions of an invisible spirit who replies with knocks ("yes") or silence ("no"). The raps seem to come from deep within the walls. We learn that Mr. Splitfoot (as the girls have named him) was murdered and his killer never brought to justice. Hot stuff on a chilly evening long before radio, television, and the Internet were available to entertain us!

We want more. So do thousands—make that millions—of people across the nation, and then across the Atlantic. Spirit communication becomes an international fascination. The Fox sisters are now celebrities, but cannot begin to meet the demand. We then do what so many others are doing. We gather around a table and invite spirits of the departed to satisfy our curiosity about "life" on the other side of death. Sometimes it seems to work, often it doesn't, but maybe next time. New methods are devised. Everybody hold hands. No, everybody place your hands on the table; it will tip when a spirit visits. Even better: use a planchette, a pencil held by a heart-shaped piece of wood on small wheels. Spirit energy will guide the pencil to write notes from the beyond. Wait—forget the planchette. We can buy a Ouija board from Sears.

But why, exactly, are we doing this? For some people it is cheap entertainment, a social occasion, and the thrill of playing at the fringes of mystery. For others though, it is a serious, even a desperate enterprise. There are grieving widows who need a word of comfort, sons and daughters who long to be forgiven, and people of deep religious sensitivity tormented by doubts about survival of death. Enough people are hopeful enough to keep spirit communication flourishing, skeptics notwithstanding. Nevertheless, there is a limit to what we can learn from yes/no responses. We have not yet discovered much about the lives of the dead or what secrets they might impart to us.

Four developments soon are transforming our innocent efforts to contact family members and friends on the other side of the grave:

- The Civil War claims more than 600,000 lives—equivalent to 6,000,000 in today's United States population. Grief is widespread and profound. These mostly young men had not been expected to die young, brutally, and far from home. The emotional need for comfort and closure is intense. Raging epidemics (e.g., cholera and typhoid) fill graveyards throughout much of the world, adding every day to the ranks of the anguished bereaved.

- We are now seeking out those who seem especially gifted in spirit communication, instead of relying on our own feeble power. We call these people *mediums* (a later generation would be renamed *channelers*). Control of the situation shifts to the medium, away from the participants. There is a marvelous upside to this professionalization: obliging spirits can visit with a trance-state medium who then passes the message along in her own or the spirit's voice. The *séance* (literally, *sitting*) in a darkened room is now a favored setting for a session with the spirits. The elite of society as well as the most humble members are devoted to the séance. Among other things, this means there is money to be made.

- Deceit, fraud, and greed invade and conquer. Bogus mediums seize the opportunity to cadge money from emotionally needy seekers of spirit communication. They conduct rigged séances, and introduce other devices and techniques to convey messages from the beyond. For example, a blank slate is mysteriously written upon by a spirit hand, or one actually sees a ghostly shape flit across the dimly lit room. These procedures are routinely exposed as fakery by sharp-eyed investigators. Nevertheless, spirit communication continues to flourish with the public and provide easy money for its practitioners. There is a radical disconnect between a bereaved person's sincere impulse to have a sense of contact with the lost loved one, and the cynical fraud perpetuated on them by bogus mediums who soon dominated the field.

- The dubious proceedings in dimly-lit séance rooms are now becoming matters of concern for two powerful societal forces: church and science. The religious establishment was at first distressed by public fascination with spirit communication. This practice is not countenanced by church dogma. It is, at the least, a distraction and, potentially, a threat to the influence of the religious establishment. The perceived threat becomes more formidable and urgent in 1859 when Charles Darwin finally gets around to publishing *On the Origin of Species*. Darwin himself is not motivated to contest church teachings; he has simply followed his abundant data where they lead. Nevertheless, the war is on. Science and its technological advances have already made significant inroads on religious explanations of how the world works. Many individuals do merge scientific acumen with religious faith. Extremists on both sides, however, are choosing Darwin's thesis as the prime battleground to determine whether religion or science should hold sway.

And so we come down to this question: are humans no more than animals who perish as do all mortal creatures, or are we favored by God with an immortal soul? Proof of survival would be proof of God and a redeeming after-world. Fail to prove survival, and who are we then, really, and with what prospects? Now begins a long, bitter, and complex struggle in which hard-nosed scientists will not admit that the survival question even deserves to be studied, while equally resolute religionists try to hold their ground without seeking too much support from fraud-ridden spiritism.

The ouiji ("yes/no") board was one of the devices employed to contact the dead when Spiritism swept much of the world. The most celebrated Séances, however, were those in which a medium gave the impression of channeling or visually producing the departed soul.

A Frustrating Quest

A small number of exceptionally able scholars attempted to study the survival question with open-minds. Deborah Blum's *Ghost Hunters* (2006) offers a masterful account of this unique enterprise and its participants. Societies for the study of psychical research were established first in England, then in the United States and other nations. Much of their limited resources were expended on the investigation of mediums. A few of their investigators (including world-class scientists) were fooled a few times, but generally they excelled in exposing the cheats. It was satisfying to establish the credibility of their project in this way, but also discouraging. Occasional medium sessions produced such remarkable results that the investigator was left shaken. "How

could she have known these obscure details of my childhood, and that secret concern I have been carrying all these years? Perhaps she *is* in contact with my father." Some of these apparent revelations might be explained by a theory was itself controversial but not as far-out as communication with the dead: the medium might have picked up the information from the mind of another living person. Yet even this explanation did not apply consistently. All in all, there was little to show for this line of inquiry. By no reasonable standard of evidence could mediums be said to have demonstrated proof of survival.

What, then, about "spirit photography"? These productions were also quickly discredited by professional photographers who demonstrated how easy it was to concoct pictures of deceased people and disembodied forms. Seeing was not necessarily believing after all.

The investigators sought other lines of inquiry such as *automatic writing*. This phenomenon occurred in a dissociative state of consciousness. The individual (almost always a woman) would not be aware of what she was writing, or, often, that she was writing at all. This technique soon was appropriated by bogus mediums, but was also practiced under control conditions by respectable personages. Again, there were episodes that suggested the participation of a deceased spirit and, again, much caution was needed to drawing that conclusion as a certainty. Eventually, automatic writing would morph into the most intricate of investigative techniques. F. W. H. Myers (1903/1975) had come as close as anybody to making sense of previous findings in his monumental two-volume work, *Human Personality and Its Survival of Bodily Death*. Did Myers invent a new method of inquiry after his own death? Some people think so. Messages started coming through to several people who did not know each other. When compared, the enigmatic—almost teasing—messages made excellent sense and were anchored in obscure literary passages well known to Myers but to few others. These *cross-correspondences* continued for several years, and included other deceased contributors. Was this all an elaborate hoax? A construction of pattern and meaning from random bits and pieces? Or was Myers actually proving survival of death by his own efforts from the other side? Material of this kind satisfied some people and drew ridicule from others. Today, few people if any have the motivation and patience to work their way through these controversial materials and the context in which they occurred.

Why not turn to the public for evidence? Did ordinary people have any experiences that are at least strongly suggestive of survival? Two surveys were conducted. The researchers culled through thousands of responses and conducted follow-ups on the most promising cases. The findings are vulnerable to critical analysis. The researchers themselves did not claim they had proven survival, but hoped they had provided enough material to encourage others to develop more refined scientific methods to study the

problem. The scientific establishment, though, still considered the subject to be undeserving of its attention and heaped scorn upon those who did take up the quest.

Is there anything in these nearly forgotten reports that might still deserve attention? The *crisis apparition* might be the best candidate. In the midst of daily life, a person unexpectedly sees somebody known to them who shouldn't be there. There is also something curious about how the person looks or is behaving. The encounter is fleeting, odd, just one of those things. Later it is learned that the person whose image was perceived had at that moment died in another part of the world and often in a manner consistent with the fleeting image. To the untrained mind, this would seem to be an inexplicable but authentic happening: a friend communicating the last moment of his or her life. What of the trained mind? The scholars who analyzed and investigated the most impressive of these reports could not draw a firm conclusion either. Where there is no clear answer, one should choose the least radical working hypothesis. The simplest alternative would be that these reports were made up or distorted—unreliable. Skeptics can certainly insist on this explanation, but that becomes increasingly difficult if one follows the investigation closely. The most radical conclusion would be that crisis apparitions demonstrate survival of death. This would be going beyond the reports , however, which described what seemed to be the apparition of a living person at the near edge of death.

The implicit conclusion after years of energetic, resourceful, and frustrating inquiry was that "There might be something there, some partial hints of authentic survival among the many deceits and disappointments encountered. But we do not have adequate evidence to meet scientific criteria or persuade educated and resolute minds."

Every now and then claims are brought forward that spirit communication has been proven through the reported experiences of a channeler. Most famous in recent times is the story of Bridey Murphy. Under hypnosis, Ruth Simmons, a twentieth-century American woman, recounted her experiences as "Bridey Murphy," who was said to have been born in Ireland in 1768 and to have died there in 1864. The book reporting this account (Bernstein, 1965) became a best seller and stimulated interest in so-called past life regression. Unfortunately, the story was later found to be a compendium of experiences Simmons had in her own everyday life, but which had emerged during the hypnotic sessions as hidden memories. Authentic-sounding memories of Ireland had slipped into her mind from a childhood visit to the World's Fair in St. Louis, where an Irish village had been recreated. There have been other reports of past lives since Bridey Murphy came and went, and the same doubts and limitations remain. "My past life" seems to function as an enabling metaphor that opens the door to memory fragments and fantasies that come together as though reports of an actual set of meaningful experiences.

The elite quest for scientific proof of survival faded away with the generation of scholars who had devoted themselves to this project. The whole enterprise had been stained somewhat by its own success in discrediting bogus mediums. Perhaps the investigators shouldn't be taken seriously either. A more fundamental was—and continues to be—the lack of a plausible explanation for findings that hint at survival. This issue has arisen repeatedly in the history of science. Those who believe that it is possible to discover adequate evidence and come up with a solid explanation for survival of death can take comfort in the fact that science has already surprised itself on many occasions. Those who hold that survival has already received adequate scientific evidence and explanation will not have an easy time of making their case.

An Apple on a String

This exploration of prime time spiritism started with the Fox sisters in 1848. Let's fast forward to October 21, 1888. Our scene is the glittering Academy of Music, one of the largest auditoriums in New York City, and on this evening it is crowded to capacity. The attraction is Margaret Fox Kane. She is hardly less the celebrity 40 years after introducing the world to Mr. Splitfoot, though seldom seen in public. The gist of her message (Kane, 1888/1987) as recorded by a newspaper reporter:

> I was the first in the field and I have the right to expose it. My sister Kate and I were very young children when this horrible deception began. . . . We were very mischievous children and wanted to terrify our dear mother, who was a good woman and easily frightened. At night, when we went to bed, we used to tie an apple to a string and move the string up and down, causing the apple to bump on the floor . . . Mother listened to this for a time. She could not understand it and did not suspect us of being capable of a trick because we were so young (p. 226).

The girls refined their art when neighbors came by and apple-dropping no longer would do the job. They then made the "wonderful discovery" that they could produce resounding raps by snapping their toes and fingers, a skill they possessed to an astounding degree. From that point on, the girls were trapped in their own success: enjoying the attention, but shamed by their deception and fearful of admitting it. The now-elderly Margaret offered more details on production of the raps, and she even took off her shoes and strolled down the aisle, rapping as loudly as a wall full of Mr. Splitfoots. To make matters perfectly clear, she stated that she had never believed in spirits and the like: it was all childish fun that had gotten out of hand.

And the audience response to these revelations? Almost all those present continued to believe in Mr. Splitfoot and other spirit manifestations despite Margaret's disavowal and dramatic demonstration. Why spoil an appealing belief just because the facts are against it?

There is a postscript, the very sort of uncomfortable incident that has kept many critical psychic investigators from closing the book completely. It is now ten years after both Fox sisters have died. Children are playing the cellar of the abandoned house where the spirit fraud introduced itself to the world. All right, you know what they found, don't you? The skeleton and tin cup of a murdered peddler whose body had finally been exposed behind a crumbling wall (Blum, 2006).

NEAR-DEATH EXPERIENCES: EVIDENCE FOR SURVIVAL?

The survival question had been in the doldrums for a while, but snapped back to renewed attention with the publication of *Life After Life* in 1975. Raymond A. Moody, Jr. listened to the experiences of people who had recovered after coming close to death, then added his own thoughts. Many additional near death experience reports (NDERs) soon came forth from people that had been reluctant to share them until Moody's book brought the phenomenon into the open.

Here is a typical case from Moody's collection:

> I was hospitalized for a severe kidney condition, and I was in a coma for approximately a week. . . . During this period when I was unconscious, I felt as though I were lifted right up, just as though I didn't have a physical body at all. A brilliant white light appeared to me. The light was so bright that I could not see through it, but going into its presence was so calming and so wonderful. There is just no experience on earth like it. In the presence of the light, the thoughts or words came into my mind: "Do you want to die?" And I replied that I didn't know since I knew nothing about death. Then the white light said, "Come over this line and you will learn." I felt that I knew where the line was in front of me, although I could not actually see it. As I went across the line, the most wonderful feelings came over me—feelings of peace, tranquility, a vanishing of all worries" (p. 56).

This report illustrates major features of the primary near-death experience (NDE). Instead of panic or despair, there is a sense of serenity and well-being. The sensation of being "lifted right up" is also one of the most striking characteristics. Known popularly as the "out-of-body experience," it is also known as the *autoscopic* experience. There is frequently a sense of journey, a going toward something. A "brilliant white light" may be discovered as the journey continues. There might also be a turning-point encounter that guides the person back to life.

The big question now arose: Does the NDER constitute proof for survival of death? Moody later stated that neither NDERs "or any sort of conventionally established methodological procedures will be able to get evidence of life after death" (Kastenbaum, 1995a, p. 95). Moody's disavowal of NDEs as proof of survival, however, did not discourage others from drawing this conclusion.

Evidence Favoring the NDE as Proof of Survival

The experience seems to have a powerful effect on many survivors, as Ring (1980, 1992) and subsequent researchers have found. Survivors of a close brush with death often have a renewed sense of purpose in life. Daily life also becomes more precious. Many survivors report that they have become less concerned about dying and death; there was something very comforting and reassuring about their close encounter. Some respondents were convinced they had been dead; therefore, their recovery proved the existence of an afterlife. These personal reports were convincing to the experiencers and to many of the people who learned of them. However, scientists and more cautious members of the public required evidence more convincing than subjective report of an altered state of consciousness.

Biomedical Attempts to Verify NDE Phenomena

Cardiologist Michael B. Sabom (1982) and his colleagues wondered if a person could make accurate observations while trapped within a horizontal, impaired, and endangered body. Sabom found that six survivors recalled details of their experiences during life-threatening episodes in surgery (from a larger set of patients, most of whom did not recall details). Each reported one or more events that could not have been obtained through guesswork or prior knowledge of cardiopulmonary resuscitation. This finding suggested that some individuals had acquired information consistent with an out-of-the-body state.

Sabom did not claim that his findings proved survival of death. Instead, he suggested that the autoscopic phenomenon could be authentic. Perhaps during this altered state a person can make accurate observations of immediate

A woman's spirit floats over her body in this visualization of an out-of-the-body experience.

reality, as well as enter into the mystical state of being often reported for NDEs. He also came up with an interesting finding that has been mostly confirmed by later studies: NDERs had no demonstrable relationship to age, gender, socioeconomic status, or the cause of the crisis (e.g., cardiac arrest, motor vehicle accident).

Sabom's first study had relied upon retrospective accounts. It would be more useful to observe a patient who was "clinically dead" (the terminology in use at the time). A woman was placed in a state of minimal functioning in preparation for brain surgery. The electrical activity of her brain was suspended, accompanied by intentional cardiac arrest, and reduction of body temperature. Upon recovering, she claimed to have been highly alert and was able to make accurate reports of things she had seen and heard (Sabom, 1998).

This was certainly an impressive experience, suggesting that there is much more to learn about the potentials of the mind and its relationship to physical conditions. But does it prove survival after death? The patient's recollections were tested against actual events that occurred in the operating room. However, there is no such direct way to test a person's account of having met a spiritual being of light, and the other subjective phenomena included in NDERs. Furthermore, the patient had an intact body to host and support her recovery. This is a luxury not available to people who have been dead and buried or cremated. Sabom did quality research in difficult situations and has given us useful information to build upon. Nevertheless, it would be a long stretch to conclude that the results have proved survival, as Sabom himself has noted.

A team of cardiologists in the Netherlands have also made a determined effort. They identified 344 consecutive patients who had been resuscitated after cardiac arrest. All these patients had lost consciousness because of insufficient blood supply and/or circulation within the brain. The patients were interviewed shortly after their resuscitation, and those who were still alive and willing to participate were interviewed again 2 years and 8 years later. Pim von Lommel and his colleagues (2001) found that NDERs were uncommon (18%).

> Furthermore, seriousness of the crisis was not related to occurrence or depth of the experience. If purely physiological factors resulting from cerebral anoxia caused NDE, most of our patients should have had this experience. Patients' medication was also unrelated to frequency of NDE. Psychological factors are unlikely to be important as fear was not associated with NDE (p. 2043).

The NDEs they did find were similar to those reported by Moody, Ring, and other researchers. They also came up with additional support for previous findings that people often feel their attitude toward life has been positively transformed by their NDE. There was also an interesting new finding made possible by the repeated interviews: Positive changes such as becoming more intuitive and having no fear of death actually became more evident years after the event. The authors suggest that the profound impact of the NDE might take years to become fully integrated in the individual's personality.

A similar study is reported by British researchers Sam Parnia and Peter Fenwick (2001, p. 10). They also found that "memories are rare after resuscitation from cardiac arrest." The relatively few memories (11% of the sample) did have some features of an NDE and were usually pleasant. There was a hint in the findings that NDEs were more common among patients who had more oxygenation and therefore better brain function during the resuscitation. These researchers tried to determine if the patients with NDEs had seen events from an out-of-body floating perspective, but, as in the Netherlands study, there were insufficient data to draw a conclusion.

There are many reports of NDEs in circulation, but investigators have found very few cases in their prospective studies—which themselves are rather few. Do NDEs conceal themselves under biomedical investigation, but then transform themselves into vivid memories? There is abundant room for speculation here.

Eliminating Other Explanations

Skeptics soon developed alternative hypotheses to explain or explain away NDERs. Glen Gabbard and Stuart Twemlow (1984) dismissed several of these alternatives by noting that:

1. NDEs are not caused by nor are they necessarily symptoms of mental illness.
2. NDEs are not related to level of education.
3. There is no evidence that NDEs occur mostly among people who previously had been fascinated by mystic or other unusual phenomena.
4. The NDE does not have much similarity to dreams. It is a different kind of mental state.

These findings suggest that NDEs cannot be easily explained away as a dream state or as a function of education or mental illness. However, there are other alternative hypotheses still to consider, as well as some problems with the data and logic of the survival interpretation.

The Case Against the NDE as Proof of Survival

There are logical as well as empirical objections to interpreting NDEs as evidence for survival:

1. Many people who return from a close encounter with death recall nothing at all or only vague and dreamlike fragments.
2. Some survivors return with nightmarish experiences. Atwater (1992) reports that these cases are more frequent than previously thought, and can be compared with visions of hell. I have collected both positive and negative reports myself (see Box 13-2).
3. NDEs occur sometimes in situations in which the individual is not in physical peril. For example, the out-of-the-body component of the NDE has also been reported frequently

> **BOX 13-2   SOME FRIGHTENING NEAR-DEATH***

- There were so many pews on each side, and each pew was filled with people wearing black robes with hoods. I couldn't see their faces but if I turned my eyes I could see the inside of the hoods were lined with red. . . . I stood there wondering where I was and what I was doing there, when a door opened to the right of the altar and out came the devil. . . . I saw that what he was pouring from the jug was fire, and I screamed, dropped the goblet, and started to run . . . (Irwin & Bramwell, 1988, p. 42).

- I was thrilled to meet this person—or was it an angel—and then all at once I saw that she or it was truly horrible. Where the eyes were supposed to be were slits, and kind of blue-green flames flickered through them, through the eye places. I can still see this demon, this whatever-it-was. With my eyes wide open, I can still see it.

- She told me to go back. I didn't want to. I said I was so happy being where I was, not that I knew where I was. I thought she was being mean to make me go back into that bloody wrecked body. I could feel myself shaking and crying. I didn't feel good any more.

* Told to the author by survivors of motor vehicle accidents, except where indicated otherwise.

in parapsychological experiments in which there is no life-threatening situation. Gabbard and Twemlow (1991) conclude that "the state of mind of the near-death subject is far more important than the state of the body" (p. 46). NDEs may be triggered by the belief that one is close to death or some other impending catastrophe.

4. Medical records reveal that many people who report NDEs actually had not come close to death. Only about half of the NDE reporters had survived a life-threatening illness or injury. Nevertheless, some patients had decided for themselves that they had been "dead" or "clinically dead." Others misinterpreted what they had been told by doctors or nurses. The researchers comment that "having had the NDE itself may have led some people to believe retrospectively that their condition must have been worse than it otherwise seemed" (Stevenson, Cook, & McClean-Rice, 1989/1990, p. 52).

5. People who had been in severe pain were more likely than others to experience a sense of distance from their bodies. Gabbard and Twemlow (1984) note that in hypnotic pain experiments, it is a common suggestion to dissociate the painful part from the body so that it is treated as "not self." Furthermore, patients who had been under anesthesia were especially likely to see brilliant lights and hear unusual sounds. These effects occur with many people who have been anesthetized, whether or not their conditions were life threatening.

6. We hear NDERs only from the survivors. There is no evidence that what happens when a person really dies "and stays dead" has any relationship to the experiences reported by those who have recovered from a life-threatening episode. There is always an observing self that categorizes the observed self as inert or dead. This split consciousness may result in the opinion that "I was dead," but there was always another "I" lively and perceptive enough to make that judgment.

Mystical, Depersonalization, and Hyperalertness Responses to Crisis

What else do people experience in crisis situations? Psychiatrist Russell Noyes, Jr. and his colleagues interviewed people who survived a variety of life-threatening crises. Three dimensions were often found: mysticism, depersonalization, and hyperalertness.

The mystical dimension of experiences close to death includes the feeling of great understanding, sharp and vivid images, revival of memories, the sense of harmony, unity, joy, and revelation. There may also be visions and strange bodily sensations. The *depersonalization* dimension includes loss of emotion, the sense of the self being detached both from the body and the world, an altered sense of time, objects appearing small and far away, strange sounds, and the body having been altered in some weird way. The *hyperalertness* dimension includes the feeling that vision and hearing have become sharper, and thoughts either more vivid or more dull and speeded up or blurred. One has an overall feeling of being mechanical in both thoughts and movements.

Hyperalertness and depersonalization help us through dangerous circumstances. Hyperalertness sharpens our ability to detect dangers and routes of escape. Depersonalization dampens the excessive emotionality that could disorganize us. We deal with a crisis more resourcefully when hyperalertness and depersonalization set us up in a cool, calm, and objective response mode. Noyes (1979) further suggests that depersonalization is a specific defense against the threat of death. The people he interviewed had been calm in frightening situations:

> but they also felt detached from what was happening. . . . *The depersonalized state is one that mimics death* [italics added]. In it a person experiences himself as empty, lifeless, and unfamiliar. In a sense he escapes death, for what has already happened cannot happen again; he cannot die, because he is already dead (p. 79).

When Do People *Not* Have NDEs? An Alternative Explanation

Ask the other side of the question—when do people in a crisis *not* have NDEs—and we discover something interesting (Kastenbaum, 1995b). First, we might expect that those who are in the most perilous physical condition should be the most likely to have intense NDEs. The available evidence, however, finds just the opposite (Parnia et al., 2001). This weakens the assumed connection between the NDE and death. It also highlights a somewhat neglected question: Precisely when does the NDE occur? Perhaps the NDE is a memory created on the way back. It is not necessarily what the person experiences at the peak of the crisis but rather an attempt to make sense of the profound, yet confusing events. The NDER, then, can be regarded as a narrative created in the aftermath of extraordinary stress, rather than a video clip of the event as it occurred (Kastenbaum, 1996).

Consider now the individual's role in the crisis situation. A driver faced with an impending collision is much more likely to make an emergency maneuver than to split off into an autoscopic experience. We engage in instrumental actions—we do something—when the circumstances permit. This is a survival mechanism: action to avoid catastrophe. I have learned from conversations with crisis survivors that the NDE is much more likely to occur when the jeopardized person had no instrumental action available. In a situation of perceived helplessness, the NDE serves a quieting, energy-conserving function. The resulting sense of serenity implies the activation of self-produced brain opiates (*endorphins*). This altered state enables body functions to continue with minimum expenditure of energy and is represented at the psychic level by comforting imagery. The imagery becomes more coherent as the individual recovers, although in retrospect it is attributed to an earlier phase of the crisis. If we can do something in a crisis situation—we do it (or at least make the effort). If there is nothing we can do to escape the danger physically, we do so by switching to a transcending state of being, with major assistance from our neural and spiritual imaging resources.

NDEs as Exercises in Religious Imagination?

Perhaps you have noticed similarities between religious conceptions of the journey of the dead and contemporary NDERs. Others would agree with you.

In *Otherworld Journeys* (1987), Carol Zaleski offers the following example:

Four days ago, I died and was taken by two angels to the height of heaven. And it was just as though I rose above not only this squalid earth, but even the sun and moon, the clouds and stars. Then I went through a gate that was brighter than normal daylight, into a place where the entire floor shone like gold and silver. The light was indescribable, and I can't tell you how vast it was (p. 58).

Salvius had been left for dead one evening on a funeral bier. He was said to have revived and, inspired by his vision, became a bishop. Zaleski concludes that there is "a fundamental kinship" between these visions (or NDEs) and the imaginative powers that we use in everyday life:

We are all, in a sense, otherworld travelers. Otherworld visions are products of the same imaginative power that is active in our ordinary ways of visualizing death; our tendency to portray ideas in concrete, embodied, and dramatic forms; the capacity of our inner states to transfigure our perception of outer landscapes; our need to internalize the cultural map of the physical universe, and our drive to experience that universe as a moral and spiritual cosmos in which we belong and have a purpose. . . . Near-death testimony is one way in which the religious imagination mediates the search for ultimate truth (p. 205).

A reading of *The Tibetan Book of the Dead* (Evans-Wentz, 2000) would provide us with further examples.

The G-LOC Problem

Still another possible explanation remains in the wind. There is a heightened interest in brain function near the end of life that could contribute to our understanding of NDEs (Parnia & Fenwick, 2002, and Chapter 3). Altered states of consciousness have also engaged the attention of many medical and psychological researchers. For example, Whinnery (1997) calls attention to the loss of consciousness that

occurs with acceleration during fighter aircraft operation (or ground-based centrifuge simulation). The *G-LOC* problem, as it is known, continues to present a challenge to fighter aviation medicine. Pilots who black out under acceleration stress are in danger for their lives. Whinnery concludes that:

The major characteristics of G-LOC experiences that are shared in common with NDEs include tunnel vision and bright lights, floating sensations, automatic movement, autoscopy, out-of-body experiences, not wanting to be disturbed, paralysis, vivid dreamlets of beautiful places, pleasurable sensations, psychological alterations of euphoria and dissociation, inclusion of friends and family, inclusion of prior memories and thoughts, the experience being very memorable (when it can be remembered), confabulation, and a strong urge to understand the experience (p. 245).

Clearly, there is much in common between typical NDE reports and the reports given by pilots who have undergone G-LOC. These similarities do not prove anything, but certainly encourage further exploration of experiential states and the physiological conditions that influence them so strongly.

What Has Been Learned from NDERs?

The NDE clearly is of interest as a remarkable human experience. But do such reports provide evidence for survival of death? One fact, at least, has become clear. Research into this question, never especially abundant and vigorous, has become nearly extinct. There has been no shortage of NDERs, nor of speculation. For whatever reasons, though, there have been precious few reports of studies directed specifically to the NDE-as-evidence-for-afterlife question. Believers continue to believe; scientists have found other things to do. *The Journal of Near Death Studies*, starved for significant new material, sadly folded its wings. But life—and perhaps death—is full of surprises, so perhaps NDERs will come our way again with something compelling to offer.

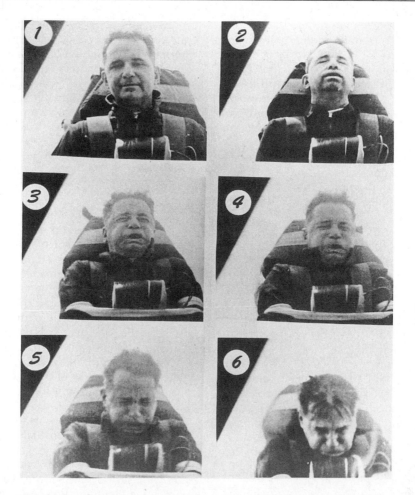

G-LOC is a physical and mental phenomenon that occurs under the acceleration stress that is being experienced here by a pilot in a centrifugal chamber. It has been suggested that near-death reports have much in common with this experience.

SHOULD WE SURVIVE DEATH?

Should we survive death? This is a question that perhaps should be asked more often. Let's begin with responses from college students to item 3 ("I think of Heaven as") in the self-quiz earlier in this chapter.

- "I really can't answer that question. That's funny, isn't it? Here I am, a good Christian

and I believe in heaven and all that, but I can't get what it's all about clear in my mind. I think my problem is in the idea of a literal heaven, a Sunday school fairytale. I can't really accept that any more, but I don't have anything to replace it."

- "You tell me! I imagine eternity as a state of perfection. No more worries, no more problems. Best of all, no more deadlines and exams! But then what? All I can imagine is God and all the rest of us posing forever for our portrait with this transcendental smile on our faces. I'd go crazy! I need to worry and rush around or I'm not really myself. It will be beautiful and peaceful. More beautiful and peaceful than anything we can know on earth. Maybe the closest would be a long and relaxed Sunday afternoon. What makes a Sunday afternoon so great, though, is that it comes after one hectic week and before another. I don't know how I would do if there was only Sunday afternoon. This is probably a dumb way to think about heaven, but it's the best I can do."

These respondents were hesitant about survival of death because the "what do we do after we get there?" image was unclear. Perhaps there is more appeal in the type of afterlife that has been envisioned by many tribal peoples: It was much like the familiar here-and-now life, with such understandable activities as hunting, fishing, preparing and enjoying feasts, outsmarting adversaries, demonstrating valor, and so forth. Such conceptions of the afterlife involve not only continuing activity but also change, risk, and danger. Intellectuals and mystics might be capable of envisioning a Christian afterlife that is neither literal nor dull. Other believers, however, are uncomfortable with a heaven that seems just too heavenly and therefore remote from their own lives and thoughts.

A more radical orientation can also be taken toward the desirability of survival. There are two main components here: (1) we do not deserve survival, and (2) the prospect of survival encourages the worst side of human nature.

The first component would be supported by all the cruelty, stupidity, greed, and pettiness that can be found in the lives of individuals and societies through the centuries. Make your own list. How many examples of genocide will you include? How many examples of fortunes being made by inflicting suffering on others? How many corporate executives deceiving the public and exploiting their own employees' retirement funds? How many examples of wanton destruction, royal whim, or bureaucratic arrogance? Perhaps *Homo sapiens* have not earned the right for survival beyond the grave. We might also

count against ourselves the ways in which we often waste time and, therefore, life. Should eternal life be granted to those who snooze or booze through earthly life? If our discretionary time is merely filled or killed, what claim dare we make on immortality?

The second argument also places the human race in a harsh light. The prospect of eternal life has been used repeatedly in the service of power, greed, and raging fanaticism. Again, we cannot help but think about the September 11, 2001, terrorists who believed that they were earning admission to paradise (a dubious assumption according to scholarly interpretations of the Qur'an). The promise of immortal blessing for those who die while slaughtering designated enemies has contributed to some of history's most ferocious episodes of violence. The moral case against survival, then, is that we might be forced to become better people and learn to make more constructive use of our time on Earth if we did not have the prospect of an afterlife as either an all-dominating or fail-safe goal.

Eastern thought and practice adds still other dimensions. The way of the Buddha, for example, differs greatly from Christian conceptions of life, death, and afterlife (Bonney, 2002). "Death," in effect, disappears for those who can attain a heightened spiritual development in which birth and beginnings, cravings and ambitions all dissolve. The character of the Buddhist survival doctrine is also distinctive in its implications for individual and social action. Militant violence against others, for example, does not flow readily from this tradition.

BUT WHAT KIND OF SURVIVAL?

Suppose that there is survival after death. Suppose, further, we are in a roomful of people who agree with this statement—but in their own ways. Here is what they might tell us:

• "Survival? Yes—as a burst of pure energy at the last moment of life. There is a discharge of electromagnetic radiation (or something like that). Does this death encode and preserve the individual's identity? Perhaps, perhaps not. It's not out the realm of possibility that this burst of electromagnetic radiation could be documented. This might be a long way from immortality, but a burst of glory—isn't that something?"

- "Have you seen a ghost? Most apparitions seem rather lost and slow-witted, not like the real people they once were, more like shadows or representations. What sometimes happens after death is that a temporary trace of the person remains in the locale. This 'person-shaped force field' is real but transient. It is not the survived person, merely his or her energy traces, and these will soon fade. Like the death flash, the ghost is a kind of survival, but not much to write home about."

- "Fading, yes, but not in the way that you have proposed. When people die they move from the realm of light to darkness. There is sad survival here, a slow fading away to poor, lost, blank characterless souls in a cosmic nightmare. The Greeks called them shades, and were none too happy about it."

- "These quaint ideas miss the real point. There is true immortality—but not for everybody. Like much else in life, survival of death is conditional. What is it conditional on? This surpasses our understanding at present—but some wise people have believed that those who develop great spiritual strength will not perish along with their bodies. The soul is not endowed with immortality: That has to be earned. Perhaps the rest of us are recycled as buttons, as Ibsen's Peer Gynt was informed after a life of self-seeking escapades."

- "Survival? How can you avoid it? We are born but to die, and die but to be reborn. Not only those of us who are at the moment human beings, but all living things (and perhaps 'inanimate' things as well) go through cycles of existence. There are many beginnings and ends: but, for most of us, no Beginning and no End."

- "We live. We die. We are judged. We are damned, or we are granted salvation. The righteous dwell forever with the Lord; those who live in ignorance or defiance will know the fires of hell. Are you listening?"

- "Human life is—or should be—a progression toward enlightenment, toward spiritual development. This does not have much to do with the external forms of religion but rather with each person's journey from ignorance to understanding, from concern with individuality and materiality to becoming part of a more universal consciousness."

- "Leaving this life produces an altered state of consciousness. Somebody survives, but not the somebody we have been all along. There are many examples of altered states as part of our life experiences, so death may be simply the most impressive of these changes."

- A person dies, of course. This always happens. And then that person just goes on with his life or with her life. This always happens, too. The next life is much like this one. Pleasures. Troubles. Dangers. Say the wrong thing or annoy the wrong person and you can get yourself killed again. What else is a person to do in the next life but be who we are and do what we do?"

All the views quoted above have been expressed at various times. The concept of the next life being essentially a continuation of the present life has been held by many tribal peoples over the centuries. By contrast, the death flash theory is based upon controversial and inconclusive experiments on electromagnetic radiation in living tissues (Slawinski, 1987), and the force-field theory seems to have been first suggested by Myers (1903/1975). Conditional immortality was proposed by one of the few twentieth-century philosophers who took the question of survival as a serious intellectual issue (Hocking, 1957). And a specialist in the study of altered states suggests that death results in—what else?—an altered state (Tart, 1990).

It is not likely that any one person would find all of these versions equally plausible or appealing. Nevertheless, we have reminded ourselves that more than one possibility has been envisioned in the ongoing scrimmage between the evident fact of death and the vast reaches of imagination and desire.

ASSISTED AND SYMBOLIC SURVIVAL

There are two other types of possible survival that are so different from those already identified that we need to give them separate attention

---

> **BOX 13-3   WE'LL NEVER FORGET WHAT'S HIS NAME: PART 1**
>
> Please fill in the blanks—
>
> _____'s great poem _____
> describes a classic example of the way in which time can cancel the symbolic immortality of a once-
> mighty person.

---

here. Symbolic immortality is the more familiar and better established of these concepts. The other type is emerging strongly in our own society today—let's call it *assisted survival*.

Symbolic Immortality

Somebody—actually, several somebodies—had carved their initials into the old desk where I did a lot of my daydreaming in Public School 35, the Bronx. Third graders before me had made at least these marks in the world. The impulse to leave an enduring mark on the world begins early in life. Times of danger intensify this need. "Kilroy was here!" became a famous phrase during World War II, scrawled on practically everything that could be scrawled upon, mostly by young men and women in the armed forces who were assigned to unfamiliar places in hazardous conditions. "Kilroy" represented those who might never return—but they had been here, meaning they had been alive, had existed, had done something.

The concept of symbolic immortality became salient through the writings of Robert Jay Lifton (1979) as he reflected upon the psychological effects of World War II. Death had become increasingly difficult to deny, and not all mourners were consoled by belief in a traditional afterlife. There was a subtle shift from talk of "soul" to "self." What was to become of the self when the body was finished? Perhaps it could live on in the memories of others. This was not a new idea. Many world cultures had ways of keeping their dead alive in sacred keepsakes and ritual. In our own society, fund-raisers persuaded wealthy people to pay for buildings that would bear their names forever.

The upsurge of interest in symbolic immortality was, in part, aroused by twentieth century mass brutality. Holocaust survivors often saw themselves as witnesses with the responsibility to bear testimony: "We saw these things happen. We knew and loved these good people who were tormented and killed!" The horrendous deaths (Leviton, 1991) of genocide were crimes against humanity that could not and should not be forgotten. It was essential to pass the memories of the victims and the atrocities on to the next generation

Engrossment in symbolic immortality can also be motivated by the desire to remain influential, after death. Even if we are secure in our faith in an afterlife, it might also be encouraging to know that we still have a vicarious role in earthly matters. Symbolic immortality might also confirm our reputations of people of exceptional merit, deserving our own halls of fame. Sometimes this postmortem reputation, set in stone, is in fact well deserved. Late in my seemingly endless graduate student days, I happened to meet an elfin and spry old man with a flowing white beard and a merry demeanor. He could have come straight from the Black Forest and any number of folktales. Rufus von Kleinschmidt lives in my memory as an extraordinary person—and I suppose I am mentioning this brief encounter because I would like to continue his symbolic immortality through you. But the former chancellor of the University of Southern California now is officially immortal through a large building that carries his name. Beautiful building, but I miss the man. There are many people who achieve symbolic immortality without seeking or realizing it. Teachers, for example, can become role models who influence their former students throughout their lives. A mentor can survive not only in memory but also as an inner representation that influences a person's life in many ways (Marwit & Lessor, 2000).

The desire for symbolic immortality can be just one part of a person's motivational repertoire, or it can become a driving and distorting force. It is natural, for example, to hope that something of one's self might live on in our children and grandchildren—but "control freak" is seldom a term of endearment. Transmitting the family genes remains the most direct method, but we should not underestimate passing some good (or fascinatingly bad) family stories that can be retold to later generations. Home videos are increasingly becoming part of that package.

The "immortality" in symbolic immortality is vulnerable to time and circumstance. The remembering people themselves die. Once-famous events and achievements become obscure. Buildings are destroyed, memorials worn down or defaced. Every generation contributes by its selective remembering and forgetting.

Assisted Immortality

Technology is opening new possibilities for symbolic immortality. Recorded images and sounds, so familiar to us now, were an historic breakthrough. The past could now be part of the present, and the present part of the future. Furthermore, some of the most brilliant inventors labored on devices that might prove or assure survival of death. Marconi made radio possible, and Edison helped to bring electricity into everyday life—yet both considered themselves failures because they couldn't come up with a working immortality machine. Perhaps technologically assisted survival is an especially attractive proposition for people who do not have a strong faith in a religion that promises an afterlife.

The following are some modes of assisted survival that are under consideration at this time. (Cryonic resuscitation is in something of a class by itself and was considered in Chapter 6.)

Clone thyself. Make a perfect copy of a document or compact disk? We do things like that all the time now. Why not duplicate ourselves? Wouldn't that be the way to go? Or, actually, not to go! Cloning is also known as "twinning," in reference to the naturally occurring process that results in identical twins. The identical twins come from genetic contributions by both parents. Experimental cloning works differently to achieve the same result. The most famous sheep since Mary's Little Lamb was created through nuclear transfer: The nucleus of a cell was removed from an adult ewe, implanted in an egg, developed into an embryo, and then placed within a surrogate ewe who became Dolly's birth, though not her biological, mother (Wilmut et al., 2001). This was neither the first nor the last laboratory production of a cloned animal. J. B. Gurdon and his colleagues had spawned swimming tadpoles by nuclear transfers (2001), and soon there were also cloned monkeys scrambling about. Research has been directed primarily toward improving crops or developing genetic fixes for life-threatening conditions. What mostly concerns us here is cloning as a possible form of assisted survival. In theory, wizards of genetic science would replicate one's own body. This would be a new and possibly improved habitat for the soul. Presumably, additional clones could be grown as the need arose and the funding held up. Such familiar concepts as "resuscitation" and "reincarnation" would need to be looked at in a different light.

BOX 13-4 WE'LL NEVER FORGET WHAT'S HIS NAME: PART 2

Percy Bysshe Shelley's great poem, *Ozymandias*, describes a classic example of the way in which time can cancel the symbolic immortality of a once-mighty person. Is this—or any—poet still remembered, or have those who reflected on symbolic immortality lost theirs as well?

The problems and questions involved are monumental. Successful cloning is difficult, and even more so if attempted with humans. There were many failures in the attempts to produce viable tadpoles and sheep. The painful issue of dealing with genetically defective infants would expand if human cloning were to be attempted.

The fundamental question, though, is whether the clone will actually be the original in all its significant respects. Yes, Clone looks like Original, and perhaps walks and talks like Original. But—hold on! Does Clone have the same life history as the Original? Did Clone grow up during the same sociohistorical period? And hold on again—has Original's consciousness been installed in Clone? Can science replicate our inner sense of self? The most perfect Clone will not be the Original if it does not experience itself and the world through the unique consciousness of the Original. If a person's consciousness does not survive, that person will not even be aware of his or her "survival." How much good is that?

Become a smart chip. Perhaps bodies are overhyped. Perhaps we would be better off without them. There are already eager minds hoping to preserve their memory and cognitive skills after death. William Gibson's futuristic novel *Neuromancer* (1994) dismissed bodies as "meat," useless burdens that we should abandon to enjoy the infinite delights of "the matrix." Margaret Wertheim (1999) cited stories in which people downloaded themselves into computers. Joslyn, Turchin, and Heylighen (1997) labeled this process as "up-loading," and suggested that:

Since user and computer system would continuously work together, they would in a sense "merge": it would become meaningless to separate the one from the other. If at a certain stage the biological individual of this symbiotic couple would die, the computational part might carry on as if nothing had happened. The individual's mind could then be said to have survived in the non-organic part of the system (pp. 1–2).

Up-loading one's self as a smart chip is still a work in progress. However, many people now enjoy sporting about in simulated cyberspace communities. They enter a virtual world such as Second Life in the form of an *avatar*. Historically, avatar is the Sanskrit word for a Hindu god who is incarnated in human form. In computer-speak, avatars are fantasy figures who are shaped by players to represent them in a digitalized proxy world. Is this taking a step away from one's mortal meat-self? Is the customized avatar a fail-safe digital replacement for the immortal soul? Or is the avatar an expendable self that one can triumphantly survive? Death in Second Life is an unsettled process at this point, still feeling its way. Most players probably continue to enjoy romps in cyberspace simulations with little interest in the death of avatars. Others, though, might be tempted to incorporate these incorporeal representatives of themselves in death-evading fantasies. Among these might well be the person who demanded a "back up copy of himself" as quoted at the beginning of this chapter.

Mail ourselves to the future. Time capsules have been around for a while. Selected objects are placed in a container to be opened by some future generation. Could this be a form of assisted survival? A commercial organization known as Highway Products, Inc. assures us that an Infinity Time Capsule is not only "the best gift you can give to your future generation" but also "your chance at immortality." The technological assist in this case is through argon, a dry, inert gas that is intended to prevent deterioration of objects by acid, oxidation, or ultraviolet light. "Each Infinity Time Capsule is then punched with a serial number that we record and keep as a record. Your valuable contents are now safe and secured from the elements until your ancestors open your Infinity Time Capsule" (p. 2).

I would definitely be intrigued if a time capsule came my way from ancestors little known to me. But would this make them immortal in any meaningful sense of the term? We come back once again to a question each person will probably have to decide: What would be a meaningful or essential form of survival—and would I make use of a technological assist, if available?

THE SUICIDE-SURVIVAL CONNECTION

When Christianity was a new sect struggling for its survival, many tried to emulate Jesus through martyrdom at the hands of the Roman authorities. A thousand years later, both Islamic and Christian warriors sought deaths that would earn them entry into their respective realms of eternal bliss. A thousand years after that—four hijacked jets headed toward a suicide mission. The idea that people who die a heroic death will find an eternal reward has been a motif in many cultures. See a production of Wagner's music drama *Der Valkyrie* and you will be treated to an imaginative reenactment of an ancient Norse legend in which fallen heroes are scooped up from the field of battle and escorted to Valhalla, a Viking warrior's version of heaven.

What about those who believe that there simply is no death? This is by far the most common response we are finding in an ongoing study of people who identify themselves with the "New Age" movement. As one respondent put it, death "is just changing clothes." What remains to be learned is whether or not suicide will be seen as an action that is unimportant, therefore not to be prevented or mourned. Some respondents have already expressed the view that what seems to be a premature and tragic death is nothing to be upset about because (a) death really isn't anything and (b) if it happened that way, why that's the way it was supposed to be. What do you think?

We have known for some time what Hamlet thinks. In that most famous of monologues (Act III, Scene 1) he begins with the question: "To be or not to be?" For a moment it looks as though death, not being, will be his answer:

and by a sleep to say we end
The heart-ache and the thousand natural shocks
That flesh is heir to, 'tis a consummation
Devoutly to be wish'd. To die, to sleep . . .

He would not continue to suffer the "natural shocks that flesh is heir to." Understandable, of course. But notice how that subtle mind proceeds to deceive himself, or to attempt deception: "'tis a consummation Devoutly to be wish'd." But is death really a consummation? If he copes differently with his ordeal, Hamlet and Ophelia might yet have each other—now there would be a consummation! The imagery of sexual fulfillment is substituted for the reality of death, making it easier to edge his way toward the grave. He continues to blur the reality of death by again reassuring

himself: "To die, to sleep." That's all death is—sleep—and who's afraid of sleep? So, he's going to pack it in then, right? Not so fast!

To sleep: perchance to dream: ay, there's the rub;
For in that sleep of death what dreams may come
When we have shuffled off this mortal coil,
Must give us pause. . . .

Hamlet pauses. In a moment he arrives at the image of bloody suicide, "When he himself might his quietus make with a bare bodkin." But there is that one troubling reason to stay his hand:

. . . the dread of something after death,
the undiscover'd country from whose bourn
No traveller returns, puzzles the will
And makes us rather bear those ills we have
Than fly to others that we know not of.

Every day there are people who confront their own "to be or not to be" dilemmas. Each person, each dilemma is unique. Nevertheless, all involve assumptions about life, death, and afterlife. Perhaps we can be wiser companions in these situations if we have explored our own undiscovered countries deeply enough to offer them a life-giving pause.

SUMMARY

Most people in most societies throughout the centuries have believed in some form of survival. Several of these belief systems were described, with particular attention to Judaic, Christian, Islamic, and Buddhist traditions. It was seen that terrorists who believe that becoming martyrs will earn them honor and pleasure in paradise are operating on fantasies that are at variance with the Qur'an. The journey of the dead as well as the heavens and hells imagined by various religious faiths are explored. Recent surveys indicate that afterlife belief remains strong in the United States, although it is declining in Europe. The baby boomer generation reports an abundance of belief: in heaven, encounters with spirits of the dead, and, to an increasing extent, reincarnation. Nevertheless, doubt and questioning has also continued since the emergence of science, with its revisionary views of life and the universe. Much of this chapter, therefore, was concerned with attempts to strengthen afterlife belief with evidence. You were asked to put your own ideas and beliefs on the line in a self-quiz. We examined near-death experience reports (NDERs) in some detail because many have often taken these reports as proof of survival. Many who have had this kind of experience report that their lives had changed—for the better—as a result. This outcome does not in itself prove survival, however. The NDE material offered as proof of survival was reviewed and critiqued. We also considered several theories that attempt to explain the NDE. These included the spiritual/survival explanation but also alternatives that interpret the NDE as (a) a split-off psychological reaction to stress, (b) a quieting, energy-conserving function when we can do nothing to extricate ourselves from a life-threatening situation, (c) an hallucination produced by psychophysiological changes, (d) an exercise in religious imagination, (e) a healing and illuminating metaphor, and, most recently, (f) a stress response that parallels the G-LOC experience of pilots subjected to extreme acceleration pressure. Next we examined another source of possible evidence for survival: the dead themselves, or their spirit representatives. This discussion included folktales, deathbed escorts, contacts made through mediums and channelers, and my personal favorite, ghosts. The tragic consequences of belief in the reality and power of ghosts was illustrated by the Ghost Dance through which some Native American peoples hoped to invoke the protection of their ancestors and raise them from the dead, but instead exposed themselves to massacre. Reincarnation, although usually associated with Asian and African belief systems, has gained a large following in the United States and other Western nations in recent years. Ian Stevenson's careful and prolific research into "evidence suggestive of reincarnation" was the center of our attention.

Before concluding, we forced ourselves to consider the question, should we survive death? This was followed by perhaps an even more unsettling question: but what kind of survival? After considering several traditional concepts of how we survive death, attention was given to symbolic immortality, cloning, and becoming a kind of "smart chip" that enters into the cosmic matrix.

REFERENCES

Agha, A. (2003). Tibetan book of the dead. In R. Kastenbaum (Ed.), *Macmillan encyclopedia of death and dying*: Vol. I (pp. 896–898) New York: Macmillan.

Alexander, B. (2003). *Rapture. A raucous tour of cloning, transhumanism, and the new era of immortality.* New York: Basic Books.

Atwater, P. M. H. (1992). Is there a Hell? Surprising observations about the near-death experience. *Journal of Near-Death Studies, 10,* 149–160.

Barrett, W. (1986). *Death-bed visions.* Northampton, MA: The Aquarian Press. (Original work published 1926.)

Bentham, J. (1832). *Last will and testament.* Westminster, UK. www.utilitarian.net/Bentham

Bernstein, W. (1965). *The search for Bridey Murphy.* Garden City, NY: Doubleday.

Bernstein, A. E. (1993). *The formation of Hell.* Ithaca, NY: Cornell University Press.

Blackmore, S. (2004). *Consciousness.* Oxford, UK: Oxford University Press.

Bonney, R. (2002). Buddhism. In R. Kastenbaum (Ed.), *Macmillan encyclopedia of death and dying*: Vol. 1 (pp. 74–80). New York: Macmillan.

Boyce, M. (1979). *Zoroastrians: Their religious beliefs and practices.* London: Routledge & Kegan Paul.

Brea, J. (January 26, 2007). 'Ghost bride' returns to haunt Chinese trio. http://news.Scotman.com/international.cfm?id-134732007

Bryant, C. (2003). Ghosts: The dead among us. In C. Bryant (Ed.), *Handbook of death and dying*: Vol. 1 (pp. 87–95). Thousand Oaks, CA: Sage.

Chen, S-C J (2007). In China: A macabre trade in ghost brides. Forbes.com

Crowe, C. (2008) *Night side of nature or ghosts and ghost seers.* Whitefish, MT: Kessinger (Original, 1846.)

Darwin, C. (1859). *On the origin of species.* London: John Murray.

Dillon, J. (2003). Reincarnation: The technology of death. In C. D. Bryant (Ed.), *Handbook of death & dying:* Vol. 1 (pp. 65–76). Thousand Oaks, CA: Sage.

Emmons, C. F. (1982). *Chinese ghosts and ESP: A study of paranormal beliefs and experiences.* Metuchen, NJ: Scarecrow.

Evans-Wentz, W. Y. (Ed.). (2000). *The Tibetan book of the dead, or the afterdeath experiences on the Bardo plane.* Oxford, UK: Oxford University Press.

Fisk, R. (2005). In the Middle East, those who are about to die believe profoundly in the afterlife. www.highbeam.com/library/doc3.asp?DOCID51G1

Flew, A. (1967). Mind-body problem. In P. Edwards (Ed.), *The encyclopedia of philosophy:* Vol. 5 (pp. 336–353). New York: Macmillan.

Freed, R. S., & Freed, S. A. (1993). *Ghosts: Life and death in North India* (Anthropological Papers, No. 72). New York: American Museum of Natural History.

Gabbard, G. O., & Twemlow, S. W. (1984). *With the eyes of the mind*. New York: Praeger.

Gabbard, G. O., & Twemlow, S. W. (1991). Do "near-death experiences" occur only near-death? *Journal of Near-Death Studies, 10,* 41–48.

Gallup Poll Survey No. GO 129321. (1999, December). CNN/USA Today.

Gibson, W. (1994). *Neuromancer*. New York: Ace Books.

Greeley, A. M., & Hout, M. (1999). Belief in life after death increasing in the United States. *American Sociological Review, 64,* 813–836.

Green, C., & McCreery, C. (1989). *Apparitions*. Oxford, UK: Institute of Psychophysical Research.

Gurdon, J. B. (2001). The birth of cloning. In M. Ruse & A. Sheppard (Eds.), *Cloning* (pp. 39–48). Amherst, NY: Prometheus.

Hanson, H. Y. (2003). Islam. In R. Kastenbaum (Ed.), *Macmillan encyclopedia of death and dying:* Vol. 1 (pp. 484–489). New York: Macmillan.

Harris, S. (2004). *The end of faith*. New York: W. W. Norton.

Hayslip, B., & Peveto. C. (2005). *Historical shifts in attitudes toward death, dying, and bereavement*. Amityville, NY: Baywood.

Hinton, D. E., Pich, V., Chean, D., & Pollack, M. H. (2005). "The ghost pushes you down": Sleep paralysis-type panic attacks in a Khmer refugee population. *Transcultural Psychiatry, 42,* 46–77.

Hittman, M. (1990). *Wovoka and the ghost dance*. Lincoln: University of Nebraska Press.

Hocking, W. E. (1957). *The meaning of immortality in human experience*. New York: Harper.

Irwin, H. J., & Bramwell, A. B. (1988). The devil in heaven: A near-death experience with both positive and negative facets. *Journal of Near-Death Experiences, 7,* 38–43.

Josyln, C., Turchin, V., & Heylighen, F. (1997). Cyberbetic immortality. Principia Cybernetica Web. www.pespmc1.vub.ac.be/CYBIMM.html

Kane, M. F. (1888). Spiritualism exposed. In P. Kurtz (Ed.), *A skeptic's handbook of parapsychology*. Buffalo, NY: Prometheus.

Kastenbaum, R. (1993). Ian Stevenson: An Omega interview. *Omega, Journal of Death and Dying, 28,* 165–182.

Kastenbaum, R. (1995a). Raymond A. Moody, Jr.: An Omega interview. *Omega, Journal of Death and Dying, 31,* 87–98.

Kastenbaum, R. (1995b). *Is there life after death?* London: Prion.

Kastenbaum, R. (1996). Near-death reports: Evidence for survival of death? In L. W. Bailey & J. Yates (Eds.), *The near-death experience reader* (pp. 245–264). New York: Routledge.

Kastenbaum, R. (1998b). Temporarily dead. *Readings, 13,* 16–21.

Kastenbaum, R. (2004). *On our way: The final passage through life and death*. Berkeley: University of California Press.

Kearl, M. C. (2002). Immortality: Symbolic. In R. Kastenbaum (Ed.), *Macmillan encyclopedia of death and dying:* Vol. 2 (pp. 461–464). New York: Macmillan.

Kelly, E. W., Greyston, B., & Stevenson, I. (1999/2000). Can experiences near death furnish evidence of life after death? *Omega, Journal of Death and Dying, 40,* 513–520.

Klugman, C. M. (2006). Dead men talking: Evidence of post death contact and continuing bonds. *Omega, Journal of Death and Dying, 53,* 249–262.

Kramer, K. P. (1988) *The sacred art of dying: How world religions understand death*. Mahwah, NJ: Paulist Press.

Lester, D., Aldridge, M., Aspenberg, C., Boyle, K., Radsniak, P., & Waldron, C. (2001/2002). What is the afterlife like? Undergraduate beliefs about the afterlife. *Omega, Journal of Death and Dying, 44,* 113–126.

Leviton, D. (1991). *Horrendous death, health, and well-being*. New York: Hemisphere.

Lifton, R. J. (1979). *The broken connection. On death and the continuity of life*. New York: Simon & Schuster.

Lommel, P. v., Wees, R. V., Meyers, V., & Elfferich, I. (2001). Near-death experience in survivors of cardiac arrest: A prospective study in The Netherlands. *Lancet, 358,* 2039–2045.

Lucretius (Titus Lucretius Carus). *On the nature of things*. (Original work 54 B.C.) In R. M. Hutchins (Ed.), *Great books of the Western world:* Vol. 12 (pp. 1–97). Chicago: Chicago University Press.

McDannel, C., & Lang, B. (1988). *Heaven. A history*. New Haven, CT: Yale University Press.

Marwit, S. J., & Lessor, C. (2000). Role of deceased mentors in the ongoing lives of proteges. *Omega, Journal of Death and Dying, 41,* 125–138.

Mehr, F. (2003). Zoroastrianism. In R. Kastenbaum (Ed.), *Macmillan encyclopedia of death and dying:* Vol. 2 (pp. 956–960). New York: Macmillan.

Miller, J. Y. (2001, August 5). AJC Southern Poll: Southerners' thoughts about death and dying are set apart by traditions and religious beliefs. *The Atlanta Journal and Constitution* online.

Moody, R. A., Jr. (1975). *Life after life*. Atlanta: Mockingbird Books.

Mooney, J. (1996). *The ghost dance*. North Dighton, MA: JG Press, Inc.

Morin, R. (2000). Do Americans believe in God? www.washingtonpost.com/wsev/politics/polls/wat/archive/wat042400/htm

Myers, F. W. H. (1975). *Human personality and its survival of bodily death* (Vols. 1–2). New York: Arno Press. (Original work published 1903.)

Newcott, B. (2007). Life after death. www.aarpmagazine.org/people/life_after_death.html

Noyes, R., Jr. (1979). Near-death experiences: Their interpretation. In R. Kastenbaum (Ed.), *Between life and death* (pp. 73–88). New York: Springer.

Osis, K. (1961). *Deathbed observations by physicians and nurses.* New York: Parapsychology Foundation.

Osis, K., & Haraldsson, E. (1977). *At the hour of death.* New York: Avon.

Parnia, S., & Fenwick, P. (2002). Near death experiences in cardiac arrest: Visions of a dying brain or visions of a new science of consciousness. *Resuscitation, 52,* 5–11.

Pew Research Center. (2008, February 25). The U.S. religious landscape survey reveals a fluid and diverse pattern of faith. http://pewresearch.org/pubs/743/united-states-religion

Reuters. (2002). Man shot dead over heaven and hell argument. www.channels.Netscape.com/ns/news/ns/story

Ring, K. (1980). *Life at death.* New York: Coward, McCann & Geoghegan.

Ring, K. (1992). *The Omega project.* New York: William Morrow.

Robinson, R. (2003). *Famous last words, fond farewells, death diatribes, and exclamations upon expiration.* New York: Workman.

Sabom, M. B. (1982). *Recollections of death.* New York: Simon & Schuster.

Sabom, M. B. (1998). *Light and death: One doctor's fascinating account of near-death experiences.* Grand Rapids, MI: Zondervan.

Sheler, J. L. (2000, January 31). Hell hath no fury. *U.S. News & World Report* online.

Siegel, R. K. (1980). The psychology of life after death. *American Psychologist, 35,* 911–931.

Slawinski, J. (1987). Electrometic radiation and the afterlife. *Journal of Near-Death Studies, 6,* 79–94.

Stevenson, I. (1974). *Twenty cases suggestive of reincarnation* (Rev. ed.). Charlottesville: University Press of Virginia.

Stevenson, I. (1997a). *Reincarnation and biology. A contribution to the etiology of birthmarks and birth defects:* Vols. 1–2. Westport, CT: Praeger.

Stevenson, I. (1997b). *Where reincarnation and biology intersect.* Westport, CT: Praeger.

Stevenson, I., Cook, C. W., & McClean-Rice, N. (1989/1990). Are persons reporting "near-death experiences" really near death? A study of medical records. *Omega, Journal of Death and Dying, 20,* 45–54.

Stevenson, I., & Greyson, B. (1996). Near-death experiences: Relevance to the question of survival after death. In L. W. Bailey & J. Yates (Eds.), *The near-death experience reader* (pp. 199–206). New Haven: Yale University Press.

Tart, C. (1990). Who survives? Implications of modern consciousness research. In G. Doore (Ed.), *What survives?* (pp. 138–152). Los Angeles: Jeremy P. Tarchers.

Taylor, R. P. (Ed.). (2000). *Death and the afterlife.* Santa Barbara, CA: ABC-CLIO.

Turner, A. K. (1993). *The history of Hell.* New York: Harcourt Brace.

Wallis, J. (2001). Continuing bonds: Relationships between the living and the dead within contemporary spiritualism. *Mortality, 6,* 127–145.

Washburn, K., & Majors, J. S. (1998). *World poetry: An anthology of verses from antiquity to our time.* New York: Norton.

Wasilewska, E. (2002). So the soul can rest—Death and afterlife in the Qur'an: Part 2. www.highbeam.com/library/doc3.asp?DOCID–161:987801358&byn

Wertheim, M. (1999). *The pearly gates of cyberspace.* New York: Norton.

Westwood, J. (2002) Gilgamesh. In R. Kastenbaum (Ed). *Macmillan encyclopedia of death and dying:* Vol. 1 (pp. 331–334). New York: Macmillan.

Whinnery, J. E. (1997). Psychophysiologic correlates of unconsciousness and near-death experiences. *Journal of Near-Death Studies, 15,* 231–258.

Wilmut, I., Schnieke, A. E., McWhir, A., Kind, A. F., & Campbell, K. H. S. (2001). Viable offspring derived from fetal and adult mammalian cells. In M. Ruse & A. Sheppard (Eds.), *Cloning* (pp. 31–38). New York: Prometheus.

Wohlberg, S. (2002). *Do all pets go to heaven?* Enuclaw, WA: Winepress Publishing.

Zaleski, C. (1987). *Otherworld journeys.* New York: Oxford University Press.

Zaleski, C. (2003, April 5). When I get to heaven: Picturing paradise. *The Christian Century Online.*

Zuckerman, P. (2004, March 1). Securalization: Europe—yes, United States—no: why has securalization occurred in Western Europe but not in the United States? *Skeptical Inquirer* online. (SICOP.org).

GLOSSARY

Autoscopic experience: Perceiving one's own body as though from above, a facet of the out-of-the-body experience.

Channeler: A person with the reputed power to communicate with the past lives of oneself or others.

Conservation theme: The afterlife is regarded as an opportunity to provide the contentment, triumph, justice, freedom, or other desired experience that did not happen in earthly life.

Depersonalization: A sense of emotional distance from one's own body and self.

Endorphins: Substances the brain produces that effect mood and awareness.

G-LOC: An altered state of consciousness produced by the stress of extreme acceleration in fighter planes or ground simulations.

Hezbollah: An Islamic resistance movement. Literally, "The Party of God."

Hyperalertness: A state of heightened attention, usually to danger signals.

Immortality: The persistence of spirit, soul, or personality after death. Not all afterlife beliefs hold that people survive death on a permanent basis; therefore, not all survival has immortal status.

Jahannam: Islamic concept of hell.

Medium: A person with the reputed power of receiving messages from the dead (earlier term for channeler).

Near-death experience (NDE): Images, perceptions, and feelings that are recalled by some people after a life-threatening episode. The near-death experience report (NDER) is the account of such experiences as shared with others.

Necromancer: A person who evokes the dead (often at cemeteries) through secret spells and rituals.

Pluralistic death: Concept that death and possible afterlife might not be the same for all living creatures under all conditions;

Psychopomp: A spirit being or messenger from God who escorts a dying person to the next life.

Reincarnation: The return of the spirit or soul in another physical form after death.

Séance: Literally, a sitting. The name given to sessions with a medium.

Yahweh: A name given to God in the Old Testament.

Zoroastrianism: An ancient religion centered in Persia that had significant influence on the later Judaic, Christian, and Islamic belief systems.

ON FURTHER THOUGHT . . .

Your Heaven:

History—right up to the present time—suggests that people have found it easier to imagine Hell. Detailed ideas about an enjoyable afterlife are found mostly in societies that conceive of the next life as being mostly similar to the life one is leaving. In the United States, most people express a belief in survival of death, but most also are vague about Heaven and what one does there all day. Perhaps Heaven is simply beyond imagining. Give it a try, though!

1. What is your best idea of what Heaven really is? Go for accuracy. What makes Heaven Heaven? Be as absolutely clear and detailed as you can.

2. What would Heaven be if you could design your own and have it come true? Again, challenge yourself to be as clear and detailed as you can. Do your friends and family have similar, or perhaps quite different, visions of Heaven? If you can get them to talk about them, proceed to the next questions.

3. What Heaven can you, your family, and friends construct together? What might this exercise tell you about what you are looking for in your life right here and now?

Where's all that fascinating and frustrating old stuff?

Books and journal articles written during the heyday of spiritism and survival research have been almost ghost-like in their appearances and disappearances. Arno Press issued a sizable set of reprint books in 1975, but these have been out of print for some time. *Phantasms of the Living,* an 1886 report of the first British Society for Psychic Research survey, is half-available at the moment through Amazon.com. *The Census of Hallucinations* (Sidgwick et al., 1889) is more or less available through reprinted excerpts from journal articles. Kessinger Publishing, www.kessinger.net, (also available through Amazon.com) is at present the most promising source for rediscovering writings that were influential in the controversy. I do recommend becoming better acquainted with the field in a general way through Blum's (2006) book already mentioned; Alfred Douglas' *Extrasensory Powers* (1976), Woodstock, NY: The Overlook Press, and my *Is There Life After Death?* (1995, revised edition), London: Prion. Whooops! That's out of print, too!

"Hmmm! Dolly needs expert medical attention. Good thing that I'm here!" Many people who choose a career of helping others first discovered this impulse in childhood.

14

HOW CAN WE HELP?

Caregiving and death education

And he was young and energetic and full of life going into it. And the pain . . . there was just this horrible pain. The next day, it made him unable to talk, and we were sitting there watching the death and there was nothing we could do.
—Quoted by Sharon R. Kaufman (2005)

I have done just about everything from long-term care to hospitals. They are all the same. It is always give more, more, more. I reached a point about a year ago where I began having anxiety attacks. . . . Working conditions are terrible. There are too many patients with critical needs and not enough help to do the things that need to be done. I felt like such a failure. . . . I felt that every day I worked the floor as a nurse I was putting my license on the line.
—Anon (2005, p. 9)

I have been a nurse for ten years. I started as an LPN and thought I would be treated better if I became an RN. Big mistake. Treated just as badly, but now I'm responsible for everything and everybody. You are blamed for everything and thanked for nothing. You may work like a dog for years, never take breaks, give it your heart, your soul, your blood, sweat and tears, and ruin your back. . . . You'll end up a bitter old person with a bad back.
—Val Salva (2005, p. 1)

I picked him up, ran out here, and laid him on the counter and called 911. And of course screamed hysterically into the phone. "Help me!" And they said they called the paramedics and they were on the way, and they want you to do CPR. And I had been trained in CPR (crying). I probably didn't do it the way I should have. I'm sure I didn't. They did stay on the line with me. I think a woman answered first, and I think they put a man on the phone. He kind of talked me through the CPR.
—Gail (as quoted by Paul C. Rosenblatt, 2000, p. 34)

In the weeks that followed Josh's [19 months old] sudden death, Toby [2$\frac{1}{2}$ years old] began to imitate all Joshua's mannerisms, including his baby talk. It was as though, in a desperate attempt to make everything better for the grown-ups, he had decided to "be" his dead brother, a notion I find particularly heart-wrenching.
—R. W. Weinbach (as quoted in Iserson, 1999, p. 136)

With little peeks over his shoulder as his mother was rolled out the door, Tristen told me when he becomes president, he's going to make a law that no one's mother will have to be carried out in a plastic bag. I told him it was a good law to make.
—Laura R. Smith (1996, p. 16)

Before he got sick, the most physical contact we would have was a warm handshake. A real blessing during that last month in the hospital was that we both felt more free to display affection. . . . I would kiss him on the forehead. I massaged his feet with lotion. I could tell he liked it. So did I.
—A man reflecting on caring for his dying father (as quoted in Chethik, 2001)

People needing help. People in a position to offer help. Many of us will be in both roles at different points in our lives. In this chapter, we focus on the support that can be provided in death-relevant situations by people with professional training, but also by friends, families, and the community at large.

The nurse at the bedside of the dying young man was suffering along with him. There would be no medical miracles to save his life. But what about his terrible pain? "At this point, he hadn't had anything, no pain medicine whatsoever. The doctor on call didn't know him, and he wasn't thinking about the long night this human being was going to have" (Kaufman, p. 44). The nurse intervened. She persuaded the doctor to shift his attention from the patient's blood pressure to his suffering. Pain medication was given. The young man relaxed, and his final hours were much less an ordeal. Care providers often find themselves in situations in which the treatment options are limited, and comfort decisions can go one way or another—or simply be ignored. This nurse is one of many experienced health care providers who have learned how to make a difference in desperate situations, but the stress continues for nurses and physicians patrolling the borderline between life and death. Many physicians as well as nurses describe themselves as so emotionally exhausted and frustrated that they would not recommend professions in the health care field to their own children (Manion, 2005). Caregiver *burnout* also places patients at a heightened risk.

The parents of young Toby and even younger Josh recognized that the surviving child's reversion to baby talk was a meaningful action. Somebody else might have dismissed Toby's behavior as silly and not have connected it with Josh's death, might even have punished the boy for being so childish. Fortunately, Toby's parents took a different approach:

It was very important then to let Toby know that we loved him for being himself, and that he did not have to "become" Josh to gain our approval. So we never admonished him for taking the role of Josh, but we did remind him often that we loved him very much (Iserson, 1999, p. 136).

It was a certified death educator and counselor in Oregon who helped 10-year-old Tristen and his 8-year-old brother Clayton through the end phase of their young mother's terminal illness. During their sixth visit together in the hospital room she started to discuss with the brothers the various times in people's lives when they have to say good-bye to places, things, and each other.

Tristen crawled up right in front of me and looked me in the eyes. "In case you didn't notice. I don't want to talk about this." His look was steady. I was so proud of him for speaking up. "Thank you, Tristen. I'm really glad you told me and I respect your need not to talk about this right now." I patted his shoulder and we went on to play with something else (Smith, 1996, pp. 13–14).

"I cried all the way home and into the night," Smith reports, but she also felt the sense of love that the dying woman, her fiancé, and her children had shared with each other (p. 16). She knew the road ahead for the children, though very difficult, had been made that much easier by loving memories.

It was not a death educator but an adult son who spent many hours by his father's bedside as the older man died of kidney failure. The son experienced a sense of closeness and closure. Journalist Neil Chethik (2001) interviewed men to learn how they dealt with the deaths of their fathers. In general, he found that sons who spent time caring for the fathers before their deaths or talking with them directly about death reported that such actions helped them in their grieving process afterward. Communication and sharing did much both to comfort the dying fathers and to help the sons go on with their lives.

Professional caregivers and community volunteers who choose to work with hospice programs try to comprehend the whole person, rather than just the terminal illness. They also usually have less need to protect themselves from the impact of dying and death (Turnipseed, 1987). We found (Kastenbaum & Schneider, 1991) that most hospice staff and volunteers call upon personal prayer—a communication just between themselves and God—to give them the strength to go on. One volunteer was speaking for many others when she told us, "I feel it is a privilege to be with a person at this vulnerable and sacred time of their lives." No respondents described themselves as discovering prayer or becoming religious as a result of their experiences with dying persons: It was the other way around. People who had already discovered prayer as a source of strength continued to do so as they encountered the challenges of hospice work. They did not ask for divine intervention or miracles in their prayers, nor did they impose these prayers on patients and families. Praying was a way of staying in touch with themselves and their deepest beliefs. Although the term was not mentioned, the volunteers seemed to have found prayer an effective means of preventing or reducing burnout.

"COMPASSIONATE FATIGUE": BURNOUT AND THE HEALTH CARE PROVIDER

Anxiety and depression have shadowed the human condition through the centuries. What is special about burnout? Maslach and Leiter (2000) provide a crisp explanation:

> Burnout is a prolonged response to chronic emotional and interpersonal stressors on the job. It is defined by the three dimensions of exhaustion, cynicism, and inefficacy. . . . Burnout clearly places the individual stress experience within a larger organizational context of people's relation to their work (p. 358).

Burnout is more likely to develop when people feel trapped in an intolerable situation over which they have little or no control. Lack of social support is one of these conditions, as identified by nurse Salva ("You are blamed for everything and thanked for nothing"). Nurse Anon feels like a failure because she cannot continue to meet the demands for "more, more, and more." After a while, even the most resolute person might experience exhaustion, cynicism, and reduced efficiency.

People in the helping professions, such as teachers, counselors, firefighters, and police officers are among those at particular risk. Nurses are often more vulnerable than physicians because they have less structural power in the situation. An alternative term, *compassion fatigue* (Figley, 1995), expresses the dilemma of health care workers who work with many chronically ill and life-threatened patients. Many health care providers have chosen their professions with the expectation of providing the best possible care to people in their times of suffering and vulnerability. Compassion fatigue develops after repeated experiences of frustration and disappointment in which circumstances have interfered with providing the needed level of care. This differs from posttraumatic stress disorder (Chapter 11) which often results from a single devastating experience, for example, being witness to an act of violence The health care provider who once looked forward to the day's challenges now, worn down by pressure-filled and frustrating situations, feels tense and apprehensive, having to make a special effort just to show up for work.

Exhaustion and other symptoms of burnout are often experienced by the people who are counted on to help other people, such as this hospital-based physician.

A traumatic experience, as in the sudden death of a student or colleague, can lead to the burnout syndrome that has been held barely in check up to that point (Tebrani, 2004).

Typical signs of burnout are listed in Table 14-1. A particular individual might not experience all these problems, and individuals also differ with respect to the most severe problems.

The burnout syndrome includes physiological, behavioral, and social elements (Lundberg, 2000). Some victims of burnout have brought their preexisting anxiety and depression into the situation. For example, hospice nurses whose own lives were stressed by trauma experiences, excessive obligations, and a painfully high degree of empathy have been found to be at greater risk for compassion fatigue (Abenroth & Flannery,

TABLE 14-1

Signs of Burnout

Most obvious signs
- Exhaustion, lack of energy, feeling rundown
- Tension headaches
- Sleep disturbances
- Appetite and digestive disturbances
- Increased errors at work
- Becoming irritable and negative
- Anger flare-ups
- Self-criticism
- Feeling helpless
- Feeling depersonalized and distant in relationships

Less obvious signs
- Reduced immune function
- Increased secretion of stress hormones
- Elevated blood pressure
- Metabolic dysfunctions

2006). Widowed nurses with limited social support also are higher risk for compassion fatigue (Ifeagwazi, 2005/2006). There is also reason for concern about the limited training in working with life-threatened patients that is made available to health care providers, thereby increasing their risk for burnout and compassion fatigue (Al-Sabwah, & Abdel-Khalek, 2005/2006)

Caregivers in Death-Salient Situations

Health care providers face even higher risk when they are responsible for the care of life-threatened or dying patients. The cultural taboo against discussing death and the philosophy of distancing and avoiding passed on from one generation of physicians to the next condemned many health care providers, as well as their patients, to isolation and denial (Kastenbaum, 2004). I saw plenty of this. The compassionate nurse who had a single car accident after one of her long-term geriatric patients died: "We were not supposed to get involved in the first place." The surgery resident who had "lost" another patient, although "I did everything right, and then she had to go off and die on me." He wasn't sure that he wanted to continue his medical career. "I'm mad at everybody," he admitted, "God, too! I must be hell to live with!" These were but two of the many health care professionals who were not prepared or supported by the system when they encountered limits, loss, and stress in the course of their work.

Research has consistently found burnout or compassionate fatigue among health care providers to life-threatened and dying patients. In her pioneering study, Mary L. S. Vachon (1987) interviewed about 600 professional caregivers from hospitals, palliative care facilities, chronic care institutions, and voluntary agencies. What was the basic source of stress for physicians, nurses, and others who care for dying patients? And how did they cope with this stress?

Her answer might surprise those who have not worked in a health care setting. The findings are crisply expressed in one of her chapter titles: "Dying Patients Are Not the Real Problem." The caregivers reported they were most stressed by their work environment and occupational roles, not by their contact with dying patients and their families. Their stresses included poor communication within the health care facility, conflicts between one unit and another, and lack of continuity as staff come and go.

Vachon's findings continue to ring true. Tense, anxious, frustrated, and exhausted caregivers have difficulty bringing their best selves to dying patients and their families. We do not have to assume that a nurse who withdraws from a dying person is motivated by her own excessive death anxieties. She might instead be caught in a role conflict (between being technical expert and a humane caregiver). It is also probable that she is trapped in a time bind created by understaffing, mixed priorities, and poor communication patterns.

A major study of hospices in the United Kingdom (Addington-Hall & Saffron, 2005) finds that about half the staff was considering leaving because of a perceived lack of respect from colleagues in other disciplines and lack of support from management. These findings are of particular concern because hospice programs give high priority to teamwork and mutual support. Reviewing a number of studies, physician Kernan Manion (2005) concludes that:

> Many doctors throughout the country are finding themselves so worn down by the overwhelming array of issues continuously confronting them in health care as to be approaching frank burnout (p. 1).

Tension increases when a new health crisis emerges. Toronto was threatened with a possible catastrophic epidemic in 2003, when cases of severe acute respiratory syndrome (SARS) were identified. There could have been widespread contagion, with many deaths in Toronto and then rapidly spreading elsewhere. The tensions already experienced by hospital staff in their everyday work were sharply increased. Nurses were the most severely affected because the peer support they relied on had been overwhelmed by the emergency response effort, and they also felt less informed and less empowered to participate in decision making (Tolomiczenko et al., 2005). As Maslach and Leiter (2000) have noted, the sense of "inefficacy"—the lack of opportunity to influence the course of events—is a major component of burnout.

Caregivers for terminally ill children are perhaps the most vulnerable to severe burnout experiences. Danai Papadatou (2006) interviewed many distressed pediatric care providers with experiences such as the following:

I think I age quickly, both biologically and psychologically, as a result of this work. Now I experience a pressure upon my heart, a constant weight that does not allow me to breathe. Now, I don't want to be close to any dying child or family. I cannot handle their suffering or my pain any more. I cannot even sit by their side, the silence seems very heavy. I have nothing to offer. Words don't come out. I cannot even give this special and tender look I once gave to my patients. If ever I give it, it's filled with despair (p. 311).

Staff Burnout: What Effects on Patients?

Does caregiver stress have negative consequences for the patients? Recent studies suggest that pressured work conditions are associated with increased patient risk. The term "vicious cycle" seems to apply. The shortage of registered nurses has been linked to stressful work conditions. Experiencing burnout, a substantial number of nurses leave hospital service, and this career option has become less attractive to new waves of students. Unfortunately, the nurses who are on duty are expected to do "more, more, and more" under increasing pressure. Larger case loads and longer shifts result in more errors on the job (Rogers et al., 2004). The exhausting schedules not only lead to more errors but also to less opportunity to attend to life-threatened patients. There is also less "down time" for nurses to reflect on and recover from stressful experiences.

Does this mean that more people die because of staff shortages and overwork? The answer is yes, according to a major study reported by the Joint Commission on Accreditation of Healthcare Organizations (Aiken et al., 2002). Key findings were:

- The risk of death increases by 7% for surgical patients for each additional patient over four in a nurse's workload.

- The risk of death increases by 31% in hospitals where nurses have a caseload of eight as compared with four patients each.
- Increased patient caseload also increased burnout, with more than two out of five nurses intending to leave their position within the next 12 months—an action that could again increase caseload and patient risk.

These explosive findings created ripples of reflection, controversy, and calls for action. It cannot be said, however, that the overwork/burnout problem has been resolved. Economic and other large-scale problems in the health care system continue to require attention. What, if anything, can individuals do to prevent or alleviate burnout?

How Can We Protect Ourselves from Burnout?

The caregiver quoted by Papadatou (2006) "never gave herself the time to process her experiences and did not seek support." Education and training programs could do more to prepare health care professionals for the challenges they will encounter. A crucial step would be to acknowledge burnout as a serious threat to the health care system at large, responsible for patient and family stress, high staff stress and turnover, and other added expenses.

An organizational solution to the organizational problems would be a logical course of action. Tahiti or the Bahamas? When your friend becomes president of the United States and offers you a choice of ambassadorships, pause a moment and say that you would rather be director of the Health Care and Finance Administration. Devote yourself to establishing a policy for health care education and practice that takes the well-being of professional staff seriously, makes it one of the crucial factors to consider. Enforce this policy immediately and find effective people who will make sure that prevention of burnout is accepted as an essential for all health care organizations. Now you can choose one of those ambassadorships!

Until your friend is elected, however, there are other useful things that can be done:

- Develop a peer network in which staff discontents and rivalries give way to whole-hearted support for all care providers. Caregivers such as the person interviewed by Papadatou would not have to be alone and isolated in their stress. Take a cue from "the voices of nursing home staff" that find ways of supporting each other behind the scenes even when the institution is not keen about facing end-of-life situations (Oliver, Porock, & Oliver, 2006). The staff's "backstage interactions" (i.e., having a closer relationship with dying residents than expected or countenanced by the administration) not only provide comfort to people who otherwise would have been isolated during their last days of life, but also fulfill the staff's need to be truly helpful.

- Develop consensus for more shared decision making. Staff with various specialties could do more listening to each other and less pulling of rank. "Empowering" achieved the status of a buzzword a few years ago but has vital meaning for caregivers; nurses, physicians, and other care providers who feel empowered to use their own knowledge, skills, and compassion are much less likely to experience burnout.

- Learn basic relaxation techniques that are useful within and beyond the work situation. Most of these techniques are simple and can be done without special equipment. They are also mostly pleasant to perform. There are many other exercises and techniques available for exploration, including "mindfulness" instruction that has already been shown to be helpful to caregivers (Bromley, 2005).

Whose Problem? Whose Need?

Care providers sometimes contribute mightily to their own stress and frustration. This situation is most likely to develop when one's own feelings are confused with those of the client. For example, a young psychologist is stewing in his own anxiety because he cannot make his aged client any younger or healthier, not even provide him with an environment more congenial than a grim state institution. The psychologist naturally assumes that the patient is even more anxious and depressed because it is his life that is becoming ever more distressful. In this state of mind, the psychologist is not especially

useful to the patient or himself. Fortunately, though, the light goes on before it is too late. I realize the old man has made peace with his situation. Just listening, I learn how he had made it through a hard life that he would not exchange with any other. "Even my bruises have bruises, but they're all mine. " Now he does not expect anything but the inevitable. That's not quite true, though. The nurses were being too much tippy-toeing around him. Nobody teased him any more. And they wouldn't give him any real food to eat, if you could call that cafeteria stuff real food. Basically, he wanted to be treated as himself and alive while still he was. This could actually be made to happen! The nurses, like the psychologist, started to feel a little more normal around the patient. Bustling, teasing, and "real" food returned.

As a psychologist, I was familiar with the concepts of *transference* and *countertransference*. Clients in psychotherapy are inclined to project their own characteristics or characteristics of important people in their lives upon their therapists, who therefore find themselves intensely loved, hated, or both. That's transference, in the psychoanalytic sense of the term. But therapists are human also, and can project their moods and motives on the clients. That's countertransference. Psychotherapists are expected to recognize both transference and countertransference and act accordingly.

I had to learn on the job that transference and countertransference also are likely to develop during interactions with life-threatened and terminally ill people. For example, a patient might remind us—not quite consciously—of somebody in our own lives with whom we have had a strong emotional attachment. Our own hidden anxieties about death might also force themselves into our caregiving activities. The result can be unfortunate, as Kelly and Varghese (2006, p. 44) illustrate:

In the case of a gravely ill or difficult patient, the clinician may experience intense feelings of frustration, helplessness, and anger toward the patient. As much as we may hate to admit to these feelings, they are not uncommon and may in fact, be unconsciously detected by the patient as a wish that he or she would die . . . Unexamined projective identification can shape the helping professional's clinical actions and responses.

Empathy is one thing; confusing another person's moods and needs with our own is another and more problematic thing.

DEATH EDUCATORS AND COUNSELORS: THE "BORDER PATROL"

Most people who serve as death educators and counselors draw upon personal experiences as well as academic and professional education. They realize that the boundary between the land of the living and the land of the dead is as subtle as the next breath we take.

Some people still have difficulty in understanding how death can be studied or taught. Others are fearful that strangers under the guise of educators and counselors might invade the sanctity of their innermost beliefs. Questions may also be raised by researchers, educators, and counselors in other fields. Is there a solid basis for this field, or does death education survey only untested assumptions and fancies? What do people derive from death education and counseling? And what should people derive?

We begin our exploration with a brief historical introduction, then examine the current scene in death education and counseling, and conclude with some observations about future prospects and challenges.

DEATH EDUCATION IN HISTORICAL PERSPECTIVE

The term death education itself and the field to which it refers did not become a recognizable part of our society until the 1960s, as noted in Chapter 4. In the broader sense, however, we have never been without some form of instruction and guidance.

From Ancient Times

Ancient documents from Tibet and dynastic Egypt offer detailed accounts of what becomes of the soul after death and what preparations can be made for a safe passage. These documents have become known in the Western world as "books of the dead." It helps if one knows the names of the underworld demons and deities and the challenges they will put to the spirits of the deceased. In dynastic Egypt, 42 gods sit in judgment as the newly dead person confesses a lifetime's worth of faults and misdeeds. One's soul is then measured against a feather: paradise is ahead if the scale balances perfectly. What happens if the soul fails to pass? In general, ancient death education, then, had much to do with how one should prepare for the ordeal of judgment after taking that last breath. In contrast, death education today often focuses on people attempting to cope with death in the midst of life (e.g., the hospice nurse, the grieving family member, the individual who has just been informed of a life-threatening disease).

Through the centuries, many images and ideas about our relationship to death have been offered. One of the most common themes has been the fleeting nature of life. Job (13:12) laments: "Man that is born of a woman is of few days, and full of trouble. He cometh forth like a flower, and is cut down: he fleeth also as a shadow, and continueth not." The Old Testament compares human life with the grass that withers and is blown away by the whirlwind. The evanescence of life is linked with the limits of human knowledge and power. Do we suppose ourselves to be lordly beings? Proverbs (27:1) quickly deflates us: "Boast not thyself of tomorrow; for thou knowest not what a day may bring forth."

It is not only the Judeo-Christian tradition that has attempted to bring awareness of our mortality to the fore. The collection of stories known as The Arabian Nights is best known for its celebration of sensuality. But death is also given eloquent attention. The following passage demonstrates how awareness of our mortality might provide the basis for a mature philosophy of life:

O sons of men,
Turn quickly and you will see death
Behind your shoulder.
Adam saw him,
Nimrod saw him
Who wound his horn in the forest,
The masters of Persia saw him.

Alexander, who wrestled with the world
And threw the world,
Turned quickly and saw death
Behind his shoulder. . . .
O sons of men,
When you give yourselves to the sweet trap
　of life
Leave one limb free for God.
The fear of death is the beginning of wisdom
And the fair things you do
Shall blow and smell like flowers
On the red and fiery day.
(Mathers, 1972, pp. 300–301)

Both the *Old Testament* and *The Arabian Nights* contrast the power of God with the powerlessness of the mortal person, but not with the same emotional tone. The troubled, fleeting shadow portrayed in the Old Testament finds neither pleasure nor solace. By contrast, the readers of Scheherazade's tales of 1,001 nights are expected to give themselves to "the sweet trap of life." What are we to do, then? Should we spend our lives lamenting and "eating worms" before the worms eat us? Or should we enjoy the sweet trap while we can, knowing full well that our pleasures and triumphs will not endure because we will not endure?

The *New Testament* introduced a radically different perspective: "Who so eateth my flesh, and drinketh my blood, hath eternal life; and I will raise him up at the last day" (John 6:54). "And this is the promise that he hath promised us, even eternal life" (John 3:15). "And the sea gave up the dead which were in it; and death and hell delivered up the dead which were in them: and they were judged every man according to their works. (Revelations 20:13–14).

In centuries to come, Christians would differ among themselves on many issues (e.g., is it faith, good works, or predestination that will ensure the triumph over death?). From the start, however, at the core of Christianity was its bold contention that man had been redeemed from death through Jesus.

The early Christian "death education lesson" advised that we do not have to sorrow our way through life, nor surrender to the "sweet trap" with the bittersweet knowledge that it will soon snap shut upon us. Instead, we should feel joyful about the life to come after this brief sojourn on earth is completed. This rousing lesson did not escape change through time, however. Other themes became salient as Christianity expanded and became more diverse. Three related themes remain influential today:

1. Death is *punishment* for Adam and Eve's disobedience (original sin doctrine).
2. Death is a *test* that separates the worthy from the unworthy: the most final of all exams.
3. Death is blessed *release* from the illusions and miseries of life.

Not all Christians subscribe to all these views. However, they have the cumulative weight of centuries behind them. Consider for example the born-again minister who paid an unexpected visit to a woman hospitalized with a terminal illness. He burst into her room with these words: "God knows what a sinner you are! Prepare yourself for the moment of judgment!" The astonished woman quietly replied, "God and I have never given each other any trouble." Undeterred, he made repeated attempts to bully the exhausted woman into confessing sins and placing her life into his hands. Upon learning of this incident, the official hospital chaplain was even more distressed than the woman who had fallen victim to this brutal intervention. Responsible death educators and counselors hold a variety of religious beliefs themselves, but they also are aware and respectful of the traditions that influence their students and clients.

The Medieval Heritage

Traditional ways of communicating about death developed in societies that differed from ours in many ways. In medieval times, for example, most people lived in small, agrarian communities. They had little education and little contact with people outside their own circle. The concepts of having "inalienable" human rights, holding one's own political and religious opinions, and being free to pursue unlimited personal interests and ambitions were unknown. People lived in low-technology societies that were fairly stable from generation to generation and that offered little protection against the forces of nature and the disasters encountered in everyday life. When darkness fell at night, few would venture out of doors, where both real and fantasy terrors lurked. Little faith could be placed in the "medical" treatments of the time that frequently caused as much suffering as the diseases themselves. Many newborn babies failed to survive into adulthood. Infections associated with childbirth, wounds, and injuries often proved fatal to adults, and epidemics periodically decimated the population. Exposure to corpses, human and animal, was commonplace. In short, death was part of almost every person's experience from childhood onward, not hidden away from view.

Medieval society's raw encounters with dying and death produced striking themes and images. The dance of death, for example, was a compelling image that was introduced by poets, artists, and performers in the thirteenth century, if not earlier. The living and the dead are portrayed as companions in a slow and solemn dance. The *danse macabre* theme often depicted death as a skeletal figure who laid claim to all mortal souls, whether low or high born (Kastenbaum, 2002). "We all look the same to Death: kings, bishops or peasants, we are all mortal beings" was part of the core message. And a powerful message this was—bearing in mind that society was highly stratified at the time, with a few "high and mighty" people lording over the masses. The powerful idea that people are created equal arose in the common person's awareness that all souls are harvested by death.

Another significant tradition arose in the fifteenth century: the use of Christian guidebooks to help people in their last days and hours of life. This has become known to historians as the *Ars moriendi* tradition—literally, the art of dying well. Most of the guidebooks were brief descriptions of rituals that should be performed as part of the deathbed scene. The earliest guidebooks relied much on cartoonish illustrations of the dying person under assault by Satan's legions while being encouraged by guardian angels to withstand temptations. Later guidebooks were more subtle and substantive in their arguments. The passage from life to death was presented as the critical test of the soul's worthiness for salvation. People were never more at risk than at the moment of death. The priest tried to help the dying person resist the assaults and temptations of the demons who hoped to consign the soul to the flames of hell.

The *Ars moriendi* guidebooks expressed some beliefs and concerns that can be observed in our own death awareness movement. These include: (1) the view that how a person dies is a significant matter, therefore, (2) some deaths are better than others, so (3) a "good death" is a real achievement, and (4) flows more readily from a life that has been lived in the recognition of mortality, with (5) the support of caring people who have also prepared themselves properly for the encounter with death.

The capstone of the *Ars moriendi* tradition was reached in 1651 with the publication of Jeremy Taylor's *Rules and Exercises of Holy Dying*. Reverend Taylor, chaplain to ruling monarch Charles II, urged a daily "refresher course" on life and death. Today we might describe this as a life review. Taylor, however, would not have us wait until we are well up in years and reluctantly aware that this final act of life is not long in coming:

> For, if we make but one general account, and never reckon till we die . . . we shall only reckon by great sums, and remember nothing but clamorous and crying sins, and never consider concerning particulars, or forget very many. . . . But if we observe all the little passages of our life . . . see everyday sins increase so fast, and virtues grow up so slow . . . we may see our evil and amend it. . . . As therefore every night we must make our bed the memorial of our grave, so let our evening thoughts be an image of the day of judgment (pp. 48–49).

Death education and counseling had to begin anew after centuries of avoidance. What is the nature of death education and counseling today? We begin with death education.

DEATH EDUCATION AND COUNSELING: THE CURRENT SCENE

We can gain a quick view of the changed scene by becoming familiar with an organization known as Association for Death Education

The medieval dance of death was more common in visual art than in actual performance. In this sixteenth-century version, Death and his messengers are respectful as they approach a king and his lady.

and Counseling (ADEC). This nonprofit organization was incorporated in 1976 to improve the quality of death education and death-related counseling (Wass, 2002). ADEC offers national training workshops and certification procedures for death educators and counselors. If you attend one of ADEC's national conferences, you will probably be impressed with the combination of maturity and dedication. What you will probably not see is the person who has read one book, attended a workshop, and is therefore eager to impose his or her ignorance upon the world. The "pop death" people who hatched in the 1970s have mostly drifted off to other enthusiasms. Today there are more human service providers who bring substantial experience and a disciplined mind to the challenges.

ADEC members usually are aware of their own death-related feelings and have experience in areas of real life concern (e.g., supporting families after the death of a child, counseling people who have tested positive for the AIDS virus, training hospice volunteers).

Some people still do put themselves forward as death educators or counselors without possessing either the personal or experiential qualifications. The minister who burst into the dying woman's hospital room was motivated by a personal agenda, not by the expressed needs of a person he had never met. The teacher who never opens the pages of peer-reviewed scholarly journals such as *Omega; Death Studies; Illness, Crisis and Loss*; and *Mortality* will be lecturing from untested assumptions and limited personal observations.

People come to this topic with a variety of needs and expectations. Students hope to add to their competencies as nurses, paramedics, social workers, counselors, or psychologists. Others have had personal experiences that give the topic special urgency. Still others are keenly interested in working with the dying or the bereaved; others have become curious about some particular facet of death (e.g., funerals or near-death experiences). Clinical skills are probably developed best in clinical situations. Classroom examples can be helpful, but case experience and supervision is also needed. "Deep learning"—an experience that is emotional as well as intellectual—often requires a series of in-depth and personal discussions that are not always possible within the classroom. It is useful, then, for all participants to recognize what can and should be accomplished in a particular course, conference, or workshop and what must be achieved in other settings.

Richard A. Kalish (1980/1981) observed that the death educator came along at a time when two of society's most important traditional roles have undergone significant change. The priest was once the dominant person who mediated our relationship to death. The physician gained increasing prestige, however, as society shifted its orientation from hopes of a better life after death to a longer and healthier life on earth. The death educator entered the scene, then, when society was no longer as enthusiastic about accepting an afterlife as substitute for a long and fulfilling life on Earth—but also at a time when society had judged that the physician did not have the "magic" either. Death educators can come into conflicts with priests and physicians when perceived as venturing into their turfs. They can also seem to be promising too much and thereby set themselves up for failure: "Death educators and counselors are treading sacred ground, and must be expected to be attacked for their errors, their vanities, any signs of greed or lust or need of power" (Kalish, 1980/1981, p. 83). Kalish's point that death educators and counselors should be aware of their role relationships with other professionals is well taken, as is the caution that they should

refrain from creating unrealistic expectations on the part of students or clients.

Effective death educators come from a variety of established fields, such as psychology, psychiatry, medical ethics, nursing, sociology, and the ministry. It is valuable to have a solid grounding in one or more substantive fields as well as particular competency in death-related topics. Death education also takes a variety of forms. Corr and Corr (2003) remind us that informal death education can occur when we learn from life experiences, as well as within family homes and church or other religious groups. They also call particular attention to teachable moments—"unplanned life events from which important lessons can be drawn" (p. 294). (Examples of teachable moments in childhood are given in Chapter 10.) Formal death education has been introduced into the curriculum of middle schools, high schools, colleges, and universities.

Adult education in death-related issues is becoming more common. Corr and Corr (2003) point out that these programs take such forms as continuing education courses, workshops, and professional conferences; clinical pastoral education; hospice training sessions; and special programs to help people cope with disasters or traumatic loss. The Widow-to-Widow Program and the Widowed Persons Service of the American Association of Retired Persons are among the community-based resources for bereavement guidance and counseling.

It would be simplistic to maintain that death education courses have the basic function of reducing death anxiety. As we have seen (Chapter 1), there is little solid information available on what constitutes the "right" level of death anxiety. Most people express only a moderate level of death anxiety most of the time. Furthermore, anxiety can serve as a signal of possible danger, part of our survival repertoire. Skilled death educators can help people distinguish between anxiety as a vigilant alarm and as a dysfunctional response that can actually obstruct effective response.

Person-to-person contact is at the core of death education, but sometimes one can recruit a little help from an instructor who has had no

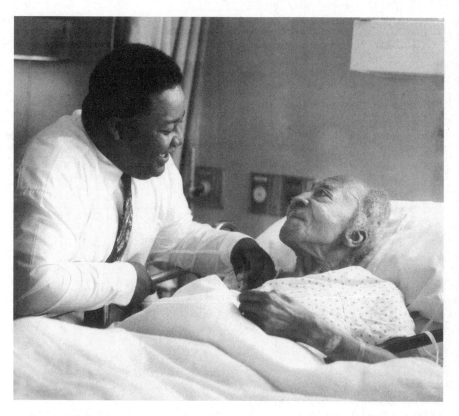

A caring relationship is often the best medicine for a terminally ill person.

birth but has been subjected to many deaths. Meet SimMan.

SimMan: An Interview with Beatrice Kastenbaum, MSN

Beatrice Kastenbaum, a pioneer in the hospice movement, is a faculty member of Arizona State University's College of Nursing and a special friend of SimMan.

INTERVIEWER: Who is SimMan?

KASTENBAUM: SimMan is a *human patient simulator.* Examine him and you will discover his physiologically correct carotid, femoral, brachial, and radial pulses. Check his blood pressure. Listen to his heart, lung, bowel, and vocal sounds—he speaks, moans, could sing, whistle, or yodel if need be.

INTERVIEWER: He breathes, too?

KASTENBAUM: He can realistically simulate all relevant airway management and patient care situations. SimMan also comes equipped with over 2,500 cardiac rhythm variants that can be monitored.

INTERVIEWER: Is he healthy?

KASTENBAUM: Healthy or end-stage dying, or anything in between. For example, sometimes he has wounds and skin lesions that need management. You can practice your skills in administering peripheral intravenous therapy in his IV training arm. If SimMan needs to have a

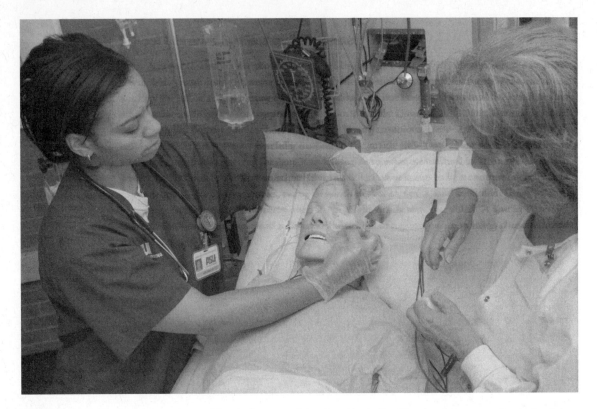

"Healthy or end-stage dying, or anything in between" *(see interview).* SimMan is a human patient simulator, here receiving attention from student and instructor at the Arizona State University School of Health and Innovation.

chest tube insertion, you can help him out in that way, too. You can apply a defibrillator if he has a cardiac emergency.

INTERVIEWER: Is he always a he?

KASTENBAUM: Not when he's being a she. There are realistic male/female genitalia for practice of urologic procedures.

INTERVIEWER: How does SimMan do what he does?

KASTENBAUM: He is integrated into a system with a patient monitor that can be operated through a PC or handheld remote controls.

INTERVIEWER: How does he decide what to say?

KASTENBAUM: His vocal responses can be prerecorded or produced spontaneously via operator microphone. In other words, SimMan can talk. He can answer questions. He can describe his pain.

INTERVIEWER: How does SimMan contribute to nurse education?

KASTENBAUM: SimMan offers the students experiences that real patients can't. He is very patient. Students can be slow and practice things over again and again. He can help them make comparisons, for instance, between different breath sounds: Is it a crackle or a wheeze? He allows students to stop midpractice to ask questions. The student can do something terribly wrong, but SimMan will come back to life and try again. SimMan is a novel experience for most students. This attracts their intention. Our students want to know, "What else can he do?" Students who are comfortable with computers and game playing learn further by creating their own scenarios and programming his responses.

INTERVIEWER: One more question: How can SimMan contribute to nursing care of life-threatened and dying patients?

KASTENBAUM: Nursing students worry about having patients die. They worry about whether they will be responsible for the death. They worry about what they will feel when the death occurs. Will they be able to stay calm and do what they should be doing? We believe that practicing the "code" situation in a simulation scenario helps to decrease some of the unknowns about what is going on and how to act. In addition, if the scenario feels real to the student, they may come to understand their own potential responses to a death. When scenarios and actual experiences are paired with self-reflection, students may be able to cope better with the stressful death-related situations they will face in the future. At least, that is my hope.

INTERVIEWER: Thank you very much. Actually I do have one more question; why is SimMan wearing my second best pair of brown shoes?

KASTENBAUM: Because they fit him perfectly, and thank you!

COUNSELING AND THE COUNSELORS

Counseling, like education, can occur under informal circumstances or as part of a systematic program. The boundary between counseling and education can also be crossed easily from either side. A classroom discussion, for example, may become transformed into an advice-sharing session to help a student decide whether or not to continue his or her practice of avoiding funerals. Similarly, a priest who is counseling the spouse of a dying person may be able to reduce anxiety by providing specific information about church beliefs and practices. In exploring counseling and the counselors, then, we are not entirely forgetting death education.

Characteristics of Professionals in the Death System

It is an article of faith that people who would help others must also be aware of their own personalities and in control of their own conflicts. Several early studies looked into this situation. Professionals representing five different fields were neither more nor less anxious than a comparison population (Morrison et al., 1981/1982). Neimeyer, Behnke, and Reiss (1983) found that the medical residents who personally felt most strongly threatened by death were also those who most often used avoidance strategies when caring for a dying patient. These were the young physicians who busied themselves in reviewing charts and finding other things to do instead of meeting their patients' needs for personal contact, information, guidance, and emotional support.

Fortunately, it is possible to improve our skills and thereby also reduce our anxieties in communicating with people in difficult situations. Attention can be given to body language as well as verbal communication. People preparing for careers in nursing, medicine, social work, and other human service fields have often found it useful to take courses and workshops to improve their communication skills.

A related question has recently received a hint of an answer. Thanatologists are the scholars, researchers, and clinicians who study death-related issues. How do they deal with death in their own lives? Feifel and Strack (2001) analyzed questionnaire responses from a sample of early (1970s) thanatologists. The authors note that these pioneering thanatologists:

> reported real apprehensions and concerns about their own death and the consequences of death. At the same time, gazing steadily at death over long periods of time does not seem to cause

morbid preoccupation or increase one's fear of mortality. Indeed, across the 15-year time interval of this survey, many participants reported a lessening fear of death, greater acceptance of death, and/or an increased appreciation of life accompanying their continued exposure to thanatology (p. 208).

The self-reported death anxiety of thanatologists was pretty much the same as the population in general. Furthermore, their lessening fear and increased acceptance over a 15-year period is also consistent with the attitudinal shift that seems to occur with many other people as they move deeper into the adult years. Many students after completing a course in death education have told me that they are still concerned about death, but feel more competent and comfortable in dealing with death-related issues—and, above everything, their appreciation of life has been enhanced.

Counseling and Psychotherapy

People do not necessarily need counseling or psychotherapy when death enters their lives (see also Chapter 11). Sometimes the needed strength can be drawn from love, friendship, a familiar environment, and one's own beliefs, values, and coping resources. Financial security and competent nursing and medical care also likely help to see the person through. Before considering counseling or therapy, then, it is usually wise to assess the total situation. Perhaps what this man needs is a more effective pain management regimen; perhaps what this woman needs is the opportunity to spend some time with the sister or brother she has not seen for years. Counseling and therapy are options that may be worth considering, but not to the neglect of the many other factors that could provide comfort and peace of mind.

Many counselors believe that one of the most important goals is to help their clients draw on their own inner strengths. A sense of helplessness can reduce an individual's ability to cope with illness, not only physically but also psychologically. The counselor can help to restore self-confidence, relaxation, and a renewed sense of still being a valuable and lovable person. This more positive psychological state can have a favorable effect on

bodily response (e.g., through improved cardiovascular circulation or more vigorous functioning of the immune system). Therapeutic touch, music therapy, guided imagery, and storytelling are among the techniques that have been used effectively (e.g., Winslade, 2001). Another promising approach has been offered by Hedtke (2002). "Reconstructing the language of grief" focuses on the way our habits of thought and speech influence the response to death and dying. For example, well-meaning friends:

> often say "I am sorry" to someone whose loved one is dead. However, . . . these words bind the grievers to an unspoken agreement about how they will proceed with their grief. This process is both produced and sanctioned to not take too long, not be too messy, not dwell on our loved one's memory, and not include public displays of extreme emotion (pp. 287–288).

Becoming more aware of such language-mediated "rules" can help to improve communication and relieve grieving people of unrealistic and burdensome expectations.

The success of any approach depends as much upon the caregiver's personality as his or her "technique." It is difficult to imagine a nervous, time-conscious, and hard-driving person achieving the same results as a firm but patient and gentle individual. Those who would provide counseling or psychotherapy in death-related situations would be wise to select an approach that is in harmony with their own personalities, as well as one that is well-grounded in the knowledge of human nature.

There is no definitive list of counseling and therapeutic approaches that can be effective in death-related situations, nor is there compelling evidence to demonstrate that one approach is generally superior to another. Furthermore, there is no reason to suppose that all dying people require such interventions. Counseling and therapy does have a place, however, in the total spectrum of services that should be available when appropriate.

HOW WE ALL CAN HELP

We all can help by realizing that *prosocial* action is well within our capabilities. Even though we live in a world where self-interest and competition are salient, we are also a species that has repeatedly demonstrated concern and compassion for others. As a matter of fact, some of our other fellow creatures have also shown this ability.

I am thinking, for example, of that alarming moment when a 3-year-old fell into the outdoor gorilla exhibit at the Brookfield Zoo in Illinois. The boy landed 18 feet down in the rock-studded pit, injured, unable to move, and probably unconscious. Binti Jua rushed over to the injured boy, with Koola, her own 16-month-old daughter, clinging to her back. The gorilla gently took the boy in her arms and brought him to a gate where he could be rescued easily. The boy survived his injuries. It turns out that Binti had been raised by humans, but it is possible that, as a good mother, she would have saved the little boy's life anyway.

Binti Jua's prosocial action is a useful reminder that murder, suicide, loss, and indifference do not tell the entire story. An aging Sigmund Freud came to the conclusion that our journey through life spins around our relationship to opposing instincts: Eros, the drive toward experience, stimulation, and love; and Thanatos, the drive toward self-destruction and death. According to Freud, the only hope for survival of the human race as well as a rewarding life for individuals is to moderate the force of Thanatos with the caring and joy of Eros (Freud, 1915, 1917). Later, Abraham Maslow (1954, 1968) would make the cogent counterargument that we do not always have to transform instinctual dangers and conflicts into positive feelings, but that the healthy and creative side of our personalities comes directly from healthy and creative experiences. Either way, there is a caring and loving side to human nature that can be called upon when we face peril and loss—as well as in our everyday interactions. Developing our own caring impulses should be a major priority for the individual and society. And, when we need a refresher course, perhaps we can call upon that outstanding death educator and counselor: Binti Jua!

One way in which we can help, then, is to recognize our potential for helping and, therefore, not feel obliged to leave everything to "experts." The experts will usually tell you that there is no substitute for the comforting presence of a family member or intimate friend. Another way in which we can help is to become more competent in communicating with each other about sudden, unexpected deaths. Communication is especially difficult because nobody really wants to break the bad news and nobody wants to hear it. There is no magic way to convert a tragic into a positive situation. Some approaches are better than other, though, in helping people start the long and difficult process of acknowledging and coping with the unexpected loss. An excellent resource is Kenneth Iserson's book, *Grave Words: Notifying Survivors about Sudden, Unexpected Deaths* (1999). IIserson provides guidelines for telephone notifications as well as direct conversations in a variety of circumstances. Iserson emphasizes the importance of clear and accurate communication to avoid adding confusion to grief:

> Although to some it may seem cruel and to others obvious, notifiers must use one of the "D" words when informing survivors about a death. "D" words include: "Died," "Death," and "Dead." For many reasons, including their own discomfort, many notifiers prefer to use euphemisms instead. The more common ones use such phrases as "passed away," "passed on," "left us," "checked out," "fatally injured," "gone," "deceased," or "expired." But it is better if you use a "D" word (Iserson, 1999, p. 43).

Another way we can help is to improve our awareness of the total family response to death. We respond to dying, grief, and loss as individuals but also as members of family constellations that often have their own styles of coping with stress. Elliott J. Rosen's *Families Facing Death* (1998) focuses on not the sudden death but the sometimes lengthy period in which family life is under stress in the anticipation of death. His observations include some facts that have not been generally appreciated, for example, the early onset of family stress:

> A family actually begins to address the prospect of loss with the very first symptoms of disease. As incredible as this may seem, when any member of a family is stricken with illness, even the mildest of physical ailment, the family automatically begins a process of adaptation to preserved threatened homeostasis. . . . If little Mary Smith

gets the sniffles, her parents may become overly solicitous, aware of every twitch of the youngster's nose. Mary may want to crawl into Mommy's lap, a behavior she had more or less abandoned, and Mommy will readily comply . . . (Rosen, 1998, p. 76).

Families sense the threat quickly and do what they can—for as long as they can—to keep things seeming and feeling "normal." The more aware we are of such family dynamics, the more likely we are to provide intelligent and effective support.

These are but a few of the ways in which we—all of us—can help each other.

SUMMARY

Often there is a feeling of helplessness when people close to us are dying or grieving. Perhaps we should just stand back and leave it all to the experts. This chapter proposes that there is much all of us can do, whether as professional care providers, family members, friends, colleagues, or neighbors. Learning how to communicate effectively—both verbally and nonverbally—is a key.

We saw that death education and counseling have their roots in ancient times. In the past, the emphasis often was on guiding people safely from one life to the next. Much of the emphasis today is on the individual and family facing death or living with grief. Common to both past and current philosophies is the belief that death is a central fact of life and deserves our most serious and enlightened attention. We cannot simply repeat the approaches taken in the past, however, because conditions of life in ancient and medieval times differ so much from our own. Nevertheless, attention to the Arabian perspective on mortality, and the Christian *Ars moriendi* guidebooks reminds us that we are not the first to face life-and-death issues.

The modern death awareness movement in the United States established itself during the 1970s with such developments as the beginnings of the Association for Death Education and Counseling. Effective death educators come from a variety of fields, including anthropology, psychology, psychiatry, medical ethics, nursing, social work, sociology, and the ministry. The scope of death education continues to expand, now reaching more people who are preparing for professional caregiving careers. Nevertheless, many human service providers (teachers, in particular) still complete their studies without preparation for helping the dying, grieving, or suicidal people they will encounter from time to time.

Professional caregivers often experience intense stress as they struggle not only to communicate with patients and families but also to cope with difficult work environments. Burnout and compassion fatigue have become major problems among nurses and physicians, increasing staff turnover and interfering with quality care. It has become clear that improved communication among caregivers is needed to reduce their frustration and anxiety. Caregivers also face the challenge of distinguishing their own needs, stresses, and impulses from those of their patients. Organizational solutions, strengthened peer support, and individual relaxation techniques can help to prevent or reduce burnout. People do not necessarily need counseling or psychotherapy when death enters their lives. Often the needed strength can be drawn from love, friendship, a familiar environment, and one's own beliefs, values, and coping resources. Financial security and competent nursing and medical care are also important.

We all can help each other when faced with death-related stress and loss. Specific examples were given about communicating in unexpected, sudden death situations and understanding family responses to life-threatening illness. Expert care providers often play a significant role, but there is no substitute for compassion and companionship shared between one person and another.

REFERENCES

Abenroth, M., & Flannery, J. (2006). Predicting the risk of compassion fatigue: A study of hospice nurses. *Journal of Hospice & Palliative Nursing, 8,* 346–356.

Addington-Hall, J. M., & Saffron, K. (2005). A national survey of health professionals and volunteers working in voluntary hospices in the UK: Staff and volunteers' experiences of working in hospices. *Palliative Medicine, 19,* 49–57.

Aiken, L. H., Clarke, S. P., Sloane, D. M., Sochalski, J., & Silber, J. H. (2002). Hospital nurse staffing and patient mortality, nurse burnout, and job dissatisfaction. *Journal of the American Medical Association, 288,* 1987–1993.

Al-Sabwah, M. N., & Abdel-Khalek, A. M. (2005/2006). Four year cross-sectional comparison of death distress among nursing college students. *Omega, Journal of Death & Dying, 52,* 237–248.

Anderson, K. A., & Gaugler, J. E. (2006/2007). The grief experiences of certified nursing assistants: Personal growth and complicated grief. *Omega, Journal of Death & Dying, 54,* 301–318.

Anonymous. (2005). Comment on "Job story." www.aboutmyjob.com/main.php3?action=displayarticle&artid=575.html

Atkins, S., & Nygaard, J. (2004). Relationship between patient mortality and nurses' level of education. *Journal of the American Medical Association, 291,* 1320–1321.

Bromley, A. (2005). Mindfulness courses reduce stress among doctors, nurses—lead to more compassionate patient care. www.virginia.edu/insideuva/2005/mindfulness.html

Chethik, N. (2001). *FatherLoss.* New York: Hyperion.

Corr, C. A., & Corr, D. M. (2003). Death education. In C. Bryant (Ed.), *Handbook of death and dying:* Vol. 1 (pp. 292–301). Thousand Oaks, CA: Sage.

Feifel, H., & Strack, S. (2001). Thanatologists view death: A 15-year perspective. *Omega, Journal of Death and Dying, 43,* 97–112.

Figley, C. R. (Ed.). (1995). *Compassion fatigue: Coping with secondary traumatic stress disorder in those who treat the traumatized.* New York: Brunner/Mazel.

Freud, S. (1915). Thoughts for the times on war and death. In *Collected works of Sigmund Freud:* Vol. 14. London: Hogarth Press.

Freud, S. (1917). Mourning and melancholia. In *Collected works of Sigmund Freud:* Vol. 14. London: Hogarth Press.

Hedtke, L. (2002). Reconstructing the language of death and grief. *Illness, Crisis & Loss, 10,* 285–293.

Ifeagwazi, C. M. (2005/2006). The influence of marital status on self-report of symptoms of psychological burnout among nurses. *Omega, Journal of Death & Dying, 52,* 359–37.

Iserson, K. V. (1999). *Grave words. Notifying survivors about sudden, unexpected deaths.* Tucson, AZ: Galen.

Kalish, R. A. (1980/1981). Death educator as deacon. *Omega, Journal of Death and Dying, 11,* 75–85.

Kastenbaum, R. (1977). We covered death today. *Death Education, 1,* 85–92.

Kastenbaum, R. (1993). Ars Moriendi. In R. Kastenbaum & B. Kastenbaum (Eds.), *Encyclopedia of death* (pp. 17–19). New York: Avon.

Kastenbaum, R. (2002). Danse macabre. In R. Kastenbaum (Ed.), *Macmillan encyclopedia of death and dying:* Vol. 1 (pp. 201–202). New York: Macmillan.

Kastenbaum, R. (2004). *On our way. The final passage through life and death.* Berkeley: University of California Press.

Kastenbaum, R., Barber, T. X., Wilson, S. G., Ryder, B. L., & Hathaway, L. B. (1981). *Old, sick and helpless: Where therapy begins.* Cambridge, MA: Ballinger.

Kastenbaum, R., & Schneider, S. (1991). Does ADEC have a prayer? A survey report. *The Forum Newsletter, 16*(5), 1, 12–13.

Kaufman, S. R. (2005). *And a time to die: How American hospitals shape the end of life.* New York: Scribner.

Kelly, B., & Varghese, F. T. N. (2006) The seduction of autonomy: Countertransference and assisted suicide. In R. S. Katz & T. A. Johnson (Eds.), *When professionals weep. Emotional and Countertransference responses in end-of-life care* (pp. 39–54). New York: Routledge.

Kempson, D. A. (2000/2001). Effects of intentional touch on complicated grief of bereaved mothers. *Omega, Journal of Death and Dying, 42,* 341–354.

Lundberg, U. (2000). Workplace stress. In G. Fink (Ed.), *Encyclopedia of stress:* Vol. 3 (pp. 684–692). New York: Academic Press.

Manion, K. (2005). The unspoken epidemic: Burnout in healthcare. www.worklifedesign.org/Resources/Burnout.pdf

Maslach, C., & Leiter, M. P. (2000). Burnout. In G. Fink (Ed.), *Encyclopedia of stress:* Vol. 1 (pp. 358–364). New York: Academic Press.

Maslow, A. H. (1954). *Motivation and personality.* New York: Harper & Row.

Maslow, A. H. (1968). *Toward a psychology of being.* New York: Van Nostrand Reinhold.

Mathers, P. (1974). (Trans.). *The book of the thousand and one nights:* Vol. 2. New York: St. Martin's.

Morrison, J. K., Vanderwyst, D., Cocozza, J., & Dowling, S. (1981/1982). Death concerns among mental health workers. *Omega, Journal of Death and Dying, 12,* 179–190.

Neimeyer, C. J., Behnke, M., & Reiss, J. (1983). Constructs and coping: Physicians' responses to patient death. *Death Education, 7,* 245–266.

Oliver, D. P., Porock, D., & Oliver, D. B. (2006). Managing the secrets of dying backstage: The voices of nursing home staff. *Omega, Journal of Death & Dying, 53,* 193–208.

Papadatou, D. (2006). Care providers' responses to the death of a child. In A. Goldman, R. Hain, & S. Lieber (Eds.), *Oxford textbook of pediatric palliative care.* Oxford: Oxford University Press.

Powell, D. (2002, November 5). Presentation, Neuroscience Society Annual Meeting, Orlando, Florida.

Riordan R. J., & Saltzer S. K. (1992). Burnout prevention among health care providers working with the terminally ill: A literature review. *Omega, Journal of Death and Dying, 25,* 17–24.

Rogers, A. E., Hwang, W. T., Scott, L. D., Aiken, L. H., & Dinges, D. F. (2004). The working hours of hospital staff nurses and patient safety. *Health Affairs, 23,* 202–212.

Rosen, E. (1998). *Families facing death* (Rev. ed.). San Francisco: Jossey-Bass.

Rosenblatt, P. C. (2000). *Parent grief. Narratives of loss and relationship.* New York: Brunner/Mazel.

Salva, V. (2005). Job story: Burnout in my 5th year . . . another nursing statistic. www.aboutmyjob.com/main. php3?action=displayarticle&artid=575.html

Schneider, S., & Kastenbaum, R. (1993). Patterns and meanings of prayer in hospice caregivers: An exploratory study. *Death Studies, 17,* 471–485.

Smith, L. R. (1996). Gillian's journey. *The Forum Newsletter* (American Association for Death Education and Counseling), *22*(1), 14–16.

Sobel, H. (Ed.). (1981). *Behavior therapy in terminal care.* Cambridge, MA: Ballinger.

Speck, P. (2000). Working with dying people: On being good enough. In A. Obholzer & V. Z. Roberts (Eds.), *The unconscious at work: Individual and organizational stress at work* (2nd ed., pp. 94–100). London: Brunner-Routledge.

Taylor, J. (1977). *The rules and exercises of holy dying.* New York: Arno Press. (Original work published 1651.)

Tebrani, N. (2004). *Workplace trauma.* Florence, KY: Routledge.

Tolomiczenko, G. S., Kahan, M., Ricci, M., Strathern, L., Jeney, C., Patterson, K., & Wilson, L. (2005). Nursing and health care management and policy. SARS: Coping with the impact at a community hospital. *Journal of Advanced Nursing, 50,* 101–110.

Turnipseed, D., Jr. (1987). Burnout among hospice nurses: An empirical assessment. *Hospice Journal, 3,* 105–119.

Vachon, M. L. S. (1987). *Occupational stress in the care of the critically ill, the dying, and the bereaved.* Washington: Hemisphere.

Vahey, D. C., Aiken, L., Sloane, D. M., & Vargas, D. (2004). Nurse burnout and patient satisfaction. *Medical Care 42*(2), (Suppl.), 57–66.

Wass. H. (2002). Death education. In R. Kastenbaum (Ed.), *Macmillan encyclopedia of death and dying:* Vol. 1 (pp. 211–218). New York: Macmillan.

Winslade, J. (2001). Putting stories to work. *The Forum* (Association for Death Education and Counseling), *27*(2), 1, 3–4.

GLOSSARY

Ars moriendi: The art of dying well. First presented in illustrated books of the fifteenth century.

Burnout: Emotional exhaustion as a result of prolonged job stress.

Compassion fatigue: A major factor in burnout for human service care providers.

Danse macabre: A visual image of personified Death leading people to their graves in a slow, dignified dance (first appearing in thirteenth century).

Human patient simulator: An interactive device in the form of an adult or child that can serve as a practice patient for nursing and medical students.

Prosocial: Thoughts, feelings, and actions that are motivated by the intention to help others.

ON FURTHER THOUGHT . . .

Useful online resources:

Association for Death Education and Counseling
www.adec.org
Bioethics.net
www.bioethics.net
Center for Death Education and Bioethics
www.uwlax.edu/sociology/cde&b
Compassionate Friends, Inc.
www.compassionatefriends.org
Hastings Center
www.thehastingscenter.org
Medline Plus Health Information
www.nlm.nih.gov/medlineplus
National Institutes of Health Bioethics Resources on the Web
www.nih.gov/sigs/bioethics/

Help wanted!

In recent years, more people have been helping more people cope with dying and grief. However, there are still large numbers of people whose distress is often neglected. These include people residing in nursing homes and geriatric facilities, and persons with mental retardation, especially if institutionalized. It is commonly thought that cognitive impairment or limitations will shield a person from anxiety and grief. This assumption is seldom tested and therefore becomes self-perpetuating. If you are or will become a human services professional, perhaps you would consider taking a leadership role in encouraging more awareness of the death-related thoughts and feelings of people with impairment and more attention to their needs. Some useful readings:

Casarett, D. J., Hirschman, K. B., & Henry, M. R. (2001) Does hospice have a role in nursing home care at the end of life? *Journal of the American Geriatric Society, 49,* 1493–1498.

Johnson, S. (2005). Living and dying in nursing homes. In K. J. Doka, B. Jennings, & C.A. Corr (Eds.), *Ethical dilemmas at the end of life* (pp. 237–250). Washington, DC: Hospice Foundation of America.

Kauffman, J. (2005). *Guidebook on helping persons with mental retardation mourn*. Amityville, N.Y.: Baywood.

Kloeppel, D., & Hollins, S. (1989). Double handicap: Mental retardation and death in the family. *Death Studies, 13,* 31–38.

Yanok, J., & Beifus, J. A. (1993). Communicating about loss and mourning: Death education for individuals with mental retardation. *Mental Retardation, 31,* 144–147.

Many members of the baby boomers and following generations have demonstrated their motivation to stay healthy with diet and exercise. There is growing public recognition of the ways in which lifestyle contributes to longevity.

chapter 15

GOOD LIFE, GOOD DEATH?

Trying to make sense of it all

Civil War soldiers were, in fact, better prepared to die than to kill, for they lived in a culture that offered many lessons in how life should end. But these lessons had to be adapted to the dramatically changed circumstances of the Civil War.
—Drew Gilpin Faust (2008, p. 6)

Esther Britt lay in an oversize casket the color of an overcast sky. She wasn't always so heavy, but relatives say a string of illnesses and unhealthy life choices pushed her weight past 350 pounds and led here Wednesday afternoon—lying at age 56 in Stevens Funeral Home. "Her body was just tired, worn out," her sister Mary Britt, 54, said. "This is better for her. Hard for us, but better for her."
—Therese Vargas (April 28, 2008)

What actually happens is that we leave it to others to make sense of our death.
—Herman H. van der Kloot Meijburg (2005, p.53)

In those days people were born in places where people lived. Astonishing, but true. I came into this world, would you believe it, in this very room. It was my parents' bedroom and their bed was over there, against that wall. I was born in that bed.
—Alexander McCall Smith (2005, p. 6)

Good to begin well, better to end well.
—Advice from a fortune cookie

An analysis of e-mail, phone calls and voice mail messages from the World Trade Center shows that at least 353 of those who died in the towers were able to reach people outside, the New York Times reported Sunday.
—Associated Press (2002)

I am inclined to think that these muscles and bones of mine would have gone off long ago to Megara or Boeotia—by the dog they would, if they had been moved only by their own idea of what was best, and if I had not chosen the better and nobler part, instead of playing truant and running away, of enduring any punishment which the state inflicts.
—A prisoner awaiting execution in 399 B.C.

"My in-laws had started to treat us like outcasts and nobody would come near us or touch us," she said, adding that she can cope with the threat of death, but not with the stigma AIDS carries.
—Quoted in Hussain (2002)

*As I walked into Dad's room I was struck by how small he looked. Above him an oscillo-scope traced the electrical activity of his heart, and chrome IV poles framed the head of his bed. The IV in his left arm was attached to a bottle of saline, and a plastic bag of antibiotic solution was piggy-backed into the tubing at his wrist. Another IV, this one a large-bore catheter that entered the subclavian vein just below the midportion of his right collarbone, was attached to a three-way stopcock valve. Through it saline was flowing at a to-keep-open rate; also attached to the stopcock was a manometer that provided measurement of central venous pressure, a guide to his volume status. The third channel led to a dopamine drip with its own infusion pump that was standing by, just in case that medication was needed to raise his blood pressure. Oxygen tubing ran from his nose. A call button was pinned to his pillow. A urine bottle hung at his bedrail. On his bedside table was a cafeteria tray with his untouched breakfast, a pitcher of water, and a menu of the next day's meals.
"Hi, Dad." I managed to say. "How are you doing?"*
—Byock (1997, p. 15)

The party is still going on. I don't want to go.
—Billie S., a woman receiving hospice home care

In the nineteenth century United States, the "good death" was a powerful and pervasive concept. How a person died was crucial to determining how well he or she had lived and what the afterlife would hold. The Civil War often violated the conditions for a good death, and it did so on an unprecedented scale. There was a profound effect on family survivors. According to historian Drew Gilpin Faust (2008, p. 208):

The nation was a survivor, too, transformed by its encounter with death, obligated by the sacrifices of its dead. The war's staggering human cost demanded a new sense of national destiny, one designed to ensure that lives had been sacrificed for appropriately lofty ends. So much suffering had to have transcendent purpose.

That Johnny Rebel and Jeremiah Union had given their young lives under horrific conditions required making good somehow. It must be that their sacrifice was itself good, noble, sacred. It was now up to the nation to live up to these

deaths that did not meet the prevailing criteria for a comforting and meaningful exit.

Esther Britt's death was not considered "good" by either her friends or herself—other than the fact that it ended a life that had become increasingly burdensome. By current standards, it was also a short life. So many other women in Southwest Virginia have been faltering toward early death from a difficult life that public health officials have become alarmed (Vargas, 2008). Life expectancy for women in communities such as Pulaski and Radford has dropped markedly nearly six years over a 16-year period: a radical decline, especially in a nation with increasing longevity. Men in this region have also been declining in life expectancy, though not to such a degree. Poor diets and smoking stand out as obvious contributors to the decline in health and longevity, but do not seem to tell the whole story. The director of the local health district identifies the area's impoverished economy as a major influence: "If you are struggling to put food on the table, you don't have time to think about prevention." Few people can afford health insurance, and the price of gas discourages visits to the doctor's office. Women might be at particular risk because they put the welfare of others above their own, as seemed to be the case with Esther Britt, a former nurse. There are no active Civil War battlefields in Virginia these days, but some people becomes "just tired, worn out" in a grinding life that terminates in what would be difficult to regard as a good death.

Dutch scholar Herman H. van der Kloot Meijburg (2005) confirms that often we do not have the opportunity to shape the end of our lives as we might choose. Statistics from The Netherlands (fairly comparable with those of the United States) indicate that only about one person in three can have much control over the way he or she dies. Most people either die suddenly and unexpectedly or slip away after an illness that was "diagnosed and treated over time, but never caused any reason for serious concern because it never culminated in a crisis whereby intervention was required" (p. 52). For about two out of three people, then, the "goodness" of a death is much dependent on the way it is interpreted by the survivors, the stories they construct. There is growing awareness that end-of-life stories have much to do with the memories and well-being of family and caregivers (Gelfand et al., 2005).

Another hint about the good death is provided by a wise and worldly woman in Alexander McCall Smith's (2005) novel, *44 Scotland Street*. She is offering guidance to a younger woman who has yet to discover who she is and where she is going. The older woman has a firm sense of place and identity: She has the security of feeling that death will complete her life within a coherent framework of experience. Why not die where she was born? That would somehow seem right.

The fortune cookie leaves a question unanswered: *How* to end well? This chapter is not the answer, for each of us must find our own. Nevertheless, we will continue to journey together through territory both familiar and unfamiliar. Much of what we have surveyed has its setting in our own society. It is also familiar

because we have looked at human interactions, children developing their ideas about the world, adults encountering challenge, the facts behind headlines and, perhaps most significantly, the workings of our own minds. These familiar landmarks have also taken on unfamiliar aspects, however. Our visit to the world of childhood revealed curiosities and anxieties about death that adults have usually assumed are not of concern to the young. The headlines have often opened the way to discovering the extent of suicide, homicide, and other destructive patterns within our society. Our minds struggle to acknowledge the reality of risk and death, while at the same time trying to protect us against a keen awareness of mortality. Furthermore, we have repeatedly found a diversity of ideas and opinions on core issues, including the nature and meaning of death.

Death sometimes makes itself known to us as a thought that curls around the edges of our minds for a moment before again disappearing. Sometimes it is the thrust of an invisible dagger we feel when we see the marks of mortal vulnerability in a person we love. Sometimes it is the bodies trapped in the crushed automobile or scattered at the scene of a mass murder. The varied contact points with aspects of death are hard to bring together within a coherent and comforting framework. It is in our nature, however, to try to make sense of our experiences.

Our unifying theme is the question: Good life, good death? I have no quarrel with the fortune cookie's message. Many people believe that a "good" life prepares the way for a "good death." This has long been a component of religious beliefs as expressed, for example, by Jeremy Taylor (1665/1970) in his *Rules and Exercises of Holy Dying*. Some have drawn the lesson that we should live each day as though our last. Buddhist philosophy emphasizes a continuous flow in which life and death move together in everything we do (Gyatso, 1985). A good death is intrinsically related to a good life because what we call "life" and what we call "death" have always been companions.

Variations on this theme have continued to develop. For example, Avery D. Weisman (1972), a pioneering psychotherapist and researcher with terminally ill people, introduced the influential concept of an *appropriate death,* that is, the death we would choose for ourselves if they really had a choice. The "good" death, then, might be very different from one person to another. Many writers focus on the importance of having lived a full and rewarding life. People who can accept their lives are thought to be more likely to experience a "good death." Partisans of this view include Erikson (1950) in his theory of lifespan development, and Tomer and Eliason (1996) in their regret theory of death anxiety.

That a good life leads to a good death is an appealing concept but not yet a firmly demonstrated fact. We will be in a better position to reflect on all these ideas as this chapter and book come to a close.

THREE PATHS TO DEATH

The people who sent messages to their loved ones from the World Trade Center (WTC) towers on September 11, 2001, the condemned prisoner in Athens, and AIDS victims in Gauhati, India, were in circumstances that raise difficult questions about a "good death."

The men and women who died in the WTC towers expected to return home for an evening with family or friends. Neither they nor their loved ones had reason to expect that their lives would come to an abrupt end. They suffered what Leviton (1991) had previously identified as a *horrendous death.* It would be difficult to find anything good about this kind of death:

- The victims had done nothing to provoke the savage attack.
- Their individuality had counted for nothing: The terrorist's goal was to compile a large body count.
- The sudden and unexpected catastrophe allowed no time for the victims to prepare themselves spiritually for the end of their lives or to make practical arrangements for their families.
- Families were shattered, burdened with grief, deprived of companionship and support, and faced with the challenge of somehow going on with life despite this tremendous blow. The report of last-minute communications

from victims to families does raise a question: Is it better to die swiftly or to become aware in advance? Most people say they would prefer to slip away from life, preferably from peaceful sleep. Awareness of imminent death is experienced as torment. Family members who received that last call from the WTC responded with shock and anxiety. Nevertheless, they cherished that last communication and used it as a transitional memory structure between the person they loved and the absence they now experience. The victims themselves were strongly motivated to make that final contact. Furthermore, the simple act of placing the call was something that one could still do—an expression of self against overwhelming catastrophe. Good to die at the WTC on 9/11? No. Good to have had that last moment to communicate with loved ones? Probably so.

- Socrates is generally considered to be the father of philosophical thought, although other insightful thinkers had preceded him. He was respected in his own time as valiant soldier, competent stone mason, and relentless seeker of truth. His death sentence was the unexpected outcome of bogus charges brought against him as payback for bruising some Athenian egos (Ahrensdorf, 1995; Kastenbaum, 2002). Socrates could have escaped execution by a few words of contrition or by boarding a ship provided by his friends while the authorities pretended not to notice. Within his prison walls, Socrates patiently reasoned with his friends about the meaning of life and death and sought to relieve their anxieties by his own serenity. When he accepted the cup of hemlock (if that's what it really was, see Ober, 1988) from the reluctant hands of a jailer, Socrates offered himself as a model for facing death with equanimity, along with his characteristic twist of humor. This was quite a bad death: miscarriage of justice, silencing one of humankind's greatest thinkers, depriving a great but troubled city-nation of an invaluable citizen. However, history also regards this episode as a sterling example of a very good death: bringing a clear and calm philosophical mind to the end of life and facing death in such a way as to affirm and fulfill all that has gone before. Despite the injustice of the situation, here was a good death that flowed from a good life.

- AIDS continues to be regarded throughout the world as a tainted pathway to death. Enlightened caregivers have had to contest with negative attitudes toward the disease and its victims. This pattern of avoidant behaviors exists both in developed nations and in countries that are struggling for stability and survival (such as much of sub-Saharan Africa). Our example comes from India, where the actual number of people infected with HIV/AIDS has been massively underestimated and where both the victims and their families are often ostracized by society, thereby impairing prevention and treatment efforts. It is estimated that there are now about 4 million HIV/AIDS cases in India, but this number could rise to 25 million within the next few years. The human side is illustrated by the woman quoted at the start of the chapter. Her family was shunned while her husband suffered and then died from AIDS, and landlords would boot them out when they learned of his condition. The whole family was rejected by society not because the husband was dying but because he was dying of AIDS. The symptoms that accompany AIDS are stressful, painful, and eventually debilitating (although controlled more adequately today in societies with the resources to do so). Rejection—"social death" at the extreme—intensifies the ordeal experienced by people with HIV/AIDS and their families.

We take now a more extended example from our own society that raises the good death/bad death issue in a different way.

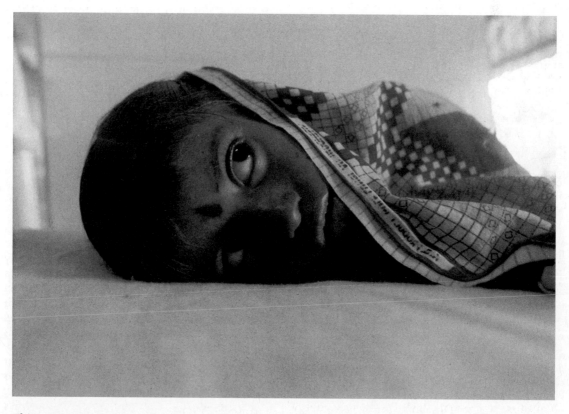

This young woman is among the many victims of AIDS in India, one of several nations that have been slow to recognize and respond to this crisis.

A FATHER DIES:
A MISSION BEGINS

Ira Byock, M.D., is founder of the American Academy of Hospice and Palliative Medicine and a leading advocate for improved care of terminally ill people. It was early in Byock's medical career that his father was struck with a fatal illness. Byock was stunned, moved, and instructed by this experience.

The hospital scene is described in the opening quotation. As a physician, Byock recognized the devices that were connected to the small-looking man in the bed. As a son, he felt disoriented by the barrier they established between his father and himself. How do you relate to a person who has become a component of a life support system? "Hi, Dad," I managed to say, "How are you doing?" Here is a situation that has confronted an increasing number of people in recent years. One could hardly feel more awkward and unnatural. We know less from the standpoint of the person connected to the life support system. Often consciousness and responsiveness are impaired, but sometimes the person can hear and understand what is being said. A scene such as this would be difficult to describe as "good death" by either the patient or the family member.

But wait—the purpose of life support systems is to support life! Byock's father recovered with the assistance of these devices and devoted nursing care. This made it possible for the family to have more time together with the father still an active participant. It might have been anything but a "good death" if he had died during this episode, but as it happened, quality care gave him a little more time to live. Situations such as these caution us against simplistic conclusions about the relationship between life support systems and the "good death."

His father's death occurred later, peacefully, at home. Byock (1997) noted:

He appeared suddenly to be relaxed, as if the work, whatever it had been, was over. He was peaceful, no longer sweating, and his breathing was easy and deep, though irregular. Mom stood touching his foot, and Anita and I sat on each side of the bed touching his arms, as he drew his last breath and left. For the next hour we continued our vigil: hugging one another, crying intermittently, grieving openly and together (p. 24).

Sy Byock seemed to experience the moment of death as a relief and release. There was no way of knowing how much awareness he had of the situation—but if he did, it would have been the loving presence of his family. A sense of unity and completion was experienced by the family itself, much different from the alienating hospital situation. The same person and the same family, then, had two very different experiences, one at the brink of death and one at the actual final moment. The death had been expected. Nevertheless, Byock, stunned, found it difficult to accept the fact that he would never see his father again. All that Byock had learned about managing terminal illness as a physician now seemed inadequate. He realized that the health care system was at war with death and, therefore, with dying people as well:

If death on the wards was macabre, in the emergency room, it was ghastly. Passings that should have been peaceful turned gruesome. Nursing homes, for example, routinely sent patients only moments away from death to the hospital by ambulance, lights and sirens blazing. By transferring the almost-dead to the emergency room, nursing homes could claim a mortality rate of nearly zero, while providing evidence to families, and any interested attorneys, that "everything possible" had been done. This bizarre scenario extended not only to sudden deaths but also to people who were unconscious, in the final moments of dying, and expected to die. Even though the medical people knew that death had arrived and any efforts would be futile, the system and their training compelled them to attempt CPR before they could pronounce someone officially dead (p. 27).

Byock is a physician who, touched by his father's death and appalled by the mismanagement of dying people in the health care system, has since contributed much to medical education and the improvement of terminal care. Futile medical procedures perpetuate the health care system's unwillingness to face the reality of dying and death and can even constitute a kind of assault on the patient in which respect and dignity lose out. The opportunity for family and patient to have time together in familiar surroundings can encourage meaningful communication and the affirmation and demonstration of loving relationships. Whatever else "the good death" might be, it is more likely to occur within a supportive interpersonal framework and without medical interventions that are both futile and alienating. We will continue to work with the

concept of "the good death" as we move along.

A SHIFT IN THE MEANING OF LIFE AND DEATH?

"Dying well" is perhaps a more accurate term than "the good death" because the emphasis is usually on what occurs while the person is still living. Nevertheless, our interpretations of death influence our attitudes toward end-of-life experiences. A person who regards death as destination and fulfillment may have a different set of expectations and priorities than one who regards death as end or outcome. Five alternative interpretations were considered in Chapter 3. These were all what might be called structural or cognitive models. Each proposed its own version of the nature of

Socrates, the gadfly of Athens, teaches his last lessons moments before he accepts the lethal cup of hemlock. The original 1787 painting by Jacques Louis David can be found in New York's Metropolitan Museum of Art.

death. We can refresh our memory with the help of Table 15-1.

TABLE 15-1
Meanings that Have Been Given to Death

- Death is an enfeebled form of life.
- Death is a continuation of life.
- Death is perpetual development.
- Death is waiting.
- Death is cycling and recycling.

Each of these interpretations has distinctive implications for how we might prepare ourselves for death. We have examined our feelings about death, especially in when we focused on anxiety, denial, and acceptance. Shifts will continue to occur as we move deeper into the twenty-first century. One of these developments is associated with the emergence of a computer-mediated society and will be considered a little later. Here we attend to the words of Billie S., the hospice patient who sighed, "The party is still going on. I don't want to go." She is not the only person who has felt this way. It seems to be a common sentiment among that most famous of generations, the baby boomers. A long life has become more attractive for many people. Throughout world history, people often feared growing old because of possible infirmity, suffering, and abandonment. The psalmist of the Old Testament records the lament: "Cast me not off in the time of old age; forsake me not when my strength faileth. Now also when I am old and greyheaded, O God, forsake me not" (Psalm 71:9).

Death was often regarded as release from infirmity, suffering, and indignity. This attitude has not been restricted to elderly people because infirmity, suffering, and indignity can occur at any age. Suicide has been one way of acting on the feeling that life can be cured only by death. Another path has been systematic degradation of health and heightened risk taking, as by the abuse of alcohol and drugs. Less obvious is the silent withdrawal from life. Activities that once were attractive now seem either out of reach or only further sources of distress. Read history at ground level—the lives of everyday people—and we encounter repeatedly the scourges of poverty, famine, illness, bereavement, oppression, and war. Life was hard and dangerous. Many people had to ask themselves, "Why go on?" even as they struggled to go on.

Lullabies, those charming and comforting songs we sing to sleeping babies, have their origins in misery so deep and pervasive that the desire to live was strenuously challenged by the temptation to get it all over with. Kalle Achte (1989) tells us that:

> lullabies originated during the centuries that most people lived in agricultural communities, did hard work, and battled against the forces of nature. Famine was an ever-present threat, and epidemics killed many people, especially young children. . . . A woman's life was especially difficult at that time. Some mothers may have felt that death offered the only release from a joyless life and continuous labor. The mother's own depression and frustration may have been crucial factors in the origins of lullabies with death themes. Perhaps overworked and depressed mothers transferred their own death wishes to the child (pp. 177–178).

An example of a death-themed lullaby:

> Today Vanyushka will die
> the funeral will be held tomorrow
> we shall bury Vanya
> and toll the big bell (p. 177).

Death-ridden lullabies became less common as the conditions of life improved for many people— and that's the point here. Life has been looking better to people fortunate enough to receive such benefits as abundant food and improved health care, and such perks as the automobile and home video. Traditional attitudes toward death were forged when for most people life was hard, dangerous, and brief. As conditions of life have improved, aging has come to seem a less fearsome prospect, and death has not seemed to lurk so ominously around every corner.

Competing models of death emerged even when life was very difficult. The ancient "death as enfeebled life" model was challenged by the new Christian doctrine that life is only an interlude of waiting for a spiritually enhanced afterlife. Believers in both models of death shared the same difficult life conditions. Their expectations differed significantly, however. The person who maintained the older belief might regard death as not so dramatically different from life. Worn down from aging and hard times, one has already lost so much, and there is not much to expect from death because the decline continues. By contrast, the Christian vision of death promised transformation. The miseries of life can be exchanged for the blessings of heaven. Death, therefore, could seem a lot more appealing than the frustrations, disappointments, sorrows, and suffering of life. This positive outlook, however, was shadowed by the fear of damnation and punishment. Perhaps a stressful life would be followed by an even more stressful experience after death. The stakes were high for Christians: salvation or damnation?

Today, fewer people seem impelled to think of death as either a terrifying punishment or release from a burdensome life. This life on Earth has attracted some of the attention formerly accorded to death. Many elderly men and women are active, vigorous, and strongly engaged with life. Attitude studies find that many elderly people are well satisfied with their lives. A retired public health officer, for example, told me that "I am finally discovering who I am after all these years, and having the time of my life. The absolute time of my life!"

We would not want to exaggerate the differences between past and present attitudes. Many people treasured life and did all they could to survive in difficult circumstances. There were also people then as well as now who "had it made" and were more interested in continuing a pleasant life than in entering a promised land after death. Nevertheless, death may be becoming less salient in everyday life (Hayslip & Peveto, 2004). We may still have our own individual mix of anxiety, denial, and acceptance and yet feel less intensely about death as either an overpowering catastrophe or a transcendent blessing.

The *regret theory* of death anxiety suggests that people who consider themselves to have full and satisfying lives are less anxious about death because they have already lived well. It might be useful, though, to remember that a life filled with stress and loss does not necessarily produce regrets. Willa T., a woman in her mid-80s, nearly blind for the past several years, put it this way:

> You can't change the past. All the bad stuff was part of all the good stuff. You can't really pick and choose. All in all, I've had more in life than I had any right to expect. But, listen, I want more. More life. I don't want to hear about "them pearly gates." I don't want to see them pearly gates any time soon. It's not that I have any problem with death. I don't. Do you understand? It's that I'm used to living and I haven't used up living. Poor Razzi was the same way. She died last night, you know, or early in the morning. I am not afraid of that happening to me, but, oh, it would be a shame, wouldn't it, to have to leave when there's so much more in front of you every day!

Within this perspective, Death is not an awesome figure, terrifying or beatific. Instead, Death is more the spoilsport who turns out the lights and says "The party's over" before we are ready to go.

The Golden Rule Revisited

"Do unto others as we would have done to ourselves." This simple guide has often proved difficult to follow. World culture has long been faced with a discordant pair of propositions. One is the *should,* as in: "we should treat each other with respect and compassion." The other is the *observational,* as in "every day I see self-interest, malice, and indifference in human interactions." This tension between ideal and reality courses through the spiritual teachings of world religions, critical decision making on the national and international level, and our own day-to-day interactions. This tension has its many twists and turns. For example, peacekeeping forces in Kosovo and East Timor had to use lethal weapons in order to prevent violence. In the domestic sphere, this kind of irony was not lost on the mother who saw her young son hit another child. "Don't hit!" she commanded, as she slapped her son. A moment later she was flushed with embarrassment. "Oh, my god—what have I done!" It can be difficult for the most well-meaning person to pursue the ideal of the golden rule when confronted with stress, complexity, and conflict.

Sometimes our failure to "do unto others" results in hurt feelings, strained relationships, missed opportunities, and the like. Sometimes a buildup of anger, distrust, or, simply, indifference to others becomes the bomb whose fuse is ignited by circumstances. The victim can be a single individual, or the 11 million Russian peasants who were systematically killed—by their own countrymen—either through starvation or murder. More than 6 million Jews, many of them loyal German citizens, were victims of the Nazi's "final solution." Both the Russian (Conquest, 1986) and the Nazi (Friedlander, 1995; Goldhagen, 1996) catastrophes had their origins in the most dangerous of all territories: the human mind. "Peasants" and "Jews" were not like us. They were subhuman and therefore were meant to be exploited, ignored, or destroyed in accordance with our own plans and aspirations. Many of those responsible for these killings felt they had done nothing wrong. So powerful is this sense of emotional insulation from the killing that people may refuse to believe what happened, even in the face of overwhelming evidence (e.g., Lifton, 1986; Lipstadt, 1994).

From so much suffering and death—what lesson stands out most clearly? *The golden rule is flagrantly disregarded, and horrendous death (Leviton, 1995) becomes a prospect when we do not feel a basic bond with other people.* The study of human development and its psychopathology reveals that we cannot take such a bonding process for granted. Infants and children who are derived of loving parents or parent surrogates often do not show the ability to form intimate relationships with others. Children growing up within dysfunctional families often have mixed experiences of affection, neglect, and cruelty that interfere with their ability to create and maintain close relationships. Whatever contributes to a loving and supportive home environment, then, in all likelihood also contributes to the development of human feeling and empathy.

There is another level of social influence, however, that can inhibit the development of emotional bonds with others. Division of the human race into *Us* and *Them* has been a common mindset throughout history. People who are regarded as belonging to the *in* group may

be respected, cherished, and protected. There is little sense of human bonding, though, for those who are regarded as outsiders. The rules of engagement may be so different that outsiders are taken to be fair prey (as in slavery or crime) and to have no claim on human rights.

It is easier to treat others as less than human if we do not actually know them. We are no longer as free to act upon images, assumptions, and stereotypes when we see for ourselves that the Others are, like us, real and unique persons. "Do unto others . . ." too often has had an escape clause. We may feel we should do right by others if they are not really Other. And Other may include a large proportion of the human race: people who speak a different language, come in a different color or gender, or simply live in the wrong side of town or even just across the symbolic turf border within the same neighborhood. Can group esteem exist without putting down other groups? Can we develop the willingness and ability to feel ourselves a part of the total human community?

Positive signs already exist. Some people have learned from the hard lessons of racial discrimination, the Holocaust, and other twentieth and twenty-first century disasters. Furthermore, the far reaches of the world now seem more within personal range for people who interact regularly through e-mail and the Internet. Many industries and corporations involve multicultural partnerships; many campuses are enriched with students and faculty of the most varied backgrounds. Travel has also developed friendships that cross over national, racial, and ethnic lines. Disasters in Bosnia, Kosovo, Turkey, Taiwan, and East Timor, for example, all had personal meanings to some of my students who, in turn, helped the rest of us to put a human face on the tragedies. Whatever enhances communication and personalization, then, should help to develop human bonds that provide some protection against horrendous death.

One powerful trend, however, has the potential for weakening our sense of deep connection with others. It might also blur our awareness of the difference between real and virtual life—and, therefore, between real death and its electronic counterfeit. We must pay another brief visit to the compelling satellite world of so-called virtual reality.

Are We Live or on Tape? The Life-and-Death Challenges of Virtual Reality

Face-to-face encounters almost completely dominated human interactions until technological innovations offered supplements, enhancements, and replacements. Photography not only altered our sense of identity but also transformed our relationship to the past, especially to loved ones, who now could still be with us just as they were. The tiny framed oval photograph of grandmother or the portrait showing the entire family as once it was became among the most cherished of possessions. Photographs provided a powerful new way for the dead to speak to the living. The emotional impact of the Civil War has remained potent through the lens of photographers, the first to offer visual evidence of a major conflict. The dead also speak to the living in the movie, *Dead Poets Society* as a teacher (Robin Williams) directs his students to study a photograph of an earlier generation of students. The intense aliveness of this vanished generation becomes a unique lesson to the present student generation. The dead were once young and full of life, just as the students of today. The lesson here: Seize the day! In this and in many other ways, the photograph has added an enduring visual context within which today's lives and deaths gain resonance.

The telephone had its own distinctive transformational effect. The human voice with all its subtle tones and inflections now could transcend distance. The pangs of separation and absence—so closely associated with bereavement—could be relieved by hearing the familiar reassuring voice. And so the process has continued, with every significant new form of communication having its effects on our symbolic relationship with both life and death. Sound recording not only revolutionized the place of music in society, but rescued conversations and speeches from being carried away in the ever-flowing river of time. "Are we live or on tape?" became a question with philosophical as well as practical implications. Does it really matter if the voice we hear is that of a person who is speaking to us in "real time" (another new concept)? The voice and message are the same if taped, and even if the speaker is deceased. The ear processes the sound in the same way (given an accurate recording), whether the message comes live, on tape, or from the living or the dead.

Another important dimension has been the remarkable new ability to shift time. Those born into the age of electronics might take this ability for granted as they TiVo a television show for later viewing. Nevertheless, shifting time is among the features that most distinguish present times from the human past. The role of time in human life was nailed by the Persian poet Omar Khayyam (1990) in the eleventh century:

The Moving Finger writes; and, having writ,
Moves on: nor all your Piety nor Wit
   Shall lure it back to cancel half a Line,
Nor all your Tears wash out a Word of it (p. 42).

Time rules, then. Operating through time, life does not give us a second chance. Errors cannot be corrected; failures cannot be repaired. No matter how clever or religious we might be, time will take its own course and, with that course, all that we hold dear, including life itself. How should we come to terms with death, given this view of time? People differed, then as now. Some, for example, attempted to prove Khayyam wrong by delving into alchemy or magic to prolong youth and life. The quest for perpetual youth was a desperate and occasionally inspired effort to bend time to human desire (Kastenbaum, 1995). Others decided to burn their candles brightly and live as intensely as they could within a shortened time-frame. Still others sought to distract themselves from the disappearing sands of time by drink or other means. Time was not fragmented into stopwatch or nanosecond measures but was regarded as the long, slow, unopposable wave that swept away kingdoms as inexorably as it did the individual's youth and life.

Time's rule has now been challenged. We can convert immediate experience to the time-insensitive format of digital encoding. Essentially, time becomes number (or its electronic equivalent). Life remains perishable in the stream of time, but episodes within life can be stored "for later viewing at our convenience."

What are the implications for our views of life and death? In earlier chapters, we saw how difficult it is for children to develop and for adults to face the basic facts of death. The popularity of the idea that death is a kind of sleep also reveals our reluctance to recognize it on its own terms. We are often grateful for any opportunity to escape the recognition of mortality even (or especially) when in jeopardy. Technology's very good tricks of recording and shifting time can play right into our preference for keeping death out of awareness. Every time we take advantage of a time-eluding technology we might be making it that much easier to blur the difference between "virtual" and "real reality."

Consider a person who has had limited primary social interaction during infancy and childhood. Place a computer in front of that person and provide access to a vast universe of images and symbols. Give that person the opportunity to manipulate the images and symbols. Allow that person the power of trashing and deleting whatever does not please. Add the attraction of game playing. And to this game playing add a personal impulse that has been stimulated by mass media society since childhood: the pleasures to be found not only in victory but in destruction.

Some of the most popular computer-mediated games are variations on the shooting galleries that were long popular in carnivals and fairs. With the embellishments of vivid graphics, one can zap the alien invaders or blast away at other life form images. The most technologically updated aliens are the latest stand-ins for The Other: people who are not like us and therefore suitable as targets for our rage, pride, and entertainment. Competing to see who can run up the highest score of targets destroyed in a computer game is an activity that comes painfully close to representing our society's aggressive edge. That the same group of people most attracted to zapping computer games also produces the most real-life killers is a connection that is as difficult to overlook as it is to interpret with any degree of confidence.

Many of us enjoy a phantom-like interaction through chat rooms. The people with whom we interact may or may not be representing themselves honestly. More significantly, it is possible to carry on this attenuated form of interaction to the neglect of real-life relationships. Notoriously complex, shifting, and sometimes "messy" are real-life relationships. Furthermore, the real people in our lives are not always available when we need them. Computer-mediated interactions are always available, though, just a mouse click away. Real-life relationships also have a way of making demands on us when we would rather not be bothered. One might often prefer the company of spirits generated or mediated in cyberspace to that of flesh-and-blood mortals. No heart stops beating when, with the touch of a finger, we trash or discard. Is it possible that our computer-bred, computer-linked person will fail to appreciate the crucial difference between the real death of real people and the pseudolethality that flourishes in virtual reality? (Doesn't mean we can't have fun avatarizing in Second Life!).

Perhaps it will become even easier with a few key strokes to endanger the lives of people we have never met. The 60 million (not a misprint) peasants who starved to death during China's catastrophic farm reform movement were not family, friends, or neighbors of the leadership. The planners and leaders did not have to see the effects of decisions they made at a distance. When bombs were first dropped on a civilian population (Guernica, Spain), there was a widespread reaction of shock and outrage. Nevertheless, aerial assault on civilian populations persisted and intensified, because those who unleashed their bombs with the push of a button or the slide of a lever could not see the faces and mangled bodies below. The same action involved in pushing a button (or clicking a mouse) can have the effect of playing a game, sending a communication, or destroying lives.

We just don't know yet if coming generations will have a firm grasp of both virtual reality and the kind of reality that is experienced by mortal beings.

There is another kind of virtual reality to explore, one whose long and influential history is seldom brought to mind: death and dying in imaginary places. We focus here on a blockbuster novel from the early sixteenth century.

UTOPIA: A BETTER DEATH IN A BETTER PLACE?

The endearingly clueless hero of Voltaire's *Candide* (1759) proclaims "This is the best of all possible worlds." A series of most unfortunate events promptly calls this judgment into question. This world actually could do with a bit of improvement. This brings us to the Utopia tradition. Plato (370 B.C.) proposed a scientifically managed society to produce and enforce moral behavior. People would just have to be good whether they liked it or not. By contrast, sensualists and slackers throughout history have imagined idyllic places where they could just loll about, enjoy delightful climate and abundant food, and treat themselves to such pleasures as they might desire. Not surprisingly, the carefree garden of delight was a more popular alternative to Plato's rigorous Republic. Centuries passed and neither version of a better world came into being. In fact, the emergence of what historians call the "early modern period" did not help matters. Saint-to-be Thomas More (1516) was incensed by the violence, hypocrisy, and injustice of his times. He thought a more rational form of government might protect individuals and fulfill the legitimate needs of the commonwealth. The people would be physically fit, and educated, and productive. With healthful activity, virtuous pleasures, and communal feeling within a just society, people would be more inclined to behave in accord with religious values. More called this new and improved society *Utopia* (1516) placed it on a distant island unknown to mapmakers and described it in some detail.

Utopia eventually became the inspiration for new communities that attempted to bring the system into palpable existence. It also became the progenitor of a robust literary tradition. Some versions have worked within More's concept; other versions have morphed into dystopias (scary and miserable) realms. Science fantasy versions of utopias and dystopias have escaped from the pages of pulp magazines to elaborate cinematic treatments. We will stick with the original here.

Why is life better in More's Utopia? The positives can perhaps best be expressed through a list of negatives:

- *No money. No deprivation.* Nobody's rich. Nobody's poor. No mansions. No slums. All Utopians receive from the commonwealth what is needed for a decent and secure living. There goes the threat of crimes of desperation or ego-driven greed. There also goes the impulse for an individual to strut, flaunt, and boast, because everybody has pretty much the same economic standing and show-offs are scorned. The commonwealth is so well organized that agriculture and other essential activities assure prosperity.
- *No private property.* No land-grab schemes. No disenfranchising one group of people for the advantage of another. No setting one's self up as a power broker by accumulating properties. Nice!
- *No lawyers.* More was one of the great lawyers of his time, so he took particular delight in excluding this profession. Without lawyers there is no constant skirmish between one interest and another, no mind-numbing tactics, no societal preoccupation with contentious cases. Utopia gets along without lawyers because the laws are few, basic, and easily understood.
- *No unemployment.* Everybody participates in the work of society, therefore avoiding the dark clouds of alienation and anomie. Busy hands and duty-focused minds are also less likely to indulge in useless and possibly uncitizen-like thoughts. The workload is not excessive, so there is plenty of time for people to improve themselves, for example, by reading good books (the only kind available), visiting museums, and the like.
- *No vice.* Utopians are schooled from early childhood in the virtues of responsibility, teamwork, and moderation. Temptation is neither stimulated nor countenanced. Visitors who might suppose Utopia to be a feast for sensual indulgence would be sorely disappointed. No frilled-up women, no stud-strutting men. No brothels, taverns, or other establishments of dubious propriety. Nothing but wall-to-wall virtue.

- *No gambling.* Can you think of any other sinful temptations? Just add them to the list of indulgences that will not be found in Utopia. Premarital sex and adultery are, of course, no-no's. Sexual activity is regarded as normal and healthy as long as it is practiced within the bonds of matrimony. People are free to choose their own mates, but both partners must have reached a sufficient level of maturity. Both must also be satisfied with the physique of their prospective mates. (How? A betrothed couple is required to view each other in nature's own garment and express their approval of the one-and-only lifelong mate to be). Another huge set of possible crimes and failings has been avoided. Utopia does not prize ascetic martyrs who mortify their flesh, and comes down hard on the few that stray from the marital path.
- *No persecution.* In More's time, a realm that was free from brutal persecution would have been greatly cherished, even if none of the other features of Utopia existed. It was not unusual for property to be seized, or for people to be imprisoned, tortured, left to die, executed, or slaughtered in large groups. Strife within Christianity was a major source of this brutality, primarily associated with the rift between the Catholic Church and the emerging Protestant Reformation. Thomas More himself would have his head separated from his shoulders at the command of his admiring friend, King Henry VIII, because he stayed true to his own religious beliefs in a conflict between church and state. The founders of Utopia knew the perils of religious intolerance. They allowed people to worship as they chose. It was expected that everybody would believe in a divinity that created and ruled the universe. People could choose their own comfortable way of worshiping this divinity, as long as they did not aggressively oppose other people's religions. Utopia was therefore mercifully free of acrimony and bloodshed between believers who called God by different names. The commonwealth's smooth-working machinery of governance also avoided armed hostilities based on opportunism, grudges, or rivals for royal succession. The blessings of peace were bestowed on Utopia. Naturally,

though, from time to time the Utopians themselves found justifications for pouncing on somebody else's realm.

Life in Utopia was purposeful and coherent. Luxury and self-indulgence were not part of the package, but it was far from a grim land. People were encouraged to participate in sports and keep themselves in excellent physical condition. There were satisfying communal meals with music and edifying conversation, pleasant places to stroll, and all of that. There were also limits on private initiative and activity. Perhaps Utopians did not think twice about the need to submit official requests in order to travel to another city—and to be observed and accompanied. Perhaps they also accepted without question a system of watchers: people who kept their eyes on other people. We might feel creepy and outraged in such circumstances, but this was the Utopian way of life and its citizens had known no other, and heard of no better.

Death in Utopia

What, then, about death in Utopia? I "visited" St. Thomas More's ideal commonwealth with that question in mind (Kastenbaum, 2005), and, again, with the related question of aging (Kastenbaum, 2008). Inflicted death is given more attention than natural passing away. We learn mostly about deaths associated with war and execution. Few people are put to death by the commonwealth. In this regard, Utopia differs appreciably from other nations at the time, reflecting More's anger at the infliction of capital punishment when the "crime" (if any) does not require so harsh a punishment. Nevertheless, the commonwealth does reserve the right to take the life of a citizen who violates a foundational principle of the society.

War was the far more common cause of inflicted death. The commonwealth was skillful in getting what it wanted without resorting to military action. Clever diplomacy usually worked. Most potential enemies realized it would be folly to invade Utopia, with its well-disciplined forces and daunting defenses. Sometimes, though, the rational thing to do was to invade another realm that was not using its resources nearly as well as Utopia could. After the inevitable victory, Utopian forces took prisoners instead of slashing throats, which was the more common practice at the time.

People did die in battle, though, and here two rather discordant notes are sounded: (1) Spare the lives of one's own citizens by hiring fierce but dispensable mercenaries, many of whom would be killed anyhow and therefore not have to be paid; (2) Affirm Utopian values by exposing whole families to battlefield death. The latter practice tells us a lot about the commonwealth's concept of the good life and the good death. When a man goes off to war:

> They place each wife alongside her husband in the line of battle . . . and all (his) children, kinsmen, and blood or marriage relations, so that those who have the most reason to help one another may be closest at hand for mutual aid. It is a matter of great reproach for either partner to come home without the other, or for a son to return after losing his father . . . hand to hand fighting is apt to be long and bitter, ending only when ever one is dead (More, 1975, p. 70).

Family values? Or commonwealth as monster? Shame avoidance is so powerful that an entire family is dispatched to its death. Utopia, the most enlightened and benign of realms, places the honor of the community above the lives of its citizens when the drums beat and the bugles blast. The state displays admirable restraint in executing so few offenders, but sacrificing entire families in battle is also considered admirable. The violent and painful death of "children, kinsmen, and blood or marriage relations" is good because it displays the values of the realm. Is it good from anybody else's perspective? *There is no other perspective.*

What of natural death in Utopia? In this compassionate realm, the sick and dying are tended by skillful physicians and comforted by priests and visitors in pleasant surroundings. People who are slipping away in final illness have consoling companions to the very end. Although More devotes only a few words to this process, it is worth observing that he does think it important to discuss the dying process; many later Utopian writers do not,

Sometimes, though, "the disease is not only incurable, but excruciatingly painful." Priests and public officials are up for this challenge.

They remind the dying person that he or she is now unfit for any of life's duties, a burden to self and others. Life is good while one can serve the community and experience pleasure. Death is good when pleasure is gone and one can no longer be of use to others. Obey the priests! They are the interpreters of God's will. It will be "a holy and pious act" to accept a potion that leads to peaceful sleep and death. Compliance is expected. Assisted death (Chapter 9) is good because it is endorsed by the commonwealth. There is disappointment all around should a dying person decline this thoughtful suggestion, but it is not imposed, and care continues to be provided until the last breath. Priests shake their heads regretfully. This person had a wonderful opportunity to affirm his or her personal virtue by affirming the virtues of the commonwealth. Fortunately, though, most people in this circumstance accepted their responsibility to die on request.

Consider now another person who has suffered much and has but more suffering in prospect. This person might be in even more distress than the one who has been firmly "invited" to die. In despair, this person decides to take her or his life (perhaps even with the same recommended potion). This sufferer does not have to be advised by priests that he or she has become a liability, a noncontributing drag on the commonwealth. A good death this must be since it is well in line with the criteria for assisted death. It will probably not surprise you, however, to learn that the person "who takes his own life without the approval of priests and senate, they consider unworthy of earth or fire, and throw his body, unburied and disgraced, into the nearest bog" (p. 60). The smooshing splash of a suicide's body in a distant bog tells us something about the less estimable side of Utopian philosophy and practice.

A Better Death in a Better Place?

Utopia has many admirable features that were remarkable for their time. It has serious claim as a model for designing a better place to live. How people die in Utopia is obviously connected with their way of life. Compassionate care for the sick and dying is consistent with obligations owed to

Yvonne Quinn takes care of her prized pet, Amoeba, a sparrow she saved 3 years ago. She thinks the bird is attracted to her blue nail polish.

citizens by the commonwealth. Assisted death also calls upon citizens to fulfill their obligations to the commonwealth. The harsh attitude toward people who take death into their own hands is paralleled by the unobtrusive but pervasive actions of the commonwealth to keep everybody "with the program." We note how this attitude reverses the situation in the United States today: Suicide is legal, not criminal, while assisted death is still caught up in controversy. For the guardians of Utopia, death is good when it conforms to the commonwealth's priorities. The person who has consented to assisted death and the person, equally suffering and failing, who chooses suicide have both escaped their pain and lifted the burden of support from society. In one instance, though, this is a virtuous death and, in the other, so despicable a death that the corpse is flagrantly dishonored. That a family should offer itself up for death in battle is an even

more obvious example of commonwealth policy taking precedence over the lives and deaths of its citizens. In a very small nutshell, then: *the good death in Utopia is the achievement of dying as a respectable citizen of the realm.* Choose to live in Utopia and enjoy the many benefits and we have also chosen to die one of the approved deaths of the realm.

The United States is not Utopia, as most of us have noticed from time to time. Nevertheless, our personal feelings about "the good death" are also influenced by cultural expectations in many ways. It is time now to look more systematically at the concepts of good and not-so-good deaths.

"THE GOOD DEATH": FANTASY OR REALITY?

What can we say now about the relationship between a life and its death? Does having lived a "good life" contribute to ending with a "good death?" And what about the reverse: Can the way a person dies alter the meaning and quality of that person's entire life? "Good death" has been kept in quotation marks to remind us that there are many opinions to choose from, including views that dismiss the whole idea of a good death. Now we can dispense with the quotation marks and get right to the central issues. We will also continue to speak of the good death, the term that has come into general usage, even though what we are really concerned with here is the way in which a life comes to its end.

Bring your own experience and judgment to the evaluation of the following propositions. You will notice that some of the propositions seem to be at odds with each other and that they draw upon different realms of observation, evidence, and belief. And so—to the challenge!

Proposition 1:We can agree that some forms of death are terrible even if we cannot always agree on what constitutes a good death. People should be spared such deaths. The terrible death is dominated by suffering. There is physical pain to the point of agony. There may also be extreme mental pain, as when a mother sees her child being killed while she herself is dying. Torture and humiliation, such as violent rape and murder in regions of subtropical Africa is still being used in campaigns to destroy victimized people spiritually as well as physically.

It is reasonable to assume that people everywhere would fear a death marked by extreme physical, mental, and spiritual suffering. However, some people have believed that suffering is a valuable experience. We should suffer because this either helps to pay for our sins or promotes our spiritual growth. This belief can be held to a lesser or greater degree. In the not so distant past, the extreme position has been used to argue against providing pain relief to women in labor, a particularly cruel example of gender discrimination. There are also contemporary examples of withholding pain relief to terminally ill people for similar reasons. However, terminally ill people today rarely see any inherent value in suffering. It is an unfortunate situation when people in a position to provide care to the dying patient have very different ideas about the value of suffering.

Proposition 2: The good death should enact the highest values held by society. Both the individual and society benefit from such a death. The individual is seen as accomplishing something of exceptional merit. Society is strengthened by having one of its members demonstrate allegiance to its values with the last breath. Utopia, as we have just seen, is one such example. Furthermore, each person's death is important as a possible test of both individual character and society's strength. This emphasis on how a person faces death contrasts sharply with the "failed machine" model that has often been implicit in medical management. The community and its health care professionals cannot turn away from a dying person if there is something important that all believe should be accomplished as life gives way to death.

But what precisely is to be accomplished at the end of life? The answer to this question varies. One of the most dramatic models is the heroic death. The person is to die bravely. The Kamikaze pilot and the Sioux warrior were among the many men who accepted combat missions in which their deaths were almost assured. In Norse mythology, the Vikings who died as battlefield heroes were rewarded with an afterlife in Valhalla. Both women and men are included among the martyrs—people who chose death rather than renounce their religious faith. The type of suicide that Durkheim described as altruistic (Chapter 7) may also belong here. The heroic death usually involves choice. Loyalty to one's people or God takes precedence over staying alive.

What the hero died *for* can be a troubling question. This was the case with Civil War soldiers who mostly did not consider themselves heroes, although they often fought bravely, and who often were not convinced that they were giving their lives for a just cause. Faust (2008, p. 270) quotes Oliver Wendell Holmes' as he attempted to make sense of the annihilation of so many youths:

> The faith is true and adorable which leads a soldier to throw away his life in obedience to a blindly accepted duty, in a cause which he little understands, in a plan of campaign of which he has no notion, under tactics of which he does not see the use.

Faust adds that "The very purposelessness of sacrifice created its purpose." Devastated by grief, the American public needed an explanation, a justification for the great slaughter. Keeping the United States united and abolishing slavery were significant justifications in historical perspective, but did not necessarily register profoundly on those in battle or visiting graveyards. Maybe, then, a death that could be called heroic because obedient to "a blindly accepted duty" was the way to wrest positive meaning from so much loss and destruction.

Heroic deaths seem to always have been exceptional and, therefore, especially admired and remembered. Not everybody has the opportunity or the ability to end his or her life in a way that dramatically affirms core social values. Many more people, however, have been able to demonstrate their social conscience by facing death with resolute allegiance to the values they cherish. For example, some cultural traditions hold that one should bear suffering in silence. I have known people who did not speak of their pain nor seek comfort and relief during their final illness. They were determined to live up to what was expected of them by tradition.

Others have acted in accordance with cultural expectations such as going off to a particular place or even assuming a particular physical position when death is near. Some traditions also expect the dying person to offer memorable last words. A striking example is that of the *jisei* or farewell verse written by Japanese Zen Buddhists monks and haiku writers. Although the tradition has varied over the centuries, it was often considered best to be sitting upright at the moment of death, using one's last words to offer a poem to those gathered around. In contrast to religious traditions in which last words are supposed to be pious, the *jisei* often is playful and surprising:

My last breath chases the first
Two whispers at play
In the garden of lost boys

And:

Tell them whatever you like
My jisei was perfect
Or I coughed up a green toad

If we embrace Proposition 2, then, we should expect to discover a great many variations—as many ideas about the good death as there are societal values. One of the most striking variations is *oppositional death*. People who have become

bitter or disillusioned may use their last words and energies in attacking society's values. For example, a hospice chaplain spoke to me soon after having left the bedside of a dying woman who had rejected him and cursed God. He was shaken by this encounter but already starting to make sense of it:

She couldn't have said anything that would have upset me more, and she knew it. Life had been a kind of poison to her for a long time, since her son, then her husband died. I think this was her getting the poison out and her using the strongest word she knew—that would be God. [A strange kind of prayer?] That's exactly what it was. A strange kind of prayer. I will go back to her—and she will take my hand.

It is likely that societal expectations influence the way we deal with the end of our lives, even if we are not attempting to achieve a particular kind of death. Experienced caregivers usually have learned to suspend their own expectations and attend instead to the cultural values that are most cherished by terminally ill people and their families. The situation can be more complex, however, in post-industrial societies where there are pluralistic beliefs and lifestyles instead of one dominating view. This has been found true, for example, in Japan as well as the United States (Long, 2003).

Proposition 3: The good death is one in which our most significant personal relationships are affirmed. These relationships may also embody societal and religious values, but it is their personal meanings that are especially cherished. Our studies of deathbed scenes, actual (Kastenbaum, 1994, 2000, 2004b) and imagined (Kastenbaum & Normand, 1990) find that relationships are usually the uppermost concern. People most often desire the companionship of those who have shared their lives through the years. This does not mean that dying people want to have all the people in their lives with them all the time. Sometimes it is enough to be with a person a time or two in order to achieve a sense of closure in the relationship. A dying father in Kaliai, a region of Western New Britain, said to his daughter: "'Ah, now that you are here I can die easily.' He then closed his eyes and within two hours he was dead" (Counts & Counts, 1985).

There are also circumstances in which the dying person may feel more comfortable by having only indirect interactions with some people because of certain tensions or concerns. Even when interpersonal contact is minimal or indirect, however, the quality of the interaction may help to affirm the value of the relationship. That one smile or handclasp might be enough to let others know that they have been appreciated.

Effective palliative care has done much to provide opportunities for continuing and affirming relationships near life's end. Relief of pain without dulling consciousness has helped people to have many quality interactions that otherwise would not have occurred. Being able to spend more time at home has also enhanced the opportunity for natural interactions.

The good death as affirmation of our most meaningful personal relationships has many implications for the way in which we have shaped our lives. People whose interpersonal relationships have been prevailingly antagonistic, conflictful, or distant are less likely to have loving companions at their sides near the end of life. Furthermore, nurses and other service providers may also find it difficult to establish caring relationships with people who have cultivated an abusive attitude toward others throughout their lives. Personal characteristics that earn the respect and affection of other people throughout the years often contribute to a warm and supportive interpersonal network at the end of life.

Proposition 4: The good death is one in which there is a transfiguring personal experience. As death approaches, one feels a profound sense of beauty, love, or understanding. The moment of death is also the peak experience of life. This construction of the good death has been with us in many forms throughout the centuries. The Moody-type near-death experience (Chapter 13) has brought renewed attention to this mystical state of being. The final pages of Tolstoy's *The Death of Ivan Ilych* (Chapter 1) provide a dramatic literary example. There are also real-life people who seem to be having powerful and distinctive experiences near the end of their lives (Kastenbaum, 1994). The medieval fascination with deathbed conversions and miracles (Aries, 1981) has not entirely lost its hold on us.

There are several frames of mind that can be associated with the good death as a transfiguring experience:

- *A sense of adventure:* "Life has been a series of adventures—why not death as well?
- *A sense of mystical awareness:* "I just know there is more to life than the everyday, so the moment of death may open these mysteries to me."
- *A sense of escaping from a disappointing life:* "This transfiguring moment will make up for the hurts and sorrows I have experienced in life."
- *A need to avoid the stressful realities of dying and separation:* "I will get myself to think only of the beauty and wonder of dying, not the physical side of it, and not the interpersonal issues."

A special case here is the impulse to risk death for the thrill of escape or an exhilarating sense of being fully alive and keen-witted at the last moment. This is among the motives people have mentioned for running with the bulls at Pamploma and for picking fights with opponents who might kill them. (Perhaps it is also a rampant impulse for ardent rollercoaster riders (Chapter 1). The dying process is usually accompanied by declining energy and function. Some people, then, are tempted to adventure themselves to possible death while still primed for an exciting experience. At the end of their lives, some people seem to be having a distinctive and powerful experience that we cannot share. The first person I observed in this situation was an old man close to death who was sitting himself up in bed with a surprising display of renewed strength. He gestured eloquently while engaging in an animated conversation with a visitor who was visible or audible only to himself. This was a serious interaction in which, apparently, important matters were being discussed and resolved. For whatever it means, all of us felt that he was not out of his mind but had taken his mind someplace else. But we didn't know. And the next time I saw a dying person seeming to interact with a "spirit visitor," I still didn't know what was happening.

Other people near death slip away as into a deeper sleep, and we may choose to interpret this also as the outer manifestation of a transfiguring state of being. But do most people die with an exalted experience? That is quite a different question, and the answer is likely to depend on whether we rely primarily upon faith and hope or on what can be learned through direct observation.

Proposition 4 remains a significant model of the good death, but one that can distract us from the "ordinary" challenges that are faced by dying people and their families. "Healthy dying" (Kastenbaum, 1979) attempts to sugarcoat the actual stress and loss experienced by many terminally ill people. The model of the good death as transfigured life is sometimes used to avoid dealing with disturbing realities. The idea of the good death as a peak experience is compelling enough on its own terms that it does not need an assist from denial.

Proposition 5: The good death is one in which people continue to be themselves as long as possible, preferably to the very end. This view is close to Weisman's (1972) concept of an appropriate death: the death a person would choose for himself or herself. It is not identical, though, because some people would prefer to take a different turning at the end of their lives (e.g., a heroic or transfiguring death).

Most of the terminally ill people in the National Hospice Demonstration Study (Chapter 6) who were asked about the last 3 days of their lives expressed a preference for a familiar routine: a day like any other, at home, with the people who meant the most to them. In a more recent study, elderly Israelis also emphasized the value they placed on continuity (Leichtentritt & Rettig, 2000). This value encompassed the funeral and memorial process as well. One respondent expressed his thoughts in this way:

> My funeral should correspond with whom I am . . . [with] the way I lived my life. My family knows I do not want them to sit Shiva over me . . . I do not wish people to mourn after me in this way—it is not who I am.

Another respondent had a different emphasis:

> I am willing to suffer a lot. I am willing to tolerate pain, but I am NOT willing to tolerate a disrespectful process. . . . I have seen funerals in my life that were disrespectful—that is exactly what I do not wish for. . . . When I said that I wish for a respectful process . . . it does not end the moment I close my eyes (p. 237).

Many people seem comfortable with the idea of ending their lives much as they have lived. This model of the good death is usually consistent with the model that emphasizes affirming one's closest interpersonal relationship. Again, the hospice movement has proved valuable in helping many people to continue being themselves through the final phase of life.

EXTINCTION: DEATH OF LIFE OR DEATH OF DEATH?

Trying to understand and come to terms with death is difficult enough. But—*extinction?* Perhaps we are ready to think about the total annihilation of life, perhaps not. Let's give it a try. We begin by consulting a man who was well accustomed to meditating on last things.

St. Paul's Cathedral, 1623

The physicians were doing what they could. As his life continued to slip away, they prepared draughts fortified with ingredients that are as well unmentioned. This failing, they next applied pigeons "to draw the vapours" from his head. Privately, he mused:

> But what have I done, either to breed or to breathe these vapours? They tell me it is my melancholy; did I infuse, did I drink in melancholy into myself? It is my thoughtfulness; was I not made to think? (p. 78).

He played with the idea of vapours even as the pigeons performed their ministrations. No, he decided, the most poisonous emanations come not from Nature's deadly creatures but from people who specialize in deceitful and mean-spirited actions. This meditation concluded with a simple message to the angel surrogates who were gathered around him: "Be a good pigeon to draw this vapour from the head and from doing any damage there."

What history remembers occurred a few days after the wine and pigeon treatments. He was edging ever closer to death but still could take pen in hand to record his thoughts. Lying abed so close to St. Paul's Cathedral (he was dean of this illustrious religious center), he could not help but hear the bells repeatedly tolling as one more soul departed this earth. Who was it this time? Will he be the next?

Anybody would be curious; it's in our nature.

Who bends not his ear to any bell which upon any occasion rings? But who can remove it from that bell which is passing a piece of himself out of this world? No man is an island, entire of himself; every man is a piece of the continent, a part of the main. If a clod be washed away by the sea, Europe is the less. . . . Any man's death diminishes me, because I am involved in mankind, and therefore never send to know for whom the bell tolls; it tolls for thee (pp. 167–168).

A world without polar bears? And without many other fellow creatures of land, sea, and air? Extinction of species is an ongoing reality. What is our responsibility, what should be our response?

This is an excerpt from the 17th of John Donne's Devotions (1623/1975), all of which are recommended to those who might be ready to consider the human condition without blinking too much. Donne knew life and death better than almost anybody. He reveled in the passion that binds lovers together, affirmed the bonds that unite all humans everywhere, and meditated on the mysterious relationship between a mortal soul and God.

All that lives should have compassion toward all that lives. In a sense, we are each other. Donne's message can help prepare us to consider extinction. Consider another implication from the same source. One of Donne's sonnets begins:

Death, be not proud, though some have
   called thee
Mighty and dreadful, for thou are not so;
For those whom thou think'st thou dost
   overthrow
Die not, poor Death, nor yet canst thou kill me.

It concludes:

One short sleep past, we wake eternally,
And Death shall be no more: Death, thou shalt
   die (p. 342).

This is an expression of the faith in the Christian promise that Donne labored to achieve through years of doubt. Whether or not one shares this faith, though, all can reflect on his confident dismissal: Death, thou shalt die. Hold on for a moment to the startling idea that death could die. Now introduce the idea of extinction. That death itself could perish becomes a less fantastic prospect. Death might die at its own hand. Every species extinguished perhaps reduces the power of death. Extinction of all life would be the supreme act of (let's call it) *thanatocide*. The Egyptians who honored the dung beetle by placing its likeness in the chest of dead pharaohs and queens had discerned that life needs death. But death also needs life.

Sigmund Freud (1920/1960) suggested that we have two basic instincts: one devoted to life (*Eros*), the other to death (*Thanatos*). This is the normal state of affairs. Eros and Thanatos scrimmage with each other throughout our lives, but the final outcome is never in doubt. The trick, thought Freud, was to keep the game going. Eros and only Eros would whirl us into a daze, and Thanatos, unrestrained, might suddenly destroy others as well as ourselves. Keep a little death in life, and enough life to counterbalance death. This facet of Freudian theory is itself nearly extinct now, but it is still another way of conveying the idea that impulses toward death are themselves inherently self-destructive or thanatocidal. Total extinction would be game, set, and match.

The Death of Species

Extinction usually refers to the destruction of an entire species or life form. Most famous perhaps is the termination of the dinosaur reign about 65 million years ago (although such estimates remain subject to revision). Mass extinctions have occurred at least five times in the distant past. It is also considered probable that there were a great many other episodes of mass extinction that did not leave enough evidence to analyze. Will there be a sixth mass extinction of life on Earth? "Look around," say the scientists, "It's going on right now." The five most documented mass extinctions are summarized in Table 15-2.

Accidents in space traffic are suspected as the cause of most of the mass-extinction episodes. Collisions with asteroids can be devastating, and there can also be major casualties from exposure to meteor showers. Tumultuous changes in earth/sea formations and extreme climactic changes might also have been involved. At least one thing is clear: All these extinctions occurred without human contrivance or influence.

Many species have lost their struggle for life apart from the mass extinctions. This process was first brought to general attention by Charles Darwin (1869/1995) in his landmark book, *On the Origin of Species by Means of Natural Selection, or the Preservation of Favoured Races in the Struggle for Life*. His observations led him to the conclusion that life forms are related to each other in a complex web of circumstances. (Echoes of Donne? No nematode is an island entire to itself.) The circumstances include everything that makes up the ecosphere

TABLE 15-2
Mass Extinctions

Geological Period	When?	Who Died?	Why?
Ordivician-Silurian	439 million years ago	85% of all species	Shifts in earth layers
Late Devonian	365 million years ago	75% of all species (marine life even more)	Asteroids, one or more
Permian-Triassic	251 million years ago	90% of marine and land vertebrates and many trees	Asteroid, volcano, falling sea levels
Late Triassic	200–214 million years ago	75% of all species; end of mammal-like reptiles	Asteroids, heavy rainfall
Cretacious	65 million years ago	Dinosaurs, 18% of land invertebrates, 47% of marine life	Asteroid near Yucatan and Siberian eruptions

(Browsimmer, 2002). Life forms have to contend both with each other and with the resources, limitations, and hazards of their environments or habitats. Over the course of years, some creatures are able to adapt themselves to their environments and continue to flourish; others are displaced or left helpless when circumstances change.

Species appeared and disappeared for millions of years by "natural selection" (or luck) long before humans came along to add our contributions to the process. Today it is our role in the continuing extinction of species that is arousing the most concern. Earlier in this book, a few examples were given, such as the frogs and vultures that are being decimated by pesticide and other agricultural or industrial residue. There are so many other examples, however, that one hardly knows where to start or stop. One example from the United States may serve to remind us of what the world has been losing in diversity of species and how our own kind has contributed:

Perhaps the most poignant of recent extinctions is the passenger pigeon, which was to be hunted into oblivion. At the beginning of the Civil War, this was one of the most successful bird species in North America, comprising an estimated 49 percent of the entire bird population. In 1870, a single flock one mile wide and 320 miles long flew over Cincinnati. In 1974 the last surviving pigeon died in that city's zoo. As of 2001, conservationists estimated that one in every six species of birds is in

decline on the continent and could wane by half by the year 2030 (Kearl, 2002, p. 278).

I have difficulty in trying to imagine that enormous flock of birds—and even greater difficulty in accepting the fact that our species contrived to eliminate theirs. What a sorry return for the good work of their feathered British kin who ministered to John Donne's vapours! Extinction occurs on such a scale and in so many ways that it does challenge our ability to take it all in. Planet Earth continues to change, change rapidly, and change in a great many ways—and, most often, in ways that are leading to the death of species that might otherwise remain our companions.

Is death of species good or bad—or does it occupy a moral zone beyond our usual ways of thinking? For the limited purposes of this book, perhaps all we can suggest is to remember that we are not alone on this planet and our own lives and deaths may be as truly connected to all life forms as the dean of St. Paul suggested while the bells continued to toll.

FROM GOOD LIFE TO GOOD DEATH: A PERSONAL STATEMENT

Welcome back, now, to our own lives. Obviously, we cannot simply choose or create a model of the good death and take it home until needed. Circumstances not completely in our control are likely to affect the conditions of our death. Furthermore, we might hesitate to shape our lives around the end of our days. There is a case to be made for enjoying each day as it comes and not burying ourselves prematurely. Perhaps there is a way of integrating a realization of death into our ongoing lives that does justice to both. And perhaps no two of us would do this in quite the same way.

Here, then, is what I try to do, based in unequal parts on what I have learned, what I don't know, and what I feel. This statement is offered only as an example that might be useful in reviewing your own approach.

- I hope to achieve an ongoing balance between awareness of risk and danger and a free and open attitude toward life. I do not want to put myself or others in jeopardy by engaging overmuch in denial, resistance, compartmentalization or other defensive strategies (Chapter 2). This awareness of possible threat to life encompasses physical, environmental, and man-made sources of danger. And yet I do not intend to crawl into a hole and pull the hole down with me. Like most other people who have been active in death-related studies, I enjoy life a lot and intend to keep doing so.

- I realize that I have a very limited ability to influence the large forces and events that influence how long people live and how they die. Nevertheless, I also notice how surprisingly many opportunities there are to do something in a positive direction. Sometimes this is as simple as listening a little more intently or offering an alternative way to deal with a situation.

- I doubt that my death will be able to make up for the mistakes and shortcomings of my life. This means that I do not rely on a ninth inning rally, although that would be exciting. (While in the ICU, I managed to stay alive by fouling off enough pitches from The Closer to stay in the game a while longer.) Instead, I feel that I have to try for a good at bat in every opportunity that comes along. That may or may not influence the final score, but nevertheless seems the best way to play the game within the decided limits of my ability.

- The Buddhist and Hindu perception of what we call life and what we call death as a co-existing flow makes a lot of sense to me.

No—not to the point that I dismiss the idea of death as the end of life as I have come to know it. But I do recognize at least some of the little births and little deaths that accompany us throughout life and from which we might be wise enough to learn.

- I know something of grief and loss, and so have some sensitivity to these feelings as they mark the faces, words, and lives of others. I try to be aware—at the right time, when it most counts—that this person with whom I am interacting may still be struggling with the pain of loss while trying to move on with life.

- I appreciate life the more. As a youth I went along pretty much assuming that life was both within and all about me and therefore could be taken for granted. Studies of dying and death, as well as personal experiences, have taught me to treasure life in all its forms. Yes, that does include the gigantic wolf spider that dropped down beside me one evening and decided I was okay while at the same time I was deciding he (she?) was okay; life in the trouble-making twinkle in an aged person's eyes; life in the open-eyed wonder of a young child; life in the here-right-now intensity of an athlete; and life in the who-cares-where-we-are engrossment of lovers. I can understand, I think, why encounters with death have soured some people on life. But it happens that death has given me—and I think many other thanatologists—an ever-fresh appreciation for life.

SUMMARY

This chapter has given us an opportunity to reflect on some of the issues we have been encountering throughout the book. We were particularly interested in the meaning of the good death and how this might relate to the ways in which we live. The Civil War resulted not only in an astounding number of casualties, but also in ways of dying that violated the nation's hopes and expectations for "the good death." Resonances from this experience remain with us today. The sharp reduction of life expectancy among women in some areas of West Virginia reveals a very different pattern in which difficult lives end in difficult deaths. Examples from

World Trade Center victims, people shunned because they have HIV/AIDS, and the way a great philosopher accepted his death also introduced us to some of the dimensions and complexities of this issue.

A physician's response to the terminal illness of his father reminded us of how much both medical management and family support influences the outcome. Ira Byock, M.D., touched by his father's death and appalled by the mismanagement of dying people in the health care system, became an effective force for the improvement of terminal care. Eliminating futile medical procedures and providing opportunity for family and patient to have time together in natural surroundings could be seen as basic steps to prepare for "the good death." We were reminded that there are limits to our ability to control the conditions of our death and that "making sense" of the end phase of life often is a challenge that is in the hands of the surviving family and friends.

More people today are enjoying long, healthy, and materially enhanced lives. Death is therefore less tempting as release from the stresses and sorrows of life (as, for example, once a major factor in the lullabies sung to babies). We also noted that "not wanting to leave the party" is a trend that stands the regret theory of death anxiety on its head. According to regret theory, people who feel they have led satisfying lives are less anxious about death. However, more people may now regret (rather than fear) death just because life seems so pleasant that it should go on and on.

An influential new sociotechnological development also commanded our attention. Computer-generated and computer-mediated imagery are providing what amounts to an alternative universe of experience and interaction. We wondered about the possible impact of virtual reality on our conceptions of life and death, and, therefore, on the meaning of a "good death." Photography, sound recording, and time-shifting technology have also contributed to a sense of mastery over the transience of the moment and the inexorable flow of time. Will people who are born with two umbilical cords—one connected to their mother, the other to a computer—have full appreciation for

real life and real death? Questions such as these were raised here in the hope of stimulating closer observation and thought.

An additional perspective was added with our exploration of death in an imagined society designed to provide a better life. Thomas More's Utopia raises provocative questions about the meaning and prospects for a "good death" in a thoroughly managed society.

Five propositions about the good death were identified: (1) We can agree that some deaths are terrible, even if we cannot always agree on what constitutes a good death; the terrible death is dominated by suffering; (2) The good death should enact the highest values held by society; here the heroic and the oppositional death were given particular attention; (3) The good death is one in which our most significant personal relationships are affirmed; (4) The good death is one in which there is a transfiguring personal experience; (5) The good death is one in which people continue to be themselves as long as possible, preferably to the very end.

We were also encouraged to reflect on both the history and future of extinction, a process that continues to destroy entire species and which human values and actions continue to influence.

In conclusion, I offered a personal statement about the good life and the good death.

REFERENCES

Achte, K. (1989). Lullabies of death. In R. Kastenbaum & B. K. Kastenbaum (Eds.), *Encyclopedia of death* (pp. 176–178). Phoenix: Arno.

Ahrensdorf, P. J. (1995). *The death of Socrates and the life of philosophy*. Albany: State University of New York Press.

Aries, P. (1981). *At the hour of our death*. New York: Knopf.

Associated Press (2002, May 27). At least 357 killed in terror attacks made phone calls. www.ap.org

Broswimmer, F. J. (2002). *Ecocide: A short history of mass extinction of species*. New York: Pluto Press.

Bulkeley, K., & Bulkley, P. (2005). *Dreaming beyond death*. Boston: Beacon Press.

Byock, I. (1997). *Dying well*. New York: Riverhead Books.

Conquest, R. (1986). *The harvest of sorrow*. New York: Oxford University Press.

Counts, D., & Counts, D. (1985). *Aging and its transformations: Moving toward death in Pacific societies*. Lanham, MD: University Press of America.

Darwin, C. (1995). *On the origin of species by means of natural selection, or the preservation of favoured races in the struggle for life.* New York: Signet Classics. (Original work published 1869.)

Donne, J. (1967). "Death be not proud." In *The complete poems of John Donne* (p. 342). Garden City, NY: Anchor. (Original work published 1633.)

Donne, J. (1975). *Devotions.* Ann Arbor: University of Michigan Press. (Original work published 1623.)

Erikson, E. H. (1950). *Childhood and society.* New York: Norton.

Faust, D. G. (2008). *The republic of suffering. Death and the American Civil War.* New York: Alfred A. Knopf.

Freud, S. (1960) *Beyond the pleasure principle.* New York: Norton. (Original work published 1920.)

Friedlander, H. (1995). *The origins of Nazi genocide.* Chapel Hill: University of North Carolina Press.

Gelfand, E. E., Raspa, R., Briller, S. H., & Schim, S. M. (Eds.). (2005). *End-of-life stories.* New York: Springer.

Goldhagen, D. J. (1996). *Hitler's willing executioners.* New York: Knopf.

Gyatso, Tenzin, the 14th Dali Lama. (1985). *Kindness, clarity, and insight.* (J. Hopkins, Trans.) Ithaca, NY: Snow Lions Publications.

Hallam, A., & Wignall, P. B. (1997). *Mass extinctions and their aftermath.* New York: Oxford University Press.

Hayslip, B., & Peveto, C. P. (2004). *Cultural changes in attitudes toward death, dying, and bereavement.* New York: Springer.

Hoffman, D. (2005, July 27). *60 Minutes.* [Television broadcast].

Hussain, W. (2002, December 1). Activist gives face to disease. Wants to make people aware others live in secrecy in India. Associated Press.

Kastenbaum, R. (1979). "Healthy dying": A paradoxical quest continues. *Journal of Social Issues, 35,* 185–206.

Kastenbaum, R. (1994). Is there an ideal deathbed scene? In I. B. Corless, B. B. Germino, & M. Pittman (Eds.), *Dying, death, and bereavement* (pp. 109–122). Boston: Jones & Bartlett.

Kastenbaum, R. (1995). *Dorian, graying: Is youth the only thing worth having?* New York: Baywood.

Kastenbaum, R. (2000). *The psychology of death* (3rd ed.). New York: Springer.

Kastenbaum, R. (2002). Socrates. In R. Kastenbaum (Ed.), *Macmillan encyclopedia of death and dying*: Vol. 2 (pp. 769–772). New York: Macmillan.

Kastenbaum, R. (2004a). Death writ large. *Death Studies, 28,* 375–392.

Kastenbaum, R. (2004b). *On our way. The final passage through life and death.* Berkeley: University of California Press.

Kastenbaum, R. (2005). Is death better in Utopia? *Illness, Crisis & Loss, 13,* 31–48.

Kastenbaum, R. (2008). Growing old in Utopia. *Journal of Aging, Humanities, and the Arts, 2,* 4–22.

Kastenbaum, R., & Normand, C. (1990). Deathbed scenes as imagined by the young and experienced by the old. *Death Studies, 14,* 201–218.

Kearl, M. (2002). Extinction. In R. Kastenbaum (Ed.), *Macmillan encyclopedia of death and dying*: Vol. 2 (pp. 275–283). New York: Macmillan.

Khayyam, O. (1990). The Rubaiyat of Omar Khayyam (E. Fitzgerald, Trans). New York: Dover. (Original work published 12th century.)

Leichtentritt, R. D., & Rettig, K. D. (2000). The good death: Reaching an inductive understanding. *Omega, Journal of Death and Dying, 41,* 221–248.

Leviton, D. (1995). Horrendous death: Linking thanatology and public health. In J. Kauffman (Ed.), *Awareness of mortality* (pp. 185–213). Amityville, NY: Baywood.

Lifton, R. J. (1986). *The Nazi doctors: Medical killing and the psychology of genocide.* New York: Basic Books.

Lipstadt, D. (1994). *Denying the Holocaust.* New York: Plume.

Long, S. O. (2003). Cultural scripts for a good death in Japan and the United States: Similarities and differences. *Social Science & Medicine, 58,* 913–928.

Meijburg, H. H. (2005). The significance of dying well. *Illness, Crisis & Loss, 13,* 49–62.

More. T. (1516/1975). *Utopia.* (Original title: *A truly golden handbook, no less beneficial than entertaining of the best state of the Commonwealth and new island of Utopia.*) New York: Norton. (Original work published 1527.)

Ober, W. B. (1988). Did Socrates die of hemlock poisoning? In *Boswell's clap & other essays. Medical analyses of literary men's afflictions.* New York: Harper & Row.

Plato. (1942a). Phaedo. In *Plato: Five great dialogues.* New York: Walter J. Black. (Original work published 370 B.C.)

Plato. (1942b). The republic. In *Plato: Five great dialogues.* New York: Walter J. Black. (Original work published 370 B.C.)

Smith, A. M. (2005). *44 Scotland Street.* New York: Anchor Books.

Taylor, J. (1970). *The rules and exercises of holy dying.* New York: Arno. (Original work published 1665.)

Tolstoy, L. (1960). *The death of Ivan Ilych.* New York: New American Library. (Original work published 1886.)

Tomer, A., & Eliason, G. (1996). Toward a comprehensive model of death anxiety. *Death Studies, 20,* 343–366.

Vargas, T. (2008, April 28). Southwest Va.'s mortality mystery. More than diet behind women's sharp life expectancy drop. *Washington Post,* p. A01.

Voltaire (1991) *Candide.* New York: Norton. (Original work published 1759.)

Weisman, A. D. (1972). *On dying and denying: A psychiatric study of terminality.* New York: Behavioral Publications.

GLOSSARY

Appropriate death: The way a person would choose to have his or her life come to an end.

Horrendous death: A premature and unexpected death caused by other people. Often violent and painful.

Jisei: In the Japanese Zen tradition, a farewell poem that one improvises just before drawing his or her last breath.

Utopia: An ideal society, as first imagined by Thomas More (1519) and since applied to many other versions. An overly optimistic plan is often called Utopian.

ON FURTHER THOUGHT . . .

- Characters die on television and in movies all the time. What comes to mind as the "most good" and "most not-good" death you have seen in either format? And what made them so good or so not-good? Perhaps this reflection will tell you a little more about your own hopes, fears, and priorities.

INDEX

PHOTO CREDITS